CW01370059

The Aston Villa Chronicles 1874 – 1924 (and after)

Volume 1 : From Nothing to the Top (1874 – 1900)

Aston Villa were the most outstanding trailblazers in football
between the 1890s and the 1920s,
and were, and are, the Pride of the Midlands.

It could also be said that the club were the
Unofficial World Champions, 1894-1900.
The club were also close to that level in 1910-1914.

This is a history of the club based on
narratives and reports written by
authoritative Villans and other reporters
who were on the spot as it happened.

The Aston Villa Chronicles 1874 – 1924 (and after)

The Aston Villa Chronicles 1874-1924 (and after)

Published by Aston Villa Limited

First published 2009

© Aston Villa Limited 2009

Text © John Lerwill 2009

The right of John Lerwill to be identified as the author of this work has been asserted in accordance with the Copyright, Design and Patents Act, 1988.

ISBN 978 0 9562861 0 9

Printed and bound in Great Britain by Advek Limited.

All rights reserved. No part of this publication may be reproduced, stored in a retrieval system, or transmitted in any form or by any means, electronic, mechanical, photocopy, recording or otherwise, without prior written permission of the copyright owner. Nor can it be circulated in any form of binding or cover other than that in which it is published and without similar condition including this condition being imposed on a subsequent purchaser.

The Aston Villa Chronicles 1874 – 1924 (and after)

"The annals of Aston Villa might fit a big tome if they were properly done."

The Villa News and Record, 23 March, 1912

In April, 1913, the *Evening News* proclaimed:

> *Aston Villa is the biggest news on the football canvas.*
> *It is, in fact, a household word –*
> *one of the few the game has produced.*
> *At the start of the League - Aston Villa.*
> *After 25 seasons - [still] Aston Villa.*

The Villa News and Record responded
- in the same month of 1913:

> *In the year of grace 2000 AD it must still be Aston Villa.*
> *We cannot imagine football without the claret and blue.*

And it was also written:

> *The Villa possessed some rare and radiant songbirds*
> *in the days of old,*
> *and they would lilt till the light grew dim*
> *and the last watchman had gone home to bed.*

The Aston Villa Chronicles 1874 – 1924 (and after)

Dedication

To George Ramsay – player, captain and administrator from 1876-1935

To Jack Urry – Aston Villa historian extraordinary from 1879-1928

and

To my patient wife.

The Aston Villa Chronicles 1874 – 1924 (and after)

Foreword

Like John Lerwill I had no choice: I was born a Villa fan. I recall reading Nick Hornsby's acclaimed book on the trials and tribulations of life as a football fan and coming up with a start when he stated that he had chosen to be an Arsenal fan. That is something incomprehensible to folk like John and me, as much as it is to the many other fans of a myriad of clubs across the land. For us our loyalty to our football club is determined not by free will but by predestination. It arises solely from our family – from family ties, family history, family identity, and family loyalty. I could no longer have supported a club other than the Villa than I could have forsworn my Englishness, renounced my name or abjured my loyalty to Birmingham. It is a fundamental part of who I am, of who my people are and of who my descendants shall be.

Many is the time when it may have seemed an easy and welcome thing to have changed my allegiance – easy and welcome that is to those who feel not the ardour of a true fan. It was not enjoyable going down the match as a nine year old to join less than 15,000 people and watch us lose 6-2 to Chelsea. It was not pleasurable standing on the Holte as relegation to the Second Division became inevitable knowing that on the Monday you would be taunted by your class mates that Aston Villa were really called Aston Vanilla because anyone could lick them. And it was not good fun when the worst thing that you could imagine happened and your club was for the first time in its history relegated to the Third Division.

So why keep going down and suffer the anguish of defeat, the misery of insults, and the despair of a lost cause? Because you had no choice. Simply that. Our Mom comes out of Whitehouse Street, Aston and is fiercely proud that she is an Aston Brummie. She was going down the match in the 1940s and told us tales of Johnny Dixon, Trevor Ford and Peter McParland. And when I felt the desolation of loss after loss she cheered me up by reminding me that in 1957 when the FA Cup winning team returned along the Aston Road North in triumph she had held me up as an eight-month old baby at the window of the club room in the 'Albion' pub to see the cup.

Then there was Our Nan. She also came out of Whitehouse Street and as a young wench in the early 1920s she had watched the likes of the prolific scorers Billy Walker and Pongo Waring, She went on to see all the greats of the pre and post-war eras. Our Nan defiantly asserted that Georgie Cummings was the only defender

The Aston Villa Chronicles 1874 – 1924 (and after)

anywhere who Stanley Matthews was afeared of; and she would always chuckle with glee recounting how when Georgie was annoyed with someone in the crowd he would show his contempt for them by turn his back and dropping his shorts so as to bare his backside. Then Our Nan would bring to mind Mush Callaghan, Frankie Moss father and son, and Joe Rutherford. In our school holidays she'd have us traipsing up Corporation Street to the sports shop of Harry Parkes with whom she would have a banter. Later in life and not long before she died, the two of us had our photo taken with one of her heroes Eric Houghton. She was chuffed with that.

Nan's husband, my Granddad Perry, was from Highgate and a staunch Blues fan but he would take our Mom down the Brummagem one week and the Villa the other. In his opinion the Villa's Gibson, Talbot and Tate made up the finest half back line in the land in the 1930s. Our Dad was also from Blues territory in Sparkbrook but was a Villa fan. We have letters from my Granddad Chinn in late 1914 from the trenches in which he writes 'well done the Blues and hard luck the Villa'. He always backed the Blues as a Birmingham team but Granddad was a Villa fan. Born in 1892, before the nineteenth century was out he and his younger brother, Bill, had walked to Aston and stood on the hill in Aston Park to catch a glimpse of the match in the new ground of Villa Park. After he joined up in 1913, Granddad saw the Villa beat Sunderland 1-0 in the FA Cup Final at the Crystal Palace and after the war he was at Stamford Bridge in 1920 when we won the cup again after beating Huddersfield 1-0.

Our Dad started going down the Villa in the 1940s and later went on to become chairman of the Aston Villa Democracy Group and the Aston Villa Shareholders Association. He always stuck up for the rights of the fans on the terraces and in the stands and we still go down the match together with our family and still drink in the 'Albion' at Aston Cross. With such a background it is not surprising that I grew up imbued with the Villa's history and a deep sense of Villa's importance as a club. In my younger days I eagerly found out all I that could about our past because that is all we seemed to have; and since then and as a social historian I have become fascinated with the origins of football as a working-class game. So it is both as a fan and as a historian that I have read John Lerwill's Villa Chronicles – and as I have done so I have been profoundly impressed on both counts.

This is a monumental piece of historical research. I know of no other work that has brought together such a wide-ranging wealth of information about one particular club. In so doing John has revealed not only the beginnings of Aston Villa but through his assiduous delving into a host of primary sources he has brought into sharp focus the start of association football in Birmingham and Britain. As such this

The Aston Villa Chronicles 1874 – 1924 (and after)

'Chronicle' will be an invaluable resource for social historians intrigued as to how and why football became not only the national game of England but also the game of the world. It will also be a precious store of material on football in Birmingham and for Villa fans it will be a treasure trove of wonderful accounts.

The task that John Lerwill set himself is one from which most historians would have blanched. He has gone through thousands of newspaper reports, programmes and other forms of evidence to let the people from the time tell the story of Aston Villa. So many books on football are compendia of facts and figures. This Chronicle is so much more than that. The facts and figures are here but most importantly so too are the lives of the footballers, the directors and the others intimately bonded with the Villa. They reach out to us through long-forgotten speeches, notes and entries. Without John they would have remained hidden from view. That is the true measure of John's labour of love – he has brought to life the early folk of Aston Villa and rescued them from obscurity. He has set the bench mark for other club historians. I hope that others take up the challenge. John, both as a Villa fan and a historian I express my admiration for what you have done.

Professor Carl Chinn, MBE

Birmingham, 2009

The Aston Villa Chronicles 1874 – 1924 (and after)

Preface and Acknowledgments

What is 'Aston Villa'?

A supporter of the club will proudly confirm that Aston Villa is an English premier football (or soccer) club, and that it is a club that has hardly ever been out of the headlines since before 1880. The club is as well-known now as it has ever been and has been at the forefront of football much longer than several of today's big English clubs.

More than 130 years have elapsed since this footballing phenomenon first came to the world's notice. When it is considered that Queen Victoria was then a little way over half-way through her reign, that the American Wild West was then still wild, and that Buffalo Bill was still a few years away from bringing his Wild West circus to perform at Birmingham, then, indeed, those early days of Aston Villa seem truly to be ancient history. That motorcars and aeroplanes were then still a futuristic dream only enhances that view.

The club is located in Aston, a suburb of Birmingham. Although Birmingham and Aston were not incorporated as one municipality until 1911, the area in and around Aston had long been considered as 'Brummie' country, and Aston Villa were seen (probably by the great majority) as not only a Birmingham team but also Birmingham's leading football club from very early on. In a presentation to the retiring chairman of Aston Villa in 1899, the Birmingham Corporation's coat of arms, as well as Aston Villa's, was emblazoned on the illuminated address, and in a photograph of the 1887 Aston Villa team, some of the players are seen to be sporting the same Birmingham Corporation coat of arms.

It was a local government re-organisation in 1903, making Aston Manor a separate council authority, that prompted the Villa's local rivals, the hitherto-named Small Heath football club, to change its name to Birmingham, seemingly on the pretext that Villa was no longer a Birmingham club! *They* thus became – by default as it were – officially the leading Birmingham club! However, their position was short-lived, as the Aston Manor district officially merged with Birmingham Corporation in 1911. It was too late to rectify what 'Small Heath' had done, though there has never been any doubt about which club had the greater following and the greater success. Aston Villa Football Club seem to have treated this incident with grace and humour; in a patriarchal kind of way.

The Aston Villa Chronicles 1874 – 1924 (and after)

Aston Villa, through its founding fathers, their inspiration, their values, and the club's successes, was a highly significant factor in making professional football what it was in the 1890s and at the start of the 20th century, and – indeed – how football has developed since. And, unlike their Birmingham neighbours, Aston Villa never had cause to change their proud name!

The Villa's name has, in fact, been a constant source of fascination to many over the years – including the Hollywood actor Tom Hanks! Villa's famed Geordie skipper at the time of the 1957 FA Cup Final – Johnny Dixon – wrote:

> It was the name Aston Villa that made me write to the club for a trial.
> Nothing to do with anything else, just the name ...

Though not the oldest soccer club extant, there is no other soccer club that is both so old *and* so rich in history over so long a period as Aston Villa, and apart from a few exceptional years, the Villa has been the predominant football club in the English Midlands since the early 1880s. In the greater Birmingham area, Aston Villa and Joseph Chamberlain[1] became the twin gods of that great and progressive locality at more-or-less the same time. And both became famous a long way outside its boundaries.

Within a decade of the creation of the club in 1874, *The Villans* (as they soon became known) were making a big impact on the football world, which, by 1885, had become a professional world, progressively replacing the great amateur trailblazers of competitive soccer in England, such as The Wanderers and The Corinthians. Amateur football, however, remained a strong force for many years to come, driven by those who played the game – as it had been in the beginning – simply for fun, and sport.

---

[1] He was – thanks to his father's stake – a major figure in the screw-making firm of Nettlefold's and Chamberlain (later Guest, Keen and Nettelfold's: GKN), but subsequently became greatly involved in Birmingham politics and the city's reconstruction and was hugely popular. Following this, he was a M.P. and major politician at Westminster until 1906. He was Colonial Secretary at the time of the Boer War (1899-1902). His sons included Neville Chamberlain, who was Prime Minister at the outbreak of World War 2, and Austen Chamberlain, another famous politician of his time.

The Aston Villa Chronicles 1874 – 1924 (and after)

A Personal Introduction

For me, my father and his father before him, and the entire Lerwill family of Birmingham, Aston Villa is and has been a great institution, and one that I have followed (initially as a result of my dad's light-hearted insistence) since my childhood days in the early 1950s. Like many supporters of those days, I inhabited the Holte End (very much in the standing-only days), and remember clearly – as a boy – being hoisted over the Villa fans' heads to be given a chance to see the match from the front. But, alas, the view from the railings was not great either, and luckily I grew to be a six-footer-plus so I could see over the heads of others! My size also qualified me for being pushed and buffeted in company with all others that braved the Holte End terracing in those days, especially in a 50,000 or 60,000 crowd!

Today, I wonder how we survived the 'Holte End Sway' and the perilous head-high encounter with the 'rattles' that many supporters carried to provide as much noisy support as possible. All this, combined with the long journey across town (and back) from Kings Heath (well, Billesley, in fact!) by bus. Saturday afternoons in the football season were truly an adventure to a young 'un!

The late '50s were a time of exuberant 'runs' in 'the Cup'. I was able to see the 1957 Cup Final (fortuitously, as we'd not long had TV!) after actually being in the crowds at Burnley and Molineux during that year's Cup run, as well as a couple of the home ties. Both of those away matches were great affairs, and particularly the Molineux semi-final against the Albion, which will go down as one of the most exciting and hard-fought matches I have ever seen Villa play, especially against local opposition. The Albion had a strong side in 1957, and had only just missed winning the 'double' in 1954. Jimmy Dugdale – then of Villa – had played in that 1954 Albion side. At that time, I had not appreciated the depth of history that surrounded both those clubs in the relatively early years of organised football, back in the 1880s and 1890s.

With my father's unavailability because of lengthy working hours, my ability to get to those matches as a 12-year-old was made possible by a great family friend and Villa season ticket holder, "Uncle George", properly known as John Downer (a.k.a. George Page, one time secretary of the South Birmingham Sunday Football League), and who so kindly subsidised many interests of mine, not just football. Years later – when he became ill – we found out that 'George Page' was a pseudonym for reasons best known to himself, and I strongly suspect (through something he once said about his knowledge of Villa history) that he chose the name from one of the Villa's original team members. A very jovial and kind-hearted man, he was a gem, and

The Aston Villa Chronicles 1874 – 1924 (and after)

knew thoroughly the reputation of Aston Villa in Scotland, where he lived for a time before the War. He was, I believe, a former player with Greenock Morton. It was probably he that saved me from a desperate plight – under pressure from my south-Birmingham schoolmates, I had very nearly switched allegiance to Birmingham City during their cup exploits of 1956, but George guided me down the right route back to Villa Park before too much harm had been done!

And then the all-night waiting for Cup tickets when Villa were on a long cup run in 1960. The queue from the Trinity Road ticket office would stretch right down the Trinity Road and round the Holte Hotel, even by 10 p.m. on the Saturday, 12 hours before the ticket office was due to open!

Although I can lay claim to having seen Danny Blanchflower[2] play and score for Villa, as well as the likes of Tommy Thompson,[3] Harry Parkes[4] and Frank Moss Jnr.,[5] I was then still a bit too young to remember very much detail from that time. Thus, Nigel Sims and Peter McParland, and then Gerry Hitchens, became my greatest heroes. The '57 Final and Johnny Dixon's last game at the end of the 1960-61 season were highly charged and poignant moments, as were the occasions of seeing my heroes thrash the likes of Charlton Athletic (by 11 goals to 1) in 1959 and Leicester City (by 8 goals to 3) in 1962. A 4-0 win over a Bobby Charlton and Dennis Law Manchester United in the 1963-64 season was another great highlight – before Villa's 'slide' started in earnest, which happened to coincide with the rise of a player by the name of George Best. The Villa Park faithful rarely saw George in the raw, so to speak, except when Villa played the United in 'the cup' – the 1970-71 League Cup semi-final against them being a wonderfully notable event for the Villans.

I remember very well the sterling efforts of managers Eric Houghton and then Joe Mercer to bring Villa back into the fold of the top clubs with very limited funds, and then the years of decline and relegation, followed by the years of rising hope and then, finally – through the management of Ron Saunders – success! All those years

---

[2] After leaving Aston Villa, he went on to lead Tottenham Hotspur to the winning of the League Championship and FA Cup in the same season (the 'double' event of 1960-61).
[3] 'Toucher' Thompson became a strike partner with the great Tom Finney at Preston North End. Between them they scored over 200 goals in 4 seasons, and Finney has since commented on his and Thompson's uncanny understanding.
[4] One of the best of Villa's non-capped players and long servant to the club.
[5] Of whom the once-famed former England centre-forward Tommy Lawton had the highest opinion.

The Aston Villa Chronicles 1874 – 1924 (and after)

of support, home and away, were never short of either frustration or elation!

Even though I left the Midlands for London in the mid-1970s, I have always followed Villa's fortunes as much as possible, including the odd visit to see Villa play at a London club's ground, or even at Villa Park. "Once a Villa fan, always a Villa fan" is the feeling amongst Villa supporters, who have seen Villa go through both bleak and wonderful days over the last 50 years and more.

Before me, my father had been a great fan, although he rarely had the time to see them at away matches. He grew up during the tail-end of Villa's great first 50 years, and Billy Walker, 'Pongo' Waring and the six-foot half-backs Gibson, Talbot and Tate ("Wind, Rain and Sleet" as they were known) became his main heroes in those early 1930s days when Villa were still creating records and constantly pushing for the championship, but somehow falling short each time. My father had the misfortune never to see Villa win a league championship – he was born at the end of the championship year of 1910, and died a few years before the 1981 championship.

Before my father, my father's father (my grandfather), who for a period actually lived just down the road from Villa's first permanent home at Perry Barr (my grandmother's home was even closer). When they married, my grandparents moved to Aston before again moving, this time to south Birmingham by 1900. He was from the Archie Hunter and John Devey playing era; a highly skilled craftsman – a cabinet maker – who greatly appreciated skilled craftsmanship in others. From those very early days, football to him was described in two five-letter words: "Aston Villa"!

I only mention the next two facts because the old days of the Villa give me a thrill anyway, and for my family to have had just a little connection with that time adds a little more of a thrill to it all.

To my great delight, in the last few years I discovered that it was a niece of my grandfather (mentioned above) who married the great Frank Moss of the 1920s, and whose sons Frank and Amos also wore the claret and blue. However, when I saw the Moss brothers play for Villa in the early '50s, I was oblivious of their relationship to our family!

A further 'turn-up' that occurred during the research for this book was the discovery that a distant relative of mine was a co-founder of Wednesbury Old Athletic – one of the Villa's great contemporaries and opponents in the very early days of 'soccer' – and was also a player for them. Further, he played against the Villa at least once in their very early matches in the 1870s. During Villa's first ten years, the results obtained against the "Old 'Uns" acted as a kind of barometer of Villa's growth, and then of the Old 'Uns' demise.

The Writer's Acknowledgments

I would like very much to pass on my sincere thanks to the staff of the British Library at the Newspaper Archives at Colindale, and at the main Library at St. Pancras, London, and to the staff of the Archives and Heritage section of the Birmingham Central Reference Library, for their efficiency and help in making it possible to view the material that has contributed to the production of this book.

Further, my very best thanks to Aston Villa Football Club for the opportunity to examine original sources in their archives; notably the club's committee minutes from the 1880s onwards. This facility was coincidental with the club's need to re-establish their archives room, so for seven months in 2007, I found myself in the wonderful position of being able to research as I sifted through and put into some kind of order the magnificent collection of records and memorabilia in the club's collection. In acknowledging the help of the club, I must give specific thanks to the various archivists that have worked there since 1981, and whose notes have helped in the research process:

> From 1981 to 1987, the part-time incumbents were Linda Fletcher and Margaret Stokes, followed by Bert Sisk (club registrar) until his sudden death in 1993. Then the historians and authors Derryck Spink and David Goodyear participated, and they were followed in turn by Reg Thacker, who remained at the helm for several years until about 2004.

My special thanks are due to long-time Villa supporter Brian Halls for bringing my attention to an article written by William McGregor, and his transcription of the same. In addition, my sincere and grateful thanks are due to the highly experienced and reputable sports journalist Rob Bishop, whose frank comments and editing of a substantial portion of my original draft were gratefully received. Many thanks are also extended to Nadine Lees at Aston Villa for her valuable work and time expended in scanning and supplying important photographs for this book, and to Nick Oldham who supplied several cartoons, especially for this book.

Lastly, I must express my indebtedness to first-class English graduate Susana Lee, whose penchant for verbal and presentation accuracy was so well applied to the final draft. My sincere thanks is happily given to those several Villa fans who read draft portions of this book, and who gave me encouragement to continue.

The Aston Villa Chronicles 1874 – 1924 (and after)

The reason for this book and its primary sources

Albion John ('Jack') Urry

He came from the Isle of Wight, received training at a Birmingham printers and then became a sports journalist.

He involved himself in many sports – notably football and cycling.

The original cause for the writing of another book on Aston Villa was as a celebration of *The Villa News and Record* (hereafter referred to as '*The Villa News*'), which, in 2006, was celebrating its 100th anniversary. But, as I imbibed the splendorous content of its pages from 1906 onwards, it became clear that there – intact – was the basis for a new detailed history of the club. From very early on, *The Villa News* had the services of one Jack Urry, who proved to be an enthusiastic local journalist that had "intimate knowledge of the club and its doings since 1879", and who thus was able to pen his memories of the Villa's very early days and since. His contributions to *The Villa News* continued into the 1920s until he died, in 1928, after nearly fifty years as a Villa man.

In an obituary on Jack in *The Villa News*, it was stated, "Probably no man knew more of the early history of the club ..." (other than George Ramsay, that is.)

It was Jack Urry (writing under the pen-name of 'Old Fogey' during the early years of *The Villa News*) who not only wrote many historical accounts of daring-do himself, but also pointed to other writers worthy of reading, and who told their own story. It was Jack Urry, it is reliably transmitted, who concocted the word '*Villan*' (to describe an Aston Villa enthusiast), and also hijacked the expression '*daisycutter*' and applied the word to the shooting style of Olly Whateley.

In many respects, this book is a celebration of the work of Jack Urry. He was a close friend of Archie Hunter and many of the early Aston Villa notables, and through his articles in *The Villa News*, ensured that Villa's early history would never be lost in its entirety. Indeed, I felt that many of Jack Urry's historical articles seemed to be addressed to a much later readership, for the years about which he wrote in such depth must have far more significance for to-day's reader; we would otherwise barely be able to imagine the football of those times. Jack Urry left a wonderful historical legacy.

The Aston Villa Chronicles 1874 – 1924 (and after)

> Though it was Jack Urry that concocted the word *Villan*, it was the cartoonist **Tom Webster** (1886-1962) that animated the character of the same name in about 1905. In this book, I use samples of his cartoon-ship, including *The Villan* (see across). Tom Webster was a railway booking clerk who won a newspaper cartoon contest in 1904 and thus joined the *Evening Despatch* and *Sports Argus*.
>
> *The Villan*
>
> He rose to national acclaim when he moved to the *Daily Mail* in 1919, and later became a friend of the famed Arsenal manager Herbert Chapman, who (it is said) was so taken with a combination of clothing worn by Webster, that it inspired Chapman to add white sleeves to Arsenal's red shirts.
>
> **Norman Edwards** (1906-2002) became cartoonist to the *Evening Despatch* and *Sports Argus* in 1921, and re-invigorated the *Villan* cartoon.

I re-directed my aim, and determined that I would write a new detailed history of Aston Villa based upon first-hand accounts, using Jack Urry's accounts as the main thread, but also using match reports and the columns of many famous writers of the time. As the book style relies so much on recordings from that period, the title of the book came to include the word 'Chronicles'.

As a result of finding many scattered and varied articles, it has been possible to quote a very detailed history of the Villa before World War One and in those immediate post-War years, including the development of the game itself before and during the period of Villa's growth. A major reason for this approach was to capture the views and opinions of the time from those who saw the action and knew the players first-hand, and whose opinions about the relative abilities of various players must be considered a true state of affairs according to those times.

I consequently spent many months at the British Library in London (and the Birmingham Central Library), reading the weekly sporting journals; the *Sporting Mail, Sports Argus, Athletic News, Sport and Play,* and the *Midland Athlete*, in addition to *The Villa News*. I very often also had the need to refer to old daily newspapers. I was also delighted to find that Jack Urry (in an earlier guise as 'Leather Stocking') was a primary contributor to the *Sport and Play* journal before the inception of *The Villa News*, and so he provided considerable continuity in his narration of the Villa history as it happened.

The Aston Villa Chronicles 1874 – 1924 (and after)

It should be noted that the Birmingham Central Reference Library has digitised virtually all copies of *The Villa News* – or will have when time allows – thus preserving a marvellous record of the club for research.

In 1907, long-serving journalist Mr. Edwin Cox, having (apparently with Jack Urry's help) done his work of shaping *The Villa News* in its first year, moved on to other things, and he was replaced by Mr. Harry H. Doe, who magnificently continued – though modified – Mr. Cox's standard. In *The Villa News*' first season, the Chelsea equivalent, *The Chelsea FC Chronicle*, stated: "The only Club Programme we have seen that we will acknowledge as superior to our own is that of Aston Villa". Pleasant but brave words from a new club still in the second division and which had just suffered what was then a huge trading deficit of £5,000! Note also that Manchester United did not launch their programme until 1910 – but I would have to say that it was not to the standard that Villa had set.

Those who steered *The Villa News* forward succeeded not only in creating an interesting picture of the state of Aston Villa Football Club at that time – and also of football in general – but also reflected the desires, frustrations and elations of the Villa Fan, whom we find not (perhaps) to be a very different creature to the Villan of today! However, in those far off days before the growth of the football stadium, there appears to have been a physically closer link between the Villa supporter and the player, and from Jack Urry's comments in particular, you can sense that the crowd liked a player who could play and also appreciate the funny side when appropriate – and the player who enjoyed his game.

A list of all the authoritative individuals (whose true identity has not been found in some cases) is as follows:

Sidney Gilbert who, as "By One of 'Em", wrote an authoritative account of Villa's history between 1874 and 1880 in a then-existing Birmingham periodical called *Saturday Night*, in 1893. This account of Villa's very early history seems to have had official blessing at the time. In conjunction with Peter Lupson's chapter on Aston Villa in his "Thank God for Football", which established some interesting matters with regard to the Villa's church-related beginnings, the *Saturday Night* series and other articles (including input from Jack Urry) provide the earliest accounts of the club up to 1880;

The aforementioned **Jack Urry**. He proved to have been a sports commentator of some repute in the Midlands stretching back to 1879 (writing under the pen-name of 'Leather Stocking' in various sports journals) with intimate knowledge of various sports apart from soccer. Cycling was of special interest to him, and on which topic he had a regular column in the

The Aston Villa Chronicles 1874 – 1924 (and after)

Sports Argus. It was Jack Urry (in his *Villa News* columns) that often urged George Ramsay to write a history of Aston Villa, as had been Ramsay's stated intention. Alas, that history – from a man steeped in many years of the Villa from the very earliest of its days, and in fact a primary cause of the club's success – did not, apparently, materialise.

I refer to Jack Urry as 'Old Fogey' in this book.

The Villa's famous old captain, **Archie Hunter.** He was interviewed for the *Birmingham Weekly Mercury* in the production of a series called *Triumphs of the Football Field*,[6] published from October, 1890 to February, 1891, that gave accounts of historic playing events during Hunter's playing career with the Villa. He was a major playing influence from 1878, and Villa's captain throughout the 1880s.

William McGregor. A vice-president of Aston Villa and Villa committee member of the multi-skilled variety, and a man who contributed hugely to the club (in time and money). He is particularly famed as 'Father of the League'. He had been involved with the Villa since 1877, and in 1904 and 1905, he published a broad history of Villa's first thirty years. He also wrote a regular column in the *Daily Gazette* and *Sports Argus* from 1904 until his death in late 1911.

Charlie Johnstone. A former Villa player in the late 1870s till the early 1880s, and was involved with the Villa as a committee-member, director and then as a vice-president. He was also once a top sprinter, and was still involved in the AAA in the early 1900s. A schoolteacher by profession, his opinions were always controversial and thought-provoking, and he was clearly one well able (through his array of talents and insight) to look at 'the bigger picture'. He wrote a column in *The Sporting Mail* from 1906. This paper was absorbed into the *Birmingham Mail* after World War One as their sports edition. He also contributed to *The Villa News*.

"Brum" (Charles Wheelwright): He started writing on all West Midlands' sports matters for the Manchester-based *Athletic News* in 1881, and was still reporting for that journal 34 years later, in 1915. He could always be relied upon to write a lively "Midlands Notes" column in that journal, in addition to first-rate football match reports. He also wrote in the *Daily Gazette* and *Sports Argus*.

"Argus Junior": He was the lead writer for the *Sports Argus* from its inception in 1897, through to the 1920s.

"Nomad" and **"Crusader":** Reporters for the *Sports Argus* on many of the Villa's matches until the 1920s.

---

[6] This series was reproduced in its entirety in a book of the same name by Sports Projects Limited, in 1997.

The Aston Villa Chronicles 1874 – 1924 (and after)

Various other great pioneers of sports journalism can be added to the list, including the then famed **"Tityrus" (James H. Catton)** of the *Athletic News* and **"Veteran" (A. G. Taylor)** of *Sport and Play* and the *Sports Argus*, and who kept notebooks on the Villa's main achievements.

Other significant journalistic contributions came from **John (Jack) Devey** and **Howard Spencer**, who were great players and captains from the early 1890s to the mid-1900s (and who also became members of the Villa Board of Directors). They wrote occasional columns in the *Sports Argus* and *The Sporting Mail*. There are also letters from other former Villa players that were published in *The Villa News* and other periodicals, and reproduced here.

Of previous publications on the Villa's history in book form, I am particularly indebted to **Fred Ward**, a sports journalist and follower of the Villa since the 1880s, who was author of the relatively short but amazingly insightful *Aston Villa* (1948), and another sports journalist and follower of the Villa in earlier days, **R. Allen** in his *All in the Day's Sport* (1946) in which there is a chapter on Aston Villa. Thanks also to **Peter Morris**, author of *Aston Villa: The History of a Great Football Club, 1874-1960*, for significant pointers and information.

In Fred Ward's book there are quotations from Howard Vaughton and Dennis Hodgetts (who were outstanding members of the 1887 cup-winning side). In Peter Morris' book, there is information obtained directly from Albert Evans, the last survivor of 'the double' winning team (1896-97), who was still alive at the time of the writing of his book. And what a 'survivor' he was, too – five times he broke a leg during his playing years (three times whilst with the Villa), and each time came back to play again, and fought for his country in World War One.

Another name that was once famous in the Villa ranks at the time of their sixth League Championship (1910), Christopher Buckley, was chairman of the Aston Villa Board of Directors at the time that Peter Morris's history was written (1960). Buckley wrote a foreword to the book – "this first complete history of Aston Villa" – and referred to his (then) 54 years' connection with the club:[7]

> I have ever been conscious of the privilege of my association with this great club, its traditions, and its conception of all that is best in Association Football. ... I am proud to recall that the story of the Villa club is probably the most colourful and inspiring of any.

Last but not least, I must include in my credits the work of **Norman Edwards**, who, from 1921 into modern times, enthralled us with his wonderful cartoonery in relation to all sports, and published a collection of his cartoon series as *The Story of*

---

[7] Player from 1906 to 1912; director from 1936 to 1965; chairman from 1955 to 1965.

The Aston Villa Chronicles 1874 – 1924 (and after)

Aston Villa in 1947.

I also commend the reader to the various wonderful histories of Aston Villa published in the 1990s, which in most respects supplement the contents of this book. Many of these are beautifully illustrated. Please also see my *Bibliography* in the Appendix for a list of important published histories.

Other reasons for this book

Certainly, part of the motivation for this book was to try to convey a sense of the times and the wonderful achievements of Aston Villa during a period when there was no adequate recording mechanism other than by the written word and primitive photography (by today's standards). The accomplishments of teams over the past (say) fifty years can be viewed on film, but the full record of the Villa's hey-day can only be transmitted through the bringing together of the various written reports. However, there are other underlying issues.

One of those "underlying issues" is that no book I had read on the Villa seemed to say much about the earliest players, apart from something about the first-ever Aston Villa team and (of course) George Ramsay and Archie Hunter, and there grew an assumption that the players of the 1870s and 1880s were for the most part inferior players – possibly on account of the absence of a league until 1888. On one occasion I had a debate with an author of one of those books who believed that Andy Hunter (Archie Hunter's brother) was not of great value, perhaps unaware that later match reports about him as a player were when he was already infected with the later stages of a killer disease. There are some that feel that the history of Aston Villa did not really start until professionalism (1885) or their first FA Cup win in 1887. Nothing could be further from the truth.

History has been described as "a bridge connecting the past with the present and pointing the road to the future".[8] Thus, if the foundations of historical fact have been improperly laid, and their memory dimmed, then the road to the future can also be distorted. Hence, the need for accuracy is certainly part of the motivation for this book, and though it may be that some inaccuracy might be found within these leaves, it will not have been without trying to make the facts as flawless as possible. It is also the recognition that there is a story to tell that can (and should) re-establish the fact that Aston Villa has been at the very forefront of the evolution of association football, and, I suggest, particularly during a most important period

---

[8] Allen Nerins, historian

The Aston Villa Chronicles 1874 – 1924 (and after)

in that evolution.

More than this. The fact that the values that permeated through the club during that important evolution were the basis of its success, and the fact that those values continue to exist (in practical form in respect of community involvement, but also in other ways) indicates the existence of a personality in the club. And, I suggest, proving that 'values' are an underpinning foundation for even an organization. An organization is still – at the end of it all – made up of people.

History is indeed an important issue – it promulgates self-awareness. Aston Villa FC always was – and is – a great club, and I trust that I have put together something that will prove to be of value and put straight a few myths that have crept into the popular history of the club, as well as enhancing the passion and splendour of the club's history.

This Book and its Structure

This book is based almost entirely on my original research findings, and contains what I felt to be the best-sourced and best quotable material. I have tried to reproduce the most worthwhile events; wherever, in fact, something interesting or humorous is worth quoting. Sometimes my quotations are lengthy, and if this is considered to be a detriment, then I apologise for it but insist that there are occasions where to quote as fully as possible are necessary – to demonstrate that the book is *a chronicle*, and not just a history book.

In fact, this is not primarily a book of statistics. Facts and figures are, of course, used throughout, but the essential intention of this book is to convey a sense of the approach, the atmosphere, the skill, and the record-breaking achievements of the Aston Villa club during its first fifty years. Yes, the Villa continued to break records after 1924, but the preceding fifty years probably represent the (to-date) greatest period of the club's history, when the club became famous world-wide. Aston Villa led the van.

The Villa News stated, on the occasion of the club's Golden Jubilee:

> Curiously enough, there has never been a dependable account of the club published, and this is remarkable when you remember the name and reputation of the Villa, for it would not be too much to say that the Aston organisation has been talked about more than any other individual football

The Aston Villa Chronicles 1874 – 1924 (and after)

club in the world.[9]

The book consists of two volumes. The period covered by both these volumes can be looked upon as five certain 'chunks':

- that of 1874 to 1888, before the League started and during which fun was very much part and parcel of the game, and the start of professionalism;

- the period between 1888 and about 1900, when the League was still in its early years of development, followed by its rapid development and the Villa's golden period;

- the period from 1900 to 1909, when Villa's 'old stars' of the golden period reached the end of their careers, the resultant team re-building and the 'levelling out' of the standard of play amongst League clubs;

- the period from 1909 to 1915, a period of great resurgence for the Villa;

- lastly, the immediate post-World War One years, when the Villa had to 'find its feet' again in the climate of a very different world than that which existed before, and the end of the club's old administration.

If any errors be found then they are mine and mine alone. All I can do is lay at the reader's feet the result of some two years almost continuous research involving a thirst for accuracy. I admit that, even now, there are one or two missing fragments of the club's history, but I believe the main part of the story is here.

I trust readers will enjoy the accounts of the Villa's early history – bringing alive what is lost to living memory – the story of a remarkable, and evolutionary, football club.

Up the Villa!

John Lerwill,
Birmingham, 2009

---

[9] Villa News & Record, 2 Feb 1924

The Aston Villa Chronicles 1874 – 1924 (and after)

Contents for the
1874-1900 Period
(Volume 1)

1. Prologue 23
2. The Development of Football 45
3. How Aston Villa Began 56
4. 1875 to 1880: On to the Birmingham Cup 68
5. More Accounts of the 'Band of Brothers' 129
6. Villa's General Progress - 1880 to 1885 139
7. Playing The Scots 169
8. More Villa Heroes (ca. 1885 to 1891) 181
9. Major Crisis Number One 188
10. Jubilee Year In More Ways Than One 200
11. Defending the FA Cup – and Reputation 216
12. Those So-called 'Friendly Matches' 227
13. William McGregor and The League 234
14. More About Villa – and Their Neighbours 241
15. 1888-1891: Finding Their Feet in the League 247
16. The Golden Years of the 1890s 294

Appendix 1. The Chief Playing Heroes, 1891 to 1915 481

The Aston Villa Chronicles 1874 – 1924 (and after)

1. Prologue

High-level English League football (not just the Premier League) today contains several teams that came to the fore earlier than the Villa – clubs 'born' soon after the start of Association Football; particularly Notts County, Stoke, Notts Forest and Sheffield Wednesday. But the Villa was the first of a group of what are today recognisable as modern 'big clubs' that were 'born' in the mid-to-late 1870s; the Villa, Bolton Wanderers, Blackburn Rovers and Everton all have a long and proud history in the top-flight. It was these teams, together with Preston North End and West Bromwich Albion, and the slightly later manifestations Sunderland and Liverpool, that were the main causes of the success of organised English football into the twentieth century. Many of today's top clubs – the likes of the Manchester clubs, Arsenal, Newcastle United, Chelsea, and 'Spurs' – came to significant prominence very much later.

Having established a substantial national reputation by the end of the 1880s, Aston Villa went on to greater achievements after the formation of the Football League in 1888. These achievements would be unparalleled for many years. Between 1893-94 and 1923-24 (27 seasons, taking into account World War One), the Villa achieved honours 17 times in the two national competitions:

    5 FA Cup wins (and once losing finalists)

    6 League Championships (and 5 times runner-up)

In the greater period between 1888-89 and 1932-33 (41 seasons, taking into account World War One), the Villa finished in the top-6 League positions on 29 occasions, and finished out of the top-10 on only three occasions.

At that time, these were great achievements. In the time before European competitions and mostly before the World Cup started, the Villa's name was the most famous in the world of football, and even until World War Two (in 1939),[10] Villa's overall playing record had still not been bettered – not even by the rising star of Arsenal. But it was the post-War Manchester United of Matt Busby that surpassed the Villa's fame, particularly after their 1958 tragedy. The great

---

[10] Ted Drake – a well-known English football international of the 1930s and later football manager – is believed to have complained that when he travelled abroad with the England team, everyone seemed to want to only know about Aston Villa!

The Aston Villa Chronicles 1874 – 1924 (and after)

Tottenham Hotspur side of 1960-63, and then more particularly Liverpool, provided serious competition to the post-Munich Manchester United, and with Arsenal re-joining the fray, the eclipse of the Villa as the greatest club was complete, in the public eye at least. However, as the club went into decline as the 1960s progressed, the memory of the great teams of Aston Villa was still alive in the collective memory of the older generation of that time.

In his "Kings of English Football" (1972), the writer John Bills identified Aston Villa, Arsenal and Manchester United as the three teams that until then had ruled the English football scene since the start of the Football League (1888). Aston Villa was his chosen leading club until 1915. In his book, Bills created a statistical comparison to form a judgment on which of the clubs had been the greatest achiever over the period until 1968. The following table is a summary of his main statistics; the 'Number of Honours' column includes appearances at the FA Cup Final and as League runners'-up, not only the winning of trophies. The Football League Cup and European successes were excluded in the analysis in order to form a 'flat playing field':

Club	Period	Number of Seasons	League Matches Played	League Points Gained	% of Possible Points	Number of Honours	Honours Over Seasons Played %
Aston Villa	1888-1915	27	890	1063	59%	17	63%
Arsenal	1919-1939	20	840	942	56%	11	55%
Man United	1946-1968	22	924	1131	61%	22	73%

This analysis, based purely on performance data, seems to confirm Manchester United as the greatest of the three clubs as of 1968, with Aston Villa not a long distance behind. *However*, in terms of overall impact on the game, taking into account that it was the Villa that were a great influence on the development of the game at an important time (from before 1888) and over the longest period, in playing method, in ground development and in sound management, it is possible to say that the Villa had had the greatest impact as a club on the foundation of the game, particularly in helping towards its rise in popularity. In fact, it would probably have been more accurate to measure Villa's performance up until 1924, particularly as by then the Arsenal had still not risen much into the firmament of success.

By the time the Arsenal had usurped the limelight in the 1930s, the game had become settled in terms of its main rules and regulations, and management

The Aston Villa Chronicles 1874 – 1924 (and after)

approach at club level and in the League and Cup competitions; but it was the Villa that had been a major part of the evolution to make it so. It was one of the Villa's greatest officials (and one of the game's leading administrators of the time) that was the prime mover in the creation of the Football League itself – the world's first football league.

Since 1968, the game has moved on into different realms. Technological, training, medical and safety developments have all taken their part in transforming the game from what it was, aided by huge financial investments and incomes since 1992. In these last 40 years, there have been three clubs that have dominated the football scene in England, those being Liverpool, Arsenal and Manchester United, though the Villa's phoenix-like rise between 1975 and 1983, and again for a period in the early 1990s, almost precipitated them once more into the forefront as one of the

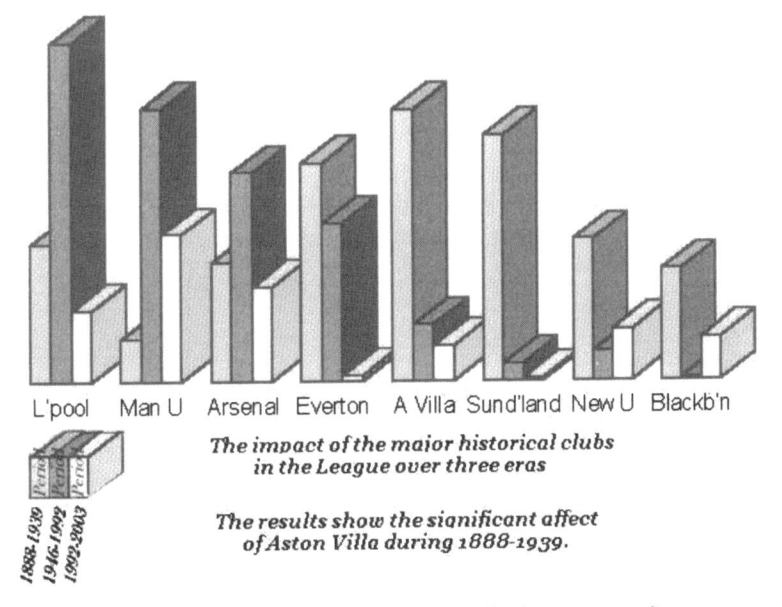

The impact of the major historical clubs in the League over three eras

The results show the significant affect of Aston Villa during 1888-1939.

(My histogram based upon League placings to 2003)

greatest modern clubs, and not essentially a Victorian/Edwardian phenomenon, as the club is often perceived. But what the Villa accomplished in those far-off days should *not* be under-valued. *In the nation's eyes, the Villa were – for their day – the equivalent of one the current top-4 clubs, and were unchallenged (fame-wise) for many years.*

The Aston Villa Chronicles 1874 – 1924 (and after)

Even today, there are those who think of Villa's success as essentially lying in pre-1900 times. That is quite an invalid perception – their *greatest* period in terms of trophies may have been in the last years of the 1890s, but for another 30 years after that they were still the most admired club. Into the 1900s, the club continued its success, but not at the same rate. Since 1900, the Villa have won the FA Cup four times, and the League Championship twice (and runner-up on several other occasions). They were the first winners of the League Cup (1961), and have won that trophy four times since. And to add to that (in no uncertain terms!), the Villa won the European Cup in 1982, followed by the European Supercup. In 2008, they were still members of an exclusively small number of five British clubs that have won the European Cup.

The Aston Villa versus Everton fixture is the most-played fixture in English high-level League football, and in days gone by a meeting of the two clubs was one to relish. In 1906, it was written:

> Everton and Aston Villa are names which at once conjure up in the minds of football enthusiasts memories of the best type of football. No clubs in the country have developed the artistry of the game with greater effect than these two famous organisations, and the lover of the pastime can look forward to a dazzling display of brilliance when they come into conflict.[11]

Other wonderful sides of that particular time included Sunderland, Liverpool and Newcastle United. Mr. Tom Watson – who was then a household name in football circles, and manager in succession of the fine Sunderland and Liverpool clubs of the 1890s and early 1900s – wrote an article that was printed in *The Villa News* in November, 1907, including the following:

> [About Aston Villa,] there is no team in England which commands a greater share of my admiration than the famous organisation which had its headquarters at Perry Barr, and now at Villa Park, Aston. I look upon 'the Villans' – to give them the appropriate title they receive from press and public – as amongst the pioneers of those improvements in the game which have raised it so high a pinnacle in popular favour...

It is probably true to say that at no time in their existence have Villa been without a great player or long-term hero in their midst; in every decade since the 1870s there have been players whose names have been on the supporters' lips as heroes. Many of those names have been famous nationally, though it is noticeable that the club's concentration on the team ethic meant that individuals were never over-glorified –

---

[11] Sports Argus 27 Jan 1906

The Aston Villa Chronicles 1874 – 1924 (and after)

though the existence of so many great players in the team (particularly in the first 50 years) meant that it was often difficult to isolate one great player. Several Villa players have been recognised as being amongst the top-100 players that played in the Football League, they being Hunter, Hardy and Clem Stephenson of the 1874-1924 period.

Significantly, even until the late 1930s, the deeds of the old Villa teams were recalled time and again, and players of the ilk of Archie Hunter, James Cowan, John Devey, Charlie Athersmith, Howard Spencer, Jimmy Crabtree, Harry Hampton, Joe Bache, Sam Hardy and Clem Stephenson long lived on in the memory of the nation. Jimmy Crabtree was, even thirty years after he played, frequently regarded as an automatic selection for the then all-time best England team. It took a world war (World War Two) for that memory to be largely erased.

There was, according to the legendary Archie Hunter, a specific element that made Aston Villa stand out from the crowd, particularly in the twenty-odd years following the time when he made his mark with Villa:

> There was one thing about the Villa, as everybody knows, I think, whoever saw us play. We had the power of making up our minds to win and when that determination was upon us the other side had got some hard work to do. ... No matter how badly we began, nobody could tell that we should redeem ourselves before the call of time.[12]

Ten years later, a lead writer in the *Sports Argus* was moved to say:

> I know no team which can play such hard practical football as the Villa; I know of no other team which can so make a set of devoted followers tear their hair in bitter despair! ... Their methods and manoeuvres are always intelligent; there is a resourcefulness about the ideas embodied in their play that is a source of unfailing interest and attractiveness to the spectators.[13]

The article went on to say that sentiment, when it came to selecting the team, had no place, however:

> There is less sentiment in the composition of the Villa directors than in that of any other club authority in England when it comes to the selection of the team week by week.

---

[12] "Triumphs of the Football Field", Birmingham Weekly Mercury, October, 1890 to February, 1891
[13] "Argus Junior" in Sports Argus 17 Feb 1900

The Aston Villa Chronicles 1874 – 1924 (and after)

Over the period 1885 to 1915, the following of the Villa rose from the then 'great' crowds of 10 or 12,000, to 40,000 or more, which figure – though a rare phenomenon in 1900 – was becoming commonplace at the grounds of some clubs (particularly Chelsea) from about 1907. The Villa always had intentions of purchasing the Aston Lower Grounds (on which Villa Park was built) when the time was ripe, and the growth of public interest (with resultant earnings heaped in their 'war chest') caused the Villa, by 1911, to purchase their ground, and then to look strongly into re-shaping the ground to accommodate at least 60,000 spectators with plans to grow to 130,000. Because of the War, that development did not materialise more fully until 1923 and after, though the full objectives were never realised.

The Builders of the Villa

No great sporting organisation could have just happened by itself. There had to be a motivating force – whether it was an individual or a posse of individuals – to get such an organisation off the ground. What is more, for many, many years, being a committee- member or a director entailed no reward in its service other than the undertaking of the task out of sheer enthusiasm. As 'Tityrus' (once editor of the *Athletic News*) put it:

> There are various kinds of leaders. It is astonishing what men will do for football. I have known of directors who have ruined themselves owing to their fascination for the game. I have known the chairman of a great club who came to an untimely end [by suicide]. ... There are those who have shortened their lives by the intensity of their feelings for the success of the team [and developed heart disease]. ...[14]

He went on, however, to pay tribute:

> ... to those who have been leaders in the larger sense, who have never spared themselves for the good of the game as a whole, who have endeavoured to take the best steps for the welfare of all football, and to keep it, whether as a pastime for amateurs, or as a spectacular sport for the delectation of the populace, honest, wholesome, and exemplary, and as a means of drawing men from the base, brutal and degrading amusements which were not unknown to their forefathers.

The Midlands had their share of "leaders in the larger sense", including J. Campbell Orr and Charlie Crump, and it must be fair to say (from their revealed

---

[14] J.A.H. Catton ('Tityrus'): "The Story of Association Football" (1926) (Classic Reprint)

The Aston Villa Chronicles 1874 – 1924 (and after)

thoughts and actions) that there were those within the walls of Aston Villa who were also imbued by the notion of a 'greater good'.

Only one of the original founding-members retained a long-term organisational involvement in the club, and during his period of involvement, further great personalities joined to develop the club's ideals and reputation. In the club's first decade and beyond, there was very much a Scottish development, both through those directly involved in the club, and the style of football that they emulated – that of Queen's Park of Glasgow, the great Scottish team of the 1870s and 1880s. As a Scot and early Villan (Charlie Johnstone) wrote:

> It is said that the first thing an Englishman does when landing on foreign soil is to solemnly pace out twenty-two yards on the most level stretch he can find, stick up three stumps, and start playing cricket. Football seems to have as great an attraction for the Scotsman. If there is not a club where he settles, he'll start one; if there is, he'll join up.[15]

The great names that were hugely influential in building up the club from the 1870s and well into the twentieth century are now introduced and briefly described in the order in which they joined the club. Further details concerning them will emerge in the detailed history that follows.

Billy Mason – 1874 to his death in 1894

As one of the first builders of the club, Billy's surname was more than suitable! A Birmingham man, he was a founder-member and player with the Villa from its inception in 1874 to 1880 (and treasurer during a portion of this period), then honorary club secretary from 1880 to 1882. For his services to the club he was presented with a scroll which referred to his "scrupulous integrity and self-abnegation" and "unremitting zeal and ardour". Afterwards, he was sometimes called upon by the club in emergency situations, particularly to act as chairman of special committees but also as a committee-member. He became the Villa's representative at the national FA, and such was his personality and "aristocratic bearing",[16] it was noted that the London members held him in awe. Billy was particularly organisationally active in the Birmingham and District FA from 1880 (becoming a vice-president) until his premature death.

---

[15] Villa News & Record, 7 Jan 1928
[16] Villa News & Record 23 Oct 1926

The Aston Villa Chronicles 1874 – 1924 (and after)

George Burrell Ramsay – 1876 to his death in 1935

Undoubtedly the greatest single influence on the growth of the club over its first 50 years, this Scot arrived in Birmingham in around 1871 to work as a clerk in a brass foundry. He was 21 years old when he came across a Villa practise match in the spring of 1876 and asked to play a game. His skill was such that he was soon appointed captain, taught the club's players how to play (and helped to guide the way for Birmingham and district football in general), led them to their first trophy win – the Birmingham Cup in 1880 – and to their first run in the FA Cup the same year.

As a player, he made an enormous contribution to the development of football in the west Midlands.

A committee member and even a chairman from 1876, in 1886[17] he became the club's first paid secretary/manager, and helped to steer Villa to their greatest triumphs. In his early years in that post, many was the time that he had to resort to extreme methods to capture a player – even the word 'kidnapping' has been used to describe this aspect of his work! A highly able and famous administrator, he retired in 1926, after 40 years in the job.

During his career he saw not just the Villa, but also football itself, grow to a stature that would have been unthinkable in the 1870s. He was very much an active part of that development. *The Villa News* (12 October 1935) remarked that:

> He was not content that Aston Villa should be noted [just] in the playing sense; his demand was that it should become an institution with a world-wide reputation for probity in sportsmanship.

George Ramsay is reported as having once said:

> " I helped to plant the seed, and I have seen a strong oak grow. "

Even until his last days, he was involved with the club as a vice-president. He died in October, 1935 (49 years after becoming club secretary and 59 years since becoming Villa's first player of note), presaging the club's first relegation to Division Two by a mere six months. Aston Villa was never relegated in his lifetime.

---

[17] Not 1884 as is often claimed

The Aston Villa Chronicles 1874 – 1924 (and after)

William McGregor – 1877 to his death in 1911

Another Scot, he also made the move from Perthshire in Scotland to work in Birmingham, and with his brother he opened a milliner's shop in Summer Lane, in 1870.

His abilities as a man of wisdom and in administration were quickly noted, and he was made a vice-president of the club from 1877 until his death in 1911. Helped by his friend Fergus Johnstone he was instrumental as a committee member during the 1880s in influencing stability within Aston Villa Football Club. Greatly trusted, he at one time held the posts of both Honorary Secretary and Honorary Treasurer, and was Chairman of Committee at the time of the Villa winning the FA Cup for the first time (1887). Towards the end of the 1880s, he recognised the need for improvements in the club's organisation, and it was he that first promoted the idea of converting the club into a limited company, though his effort was at first watered-down by the committee. It was not until the Football League had grown a little that his fellow club members saw the logic of making the club into a limited company. 'Mac' was not active in the management of the club after February, 1893, when he announced his refusal to be considered for future office, though he remained ever involved in helping the club in various projects and tasks.

He was a man of fertile imagination whose ideas for Aston Villa and football in general were constantly appreciated by all who knew him. In later years, it was written of him:

> He is a safe guide on almost all points, though he will not move until he sees his way clearly. Legislation in a hurry or without clear cause was ever distasteful to him. He would prefer to let a bad phase of the game have rope enough until it hanged itself, unless it was so bad that his love of fair-play and of the freedom of the player compelled him to strike. Then he would strike, and with force.[18]

Following his personal 'nudge' towards the establishment of professional football in 1885, he is most famous for his work in establishing the Football League (his "fixity of fixtures"), becoming its first chairman in 1888 with the post then transforming into 'president' – until 1893). He remained a life-member of the League's Management Committee. He was also still actively working for the Football Association weeks before his death. His passing, in 1911, was greatly mourned.

---

[18] Football and The Men Who Made It (1905)

The Aston Villa Chronicles 1874 – 1924 (and after)

Archie Hunter – 1878 to his death in 1894

Yet another Scot, he first started playing rugby as a full-back, but when he found out about association football, he joined Ayr Thistle (again as full-back), for which he became captain at the age of 16! When he left for Birmingham in 1878, the Thistle club gave him a gold ring and an 'Albert chain' as a 'thank you' for his services.

Archie Hunter almost always played at centre-forward for the Villa, though he had a 'play-anywhere' capability, and was club captain for much of the next ten years from 1880, when aged 21. With his younger brother Andy, Archie Hunter laid down the method of play and how to play, but Archie's greatest fame was as club captain.

The devotion towards him from his players was well-known, so it is perhaps interesting that he revealed something of his overall attitude and magnanimity in 1890-91:

> The team, however it is composed, must play as a team and not as a gathering of different men out of harmony with each other. I always tried to foster good feeling in Aston Villa and I think we were one of the merriest and happiest teams in the country. For myself, I never bothered my head about the country a man came from as long as we had good players and good fellows amongst us, it mattered not whether they were English, Scotch or Welsh.[19]

Archie also referred to the difficulties incurred as a captain in those days if he was of the disposition to apply himself conscientiously to that task:

> … a man finds it difficult to do his best work while he has got to look after a team, pull the men together, guide them, see that they don't get scattered and make certain of their taking every advantage, as it comes. I can tell you it is a hard job and there is the danger that in looking after the organisation of his forces the captain will be unable to play a good game himself.

However, his skill was also 'world famous'. Even in 1919 it was said that there had scarcely been a better centre-forward and that his level of dribbling was something that could no longer be seen (in 1919).[20]

Tragically, Archie Hunter was taken very ill while playing for Villa against Everton at the start of 1890 (in the second season of the League) and never fully recovered; already past his prime as a player, he certainly did not play again. After continuing to be of service to the club as a match umpire and

---

[19] "Triumphs of the Football Field", Birmingham Weekly Mercury, October, 1890 to February, 1891
[20] Villa News & Record 13/15 Sep 1919 – Based on an extract from *All Sports Weekly*

The Aston Villa Chronicles 1874 – 1924 (and after)

committee-man, he died four years later (still a young man), a few months after Villa won their first League Championship. William McGregor recorded that as he lay in his death-bed, he asked to be placed closer to his window in order to see the crowds flock to his beloved Wellington Road ground, less than three years before the club moved to Villa Park.

Fred Rinder – 1881 to 1925 and 1936 to his death in 1938

Born in Liverpool in 1858 in his own words he was, "born in Lancashire, developed in Yorkshire, polished in London and finished off in Birmingham". He arrived in Birmingham in 1877 to work in the City Surveyor's Department (and was thus part of the city redevelopment sparked by Joseph Chamberlain), and this explains his capability with regard to his involvement in the ground developments at both Perry Barr and Villa Park. He certainly had intimate involvement in the original building and all modifications to Villa Park.

Soon after arriving he became associated with the Villa, and became a member of the club in 1881. He went on to develop considerable business acumen to maximise the club's financial clout, and vehemently opposed the maximum wage following its introduction in 1902 and took the FA and the League to task over this and many issues. His reputation was that of an autocrat; he worked to firm principles of what was 'right', and yet was also known as a champion of players' causes. Apt to be too coldly logical in his earlier days, he mellowed a good deal as the years went on.

His approach was important to the club at a time when football was not yet fully 'on its feet' in the early 1890s, despite the existence of the League. Appointed financial secretary in 1893, and director on the club's incorporation in 1896, he became chairman of the club in 1898. His chairmanship lasted until 1925. He was an energetic and imaginative worker for the Villa, and it is recorded that he was not averse to 'going down the pit' to sign up a needed player. Steve Smith, a coalminer and one of Villa's stars of the 1890s, was one such signing.

He was a member of the Football League Management Committee from 1917, and vice-president three times in the 1930s.

After various club failings in the mid-1930s, he came back into the club as a director in 1936, but died at the end of 1938 after playing a big part in getting the club back 'on stream'. Fred Rinder thus died whilst holding an important role in the club more than 45 years since first becoming involved in the club's administration.

In his obituary in *The Villa News* on the last day of 1938, it was stated that "he assumed high and onerous responsibilities alike in connection with the

The Aston Villa Chronicles 1874 – 1924 (and after)

Football Association and the Football League. He was an indefatigable member of the International Selection Committee, and was often placed in charge of representative sides. ... Yes, we have lost a big man, a man with a powerful brain and a large mind. We may never quite see his equal again ...".

John Devey- 1891 to 1934

A Brummie, this man captained the Villa through two Cup wins and five League Championships in eight years as skipper, after joining the club in March, 1891. He was a fitting successor as captain to the great Archie Hunter and many wonder how it was that he only obtained two international 'caps', though the long-term presence of Steve Bloomer was a main contributory factor to this injustice. His right-wing club partnership with Charlie Athersmith became legendary. Devey was an assistant to Joe Grierson after his playing retirement in 1902, and soon became a highly able director of the club, a post he held until September, 1934.

Howard Spencer – 1892 to 1936

Dubbed 'Prince of Full-backs', Howard Spencer – another Brummie – was one of the greatest defenders to play for Aston Villa, and possibly the classiest full-back of all before World War One. After being groomed at Birchfield Trinity by former Villa hero Arthur Brown, he played for the Villa junior team as an amateur in 1892. A professional from 1894, he played in the great teams of the later 1890s and was captain of the cup-winning side in 1905. He also captained his country, one of only three Aston Villa players to do so, and won three FA Cup Winners' medals – the only Villa player to do so. He played his last game in 1907 and in 1909 became an Aston Villa director – just in time for the resurgence of the Villa that lasted to the Great War. He remained a director until 1936.

Joe Grierson- 1893 to 1915

Another Scot, hailing from Dumfries, he was 'poached' from the strangely-titled Middlesbrough Ironopolis club. He made an immediate impact as the Villa's trainer, and had the single honour of training every one of Aston Villa's six League Championship winning sides (and five sides finishing as runner-up) during the 1893-1915 period. In addition, the

Villa had four FA Cup triumphs during his tenure as trainer.

Affectionately known as "Old Joe" by the players, it was said: "Slackers he cannot stand; the malingerer is to him an abomination, and his remarks to such are pungent and to the point; but to the honest trier, Joe is a well of wisdom, and a true friend."[21] It was also said, "Unlike some trainers, he is a great believer in making his man happy first and then training them afterwards. ... A great believer in the punching ball, ... one of the finest methods of keeping a man fit."[22]

"A cute judge of human nature, with a wonderful knowledge of physical demands." He was a champion runner – his favourite distances were 100 yards and 120 yards, but he also did well in the quarter-mile and half-mile.[23]

Freddie Miles and Harry Cooch – both players who trained under Grierson – became successful trainers at Villa Park after World War One.

Other Significant Personalities

Jack Hughes – Primarily remembered as being one of four who met to discuss the potential for the foundation of a football club (Aston Villa), and who scored the first-ever goal for the club. However, his playing days and his connection with the Villa far exceeded the other members in that initiating quartet, and he subsequently acted for the club as 'umpire' until 1882. The earliest history of the club as detailed in this book comes from a talk given by Jack Hughes, who actively supported the club into the twentieth century. In 1900, he was the only remaining member of the club that had been connected with the original founding Wesleyan Chapel.

Fergus Johnstone – Another Scot, he was a Villa vice-president from 1877 for about ten years, a great friend of the club and of William McGregor during a period of great crisis at the club in the mid-1880s.

Charlie Johnstone (Fergus Johnstone's son) – "A schoolmaster of considerable reputation"[24] (becoming headmaster at Jenkins Street school, Aston, and famed as a disciplinarian, though remembered with fondness by his pupils), he was an exceedingly good athlete. In the Midlands, he was bettered in his time in the 100 yards only by Villa's Tom Pank. He played for the Villa for a few years from 1877, and, "being a talker of great industry", it was he (according to Jack Urry[25] and confirmed by Charlie) who was a

---

[21] Charlie Johnstone in his column in The Sporting Mail 30 Aug 1913
[22] Midland Express 7 Mar 1903
[23] Villa News & Record 7 Jan 1911
[24] Villa News & Record 11 Oct 1913
[25] Villa News & Record 11 Oct 1919

significant influence on Archie Hunter to cause him to join the Villa. Charlie remained closely-linked to the Villa for the most part of the rest of his long life, including an important period as director – a committee man from 1892, he was one of the first directors of Aston Villa Football Club Limited in 1896, of which there were, initially, four. It was he, with Fred Rinder, who secured the deal with Henry Flower to obtain the Lower Grounds (Villa Park) as the Villa's new home. A man of many ideas, he proposed a players' bonus system that was adopted by the club in the late 1890s, and had strong views about training and coaching methods. He resigned his directorship in 1900, but he was subsequently always vocal at Villa's AGMs, and later became vice-president. He retired to Scotland in the mid-1920s, and died there in 1941.

Josiah Margoschis - A member of the club since the late 1870s, and a committee-man during the early 1890s, Jo. ('Mar') Margoschis was the first chairman of the re-formed Aston Villa 'Limited' in 1896, and retained that position through the 'double' season, the move to Villa Park, and to 1898, when he resigned on health grounds. He was subsequently made vice-president. 'Mar' was considerably involved in charitable activities undertaken by the club. A tobacconist, he was fond of new technology and used his shop window in Constitution Hill to display the telegraphed status of Villa's away matches.

Joseph Ansell – President of the club from 1893 till his death in 1923. Formerly the club's legal advisor (but did not always charge for his services, such was his affection for the club and its management), he continued in that role through his presidency.

George Kynoch – Founder and owner of the nearby munitions factory, and thus provider of employment to many Astonians. He was MP for Aston for a while, and was president of the club from 1885 to 1888. Shortly afterwards, he left England for South Africa. For a time, he was a considerable financial benefactor to the club, particularly in his funding of social and celebratory occasions.

The Aston Villa Chronicles 1874 – 1924 (and after)

Significant Dates in Villa History to 1924

The Formative Period (1874-81)

1874	The club's church-based inception.
1876	George Ramsay joined the club, greatly influenced the club's playing style, and was made captain. Also investment in the club's first permanent ground at Perry Bar.
1877	William McGregor became vice-president of Aston Villa.
1878	Archie Hunter joined the club, and, as Ramsay had done, greatly influenced the club's playing style. But his captaincy (from 1880) was his main contribution.
1880	**Villa's first trophy was won (the Birmingham Cup)**, followed by George Ramsay's playing retirement through injury, and Archie Hunter's election as captain.
1881	The first visit of Queens Park's first team to the Villa's ground at Perry Barr, which further influenced Villa's playing style.

A National Entity (1881-93)

1882	Villa's first England internationals: Vaughton and Brown.
1885	Professionalism became legal, and the club became professional.
1886	The first major reform of the management of the club led by William McGregor, with George Ramsay appointed as the first paid secretary/manager at the club
1887	**FA Cup Winners**; Villa's first national trophy. Claret and Light Blue became the club's colours.
1888	The Football League was established, primarily through the work of Villa vice-president and former primary committee-official William McGregor, with the Villa as a founder-member and runner-up in the League's first season.
1889	William McGregor put forward a proposal to reorganise the club as a limited company. An incorporation without profits was the outcome.
1890	The enforced retirement of Archie Hunter.
1892	FA Cup Finalists. Appointment of John Devey as captain.
1893	William McGregor's second attempt at pushing through a reorganisation of the club as a limited company. What ensued was a second radical re-organisation of the club's administration. Appointment of Joe Grierson as trainer.

The Aston Villa Chronicles 1874 – 1924 (and after)

The Golden Era (1894-1924)

1894	**League Champions** for the first-time; death of both Billy Mason (a significant club founder) and Archie Hunter.
1895	**FA Cup Winners.**
1896	**League Champions** and Aston Villa became a limited company.
1897	**Winners of the FA Cup and League Championship in one season (the 'double')**, and move of headquarters from Perry Bar to Aston Lower Grounds (Villa Park).
1898	Fred Rinder became chairman of the club.
1899	**League Champions,** the season ending spectacularly.
1900	**League Champions.**
1905	**FA Cup Winners.**
1910	**League Champions.**
1911	Villa missed out on a seventh championship on the last game of the season. Freehold acquisition of Aston Lower Grounds (Villa Park). Death of William McGregor.
1913	**FA Cup Winners** and, in finishing runners-up in the league, came close to winning a second 'double'.
1914	Major ground improvement starts.
1915	Football competition was halted between 1915 and 1919 (World War 1); Joe Grierson retired.
1920	**FA Cup Winners** under Freddie Miles as the club's new trainer.
1923	Opening of the then new Trinity Road stand. *This building was demolished and rebuilt during season 2000-01.*
1924	FA Cup Finalists.

In 1925, Fred Rinder's tenure as chairman and member of the Board came to an end. The following year, George Ramsay retired.

At 1924, of the 12 clubs that first entered the League in 1888, only the Villa, Everton and Blackburn Rovers had not at some point been relegated, though all three clubs would be relegated in the 1930s. Those three clubs have the record of being the only original members of the Football League that also became founder-members of the Premier League, in 1992.

A further feat of the Villa during this time was that having themselves won the League Championship and the Cup in the same season (the 'double') in 1897 – and only the second club to do so – it was they who prevented Newcastle United from achieving the same in the Cup Final of 1905, and then Sunderland in 1913. Much later, in 1957, the Villa also prevented Manchester United from achieving that record by beating them in the Cup Final.

The 'double' was not achieved again, after Villa's accomplishment, until 1961, by Tottenham Hotspur. To do so that season, Spurs had to beat the Villa on the way to winning the Cup. That Spurs side was captained by a former Villa favourite and a great talent, Danny Blanchflower. By this time, European football was becoming the order of the day for the successful teams, and national success at the League and Cup level (very slowly) became of lesser importance.

Villa's Influence on Football

William McGregor wrote, in 1905:

> If there is a club in the country which deserves to be dubbed the greatest (and the matter is one of some delicacy) few will deny the right of Aston Villa to share the highest niche of fame with even the most historic of other aspirants. For brilliancy and, at the same time, for consistency of achievement, for activity in philanthropic enterprise, for astuteness of management and for general alertness, the superiors of Aston Villa cannot be found. They may have rivals of equal worth, but in all the characteristics named, they have never been surpassed. ...[26]

A somewhat biased viewpoint, perhaps, but others also were full of praise for the role of Aston Villa in many respects, and the club's popularity was enormous. In March, 1907, Villa made a League visit to Newcastle, and *The Villa News* reported that Villa turned out on the pitch a few minutes in advance of the home players. The Villa team was "met with a reception that was distinctly flattering, and it really did one good to note the genuine ring of the cheers of welcome." Around that time Newcastle were a 'top dog' amongst English clubs.

There was no need to take William McGregor's word on the matter of the Villa's status and achievements. A Cup visit by the Villa to Manchester United in February, 1911 (less than twelve months after Villa's sixth championship success) elicited this comment in the club's new official programme:

> However conspicuous other clubs may appear for a season or so, there is no bedimming the splendid record of Aston Villa, who are rightly regarded as

---

[26] In 'The Romance of Aston Villa', The Book of Football, 1905

the elite of the football world. ... their playing record is easily the best in the country.

The Villa were strong in all departments, as Mr. William Isaia Bassett ('Billy' Bassett, the former great Albion winger) indicated in 1910:

> Aston Villa Reserves always play good football when I see them; in fact it seems ridiculous, in one sense, to speak of them as 'reserves'. I always look upon them as a First League team.[27]

In respect of Mr. McGregor's comment concerning "philanthropic enterprise", those words were uttered in the days of no government-sponsored social benefits nor health service, and the Villa were indeed at the forefront of support for care in the community – as indeed were other football clubs. Many were the charitable projects that Jo. Margoschis was involved with – invariably with the support of Messrs. McGregor, Ramsay and Rinder. Their benevolence caused Charlie Johnstone to remark:

> There is such an air of conscious rectitude and cold-blooded goodness about their [the directors'] doings, that one has an insane desire, metaphorically, to kick them for being so good and correct![28]

Mr. William Pickford made a contribution to *The Sporting Mail* that was reproduced in *The Villa News* in January, 1907. A respected sportswriter of the day, he contributed to quality sports periodicals such as *The Athletic News*, but he became more famous as co-author of the publication "Association Football and The Men Who Made It" (1905) and as a servant of the FA and its president in the late 1930s. Please note that references to "Birmingham" in his article are to the general place, *not* a specific club!:

> Looking at Birmingham in football from the distance of the South, it has been our nearest professional club centre. In the dark days when there was no decent football to be watched in the South other than the Corinthians, or chance holiday matches by touring teams, Birmingham, having the nearest class club, took a great place in the affections of the public. A trip to the Onion Fair meant a peep at the Villa, and I have no hesitation in saying that the Aston club stood with the Southern footballer for all that was best in the professional game. This is something to say. Moreover, the influence of Birmingham, in the 1890s at least, pervaded the South. In remote towns – nay, in the Metropolis itself – a man had only to say that he had played for

---

[27] In his column in The Sporting Mail 9 Apr 1910
[28] Charlie Johnstone, in his column in The Sporting Mail 2 Nov 1907

The Aston Villa Chronicles 1874 – 1924 (and after)

Aston Villa to be taken at his face value. It became almost a stock joke, but though some unworthy fellows tried to make capital out of having lived in 'Brum', the Villa were never deposed from their high pedestal. Archie and Andy Hunter, Dennis Hodgetts and Howard Vaughton were our earlier heroes, Reynolds, Athersmith and Crabtree [*no John Devey mentioned!*] of the middle period and Howard Spencer of the present. Nor did the South wax any less enthusiastic at one time over the Albion. They talk to this day [in 1906-07] of the Bassett-McLeod wing and remember the whipping that the Albion gave proud Preston in 1888.[29]

Even at a time when Villa's trophy-winning was at a relatively low ebb, William McGregor recorded:[30]

" *It was reckoned that thousands preferred going to see the Villa and Chelsea match instead of going to witness the final at the Palace last season [1907-08], both matches being played on the same day. The Villa are the most popular provincial club that visit the Metropolis.* "

But there was more modelling of play after the scientific plan of the Villa than after the dash and brilliancy of the Albion. And why? The Villa methods were ever more delightful, more skilful – taking the whole team – and more successful; and nothing, they say, succeeds like success. Moreover, 'clean' football always makes the best impression, and in the matter of honest sport, without more than the natural erring man's tincture of wickedness, Aston Villa were the Southerners' model and type of the game.

The South might easily have had a worse type, but it stands to the credit of the Aston club that from first to last it has set a high standard both of play and football management. A club – one might term it – with a conscience is bound to exercise a wise influence on others. And in the Villa we find … a club that has a clean and honourable record – law-abiding, progressive, and up-to-date. It points a moral when we find a leading London writer discussing in a recent article the question as to which Southern club is the 'Villa of the South'!

---

[29] In the FA Cup Final of that year. But Albion also whipped Preston in the previous year's semi-final.
[30] In his column in Sports Argus 19 Sep 1908

The Aston Villa Chronicles 1874 – 1924 (and after)

The Downside

To give the impression that the Villa of old were an always-successful side that never knew the meaning of doubt, and never lacked motivation, or didn't at some point have villainy (not just *villany*!) afoot within its portals, would be totally wrong. This book will bring to light the major occurrences of 'growing pains' within the club, but rarely has there been such an organisation that has been able to renew itself from its calamities, and each time, it would seem, then gone on from strength to strength.

On the pitch, things were not always as they have since been perceived to be; it was not always success and happiness. But what kind of failure was it when a reporter could state (in 1900, when Villa were noted for their scoring achievements!): "The Villa ... get such endless [scoring] opportunities, but what percentage of their opportunities do they turn to good account? A very small one, indeed!" And as confirmed by 'Brum':

> There has never been a time in my football history (and that embraces a quarter of a century), when Aston Villa have not been a clever side in midfield. Their faults have usually been lack of dash and irresolution in front of goal ...[31]

In other words, the Villa's main playing failure was in their inability – or lack of will – to turn opportunities into more goals, and this seemed to be an endemic weakness – it went on from one generation of players to another. A fictional dialogue on this matter and the matter of consistency, between fictional Villans named as Jim and Bill, appeared in *The Villa News* in 1908:

> Bill: "...I don't deny the cleverness and other good stuff that is in Aston Villa, Jim, but I do think they ought to be a bit more consistent."
>
> "You may be right about that, Bill," said the older footballer, "... but it's always been a characteristic of theirs. It was so in Archie Hunter's days; it was even in the middle and late [eighteen-]nineties, when they made such a reputation for themselves and I suppose that a failing of this sort will stick to them, whoever comes and goes in the eleven, like birth-marks stick to people - all the time. Helps to make their displays more varied, Bill, d'yer see? It would never do for them to be right on the top of their form, or their play would get what they call monotonous, wouldn't it?"

---

[31] Athletic News 2 Jan 1905

The Aston Villa Chronicles 1874 – 1924 (and after)

"Not to me, it wouldn't," said Bill, with a laugh, "nor to a lot more. Perhaps some season or other, if I live long enough, I shall see the Villa play three tip-top matches in succession, but I'm blest if I've ever seen it yet, and when I do I shall be a good deal older. What puzzles me, Jim, is this: Football players are paid to do certain things like other people. Well, the majority of professionals act up their profession consistently - say, for instance, actors. What would be said of some of the first-raters if one night they played their parts, humorous or tragic, in a manner that brought down the house, as the saying is, and the next practically made fools of themselves, wholly or partly to the disgust of the audience? What d'yer think the newspapers would say? Think they'd make excuses for that sort of inconsistency?"

"Ha! That's all right my young friend," answered Jim: "but football ain't a theoretical game, and can't be performed by rule, so to speak. It mostly depends upon circumstances; and though I'll admit that few of the team play with anything like the consistency which might be expected, don't forget that opposing excellence very often takes away from the brilliance of the other side. D'yer twig what I mean?"

"No, I'm blamed if I do," said Bill, "nor do I understand why there should be all the cost of up-and-down form. Fact is, Jim, you know the Villa didn't play anything like a good game against Leicester Fosse, and, like so many of their partisans, you're trying to make excuses for them. You know that the defence was, with the exception of George, unsound; that the half-backs were not so good as they ought to have been; that the forwards were seldom together, even if they were sometimes damned clever; and the result of the match was a great disappointment to the people who saw it, especially after what they had seen against Manchester. I grant you that no team can play right up to first-rate form every time; but, hang it, there's a difference between the top and pretty nearly the bottom round of the ladder, and I say again that the display against Leicester Fosse was not worthy of the team's reputation."

"Have your own way, Bill," said Jim resignedly; "perhaps you'll live all the longer for it; but you ain't giving the strangers fair play while you're lolloping it on the Villa chaps; and they managed to draw the game anyhow."

"Yes!", growled Bill, "but everybody said they were going to win; and there were times when they were darn near losing. Perhaps they'll do better against Notts County next week?" [They didn't: it was another draw!]

"Should think they would, my son; but take my tip; and be satisfied with little points when you can't have big ones, and drop the idea that any set of players can do just exactly as you want 'em to. 'Taint in human nature - at least, not in the football part of it. Keep your pecker up ... So long!"

The Aston Villa Chronicles 1874 – 1924 (and after)

Monetary Values in the Period Covered by this Book

Throughout this book, reference is made to monetary sums in pounds (sterling) in relation to player purchases, 'gate' receipts and profit.[32] Please note that those sums of money are quoted as they were at the time; the value of the pound depreciated hardly at all in the decades up to World War One. The value of the pound (sterling) in 1900 should be taken as about £70 in year 2000 money.[33] However, a multiplier of 70 does not successfully equate to modern day values! Others have reckoned that the average urban working-class man's wage in those times – £1 per week – is equivalent to £150 today. A middle-class professional worker would then earn about £6 per week. So, though the star footballer (at £4 per week from 1902) was quite highly paid according to the time, he was not paid above the then typical professional worker.

---

[32] In pre-decimalisation days (1971), pounds were made up of shillings and pence, and not just pence as is the case today. There were 20 shillings to the pound and 12 pence to the shilling. Sixpence (or six pennies) were equivalent to 2.5 pence in today's system; one shilling would be equivalent to 5 pence (today). An added complexity in the monetary system in those pre-decimalisation days was the use of 'guineas' - £1 1s. 0d. being the value of one guinea.

[33] 2003 UK Parliamentary Research paper: Inflation: the value of the pound, 1750-2002

The Aston Villa Chronicles 1874 – 1924 (and after)

2. The Development of Football

To put Aston Villa's history into context perhaps needs a preliminary general description of how Association Football – or 'soccer' – developed. It took until the late 1880s before soccer evolved into anything like the game that we know today, and even after then and before 1925, the game went through other transformations. The game has gone through many detailed changes since, but by 1925 the fundamentals of the game had been settled.

Early Developments

Football in Britain is an ancient sport that preceded even King Edward III's edict of 1389 that forbade the playing of football on account of its interference with the practise of archery. Even that renowned man of verse and drama, and erstwhile Midlander – who would surely have been a Villa supporter! – William Shakespeare, mentions football twice in his works:

The Comedy of Errors: Act 2, Scene 1

> Dromio of Ephesus:
>> *Am I so round with you as you with me,*
>> *That like a football you do spurn me thus?*
>> *You spurn me hence, and he will spurn me hither:*
>> *If I last in this service, you must case me in leather.*

King Lear: Act 1, Scene 4

> Kent:
>> *Nor tripped neither, you base football player.*

However, the very start was (for all practical purposes) the matter of how Association Football itself developed from the primitive football days, when rugby and soccer were yet to be distinguished and led to bruising encounters. It seems that Sir Walter Scott recorded the details of such a primitive match between the people of the Dale of Yarrow and those of the Parish of Selkirk, which took place on 4 December, 1815.[34]

A Frenchman, passing through Derby in 1829, when observing a football match, remarked, "If Englishmen call this 'playing', what do they call 'fighting'?"[35]

---

[34] Scott's account was re-printed in an article by Wm McGregor, Sports Argus 15 Sep 1906
[35] Sports Argus 1 Oct 1904

The Aston Villa Chronicles 1874 – 1924 (and after)

In the *Athletic News* of 15 January, 1879, there was printed a reminiscence of a match played in 1855, which stated, amidst the details of the match – long before the advent of shin-guards:

> The boots worn by the majority were formidable in the extreme, the soles being covered with the customary large hob-nails, and I shuddered at the thought of getting a kick on my shins instead of the ball.

The origin of shin-guards came about in 1874, when 'hacking' was rife in the game. Fred Ward wrote: "if an opponent's leg was in your way, and there was a doubt about you getting the ball, you could just remove that leg and get along with the ball."[36]

Old Fogey added:

> Those were the times when the players used to go for the ball practically regardless of consequences, and when they couldn't take their gruel standing up, they used to crawl away with it. …. They rested all day on Sunday, and sometimes had to hobble to work on Monday.[37]

Archie Hunter added to the stories of those early days of organised football:

> It used to be very amusing at one time … to see the backs fall down in the field and cause their opponents to fly headlong over them … You see your opponent advancing at top speed with the ball and instead of trying to take the leather from him you drop suddenly upon your knee and over he goes … It was highly dangerous … and thus a rule was properly passed prohibiting it.[38]

Old Fogey wrote this general account of soccer's development from the mid-1800s and into the 20th century:

> [In the 1850s] 'Socker' (of a kind) was played regularly in Steeldom [Sheffield] and was indeed intensely popular there, long before it became more than crudely known in the Midlands. First, from Sheffield it drifted down South, and London and the Universities took it up and started to 'refine it' in their way, and unquestionably handled it in a manner that made it more likeable to the public taste; then it went to Scotland, permeated Lancashire and at length obsessed the Midlands.

---

[36] In his book on Aston Villa (1948)
[37] Villa News & Record 30 Nov 1912 – "The Old Game"
[38] "Triumphs of the Football Field", Birmingham Weekly Mercury, October, 1890 to February, 1891

The Aston Villa Chronicles 1874 – 1924 (and after)

[The offside rule was introduced in the 1870s. Until then,] the football race was to the strong rather than scientific, and the pastime was more conspicuous for form and speed than for skill and pretty pedipulation.

Those amongst us who remember the game when it was played under 'Sheffield Rules'[39] will recollect the violent and prolonged scrimmages which used to take place under the shadow of the goalposts, the individualistic character of the play, and the utter selfishness in which the more able men were wont to indulge.

It was an entirely different game to that which we see today [in 1908], for there was hardly any idea of passing; long kicks and strenuous rushes, with occasional dribbles by conspicuously clever people were the order of the play, and the poor old custodian used to see heaps of trouble. For, generally speaking, all of the forwards… [were] deputed to attend to the man between the sticks, and immediately the ball verged in his direction, so surely did this pulverising scout make tracks for the goalkeeper, and when the shooting came or a raid took place, the chap who was supposed to hold the fort was bundled over, knocked flying through his goal, or horizontalised with two or three of the attacking party sitting heavily on his chest, what time the other folk garnered points [i.e. goals]![40]

As to the source of quality football, Old Fogey commented:

… it must be confessed that the Scots were the people who mostly taught us to play football in the combinative and scientific way we see it at its best [in the years to 1926]. … [Some would gnash their teeth] and remind me of the great 'public school' elevens such as the Old Etonians, the Old Carthusians, and others of what may be termed the helter-skelter variety. They were good to see, but they were no respecter of persons, and they always appeared to me a collection of eleven men waiting for the ball, and when any one of them got it, he made off for goal 'on his own' without remembering (except by accident) that he had any comrades.[41]

Old Fogey also alluded to the rough nature of the 'public schools' play that would, in later years, automatically invoke the referee's whistle and hoots of protest from the crowd. That style was supplanted by the methodical game of the Scots during the

---

[39] "They were written in a garden shed on 24 October 1857 at the formation of Sheffield FC by pioneers of the sport Nathaniel Creswick and William Prest. [These laws] allowed the ball to be headed for the first time, introduced wooden crossbars, free kicks, corners *and the idea of floodlights*." (*The Independent*, 8 November 2007)
[40] Villa News & Record 15 Feb 1908 – "The Development of Football"
[41] Villa News & Record 5 and 6 Apr 1926 ("Some More Villa History")

The Aston Villa Chronicles 1874 – 1924 (and after)

1870s and 1880s. Old Fogey later added:

> Football is played half as fast again as it was twenty years ago [early 1880s]: there is very little of the clever deliberation about it that marked the movements of the giants of old; and I am not traducing the ancient exponents of the pastime when I say that if it were possible to put an eleven of them today in the field in all their pristine vigour, a modern side would make hares of them.
>
> The game as played today [i.e. in 1910] is a kaleidoscopic dazzle compared to the comparatively gently moving mosaic we witnessed when the amateur reigned and the professional was not yet.
>
> Year by year it has been, to use a motoring expression, 'speeded up', till it has grown into an almost feverish sparkle; and old inhabitants who watched the perhaps prettier, and certainly more leisurely 'carpet-weaving' that went on in Archie Hunter's palmy days, are sometimes amazed at the prodigious pace and power which has been introduced.[42]

Old Fogey also wrote this overview on the growth of the sport:

> The unpolished novice started copying his more finished comrade, and if these were real and loyal club fellows they very soon coalesced, and a first-rate man or two not only served to lever the whole 'leven, so to speak; but attracted other players with ambitions and ability.
>
> Nearly every club started like that, and particularly this may be said of the Villa, the Albion, and one or two other organisations which still flourish.
>
> When the friends of the players told *their* friends about the doings of the 'boys', the latter were attracted, and they in their turn chattered about the joyance of certain spectacles in the football line, so that quite a little crowd assembled to witness the deeds of derring-do of the young and enthusiastic striplings.
>
> Then the generous-hearted subscribed to their expenses in the matters of rent, outfit, and care of the ground; and then Mr. Mammon insinuated himself into the hon. secretary's brainpan, and suggested [chargeable] admission to the field — always a 'small' charge at first, mark you, with the residue (if any) to some charitable object.
>
> After that the desire for publicity grew, and so there sprang up certain journals (mostly of the amateur persuasion), and criticism became the order of the day; though tentatively a sort of running account of the game was tried, and 'personal' remarks were not ventured upon for a start.

---

[42] Villa News & Record 31 Dec 1910 (Old Fogey)

The Aston Villa Chronicles 1874 – 1924 (and after)

> But they came eventually, and sometimes grew virulent — so much so, indeed, that I could give a good many instances where the scribe was threatened with grave and painful consequences. These criticisms were sometimes piquant and often picturesque, and there was developed a style of football writing which has continued even unto this day; though I make no doubt that the modern critic fancies himself a much more able chap than any of those who started the game.
>
> Anyhow, I frequently hap upon expressions and phrases which were coined from an original mint a quarter of a century and more ago, and feel quite delighted to renew the acquaintance of old friends. All this, of course, naturally put the players on their mettle; and then came the invasion of the daily press, when all the spade-work of the enthusiasts had made easy digging for the monopolists.
>
> 'Gates' grew tremendously, and with the 'gates' came the exploitation of the players.
>
> Local heart-burnings and tribal jealousies were high and rife, and 'missionary' work became the duty — and very often the delight — of partisans and those who desire the triumph of their team at almost any cost.
>
> That, roughly put, is how spectacular football grew in the Midlands, and it was much the same elsewhere, till it was solidified and systematised with the advent of the League, the brain-child of Mr. William McGregor, and unquestionably the salvation of the game from a public point of view.

Charlie Johnstone wrote[43] that in 1872 he had not even heard of Association Football. "Football was then played mainly by public schoolboys, 'Varsity men and the professional or semi-professional classes. It was not until 1874, at Aston Park, that I had my earliest view of the strange new game." He went on to comment on the development of arbitration in match disputes, stating that in the late 1870s, referees – or umpires – were unknown; instead, the two captains settled all disputed points:

> The next step was the evolution of the club umpire... Jack Hughes... was our umpire [from 1878 to 1882]. What he could not fish the other man into was not worth having! Then came two umpires, each responsible for the play in his own half, with a referee who only gave decisions when appealed to.[44]

Then came the referee as is now known, but also with the two club umpires (linesmen).

---

[43] In his column in The Sporting Mail 8 Nov 1913
[44] In his column in The Sporting Mail 24 Nov 1906

The Aston Villa Chronicles 1874 – 1924 (and after)

Late 19th Century Developments, and Since

With regard to how the game was played back in the 1880s and 1890s, perhaps it would be useful to make some comparisons. The game was played somewhat differently in a number of respects, but many of the significant changes since that time (not the fundamentals of the game) have only come about since the early 1960s. Other changes have been more cosmetic in nature.

Possibly the most significant differences in the game concern the team formation; in the earliest days of 'soccer', there was in fact little sense of organisation – the play was essentially a charge by virtually the whole team, but gradually the idea of having backs and half-backs came into being. The formation of two full backs, two half-backs and six forwards (with two centre-forwards) became common – but it was not the only system. Some teams – including the Villa – modified this to one full-back and three half-backs, but after their initial encounter with Queen's Park in 1881, Villa relaxed that tendency, especially against clever sides, but it was not until April, 1883 that the use of two full-backs – but with two half-backs – was formally ratified by the Villa Committee. Then, from the mid/late 1880s to the early 1960s (in Britain), the accepted 'formation' was two full-backs, three half-backs, and five forwards, with the right-hand 'pair' of forwards working as a unit, as would the left-hand pair. The centre-half, however, was originally not the defensive player that we know of today.

The two extreme right and left-side forwards were known as 'wingers' and generally played in those positions because of their pace and ability to beat defenders with speed and trickery, in addition to being able to centre the ball well. This formation, in reality, was not so fixed as may be thought, as the half-back line in particular had to work in concert with the forwards, and 'triangulation' was the system often used by the scientific sides in the linkage between half-backs and forwards.

A good centre-forward would be regarded as one who would 'feed' the wings when he received the ball in a deep position, and, hopefully, capitalise when the winger would centre the ball into the goal. Harry Hampton was of that ilk, but such was his energy, he was often seen helping in defence. If the team was reduced to 10 men for some reason, he was sometimes re-positioned at centre-half. And this was a player who also managed to score 242 goals for the Villa! It was later on that the centre-forward would primarily be regarded as a goalscorer/striker.

This then, was the accepted formation of a football team from the later 1880s until the 1960s:

The Aston Villa Chronicles 1874 – 1924 (and after)

Goalkeeper

Right-back   Left-back

Right-half   Centre-half   Left-half

Outside-right   Inside-right   Centre-forward   Inside-left   Outside-left

It was generally true that if a team had a strong half-back line (allied to an otherwise skilful side), then the team would be likely contenders for some kind of honours. This maxim seemed to prove itself time and time again; certainly the Villa's best and most successful teams were strong at half-back. Today, we think of 'midfield' being a key area for a successful team, and that corresponds to the thoughts about the half-backs of earlier times. G. O. Smith, a great amateur player, and captain of England in the late 1890s, wrote:

> A half-back must be possessed of almost every quality that football requires; he must be as a good a tackler and as sure a kick as a back, and must dribble and pass with equal skill to a forward. He must be able to head well, and be a good shot at goal, as on wet grounds an opportunity often occurs for him to put in a shot; he must, too, be quick and active, since his work is offensive and defensive, and he must be with his forwards when they are attacking, and with his backs when they are, in turn, attacked; in fine, a half-back must be everywhere, and if he is slow he will be unable to fulfil all that his position demands.[45]

Perhaps the same could be said today of a midfielder. Note that Smith's description of the half-back applied equally to the centre-half of those days.

Villa had centre-halves such as Cowan (1890s), Buckley (1906-1912), Harrop (1910s) and Barson (early 1920s), who, with their colleagues at wing-half, achieved all that was required according to Smith's specification, but the job of the centre-half was later reduced to being a more defensive role – more the 'centre-back' of today, whose upfield involvement tends to be restricted to dead-ball situations (free-kicks and corner-kicks). In fact, the main change in the centre-half's style eventually came about following a change in the offside law that came about in 1925. Herbert Chapman, already a League winning manager with Huddersfield, and soon to start an even better record with Arsenal, is said to have taken the advice of star player Charlie Buchan to be the first to start the new fashion in making the centre-half a 'stopper' defender, and moved the two full-backs out wider, to cover the wings. Deprecating this approach, R. Allen wrote:

---

[45] Quoted in Sports Argus 1 Oct 1898

The Aston Villa Chronicles 1874 – 1924 (and after)

> [The] dominating Frank Barson and Christopher Buckley were centre-half backs of the classic touches, who, against the modern [i.e. late 1920s-onwards] development of centre-half back tactics, did the whole of the job instead of remaining with the backs and waiting for the game to come to them. [46]

It is extremely difficult to compare star Villa centre-halves (or centre-backs) of different eras. The styles and duties of the 1890s' star James Cowan, and the 1990s' star Paul McGrath were quite different, though McGrath was seen to have the occasional sortie upfield.

As a hangover from the earlier times of football, charging the goalkeeper was also very much tolerated. Until quite recently, a goal could be scored by an attacker barging the goalkeeper into the net – as was seen in the televised 1958 cup final – provided the keeper was in possession of the ball. Early twentieth century match reports contained descriptions of the keeper being barged into the net, a skill of which Harry Hampton was master – a proposition that would certainly not be tolerated these days!

With regard to how the goalkeeper was treated:

> In olden times, a forward was told to act as a human battering ram. His duty was to bundle the keeper through the goal as soon as the ball was anywhere in the vicinity of the posts. The keeper defended himself in various ingenious ways. Sometimes he would punch the ball with one hand and the attacker with the other; sometimes he would duck and throw him over his shoulder, or he would raise a knee for his delectation!
>
> This came to be regarded as somewhat dangerous and barbarous, so the keeper has been provided with a marked-out space called the goal-area, in which he must not be charged except when actually charging the ball. [47]

Shoulder charging (not just on the goalkeeper) was part and parcel of the game in the early days, and has never truly disappeared. Even in the early 1900s, however, robust charges were frowned upon by many referees. This seems to have led to underhand fouling (shirt-tugging etc) which even today is regularly witnessed.

It was remarked upon that, in the early days of football, referees were quite lenient:

> … if the charge was a trifle more energetic than intended [then] 'sorry, old chap', and on with the play! The man bowled over did not dream of

---

[46] "All in the Day's Sport" (Ch.3) (1946)
[47] Charlie Johnstone in his column in The Sporting Mail 12 Nov 1910

The Aston Villa Chronicles 1874 – 1924 (and after)

resenting it. ....[48]

Football boots and the ball were very much a different pattern to the modern form, being made of leather and needing much more maintenance. The heading of a thoroughly rain-soaked laced leather football is an experience that will soon be gone from the living reservoir of human memory.

It was not until the 1960s that players often had multiple roles. Previously, for example, a full-back was generally purely a defensive player, although there were exceptions to the rule such as Stan Lynn of the 1950s and '60s, who scored many notable goals for the Villa and then Birmingham City, and holds the Villa goals record for a full-back. He even once scored a hat-trick in a match, though two of those were penalty kicks. The term 'wing-back' was very much a later connotation. However, there were some teams in the earlier days that were good enough, tactically, to organise themselves so that the team defended as a unit, and also attacked as a unit, as appropriate.

Some attempt at comparison between the play of the old era and as it is now is inevitable, but without having been there in those days of yore, how can one truly compare? Well, on this issue my highly-respected virtual friend of the 'Villa List' (a mailing list on the Internet), Steve Wade, made this observation:

> I would say that the physical difference between Villa's elite athletes and the watching crowd would have been greater than it is now. I can only imagine that for the working class (especially non-skilled) it must have been like watching Greek gods in action to see the Villa then.
>
> There's no doubt in my mind that footballers would have represented the genetic and nutritional elite of the working classes and of course still do but possibly to a lesser extent.
>
> These days the gene-pool is a lot bigger and average heights and weights have definitely increased. These days being six foot is quite unremarkable (we have to be reminded that Beckham and Ronaldo are six-footers).
>
> I have little doubt that today's footballers would be by far the physical superiors to the early teams but as the Villa's creaking Old Boys prove every time they slaughter some amateurs, the game is probably more about brains than brawn, and the outstanding players of any era would be outstanding in others.
>
> But I suspect that the game has changed so much over the years, that it has to be considered an entirely different game to those early decades. One can

---

[48] Charlie Johnstone in his column in The Sporting Mail 29 Sep 1906

The Aston Villa Chronicles 1874 – 1924 (and after)

wonder at the ability of the players to deal with the weight of the old ball but you can't have it both ways - the heavy ball must have slowed the game down. But faster is not better, I hear you say.

I have little doubt that a modern team would beat any of the late and greats.

It is very difficult to argue with Steve on his point of view. Old Fogey (in 1908) may have spoken about how fast the game had then become, but whether it was as fast as it is now is perhaps open to question. That players could do marvellous tricks with the old (more firm, and sometimes heavy) ball, however, seems beyond doubt, especially as there are many that survive who can recall the skills of Matthews, Finney, Shackleton, Haynes, Blanchflower, Bobby Charlton, and a certain George Best. And that's not even talking of the great Magyar and Brazilian sides, and of Real Madrid of the late 1950s.

Near the end of Old Fogey's life in the mid-1920s, there were still a fair number that attended at Villa Park who remembered the old days at Perry Barr. Old Fogey wrote many accounts of those old days, and was not slow to mention that those old supporters' eyes would sparkle at the particular mention of Archie Hunter's captaincy, and also the 'double' side of 1896-97. No matter how much football had developed by the 1920s, the quality of the old ones was at that time still a standard that people talked of in fondness, as though the play in those days was the epitome of everything that had been the finest in association football.

─ · ─ · ─ · ─ · ─ · ─ · ─ ·

One very new aspect of the game came about (in the League) only in the mid-1960s: the substitute. When first introduced, only one substitute was allowed and could only be used in case of severe injury, but soon the rule was also used tactically. In the earlier days of football, a serious injury (which was very frequent) meant that a team had to rely on the players left on the field, and going by reports of matches in the early days it seems that reduction of the side by one player did not often, by itself, create undue cause for concern that the match might be lost.[49] However, the incidence of players having to permanently leave the field, or becoming a 'passenger' on the wing, was very high, and the eventual final 'nudge' towards the introduction of substitutes probably came about as a result of a series of injuries in FA Cup Finals in the 1950s – particularly the severe injuries to goalkeepers Bert Trautmann (1956) and Ray Wood (1957), and in a number of outfield situations.

---

[49] In a 1920s match, Villa were leading 2-0 when they lost a player, but still won 7-1.

The Aston Villa Chronicles 1874 – 1924 (and after)

Other major differences implemented in the 1980s concern the change of the number of points for a win (increased from two to three), and that 'goal difference' instead of 'goal average' would be used to distinguish between teams on the same number of points.

There was another interesting facet in the old days – at least as far as Villa was concerned until quite late on. That is that the captain appears to have had more responsibility. There are innumerable cases reported where the captain made on-the-pitch decisions on who should play where – especially if someone was being tried in a new position and was not making sufficient impact, or in the case of a serious injury to a player and a reformation of the team was imposed. This arrangement probably suited the situation (as in Villa's case until the 1930s) where the team was decided upon by a committee, and no specific team manager or coach with responsibility was officially appointed, other than the club manager/secretary and trainer.

The Aston Villa Chronicles 1874 – 1924 (and after)

3. How Aston Villa Began

It was the late Mr. G. L. Wilson[50] who proved that in the 19th century, the area of Lozells where Villa Road, Lozells Road and Heathfield Road joined was known as "Aston Villa" – so-called after a large Georgian house of that name (a type called a 'villa') which stood at the junction of Lozells Road and Heathfield Road.[51]

Just prior to the FA Cup Final of 1905, the editor of the Manchester publication, the *Athletic News*, went so far as to say that *every* schoolboy knew the story of Aston Villa and their Wesleyan roots.

Not just Birmingham schoolboys, and not even just Midlands' schoolboys, but *all* schoolboys!

Such was the fame of the Villa in those days.

In 1850, the 'Aston Villa Wesleyan Chapel' came to be established close by. This was followed by a more substantial building in 1865 that remained a Methodist Chapel until 1962. From that Chapel was started the cricket club, followed two years later (in 1874) by the football club. Both entities were formed from the Bible Class of the Chapel run by Mr. H. H. Hartshorne,[52] who became the football club's first president.

It was written, in 1946, by a sportsman of forty years pedigree in watching the Villa:

> If Aston Villa had not, for more than seventy years, stuck tenaciously to the ideals born in a Sunday school class, nurtured and developed by a succession of officials and players, never completely swamped by the modern crazes for figures and quick results, the youngest player in their reserve side would not have had justification for sticking his chest out, whatever story the figures told.[53]

Although this statement probably does not sum up all the reasons for Villa's success, it possibly provides some indication of how much emphasis was put on ideals from the very start.

---

[50] Who happened to live in the same small street at Warwick as a cousin of mine, after moving from Erdington. Mr. Wilson's father (and perhaps G. L. Wilson himself) was very much involved with the early Wesleyan Chapel at Aston Villa.
[51] Aston Villa is named in Robins 1824 map as standing at the junction of Lozells Road and Heathfield Road. The house named Aston Villa became the Villa Cross 'pub'. The original building was replaced by a new 'pub' in 1937.
[52] Villa News & Record & Record 25 Jan 1913
[53] R. Allen, in "All in The Day's Sport" (Chapter 3 on Aston Villa) (1946)

The Aston Villa Chronicles 1874 – 1924 (and after)

> After Aston Villa won the Cup in 1897 – and thus having also won the 'double' that season – Joseph Ansell, the then Villa president, stated:
>
> " Football, and Aston Villa in particular, have done as much as any temperance movement to keep working men out of the public houses. "

A lot of the initial momentum came from the developing ethos of service and striving that became part of 19th century Christianity. In many areas of England, organised football evolved as a Christian development to divert youths from gang-fights and drunkenness as a method to instil finer qualities of character – fair play, teamwork, unselfishness and self-control. From the earliest days at Aston Villa, emphasis was placed upon teamwork and togetherness, and the club was led by several men of great character.

However, the launch of 'Aston Villa (Wesleyan) Football Club' – as the club was initially called – had first to be given approval, as Peter Lupson states:

> The new minister, the Reverend Robert Balshaw, and the new circuit superintendent, the Reverend William Williams, would have to be approached. Fortunately, Balshaw, a man known for his great humility and kindness, and Williams, a warm approachable Welshman, were supportive.[54]

The Villa was a seed that, with the coming of individuals of great skill and character, gradually grew into a sapling before becoming a well-rooted tree – and in the process finding world-wide fame. It was even the time before the term *Villan* had been concocted, and when eventually that 'word' first came into circulation (through the word art of Old Fogey – Jack Urry), the worry was that the term sounded so vulgar that it might blacken the name of the Villa![55]

The Very Start

It is possible that the sewing of the seed of football in the minds of the young men of Aston Villa began a little earlier than many have imagined. I was recently privy to a portion of the family history of a Phillips family, where it refers to Harry Phillips (1843-1932) who was apparently head of Lozells Street Boys' School in the period 1870 onwards. Now it seems that he was keen on athletic sports, and went so far as to promote Association Football at the school and encouraged the pupils to further that interest in 'old boys' teams. The family history asserts that it was as a result of this effort of Harry's (and his brother Edward) that old boys of Lozells Street School

---

[54] In "Thank God for Football" (Peter Lupson, 2006)
[55] Villa News & Record Christmas 1923 – "Some Famous Players"

The Aston Villa Chronicles 1874 – 1924 (and after)

came to form Aston Villa FC.

Well, it is quite likely that some of those old boys did participate in the formation of Aston Villa FC, but perhaps not quite in the way that that family history suggests, although it is of great interest to note that perhaps some players did have 'soccer' skills before they came to form the Villa.

The story of how the Villa came into being and its early development was given as a talk by a founding member and player with the club, **Jack Hughes**, to the Old Villans Society on Monday, 4 December, 1899. The talk was reported in the *Sports Argus* later that week. Hughes briefly related the Wesleyan church connection, and how the cricket club was formed,[56] and the next part of Jack Hughes' talk was reported as follows:

> In February of that year [1874], a few members of the cricket club went to see a football match at Heathfield Road, Handsworth. The competing teams were the Handsworth Rugby Club and the [Moseley] Grasshoppers. **[Billy] Mason** was then playing for the Grasshoppers and the cricketers were anxious to see what the game then played was like.
>
> They were favourably impressed with it, and after its finish they met in conference under the glimmer of a gas lamp at [Villa][57] Cross.

Jack Hughes

The delegation that met under the gas lamp – **W. H. Price, W. Scattergood, Jack Hughes** and **George Matthews** – were the prime acknowledged 'movers' of the fledgling football club, but they did not do so without considerable help from Billy Mason, as mentioned. It is possible that he was Villa's first but unofficial (honorary) secretary in between 1874 and 1876, when the Villa held their first AGM. Then, the first official (honorary) secretary – D. J. Stephens it would seem – was elected. It *is* certain that Mason became honorary secretary in 1881 after he ceased

---

[56] The cricket club founders were given as: W. Scattergood, G. Matthews, W. Price, J. Hughes, W. Weiss, W. Davis, W. Griffiths, F. Knight, C. Midgley, J. Swimgrood, C. Foster, T. Fraggart.

[57] The *Sports Argus* report actually says "Aston Cross", but I feel that the reporter must have mistyped his report, as all other reports as to the whereabouts of that meeting specifically state Villa Cross, particularly that the meeting was in the aforementioned Heathfield Road. It is certainly more logical that the meeting would have been in the Villa Cross area, that being the locality of their church, and the report also states that the meeting took place at the finish of the match they had witnessed nearby.

The Aston Villa Chronicles 1874 – 1924 (and after)

playing and that he was Hon. Treasurer before that. It is also a fact that Billy Mason was one of only two players to bridge the very start of the club and the winning of their first trophy in 1880; the other of the two was **E. B. ("Teddy") Lee**, who became the last playing survivor of the original team, and whose play grew magnificently, in step with his club. The report on Hughes' talk continued:

> [Under the gaslamp] the features of the game were discussed, and with one accord they decided to start on the Association game the following Saturday. Thus humbly was how the mighty Aston Villa born. Their resolution they gave effect to when they played a practise game on a plot of land at Westminster Road, exactly where the church now stands. After the game, fifteen players subscribed one shilling each[58] – the first funds into the coffers of the Aston Villa. [When this occurred appears to have been the first week in March, 1874, as reported fifty years later.[59]]

The fifteen who thus laid the foundations of the club will undoubtedly prove of interest now:

W. Scattergood, G. Matthews, W. Price, W. Mason, J. Hughes, W. Weiss, E. B. Lee, F. Knight, C. Midgley, W. Such, H. Matthews, W. Sothers, G. Page, A. Robins, G. Greaves.

The new football club practised assiduously, and after a time they found themselves in a position to take on matches. Their first opponents were Aston St. Mary's. The first half of the game was played under Rugby rules ... The second half was under 'Socker' rules, and while no scoring occurred in the first period, a goal was notched for Villa in the second by Mr. J. Hughes. They won by this goal to nothing.

The first-ever Villa team formation according to Norman Edwards and A. G. Taylor (an early journalist).

---

[58] Equivalent to five new pence, but about 3 pounds and 50 pence each in 2006 values.
[59] Sports Argus 1 Mar 1924

The Aston Villa Chronicles 1874 – 1924 (and after)

With the exception of H. Whateley in place of G. Greaves,[60] the fifteen who played in the first match are the same fifteen quoted by Jack Hughes as those who "laid the foundations of the club". Of course, when the first match was played it is not inconceivable that one of the founders might have had an enforced absence from the team and had to be substituted.

The ground for that first match was loaned by a local land-owner, 'Mr. Wilson', according to both A. G. Taylor and the *Birmingham Daily Gazette*, 4 April 1887. A. G. Taylor, Norman Edwards and other authors further state that that match was played in March, 1874, but it has to be admitted that there is a doubt, as there are a number of articles that refer to October, 1874 as the occasion of the first match. However, in the several documents and publications I have seen written by early scribes, there is no indication that the first match could have been after October, 1874. All the indications are that the first match must have taken place in 1874. Further, as it is also thought that only one match was played in their first season, and as the season in those days finished at the end of March, then March, 1874 as the occasion of the first match (as stated by Taylor and Edwards) gains credence, especially as we know that at least one other match was played in the next (1874-75) season.

That first match against St. Mary's was a very fiercely contested game during the first half (when Rugby rules were played). The Villans held their own against the Saints, as when half-time was called, neither side had scored. At the Association game, in the second half, the Villa had a bit the best of matters. Jack Hughes' reported account continued:

> For some time most of the matches were played with the fifteen men on each side, but ultimately that number was reduced to eleven. Among the other matches played were those with Aston Unity, Walsall Albion, St. Mary's and St. George's. Blank Saturdays were spent in practise games, for the early Villans appreciated the advantage of training,[61] and knew that unless they did so they would never become masters of the game. A defeat of three goals to one at the hands of Wednesbury Old Athletic, a sturdy lot, spurred them on, and they resolved that they would win or die. ...

---

[60] According to *Aston Villa: The History of a Great Football Club, 1874-1960*, by Peter Morris, and *Aston Villa, 1874-1998*, by Graham McColl, and also by Norman Edwards (the cartoonist, who apparently did much research for his cartoon series on the Villa history) in the *Evening Despatch* in 1946.

[61] "Training" in this context clearly means learning about and practising the game, apart from the physical training.

The Aston Villa Chronicles 1874 – 1924 (and after)

Villa's first match does not appear to have been reported in the press (who, typically, had not as yet taken to the game). The first published report of a Villa match seems to be a short account in the *Birmingham Morning News* (of the January 12, 1875) concerning a match between Aston Park Unity (later to be called Aston Unity) and the Villa the preceding Saturday. This was a 14-a-side match under Sheffield Rules, with Villa's team now composed of the following players:

G. Matthews (captain[62]), W. Price, J. Hughes, McBean, A. Walters, W. Scattergood, H. Matthews, E. Lee, A. Robbins, G. Mason, Weiss, C. Midgely, T. F. Smith, and Lewis.

The match, having started late, was finished "when darkness stopped the game". In a hard-fought match that went "slightly in favour of the Unity", the Villa lost 0-1, with Matthews, Price and Mason being Villa's men of the match. Before Unity had scored, Villa had a goal disallowed in the first half "owing to one of their side having 'fouled' the ball". Thus began a regular meeting of two clubs that would soon vie for supremacy in Aston and district.

At this time, there was precious little reporting of matches in the local press, the *Birmingham Morning News* being a welcome exception in that they reported anything at all, but even in that newspaper reports were few and far between. What local 'soccer' reports appeared seemed to mainly concern Calthorpe (initially known as the Birmingham Clerks AFC) and Aston (Park) Unity as probably two of the leading teams of the district at that time, and hence probably the cause of how the report on the match involving the Villa appeared; it is to be noted that the Villa did fairly well against these opponents. But accounts of the Villa against (presumably) lesser quality opposition do not seem to exist. It would appear that it was some time before the Villa were again referred to in the press.

So, Jack Hughes clearly pointed to 15-a-side matches (and other formations) as being a regular event for some time. Jack Hughes went on to give a longer account in his talk that evening, but it skipped over many details of the 1870s. Fortunately, there proved to be an even finer, and more detailed account, of those inaugural years by way of a weekly series in the Birmingham-published *Saturday Night* during the months of April to July, 1893. The author of that series wrote at its end:

---

[62] Obviously having replaced W. H. Price as captain by this time.

The Aston Villa Chronicles 1874 – 1924 (and after)

There was admitted by all a big gap lying between the far back times and the later days when the fame and prowess of Aston Villa was in all mouths. It was known that the club had been started so many years ago, that so and so and so and so had been prominently connected with it, that it was an uphill fight and yet had emerged to the front …

[And it emerged] from the lips of one, the most prominent of the Perry Barr officials, the complimentary remark that this was the best [early] history of the Villa club that had been penned.

The next chapter is based upon that series of *Saturday Night* articles, but is not a verbatim transcript of the highly detailed version that was published. The first of those articles gave its own account on the general development of football, and went on to pick up from Jack Hughes' report of the first (15-a-side) match against St. Mary's.

The rest of the story for the period to 1880 continues from that historic first match, with additional comments from other significant writers of later years (including William McGregor, Old Fogey, Archie Hunter and Charlie Johnstone), woven into the story from the *Saturday Night* series of articles.

The detail of that period reveals how the pieces of the jigsaw to club success were gradually pieced together, so that by 1880 it could be seen that a star had risen in this still new sport. By 1880, the Villa had still not caught the eye of the nation to any great degree, but in the Birmingham district it became a star of such ability and brotherly reputation that many worthy players in the area were quickly attracted to it, and these players of ability added the 'lift' necessary for the Villa to compete at the national level.

Firstly, a description is needed of the Aston Lower Grounds. This venue was to be the scene of many a fine contest in the local Cup competitions, many of them involving the Villa.

What is more, these grounds were destined to be the eventual permanent home of the Aston Villa Football Club.

The Aston Villa Chronicles 1874 – 1924 (and after)

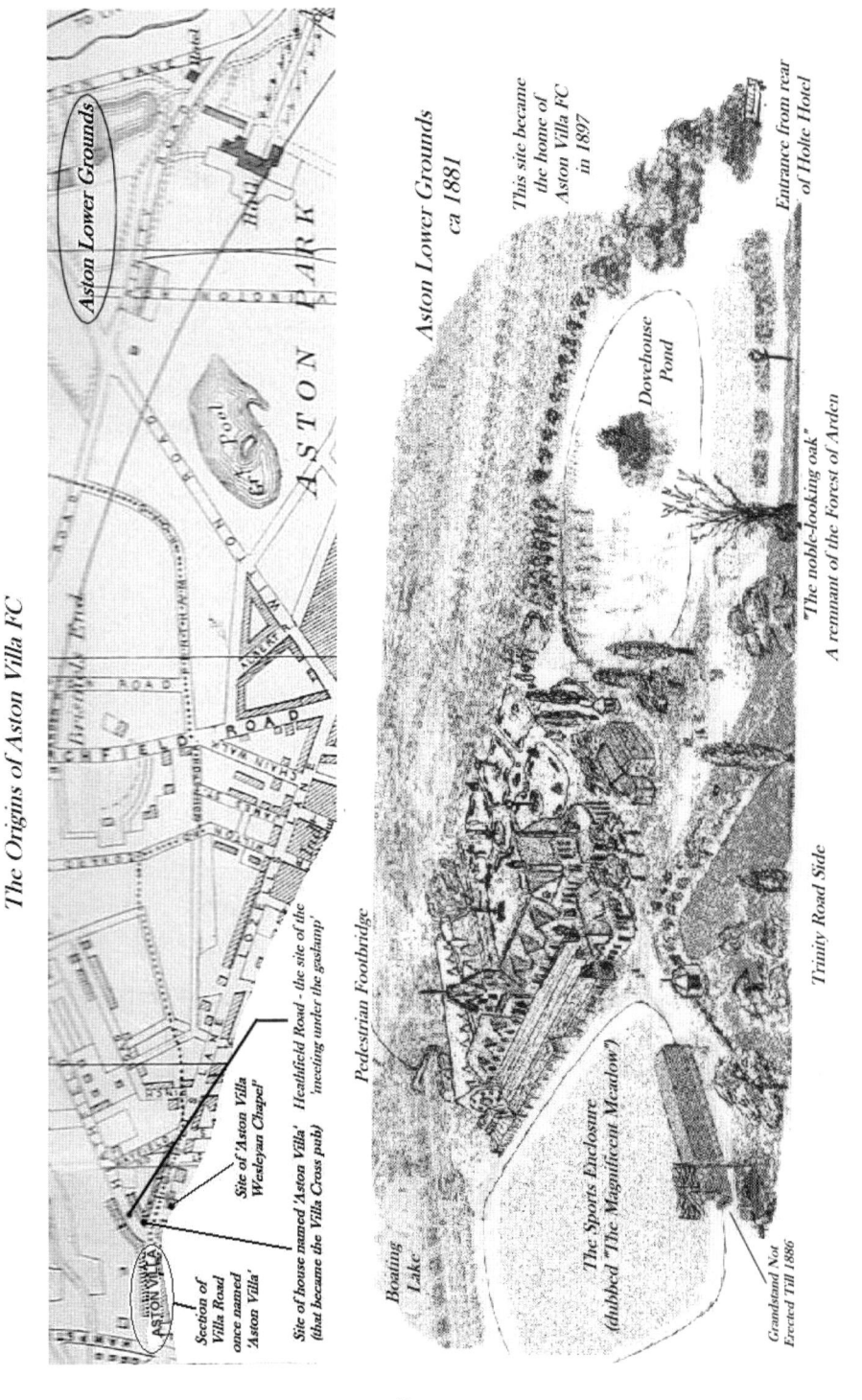

The Origins of Aston Villa FC

- Section of Villa Road once named 'Aston Villa'
- Site of house named 'Aston Villa' (that became the Villa Cross pub)
- Site of 'Aston Villa Wesleyan Chapel'
- Heathfield Road - the site of the 'meeting under the gaslamp'
- Aston Lower Grounds

Aston Lower Grounds ca 1881

- 'This site became the home of Aston Villa FC in 1897'
- Dovehouse Pond
- Entrance from rear of Holte Hotel
- "The noble-looking oak" A remnant of the Forest of Arden
- Trinity Road Side
- The Sports Enclosure (dubbed "The Magnificent Meadow")
- Boating Lake
- Pedestrian Footbridge
- Grandstand Not Erected Till 1886

63

The Aston Villa Chronicles 1874 – 1924 (and after)

The Aston Lower Grounds

These grounds were a central feature of west Midlands' outdoor activities – both as a sports centre and as pleasure grounds – for some thirty years. Over-commercialisation of the site after it had passed into new hands gradually saw its demise, and then it became the opportunity that Aston Villa sought for a new permanent ground. The greater part of 'the Lower Grounds' became known as Villa Park.

The Grounds as they were are described in Showell's Dictionary of Birmingham (1888):

> The most beautiful pleasure grounds in the Midland counties, cover 31 acres, and were originally nothing more than the kitchen and private gardens and the fish-ponds belonging to Aston Hall, and were purchased at the sale in 1818 by the Warwick bankers, who let them to Mr. H.G. Quilter ... Adding to its attractions year by year, Mr. Quilter remained on the ground until 1878, when a limited liability company was formed to take to the hotel and premises, building an aquarium 320 feet long by 54 feet wide, an assembly-room, 220 feet long, by 91 feet wide, and otherwise catering for the comfort of their visitors, 10,000 of whom can be now entertained and amused under shelter, in case of wet weather. Mr. Quilter [recently had the property sold, and] is now in private hands. The visitors to the Lower Grounds since 1864 have averaged 280,000 per annum.

The Grounds consisted of gardens, a pond and a menagerie of animals. A theatre – called the Holte – was added in 1879. The Aston Lower Grounds were the scene of musical recitals and many popular events, including fairs. Magnificent spectacles were staged in the 1880s, depicting events such as the eruption of Vesuvius and the Battle of Alexandria. The 'Cavern of Mysteries' was a particular success.

On the day of November the fifth 1887, possibly the most famous name in American cowboy history – Buffalo Bill – was presenting his touring Wild West Show at Aston Lower Grounds. His show included over two hundred horses, mules, buffalos, prairie elk, cowboys and Indians, and the famous Deadwood Stage. However, on that day, Aston Villa were playing at Small Heath Alliance, where Villa won 4-0 in the FA Cup, and Buffalo Bill performed to his lowest crowd ever as a result of the counter-attraction!

Adjacent to (and part of) the Grounds was a sports field, popularly known as 'The Lower Grounds Meadow'. It was thought in the 1870s and '80s that the "meadow" was "one of the prettiest places in England". George Kynoch – once president of the

The Aston Villa Chronicles 1874 – 1924 (and after)

Villa – referred to it as "the magnificent meadow".[63] It was one of the major sports centres of the Midlands.

In 1884, an England XI met the Australians here, at cricket, and the legendary Dr. W. G. Grace displayed his cricketing skills at the Grounds. The Grounds were once home to the Warwickshire County Cricket Club and also to clubs such as the Birmingham Football and Cricket Club, and then the Excelsior football club. There was also an athletics track that enclosed the sports pitch. The track was made up of red ash, 501 yards in length, near rectangular in shape, and went around the cricket/football pitch.

The Lower Grounds Meadow became the venue for all important local football matches in the 1880s, such as the semi-finals and finals of the Birmingham Cup and the Lord Mayor's Charity Shield, both of which Aston Villa carried off numerous times. The FA Cup Semi Finals of 1884 and 1886 were also staged here, and other major sporting events, such as the AAA championships, and important cycling events.

In August, 1888, the area of the Sports Ground (the 'Magnificent Meadow') was put up for sale with a plan to build houses on the hallowe'ed grounds. There was a movement to have this process reversed, and for the grounds to be properly managed, but clearly that attempt failed, and a housing estate was soon built on the famous enclosure.

The Villa News once described the popularity of the Grounds:

> There had always been a large contingent of Black Country folk who had favoured the famous old and beautiful grounds, and Sundays were gala days with these people, and they came in thousands and in all sorts of horsed vehicles (you might have seen 16 in a large trap or cart behind the horse), and they were still catered for by the Sunday concerts which were held all the year round in the Great Hall … . After the old meadow had been cut up into building lots, another cinder track was built on the land where the Villa [Trinity Road stand lies], and for a time this racing path grew popular …[64]

When Aston Villa came to take up a lease on the remainder of the Grounds in 1896, the old 'Meadow' had already gone, and the new 'Villa Park' was built over and around the remaining pond. The 'Aquarium' and 'Dining Rooms' building were taken up for use for various purposes, including use as offices. Those buildings were

---
[63] Villa News & Record 23 Nov 1907
[64] Villa News & Record 27 Dec 1924

The Aston Villa Chronicles 1874 – 1924 (and after)

eventually demolished for ground development at the Witton End in 1981.

The diagram below shows the Lower Grounds as copied by Norman Edwards from the plan in the 1882 Hammonds' Guide.

The once-named Holte Hotel (now 'the Holte') – listed in 1875 as present at the onset of Aston Villa – is all that remains of Henry Quilter's fine establishment. The Holte Hotel has been the scene of many local sports' celebrations over the years, although after 1897 the celebratory events there were entirely Aston Villa orientated. It was extended and refurbished in 1897, and, again (eventually) in 2007, by the recent purchaser of Aston Villa and the Holte, Mr. Lerner.

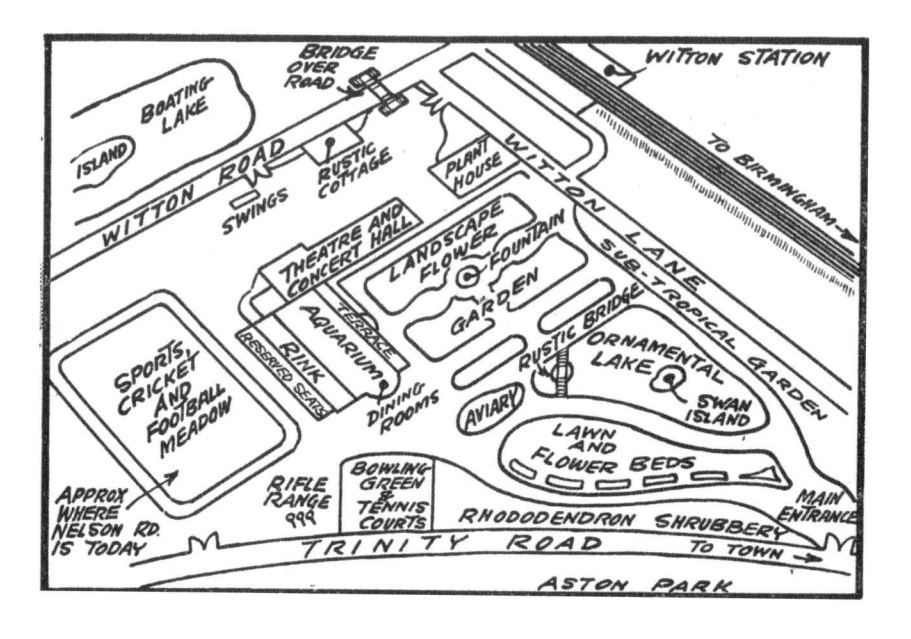

The Aston Villa Chronicles 1874 – 1924 (and after)

A Winter's Scene at the Lower Grounds

At Birmingham on New Year's day in 1887, it was a very wintry scene with ten degrees of frost, and fog. Frustrated by the dearth of football to report on, Old Fogey (on duty for the *Sport and Play* periodical) took himself to the Aston Lower Grounds to enjoy some skating on Dovehouse Pond (partly the future football pitch at Villa Park). He wrote this description of his view at the Lower Grounds that day:

> Like a transformation scene, only ever so much more lovely and enchanting, the fog cleared off, and a bright gleam of red wintry sunshine made the prettiest and most interesting picture I have seen for a long time.
>
> Everywhere the trees were hung with festoons of silvery white lace that sparkled and glittered in the sun's rays, and every little twig and branch was a beautiful picture in itself. Not a leaf had been missed, and as the frost was intense, some of the effects, such as the holly and firs, were simply wonderful in their beauty.
>
> As one stood at the bottom end of the pool,[65] and looked toward the island, and saw the red glint of the sunshine on the bright blades of the skates as the wearers glanced to and fro to the rhythmic ring of the steel on the ice, one felt sorry to leave such a scene and surroundings, especially as there were some splendid girls on blades, and if there is a sight worth looking at it is to see a lady skater who knows her business.

---

[65] Towards what is now the Holte End!

The Aston Villa Chronicles 1874 – 1924 (and after)

4. 1875 to 1880: On to the Birmingham Cup

Up to the time when the *Saturday Night* series of articles was printed in 1893, there was a dearth of information on how the club had started and found its way. In fact, it seems that no one since then has written as much about those first half-dozen and highly significant years, when the club was almost unknown outside the Midlands region, and might have gone the way of many early clubs – out of sight.

Although many of the faces of the early team faded from view, there were a few of them still to be seen round and about in the early 1890s. Scattergood had afterwards thrown in his lot with the Aston Clifton football club, while Weiss went "far over the sea in the land of the West". Compared to a scientific player of later days, Billy Weiss might perhaps have made an indifferent show, but it was said he was one of the sweetest singers amongst the 'Villa choir', an attribute in those early days that was as much welcomed as a player's footballing ability. H. Matthews was a commercial traveller; W. Such, a brother-in-law of Herr Weiss, also left for the place "over the herring pond", while Charlie Midgley – an early secretary of the club – eventually left for London. Teddy Lee, Jack Hughes, W. H. Price and G. Matthews were still to be seen in Birmingham.

> " ... only a few of the old hands know what a band of brothers the original Aston Villa players were ... "
>
> *- William McGregor (1904)*

Sadly, W. H. Price (a co-founder and Villa's first captain) seems to have fallen on hard times by late 1889,[66] as he applied to the Villa committee for assistance in November of that year. The committee (the minutes refer to Price as simply "a former player") asked their secretary to investigate and give £2 maximum. Applications for assistance from old players became an increasing phenomenon as time passed and as Villa continued to thrive, and the Villa were always mindful of helping their former stalwarts and their families.

Time and circumstances dealt more harshly with some of those old once-familiar faces, while others tasted of Life's prosperity. But whatever came to be their position, the old Villans were drawn together by a common bond of sympathy when

---

[66] Perhaps somewhat surprisingly, as Peter Lupson's research discovered that Price (like his father) worked as a craftsman in the Jewellery Quarter.

The Aston Villa Chronicles 1874 – 1924 (and after)

looking back with lingering regretful pleasure to the football experiences of the past.

The "insignificant little pot" – as the small FA Cup was once dubbed[67] – was a far-off thing of beauty then, as it rested in the proud custody of clubs such as Oxford University, while the newspapers (as has already been discovered) had not condescended to notice in any way but the briefest such a trifling pastime as football. Imagine, if you can, George Ramsay sitting down after a match to carefully write out a short report of the game for Monday's 'Post' or 'Mail'. He would then write, in polite submission to the power of the editor:

> "... the insertion of which will be esteemed a great favour by Yours respectfully ...".

That was the situation in those very early days of the club, when football was a dead letter in the land; a game played by a few devotees who were regarded as hopeless maniacs by the unbiased and dispassionate majority.

Charlie Johnstone wrote of one such early attempt to spread the 'Gospel of Aston Villa' via the medium of a match report. The occasion was Villa's first defeat of Saltley College by two goals to nil in 1876-77. Indeed, that was then a matter for spreading the news far and wide, for such had been the power and reputation of Saltley College in local football circles. Following the match, there was the usual dinner and jollification (which was part and parcel of the club's activities in those days), and then Charlie, Billy Mason and George Ramsay got together to write the report, intended for the *Birmingham Mail*. Charlie stated:

> Three hours of strenuous endeavour produced an exhaustive account, which a deputation of two were authorised to present to the august editor of the 'Mail' on the following morning. I think we got as far as the local sub-editor; there were explanations [requested] as to the status of the club, and we withdrew to await the proud moment when our great literary effort should strike the public eye. After much searching in the evening edition we found it - six lines in an obscure corner of the paper![68]

---

[67] At 19 ounces, the FA Cup was superseded in size by the Birmingham Cup (which was 25 ounces)!
[68] In his column in The Sporting Mail 20 Oct 1906

The Aston Villa Chronicles 1874 – 1924 (and after)

In those late-1870s' days, Charlie Crump of the Wolverhampton-based Stafford Road club – a predominant west Midlands team of the time - was a great exponent of the old method of football - the 'battering ram' policy. He eventually became president of the Birmingham and District FA, and on attaining that elevated position then developed quite a different perspective on how football should be played! But in the early days, encounters on the pitch between he and Teddy Lee were episodes to be ever remembered and laughed over when the old cronies got together and revived the past.

Then, in the old teams, there was always a 'strong man' who spent an independent free-lance sort of existence during the progress of the match. He was selected in no particular position, but was supposed to roam from flower to flower, as it were. If any of the players found an opponent too much for them, or had a score to pay off, they passed the word along for the 'minder', who took the earliest possible chance of avenging them.

Billy Weiss used to be the Villa 'minder', and his favourite boast was that he had never been 'upset' (i.e. physically turned over). However the pitcher went once too often at last, and on one memorable occasion the champion was overthrown. Burning with the disgrace of his downfall, Weiss speedily retaliated on his opponent, although the ball was – metaphorically speaking – miles away, exclaiming, as he gracefully turned his rival upside down, "There now, we're quits!"

Yellow card? Red card? Nothing of the kind in those days!

Season 1875-76

It would seem that Aston Villa's first full season (1874-75) was a haphazard affair, and significant details about that time appear to be lost, apart from the single report revealed earlier, against Aston Unity. In season 1875-76, however, a regular list of fixtures were arranged and played off. Figuring among the Villa antagonists were Aston Unity, Stafford Road, Wednesbury Old Athletic, Grasshoppers, St. George's, and St. Mary's. All of those clubs were then at the forefront in first-class soccer in the West Midlands area.

Jack Hughes' younger brother **Charlie Hughes**, who was first associated through the cricket club and used to accompany brother Jack to those matches and act as scorer, wrote:

The Aston Villa Chronicles 1874 – 1924 (and after)

> My first match with the Aston Villa Football Club was against Wednesbury Old Athletic on Aston Park by the side of Trinity Road. I was 15 years of age when I played in that game, so, you see, I had something to do against those burly fellows, who beat us by three goals. We played several matches on Aston Park...[69]

The match he refers to appears to have been the first of the season, and the first of those matches played on Aston Park. The team were evidently at that stage very far indeed from being fliers, for their efforts, however well-intended, were not productive of much success. Stafford Road – boldly bearded in their Wolverhampton den – was another formidable opponent, and our aspiring visitors were taken in and done for to the tune of 0-7. At this point, the future of the Villa did not look very bright, but the tide was soon to turn.

The Birmingham and District FA

This was also the year when two of the local game's then most respected players, Messrs. J. Campbell Orr (Calthorpe) and Sam Durban (Aston Unity), called a meeting of delegates to form the Birmingham and District Football Association. The first meeting on 8 December, 1875 was attended by Messrs. Scattergood and J. Hughes as representatives of the Villa. However, the Birmingham and District FA did not commence active operations until the following season, when the Birmingham (Senior) Cup competition was inaugurated. Although the Villans themselves had not made any marked perceptible progress, there was every sign that the game itself was taking root and widening its popularity in the district.

A map of the main early footballing centres of the Birmingham & District

Villa, our ball-kicking novices of the Midlands, were simply hopelessly floundering in the elementary stages of the new science. None of our clubs had properly grasped the real principle of the game, and there was no one to teach them. Beyond a wild lungeous kick, and a clumsy, madheaded rush for goal, football proper was unknown to the natives. No club was more in need of instruction than the Villa, for probably no club in the district was then lower down in the scale.

---

[69] Villa News & Record 28 Dec 1908 – "Makers of Villa History"

The Aston Villa Chronicles 1874 – 1924 (and after)

The Arrival of GBR

The Midlands were waiting for the arrival of the football missionary to lighten their darkness. The game was ripe for the Man, and the Man came! He may not have driven up in a chariot and four, greeted with the inspiring strains of "See the conquering hero comes", but modest and unpretentious as his advent may have been, he was destined to make a big mark on the football records of the district. When the Villans were at practise at the Aston Upper Grounds, their performances (to the eye of the cultured player) were, doubtless, very far from satisfactory.

It would seem that it was in the winter of 1875-76 that a dapper little stranger, who spoke with a very pronounced Glaswegian cut, stood among the small crowd of watchers. He was quite unknown, and would in all probability have remained so, had he not presently occasioned a grand sensation by asking if he could be allowed to participate in the game. This favour being acceded to (after lengthy negotiation in view of the stranger's strong accent!), the young Scot joined in the sport with results that were most bewildering and surprising. Dribbling was a completely unknown art to those primitive Villans, so that when the stranger proceeded to give them a few practical illustrations of the same, bewilderment was quickly followed by delight and inspiration.

The youth was a perfect revelation to them when, with the ball at his toe, he wriggled through them all like an eel, time after time carrying the leather unchecked from one goal to the other. Numerical superiority and brute strength were, alike, useless. Nothing could be done with the man who never waited to be knocked down, slipped every surge, seemed to use his feet as if they were hands and literally danced round his opponents when and ever he liked. Here indeed was a treasure to be captured without delay, and no time was lost in persuading 'Scotty' to throw in his lot with Aston Villa, by whom he was speedily elected captain.

The advent of Mr. **George Burrell Ramsay** marked an important stage in the history of the Aston Villa club, for from this appearance the organisation travelled up the ladder by leaps and bounds. Mr. Ramsay, prior to being called to Birmingham by business engagements, had been a member of a Glasgow football dub known as the Oxford, a team that had won some considerable share of fame by thrice drawing with Glasgow Rangers in the Scottish cup-ties. In one of those matches, George Ramsay had his nose broken. In later life, he recalled: "I got my nose pulled round all right. Someone put a pencil up it and drew it round again, and I went on playing merrily!"

The Aston Villa Chronicles 1874 – 1924 (and after)

Under Ramsay's captaincy the Villa quickly made their presence felt in the football world, and it was not until after 1879-80, once the team had received the Birmingham Cup, that the popular little Scot resigned the reins of captaincy to another fellow-countryman, whose fame in the land was destined to be greater than even that of his predecessor. However, until then, it was the wonderful skill of Ramsay that naturally attracted a large amount of interest in the district, and so gave a great impetus to the game. The influence of Aston Villa on football in the district started from this point. As Old Fogey put it:

> ... it may be truthfully said that he started a new era in the club life of the Midlands, and thereby led the van by popularising the game ... There is little doubt that the coming of George Ramsay not only quickened the [development of the] Villa itself, but had a very large effect on the clubs whose knowledge of one another's doings ran like quicksilver through their ranks, and who were desirous of emulating the deeds of the young Scot ...[70]

Meanwhile, the Villa had taken that gruelling defeat at Stafford Road very much to heart, and were burning to wipe out the stigma of so great a disaster. The arrival of Ramsay on the scene was most opportune, for he was in time to assist them in the return match with Mr. Crump's pets. The Wolverhampton team were very disagreeably surprised by the great improvement evinced by their old opponents, having regarded the match as rather a soft match for them. The presence, influence, and play of the new man infused fresh life and pluck into the Brums, who, playing a perfect demon game, gave Stafford Road a fair tying up, and were most unlucky indeed to lose. As things turned out, however, there were no bones broken, for the Villa had every right to claim a moral victory, having reduced a 0 to 7 reverse to the narrow margin of 0-1. Years later, George Ramsay recalled that after the match the Villa team were allocated just one bucket of water with which to wash themselves.

G. B. Ramsay was the hero of the hour, his football feats being on every tongue in the area. Several attempts were made, of course, to annex him by other clubs, but without avail, as he decided to remain true to the team with which he had cast in his lot.

From 1877 to 1879, GBR went on to take part in all representative matches of the Birmingham Association, and in one match against Wales, he gave such a fine exhibition he was promptly invited by the Welsh Association to play for them in the then classic annual fixture against Glasgow![71] George Ramsay himself gave an

---

[70] Villa News & Record 3 Nov 1923
[71] Villa News & Record Christmas, 1907 – from an article by "Old Fogey"

The Aston Villa Chronicles 1874 – 1924 (and after)

account of that affair:

> We played one match with North Wales at Ruabon. I was captain that day. ... At the end of the game [their team captain] came to me and said: 'How the devil you have got past me I don't know; no one has ever done it before as you have done it. We have got to go to Glasgow ... in a fortnight's time; will you play [for us]? ...'
>
> As I thought it would be a good chance of getting home, I consented. I scored a goal and several of the Queen's Park men who knew me well wanted to know what I was doing playing for Wales. I just smiled, and so did they.[72]

Unfortunately for GBR he did not get a free holiday in his home-land. He never received the ten pounds expenses he was due to receive to cover his costs; "All the money has gone", they said!

George Ramsay proved to be a leader of credit and renown, and a bit of a martinet on the field; he also played with much nerve and abandon, and received, naturally, a good many bumps in consequence.

The football fever had fairly caught on among the Villans, and the cricket section was having a rather bad time. In so languishing a condition was the summer department that in 1876 it was only with the greatest difficulty that the fixtures were fulfilled, and the summer of 1876 was almost exclusively taken up for football practice. Jack Hughes, as part of the talk partly recounted earlier in this chapter, was reported as saying:

> The players suffered from the football fever, and while under the effects of that complaint, the Villans gave but little attention to cricket! Whenever they started practising the summer game, someone would disturb their peace of mind by throwing a football among the players. The sight of that would prove too much, and then it was off with the love – cricket; and on with the new love – football! They were all badly smitten by the football craze.

Hitherto, the football team had not been successful on the field, and there was a general desire on the part of the members to make a step to the front in the following winter. Under the careful, energetic, coaching of their new captain, the players therefore threw themselves into the work of preparation, with hearty enthusiasm and spirit. All kinds of athletic exercises were freely resorted to, such as jumping, running, throwing the hammer, and gymnastics. A lot of hard work was perseveringly got through by the old Villans, the self-denial practised in order to

---

[72] Villa News & Record 7 Jan 1928

The Aston Villa Chronicles 1874 – 1924 (and after)

achieve this end speaking volumes for the resolve and earnestness of the members.

It was in this summer that the brothers Lindsay first became connected with Aston Villa. They hailed from the north of Scotland, having been called down to Birmingham to fulfil business engagements, as a great many Scots did, and Birmingham was greatly expanding in those days. Jemmy Lindsay was a splendid back, while his brother Billy officiated with fair average ability at half. When, in the following season, the Villa first rose to the dignity of taking a 'gate', Billy Lindsay was the hero who purchased a bottle of gum and started on a tour round the district, posting the football bills on the lamp-posts as he went.

Up until this time, Aston Villa had enjoyed but a sort of vagrant existence, having, as it were, no visible means of support, and being without the joys and comforts of a home. The time was now rapidly approaching when this unsettled, precarious state of things was to cease. The executive had long realised the fact that it was highly essential to future Villa success that a good private ground should be secured, with the least possible delay. Many protracted and earnest debates ensued on this important subject, and eventually negotiations were opened and overtures made which finally resulted in Aston Villa being established at Perry Barr, 'Prepared' for the season 1876-77. This was another credit to Mr. Ramsay, who one day had taken a walk with J. Lindsay, and came across this field at Wellington Road, and found it to their liking. As William McGregor put it:

> Mr. Ramsay's glib tongue prevailed upon the occupier to let it to the club for the season at a rental of £5, but in the following year the owner sternly demanded £8, and this was paid – cheerfully, no doubt, for the Villa realised that they had found an advantageous pitch. Then £10 was demanded, and by this time the Villa desired a fixity of tenure, so they approached the owners, the Bridge Trust school trustees, and obtained a three years' lease but they had to pay £60 per annum for the privilege. By stages the rent was advanced to £80,[73] £120, £150 and finally £200 per annum. Still the trustees were not satisfied and then it was that the big scheme which resulted in the construction of Villa Park was embarked upon.[74]

---

[73] It was held at that level (£80) for a number of years until Villa gained success in the FA Cup, followed by the formation of the League, which the Bridge Trust saw as a big revenue-earner.

[74] C.B Fry's Magazine of Action and Outdoor Life Vol 2 Oct 1904 to Mar 1905 p.39 *et seq*

The Aston Villa Chronicles 1874 – 1924 (and after)

But about that eventful first year at Perry Barr, Jack Hughes was reported as saying:

> ... their joy was unbounded when George Ramsay told them that there was a prospect of a pitch being secured at Wellington Road, Perry Barr. [Later,] their delight was unlimited when they were informed that the lease for the ground had been signed.
>
> When they got the ground, however, there was much to be done. It had to be laid out, goals fixed up and other things done, but every member lent assistance, and soon everything was in ship-shape order.

Of course, the field was very different then compared to what it became by the 1890s, though it did not entirely lose its rustic charm. In those days, there were trees growing round it here and there, even encroaching upon the playing portion. The ground was also ornamented during the first season with a hayrick, which being situated within the bounds of play was the occasion of much merriment and diversion to the home players and bewilderment to the visitors, who could not understand where the ball had gone to when it was passed out of sight and returned on the other side!

Season 1876-77

The club held its first AGM in 1876, and the Villa officials for 1876-77, in this the first Perry Barr year, were:

Captain, G. B. Ramsay; Vice-captain, W. B, Mason; Treasurer, W. H. Price; Hon Sec., D. J. Stevens. The committee comprised Messrs. W. Weiss, E. B. Lee, J. Hughes, E. C. Bishop, and W. Lindsay. Later on in the season Mr. Stephens resigned his secretarial duties in favour of C. H. Midgley. The president at this stage was probably still Mr. Hartshorne of the Aston Villa Wesleyan Chapel.

Mr. George Kynoch, founder of the local armaments factory and looked upon with veneration for the employment his company gave the populace, was a very early supporter of the Villa club. In their first season at Perry Barr, the Pets were honoured by the patronage of the popular crowned king of Aston, who with his wife used to do a round of the field on horseback, while the game was in progress. Nearly a decade later Mr. Kynoch became president of the club, but in-between time, he gave the club great patronage and was always ready to dig deep into his pockets at times of festivity, in particular as host when opposing teams from afar came to call.

The Aston Villa Chronicles 1874 – 1924 (and after)

In time, the space around the Perry Barr touchlines meant that the more affluent football enthusiasts could bring their carriages onto the ground via a special entrance and park them around the pitch. George Kynoch took full advantage of these prototype executive boxes. For the masses, however, facilities were rather more basic!

> Old Fogey once remarked that it was during the twenty-one years or so that the Villa occupied their Wellington Road premises that Association Football became, gradually, a great sporting institution in the country. Football did not grow, as some imagined, by leaps and bounds into the public's favour; it was only by quiet progress and demonstration that the game became worthy.

The club colours and outfit at that time was a royal blue cap and stockings, scarlet and royal blue striped jersey and white knicks, from which it will be gathered that the Perry Pets of those days were things of beauty and joys for ever, when decked out in their war paint. A strong fixture card was compiled, with first and second teams being well catered for. The first team list included all the chief local clubs, including Wednesbury Town, Stafford Road, Wednesbury Old Athletic, Saltley College, Aston Park Unity, Victoria Swifts, Calthorpe, West Bromwich, Harborne, Coventry Royal, and Wednesbury Old Park.

The membership list had been very considerably augmented during the summer months, while the move to the new ground attracted additional players. Most noticeable among the latest recruits was little **Sam Law**, the player who was to render such veteran service for the club in the half-back department. Unusually, Sam was already the father of a family before he started playing. Attracted by curiosity to the scene of one of the Villa's practices, he was persuaded to join in, and soon became a victim to the all-pervading contagion. He took to the game simply like a duck takes to water, and, after playing once or twice in the second team, was promptly drafted on to the senior eleven, where he was not long in making a name for himself. His favourite position was centre field, midway between the halves and forwards – quarter-back it was called – and here Sam Law's speedy trickery and invincible tackling proved of invaluable use to his clubmates. Old Fogey described[75] how every time Villa scored, "he turned Catherine Wheels like one o'clock!" Old Fogey also said:

---

[75] Villa News and Record 14 Sep 1912

The Aston Villa Chronicles 1874 – 1924 (and after)

> What made him more conspicuous than the ordinary run of footballers was the fact that he sported mutton-chop whiskers, and these being a pronounced tinge of auburn, he darted about the field at Perry Barr and elsewhere like a ray of shining light.
>
> He seemed to bounce as easily as an India-rubber ball, and his tackling was clever, persistent and clean; indeed, Law was a gentleman of the first persuasion on the field, and could win and lose with uncommonly good grace.

The next stalwart at half-back was **E. B. (Teddy) Lee.** But he was not a new player – he was one of the original members of the Villa. Old Fogey said of him:

> He was a sportsman of the first water, and a most lovable chap. His delight in the club was hearty and unaffected, and every one of his comrades was a hero in his eyes. As a player he was zealous and capable, whole-hearted and efficient; but it would be flattering his memory too highly to say that he was as brilliant a half-back as Tom Pank or Sam Law in his own day, or as James Cowan or Andrew Ducat of middle and modern generations [i.e. 1890s through to the 1910s]; but he was always a valuable man on a side because his virility and tremendous love for the game inspired his comrades, and his boyish spirits and mental elasticity gave a sort of 'life' to the team which, so to speak, gladdened it; for Teddy Lee possessed the fine flower of comradeship, and he was a very loyal club man.
>
> I don't think I ever saw a finer loser. Of course he liked to win, and rejoiced greatly thereat; but he could always laugh on both sides of his face if the Villa flag was temporarily lowered, and they had to doff their plumes to a finer combination. I have seen Teddy Lee stand and laugh at an opponent who had just beaten him for the ball; and he would go up to him during a pause in the game and say 'I say, old chap; that was jolly clever – you might explain to me how it was done.' He had a way with him, as they said of Father O'Flynn; and, so long as the game was played honourably and fairly, I really think he had as much respect for those against him as he had regard for his own mates. There was something really 'big' about Teddy Lee; he had all the fine qualities of a natural gentleman, for while he admired and praised the shining points of a player, he passed by or ignored the baser sort of tricks which even in those days were not uncommon …
>
> I do not exaggerate when I say that he very materially helped to imbue the Villa with the jolly spirit of sporting Bohemianism which had such a splendid effect on its fortunes in its days of upspringing, and I am sure his influence was greater than he knew. [76]

---

[76] Villa News and Record 2 Apr 1920 ("Makers of the Villa" by Old Fogey)

The Aston Villa Chronicles 1874 – 1924 (and after)

Lee continued playing for nearly a decade and was a celebrity: "Teddy always has a good game in those brown nicks of his. May they never wear out!"[77] He went to Cape Colony some years later, and died there in about 1903, whilst still in his forties.

Another afterwards famous player and half-back came to light about this time (as a result of an introduction by Teddy Lee) in the person of **Tom Pank**, whose magnificent sprinting abilities were fated to be the delight and admiration of habitués of Midland athletic tracks.

Lee, Pank and Law, on their day, were about as fine a half-back trio as one could wish to see. The many successful struggles of "Evergreen Sammy" Law, with opponents twice his size produced no end of mirth and jubilation to Perry Barr supporters.

Cartwright, who joined the Perry Barr team, was also connected with the Birmingham Club,[78] the organisation that played at Aston Lower Grounds and numbered in its ranks such men as George and Charlie Quilter, Joseph Cofield, George Pears, Captain Walker, Webster, and Hiram Slack. Cartwright used to usually play centre or inside on the wing, and was very partial to odd coloured stockings, his legs on the field of play often wearing a grotesque appearance in consequence.

Changes were pretty frequently made in the composition of the eleven for this season, but still they were not of a sweeping character, and the following names can be taken as a fair sample of an average Villa team in 1876-77. This is the team that played in the memorable Birmingham Cup-tie with Tipton (an account of which is given later) and is interesting in that it was a 2-3-5 formation:

Goal: *Weiss*; Backs: *W. H. Price, W. Taylor*; Half-backs: *W. Lindsay, E. B. Lee, S. Law*; Forwards: *Ramsay, W. B. Mason, Cartwright, J. Hughes, W. Such*.

The first matches at Perry Barr

The Villa opened their campaign at their new Wellington Road ground against Wednesbury Town on 30 September, 1876. The two Knowles (G. R. and B. C.) were members of this team, which was afterwards known as Wednesbury Strollers, captained by Tom Bryan, and assisted by Alf Harvey, both of whom later joined the Villa. The Blackcountry men were a hard dashing lot, and it took the Villans all their

---

[77] Midland Athlete 24 Jan 1883
[78] Actually called the Birmingham Cricket and Football Club

time to win. The systematic training of the preceding summer, however, told its tale, and at call of time the Villa finished victors of a desperately contested game by the narrow margin of one goal.

Hitherto, the Perry Barr team had not known the luxury of a 'gate', with the exception of the one on their Wilson Road field, which had afforded fine reserved seating accommodation and occasionally stood duty for a goal itself. On their arrival at Wellington Road, the Villans were now the proud recipients of a real live 'gate'. There was not much of it, it is true, but there it was, such as it was, a genuine 'gate'. Messrs. W. B. Mason and W. Sothers were honoured with the solemn task of collecting the Villa toll for the first time, and at the conclusion of the operation their pockets were as light as their hearts, the enthusiasm of the public only having proved equal to 5s. 3d.[79] It wasn't much, but it was a beginning, and a heap better, after all, than that first Birmingham Association Charity match at Tipton, when the proceeds amounted to the magnificent sum of two shillings and fourpence!

The second match of the season was played at Wolverhampton (the Stafford Road club), where the Villans exhibited still further proof of the improvement which George Ramsay had wrought among them by holding their own from start to finish, the game ending in a draw of one goal each. Wednesbury Old Athletic signalled their first appearance at Perry Barr by snatching a goal victory, but later on at Wednesbury were only able to draw with their Birmingham visitors. Saltley College next administered a gruelling defeat of five goals to the Villa at Saltley. On this occasion the Villa were short of several of their best men, and off-colour as well. The tables were turned later in the season, when the Collegians were well beaten, 2-0. Next on the list, however, came the Tipton Cup tie, with regard to which a few explanatory notes may not be out of place.

The football season of 1876-77 was a most important one in the annals of the local game, for from that year dates the commencement of the Birmingham and District Association and its labours. The body in question had been established twelve months before (as previously documented), but the work done during that period had only been of a brief and preliminary character. In this winter, however, football organisation was started in real earnest by the institution of the Birmingham (Senior) Cup competition.

---

[79] According to William McGregor; a different figure was quoted in the *Saturday Night* account.

The Aston Villa Chronicles 1874 – 1924 (and after)

The Association opened the winter with a membership of sixteen clubs.[80] The secretary was in the happy position of being able to report a balance in hand of £2 14s. 9d., and the following clubs announced their intention of playing for the Cup: Stafford Road, Wednesbury Old Athletic, Wednesbury Town, Calthorpe, Aston Villa, Aston Park Unity, Elwell's, Saltley College, St. George's, Harborne, Cannock, West Bromwich, Harold, Royal, Tipton, and Wednesbury Old Park.

The previously-referred-to Birmingham Club was not included in the list of combatants for the Birmingham Cup. Nevertheless, the Birmingham Club was one of those clubs that Villa had to dispose of to be recognised as the best in the Birmingham area; but that was to be later. William McGregor was to say: "… the club at Aston Lower Grounds, which was dignified with the proud title of the Birmingham Cricket and Football Club, had a splendid meadow and indulgent patronage."

The Tipton Cup-tie

Tipton, Villa's first opponents in the Birmingham Cup, were not too high in its standing as a club. Nevertheless, Tipton had a formidable team as far as weight, dash and determination were concerned, but they had very little science. The two Peacocks and Haines were the shining lights of the Tipton eleven, the two former playing a very powerful game at back. The Villans were most anxious to win this match and do well in the Cup, and every nerve was strained to turn out fit and well. Players then had to fulfil business duties as well, and often great difficulty was experienced in getting away from work early on Saturday. There was no comfortable dressing-room then at Perry Barr, the players having to dress at home and come down to the ground in their kit. The Villa, in spite of everything, succeeded in getting a good representative team on the field, despite the absence of Tom Pank.

It was a dreadfully rough game, that cup-tie. The Peacocks put their all in, and the lighter Villans were soon railing about like ninepins. Nevertheless, the Brums performed bravely, and were very often dangerous. Tipton scored one goal, but the Villa got the ball through twice. The referee was, however, "agin 'em", as a man in the crowd would have said, and therefore Tipton won by that one goal.

---

[80] The governing section being selected as follows: President, C. Crump (Stafford Road); Vice-presidents, J. Carson (Calthorpe) and F. Hackwood (Wednesbury Town); Treasurer, F. Bagnall (St. George's); Hon. secretary, J. C. Orr (Calthorpe).

The Aston Villa Chronicles 1874 – 1924 (and after)

The losers were very raw over this result and appealed to the Association, only to have their protest ruled out of order as being "frivolous". The Perry Barr folks could not see it in that light. The Tipton disaster, however mortifying at the time, did the club good, for they strove more determinedly than before to make their mark during the remainder of that season. The Tiptonians were visited toward the end of the same winter, and were handsomely defeated, 2-0.

The Inaugural Birmingham Cup Final

Meanwhile, the inaugural Birmingham Cup competition was fought out to the bitter end, the finalists being Wednesbury Old Athletic and Stafford Road (of Wolverhampton). The deciding struggle took place on the Calthorpe ground, Bristol Road on March 21, 1877. So great was the interest felt in this final tie that a then outstanding crowd of 2,000 gathered together to witness the fight. They had not got turnstiles in those days, and the 'wall ticket' system flourished, for £15 was all that was taken at the gate. A general impression prevailed that the two teams were well matched and that a fine finish should result. The prophets for once were right as Wednesbury beat Stafford by just 3 goals to 2.

The referee for this final and the 1878 Birmingham Cup Final was George Ramsay.

More Scots Arrive

Among the two thousand odd spectators who witnessed the match which decided the first home of the Birmingham Cup, was a gentleman who was destined to afterwards write his name indelibly down on the records of the Aston Villa Club. He was to be prominently associated with their future movements, was to evolve and organise their most important and critical new departures, and who was, in fact, to provide the very blood, bone and sinew without which the Perry Barr club – brilliant as were the players – would have been totally unable to obtain that high honoured position and tone in the football world which they came to occupy. While the Ramsays, Hunters, and all the grand array of Villa talent won the club undying fame upon the field of play in the club's first years, it was left to the enviable lot of gentlemen of the McGregor stamp to reap the harvest of the quiet eye over the football council board.

Mr. **William McGregor** (affectionately known as 'Mac') was one of the crowd at that

The Aston Villa Chronicles 1874 – 1924 (and after)

first Birmingham Cup final, and subsequently witnessed every deciding tie up to 1893, when a business engagement at Burton deprived him of the opportunity of keeping up his unique unbroken record. In 1877, the big-bearded, genial Scot had not then identified himself with any particular club and indeed was, comparatively speaking, unknown beyond being seen as a gentleman who was often among the small crowd of spectators who attended the Calthorpe and Birmingham matches at Bristol Road and Aston Lower Grounds. Another significant gentleman present at Bristol Road at that final was Mr. **Fergus Johnstone**.

The Stafford Road players were dressed in the familiar Queen's Park colours and looked so much nicer and neater than their opponents to the artistic draper's eye that Mr. McGregor speedily installed them as his special favourites, and hoped they would win - which they didn't!

On first coming to Birmingham from far off Perth, Mr. McGregor, under the impression that only the Rugby game was played here, did not interest himself in football matters.[81] Later, on hearing of the Calthorpe club, he started to attend their matches, afterwards dividing his favours pretty evenly between the Calthorpe club at Bristol Road and the 'Birmingham Club' at the Lower Grounds.

Queen's Park second team, captained by Davie Anderson (afterwards of the Villa), twice came down to play Calthorpe. The Brums whipped up special teams for these occasions, but the Scots were too strong for them. The crack of the Queen's Park forwards was a player named Fred Smith, a really magnificent dribbler who, strange to say, was an Englishman, being a native of the Potteries. Even in those days, local talent was evidently not to be despised, and the great Scottish clubs were not above profiting from the skill of their English neighbours.

Mr, McGregor saw many matches, too, at the Lower Grounds, when the Birmingham Club played Sheffield Wednesday, Heeley, and the Nottingham clubs. Players used to be borrowed indiscriminately then, and visitors to the Lower never knew exactly who they were going to play against. The Lytteltons occasionally assisted Birmingham, who were notoriously unpunctual in their home engagements.

---

[81] In his own country he had been an ardent athlete, and active member of the Peep o' Day cricket club, an organisation that used to pitch their stumps at six o'clock in the morning on the broad breezy Inch of Perth. He was also one of the best shots of the First Perthshire Volunteers' Brigade.

The Aston Villa Chronicles 1874 – 1924 (and after)

> On the matter of unpunctuality at the Lower Grounds, a letter (the first of many) appeared in a local paper, complaining of the Birmingham Club's late starts and signed 'Looker On'. When Mac (who was thought to have written the letters) 'innocently' asked the Birmingham men if they knew the author, he was told, "Oh, some blanked fool or other!"
>
> *A Lion's Fun*

The following is a personal account of how William McGregor came to be involved in the Villa and with George Ramsay. This account was published barely more than two months before 'Mac' died:

> The grounds I used to attend [in early 1877, probably] were the old Aston Lower Grounds to witness the Birmingham Club (or more commonly named 'Quilters' Club'). I was also a regular spectator at Bristol Road, when the Calthorpe Club were playing at home.
>
> From a spectator I met on the Bristol Road enclosure I learned there was a good club playing at Perry Barr, named Aston Villa, and that there were one or two Scots playing with it. I took to wandering to this rural spot when there were matches there, though in those days there were many vacant Saturdays. However, I became a regular habitué of the olden classic ground, and a decided 'Villan'. I think I can see now the little, dapper, well-built laddie [George Ramsay], with a black and red striped cap, red and blue-hooped jersey, and the same coloured stockings, getting hold of the ball on the extreme wing well within his own territory, and going off like streaked lightning, wiggling, waggling past opponents, one after another, and finally landing the ball 'between the sticks'. These were the days of the art of dribbling; and George was the past master of the cult...
>
> I was made, along with the late Mr. Fergus Johnstone,[82] a vice-president of the club in 1877, and still retain that honour. Well, shortly after my appointment, Mr. Ramsay called upon me and asked me to attend one of their committee meetings as they had some knotty point to settle. ... This was my first introduction to football management. The meetings were then held at the home of the now veteran Sam Law, in William Street, Lozells. ... In those days, I remember, it was a difficult matter to get a player to stand down, even though he was suffering from a cold or injury – all of them were

---

[82] Charlie Johnstone remembered these two vice-presidents "on committee, when they united to curb the autocracy of the late George Kynoch [the Villa president in 1885-88]." (in The Sporting Mail 23 Dec 1911)

The Aston Villa Chronicles 1874 – 1924 (and after)

so keen and eager to take part in the Saturday's game.[83]

The association between 'Mac' and George Ramsay developed as they both attended the services at the Aston Villa Wesleyan Chapel, when they would afterwards sit and discuss football for hours together, and many a scheme was suggested and subsequently took root. Those schemes included improvements to the ground that went at a faster rate than the 'gate' seemed to allow, but the Villa prospered in their play and thus the 'gate' was rarely a problem. As time went on, the spectacle of the play of the Villa (off-days excepted) was always going to bring sufficient crowds.[84]

But, of the early days at Perry Barr, 'Mac' wrote: "We had not many spectators at the Villa's games when I first became interested in their doings. More than once Ramsay's brother and I have been the only pair. But the fame of George Ramsay soon spread."

'Mac' was - at various times - vice-president, hon. treasurer, hon. secretary, committeeman, chair of committee, and auditor. While for years he worked for the club, earning the greatest admiration and respect for the technical ability and sterling impartiality he exhibited, it used to be a common grumble among Villa supporters that, "Mac's too fair for an umpire", when he took that role. But goodness knows how Aston Villa would have fared without the aid of their 'Football Father' who, by the late-1880s, was regarded as by far the most able football administrator in the Midlands, if not in the country.

The Breast Plate Incident

Let us now return once more to the season of 1876-77, when the greatest rivalry existed between the Villa and Aston Park Unity, as they were then called.[85]

In the previous winter, the Unity had beaten the Villans, though the former were not so successful this year. The games between the two teams were of a most close and desperate character. Party feeling ran very high on these occasions, no mercy being shown by either side. It was at one of these aforesaid struggles to the death that the "breast plate incident" occurred. The match in question was played at Perry Barr,

---

[83] Villa News & Record 7 Oct 1911
[84] Villa News & Record 3 Nov 1923 - "Some Famous Players"
[85] They were playing at that time in a field adjoining the Lower Grounds, and men such as Messrs. T. Atkins, Hundy, S. Durban, and Jack Brown were in the team. Jack Brown was Arthur Brown's elder brother, the younger Brown being this season engaged winning his spurs in the Florence team, along with several other youngsters who were afterwards to make a big name for themselves.

The Aston Villa Chronicles 1874 – 1924 (and after)

and among the Villa players was J. H. ('Jack') Eaves, who played half-back that afternoon and previous to the kick-off, he had been heard to make some darkly significant hint about the bad time he was going to give the Unity. Jack was a man of his word, for he seemed to mow the enemy down like grass that day. He appeared bullet proof, every charge made at him being fruitless, the aggressors recoiling from his form as from a brick wall. Great merriment was made later when it was discerned that Eaves' success was mainly down to a breast-plate made of padding which he had worn during the match!

Here are two newspaper reports of Villa matches in their first Perry Barr season. The Old Athletic's initial visit to Wellington Road is reported here, together with that disastrous Villa trip to Saltley. Note the use of twelve players per team.

WEDNESBURY OLD ATHLETIC v. ASTON VILLA

The match between the above clubs took place on Saturday upon the ground of the latter club at Perry Barr. The Athletic won the toss, electing to kick against the wind, which blew rather strong. They commenced by Villa's spirited attack upon the visitors quarters. Some fast play ensued until half-time was called, the visitors taking a decided advantage, keeping the ball close in their opponents quarters. After half time play became very quick and strong, E. Holmes eventually passing the ball through, and scoring for the Athletic for one goal to none. The fine play of E. Holmes of the W. O. A. C. was generally praised, and deserved special commendation. Ramsey, for the Villa, played a first-class game.

Wednesbury Old Athletic in 1877

The Aston Villa Chronicles 1874 – 1924 (and after)

W. O. A. C.: *Holmes, Zeally, Skidmore, Hatfield, Wills (forwards), S. Page (captain), Stokes, and C. Hatfield (half-backs), Knight, Rotton and Moore (backs), Jackson (goal).*

Aston Villa (list of players only): *Ramsay (captain), Lindsay, Stephens, Weiss, Price, Law, Page, J. Lindsay, Such, Lee, Hughes, Dutsen.*

SALTLEY COLLEGE v. ASTON VILLA

The match between the above teams was played on the College ground on Saturday, and after a pleasant game resulted in a victory for the home team by five goals to nothing. In the first half of the game the play was pretty equal, the ball remaining for an equal time in the close vicinity of each goal. A disputed goal – afterwards allowed – was obtained by Fewkes for Saltley. The Villa made two exceedingly dangerous shots for goal in this part of the game, but the excellent play of Hooke, in goal, proved equal to the occasion, and neither shot was successful. On changing ends at half-time, Saltley appeared to better advantage, two goals being obtained by Fraizier in the first half-hour. After a hard struggle on both sides, the home team, during a scrimmage, again managed to lodge the ball under the tape, and, within the last five minutes, another goal was obtained by Fewkes. The admirable manner in which the ball was passed from one player to another was noticeable in both teams. For Saltley, Pugh, Fewkes, Bird, and Johnstone played exceedingly well; and Hughes, Lindsay and Such rendered good service for the Villa. The teams were as follows:

Saltley: *Pugh, Bird, McIvor, Brazier, and Fewkes, forwards; Johnstone, Davies, and Hodges, half-backs: Swallow, Jeavons, and W. Thompson, backs; Hooke, goal.*

Aston Villa: *Such, Lee, Law, Mason, Hughes. W. Lindsay, forwards; Stephens, quarter-back; Wise and Taylor, half-backs; Matthews, goal; Price and Lindsay backs.*

The first season at Perry Barr was eventually a memorable success, denoting as it did the vast improvement effected on the team.

The Aston Villa Chronicles 1874 – 1924 (and after)

1876-77 Results			
Sep	30th H Wednesbury Town	1-0
Oct	14th A Stafford Road	1-1
	21st H Wednesbury Old Athletic	0-1
Nov	4th A Saltley College	0-5
	18th H Tipton (BC)	0-1
	25th A Burton (Allsop's)	0-1
Dec	2nd H Wednesbury Old Park	2-0
	9th A Royal	1-1
	16th A West Bromwich*	0-1
	23rd H Calthorpe	0-0
	26th H Aston Park Unity	0-0
	30th H West Bromwich*	2-0

Jan	6th (unknown)	1-1
	13th H Coventry	4-0
	20th A Wednesbury Old Park	1-1
Feb	3rd A Aston Park Unity	2-2
	10th H Stafford Road	0-2
	17th H Saltley College	2-0
	24th A Victoria Swifts	1-0
Mar	10th A Tipton	2-0
	17th H St. George's Athletic	3-0
Apr	2nd H Aston Park Unity	2-0
Played 22; 9 won, 6 lost, 7 drawn, goals 25-17
*this "West Bromwich" is not the Albion

Legend (all tables): (BC) – Birmingham Cup; (SC) – Staffs Cup; (FAC) – FA Cup.

The Birmingham and District FA

It was in this winter that the first representative match in connection with the Birmingham and District Football Association was played. The game in question took place at the Crankhall Grounds, Wednesbury, before about 500 spectators, and between teams selected from Birmingham and District. The following were the teams:

> **Birmingham**: *Messrs. Carson, capt., J. C. Orr, Maddock and Westwood (Calthorpe), S. Durban and Brown (Aston Park Unity), W. B. Mason, J. Hughes and W. H. Price (Aston Villa), Thompson, O'Connor and Johnson (Saltley College).*
>
> **District**: *Messrs. G. R. Knowles, capt., and B. C. Knowles (Wednesbury Town), Ludlam, Davis, and Whitehouse (Stafford Road), Peacock and Haines (Tipton), Zealey, Johnson and S. Page (Wednesbury Old Athletic), Harold and Benbow (West Bromwich).*

As usual in those days, the newspapers gave little space on football as will be seen in the following journalistic special on the match. This is the entire match report:

> The Birmingham captain, having won the toss elected to play up hill with the wind. Mr. G. R. Knowles kicked off for the District at a quarter past four, and after a fast and good game, the match ended in favour of the District by one goal to nothing.

The Aston Villa Chronicles 1874 – 1924 (and after)

The inter-Association matches between Birmingham and Sheffield were also played during the progress of this season, Birmingham winning the first 1-0 and losing the second 3-0.

Season 1877-78

In the summer of 1877, the A.V.F.C. members decided to hold a private athletic meeting at Perry Barr. There was no big balance at the bank to fall back on then, and patrons were few and far between. The Villans had to trust to a whip round among themselves to provide prizes such as sticks, pipes, etc.

The gathering was favoured with bright sunny weather, and passed off most successfully. Tom Pank there gave early promise of his budding ability by winning his first race, the quarter mile handicap. Pank figured in scratch, giving as much as 50 yards. There were 23 runners, with Jack Hughes coming in second. Pank also won the sprint that same afternoon, and from this little unpretentious meeting he directly afterwards blossomed out onto the leading Midland athletic grounds, simply sweeping the prize board.

Encouraged by the large amount of success that had rewarded their efforts in the past, the fellows opened their new campaign with the utmost enthusiasm and hopefulness. The following was the list of officers for 1877-78:

President: Rev. C. S. Beechcroft, M.A.;[86] captain, G. B. Ramsay; vice-captain, J. Hughes; second team captain, H. Matthews; deputy-captain. T. Pank; Financial Secretary, E. B. Lee; Hon. Secretary, C. H. Midgley, Finch Road, Handsworth. Committee: Messrs. W. Weiss, J.H. Eaves, A. Westwood, and W. Sothers.

That the sanguine anticipations felt by A.V.F.C. members were most thoroughly realised is most conclusively proved by the victories of the second Perry Barr year, when so numerous and ardent were the members that both second and third teams were run and with highly satisfactory results.

---

[86] He probably succeeded H. H. Hartshorne at this point. According to "Thank God for Football" (Peter Lupson), the Rev. Beechcroft was born in Lowestoft and resided in Wellington (Shrops), where he served as a churchman. He remained president of the Villa for one year, on which he left for Chorley, Lancs. How the Reverend became president of the Villa is unknown! His leaving the post seems to have ended the formal link between the Villa and the Wesleyan movement from which they were spawned.

The Aston Villa Chronicles 1874 – 1924 (and after)

This season showed an improved class of fixtures, and an increased membership. The Villa were beginning to make their presence felt, although as yet the Birmingham Club at Aston Lower Grounds rather dwarfed the Perry Barr men, who, try as they would, could not get the 'swells' to take them on.

Up to this season of 1877-78, the club was quite unable to fill the goalkeeper position with complete satisfaction, and although several smart reliable players were at different times tried, the Villa remained without a thoroughly efficient custodian until they secured the truly valuable services of George Copley, the Saltley College champion. Meanwhile, W. Weiss, W. Sothers and Matthews were in turn deputed to guard the posts, while later on in the season Squires went under the bar. J. Lindsay had returned to bonnie Scotland.

It was probably that season that W. L. ("Llew") Summers came in as a back, with Harry Simmonds also arriving as a back in the second team. Billy Crossland also began with Villa in the second team that season.

Another position which gave the executive great anxiety was the one of centre forward. For some time, Sammy Law was entrusted with the task of combining the wings, and acquitted himself at times with great credit. W. Lindsay was also tried in that post, as was George Page, who, by the way, played centre in the St. George's Cup tie. Turning to the forwards, Jack Hughes, catching a severe cold about the date of the Burton Robin Hoods' match, dropped out of the position on the left-wing, a task he had (in company with W. Such) filled so satisfactorily. Charlie Hughes, a brother of the aforementioned Jack, took up the vacancy, but Such joining Aston Unity, the left had once more to be attended to, George Stock being placed alongside C. Hughes. Both these two forwards had been drafted from the second team.

Meanwhile, as the old original members of the eleven were in the natural order of things falling one by one out of the team, George Ramsay and Billy Mason continued to hold their position unchallenged on the right wing. The Scot was beyond question the best forward of his day in the district, his brilliant performances, both for his club and for the Birmingham Association, earning him universal and well-deserved praise. Billy Mason, being both fast and dashing, with weight on his side, proved an invaluable partner to his captain, the right wing play standing out as a special feature of the Villa games. Other members of the team might come and go, but the invincible right wing combination went on, if not like Tennyson's brook "for ever", at any rate until the completion of the 1879-80 season at the end of which the Villa landed the coveted Birmingham Cup.

The Aston Villa Chronicles 1874 – 1924 (and after)

In 1877-78, and having got through the first round of the Birmingham Cup, the Villa made special efforts to get into form for the next round against Saltley College, whose prowess they had every reason to respect and fear. The gruelling received a few weeks previously at Saltley might have somewhat prepared their minds for the worst, but still, notwithstanding this, the Wellington Roadsters entertained hopes of victory. The chances of the team were, however, severely handicapped on the day by the fact that many of the players had to rush right away from business in cabs to the ground in order to be in time, and therefore could not have been in a condition to do themselves justice. Be that as it may, the College won, and it was heard that the Villans who took part in that match themselves admitted that Saltley deserved their triumph, and were certainly, on the day's play, the better team. It was the two wingers, Goodyear and Jeavons, who did most of the mischief for Saltley that day. One of the Collegians later in the season joined Aston Villa, played for them for years, and by the 1890s became a respected member of their executive. He was **C. S. (Charlie) Johnstone**.

The football records of Saltley College in those days were enriched by the names of some of Birmingham and District's best players.[87] The students of those times were always brimful of muscular vigour and enthusiasm, and were ever to be found somewhere to the front, or thereabouts, in the field of outdoor-sport. The Collegians were able at times to turn out a really fine team as far as football went then, but although on one memorable occasion they ran up for the Birmingham Cup, they were never able to gain any significant success. The reason for this lay in the fact that the students were a migratory crew, and the arrival of the Christmas vacation invariably resulted in the exodus of the many who had done their time as students. The advent of the new year found the College busily engaged in the heartbreaking task of filling the seven or eight vacancies in the eleven, and thus virtually start all over again. Only three of the men who defeated the Villa remained at the College after Christmas.

---

[87] Among the better known may be instanced such men as H. B. Goodyear, J. H. Wynn, C. S. Johnstone, D. Rutherford, J. Hollyhead, E. Johnson, G. Copley, and J. Brodie, to say nothing of J. O'Connor, Comberledge, Jeavons, and many others, recollections of whom had long gone even by the 1890s. There are some remembrances of those olden cracks that stayed with the seers for their lifetime. Instances include Teddy Johnson's magnetic run at the Lower Grounds against London, while George Copley's burly figure and brown-bearded good-humoured face long held a cherished corner in the mental picture gallery of his fans. Dashing, brilliant John Brodie provided another striking proof of the class of football material turned out from Saltley College.

The Aston Villa Chronicles 1874 – 1924 (and after)

Among the absentees was C. S. Johnstone, who, previous to leaving Saltley, had decided to throw in his lot with Aston Villa. He joined the Perry Barr club in the new year, and first played left half-back against West Bromwich on January 19.

Charlie Johnstone had commenced football in around 1874 when a pupil teacher at St. Mary's, Aston Brook. Originally the Saints played hockey, but Johnstone, once he had unearthed a Rugby football case, a bladder was obtained, and the lads, liking the new sport better than the old, soon took to the ball-kicking game. Once at Saltley, Johnstone played both half-back and forward with equal success. He had assisted Saltley on each occasion they defeated the Villa in 1877, but from the beginning of 1878, to 1882, he played under the Perry Barr flag. He was a very useful man, performing sometimes at half-back and sometimes forward on either wing. He played half-back in the Sheffield Heeley match (see below), and he was well remembered for a very smart left wing game he played in a Staffordshire Cup tie in 1880.

Johnstone made his first appearance on the athletic track under the auspices of Aston Villa in their summer sports of 1878, conclusively proving his sprinting ability by winning three races. At the same meeting, his younger brother, J. F. Johnstone, added the first prize of the scholars' quarter to the family plate. Charlie took part in the Amateur Athletic Championships at the Lower Grounds when the Yankees 'invaded' the event. He was a splendid handicap runner.

An Important Progress Indicator

Let us pass on to another Perry Barr match of that season, the game that may be regarded as the pick of the bunch, the Sheffield Heeley encounter, which took place on April 22 at Wellington Road. At that time, the Blades were unquestionably monarchs of all they surveyed in the provinces, and it was only with the greatest difficulty that Heeley, then one of the best of the Sheffield clubs from the birthplace of 'modern' football, was prevailed upon to give the young Birmingham organisation a place on their fixture card. The capital victory achieved by the Villa was of course, considerably reduced in value by reason of the fact that the Blades were represented rather indifferently. Still there were some real good 'uns in the visitors' team, amongst them being an old friend, once of Wednesbury renown, Alf Woodcock. Here is a report of the match, scissored from one of the papers of the day, the *Athletic News*:

The Aston Villa Chronicles 1874 – 1924 (and after)

ASTON VILLA v. HEELEY

This match was played on Monday, on the ground of the former club, at Wellington Road, Perry Barr. A good muster of the followers of the sport assembled to witness the sport. Play commenced at three o'clock, the Heeley men starting off. The Aston Villa brought a strong team into the field, while the Heeley Club were but poorly represented, which will in a great measure account for the defeat they sustained. From the outset of the game the visitors, though playing with great pluck and determination, were evidently outclassed both in pace and precision of kicking, consequently all calculations as to the relative merits of the two teams were upset, the general impression being that the Heeley players, coming from the hotbed of football, would win easily. Davis, for the Aston Villa, always merry, excelled all his previous essays, and to his fine play, together with that of Ramsay, may be due the decisive victory they obtained of four goals to nothing (and one disputed, through "off-side" being claimed and allowed) in favour of the Aston Villa, being the result. For the visitors, Pattison and the two Tomlinsons tried hard to avert defeat. The following were the players:

Aston Villa: *Squires, goal; Weiss and Taylor, backs; C. S. Johnstone, Lee and Evans, half-backs; Ramsay(capt.), Mason, Law, O'Connor and E. Davis, forwards.*

Heeley: *G. Barringham, goal; Thomson and Barringham, backs; T. A, Tomlinson and W. Moss, half-backs; J. Deans (capt.), Pattison, J. Wild, Martin, J. Tomlinson, and A. Woodcock forwards.*

The reference to "E. Davis" in this report highlights the first appearance in Villa colours of one **Eli Davis**, who now added to Villa's left-wing some greater balance to what was happening on the right. We must pause, once again, to endeavour to do something like justice to the sterling abilities of the famous left-wing "corner-man".

Eli Davis was between sixteen and seventeen years of age before he began kicking the leather, but having once started, took to the pastime like the proverbial duck to water. His first club was the Florence, a very clever young Aston team, containing in its ranks such men as Arthur Brown, Charlie Allen, W. and T. Dutton (afterwards of Excelsior) and Joe and Nathan Taylor. Howard Vaughton was also a member, although he only occasionally gave the club his assistance on the field. Davis had always been associated with the left wing, for he commenced his football in that position with the Florence and held it to the end of his career. The club was a very smart team, for they inflicted defeats, among others, upon Aston Unity, Walsall Victoria Swifts, Rushall Rovers and a St. George's team including in its composition half its first eleven. The Florence were particularly proud of their Aston Unity triumph. The game took place on the Aston Park match-ground, and the final score

The Aston Villa Chronicles 1874 – 1924 (and after)

was 2-1. Eli Davis brought away the marks of a nasty kick to remind him of that famous victory.

In those old amateur times, players were not confined to any special club, but roamed about as they liked and were often members of several teams. The abilities of Eli Davis were very quickly appreciated by the then powerful Birmingham Club into whose forward ranks he migrated. The Lower Grounds organisation was then made up of something like the following:

> *Charlie Quilter, goal; Captain Brindley and Wilkinson or Dick Evans, backs; Tom Bryan, Will Evans, Hiram Slack or George Pears, half-backs; F. Bill, Nicholls, Harry Webster, George Quilter, Howard Vaughton, J. R. Riddell, Alf. Harvey, or Eli Davis, forwards.*

J. R. Riddell was an elder brother of Tom of that ilk (later of the Villa), and afterwards, being scholastically engaged in the West, organised a Gloucester County Team which came down and played Villa some years later. Captain Brindley was a fine player, while Frank Bill, the Handsworth Wood cricketer, was very prominent as a right-wing forward. Fixtures were made with all the leading provincial clubs; the Sheffield, Nottingham, Derby, Burton, and Shrewsbury clubs being conspicuous on the list. The Birmingham team on one occasion entered for the Sheffield Cup, and were put out 3-0 by Sheffield Exchange, at the Lower Grounds. Davis took part in this match, and, indeed, in all the principal games during his membership, and his displays, especially in some of the Nottingham contests, were generally admired.

The following story is well worth telling here as an example of the free and easy manner in which fixtures were fulfilled then, including cup-ties. The Welsh Druids club, being drawn with Shropshire Wanderers in the English (FA Cup) ties, borrowed assistance from the Birmingham Club, and Tom Bryan scored the winning goal for them. In the next round the Welshmen were pitted against Royal Engineers, and Kendrick (of the Druids) wrote to Charlie Quilter, stating his intention of scratching as he could not get a team together for the London journey. Quilter wrote back, pledging himself to provide the Ancient Ones with a team.

When the eventful day arrived the Druids had only one Welshman in the whole lot. The afterwards famous Andy Watson (then belonging to a small Glasgow club) played full back by himself, while the rest of "the Druids" were made up of Birmingham men, among whom were O. and G. Quilter, Hiram Slack, H. Webster. F. Bill, W. J. Nicholls, Tom Bryan, and Eli Davis. It was a big ordeal, facing these redoubtable Engineers, who afterwards won the Cup. Hardly had the ball been started when there was a terrific cry of "Line up Sappers!" and before the Druids

The Aston Villa Chronicles 1874 – 1924 (and after)

(ahem, the revised Birmingham edition) knew where they were, the leather had been driven through their goal. The final damages were about 7 to 0 and the Druids' impostors journeyed home sadder, if not wiser, men.

Eli Davis also became a member of the Wednesbury Strollers' club, in which Tom Bryan, the two Knowles, Alf Harvey and Job Edwards also played. Fred Hackwood was Honorary Secretary, and a right good one too. Right through the season of 1877-78 Eli Davis played for the Strollers in Birmingham Cup ties. He was one of the team that put Saltley out, and took part in the final tie when Shrewsbury won. The Strollers were very dissatisfied over the result, as they considered they had the best of the play. The referee, after making some errors as to time, caused the teams to re-enter the field after the whistle had blown, and resume play. Davis held the record for Birmingham finals; he played for Strollers in 1878, and then for Aston Villa in no less than six final ties.

Although Eli Davis first assisted Villa in the spring of 1878, he was not a regular playing member until 1878-79. He then remained with the Perry Barr club until 1885-86, retiring from active service the season before the Villans first won the FA Cup. Times without number were his abilities recognised by the Birmingham Association, on whose left wing he was for a long time a permanent fixture. Eli Davis never played better than in 1880-81, when it was only by a piece of ill-luck that he missed his England cap. Hawtrey's magnificent goalkeeping for London robbed Birmingham of victory, and just in that particular match, when the eyes of the Association judges were on Davis, the very clever left-winger failed to exhibit his accustomed skill, and thus lost his chance of the honour he so thoroughly deserved. Supporters of the Villa never forgot the splendid see-saw play of the old left-wing when Davis and Vaughton were at their best.

Eli was always a worker from start to finish with any amount of dash and determination. Away he would go up the left, passing man after man. "Centre, Eli, centre!" would be the cry, but it was premature. "Why didn't he cross it? He'll lose the ball!" some would exclaim as the forward sped to his favourite spot by the corner flag, pursued by his opponents. It seemed any odds against an accurate centre at such an angle, but presently the leather came sailing triumphantly up out of the corner, curling right into the goalmouth with unerring precision. It was Eli's favourite stroke. However, William McGregor referred to how they tried to change Eli's style:

> Eli Davis ... was a fine forward, and no man ever centred a ball better; that will be conceded by all who saw him play. But he had a weakness ... of getting

The Aston Villa Chronicles 1874 – 1924 (and after)

> right into the corner and there occasionally losing the ball. Flags were put at intervals down the touchline in those days, and Andy [Hunter] had one of these placed at a certain distance from the goal-line. The understanding was that Eli was not to pass that post; when he reached it he must centre. Andy was always waiting for the centre, which he knew would be placed with beautiful accuracy and many a goal to the Villa resulted from that compact.[88]

Old Fogey later commented:

> [He was] very fast and skilful, he was for many years the Villa's famous left winger. ... Dark and rather fragile, he never condescended to 'bumping', and if antagonists started bashing him about, his fiery untamed skipper used to wander across and 'see to things' and it was always pretty bad for the basher, for Eli was a great pal of Hunter's.[89]

Eli Davis had also strong athletic as well as football claims upon the sporting public, for it is said that in conjunction with Charlie Hall, Tom Pank, W. Davies and T. Steanes, he helped to found the famous Birchfield Harriers. Charlie Hall, a Villa player before the 1878-79 season, was honorary secretary of the Harriers by 1880, and it is likely that the aforementioned group were those that met at Wheeler Street Sunday School in Lozells[90] to form the Harriers. Eli himself won many running events both across country and on the path, being a rare good man at any distance from a quarter to ten miles.

---

[88] C.B Fry's Magazine of Action and Outdoor Life Vol 2 Oct 1904 to Mar 1905 p.39 *et seq*
[89] Villa News & Record 17 Apr 1908 – "Some Forwards of Renown"
[90] Perhaps coincidentally, this appears to be the Congregational Church that William McGregor started attending at some point (perhaps around 1880).

The Aston Villa Chronicles 1874 – 1924 (and after)

			1877-78 Results						
Oct	6th	H	Brownhills	8-0	Jan	19th	A	West Bromwich	4-0
	13th	A	Stafford Road	0-2		26th	H	Burton Robin Hood	8-0
	20th	A	Coventry	3-0	Feb	16th	H	Calthorpe	4-2
	27th	H	Wednesbury Old Ath.	3-3		23rd	A	Burton Robin Hood	4-1
Nov	3rd	A	St. George's (BC)	2-0	Mar	2nd	H	St. George's	6-0
	10th	A	Saltley College	0-4	Apr	22nd	H	Sheffield (Heeley)	4-0
	17th	H	West Bromwich	1-1		23rd	H	St. George's	9-0
Dec	1st	H	Coventry	8-0					
	22nd	H	Saltley College (BC)	1-4				Played 17, 12 won, 3 lost, 2 drawn;	
	29th	H	Burton (Allsopp's)	6-0				goals 74-14.	

The Birmingham and District FA

In the season 1877-78 Birmingham took part in three inter-Association matches. On December 1, a team captained by Mr. Crump journeyed to the Metropolis and on Kennington Oval paid the penalty of their rashness to the dispiriting extent of 11-0. London had put a fine team on the field containing no less than seven international players. The Cockneys then brought down a less formidable lot to Birmingham on January 12, when Brum was more strongly represented and a fine game resulted. The following were the teams:

> **London** (White): *C. E. Hart (Ramblers), goal; J. Fox (Hawks) and C. E. Leeds (South Northwood), backs; B. G. Jarrett (Old Harrovians) and N. C. Bailey (Clapham Rovers), half-backs; P. Fairclough (Old Foresters) and F. W. Watkins (Herts Rangers) right side forwards; F. Barry (Old Foresters) and W. Buchanan (Clapham Rovers) centre forwards; H. Sedgwick (Clapham Rovers) and H. de St. Jarrett (Clapham Rovers) left forwards.*
>
> **Birmingham** (Maroon) *J. Carson (Calthorpe) goal; A. T. Ward (Stafford Road) and E. Jones (Shrewsbury) backs; H. V. Chapman (Shrewsbury) and A. E. Daniell (Calthorpe), half-backs; D. Tonks (Elwells), G. B. Ramsay (Aston Villa) right-side forwards; C. Crump (Stafford Road) and A. H. Edwards (Shrewsbury), centre forwards; H. C. Goodyear (Saltley College) and J. Wynn (Saltley College) left forwards.*

The Birmingham men played a very plucky and determined game, and although the Londoners (thanks to Fairclough) got the ball through once and won 1 to 0, the locals had quite an equal share of the action. The hero of the match was the Aston Villa captain, whose play on the right wing was the theme of general admiration. So great indeed was the enthusiasm of the crowd that at the finish of the game, George Ramsay was appropriated bodily by his admirers, and carried shoulder high from the field.

The last inter-association match of the season was played on the Aston Unity ground against a strong representative Sheffield eleven. As one of the Birmingham backs failed to turn up, Tom Butler of the Aston Unity was pressed into service and came off with flying colours. George Ramsay played on the right with good old Roland Morley. Sprott, and Hawley played centre, and Goodyear and Wynn were on the left.

There was evidently a wide margin between Birmingham and Sheffield football, for the locals, however gamely they strove, could do nothing against the superior play of the Sheffield team and were decisively beaten by 5 to 0, despite the inclusion of players such as George Ramsay. The *Daily Gazette* declared that: "It was an exceedingly plucky venture on the part of a young association like Birmingham to challenge the formidable team of the cutlery town ..."

The best of the Midlands was yet afar off, but not so distantly, for pluck and perseverance were rapidly bridging the gulf that lay between mediocrity and excellence. The advent of another leader, greater than his brilliant predecessor, was in a few months to be hailed with jubilation, and the appearance of the Ayr Thistle jersey at Perry Barr to mark the advance of a new era, rich with the fairest promise of success, both for Midland football and for Aston Villa.

Season 1878-79

The Villa officials for this season were:[91]

Captain, G. B. Ramsay; Vice-captain, S. Law; second team captain, T. Pank; deputy-captain, H. Matthews; Treasurer, W. B. Mason; Hon Sec., C. H. Midgley. The committee comprised Messrs. W. G. Sothers, J. Hughes, C. S. Johnstone, E. B. Lee, and W. Jones.

As far as the presidency is concerned, duties to the church took the Rev. C. S. Beechcroft elsewhere, and it is likely that it was at this juncture that the club's formal link with the Aston Villa Wesleyan Chapel was severed. It was probably also the occasion (or soon after) that Mr. W. M. Ellis, J.P. took over the mantle as president.

---

[91] Apparently from a 1878-79 membership card held by Tom Mason (an ex-player and Villa vice-president in 1935, when these details were published in a newspaper article (unknown newspaper).

The Aston Villa Chronicles 1874 – 1924 (and after)

The Villa's Lion – facing a different direction to today's version, and to the one used after 1880 – had been introduced by October, 1878 (see image), as it was to be seen on the club's notepaper and envelopes of that time. The motto ("Prepared") and the Lion would have been introduced by the Scottish contingent at the Villa, in particular George Ramsay and William McGregor. A Lion then appeared on the Villa jerseys, as Charlie Johnstone explained:

It came about because I was, when I joined Aston Villa, the happy possessor of a black jersey, for which I had just paid seven shillings and sixpence. You do not see the connection? Well, you must know that as an amateur club the first point for consideration is the club colours. The first colours were stripes – horizontal, black and white. They were pretty well worn out, and, besides, everyone wore stripes and we had aspirations, even in those days.

So we decided on a self-colour. For obvious reasons, I suggested black, and black it was. That was too sombre, and as our president, George Kynoch, our two vice-presidents, Fergus Johnstone and William McGregor, and our captain, George Ramsay, were Scots, and as there was a strong Scots element in the club, we adopted the Scottish Lion as a relief, which was forthwith emblazoned on our shirts by Miss Midgeley, our [then] secretary's sister. Alas, our lion had no chance with the washing lady. He became pale and anaemic, so 'Mac' was deputed to send to Scotland for thirteen lions on yellow shields proper, which could be attached and detached at will.

They came – about the size of a dessert plate! When they were duly attached – you could hardly see the man for the lion – we were each as self-conscious as a bride in a wedding-dress. We went on the field but the gorgeous lion got us down; we had a most awful whacking, and the lion was relegated to the club note-paper and flags! [92]

The lion badge – at an appropriate size! – was not re-introduced on the Villa's playing shirts again until shortly after the start of Villa's cup run in 1957, and clearly had as much beneficial affect as it had nearly eighty years before. Its re-introduction on the team's shirts was discussed by the then Villa Committee as long ago as 1894, but it was not then pursued. A lion badge has been retained on the kit ever since 1957 – in different forms.

---

[92] In his column in The Sporting Mail 17 Dec 1910

The Aston Villa Chronicles 1874 – 1924 (and after)

Yet Another Scottish Development

The point has been reached in this growing drama where the audience – in ever-growing numbers – had taken to the Perry Barr performers, and had begun to entertain hopes of even better things to come. Metaphorically speaking, the first act is over, and the stalls stroll out to the bar while the gallery crack their nuts and suck their oranges – or sip something stronger – as they sit. In this interval for refreshments, it is time to ruminate on the steady progress of the young triers. Something seems to be missing - perhaps a little fresh blood, a little more class; something 'more' is needed to ensure success. But look, the band are hard at it, the curtain lifts, and, amidst the inspiring strains of the music and the swirl of the stage mist, the hero at last treads the boards – the Villa trump card for 1878-79 – one **Archie Hunter**, who arrived in Birmingham, August 8, 1878, a youth of 19. Dame Fortune, ever smiling on the brave, once more designed to interpose in favour of the Villa.

It will be recalled that when George Ramsay landed in Midlandopolis, it was only by the merest chance that he had eventually cast in his lot with the Aston club. Well, Archie Hunter came to the Perry Barr fold in much the same casual way. Archie, having come into contact with J. Campbell Orr and the Calthorpe team when they played Ayr Thistle as part of their tour in Scotland,[93] wanted to find the Calthorpe team now he had arrived in Birmingham.

Fortunately, at Archie's place of work was a man named Uzzel. The latter happened to be an enthusiastic follower of the Wellington Road team, and hearing that the young Scot was a football player, used all his endeavours to persuade him to give Perry Barr a try. At first, it seems, Uzzel was not successful, as Charlie Johnstone later recounted:

> I was then a regular member of the team, and we used to foregather together in the evenings at Bert Hibell's, on the corner of the Chain Walk. He had a tobacconists' shop and a big room upstairs. There I met a little chap named Uzzel, who told me that a fine young Scotsman, captain of the Ayr Thistle, had come to their place – Graham's, St. Paul's Square – to learn factoring. Archie would not come down to Perry Barr at Uzzel's invitation, but started out to find Calthorpe. Fortunately, he did not succeed, and the following Saturday morning I captured him, took him home to dinner, and thence to Perry Barr.

---

[93] The first Birmingham club to do so.

The Aston Villa Chronicles 1874 – 1924 (and after)

> He said he played back, so in choosing sides we arranged that he should play on the opposite side to Ramsay, Mason and myself. After stopping us all a time or two, and sending me flying with that famous hip of his, we decided we had found a gem.[94]

However, because Harry Simmonds was the established back, Archie was subsequently tried at centre, and that is how his long reign in that position started. Hunter only played twice in the full-back position for Villa after leaving Scotland. He took his place from the first among the Villa forwards (though, when the occasion demanded it, also played at half-back), and speedily made himself the very keystone of the vanguard. Verily it is better to be born lucky than rich! The gods of old looked kindly down on Perry Barr.

The importance of the new capture was very rapidly seen, and the ability of the latest acquisition invested the Villa's September practises with additional interest. His style and approach to the game was so advanced that football enthusiasts rolled up in great numbers to get a glimpse of the young stranger from whom so much was expected in the coming season.

Brilliancy and unselfishness were the leading characteristics of his style. With the ability to dribble superbly, he passed to an inch, and even at times overdid this in his desire to practically illustrate the advantage of combination; football is a team game, after all. It was said that he was often seen to have a total disregard of self, and transfer the leather to a comrade close to goal, when ninety-nine men out of a hundred could not have resisted having a go for themselves. In fact, he could shoot splendidly, and despite his physical advantage, depended almost invariably upon his scientific knowledge of the game to extricate himself from difficult positions. Occasionally though, after having sustained a specially severe course of shoulder and kicking persecution, the Scot would go so far as to retaliate on the enemy with their own methods, and invariably get his own back. This happened very occasionally, however, for a more gentlemanly polished forward never toed a ball in those days.

As an exponent of the passing game, he was unequalled, but his merits as a player, great as they were, sunk into comparative insignificance before his abilities as a leader. A better captain than Archie Hunter never trod a football field. In his happiest days, he had an influence and control over the Villa team that can only be described as magnetic. As Billy Crossland once said of his skipper, "You've got

---

[94] Villa News & Record, 7 Jan 1928 – "The Coming of the Scots"

The Aston Villa Chronicles 1874 – 1924 (and after)

somehow to do what Archie tells you, and you can't help working when he's on the job!"

In his latter days as a player, Archie lost much of his skill, but Aston Villa were never without a magnificent leader while the old boss retained his place in the team. After his enforced retirement from active service, the Villa had to wait a while before they found a successor really fit to stand in Archie Hunter's shoes.

The Season's Play

The season of 1878-79, already rendered memorable by the appearance of Archie Hunter on the scene, was of itself a stirring, eventful, winter for Aston Villa. Archie Hunter's first match with Aston Villa was that first game of the season 1878-79, when the Villans tripped it merrily over to Burton to antagonise the Robin Hoods of that ilk. The outlaws in question were a heavy, resolute, lot, and whatever they lacked in science was simply atoned for by determination and force.

A most disastrous start was made from the outset, as Charlie Midgley (the secretary of the time) was unfortunately left behind on the New Street platform with the tickets in his possession. In consequence of this mishap, Jack Hughes had to be brought into active service as umpire, an office he continued to hold for a long time with credit to himself and his club. The ground was a fearful one, its erratic undulations reminding one more of a ploughed field than a football meadow. This was not the worst, however, for the style of game played by Robin Hood's men was even more execrable than the pitch. The home team's chief idea of leather chasing appeared to be pushing over as many opponents as possible. Hunter, hopelessly handicapped by the ground, made a far from promising début, and was continually shadowed throughout the game by a burly opponent who went for him on every possible occasion, with a ferocity that was positively appalling. Although the visitors were altogether outweighed, they managed somehow to hold their own as far as scoring went.

Archie Hunter himself intervenes to give his perspective to the story of this barbarous encounter:

> ... It was quite evident to us from the beginning that nobody in Burton wanted us to win that match and that they were determined to do their best to prevent us scoring ... When we scored our first goal the blood of the Robin Hoods began to get up ... the wrath of the spectators was as a consuming fire.

The Aston Villa Chronicles 1874 – 1924 (and after)

> ... They [the spectators] got between the goal posts, some hundreds of them, forming a solid background and presently, when a shot was made, the ball rebounded back into play and the Robin Hood claimed that no goal had been scored ... we disagreed ... the umpire would not allow the goal, so, as a protest, we left the field.
>
> I was not sorry to get away, for during the course of the game one of the Burton players had so far lost control of himself that he made sudden dashes in my direction and chased me all over the field. He had his sleeves turned up and every time he came near me he doubled up his fists in a very ominous manner. I thought he meant business, but fortunately, I was able to avoid him and escaped with my life ... I suppose I hadn't let him take the ball away from me, you see, and had been making rings round him. He was evidently a disappointed man. ...[95]

The luckless Brums, reaching the dressing room with the greatest difficulty, were locked up for safety for fully an hour and a half until the howling mob outside had dispersed. The proceedings were rendered still more exciting when a ponderous Burton player, under the influence of excitement, came up to the Villa room and expressed his desire to fight the biggest man among 'em. This description could justly only apply to Billy Weiss, but fortunately, before belligerent operations were commenced, the Burton captain turned up and successfully called his man to order.

Thanks in a great measure to the strenuous efforts of one of the Robin Hoods - a player named Owen - the Villans escaped with whole skins to the railway station, carrying back home with them memories of Burton too unpleasant to easily be forgotten.

Archie's first match at Perry Barr was on the following Saturday against Rushall Rovers. The latter team, who were at one time regarded in some quarters as dark horses for the Birmingham Cup, came to grief against the Old Athletic, and quickly dropped out of local notice though they were a very promising lot. The Villa did not, however, have much trouble in winning. After easy success in their third match against Shrewsbury Engineers, the Villa's fourth match of the season was a memorable Birmingham Cup tie with Aston Unity.

It will be remembered that the Villa and Unity had been from the first great rivals, and when the fortunes of war threw them together for the local Cup, there was no end of local excitement. The Perry Barr men considered themselves quite good

---

[95] "Triumphs of the Football Field", Birmingham Weekly Mercury, October, 1890 to February, 1891

The Aston Villa Chronicles 1874 – 1924 (and after)

enough to win, even though the game was played at the Unity's ground at Aston Lane, while the Unity were quite as confident of their ability to successfully emerge from the tie. The match proved a very close and interesting struggle. Mr. J. R. Riddell (of the Birmingham Club) officiated as referee, while the later Villan and England international Arthur Brown was at the time a member of the Unity team. The game was a very stubborn and rough one.

> The newspapers of the day reported that the play was very rough, and so the Birmingham FA called in the participating players to hear their account of the match. In unison, the players avowed that it was a pleasant and enjoyable game, and so the FA wrote to the press to put them right on the matter![96]
>
> *A Lion's Fun*

Neither eleven had anything to give away, and they went at it hammer and tongs without fear or favour. Archie Hunter was in splendid trim, his dodgy runs, passing and shooting being a continual source of annoyance and trouble to the Unity backs. Whatever there was of bad luck to be had, the Villa had it that day. The fates were against the Wellington Road men who, after a fierce game, during which they fully held their own on the field, were again ejected from the cup-ties by the narrow margin of 2 to 1.

The losers heard afterwards, to their bitter mortification, that another goal would have been allowed them had an appeal been made to the referee. It was in a large measure due to Arthur Brown's brilliant performance that the Unity proved successful.

The start of 'Captain' Archie Hunter's career with Villa was in October, 1878. However, in the following month, Hunter – presumably playing as a guest – played for the Birmingham Club at Aston Lower Grounds in a team composed of the following:

> *C H Quilter; Hon. R Lyttelton, T. Butler; B W Stevens, C Allen; G R Quilter, F. Bill, H (Henry) Webster, Archie Hunter, J R Riddell, Howard Vaughton.* [97]

It should be noted that Howard Vaughton did not join the Villa until 1880. The Quilters, it would seem, were a famous pair of brothers in those days down at the Lower Grounds' meadow. And no wonder, as they were the sons of the proprietor of the entertainments at Aston Lower Grounds, Henry Quilter. They remained at the Grounds until the gentleman from the Brighton Marina (Mr. Reeves-Smith) took

---

[96] Sir Frederick Wall "50 Years of Football 1884-1934" (Classic Reprint)
[97] Villa News & Record 15 Sep 1906

The Aston Villa Chronicles 1874 – 1924 (and after)

over management of the site. The Quilters then went to South Africa.

> It was in October, 1878, that the first football matches took place "by electric light". The first at the Aston Lower Grounds was on the 28 October.[98] A number of such matches soon followed, though the technology was still highly primitive.
>
> The *Athletic News* later commented (6 November): "It is a most interesting baby, and promises when it is grown up to cut a very notable figure in the world."

Though the Villa again failed in the cup-ties, they, by twice beating the Birmingham Club, won the championship of the town. In addition to this achievement, they held their own with both the other powerful district cracks, Stafford Road and Old Athletic.

The Birmingham Club had for some time enjoyed the reputation of being the best club in the town. How this came to be the case seems a little strange, for, at the very end of 1877, they lost on their own ground to the country town of Hagley by the impressive score of 5 goals to 2, after tying 2 goals apiece at half-time. The Hagley team was notable for the inclusion of four members of the Lyttelton family, all described by the gentlemanly title of "Hon." These were sons of the fourth Baron Lyttelton of Frankley, amongst whom was Alfred Lyttelton who became the first man to play for England at both football and cricket; he also became a noted politician. The late entertainer Humphrey Lyttelton was a great-nephew of Alfred.

The Birmingham Club met a strong Nottingham team just two months later at the Lower Grounds, and drew one apiece in an exciting match. The *Daily Gazette* noted that the teams dined in the Holte Hotel in the evening. However, this event was a return match to one played at Nottingham, where the score was again 1-1, and it was decided to play a third – at the Lower Grounds – to determine which was the better team. On the 9 March 1878, the Birmingham Club – including Howard Vaughton and Eli Davis – received their come-uppance by the margin of three to nil, and it was reported they were fortunate to get away with that scoreline. But at least they again dined at the Holte Hotel!

For a considerable period, the Villa had been itching for an opportunity of tackling the Birmingham 'toffs', who held, or pretended to hold, their Perry Barr rivals most lightly. It was not until this season that the two clubs met. The first engagement took place at the Lower Grounds when the starch was completely taken out of the

---

[98] Showell's Dictionary of Birmingham

The Aston Villa Chronicles 1874 – 1924 (and after)

Birmingham men, who had to admit themselves fairly and squarely beaten. Ramsay, Archie Hunter, Stock, and Charlie Hughes were in fine form for the Villa, their forward play altogether demoralising the enemy. Although the official score was only 2 to 1 in favour of the Wellington Roadsters, the leather was put no less than five times through the Birmingham goal. The Villa victory was a most popular one with the crowd and totally unexpected by the losers.

The return fixture at Perry Barr, which came off five weeks later, naturally attracted even more interest than the first game, for Birmingham on this occasion could be depended upon to make a special effort towards wiping out the stigma of defeat, while the Villans were equally determined to keep their ends up at any cost.

Much regret and no small amount of apprehension was felt by the Villa and their supporters at the unavoidable absence of George Ramsay, who was not able to give his valuable service on this occasion. The two teams faced out as follows:

> **Villa**: *Hill goal; L. Summers, back; Lee, Johnstone, and McBean, halves; Mason, Crossland, Archie Hunter, Law, Charlie Hughes, and Stock, forwards.*
>
> **'The Birmingham Club'**: *Captain Walker, goal; T. Butler and Stevens, backs; C. Allen and Evans, halves; Eli Davis, A. Harvey, Bill, Howard Vaughton, Riddell, and C. Durban, forwards.*

In fact, the result of this match settled conclusively the question of premiership, for once more were Birmingham defeated by Aston. The game itself was a splendidly contested one. The Villa lost the toss, and after fifteen minutes' play, Hunter put in a splendid run culminating with a shot which was only temporarily averted with the greatest difficulty by Walker. Thereupon Mason, running up, planted the leather safely through goal. Matters remained in this position on changing over. Summers was as steady as a rock at back, while Hunter's brilliant flights continuously embarrassed the visitors' defence. Before the second half was over, Law again eluded the vigilance of Walker, the Villa thus gaining the day by 2 to nil.

The Visit of 'QP' Seconds

Another great day indeed for Perry Barr was the occasion in the same season when the famed Queen's Park club of Glasgow sent a team to Wellington Road. However, the Villa were then very low down in the order of merit, while Glasgow was in the very hey-day of its success and there had been no end of trouble to get this match on, the persevering efforts of G. B. Ramsay eventually proving equal to the task of bringing down a second edition of the 'Spiders'.

The Aston Villa Chronicles 1874 – 1924 (and after)

"We'll send you our second eleven down," said Charlie Campbell, "and if you manage to beat them, it will be quite time then to talk about first team fixtures." The Villa had to be content, as they should have been, with the offer made them. So it was arranged for the Queen's Park seconds to come down, and everybody looked forward to the coming match with the liveliest interest, for the fixture was one regarded as of the utmost importance.

Prior to the day of battle, frost and snow set in, and the ground was in a terrible condition the night before, when a special emergency committee of the club was held, at which various and many were the devices proposed to get the field into playable condition for the morrow. The most elaborate calculations were made as to how many men and carts would be required, but the best laid plans of mice and men were of little use, for the feathery flakes recommenced falling in the night, and when morning came, the Perry Barr meadow was four or five inches under snow. All that was possible to be done in so short a time was done to improve matters; a straight path was cleared from goal to goal, but the other playing portions of the field were in a fearful state. As if this in itself were not quite enough to destroy any hope of a decent gate, the Birmingham Club had got a big fixture at the Lower Grounds with Edinburgh University, so what with the weather and rival attractions combined, the Villans were fairly in 'Queer Street'. QP were touring at the time, and had played at Stoke on the Saturday, and came from there to fulfil their Monday fixture with the Villans. The following were the teams:

> **Villa**: *Hill, goal; Llew Summers, back; McBean, Jones, and Lee, half-backs; Ramsay, Mason, Archie Hunter, Law, Charlie Hughes, and Stock, forwards.*
>
> **Queens Park (second team)**: *Mossman, goal; O'Brien and Taylor, backs; Davie Anderson, and Mitchell, half-backs; McTavish, Smith, Brand, Eddie Fraser, McGill, and R. Fraser, forwards.*

As Charlie Hughes commented years later, QP's team was not such a bad second eleven, as Eddie Fraser soon after received a Scottish 'cap', and Davie Anderson afterwards became a Villan.

The game itself was almost entirely spoilt by the weather, but it was close and exciting. The Villa playing downhill in the first half, held the advantage, and had considerably the best of matters during the first quarter of an hour. At the end of that period, Charlie Hughes drew first blood for the homesters, and at half-time the Brums led 1-0. After changing over, Scottish stamina began to tell its tale, and the Villa seemed jaded and worn compared to their opponents, who pegged manfully at it right to the finish, as fresh as paint. Twenty minutes after the restart, a fine run by

The Aston Villa Chronicles 1874 – 1924 (and after)

Smith and McTavish enabled Brand to equalise. The game was fiercely contested, Queens Park being the chief aggressors, until ten minutes from time when the Glasgow men obtained another goal and thus won, 1 to 2.

It was reported by the *Athletic News* that a substitution was allowed when Eddie Fraser was injured – "a good-natured concession which the Birmingham men had reason to regret."

With regard to the composition of the Villa team, Hill was a very good goalkeeper, and played heroically against the QP. He was a tall, quick fellow who had been playing with the Birmingham Club. McBean used to play with Billy Mason in the old Moseley Grasshoppers. Llew Summers and George Stock have been mentioned before; Stock and Charlie Hughes played together on the left wing throughout this season and were most successful, considering their lightness, both in weight and years.

The Perry Barr Ground

The Perry Barr ground had undergone many alterations and improvements since the Villans first began to disport themselves upon it. Originally there was a hedge round the field with gaps in, through which the free-order brigade could watch the game at their leisure. In 1878, the hedge was cut down and a substantial boarding substituted. That hoarding was still present in 1893.

One aspect of the Perry Barr ground proved very difficult to change, and that was its hill. A few years later, it was referred to as: "The celebrated hill at Perry Barr, which ought by this time to have become enshrined in football lore!"[99] But the drainage the slope facilitated was its plus point: "The Villa ground is usually in good condition and probably less permanently affected by rain than any of our other club grounds ..."[100]

Trees also grew on the meadow, and of course interfered with the play. Ropes had to be fastened round from tree to tree in order to keep the spectators back when a match was on. An arrangement of this character could be but of an unsatisfactory nature for the pressure on the folks resulted in the barriers breaking down. Further, a couple of the trees that adorned the Perry Barr field of old were close together, and in the early days, if ever the artful wily Weiss succeeded in getting his man

---

[99] Midland Athlete 30 Dec 1882. The Villa committee did make attempts to level the ground over the ensuing years.
[100] Midland Athlete 31 Jan 1883

The Aston Villa Chronicles 1874 – 1924 (and after)

'sandwiched' there, it was most unhealthy for him. Eventually the trees on the field were cut down, but even then the stumps remained, an eyesore and annoyance to players and spectators.

How the Tree Stumps were Removed

The tree stumps, however, at last in their turn disappeared, but the manner by which they did so was at the time enveloped in mystery. Their disappearance turned out to be just one of a number of examples of constructive skulduggery attributed to George Ramsay, even in his reign as club secretary/manager from 1886 – in his earlier years at least.

One dark night or early morning – it matters not which – the denizens of Perry Barr were frightened most out of their wits by a terrible explosion which occurred in their neighbourhood. At first, it was naturally thought that the Kynoch armaments factory was in a state of combustion, but this impression was soon proved to be erroneous.

Finally, an inspection of the Villa field showed that the obnoxious stumps had been blown up out of the ground by means of dynamite cartridges. No clue to the identity of the miscreants could be found, and it was not until a very long time afterwards that the truth of this matter came out. Two individuals only were responsible for the act, viz. George Ramsay and an accomplice rejoicing in the cognomen of Jones. Ramsay lodged opposite the ground at the time, and it was to him that Jones suggested the committal of the act. A suitable occasion was chosen, and it must have been a sight for gods and men to see GBR and the immortal Jones making tracks across country for the main road, in mortal fear lest the fuse should not last long enough to enable them to get clear away!

by Nick Oldham

When barriers were eventually erected at the ground, the measurements were most carefully made by the Villa captain (George Ramsay). A dressing room was built next; Mr. Walter Bowen (of the Crown and Cushion) agreed to provide the latter structure on the condition that the club allowed him to use half of it for refreshment

The Aston Villa Chronicles 1874 – 1924 (and after)

purposes. Prior to this, the team had had to dress at Bowen's, which was a great inconvenience especially in inclement weather.

The Birmingham FA and Inter-association Matches

The Birmingham Association had certainly been having a very bad time in the past, and their days of adversity were by no means over. A visit to Kennington Oval on November 30, 1878, ended in a mauling of eight goals to nil in favour of the Londoners. Fortunately, on this occasion, no members of the Villa club were on duty. Despite the severity of this reverse, Birmingham came up smiling at Sheffield on December 14. This was the first Association contest in which Arthur James – the celebrated Small Heath forward – took part.

The Scottish Counties were then tackled at Hampden Park in January 1879, when Aston Villa were again unrepresented in the Birmingham eleven, although two future members of the Perry Barr team, Eli Davis and Alf Harvey took part (as had Arthur Brown in the London debacle). The above match was played in an ocean of mud, with the Scots winning 7 to 1.

London visited on February 8, and Birmingham once more saw deep trouble, the Cockneys winning 7 to 0. This was the first inter-association match in which Archie Hunter took part, the Villan playing centre, along with J. Whitehead of Stafford Road, in the days when six forwards were played.

Hitherto, the history of the Birmingham Association had been disastrous, but their time was coming.

1878-79 Results

Oct	12th	A	Burton Robin Hood	1-1	Feb	1st	H St. George's	0-0
	19th	H	Rushall Rovers	4-0		8th	A Nottingham Sneinton W.	4-2
	26th	H	Shrewsbury Engineers	6-2		15th	H Aston Unity	2-0
Nov	2nd	A	Aston Unity (BC)	1-2		22nd	H Arcadians	8-0
	16th	H	West Bromwich	2-1	Mar	22nd	A Stafford Road	1-0
	23rd	A	The Birmingham Club	2-1	Apr	6th	H Wednesbury Old Athletic	3-0
	30th	A	Wednesbury Old Athletic	2-3	May	3rd	A Stoke	1-1
Dec	7th	H	Nottingham Sneinton W.	3-0				
Jan	11th	A	West Bromwich	2-0				
	20th	H	Quuens Park (2nd Team)	1-2				

Also 25th H The Birmingham Club 2-0.

Played 18, 12 Won, 3 Lost, 3 Drawn; Goals 45-15.

The Aston Villa Chronicles 1874 – 1924 (and after)

Season 1879-80 : The Villa's First Trophy

Telling the story of the development of the Birmingham Association is but to provide a back-cloth to the scene in which Villa's development proved to be in concert with that of the Birmingham Association. The Association and the club were rising to fame side by side, so securely linked together by the chains of common interest and brotherhood as to render their separation a matter involving a certain amount of injustice to both.

The Birmingham Association opened their season on Saturday, November 15, when a team was sent to London composed as follows (again, at this stage, not showing representation from the Villa):

> *Ray, Selman, and J. Whitehead (Stafford Road), Gathers, Wignall, and W. Shaw (Derby), G.H. Holden and J. Reeves (Old Athletic), T. Bryan (Wednesbury Strollers), Arthur Brown (Aston Unity), and E. Johnson (Saltley College).*

The Brum side performed with rare dash and determination and met their reward, winning 2 to 1. Thus, at the fifth time of asking, and after having accumulatively lost by 27 goals to 0, Birmingham gained its first victory over London.

A fortnight later the Sheffielders paid Birmingham a visit, the match coming off at Perry Barr. Harry Simmonds, the Villa back, was played at the exclusion of Gathers, the team being otherwise identical with the one that had beaten London. The Blades were powerfully represented, and a red-hot game ensued, honours being divided at two goals each. Alf Woodcock, afterwards associated with the revival of Wednesbury Town, played centre for Sheffield.

As fine a game as a footballer could wish to see was the encounter which took place at the Lower Grounds, January 17, 1880, between the Birmingham Association and the Scottish Counties. Harry Simmonds again played, and was partnered by A. T. Ward (Newport), while Arthur Brown's place at centre was occupied by Archie Hunter. The Scots ultimately won by 3 to 2, but the game was splendid throughout, reflecting equal credit upon victors and vanquished alike.

In the return match in February against the London Association, at Aston Lower Grounds, there was great excitement in the second half as the Brums sought to reduce the deficit of two goals that had carried over from the first half. Archie Hunter was in great form that day, but the chief honours on this occasion were certainly carried off by Teddy Johnson, the Saltley College captain, whose electric runs that afternoon chiefly contributed to Birmingham's eventual success. *From 0-2 down at half-time, Birmingham scored a magnificent triumph by 5 to 2.*

The Aston Villa Chronicles 1874 – 1924 (and after)

The Daily Gazette stated that "[Sammy] Law has proved the best half-back who has yet played for the Birmingham Association", and that this match would "long be remembered... [as that] which placed the Birmingham association beyond doubt in the front position among exponents of the dribbling game."

The Villa, on their part, would be even more strongly represented in the Birmingham side in future years, in matches against London and Lancashire amongst others, with as many as seven or nine of their players in the side. On this occasion, four of the Birmingham FA team were Villa men; Harry Simmonds, Sam Law, Archie Hunter – and his hitherto unmentioned brother, **Andy Hunter**.

It never rains, but it pours, and Aston Villa were certainly very fortunate in those days. The appearance of Archie Hunter on the scene had greatly strengthened their forces, but still better luck befell them in the early autumn of 1879, when the tall, fair, yellow-haired Andy of that ilk, joined his brother, and his brother's club.

Andy Hunter came down to Birmingham from that powerful Glasgow club the Third Lanark, in whose forward ranks he had been playing on the right wing. According to William McGregor, Andy Hunter was the best right-winger in Scotland. Previous to his time at Third Lanark, however, the young Scot had received no inconsiderable amount of practice and training in a little Glasgow team entitled the Lancelot. Among other men connected with that marvellous little junior club, was Hugh McIntyre, the afterwards celebrated captain of Blackburn Rovers. McIntyre joined Glasgow Rangers, and Andy Hunter – about the same time – threw in his lot with the Third Lanark, eventually being called away to Birmingham by the exigencies of business. The Perry Pets were thus again favoured by the smiles of Dame Fortune, for the new man was a genuine brilliancy from whose services the team were to largely benefit.

As a right wing forward it was open to question at the time of writing (in 1893) if Andy Hunter had ever been rivalled; like his brother, in circumstances of the utmost difficulty, he possessed wonderful control over the ball. Old Fogey said:

> He had the knack of keeping the ball uncommonly close, and a most deft trick of dragging [the ball] after him; and he would make rings round a knot of defenders in the right corner, and suddenly you would see the ball 'plopped' into the centre with most of the defenders flabbergasted at the manner in which it had arrived there. He was not a speedy player, yet he could cover the ground in a way that made defenders gasp, and his centres were so cool and

The Aston Villa Chronicles 1874 – 1924 (and after)

accurate ...[101]

It was never possible to flurry Andy, for he was not a man to outwardly turn a hair over trifles, taking things as they came with that easy nonchalant *sang-froid* so characteristic of him. He was a man who could always be depended upon to keep his head in times of football peril, and whose cool ready resource on many occasions restored the flagging confidence and drooping hearts of his club mates, and turned impending disaster into unexpected victory. He was remembered for his part in the FA Cup-tie at Nottingham when the 'long-arm' episode cropped up.[102] A quarter of an hour from time, when the Villa, two goals behind, were dispiritedly striving against odds it was by the means of two truly magnificent runs on the part of the Scot that the game was once more placed on a level footing (about this event, more will follow).

Many years later, William McGregor wrote:

> Andy Hunter was a fine, heady player. He made a science of the game and had no superior as an outside right. When a member of Third Lanark he was said to be the best of his day. John Hunter, another brother, also played for Third Lanark. All died of consumption [tuberculosis]. I doubt if three more talented brothers have ever been connected with football. Andy Hunter was at my business place for several years, and the game was rarely out of his mind. He would illustrate his theories with diagrams, and some of them are still to be seen sketched in pencil on the wood of the drawers at my place.[103]

Andy Hunter, said McGregor, was an accomplice to his brother Archie in the development of Villa's passing game. Andy's first match for Aston Villa was in the Staffordshire Cup tie at Walsall with the Swifts, October 18, 1879, when the Villa won splendidly by 7 to 1. From this time until the close of the season 1883-84, he was an active playing member of the club.

It was said that Perry Barr never since witnessed such lovely centres and corners as those grand kicks emanating from Andy Hunter. It was a perfect revelation to see him plant the ball leisurely down at the corner flag, and without any apparent effort, drop it splendidly right into the goalmouth. If Andy had got one weakness more than another it was that knee of his! Suddenly, in the midst of an exciting scrimmage, you would see him stop short with a limp, whereupon a comrade -

---

[101] Villa News & Record 1 Dec 1923 ("Some Famous Players")
[102] A noted FA Cup-tie against Notts County in 1883 (described later)
[103] C.B Fry's Magazine of Action and Outdoor Life Vol 2 Oct 1904 to Mar 1905 p.39 *et seq*

The Aston Villa Chronicles 1874 – 1924 (and after)

usually his brother - would run up to assist him. "All right," the knowing one would observe to the ignoramus in the crowd who wanted to know, "it's only Andy's knee out, he'll be at it again in a minute." And when the club-mate had re-arranged the refractory joint, the player was soon in the thick of it once more.

This is how William McGregor came to call Andy his "double-jointed man". He could not possibly be bettered when he was at his best, and yet at times, especially towards the latter end of his football career, he appeared dreadfully slow and inactive, thereby earning among those who knew not the true facts of the case, the character of being lazy.

Poor Andy! There is little doubt that the germs of that disease which finally carried him off were busily at work, undermining his system even at the period when he first came down to Birmingham. Even in those early days he would sometimes complain about the strange weariness that occasionally oppressed him, but Andy Hunter was too undemonstrative to make much about his ailings, and injustice was in consequence often done by ignorant critics. When Andy ultimately passed away, he left behind him scores of sorrowing friends to mourn the loss of a brilliant football player, and as honest a fellow as ever drew the breath of Heaven.

The Season's Play

The Villans, with the advent of Archie Hunter, had come to the front with a run, as has been fully shown by the fine outcome of the season 1878-79, when out of 18 matches, only three were lost. The winter of 1879-80 found the Perry Pets still more on the job, this year's effort evincing a further continuation and improvement over their previous successes. The addition of such shining lights to the ranks as Andy Hunter and Eli Davis, to say nothing of the sturdy Harry Simmonds, of course, in large measure accounted for the raised excellence of the team, and with the consequent increase of their triumphs, the Wellington Road organisation had certainly every reason to regard with pride a record of 26 games played, out of which but two were lost, a highly victorious season which was grandly topped off by the capture of that long awaited Birmingham Cup.

The Villa had had no luck in the competition until that winter, the chronicle of which is about to be laid before the reader. In the first year's Birmingham tie with Tipton, the referee was Harry Matthews, a Villa man himself. Under ordinary circumstances, this would be considered as a bit in the favour of Perry Barr, but Matthews happened to be a scrupulously fair, honourable young man, with a soul

The Aston Villa Chronicles 1874 – 1924 (and after)

above prejudiced interests on such an occasion as that. So roughly impartial was the referee that he actually gave Tipton the goal that won the match, although it was strongly protested against, and, in the opinion of a majority of the spectators, not a legitimate point. The Aston Unity cup-tie in the next season was a very unpleasant one, and the official result, to say the least of it, was very open to doubt. However, be that as it may, the Birmingham pot was at last landed, at the fourth time of asking.

The game of football had, by this time, got a firm grip on the public, who began to attend matches in larger numbers and to wax even more enthusiastically than before. The season's gate money and receipts went up, the gate's takings for the season of 1879-80 being £173 1s 4d, as against the £42 17s 10d of the previous year. The total income was £235 11s 9d, to the £73 11s 10d of the winter before. There was now a cheerful absence of that "loans from members" which had appeared on the previous balance sheet, an entry that had hitherto been necessary to keep the club going. Amongst the list of donors from those far-off days was included a familiar name in the shape of Mr. **J. E. Margoschis**, a later member of the committee, and the first chairman of Aston Villa Limited when that was created in 1896, and later still, vice-president. He was a gentleman who, from the time he joined the club, gave it his most valuable assistance and most unswerving devotion.

Meanwhile there is no doubt that the club had lost a splendid honorary secretary in Mr. C. H. Midgley, who, owing to pressure of business duties away, was unable to give the Villa the benefit of his valuable services any longer. He had fulfilled the functions of his office with masterly activity, promptitude and tact, and well-deserved the very best wishes of those he had served so faithfully and well. Fortunately, the Villans were able to replace their Mr. Midgley with a fine successor in the form of Mr. Billy Mason, though a Mr. W. Jones was Mr. Midgley's immediate successor. Before long, however, Billy Mason took over the reins.

The general composition of the Perry Barr eleven during this highly successful season should prove some matter of interest. In their opening match, a young player named Clements kept goal. He was quickly succeeded in that position by Ball, who did the bulk of the work between the sticks during that winter - and did it well. Harry Simmonds, who, by assiduous practising and perseverance, had earned a big name in the second team the year before, was now drafted out into the first eleven, where he soon made his mark, and he earned the soubriquet "Cartwheel Simmonds" on account of his long, sweeping, kick. Harry Simmonds was a rare good back on his day, and under his coaching a brilliant little brother, who turned out two years later

The Aston Villa Chronicles 1874 – 1924 (and after)

against Goldenhill in a Staffordshire Cup-tie, fairly eclipsed the old 'un, good as he was. That brother was **Joe Simmonds**, whose famous and distinctive red cap carried its dashing owner successfully through the cleverest of Villa's feats in the 1880s.

J. H. Ball, the above-mentioned man 'between-the-sticks' in those days in 1880, wrote a letter to *The Villa News* describing himself and that period:

> Up to 1877, my football was all Rugby Union, mostly in London. On moving to Birmingham I joined, later, a small club called the Arcadians, which for long – and at length obtained – the honour of a match with the Villa. I played goal, my Rugby practice suiting me for this position, although some experts considered that, being only 5' 6" in height, I was too short for the job. However, the Villa only beat us one to nothing, and the Arcadians were mighty cock-a-hoopy and wanted a return match, in which, I *think*, we made a draw of one each... Anyway, Geo. Ramsay, Mason, and Archie Hunter all came to me after the match, and asked me to play for the Villa. I was a 'prood mon the day, ye ken!' and remember that my club felt mightily complimented, too.
>
> I played in every match of the season '79-'80 (barring only an excursion of the club to Scotland), and only once were three goals scored against us, and only once did we lose a match, i.e. the very last – the final of the Staffordshire cup, at Stoke – and in that Eli Davis was hurt in the first fifteen minutes and was useless afterwards, and Andy Hunter's knee was failing him every time he got a hard run. Archie blew me up sky high, as was his wont; but I thought the fault lay with anyone but me. I played the first few matches of '80-'81, but then moved to Coventry, and had to resign.
>
> ... Harry Simmonds was generally [the] back in my time – a big kicker, but a bull-at-a-gate man from a keeper's point of view – and many more goals would have been scored against us but for the constant and untiring watchfulness of that pair of pearls among half-backs, Sammy Law and Teddy Lee. Next to Archie Hunter, Law was the darling of the crowd always. I have seen many League matches, but I do not remember any better men in their places than those three; and Eli Davis, as a winger, has had few superiors.
>
> ...I have seen hotter matches in those old amateur days than ever since. There was so strong a personal feeling with teams then, while your League teams always seem to me to be too disinterested, too bally impartial, except among a few old foes. Our matches with [Wednesbury] Old Athletic, Walsall Swifts and Aston Unity were as hot as they make 'em, and with the Unity, especially,

The Aston Villa Chronicles 1874 – 1924 (and after)

there were always 'wigs on the green'.[104]

Old Fogey described Ball as:

> ... an adventurous, black-haired devil-may-care young fellow, nimble as a cat, plucky as a pirate, and a custodian of rare ability, though his impetuosity often found the fort unattended! ... But if he let a lot through, he saved a lot which a less talented man would have missed ...[105]

It was this season that Law began to display an excellence at half-back that had previously been shown in the forward line. As a tackler, when at close quarters with his man, Sammy was unbeatable, and to see him fairly walk round some of the Nottingham giants was a caution to snakes!

Meanwhile, Teddy Lee and Tom Pank remained fixtures in the half-back division - not to be improved upon, and, therefore, not to be removed. Charlie Johnstone remained in service usually at left half-back or left forward. Among the forwards, Ramsay and Mason still held their position, but the clever little lefts of the previous season, Charlie Hughes and Stock, dropped out gradually, making room for the even more clever Eli Davis and Andy Hunter.

Billy Crossland also came out of his second team shell and rendered doughty service from the first. He was a dashing forward who was fearless and very partial to goalkeepers! That was a feeling far from reciprocal on the part of the custodians, who often got to know too much of him in times of scrimmage.

Taking Stock of Progress

Let us now take ourselves from the council chamber to the battlefield and see how many brave victories were won. The Wellington Road season opened in 1879-80 on Saturday October 4, when the Villa's great local rivals, the Birmingham Club, were antagonised once more. The Villa, it will be remembered, had worsted the Lower Grounds swells twice in succession in the previous season. As would be expected, there was a very good attendance, and the rival spirit ran high. Birmingham had whipped their very strongest possible eleven onto the field, but sadly missed Eli Davis, who now figured on the side of the Villans.

---

[104] Villa News & Record 2 Jan 1909 – Ball was running his own business in Barcelona, as an engineer, when he wrote this piece some 30 years after the event.
[105] Villa News & Record 30 Apr 1924 ("Some Famous Players")

The Aston Villa Chronicles 1874 – 1924 (and after)

Here are the teams:

'The Birmingham Club': *Hill, goal; Stevens and Quilter, backs; Evans and Dutton, half-backs; Tomkinson, J. R. Riddell, Tate, Howard Vaughton, Riddell and Brown, forwards.*

Villa: *Clements, goal; H. Simmonds, back; T. Pank, Lee and Law, half-backs; Archie and Andy Hunter, Ramsay, Mason, Eli Davis, and Law, forwards.*

The visitors were on their mettle in the first half and did a lot of pressing for nothing. The homesters had some luck up to half-time, but on changing ends Birmingham had shot their bolt, and the Villa, strongly aggressive all through, ran out winners of a fine game by 4 goals to 1. Hill kept goal splendidly for the defeated heroes, who could not lay their defeat at his door. The two Hunters, Eli Davis, Lee and Law played in specially strong form for the winners, who were beyond question the better team. It was now past dispute as to the question of superiority between Perry Barr and the Lower Grounds, for the former had scored wins in all three meetings between them. The rivals never encountered each other again, and the Birmingham club members and players seemed unable to hold their heads up any more after this last disaster, for the organisation fell away almost immediately, and did very little, if anything, to justify the remainder of its existence.

According to press reports of that time, the Villa's second match at Perry Barr in 1879-80 attracted about a thousand spectators. Stoke were then at the top of the North Staffordshire tree, and were holders for the second successive year of the county trophy. Villa's substantial win of 4 to 1, therefore, only underlines their rapid growth at this time. Indeed, the Stoke team came back to Perry Barr a month later to play in the very Staffordshire Cup of which they were the holders, and Villa – now playing in front of a depleted Perry Barr audience, the Villa being so much the favourites – ran out this time by 6 goals to 2.

At the time the Villa won comprehensively against Excelsior (8-1) in the Birmingham Cup, Wednesbury Old Athletic played and lost 1-2 to Small Heath Alliance in the same trophy (SHA were then thought of as "small beer"), and on WOA's own ground! The Old 'Uns England international, George Holden, later made the remark that they only had two sober players on the field as they had spent the morning celebrating a team-mate's wedding!

The Aston Villa Chronicles 1874 – 1924 (and after)

Into the FA Cup for the First Time

The Villa that season pursued no less than three cups – the two local ones and, for the first time, the then-called "English Cup", the FA Cup. The November FA Cup tie against Stafford Road was a very close and exciting game, the Wolverhampton men being fairly on their mettle. Finally the Villans returned home after having had none the best of a drawn game on frozen ground. The replayed match at Perry Barr, a week or two later, was another rare fight, Mr. Crump's men on this occasion being compelled to bite the dust in a very exciting game, they scoring their consolation goal with only a few minutes to go in Villa's 3-1 win. Wednesbury Strollers then played the Villa a splendid game in the Staffordshire Cup tie, being only beaten by the odd goal in five.

There was very great trepidation in the Villa ranks when the fact became known that the Perry Pets had been drawn for the Birmingham Cup with Newport, and, moreover, were compelled by the fortune of war to journey into Shropshire. The fame of Newport's great captain and back, A. T. Ward, had many times rung in the ears of the Birmingham crowd; and it was felt by the majority that the Villa would have to be at their very best to bring off a victory against the Salopian cracks. A local journal of those days was especially doleful over the prospect, very confidently favouring the chances of Newport. It was only a false alarm after all, for the Brums completely outclassed their burly opponents 7-0, Ward being the bright particular star of a heavy slogging eleven. The news of this, to many a totally unexpected victory, raised anew the brightest anticipations as to the capture of both the Birmingham and Staffordshire trophies.

The Birmingham Cup-tie against Unity was one of those matches that spectators and players would never be likely to forget. The rivalry between the two teams was of a most pronounced character, the Villa men burning under a sense of injustice in connection with the Cup-tie of the previous winter. The Aston Lower Grounds was the scene of action, and a big crowd collected together to see the fun. The teams lined out as follows:

> **Villa**: *Ball, goal; H. Simmonds, back; Lee, Pank, and Law, half-backs; Mason, "Centre", Hunter, E. Davis, C. S. Johnstone, forwards.*
>
> **Unity**: *T. Bailey, goal; Thomas and Thompson, backs; Hundy and Durban, half-backs; C. Durban, Ashford, Lawrence, Ogden and Such, forwards.*

In those days, the proper name of both the Hunters was often suppressed for business reasons. Archie would figure in the papers as "Centre" and Andy as

The Aston Villa Chronicles 1874 – 1924 (and after)

"Wright." As William McGregor once stated:

> Football was not popular with employers, and young fellows could not count upon any indulgence when they wanted to get to a special match. I could tell some queer tales of the way in which we used to scheme and contrive to get Archie with us. He was in business in Ludgate Hill and we used to have a brake waiting for him round a convenient corner. Archie would rush out the moment he gained his freedom, jump into the brake, and away it would go to Perry Barr, or whatever local ground the game was fixed for. His employer was a Presbyterian elder, and for a considerable time Archie did not play in his real name; he figured in the papers as A. Centre.
>
> Once, Mr. Jones, the Villa secretary, got Archie into serious trouble. He sent a post-card to his business place which ran: 'Brake will leave the Great Western Hotel for Walsall at two sharp. Hurroo boys!' The levity of the message and the mention of a licensed house gave serious offence to Archie's master. Once when we played at Nottingham we chartered a special train in order that we might have Archie with us.[106]

By the facial expressions of the two sides, it was very evident from the start that only strict business was meant. The respective supporters howled themselves hoarse during the progress of the game which was, as may be guessed, far from a pleasant engagement – there was too much at stake; too many club jealousies and rivalries for that. The two elevens were ancient enemies, and had always been at one another's throats. The local papers of the time reporting this match were very severe upon the Unity for their rough play, and some of the censure was, doubtless, well-deserved; but, on the other hand, a lot of it was exaggerated and out of place. When old foes - as the Villa and Unity were - met in important Cup ties, neither side could be expected to play parlour football, and to do them full justice they didn't, but went at it hammer and tongs, from start to finish. There was no mercy given, or taken, and a lot of unnecessary bumping was, of course, the result. The Unity were certainly the first offenders in this respect, but quickly found in the Villa ready imitators.

> The Perry Barr men were having, if anything, the best of the play, although they utterly failed to elude the vigilance of burly Tom Bailey who was simply invulnerable between the sticks. The first half was rapidly slipping away, and neither goal had as yet been captured. Only a few minutes had to elapse before the change-over, when a great disaster befell the Villa team. Davis,

---

[106] C.B Fry's Magazine of Action and Outdoor Life Vol 2 Oct 1904 to Mar 1905 p.39 *et seq*

who had been most pressing in his attacks on the Unity stronghold, receiving a determined charge from one of the defenders, was suddenly seen to fall heavily to the ground. An examination revealed the unfortunate fact that the arm of the crippled player was dislocated. Playing with only ten men, the Wellington Roadsters were severely handicapped and, for a time, disorganised. However, when the whistle blew for the interval, no goals had been scored on either side.

The battle in the second half was a terribly fierce one. At first the Villa couldn't shake off the depressing influence of Eli Davis' absence, but they rallied splendidly as the game progressed, and although short-handed, they had quite as much, if not more, of the play. Then, early in the second half, Archie Hunter also received a kick on the knee that effectively crippled him for the rest of the game. Nevertheless, when they could, the Villa forwards were giving Tom Bailey a rare peppering, his keeping being a complete revelation to the spectators.

With only a few minutes remaining it was still pointless. The Villans were still pressing like mad, and a drawn game was inevitable. Then Charlie Johnstone, on the left wing, gained possession of the ball, and after a short, sharp burst transferred over to Archie Hunter. The judicious centre had a fine chance of scoring, but seeing captain G. B. Ramsay was in a better position, promptly sent the leather along to him, and with a fast oblique screw shot, GBR scored the only goal of the match, amidst a scene of the wildest excitement and enthusiasm.[107]

Eli Davis was conveyed to the General Hospital, where he remained an inpatient until the Staffordshire final at Stoke. On that eventful day, the plucky man, burning to help his club against the Old Athletic, came out of the Hospital with his arm in a sling, journeyed to Stoke, and took his place on the pitch, crippled as he was.

The Villa landed up in two finals, their record up to date reading:

21 played, 18 won, 3 drawn, 0 lost; goals, 80 to 25.

Meanwhile, Saltley College had worked their way into the semi-final of the Birmingham Cup, where they encountered Derby, who had defeated Saltley, but, having foolishly played two ineligible men, were disqualified by the Association. Saltley thus qualified for the final. Wednesbury Old Athletic, smarting under that Small Heath reverse, were now going great guns in the Staffordshire Cup itself, running right up to the final tie, so that victories over Wednesbury and Saltley were

---

[107] Report from the 'Saturday Night' series of articles (1893)

The Aston Villa Chronicles 1874 – 1924 (and after)

necessary if Aston Villa were to be the winners of both these trophies.

The Perry Pets had resigned all hope that season of winning FA Cup renown, concentrating all their energies on the local ties. After knocking Stafford Road out of the national competition, the Villa eleven, drawn with Oxford University, wisely decided to scratch, influenced, no doubt, by that gruelling 8-0 defeat which the Dark Blues had inflicted upon the Birmingham Club at the Lower Grounds in the previous round. William McGregor many years later said[108] that the club finances were too stretched to make the away tie, and also[109] that significant Villa players could not get away from business in time to travel so far, but it is probable that all the reasons played a part in Villa's decision to scratch.

Against the Old 'Uns in the Staffordshire final, several of the Villa team were not in a fit state to play, particularly, of course, Eli Davis. But, notwithstanding this, the Villans strove gamely on against a resolute and heavier class than themselves. It was a neck and neck fight throughout, and honours were fairly even when time was called, and the Old Athletic were hailed winners by 2-1.

Birmingham Cup Winners!

All concentration was now on the Birmingham Cup. Fully six thousand spectators assembled at the Lower Grounds to witness the Final which took place the following Saturday, April 3. *The Daily Gazette's* report of the game went as follows:

> That weather on Saturday was all that could be desired... and as the match had excited a good deal of speculation among the votaries of the dribbling game, a large number of persons flocked to the Lower Grounds to witness the tussle.
>
> Shortly after the advertised time, the ball was set rolling, Saltley College having the advantage of a steady wind which blew from goal to goal. Playing with great dash, the Villa forwards made a sharp raid on their opponents' territory, but were well held by the College backs. The College, in turn, had several good runs along the wings, and with varying fortune the game progressed for about half-an-hour without either team scoring.
>
> Archie Hunter [then] came away in midfield, and after a pretty, dodging run, judiciously passed the ball across to Eli Davis, and that player, with a fine screw kick, sent the leather flying through the College goal. It was not long,

---

[108] The 'W. McGregor' column in Sports Argus 29 Jan 1910
[109] The 'W. McGregor' column in Sports Argus 6 Feb 1909

however, before matters were again made equal. The kick-off was well followed up by the College forwards, Johnson heading the attack, and in a determined scrimmage which resulted in front of the Villa's goal, Egan managed to put the ball through the posts amid loud cheers. From this point till half-time, the College youths had certainly the best of the game, but all their efforts to increase their score were neutralised by the stubborn defence of the Villa backs.

Change of ends gave the Villa the aid of the wind, and they were not long in profiting by it. No sooner was the ball kicked-off then Archie Hunter essayed a long shot which just grazed the bar of the goal, and he followed that up with a header, which the College keeper had difficulty in averting. The kick-off from goal did not improve the College prospects, for the Villa forwards, acting in unison, again came down on the citadel, and this time, after a stiff struggle with the College backs, Ramsay got an opening, and scored the second goal for his team. A third [goal] soon followed, for Davis, getting on the ball from the kick-off, put on a fine run on the left wing, which he finished with a beautiful centre right across the goalmouth to Ramsay. That player, over-reaching himself, wisely allowed Mason to step in, and a shot by him sent the ball whizzing through the goal despite the vigilance of the custodian.

Again, the game was resumed, but both sides fell off greatly in their play, a want of combination in the forward divisions being clearly observable. The consequence was that although the Villa forwards had many chances of scoring, they did not profit by them, and on the other side, Johnson, who played in grand style, lacked support when he made one of his fine dodging runs.

This was the fourth occasion of the Birmingham Cup Final, and the first time it was won by a Birmingham team. The Villa's first success was greatly celebrated, and the team were invited to a special celebration, about which Charlie Johnstone reported:

[The celebration] began on the Friday evening, and after our respected and eminently respectable vice-presidents – McGregor and my late father, Fergus Johnstone – had retired, we continued the celebration until somewhere about the following Monday morning![110]

The season came to an end with George Copley's superb goalkeeping in the Birmingham Cup Final being the talk of the Midlands, while the magnificent passing among the Villa forwards was something, when seen, never to be forgotten.

---

[110] In his column in The Sporting Mail 3 Sep 1910

The Aston Villa Chronicles 1874 – 1924 (and after)

Aston Villa – Birmingham Cup Winners, 1880
Back row: Jack Hughes (Umpire), Wm. McGregor (V-president),
Billy Mason, Teddy Lee, Harry Simmonds, Tom Pank, Eli Davis,
Fergus Johnstone (V-president), H. Jeffries (Hon. Treasurer)
Middle Row: Andy Hunter, Geo. Ramsay (Captain), W.M. Ellis (President),
Archie Hunter, Charlie Johnstone
On Ground: Sammy Law, John Ball (goalkeeper)

The enforced retirement, through injury, of George Ramsay (the result of an accident sustained in a match played under primitive floodlighting against Notts Forest at Aston Lower Grounds) was a cause for sorrow, but George Ramsay had not finished his task at Aston Villa by a long chalk! In addition, the retirement of Billy Mason as a player was also tinged with sadness, though he subsequently became honorary secretary for two years, and was always closely involved with the club to the end of his days.

However, the stage was set for Villa's continued growth. In Archie Hunter, the Villa had a magnificent captain for the 1880s, and he and his brother Andy were central to the development of the Villa and earned the following tributes, written (at different times) by Old Fogey for *The Villa News* and *Sport and Play*:

> There have been players as clever – perhaps even more brilliant in an individual way – as Archie Hunter; but never one in the Villa Club who had such a commanding personality, and who could imbue his comrades with the same earnestness and strenuousity that he himself possessed. When he went on to the field of play, he was not only captain of his side, he was their leader and their emperor! They were... his vassals, and sometimes... he was rather a stern taskmaster, for he played very hard indeed to win always, and he expected others to do the same. If they did not, they heard about it. ... With

The Aston Villa Chronicles 1874 – 1924 (and after)

all his robustness and his style of brushing aside all opposition in the most pronounced fashion, Archie Hunter was never known to perform an unworthy action on the field. The man's nature was above it, for he was a sportsman from the crown of his fair head to his heels...

... if a comrade got hurt in the fray, Archie had consideration, kept the ball away from that quarter, or went over and rendered help, as he was so well capable of doing. On the other hand, he absolutely trusted the strong men in his side, and this confidence by their skipper made them stronger still, and they would follow his fine example of helping a weaker brother when the opportunity arose.

He was an inspiration to his 'boys', and they played to him and he to them like a band of brothers. Archie's favourite song was a Scottish ditty which commenced something like this:-

I ye mind the lang, lang syne

When the summer days were prime,

And we rose with the lark in the morning.

- and he would troll it forth with a voice that made the rafters ring, and his comrades would 'let it go' with a swing and a resonance that are seldom heard in football circles now [in 1907].[111]

They made him a present of a handsome gold watch and a purse once, and there were good times that evening; and for a few months he returned to Ayr, but the Villa found they could not do without him, and he came back and set up in business, along with Andrew... at Six Ways.

On his brother, Andy:

Only overtopped by his fiercer brother was Andrew Hunter – an altogether lovable and gentle fellow; to know him was a sincere pleasure, and to watch him play his best games ... was a revelation in the science of football. He was one of the closest and cleverest dribblers I have ever seen, and the manner in which he could beat one opponent after another, and then centre truly and well to a comrade nicely placed was a rare and radiant treat.[112]

There was no prettier or more attractive and dangerous forward than he in the country. Many a time he has brought off screw shots from the right which

---

[111] Concerning after-match proceedings: "the Villa possessed some rare and radiant songbirds in the days of old, and they would lilt till the light grew dim and the last watchman had gone home to bed." (Villa News & Record 9 Nov 1907 – "A Long Time Ago")

[112] Villa News & Record 17 Apr 1908 – "Some Forwards of Renown"

The Aston Villa Chronicles 1874 – 1924 (and after)

have surely puzzled and sometimes beaten an opposing goalkeeper, and I don't think he ever had an equal in the art of tying two or three half-backs and backs in a knot in the corner of a field, and then coolly centring the ball when he had extricated himself.

Ask any of his old comrades what their opinion of Andy Hunter was, and they will speak with loving regard of the man who taught so many of them the art of playing football. When he first came amongst us, he was nothing short of a wonderful revelation...[113]

Charlie Johnstone wrote various insights concerning the early years in his regular column in *The Sporting Mail*. On the manner of team selection back then:

... we played cricket till about the middle of September; oiled our bats, had a [football] practise match or two, elected a committee and a captain – and [then] sailed in to play somebody! The actual selection of the team was a thing never to be forgotten. We were all players, and we were like cricket captains who fancy their own bowling! The goalkeeper was always a certainty; then the fun began! Each was weighed up in turn by the rest, and candid criticisms were uttered which would do some of our modern professionals a deal of good. It was an excellent tonic for swelled heads![114]

Recalling players able to use resourcefulness when needed, Charlie wrote:

In a scrimmage within the goalmouth – against Stoke I believe – Archie Hunter, with his back to the goal and no chance of getting his foot to the ball to back-heel it, caught it between his legs, and threw himself backwards through the goal! Howard Vaughton and [much later] John Campbell have on occasions shown equal presence of mind and resourcefulness.[115]

About the close physical proximity between spectators and players:

I remember playing against Stafford Road [on their ground]. I had skipped through the defence on several occasions, and just on 'time', an excited spectator rushed out to charge me as I was dribbling down the wing. I promptly punched him! The result was disastrous. The crowd came for us, and for ten minutes we had as lively a little scrimmage as ever one could imagine! Led by Archie Hunter, we steadily fought our way towards ... where we dressed, and Eli Davis, Will Mason, and ever our staid and sober secretary, with Sam Law, Teddy Lee and all the rest, punched away like Trojans. Captain Crump and his merry men [the Stafford Road players] came

---

[113] Sport and Play 11 Sep 1888
[114] In The Sporting Mail 1 Sep 1906
[115] In his column in The Sporting Mail 1 Feb 1908

to the rescue and we were soon safe inside, where, after repairs, we did ample justice to the hospitality of the Wulfrunians.[116]

On the matter of training, Charlie narrated the following incident:

> On special occasions the team had training at Perry Barr. We generally had it on Wednesday night – that gave us time to get over it by Saturday! We stripped at the Crown and Cushion and sometimes trotted round the field and sometimes as far as the Scot's Arms and back. One very dark night, Tom Simmonds, who was the pace-maker, headed straight into a ditch, and most of us followed! What a yell and splutter there was! ... After the run and rub-down, we had a leg of mutton supper followed by a real Villa sing-song ... It was very jolly and kept us together.[117]

And regarding that matter of conviviality and singing:

> Billy Watts, Tommy Horton, Billy Crossland and Fred Dawson – I believe all these were members of Trinity Church choir, and played for the choristers' club [and joined Villa in about 1878 or 1879]. ... Every one of them had an excellent voice, and under the leadership of Billy Weiss, the Villa in those days were as famous for after-dinner harmony as they were for their football![118]

Tom Mason (brother of Billy Mason), who was himself one time goalkeeper for the Villa, and much later a vice-president of the club, wrote of those times:

> Aston Villa of that day was made what it was by the brotherly affection with which each man regarded the other, and that affection has never ceased. Our eyes sparkle as we shake hands with an old one, and memories crowd upon us, and our voices grow thick with emotion as we think of those who have past from our midst...[119]

---

[116] In his column in The Sporting Mail 20 Oct 1906
[117] In his column in The Sporting Mail 5 Jan 1907
[118] In his column in The Sporting Mail 13 Sep 1913
[119] In 'Nomad's column in Sports Argus 1 Dec 1900

The Aston Villa Chronicles 1874 – 1924 (and after)

1879-80 Results							
Oct	4th	H	The Birmingham Club	4-1	24th H Stafford Rd (FAC Replay)		3-1
	11th	H	Stoke	4-1	31st H Wednesbury St (SC)		3-2
	18th	A	Walsall Swifts (SC)	7-1	Feb 14th A Newport (BC)		7-0
	25th	H	Notts Wanderers	3-2	28th N Aston Unity (BC)		1-0
Nov	1st	A	Stafford Road	4-1	Mar 13th N Golden Hill (SC semi)		9-1
	8th	A	Stoke	1-1	20th N Walsall Swifts (BC semi)		2-1
	15th	H	Park Grove, Glasgow	4-2	27th N W O A (SC Final)		1-2
	22nd	H	Excelsior (BC)	8-1	Apr 3rd N Saltley College (BC Final)		3-1
Dec	6th	H	Stoke (SC)	6-2	17th H Zulus**		3-1
	13th	A	Stafford Road (FAC)	1-1	24th A Elwells		1-1
	20th	A	Walsall Town	2-1	May 29th A Walsall Swifts*		1-2
	26th	H	St. George's	2-1	Played 26, 20 won, 2 lost, 4 drawn;		
	27th	H	Stoke	2-2	Goals 89-32.		
Jan	3rd	H	Aston Unity	4-3	*Benefit re: Birchills Ironworks explosion		
	10th	A	Calthorpe	3-1	**An extraordinary match against a make-believe Zulu team – the opposition was made up to look like them.		

A 'prank'

On the occasion of Dudley Fair [in about 1880], four of us – Teddy Lee, Archie Hunter, Charlie Hall (hon. sec. of the Birchfield Harriers at the time) and the writer – went over to the Fair, had a merry afternoon and evening, and decided to walk home. We got as far as Soho Road, Handsworth, about the hour when the midnight chimes were ringing, and as we were very tired, and a stray four-wheeler came along, we chartered it for the Six Ways, Aston, a neighbourhood we all lived in at the time. As we were jogging comfortably along we discovered that none of us had any money; we had left it all at Dudley.

What was to be done? Teddy Lee suggested the only thing to do to prevent a row was to 'vamoose', and if you had been in the Lozells Road that night you might have observed four folk drop quietly out of that growler at different points while the jarvey [a hackney coachman] went happily and slumberously on. They disappeared up side streets, and got home by devious roads, but not via Six Ways. What the driver said when he arrived I never knew; but for the sake of the reputations of the party, let me add that we saw that jarvey when our purses were replenished, and squared things up satisfactorily.[120]

A Lion's Fun

---

[120] Villa News and Record 2 Apr 1920 - "Makers of the Villa" by Old Fogey

The Aston Villa Chronicles 1874 – 1924 (and after)

5. More Accounts of the 'Band of Brothers'

Now, with the inclusion of the Hunter brothers and Eli Davis, and having garnered their first trophy, other fine local players were attracted by the rising star of the Birmingham area. These included little Joey Simmonds at full-back, and Ollie Whateley (the 'daisy-cutter'), while in the half-back division came Charlie Apperley, who performed with lynx-eyed vigilance and cat-like agility. And, of course, Arthur Brown and Howard Vaughton, and (later on) Arthur's brother, Albert. As William McGregor once wrote:

> There was an interesting period of the Villa's history when Ollie Whateley and Albert Brown played on the right, with Howard Vaughton and Eli Davis on the left and Archie Hunter in the centre. Arthur Brown and Howard Vaughton were the first Villa men to be capped against Scotland – both playing in the season of 1882 – Whateley played in the following season. Arthur Brown was a quaint and brilliant dribbler, and Vaughton was a charming player to watch. He and Dennis Hodgetts afterwards made an historic wing; he was the embodiment of unselfishness, and was the idol of the crowd. First class as a footballer, cricketer, racing cyclist, skater and hockey player, Howard Vaughton, one of nature's gentlemen, ranks as the most versatile and most popular sportsmen Birmingham has produced. He went on playing with the Villa until they won the FA Cup in 1887. Ollie Whateley was another hero. I make no exception when I say that Ollie was the deadliest shot I ever watched. The ball flew from his toe with incredible velocity and never rose an inch from the ground.[121] ... He was a prolific goalscorer for his club and the Birmingham Association.[122]

'Mac' also wrote (warmly) of Ollie: "He had all the eccentricity of the Bohemian spirit one reads about in novels. He was the most careless dare-devil young fellow I ever met. Volumes could be written about his escapades when touring with the Villa."[123]

About **Oliver Whateley** ("the daisy-cutter"): In a Mayor's Cup match against the Albion, Whateley early on had scuffed two chances, and a foremost Albion voice shouted out, "where is your wonderful daisy-cutter?!" and other scornful remarks. But it was not long before Whateley had redeemed himself with two of his specials

---

[121] Hence his title of "the Daisy Cutter", as given by Jack Urry.
[122] C.B Fry's Magazine of Action and Outdoor Life Vol 2 Oct 1904 to Mar 1905 p.39 *et seq*
[123] In his column in the Sports Argus 14 Oct 1911

that silenced the scorners – more so when Villa won 5-1![124]

> Goalkeepers of that generation will still tell you ... that he was the greatest terror they faced in first-class clubs. [He would] send in shots at difficult angles with amazing speed and certainty, and it was a striking feature about them that they hardly ever left 'the carpet'. Beyond that, they often swerved so much that they fairly flabbergasted the finest keepers, and the spin on the ball often meant goals when the shot was intercepted. It was an actual fact that he could put 'side' on a ball like a billiard player... but, of course, not to such an extent.[125]

As late as 1923, after having seen the galaxy of Villa stars in the 1890s and since, Old Fogey was able to say about Whateley, "When he was at his best ... his display was of the kind known as 'tip-top' and he was, *without exception*, the deadliest shooter Aston Villa ever had ..."[126] (my italics). Old Fogey (in the same article) went on to describe Whateley:

> How smilingly he could take a beating, and congratulate the other chaps; how he detested dirty tricks on the field, and how he threatened to punch the head of the great Nicholas Ross [of Preston North End] if he repeated a transgression of the rules of fair play ...

Whateley – "the life and soul of the Villa team, being a good singer, one who could play the piano as well and was always a merry, good-tempered comrade", according to Archie Hunter[127] – retired from football in 1888. In 1908 his home was in Putney, London, the house being named – "Aston Villa"! Ollie was a commercial artist and frequently advertised his business in *The Villa News* from its inception. His brother **Harry Whateley** also played for the Villa in earlier days. They were sons of James Whateley, a Birmingham councillor for 21 years during Joseph Chamberlain's active time in the municipality.

A lengthy – but pertinent – letter from Ollie Whateley himself, dated 19 September, 1908, went:

> It was in 1880 that Archie and Andy Hunter one evening called at my firm's place, at the instruction, I believe, of George Ramsay, and asked me to join the Villa. I remember being immensely flattered, and merrily go with them to

---

[124] Villa News & Record 17 Apr 1908 – "Some Forwards of Renown"
[125] Villa News & Record 18 Dec 1909 – "A Wounded Veteran"
[126] Villa News & Record 1 Dec 1923 – "Some Famous Players"
[127] "Triumphs of the Football Field", Birmingham Weekly Mercury, October, 1890 to February, 1891

The Aston Villa Chronicles 1874 – 1924 (and after)

Perry Barr. I was then only 18 years old. On the way we picked up George, who was then just as keen on Aston Villa's success as now. This meeting of three braw Scotties and one Englander boy resulted in my becoming a perfect Villan! I had previously been an Aston Unitarian – with happy memories of Charley and poor old Sam Durban. I remember my first game with Aston Villa was against Walsall – and my last, I thought it would be at the time, for I played a most rotten game.

However, I was tried again the following Saturday against a kind of Corinthian Scotch side – Pollock Shields – including that great player, Geordie Kerr. Here I was more my own self, and finding the great Geordie was human, and that I could give him moments of irritation, became pretty confident. From thence onward I missed very few matches. Indeed, I may claim that I never, *never*, neglected Aston Villa for business. It did me so much good to be in the open air.

I had a lot of practice in the gentle art of shooting at goal, for my partners, Andy Hunter (hats off!) and that Admirable Crichton of sport, Howard Vaughton, seemed to find extraordinary joy in doing all the work, taking all the bumps, and staggering down the field, just to give me the ball to hammer through the hole. They *never* seemed tired of these gymnastics, so I let them do it most times, fearing their anger if I worked. Archie, Arthur Brown and Eli Davis had something to say in those times – especially the dear old captain, whose command of Queen's Scottish was wide, varied and sonorous. Yes, I have quite a keen recollection of a small knot of 'choristers', with terrible, raucous advice as to what to do, when to do it, and how to do it. I can even now, in my dreams, hear the united howl if a person on the opposing side mildly saved me the trouble of shooting by diverting the ball in another direction. Just as if *I* was going to run hard after a football. But I don't often have such nightmares.

We were indeed a great and magnificent team – when we won – and a dissipated rotten lot of ruffians when we lost. I believe there are even nowadays similar views about decent teams – What? Bless 'em! I think I enjoyed the games against the Universities (Oxford and Cambridge) better than most – and what a great team Cambridge had with Cobbold and Co. Cobbold was, without doubt, the finest player I ever fell over. It was not a bit of use me charging him. He didn't even seem annoyed, which was frightfully provoking; so we let him have the ball and sulked. They played the usual public schoolboy game … of spreadeagling over the field, and giving opponents a chance of breaking through halfway down the field, with a long and exciting run on one's own. Spectacularly brilliant, but expensive to them nearly always.

The Aston Villa Chronicles 1874 – 1924 (and after)

> By the way, non-players of the game can never experience that joy of breaking through opponents and finding a clear field of about fifty yards to 'scorch' like the very deuce towards the solitary individual (between two sticks) keeping goal. One cannot hear a sound, and wonders whether the whistle has blown – or something happened: but on one rustles till the 'let-fly moment,' and then! ... The fearful shriek when you miss the goal by a street's breadth. You see your way clearly then but feel very tired, and anxious to die at once and 'have done' with such a wicked world...
>
> I can still hear Charlie Crump's silver oratory – still see the future Father of the League's [McGregor] handsome bearded face – still remember every hair of Howard's incipient but beautifully-groomed 'tache, and hear his sweet refrain about the 'Good young man who died, my friends.' Also I call to mind those dear old sweet singers and players, Billy Watts, Tommy Horton and Billy Crossland; Jack Urry, the first person to coin the since much-used word 'Daisy-cutter'; poor Billy Mason's (hats off!) flowing locks, and all the boys of the old brigade whom it was my huge luck to know, and sadness to miss nowadays.
>
> I finished my football career with a crocked knee – a fact that I often acutely know even now 'when the stormy winds do blow'; but I shall never finish remembering my old, old friends, and 'standing by' the magic words, Aston Villa, until my heart is quite crocked – and 'wha kens'? I may even then still have a chat with those old comrades who have gone aloft. Here's luck to you all – players, spectators, excellent managers and every-one interested in the claret and light blue colours – which, I may remind you, were designed by my humble self, the 'Daisy-cutter' of ancient memory! [128]

At the time Olly wrote that letter, he was suffering from a malignant cancer on his face. Perhaps his melancholy was made more pronounced by his condition.

His 1926 obituary in *The Villa News* stated:

> 'Olly' Whateley will always have a place in the annals of football, not only for the quality of his play, which was always high, but for his sterling character, his fine generosity, and his first-rate standard of sportsmanship. [129]

Capped twice for England in 1883, he was Villa's third England international.

---

[128] Villa News & Record 17 Oct 1908 – "Makers of Villa History"
[129] Villa News & Record 30 Oct 1926

The Aston Villa Chronicles 1874 – 1924 (and after)

There now follows a description of hitherto little-described players that were with the Villa to the mid-1880s, in the approximate order in which they joined the club.

Sam Law[130] joined Villa in 1875 and played in the first match at the Perry Barr ground, just when Villa began to assume a position among the older and bigger clubs of the neighbourhood. Several times selected for the Birmingham Association matches and for Staffs. vs. Lancs. at Stoke, where he scored all four goals for his side. This earned him the soubriquet of "The Evergreen".

In 1882, he was selected for all the Birmingham Association matches. N.C. Bailey was a great star of the football firmament then, and when Bailey was ill, Lee was selected to fill his place in the England trial match for the team to play Scotland. Law played well enough to give hope that he might be selected, but Bailey recovered in time.

In the 1880 Birmingham Cup, Law had to be fetched out of bed and taken by cab as he was suffering a carbuncle on his right leg. The head of this was kicked off after a few minutes into the match! One of many "players of grit in those days", Law played through the match to the finish.

Law was a great favourite of Archie Hunter and used to look after him "like a father". Law ceased active play in 1883. He was the first of the Villa players to have a benefit – vs. Walsall Swifts. Though it rained all day, his popularity ensured the raising of £40 – even at the time of writing (in 1908) it was considered "quite a big sum in those days."

Tom Pank[131] joined Villa in the season of 1875-76. He played right through to 1882. He was described as a brilliant half-back and was regularly chosen for the Birmingham Association matches, and always shone in them.

He never played finer football than in the historic matches with Notts County:

> On one occasion at Perry Barr, when another goal meant the decision of the match... with only a minute or two left to play... Harry Cursham, the crack Notts sprinter, had got clean away with a clear field, and it simply looked any odds on his scoring; but Tommy Pank was after him like a skimming swallow... [and] overtook the leonine Notts man just as he had steadied himself to shoot, and bundled him over neck and crop, whereat there was a shout that reverberated even into the walls of Birmingham. Cursham didn't

---

[130] Villa News & Record 18 Jan 1908 – "Makers of Villa History"
[131] Villa News & Record 4 Jan 1908 – "Makers of Villa History"

The Aston Villa Chronicles 1874 – 1924 (and after)

like it, [but] in those days the referee didn't mind!

Pank's fame as a sprinter was even higher than that as a footballer. "With the sole exception of Charlie Johnstone, he is probably the best sprinter that has ever been reared in the Midlands [to 1908]."

The statuette that graced the apex of the Mayor of Birmingham Charity Cup was modelled from Pank's form by Mr. George Moore, once a prominent Villan himself.

Charlie Hobson[132] (goalkeeper): "[He] was like a cat; he would twist and turn everywhere. He studied the art of goalkeeping and left nothing to chance." The writer of that text (in 1900) considered that Hobson was better, even, than the Villa keeper of that time, Billy George, who many were want to rank as the best keeper before Sam Hardy. Hobson joined Villa after his remarkable performance for Walsall Swifts against the Villa in the 1881 Birmingham Cup final, and gave way to Jimmy Warner in 1886.

Joe Simmonds[133] (full-back): 5' 3" tall. "I have heard his captain roar out instructions to him to keep his place, and directly after double himself up with laughter as he watched his courageous little back chase some big fellow half-way round the field and rob him of the ball."

Definitely not a highly cultured full-back – and having a 'short fuse' – he was a product of the times when football was more hurly-burly. Old Fogey described him as:

> A really great back, with a heart like a lion, a rush on him like a rhinoceros, and an utter inability to see anything between himself and the ball. He was a two-footed kicker almost up to the standard of ... Tom Smart [of the 1920s], and nine out of ten of his rushes were well-timed; the tenth often missed its mark – which is a good average, but sometimes led to disaster! When you watched Joe Simmonds, you wanted to either cheer or swear; you generally cheered. ... [He was] a wonderful favourite with the public.[134]

He was a great servant to the club through virtually all the 1880s and played in Villa's first FA Cup triumph, in 1887, a match in which he was outstanding according to many match reports, and (according to Old Fogey) the London spectators at the final fell in love with him! But it was once said of him: "[Simmonds] perhaps has had more said for and against him than any other back in

---

[132] 'Nomad' in the Sports Argus 10 Nov 1900
[133] Villa News & Record 4 Apr 1908 – "Some Villa Defenders"
[134] Villa News & Record 2 Apr 1924 – "Some Famous Villa Players"

The Aston Villa Chronicles 1874 – 1924 (and after)

the world!"[135]

More than 20 years later, he was still giving his all in football matches for charity.

Tommy Riddell[136] (full-back): 6' 4" tall. "His headwork was nothing short of weird, and he would cast his lower extremities about like a daddy-long-legs".

William McGregor narrated the following story about 'Tommy':

> Tommy Riddell was a boisterous character in his Villa days, and sowed a few 'wild oats'. Mr. Fergus Johnstone took a great interest in Tommy and gave him many lectures. On one occasion, when Tommy had been up to one of his tricks, Mr. Johnstone, in serious tones, said, 'Now, Tommy, you have a guid mither, and perhaps some day you will reform'. 'Ah, someday I will', replied Tommy, 'and take her some Aberdeen haddies!'[137]
>
> Tommy was a vigorous player and had many faults, but he always played a gentlemanly game, and was greatly respected as a player.[138]

When Riddell Absconded...

Footballers were then keen to go were the action of the moment was, regardless of which club they were affiliated to, and Tommy Riddell was no exception. A story was told of how, even though he was signed up for the Villa, he'd heard that Excelsior (then a club of good standing – they played at Aston Lower Grounds for a while and John Devey played for them at one point) were going to play Preston North End at Deepdale, and Riddell wanted to play. This was, of course, a big match for Excelsior.

The Villa got wind of this, and the Villa secretary lured him away from Excelsior and by cab made for the Crown and Cushion, at the corner of Wellington Road. Riddell, on seeing the pub, grasped what was afoot and when the secretary got out of the cab, Riddell got out the other side and "disappeared into the wilds of Aston Lane". He then spent long hours on the run, firstly at a prayer meeting and then at other places of seclusion until the early morning of the following day, which was the day of departure to Preston. He thus made his way to Stephenson Place, and the Excelsior team (minus their keeper, who had not made the train) travelled to Preston.

---

[135] Sport and Play 5 Sep 1887
[136] Villa News & Record 4 Apr 1908 – "Some Villa Defenders"
[137] Cannabis.
[138] The 'W. McGregor' column in the Sports Argus, 12 Nov 1910

The Aston Villa Chronicles 1874 – 1924 (and after)

> At the start of the match, being without their keeper, Riddell went into goal, and when a long shot came in, his heading tendency took over instead of his hands, but did not prevent the ball going into the net! However, Excelsior's keeper did turn up, put in a great performance, and Excelsior went down to 'The Invincibles' by just one goal to two. [139]

Riddell's judgment was superb and he lasted several seasons. Riddell was known as 'The Telescopic Neck' owing to a way in which he had of shooting his head out towards the ball when the goal was in danger."[140]

Tom was Joey Simmonds' partner in the back division, "and generally stayed at home and safely defended the citadel while his smaller comrade paid visits abroad and then hurried home again!"[141]

Arthur Brown:[142] (forward and half-back) "One of the best men who ever played for Aston Villa" and (with Howard Vaughton) was Villa's first England international (1882). He was "a great power in the Villa attack for six or seven years. He had a very deft and clever way of scoring goals, always with an exceedingly quick eye for an opening – and some of his [goals] were quite dazzling in their pace and unexpectedness; while he was the hardest player (for his inches) to knock or shift off a ball I have ever seen... When Arthur Brown had once got the leather under control, you'd see all his vanguard comrades make a bee-line for the other fellows' goal, and if they didn't score they generally contrived to get close enough to make us all gasp..."

"Arthur Brown first played for a club named the Florence on Aston Park, an organisation which had the honour of turning out some wonderfully good men, including Eli Davis... and Howard Vaughton."

Arthur then played for Aston Unity before joining the Villa. This was a result of marking Archie Hunter in a match and catching attention as a result of his performance. He played his first game for the Villa at Newport in a cup-tie, *and* in a cup-tie at Perry Barr the same afternoon!

"He played in every position in the team bar goal, but was always a wonderfully fine lieutenant to Archie Hunter, for the two used to play to one another in great style,

---

[139] 'Nomad' in the Sports Argus 28 Jul 1900
[140] "Triumphs of the Football Field", Birmingham Weekly Mercury, October, 1890 to February, 1891
[141] Villa News & Record 2 Apr 1924 – "Some Famous Villa Players"
[142] Villa News & Record 14 Mar 1908 – "Old Villa Players"

and if ever a pair knew the game it was surely this couple, and the manner in which their comrades helped them, and they did ditto for their comrades, was a sight for tired eyes."

Arthur Brown eventually went to Birchfield Trinity, where he helped to train Howard Spencer.

O. Howard Vaughton:[143] (forward) Born 1861, he started his football career with Waterloo FC in 1875 and played regularly at Aston Park. After winning virtually every away match that season, the club broke up. He then joined the Birmingham Club – then 'the' organisation of the Midlands – in 1876.

After joining Villa in 1880, he played for the Birmingham FA vs. London in 1882 and also played that year for the first time for England, in company with Arthur Brown.

For many years he played inside-left with Eli Davis till the introduction of the clever Welshman Roberts [at inside-left], when he went to the right with Whateley. The pair could fool any defence in the country. Later, he went back to the left to work with Dennis Hodgetts. Vaughton, when it came to scoring goals, was noted for his intelligent anticipation.

Vaughton was said to be highly popular with the Villa supporters, and remained a popular figure right through to the 1930s, having been made President in 1925. He stood down shortly afterwards, but continued as a vice-president.

He was a leading sportsman in other fields as well – including swimming, cycling and skating (wheels and blades)! Even until the 1920s he was a member of the managing committee of the Warwickshire County Cricket Club, and was as well-known to the younger generation of that time as the older generation from the 1880s, which once saw him being bowled out by the legendary Dr. W. G. Grace.

Charlie Apperley (half-back) was another valuable member of the Villa team, and in his short career was chosen for several big Association matches in the days when it was a great honour to be so chosen. He was forced to relinquish first-class football as a result of an accident in the Trossachs whilst on tour (as told elsewhere), when he damaged his leg too badly to continue playing, and shortly afterwards went to South Africa, where he was still residing in 1920 and where he was "big in football".

---

[143] Villa News & Record 25 Dec 1908 – from an article by "Old Fogey"

The Aston Villa Chronicles 1874 – 1924 (and after)

David Anderson[144] (former skipper of 'QP' seconds), was a fine addition. A half-back who came to Birmingham as a traveller for George Kynoch, [who became] President of Aston Villa. He had a trick of booting the ball with the side of his foot, and never a more accurate passer for Aston Villa. Socially, he knew every song by Burns and had a beautiful tenor voice. He left for South Africa in 1883.

'Freddy' Dawson:[145] "Archie Hunter's despair as an inside-left but his pride and glory as centre-half-back." He was another player who often demonstrated a 'short fuse'.

About Freddy Dawson

The Villa were playing Cambridge University at Perry Barr and the great Cobbold (one of the finest dribblers ever seen) was centre-forward with Freddy up against him. The Villa man wore no shinguards, out of compliment to the 'Varsity men, and after 20 minutes had been hacked (accidentally, of course) about as many times, till his right shin bone was about as serrated as the business side of a saw.

Every time Cobbold kicked him, he said, 'Beg pardon!' and Dawson took it smiling. Until he got rather a vicious one and then he said (for he had a brusque way): 'Look here, Cobbold; I've stood it long enough. If you kick me again, something'll happen.' Cobbold stared, took no further notice and not long after, Freddy got another, with the usual apology... A little later, Cobbold, Dawson and ball arrived at one spot together, and the Villa man kicked the ball and the Cambridge player up in the air at the same time... and as he lay on the ground, Freddy Dawson glared at him and ejaculated, 'I beg your pardon!'...

A Lion's Fun

---

[144] Villa News & Record 11 Apr 1908 – "The Middle Line"
[145] Villa News & Record 11 Apr 1908 – "The Middle Line"

6. Villa's General Progress - 1880 to 1885

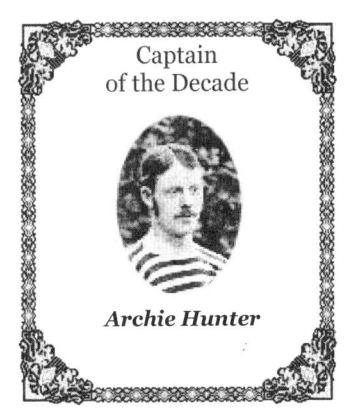

Captain of the Decade
Archie Hunter

In September and October 1877, the *Athletic News* had listed some 250 football clubs' addresses nation-wide, but though the list included Wednesbury Old Athletic, Calthorpe, Aston Unity and Saltley College, Aston Villa were not to be found in that list. By 1880, however, the Villa had become, arguably, the leading team of the locality, heading a list of other clubs that included Wednesbury Old Athletic, Stafford Road, Saltley College, Wednesbury Strollers and Walsall Swifts.[146] Other famous clubs of the time were Walsall Town, Calthorpe, Aston Unity, Excelsior and Mitchell St. George's. The previously famed 'Birmingham Club' was on a road to extinction.

Over the next few years, the Villa left the other pioneer west Midlands' teams in their wake, but West Bromwich Albion and Wolverhampton Wanderers also came up strongly, the Wolves replacing Stafford Road as the leading club of that locality. The fact was also that Villa now were able to 'pull' virtually all the best talent in the district, and several former illustrious opponents were soon found to be playing in the Villa ranks. As the 1880s proceeded, it almost became an axiom that once a local player had made a certain mark then his next step would be to sign for the Villa. The Villa's influence on the locality was starting to be huge, and by November, 1883, there was another development – Villa created a *fourth* team – the Colts – to bring on young players.

In those pre-League days, 'friendly' matches were hugely beneficial as a method of obtaining funds for charity and other good causes, as well as improving the financial standing of the club, but certain fixtures – such as the annual one against Nottingham Forest – were greatly looked forward to. They were also an occasion to show hospitality, and William McGregor remembered one 'friendly' at Oxford University:

---

[146] Villa News & Record 12 Oct 1907

The Aston Villa Chronicles 1874 – 1924 (and after)

> The 'Varsity men used to treat us most handsomely. Lunch was provided for us on arrival, and didn't some of our men – 'Little Redcap' [Joe Simmonds] for instance! – tuck in at that feed! Simmonds, it was said, ate a whole chicken![147]

By early 1881, the Villans' ambitions started to reach out further to play their 'friendlies'. Having played a successful match against Hearts (of Edinburgh) at Perry Barr, the Villa then played against two of the leading Lancashire clubs of that time – Darwen and Blackburn Rovers. The first of those matches (against Darwen) was at Perry Barr, shortly after followed by the visit of Blackburn Rovers. That first match against the Rovers is perhaps the oldest meeting between any of the clubs still in the top draw of league football – between Lanacshire and Midlands' sides at least. In April, 1881 the Villa made the return trip to play the Rovers.

The popularity of football in the Birmingham area was increasing apace, with crowds of greater than 5,000 becoming a regular event, and five-figure 'gates' were not infrequent either. That may seem a puny figure now, but at that time, it was seen as a big achievement, remembering also that Villa's Perry Barr ground, even after improvements, was later found to be very difficult to monitor if the gate reached 20,000. That size of gate (especially when it was exceeded in 1888) was undreamed of before, and there had been no experience of how to cope with it. The Aston Lower Grounds 'meadow' (where many local cup finals were held, and two FA Cup semi-finals) was incapable of holding more than about 15,000 spectators.

Wednesbury Old Athletic (the Old 'Uns) were a strong team that Villa had many battles with early on. Charlie Johnstone reflected on the Old 'Uns club when in their prime:[148]

> Sam Page, Billy Moon and [the England international] George Holden were shining lights. There was no attempt at superficial cleverness. The backs kicked hard, the half-backs tackled determinedly, and followed up their forwards. The forwards passed wide and well forward, and went straight for goal. They were a big, speedy lot and difficult to knock off the ball. They waited for no certain openings, but let drive hard on every possible occasion.

---

[147] From his column in Sports Argus 27 Dec 1909
[148] In his column in The Sporting Mail 18 Dec 1909. The Old 'Uns seem to have started up shortly after the Villa, but had got into a quicker stride by winning the 'Birmingham Cup' in its first year, 1877, and again in 1879, being semi-finalists in 1878.

The Aston Villa Chronicles 1874 – 1924 (and after)

> **In matches with the Old 'Uns, feelings often ran high!**
>
> Once... one of us had floored the redoubtable Roland Morley, their famous centre-forward, and immediately an irate female admirer of his rushed over the touch line and incontinently banged the nearest Villa player over the head with her umbrella! A more surprised man I never saw! ...[149]
>
> *A Lion's Fun*

Cup Matches from Season 1880-81

In the process of defending the Birmingham Cup they had won the previous year, and after again beating Newport on their ground, this time 6-0, a 10-1 home win over Sutton Coldfield and a bye in the third round, the Villa met the Old 'Uns in the quarter finals at the Lower Grounds (19 March, 1881), attracting a crowd of 15,000.[150]

Inside the first two minutes, "Archie Hunter burst like a fair-haired bison through the Athletic's ranks and sent the ball flying under the bar". 1-0 to Villa.

Later, "Eli Davis plumped the ball down at the feet of Archie Hunter, who deftly turned it over to a romping forward known as Billy Crossland, who slapped it straight into [the keeper's] chest, and arrived on top of the ball so that all three of them rolled over and over together through the goal!" 2-0, after about 15 minutes.

"You never saw such a scene as ensued! Many a chapeau was lost for evermore; a human-laden shed on the west side of the ground broke down with a crash and illuminated the grim 'ashes to ashes' phrase as the dust arose in the air! I saw an old lady tear her bonnet off and wave it wildly in the air by the strings, ... and I had to put a protecting arm around your former editor[151] to prevent him toppling off the wall [on which they'd climbed]."

The Old 'Uns lost their equilibrium as a result, and further goals came from Crossland (again), the two Hunters and Vaughton in the 6-0 win.[152]

"Up to that time it was unquestionably the greatest thing the Villa had done, for the Old 'Uns were a real power in the football land".

---

[149] In Charlie Johnstone's column in The Sporting Mail 2 Apr 1910
[150] Villa News & Record 23 Nov 1907
[151] Villa News & Record editor during 1906-07, Edwin Cox.
[152] In a letter from J.H. Ball in January 1909, Ball (the Villa keeper) wrote that even after Villa scored their second "the first half was the busiest I ever had between the posts."

The Aston Villa Chronicles 1874 – 1924 (and after)

The Final

To add to the nail-biting at the Lower Grounds, an accident on the road had delayed the start of that match until four o'clock; and Andy Hunter had slipped his knee-cap just before the match started, and thereon played with caution.

Incredibly, Villa *lost* 0-1 to Walsall Swifts! This was after the most one-sided encounter the reporter had ever seen. For this encounter the Villa team was:

Copley; Simmonds; Lee, Pank, Law;
Andy Hunter, Crossland, Archie Hunter, Arthur Brown, Vaughton, Davis.

After scoring their goal on 20 minutes, the Swifts reverted to 7 backs and 3 forwards, and plumped for solid defence! The Swifts (believed to have one of the best defences in Britain at that time) were bombarded until the Villa were pumped out, but the Swifts' keeper Charlie Hobson and his defence held.

> 'Nomad' in the *Sports Argus* wrote:
> "George Ramsay almost cried that afternoon; I believe he *did* cry!"[153]

The very next week, the Villa obtained some satisfaction against the Swifts by substantially beating them in the Staffordshire Cup Final, but the Birmingham Cup was always the local trophy that the Villa had most pride in. Between 1880 and 1912, the Villa won that trophy 18 times, though by the 1900s its status had begun to fall off considerably, and the Villa's second team was commissioned to play for it.

The F.A. Cup

The Villa News, in Villa's jubilee year of 1924, stated:

> There is little doubt that the [F.A.] Cup contests were one of the sure foundations of the Villa's reputation, for though the club rapidly won its way to the front rank of local talent, it was felt that national fame was necessary, and the Villa team very gallantly responded to this ambition. Good judges of football ... foretold great things of the Perry Barr club if they could retain, improve and polish the talent they undoubtedly possessed ...[154]

---

[153] 'Nomad' in Sports Argus 10 Nov 1900
[154] Villa News & Record, 6 & 8 Sep 1924

The Aston Villa Chronicles 1874 – 1924 (and after)

Villa's first encounter in the FA Cup in the 1880-81 season was a 5-3 home win over local Wednesbury Strollers. It was stated that it was a hard-fought match against a side of some repute at the time, but further details of the match and names of scorers seem to be unreported.

The next round was at Nottingham Forest, and Villa's popularity at that time (by now Arthur Brown and Howard Vaughton had joined Villa's ranks) is notable by the fact that special trains were provided to take 3,000 fans, who saw their team's extra pace in sodden conditions take them through by 2-1 "after really magnificent play on both sides" (*Daily Gazette*).

In the next round it was to Nottingham again, against the County, and a 3-1 win. After those magnificent two away wins, with Andy Hunter scoring three of the goals, and away from home to boot, hopes were greatly raised. However, William McGregor recorded that:

> [T]he renowned Stafford Road club, led by Mr. Charles Crump, gave Villa their quietus that season for Association Cup honours. The match was played at the old Perry Barr ground and proved to be a most exciting affair. The home forwards were the more clever, but the defence of the visitors was very strong and resolute. In the end Villa were defeated by three goals to two [Vaughton scored both Villa's goals; Andy Hunter was not available for this match]. One of the Wolverhampton players named Turton raised the ire of the spectators by playing a rough game. He was mobbed in coming off the ground, and, with difficulty, got to the dressing room in safety. I have reason to remember the circumstance, as in going to his help I was surrounded, and after the player was safely secured, I found the corner of my long overcoat in my side pocket with my purse gone. I have never carried a purse since then![155]

In that match in February 1881, the score was 1-1 at half-time after Stafford Road had taken the lead, but Villa went 2-1 ahead after half-time. "From this point, they fell off rapidly..." wrote the *Daily Gazette*, "... and lacked that dash and spirit that formerly characterised their play", although Villa came close to equalising near the end of the game. However, it was stated in *The Villa News* many years later (1924) that the real reason why Villa's play fell off was because of the knocks the Villa players received. The Villa were one match short of reaching the quarter-finals that year, and only in their second season in the FA Cup.

---

[155] From his column in Sports Argus 6 Feb 1909

The Aston Villa Chronicles 1874 – 1924 (and after)

It was at the end of this season that Archie Hunter returned to Ayr, but promising to return when needed (and when possible) for important matches. However, his return to Ayr was ostensibly for good after a magnificent presentation and send-off, but that situation – thank fully – was not to last.

Another significant change in the Villa's executive was the re-appearance of Billy Mason, this time as honorary secretary, an appointment that proved to be totally appropriate for a club that was now developing on a national scale. In Billy Mason's heart was not only the interests of the Villa, but of the Birmingham and District FA, in whose ranks he also sat, and for which he was later to take on much more responsibility (unpaid, of course).

In the club's annual report of 1881, and presented at the AGM held at the Crown and Cushion, Mason wrote, in the light of Archie's departure:

> I sincerely trust that we shall all see the necessity of binding ourselves more closely together, and if the players will endeavour to emulate the actions of their late captain [i.e. Archie Hunter], we shall not only retain the high position we have already gained in the football world, but probably succeed in improving it.

These were brave words from Billy Mason, but it soon became obvious that a successor to Archie's leadership could not readily be found.

1880-81 Results

Oct 2nd	H	Notts Forest	2-0
9th	H	Derby County	4-0
16th	H	Walsall Swifts	4-0
23rd	A	Stafford Road	2-1
30th	H	Wednesbury Str. (FAC)	5-3
Nov 6th+	A	Newport (Shrops) (BC)	6-0
6th+	H	Elwell's (SC)	3-2
13th	A	Notts Forest	2-0
27th	H	Stafford Road	4-1
Dec 4th	A	Notts Forest (FAC)	2-1
11th	H	Wednesbury Strollers	2-1
18th	H	Sutton (BC)	10-1
Jan 1st	H	Hearts (Scotland)	4-2
8th	H	Darwen	4-0
15th	H	Fenton (SC)*	14-0
29th	H	Blackburn Rovers	4-3
Feb 12th	A	Notts County (FAC)	3-1
19th	H	Stafford Road (FAC)	2-3
26th	H	Golden Hill (SC semi)	4-1
Mar 19th	N	Wednesbury O A (BC)	6-0
Apr 2nd	N	West Bromwich (BC semi)	2-0
9th	N	Walsall Swifts (BC Final)	0-1
16th	N	Walsall Swifts (SC Final)	4-1
18th	A	Blackburn Rovers	0-3

Played 24, 21 won, 3 lost, 0 drawn; Goals 93-23

+ These matches were played a.m. and p.m. the same day, the first in Shropshire and the second at Perry Barr.
* Andy Hunter scored 7 (seven) in this match

The Aston Villa Chronicles 1874 – 1924 (and after)

Season 1881-82

The development of Aston Villa was an on-going matter. The raising of the Villa's flag was an all-important issue to all those connected with the club, and they thought through the many ways by which the club could raise its standing.

Old Fogey commented in 1907 about his own work as a journalist and his observations on the growth of the Villa and its Scottish connections:

> I always seemed to manufacture easier 'copy' concerning the old Perry Barr club than any other, for there always seemed to be more fun, adventure and 'zip' about their play than the others.
>
> ... the main reason for the practically continuous success of Villa since 1880 has been the good faith they have kept with the public and their friends, and the first-rate football they have provided during all those years.
>
> One of the chief characteristics of the Villa... has been the Scottish element which have leavened it almost from the beginning. (e.g. the players: Ramsay, the Hunters, Charlie Johnstone, David Anderson, Kenneth Wilson, Billy Dickson, Andrew Watson, John Campbell, Jimmy Brown, George Campbell, Jas. Cowan, George Russell, Archie Goodall). Nor will two of the best friends the club had in the ancient days – Wm. McGregor and Fergus Johnstone – be ever forgotten.
>
> The leavening of the Villa team with Scottish blood came just at the right time, when Scotland undoubtedly led the van – and led it easily too – in Association football, and they did a tremendous job in making the game so wonderfully popular from the scenic standpoint... They were marvellous adepts at the passing and dribbling codes.[156]

At the end of his final paragraph, Old Fogey implied that it was the introduction of passing that changed the game from the selfish 'go for goal' approach. In the earlier '80s, Scottish football was still the major influence, and the club to measure against was Queen's Park of Glasgow. "[Villa] were the first of all the English clubs to adopt Scottish tactics in football, and it is no secret that the Queen's Park of Glasgow were their example and their shining lights."[157]

For the first-ever international match between Scotland and England in 1872, Queen's Park supplied their entire team as the Scottish representative side! Queen's Park were at their peak towards the end of the 1870s and start of the 1880s, just when football in the Midlands was growing by leaps and bounds in popular favour.

---
[156] Villa News & Record 26 Oct 1907 – "Notes of Yore"
[157] Villa News & Record 17 Apr 1908 – "Some Forwards of Renown"

The Aston Villa Chronicles 1874 – 1924 (and after)

'QP' had been unbeaten in the previous four years, according to the *Daily Gazette*.

> **FOOTBALL. FOOTBALL.**
>
> **ASTON VILLA**
> v.
> **WEDNESBURY OLD ATHLETIC,**
>
> On Saturday Next, Oct. 15, 1881,
> AT PERRY BARR.
> Kick-off at 3-30 p.m.
> ADMISSION—THREEPENCE.
> RESERVED 6d. EXTRA.
>
> ---
>
> On Thursday, Oct. 20, 1881,
>
> **QUEEN'S PARK F.C.**
> (GLASGOW),
> v.
> **ASTON VILLA**
>
> The Committee have much pleasure in announcing that they have completed arrangements with the Queen's Park (for Thursday, October 20th), Notts. Forest (English Cup Tie, Nov. 5th), Notts. County, Darwen, Blackburn Rovers, Walsall Swifts, Old Athletic, Norfolk County, Sheffield Town, Derby Town, etc., for matches at Perry Barr. Season Tickets to admit Lady and Gentleman, 4s.6d. each. May be had from
> Mr. W. MARGOSCHIS, Constitution Hill.
> Mr. W. J. BOWEN, Perry Parr.
> Mr. W. McGREGOR, 310, Summer Lane.
> Messrs. HIBELL & PRICE, Lozells Road.
> or any Member of the Committee.
> Hon. Sec., W. B. MASON,
> Edgbaston Road, Moseley.
>
> Ad from
> *The Midland Athlete*

The Villa had now (at October, 1881) gained sufficient repute that the QP club felt that they could condescend to provide their first-team presence at Perry Barr, a decision much influenced by George Ramsay's friendship with many at QP. To catch a glimpse of how the Scots influenced the Scots (so to speak, as the Villa themselves were imbued with 'em!), the following is a synopsis of Old Fogey's description of Villa's first experience against Queen's Park's first team.

The 'inner circle' were agog with excitement to see the past masters of the game [at Perry Barr], and hoping against hope that the local lads would be good enough to beat them. Billy Mason was honorary secretary at the time and he tried to boom the match all he could, but at that period the daily press took less notice of a football match than of a rabbit-coursing scramble ... 'the muddy oafs'[158] had to depend upon the sporting press, who worked very hard in those far-off days for the popularity of the pastime, and got chucked aside like a battered old plug hat when the daily press found out that more or less picturesque reporting would 'pay'. The *Daily Gazette* (W. G. Anderson) was an exception – providing 'excellent reports of Villa matches'.

The match was held on October 20 1881 – the Onion Fair holiday - in front of a 4,000 'gate' in glorious autumn weather. Before the game was 10 minutes old, their belief in the inviolability of the Villa was knocked all to smithereens!

Villa (1-3-6): *Copley; Joe Simmonds; E. Lee, S.Law, Arthur Brown; Oliver Whateley, Andy Hunter, Archie Hunter, W.Crossland, H.Vaughton, Eli Davis. Jack Hughes umpired for the Villa.*

The Queen's Park team included:

> Charles Campbell (captain): "One of the greatest centre-halves who ever kicked a ball or unceremoniously bundled a man over – for they charged to some tune in those days."

---

[158] Alluding to a line in Rudyard Kipling's 'The Islanders' (1902): "With the flannelled fools at the wicket or the muddied oafs at the goals…"

The Aston Villa Chronicles 1874 – 1924 (and after)

'Geordie' Kerr: "Perhaps the finest ever Scottish centre-forward [pre-1907]."

Queen's Park won 4-0 and worth a lot more, but behaved themselves as 'guests'! They made Villa look schoolboy-ish by comparison.

> For the first time in their lives, Birmingham people saw absolutely classy football, and they were amazed. Their disappointment gave way to admiration at the deftness of the dribbling, the pace and precision of the passing, the defiance and daring of the defence – the general altogether-ness and splendid ability of the team as a whole. Why, they made mosaics on that meadow, and they fairly flabbergasted the home crew, who did a tremendous amount of running about for nothing that afternoon. Puzzling passing was done either deliberately or swiftly, as the humour seized the Queen's Park man, and ever and anon would come a shot like a lightning flash…
>
> The Villa tried to get on terms, and now and then would display sparkle from which hope was born [– *until Queen's Park got the ball back!*] Aubern-whiskered Sammy Law and enterprising Joe Simmonds would sail in and make matters lively for a minute or two; or Archie Hunter would lead a raid with brother Andy, Whateley and Howard Vaughton, and Arthur Brown in sleuth-hand attendance…
>
> Villa learnt their lesson exceedingly well, for it is not too much to say that from that day forward, the 'class' of Perry Barr football very greatly improved, as many of the local clubs – and the majority of those that came from far off – found to their cost. There were individual members of the Villa team as brilliant as any of those on the QP side, but when it came to cohesion – playing the game in the lump, so to speak – they had much to learn from the Clydeside eleven, and they proceeded to do so. [159]

QP played with two full-backs, and it was apparently as a result of this match that the Villa concluded that it was vital to play two full-backs to combat a clever forward line, instead of just the one as had been Villa's practise (at least since Archie Hunter arrived). The Villa, therefore, did not go over to two full-backs in every match at that time – it depended on whether their opponents had "a clever forward line". And when two backs were played, Villa played with two half-backs and six forwards. The six forwards' strategy continued for awhile yet, even though some other teams were going over to three half-backs and five forwards.

---

[159] Villa News & Record 9 Nov 1907 – "A Long Time Ago"

The Aston Villa Chronicles 1874 – 1924 (and after)

Charlie Johnstone continues the story of the outcome:

> The seed sown did not fall on stony ground; we took our object lesson seriously to heart, we practised sedulously both individually and collectively, and discussed problems in tactics and combination. The whole tone of the club was influenced by 'QP' methods and ideals, and I have no doubt in my mind that its subsequent success has been largely due to these early lessons.
>
> The social side was equally sharing, and life-long friendships were formed. Those of you who have enjoyed the hospitality of a Burns' dinner can imagine what a host George Kynoch [from 1885, Villa's president] made, when, as an exiled Scot, he was entertaining 'chiels frae Glasgae!' I often wonder what the douce serious men of affairs in both cities think now, when they recall the mad pranks they played when we explored the mysteries of the Onion Fair. However, those days are past. The stern commercialism of league matches has killed the joyousness of football and with it initiative in the game itself. [160]

The following March (1882), Glasgow Rangers paid a visit to Perry Barr, a match that the Villans won 3-2, including a magnificent winner from distance by Tom Bryan. It was noted by the *Daily Gazette* that there followed "a liberal repast" provided by George Kynoch, with the assemblage including members of the Excelsior club and other friends, totalling 120 in all. The odd thing about the match itself was a 15-minute dispute as to whether a throw-in had been thrown straight, according to Scottish rules!

The FA Cup competition started in November, and the two ancient Nottingham clubs were again Villa's opponents in the FA Cup, and in the same sequence. This time, however, Villa were drawn at home on both occasions. The first tie, against the Forest, was well-won 4-1 by the Villa in quagmire conditions, but the referee disallowed another five 'goals' for offside when far removed from the play!

The next round against the County led to three matches before a result was obtained, again 4-1 to Villa, after two 2-2 draws. The first of these draws went to extra time, and "the excitement [amongst the 10,000 spectators] got to such a pitch that umbrellas, hats, sticks etc. were scattered in all directions". But the match still finished a draw, and a replay at Nottingham. Law and Crossland were both on the sick list, and Vaughton was an uncertain starter. Archie was away in Scotland and "the spirits of the Brummagemites sank to a very low ebb ... Their only hope lay with Archie Hunter". He was contacted and secured forthwith, and proceeded to play one

---

[160] In his column in The Sporting Mail 22 Oct 1910

The Aston Villa Chronicles 1874 – 1924 (and after)

of his best games. He also scored what seemed the winner after "a clever piece of dribbling" and a tremendous shot that went through the goal at high velocity and hit the pavilion forty yards away. But with three or four minutes left, the County equalised, "amidst a scene of the greatest excitement and confusion."

The final match was played in front of an estimated 12,000 spectators at Perry Barr. The *Daily Gazette* reported: "Archie Hunter showed up his old form again, his tricky dribbling and accurate passing being a real treat to witness." When Archie scored the opening goal, "the Villa skipper brought down a tumult of applause."

Next up in the FA Cup, though, were Villa's auld enemy, the Old 'Uns, at their ground in January. They were very anxious to regain some pride following Villa's demolition of their team in the semi-final of the Birmingham Cup the previous season, and, with Villa missing both Andy Hunter and Eli Davis, the Old 'Uns ran out the winners this time, by four goals to two, in front of a crowd probably numbering 8,000. This was after Villa had twice taken the lead, but Villa's wingers were badly missed that day.

In the Final of the Birmingham Cup, the Villa re-established themselves as champions of the district by gaining revenge over the Old 'Uns by 2-1 at the Lower Grounds on 1st April. This was the Villa's second win of the trophy and in front of a 10,000 crowd. However, Archie Hunter immediately returned to Scotland after this match, and was reported as taking part in the Ayr match versus Queen's Park the following week, Ayr winning 2-1.

Aston Villa – Birmingham Cup Winners, 1882 (photo at the Lower Grounds)

Back row: -------, Wm. McGregor (V-president),
Andy Hunter, ---, ---, ---, Archie Hunter, Lee, Pank, Eli Davis, ---, H. Jeffries (Hon. Treasurer)
Middle Row: Whateley, Arthur Brown, W.M. Ellis (President), ---, Law,
On Ground: ---, H. Vaughton.
*Copley (gk) and Anderson would be two of the unidentified players;
the named players are those that played in the 1882 B'ham Cup Final.*

The Aston Villa Chronicles 1874 – 1924 (and after)

As the 1880s wore on, the Villa developed a strong hold on the Birmingham Cup and also started to have a stronger presence in the FA Cup. It is noteworthy that at the annual dinner of the Birmingham & District FA in June, 1882, Alderman Joseph Chamberlain was presiding, indicating the status that football now held in the district.

England Internationals

In 1882, Arthur Brown and Howard Vaughton became the Villa's first two England international players. They first played for England against Ireland at Belfast in February, 1882, when England won 13-0. Vaughton scored five and Brown scored four. The next month, these two played for England versus Scotland at Glasgow where England lost 1-5, Vaughton scoring England's only goal to equalise (to 1-1). Below is a photo of that team. Brown and Vaughton played in the next game against Wales, when England lost 3-5 at Kennington Oval; neither scored.

England team vs Scotland, 1882 (players only; 2-2-6 formation)

Back row: Alfred Jones (RB, Walsall Swifts), Harry Swepstone (GK), Ed. Parry (CH), John Hunter (LH), Harry Cursham (OR, Notts County), Haydock Greenwood (LB)
Middle Row: Ed. Bambridge (IL, Walsall Swifts), Norman Bailey (Right CF, Clapham R.), Wm. Mosforth (OL)
On Ground: H. Vaughton (IR), Arthur Brown (CF) (both Aston Villa)

The Aston Villa Chronicles 1874 – 1924 (and after)

Season 1882-83

Again, the season started without Archie Hunter. Obviously, the Villa were not happy – who else could lead the team on to greater things? A most cordial letter from Sam Richardson (the new club secretary) was posted in the September, as soon as the Villa had observed that leadership in the team was sadly awry.

> My Dear Archie,
>
> I am happy to have to write you inviting you to our Annual Dinner & Photographic Group at the Lower Grounds, Aston, on Saturday, Sept. 16th. The same afternoon we play a match with Walsall Town for the benefit of your old chums, the Birchfield Harriers. I am also pleased to write you because I want a straight chat this way with you, relative to the future! We have had one or two Sub Committee meetings relative to the Captaincy of the 1st Team for the season 1882-83, and we feel assured that if you come amongst us our past success is not only retained but we [will] take a still higher position! Now this brings me to the main point in this question - we cannot see our way to a business that will keep two of you and pay exp's as well out of the profits, but we can see a very good opening for a Gentleman's Outfitting Department - for all kinds of athletic garments and perhaps add cigars etc. that would provide for one etc. So that the question is, can you arrange matters between yourselves? Can Andy or yourself find a situation for the day time and then assist in the trade in the evening? or can you get a good agency or two? I think if one stops in the business - with your sister to help - and the other takes a situation for a time, until your business grows, you will find such a lift in life, as few people have the offer of! Without pledging the club, I believe I can safely say, we are prepared to take a place, near Snow Hill, in the main thoroughfare and fit it suitably for Andy and your sister and yourself to be together and to lend for stock from £150 to £200. Now is that [at] all likely to meet your views! Let me have a straight answer - telling me just your opinion as though I were your brother.
>
> Yours truly,
> Sam'l Richardson

And so it was that the Villa provided the loan in question, and Archie and Andy set up business.

The Aston Villa Chronicles 1874 – 1924 (and after)

> The "new secretary" – Sam Richardson – was a teacher, described in *The Villa News*[161] as: "[A] lively and breezy pedagogue ... [H]e could talk the leg off an iron pot, and his recitations were the pride of the club." It was said that at his school, "Aston Villa deeds and prospects formed half the scholastic curriculum."
>
> Sam's letter to Notts County (Harry Cursham) in early October illustrates the respect between clubs in those days. At the same time, the letter was probably trying to get County to overcome their notoriety as poor time-keepers, and perhaps also indicating an attempt at trying to soften the 'needle' that was developing between the two clubs!:
>
>> Please not forget our fixture for Sat. next – here – kick-off at 3.30 promptly – gate halved as usual?
>>
>> Would you arrange if possible to take tea with us – or other refreshment – and to spend an hour or so with our team?
>>
>> Hoping for fine weather and a good game.

The Villa then went on that season to work their way through four rounds of the FA Cup to the quarter-finals, including the beating of both Walsall Swifts and Wednesbury Old Athletic by 4-1. A report in the *Athletic News* on the Swifts match in October 1882 included an observation on Howard Vaughton:

> To see him skip and dance around opponents as big again as himself was a pretty sight ... On this occasion he partnered Andy Hunter, the pair of them treating the visitors to splendid cool passing and laughable tricks of all descriptions.

The report continued:

> Roberts and Davis electrified the spectators with a succession of dodges and old-fashioned tricks that one seldom sees on the football field ... it generally came when least expected.
>
> [Archie Hunter] was a splendid captain in this match, [this appearance coinciding with his re-emergence in Birmingham after being in Scotland for some time. Clarke (in goal) had replaced Tom Mason for this match, and] came off with flying colours.

The match against the Old 'Uns in November saw Villa changing to a two-back system (but continuing with two half-backs; a 2-2-6 system). The match reporter stated "it is far more effective and far safer." The decision to do this was taken at the

---

[161] Villa News and Record 23 Oct 1926

The Aston Villa Chronicles 1874 – 1924 (and after)

full committee meeting on 14 November, following a proposal by Eli Davis.[162]

> [The match was played on a snow-covered but firm pitch, and it was the Old 'Uns that scored first after Villa had been doing nothing but giving them a pasting for twenty minutes!]
>
> When the Athletic did get away ... they scored ... amid screams of delight from the blackcountrymen, and quite a 'kit' of 'wormers'[163] were despatched to bear the glad tidings to Wednesbury!
>
> [That celebration was premature. Villa, undaunted, persevered in their work, and it was Archie that at length gained the equaliser as a result of a fine return pass from Harvey. That goal produced a "terrific shout from the Brums". From then on it was a case of Villa maintaining a siege with the occasional Athletic breakaway, and the Villa adding sufficient goals to complete a comfortable result.]

The report stated that both Harvey and Apperley had a magnificent game at half-back, with Apperley stopping George Holden time and time again. Archie Hunter, Vaughton and Brown were prolific in attack. It was noted as well that Brown had a sort of roaming commission at half-back.

The next match produced a 3-1 win against another auld enemy, Aston Unity, a match in which Joe Simmonds twice "brought down the house" with clever defensive work, with the Villa – as very often reported – hesitant in front of the opponents' goal and consequently spurning the goal opportunities that came to them.[164]

The fourth tie at Perry Barr (all so far had been played at home) was against Walsall Town, a match where "the supremacy of the district had to be decided" (*Midland Athlete*) as Walsall had recently beaten both Blackburn Rovers (coming to the peak of their glory) and Sheffield Wednesday.

> [A gale greeted the teams and the spectators, who] were rewarded for their pluck by seeing their head-gear floating about in an upper stratum of air, and whirled and tossed about preparatory to settling down, in most cases in a handy pool of water.
>
> [The game itself was one of almost continuous attack by the Villa, and grim defensive work by Walsall, with occasional breakaways by them. Vaughton

---

[162] The matter came up again for discussion on the following 2nd April, but the case for a 2-back system was won by a 7-5 vote.
[163] Pigeons, presumably.
[164] Midland Athlete 10 Jan 1883

opened the scoring by converting Whateley's pass "amidst the wildest uproar". The second half was particularly difficult as Villa played upfield against the gale and the stalwart defence, but Archie nevertheless secured the winner.]

[Villa eventually ran out 2-1 winners, and] the winning team received quite an ovation on leaving the ground.

The 'Long Arm' Game

It now required the Villa to win yet again against Notts County, but this time to reach the semi-finals, and on 3 March 1883, the match took place at Nottingham "beneath the castle walls". This meeting proved to be the "infamous incident of the long arm" which caused Villa to be "robbed" of further progress, and this incident would be talked of for many years afterwards. It was as a result of incidents such as this that the penalty kick rule was introduced in 1891.[165] It was also the case that the goalkeeper in those days wore the same jersey as his colleagues, and not being otherwise easily distinguishable, who made a save with his hands was not always clear. The practise of the keeper wearing a different jersey did not take effect until 1909.

Some 15,000 spectators were thought to have been present at this match. It was thought doubtful (at that time) that so many supporters (thought to be 3,000) had before travelled away to give their team support.

Villa: Mason; Lee, Simmonds, David Anderson, Apperley,

Andy Hunter, Whateley, Archie Hunter, Arthur Brown, Vaughton, Eli Davis.

It was reported in the *Midland Athlete* that the visitors looked quite diminutive compared to the gigantic proportions of the Notts players, Gunn's prodigious frame towering far above their heads. The following is Old Fogey's account of the match:

> By [a] series of extraordinarily lucky incidents, Notts were three goals to the good at half-time, and the gentle Trent 'Lambs' – oh, Lord, how did they bleat! But the Villa bucked up amazingly after the Passover, and by sheer superiority and zeal they drew level 20 minutes before the end came. I remember well Arthur Brown scoring that third goal, for when they were returning to the centre, he sprang on Archie Hunter's shoulders, who bore

---

[165] John Lewis (former referee, in his column in The Sporting Mail 15 Feb 1913) stated that originally the penalty area was a 12-yards line that went right across the pitch – i.e. that the penalty area was of pitch width. Only a decade later was the current penalty area format adopted.

The Aston Villa Chronicles 1874 – 1924 (and after)

the little man proudly down the meadow. After that, it was pandemonium, and little else. So wild and excited did the Notts spectators become that they broke into play all round the ground, turned the press-men pell-mell out of their pen, and went mad generally.

I remember talking to Howard Vaughton on the field, twenty yards inside the line, and we both remarked that the game would count for nothing, when there was a sudden burst by Notts, and lengthy William Gunn[166] got away and scored a beautiful goal, which made the Trentsiders wilder than ever [4-3 to them]. By this time all four corners of the field were invaded, and the wing men had to thread their way through the flying crowd... Presently the Villa were away in a desperate rush, with every man-jack of them going like Trojans for the goal, and [Archie] Hunter got the ball and shot like a cannon. The ball bounced off the custodian, and hovered close to goal, while Vaughton and Whateley made a bee-line for the keeper, jamming him up against the post. The ball came to David Anderson, and a pretty overhead shot was going through the right corner of the goal, when *a long arm* arose and knocked it back into play, and a Notts defender promptly kicked it out of bounds. The [final] whistle went just afterwards...

I said at the time it was robbery ... From that episode commenced the agitation for penalising the offending side for such foul tactics; but the Villa were unfairly dealt with then, for, after a so-called enquiry, the match was allowed to stand, and Notts County were knocked out in the semi-final by Old Etonians, whereat every Villa fan most heartily chuckled.[167]

Fred Ward quoted a newspaper report at the time of that 'Long Arm' game. It said: "Howard Vaughton [played] with a calmness and subtlety that was an amazing feature of the play in this maelstrom of football frenzies could have found time to devise."[168] However, the *Midland Athlete* thought that Gunn was the best player on the field "in a sea of talent", with Joe Simmonds "an immense power". Others thought that Andy Hunter had a great game.

---

[166] Gunn was over six feet four inches in his stocking feet – then a more rare sight – and "he had thighs like baulks of timber, and about as hard. ... Joe Simmonds tried him once at Perry Barr, launching himself, so to speak, at the Forest tree, and for the remainder of the game, the red-capped bounder was crumpled up and done for."
(Villa News & Record 12 Sep 1906)
[167] Villa News & Record 22 Feb 1908
[168] In his publication 'Aston Villa' (1948)

The Aston Villa Chronicles 1874 – 1924 (and after)

Double Figures. In fact, Double Double Figures!

In the Birmingham Cup that year, Villa broke scoring record after scoring record. One cup-tie produced the highest Villa score ever, and that was the match against Small Heath Swifts (*not the Alliance*, as some would have it!) at Perry Barr on 13 January, 1883.

Hitherto unknown, the Swifts created a reputation for themselves as a result of beating a lot of neighbours. Their reputation gained some credence by their (wrongly) supposed connection with the then Small Heath Alliance, and they fancied their chances against Villa. So, as fame of these Swifts had got to the Villa, caution was taken to play their strongest side.

When the day came, the referee failed to turn up. Old Fogey was asked by Archie Hunter to officiate, but a Small Heath supporter protested on the grounds that "the game was likely to be a close one … it ought to be an unbiased person." Forthwith, another referee was found.

21 – 0 !   **Villa**: *Mason; Simmonds, Harvey; Anderson, Apperley; Whateley, Andy Hunter, Archie Hunter, Arthur Brown, Vaughton, Eli Davis.*

> [Half-an-hour before the match it began to rain, and as time went on the rain became harder and harder. This resulted in a small 'gate' turning up.] For about three minutes, the Swifts made a tremendous sort of 'splash' (both literally and figuratively), and once, they actually got within striking distance … Joe Simmonds sent them down the field again, and they never came back till half-time, when, of course, they were 'at home' that end.
>
> They were compelled to stay at both ends – and, oh, how it rained; rained water and shots and goals and trouble; and the protesting gentleman from Small Heath lowered his 'aughty 'ead and got in out of the wet…
>
> When the Villa found out what sort of opponents they really had, they went in for 'larks' and it was almost pitiful to see the feeble struggle the Swifts made to stem the tide of disaster… The faster the water came down, the greater grew the score against the Swifts." This – that was supposed to have been a close game – amounted to a score of 9-0 in favour of the Villa – by half-time!
>
> Arthur Brown … had a sort of field day and kept giving the ball to other fellows to shoot, and they didn't forget to hammer it in." But their keeper was of better mettle than the players in front of him: "He had a most uncomfortable and fearfully busy time, and the poor chap looked tired

enough when they changed ends, though worse was to follow.

It kept on raining, and was persistently peppering down when coffee-time came and went, so that it was a drenched twenty-two who resumed the battle... But what was fun to the Villa was death to the reputation of Small Heath Swifts... [Villa's keeper Tom Mason] borrowed a bucket, turned it up and sat on the bottom thereof in the centre ring of the field, watching his comrades slanting in the ball from all quarters, only shifting his seat a little when the teams trooped down to kick off from the centre!

[So many goals were scored until] the Villa keeper... [kicked] through the twenty-first! Several times during the second half the Villa men were called to the bar for hot drinks, and there never was such a football farce played at Perry... the curious thing about it being that directly the match was over, the rain ceased! ... [If] it had not been for a particularly lively keeper, the 21-0 score might have been doubled![169]

The *Midland Athlete* added that it was Archie Hunter who went into goal once the 20-0 had been reached, and he kept "goal in the middle of the field with a hat on that was much too small for him, and looking disconsolate and lonely" whilst keeper Tom Mason was upfield trying his luck.

Having got into the total attack 'groove', Villa were not going to be easily shifted, and when they came up against Aston Unity in the next

16 – 0 !

round of the Birmingham Cup in February, goals, goals and goals were again the order of the day. *Sixteen of them!* Yes, Villa won 16-0, and thus produced a total of 37 goals in two successive games in the same competition. Arthur Brown bagged nine (9) in this match, whilst Dawson weighed in with four. Arthur Brown's total exceeded the seven that Andy Hunter once scored against Fenton. Again – strangely enough – the match was played in a downfall of rain!

One or two of the Unity officials looked limp and woebegone, though perhaps the rain had something to do with this! But some of the countenances I saw haunt me now," wrote the *Midland Athlete* reporter, "and I am sure if the Villa people could have seen the looks of awful dismay and misery I saw, pity would have prevented them doing so much!

Villa then went on to beat St. George's (whose team included a certain Denny Hodgetts) 4-1 in thickly falling snow in the semi-final at the Lower Grounds in March, and then again came up against Wednesbury Old Athletic in the final at the

---

[169] Distilled from Villa News & Record & Record 11 Jan 1908

The Aston Villa Chronicles 1874 – 1924 (and after)

Lower Grounds, whom they beat 3-2 in front of up to 9,000 spectators.

The Final against the Old 'Uns was certainly the closest run thing of all the rounds in that competition that year, but it was not a match to enthuse over, according to reports. The match was played on a hard ground under a hot sun on 7 April, and it was reported of Archie Hunter: "A greater portion than usual of his energies was spent in trying to keep his men up to mark; Whateley, Roberts, Davis and Anderson coming in for no small share of his commands." Indeed, the Villa opened the match as though they did not care much about the result, but as soon as several of the Old 'Uns had pushed the Villa keeper into the net and obtained the lead, "[Villa] suddenly woke up, played for 10 minutes in tip-top style, scored a trio of goals, and then went off into slumber again." Villa did just enough by the end to win through.

This series of results in the Birmingham Cup competition that season yielded a total of 53 goals for and 4 against, in six successive Birmingham Cup matches!

A special poster - in Shakespearean style - was put out in red and black print to advertise the Final:

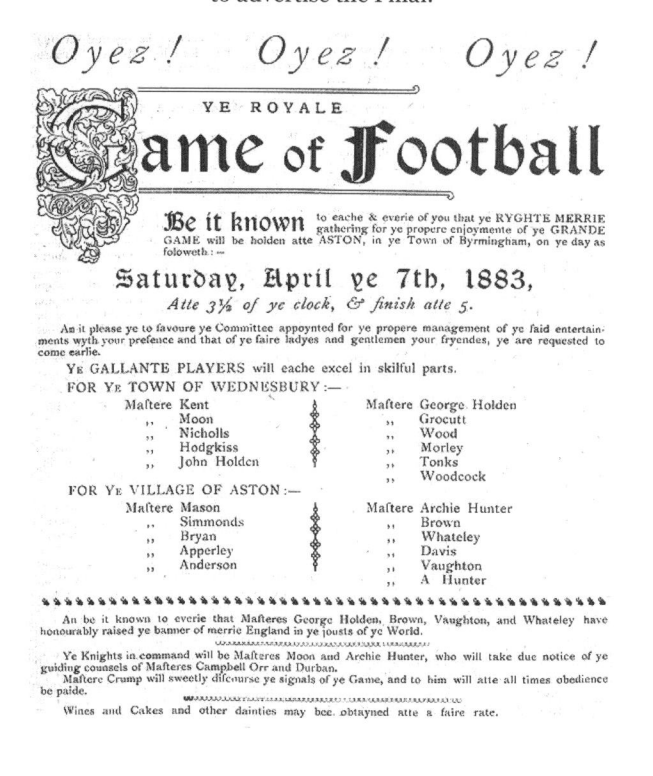

Oyez! Oyez! Oyez!

YE ROYALE Game of Football

Be it known to eache & everie of you that ye RYGHTE MERRIE gathering for ye propere enjoymente of ye GRANDE GAME will be holden atte ASTON, in ye Town of Byrmingham, on ye day as foloweth:—

Saturday, April ye 7th, 1883,

Atte 3½ of ye clock, & finish atte 5.

An it please ye to favoure ye Committee appoynted for ye propere management of ye faid entertainments wyth your prefence and that of ye faire ladyes and gentlemen your fryendes, ye are requested to come earlie.

YE GALLANTE PLAYERS will eache excel in skilful parts.

FOR YE TOWN OF WEDNESBURY:—

Maftere Kent	Maftere George Holden
,, Moon	,, Grocutt
,, Nicholls	,, Wood
,, Hodgkiss	,, Morley
,, John Holden	,, Tonks
	,, Woodcock

FOR YE VILLAGE OF ASTON:—

Maftere Mason	Maftere Archie Hunter
,, Simmonds	,, Brown
,, Bryan	,, Whateley
,, Apperley	,, Davis
,, Anderson	,, Vaughton
	,, A. Hunter

An be it known to everie that Mafteres George Holden, Brown, Vaughton, and Whateley have honourably raised ye banner of merrie England in ye joufts of ye World.

Ye Knights in command will be Mafteres Moon and Archie Hunter, who will take due notice of ye guiding counsels of Mafteres Campbell Orr and Durban.

Maftere Crump will sweetly difcourse ye signals of ye Game, and to him will atte all times obedience be paide.

Wines and Cakes and other dainties may bee obtayned atte a faire rate.

The Aston Villa Chronicles 1874 – 1924 (and after)

In the following picture taken of the **Birmingham and Distirct FA** representative side from *The Villa News*, 5 May, 1923, the year of its occasion is given as 1882. However, because Tom Bryan (central in the picture) was not a member of the Villa team until the 1882-83 season, I put this team picture as taken during that season. Note Billy Mason as Vice-president.

Back row: J.Campbell Orr (Hon. Treasurer), Billy Mason (V-president), H.Evans (Derby Midland), J.Arnall (V-president), J.Cofield (Hon. Sec.);
Middle Row: George Holden (WOA), Arthur James (Small Heath A.), Tom Bryan (Capt., Aston Villa), Alf.Harvey (A. Villa), H.Vaughton (A.Villa), Charles Crump (President);
On Ground: Sam Law (A. Villa), Arthur Brown (A. Villa), Eli Davis (A. Villa), W.Yates (Walsall Swifts).

In the Lord Mayor's Charity Final on 12 May, "with the wind in their favour, and with a dash and go that surprised even their friends", Villa returned to high-scoring ways and beat Walsall Swifts 8-0. Three-up after seven minutes, "[with] passing being simply perfection", Villa were five up after thirty minutes before they showed signs of slowing down. The Swifts then came back strongly in the second half, having got over the shock, but Dawson and Apperley put a stop to their pretensions and Villa cantered through. Archie Hunter "was playing as a sort of three-quarter-half-back-centre-forward, and the way he stopped rushes and skilfully fed the other forwards was a sight to see."[170]

---

[170] This sounds like a "deep-lying centre-forward" of the Ronnie Allen mould (for the Albion) in the 1950s.

The Aston Villa Chronicles 1874 – 1924 (and after)

How Villa's Nose Was Put Out of Joint

Thus both Aston Unity and Walsall Swifts, hitherto amongst the strongest teams of the Birmingham District, were taken down by much more than a peg or two that season. But that is not how it seemed matters would turn out at the latter end of 1882, when the Villa – by now regarded as the "premier club of the Midlands" – played West Bromwich Albion in the other cup they entered, the Staffordshire Cup. Remarkably, Villa were defeated 1-0 "by a team [the Albion], who, until a year or so ago, was virtually unknown to the football world." The result seemed so unlikely that, "for a time the Villa partisans … regarded it as an idle rouse instigated by some ill-minded and prejudiced person", wrote "Brum" in the *Athletic News*. The reporter said that Villa had, in fact, sufficient of the play to win, but were "guilty of too much show play to the gallery". Villa protested that the result was invalid owing to an intrusion of spectators onto the pitch, thus impeding their progress, but that appeal came to nought.

Season 1883-84

The Albion had signalled their appearance as opponents that were to be respected, but in this next season Villa still had not learnt their lesson properly, and again it was in the Staffordshire Cup. The Villa team that played the Albion that day was:

Clarke; Stevens, Law; Dawson, Lee;
Archie Hunter, Crossland, Horton, Eli Davis, Steer, Vaughton.[171]

[In the latter part of December, 1883, the Villa first team was due to be playing Notts Forest "in an ordinary match" and the second team was deputed to meet Albion in a Staffordshire Cup-tie at Perry Barr. It was a bitterly cold, frosty, blizzardy day and a telegraph 'wire' from Trentside announced that the entire Forest side was unfit to play. So, the first team stayed to watch the second team "knock out the rising young gentlemen from over the way." The match was not an easy one, though, as the Throstles had beaten Wednesbury O. A. in a Birmingham cup-tie on "the old magnificent meadow at Aston Lower Grounds" a week or two before. This being the case, one or two of the 'Firsts' decided to help out the youngsters. In any case,] Archie Hunter could not be kept out of football if there was any going – he bossed the show – but in the first half he and his colleagues got rather a fright for when ends were changed one side had scored three goals to nothing – and

---

[171] Villa News & Record 14 Feb 1914

The Aston Villa Chronicles 1874 – 1924 (and after)

it wasn't the Villa!

There was a council of war conducted by the 'general' and tactics were altered so that the side played up finely to the brawny Scot, and off on his own bat he notched that much-needed trio of points [i.e. goals]." It had been a very hard struggle to retrieve the situation and Archie said to Old Fogey afterwards, "Look here, old man; that lot of lads will take a deal of whacking, and they're the most promising eleven I've seen for many a day.

[The replay on the following Saturday (Christmas Eve) was] on that awful pitch known as the Four Acres, where a kind of small precipice ran athwart the field about fifteen yards from the lower goal, and if a man got a clear chance from the brow of that declivity, Old Harry himself couldn't have stopped a well-directed shot, for the ball came with the velocity of a cannonball, and the home forwards [the Albion] didn't half know the trick of it.

There was a frosty fog, a viciously hard ground, and a great deal of temporary aberration of good temper ... [and] excitement was at fever-heat all the way through the match." The young Albion side were determined to show their worth "and the ambition and enterprise of real rising talent will carry a team far, especially when every man jack in the eleven has a strong and abiding faith in his comrades...

[Half-way in the match, a man called *Aston* scored for the Albion! But Villa could not score, try as they did. The Villa fans left the ground] vexed but somewhat compensated by the undoubted fact that a new constellation had risen above the horizon of the football firmament, and the West Bromwich Albion [team] were foemen worthy to be reckoned with in the coming days.[172]

That Albion team went on to win the Staffordshire Cup that year.

The result of that Christmas meeting against the Albion proved merely to be an interval between two joys in terms of results, as will be seen in the following two FA Cup reports. In the first of these matches, Villa were drawn against Walsall Swifts at "The Chuckery", 10 November, 1883, and, won 5-1.

Villa: *Vale; Riddell, Simmonds, Apperley, Price, Dawson, Whateley, Vaughton, Archie Hunter, Roberts, Davis.*

Scorers: Hunter (2), Vaughton, Roberts, and an own goal.

---

[172] Villa News & Record 4 Jan 1908

The Aston Villa Chronicles 1874 – 1924 (and after)

The aftermath of the match, however, was a little more painful.

> [Following the one-sided match,] the team and some friends returned in a wagonette, and when the vehicle, after being 'booed' vigorously on several points of the journey, was driven by some waste ground, a big knot of roughs with missiles in their grimy fists were observed to make ready, and we knew we had to run a pretty dangerous gauntlet, for in those days the fringe of the crowd took a most material form.
>
> The driver bowed his head and whipped up his horses, and every man on board ducked swiftly before the coming storm. It came in the shape of stones, turf, brickbats, clinkers and every other kind of horror that waste ground can supply, and we had a very perilous passage, for the rain of boomerangs hurtled through the air, and several of the folk got pretty badly hit. I felt a concussion in the small of my back, and found afterwards that the iron rail had been badly bent by a brick, which, had it not been for the protection, might have ended my pilgrimage on this mundane sphere; and then I heard a gasp from George Ramsay, who sat by my side, and saw the blood running in a stream down his face from a nasty wound in the head [from which he recovered, it looking worse than it was in reality].[174]

> **A Lion's Fun**
>
> In a Villa-Albion match of long ago, the centre-half on the Albion side was a man named Bunn – known locally as 'Bunny'. He was a thorn in the side of Archie Hunter; he shadowed him and frustrated his every move. More a question of 'Bunny hunting Hunter'!
>
> In the evening, the teams met at supper, rabbit being part of the menu. Archie was offered this rabbit, but he ruefully shook his head with a sly glance at Bunn, and responded: "No thanks. I've had a surfeit of Bunny today!"[173]

The foregoing behaviour was a regular thing in those days – a gauntlet that often had to be run. Old foes Stafford Road were next up in the FA Cup, and in their 5-0 annihilation, the scene was described as follows by the *Midland Athlete* reporter:

> That field at Tattenhall Road, Wolverhampton, is about the worst I ever saw. It was vile; the players very often being up to their knees in mud and water ... [Nevertheless,] Archie ploughed about in the mud in his usual indefatigable fashion.

---

[173] Sports Argus 10 Dec 1898. Archie Hunter (in 'Triumphs of the Football Field') mentions the abilities of Bunn in frustrating his (Archie's) best moves.
[174] Villa News & Record Christmas, 1907 (Old Fogey)

The Aston Villa Chronicles 1874 – 1924 (and after)

It was a comical sight to see Tommy [Riddell] trying to pull one of his long legs out of the quagmire and the sorrowful countenance he displayed when he got an unlucky tumble. You see, he carried such a lot away with him when he arose!

Arthur Brown might have been observed after the match in a pond close by, having a bath!

In the next round of the FA Cup, the Old 'Uns were again encountered. This is a picturesque account of that occasion on 29 December, 1883, resulting in a 7-4 win to the Villa.

Villa: *Clark,[175] Price, Riddell; Dawson, Apperley; Whateley, Vaughton, Archie Hunter, Arthur Brown, Roberts, Davis.*

The match was at what used to be known as Elwell's Ground, belonging to the big factory of that name near Bescot Junction... Of all the ungodly places first-class football was ever played at, surely that was the most unpicturesque!

Well, Elwell's Ground, so far as I remember it, lay between two swamps or reservoirs, and at a little distance there was a pit bank that shut out all the rest of the world on the south side, and on the north it was bounded by the aforementioned factory and probably the ugliest and draughtiest railway station in the wide, wide, world. It was as bleak as a Russian Steppe, and when the rain came down in slanting sheets or the ghostly fog hung about the grimy lands and deluged meadows ...

It was a green Yule, and the grass was soggy, so that the players had some difficulty in extricating themselves from their hoof-prints; the majority of the company, including the expositionists, were, so to speak, a bit 'Christmassy' in feeling; and you never heard such a row as they kicked up in all your natural... I recollect George and Jack Holden, Grocutt, Kent and Roland Morley in their [Old 'Uns] side...

The Villa went off at a rush, and before the Old 'Uns knew where they were the Perry Barr brigade were three to nothing in front! Crow?! The Astonians made noise enough to raise the Ancient Britons from their graves; but before long they were destined to laugh on the other side of their mouths, for before half-time, the Wednesbury boys had not only drawn level but actually got one [in] front, so that when the Passover came, the tumult and the shouting was all for the Old Athletic, and the Villa chaps looked very glum indeed.

---

[175] Archie Vale played in goal in all other FA cup games that season.

The Aston Villa Chronicles 1874 – 1924 (and after)

They went on looking glum for a good while, too, for the Aston defence seemed to have gone all to blazes, and the grimy pitmen and coalheavers 'got their own back' in tremendous style when it came to chaff that did not have much [banter] about it. Therefore, when there was only 20 minutes to go, and with the Athletic still pressing, there seemed every chance that the Villa were going to be kicked clear out of the Cup. Then, presto! There came a marvellous change! Archie Hunter rolled up his sleeves, began calling on his boys to follow, and as if new life and strength had suddenly been infused into them the Villa became aggressors instead of three-parts beaten defenders, and the long and sad-looking Kent, the [Old 'Uns] custodian, had probably the most sultry time of his life. It was great to see the Villa come round and conquer in the truly wonderful manner they did.[176]

The Wednesbury folks, disappointed though they were, after having their hopes raised so high, could not but acknowledge the superior skills and lasting prowess of the lads from Perry Barr... I remember George Holden saying to me, as he left the field, all tired and steaming, and perhaps a little bitter at the stings of defeat, "The score is a fine testimonial to the goalkeeping;" and genial old Archie slapping him on the back, and saying, "Never mind, George lad; we've all got to lose sometime; maybe our turn to-morrow. Come awa', and ha'e a wee drappie!" [And off went the skippers.]

We followed them to a cosy inn – I think it was the Horse and Jockey – where we had tea, followed by mulled ale, many songs, and we followed with much jollification. Anyway, there was a good deal of chatter, argument, prophesying, and merriment and as I think the scene over again, the very lines of Longfellow come to me as they came long ago:

How they laughed and stamped and pounded,
Till the tavern roof resounded,
And the host looked astounded,
As they drank the ale!

Old Athletic did not have a very long life as a first-rate club after that, for not only were the good men growing old, with none of the same calibre to replace them, but the Albion were looming rapidly up over the horizon, and ere many seasons had elapsed they completely eclipsed the Old 'Uns.[177] [178]

---

[176] Vaughton scored three with Hunter getting the fourth of the half. 7-4!
[177] Villa News & Record 26 Dec 1908
[178] Note: In January 1886-87, on the way to winning the FA Cup for the first time, Villa beat the Old 'Uns 13-0 at Perry Barr. They later joined the Birmingham League, and frequently played Villa's reserve team. However, in 1924, after years propping up the Birmingham League, the Old 'Uns retired from that League.

The Aston Villa Chronicles 1874 – 1924 (and after)

In the next round the following month (January, 1884), Villa found their Bannockburn. In those days, the FA Cup was competed for by teams from all around the British Isles, and for this match they had to travel to meet the great Queen's Park (Glasgow), and there – to their infinite sorrow – they were very soundly beaten, 1-6; this after the Villans had entertained the thought that they would win. Old Fogey narrated that at least the Villa forwards matched QP's, but the QP team all-round was a fine one – on their own ground in particular. QP subsequently got to the FA Cup Final, but lost against Blackburn Rovers. At least Vaughton had the satisfaction of scoring Villa's solitary goal, as well as scoring in all the FA Cup matches that season – including a hat-trick against the Old 'Uns.

In the Birmingham Cup, the Villa won the most one-sided Final in the competition's history against Walsall Swifts, the result, however, being a modest 4-0.

> In the Birmingham Cup Final, The Villa's second goal so upset the Swifts' skipper that he ordered the keeper (Sheldon) to play upfield. However, Sheldon refused to do so, and left the field instead, to applause from a section of the crowd! The skipper put himself in goal, but the ten men conceded more goals.[179]

> It was in 1883-84 that J. Campbell Orr described the Villa forwards as:
>> ... that long unbroken line which forms such a prominent feature of the Villa play... Their old style of rushing down together in a body.[180]
>
> Old Fogey described Villa's play in this way:
>> When [Archie Hunter] was leading his men to the attack, his line was formed like a crescent, with the wings as the extreme points, and he in the centre, always ready for the inward passes which were often as unerring as his outward thrusts had been ...[181]

---

[179] The History of the Birmingham Cup (Carr)
[180] A significant officer in the local FA, Campbell Orr was a founder-member of the Calthorpe club in 1873, and was the chief football critic of the Midland Athlete, a journal that was begun in 1879. From the time of the journal's foundation, he predicted the success of Aston Villa.
[181] Villa News & Record 17 Nov 1923

The Aston Villa Chronicles 1874 – 1924 (and after)

Season 1884-85

From 1880 up until now, the Villa had been making further great strides. They had achieved consistency in the FA Cup and had established a national reputation. They also would have dominated the game in the west Midlands – but a real threat to their local status had emerged in the form of West Bromwich Albion, who were soon to be achieving great things in the national (FA) Cup. And – what was worse for the Villa – the Albion were using the Villa all too often as a stepping stone to success.

Nevertheless, the requests for fixtures with the Villa were flooding in to secretary Sam Richardson, and he performed the welcome task of weeding out the best matches for the Villa.

It was, however, a time for re-building the Villa, as their old stars – the entire half-back department of Lee, Law and Pank in fact! – went into retirement. And there was further disturbing news about another well-loved and old star.

Andy Hunter

In an earlier chapter, it was recounted how Andy Hunter was laid dangerously low by a creeping illness, and how the decision was taken to raise a fund to send him to Australia to improve his health. In 1884, it was minuted by the FA that:

> An Associationist of renown, Andy Hunter, being compelled to take a sea voyage ... your committee are proud to see how his club, Aston Villa, has recognised his merit, and they hope to be permitted to supplement the proceeds of his benefit match by a donation.[182]

On 25 August, the Villa Committee noted that Andy hoped to sail on the 20 September. An application having been made to the club, it was resolved to send a further sum of £20 at the earliest opportunity. On 2 September, it was noted that receipts (including those from a benefit match) into the Andy Hunter Fund had grossed £94; the committee decided to make up the sum to £100. The altruism behind the Fund and his sending off is unquestionable, but Andy was to die in Australia without seeing his brother again.

---

[182] Quoted in Sports Argus 13 Apr 1907

The Aston Villa Chronicles 1874 – 1924 (and after)

Archie Hunter made a mention[183] that a third brother (John) was good at football. He also mentioned that at that time he was the only one left of four brothers. When he made that statement, disease had already taken hold of Archie, the last remaining brother.

The Season's Play

As Archie Hunter put it:

> The season had its notable reverses as well as its triumphs and you will be occasionally astonished to hear of a big victory one week being followed a week later by a defeat for the Villa at the hands of what we should [in 1890] consider an inferior combination.[184]

One of the season's outstanding matches at Perry Barr, in fact, resulted in a draw. The visitors on October 4, 1884 were Bolton Wanderers, and at that time (according to Archie) they and the Villa "were about equally matched". In this, the third meeting between the clubs, the match was very intense; Bolton took a first half lead which Villa equalised shortly after the interval, and then began a 'battle-royal' to achieve the winner. Just when a draw seemed the inevitable result with seconds remaining, it was Bolton that obtained the winner. A month later, the return match ended in a 1-4 defeat for the Villa.

In between these two matches, however, the Villa met the FA Cup-holders (Blackburn Rovers, who had beaten Villa's winning opponents, QP, in the final) at Perry Barr, a match that attracted a great deal of attention and one that Villa were determined to win. The Villa in fact went off in great gusto, and sent in many shots that the Rovers dealt with in fine style. Even better, Villa scored two goals in rapid time, both of which Albert Brown had much to do with. The match was hotly fought without further score until ten minutes from time, when a miskick gave Rovers a chance, which they took. That goal of theirs set up matters for a very tough scrap for the last few minutes, but Villa ran out winners by 2-1. Archie said: "On leaving the field a huge friendly reception awaited us and we departed with the cheers of the great concourse still ringing in our ears."

---

[183] "Triumphs of the Football Field", Birmingham Weekly Mercury, October, 1890 to February, 1891
[184] "Triumphs of the Football Field", Birmingham Weekly Mercury, October, 1890 to February, 1891

The Aston Villa Chronicles 1874 – 1924 (and after)

Having achieved straight-forward wins over Wednesbury Town and Walsall Town in the first two rounds of the FA Cup, the third round brought the Villa up against the Albion, at home, on 3 January. The Albion keeper (Roberts) played a 'blinder', and an "exceedingly good" game finished 0-0, with extra time not being possible because of bad light. A week later, there was a replay at the treacherous Stoney Lane ground in front of a crowd of 10,000, even though the conditions were very rainy and slushy. It was reported that Villa had the best of the play, but conceded a goal after only eight minutes, and yet another before half-time. The Albion goal was under a veritable siege in the second half, but they broke away and scored yet another, to make it 0-3 at the finish. "Several of the home team were carried shoulder high from the ground!"

Blackburn Rovers – the eventual winners (again) of the FA Cup that year – beat the Albion in the quarter-finals, but the next year (1886), both those teams reached the Final, and the Rovers only beat the Albion after a replay. The Albion came so close to becoming the first Midlands club to win the trophy in 1886.

In the Lord Mayor's Charity Cup Final, again the Albion won (1-2) against the Villa – to great acclaim from the press. 'Brum' said: "I did not believe the Albion capable of playing such a really fine game …", and they won with four second-teamers in their ranks. In the Birmingham Cup, the Villa managed to avoid the Albion and went on to win the trophy, beating Walsall Swifts 2-0 in the final, after beating the Old 'Uns 5-0 in the semi-final.

It was as a result of this Cup win (for the fourth year on the trot) that Villa were awarded the Cup outright, and the club made it available for competition amongst the Birmingham Schools in aid of the Children's Hospital. In recent years, this, the original Birmingham Cup, was retrieved by the club, and a substitute provided.

A mixed season ended with a painful result on 9 May that was something of a shock to the Perry Barr faithful: Aston Villa 1 Preston North End 5.

A crisis of some kind was developing for the Villa, and over the next two seasons some dramatic changes took place, mostly within the club but also in the game in general. In particular, in the middle of the 1884-85 season, the developing matter of professionalism came to a head, and by the following summer, professionalism was legal.

Hitherto, much control of the club was effectively in the players' hands, and in the transfer to professionalism, some problems were incurred concerning this.

The Aston Villa Chronicles 1874 – 1924 (and after)

7. Playing The Scots

The Villa, already composed of many Scots amongst their executive and playing staff, had decided by 1880 on learning from the best teams in the British Isles. The best football was then being played in Scotland, where there were many worthy teams such as Third Lanark, Renton, the Rangers and Heart of Midlothian (Hearts). But the best team there to learn from was Queen's Park of Glasgow, who ruled Scottish football during the 1870s. In the first England versus Scotland match in 1872, the entire Scottish team was selected from Queens Park.

The Villa had obtained sufficient status for the Queen's Park first team to visit Perry Barr in October, 1881 (as previously reported), when great lessons were learnt by the Villa. The fixture against 'QP' then became an annual affair.

On 26 October 1882, on the occasion of QP's second visit, there was a marginal improvement to the score, they winning by 1-3. Attendance at the match was "enormous", supplemented by Scots resident in Birmingham. The *Athletic News* reported:

> The play of the Villa forwards till within almost ten yards of the opposition goal was perfection, but when in front of goal their efforts were altogether unworthy of such a crack team. [Villa's half-backs Bryan, Anderson and Apperley played a grand game, while Andy Hunter and Whateley played the best combined game].

The second half was played under Scottish Rules, meaning that the throw-in was to be taken overhead with both hands on the ball, and straight, as in a Rugby line-out. "Not at all pretty to look at", it was reported! The English game at that time played a one-arm throw-in, but the law soon changed.

On 25 October, 1883 the margin was cut to 0-1 to QP, after a goal-less first half, the goal being scored near the end. The match was described by the *Midland Athlete*'s reporter as:

"The best exposition of the game that has ever taken place in the district", the match played in a "soaking, steamy, muggy sort of afternoon." That day the Villa did everything but score, and it was reported: "QP may thank their lucky stars that they walked off the field victorious", with the comment that "even the Scotch team does not contain such a wonderfully deft and brilliant tackler as Charlie Apperley." And, "in Riddell, [Villa] have got a power in the defending art that they never possessed before … his headwork … was better even than Campbell's, that prince of headers."

The Aston Villa Chronicles 1874 – 1924 (and after)

The reporter significantly added: "There can be no doubt that the Perry Barr club possess the finest string of forwards in the kingdom."

At the dinner following the match, an almost apologetic speech was made by the QP's skipper. This was followed by a concert with clever recitations and fine songs "under the genial presidency of Mr. W. M. Ellis."

Significantly, it was written: "The best of good fellowship exists between the organisations, and a whole crowd of players and their friends saw the Scottish team steam out of New Street at half-past ten the same night, the cheering being long and loud."

However, the Villa's strength at home – compared with their relative inability when playing far away – shone through when, in the FA Cup, they were walloped 1-6 at Queen's Park[185] in the following January (1884). Villa's team on that day (Vaughton scored for Villa) was:

Vale; Riddell, Simmonds; Apperley, Dawson;

Whateley, Vaughton, Arthur Brown, Archie Hunter, Roberts, Davis.

Despite the score-line, it was regarded a plucky attempt by the Villa, but Hunter stated, "The opinion after the match was that nothing could beat Queen's Park".

> Of that occasion, William McGregor had a tale to tell:
>
>> There was a humorous incident in connection with the great cup-tie between Villa and Queen's Park. Mr Margoschis, a member of the Villa committee, was in the habit of wiring news to be displayed in his shop window. On the Saturday morning he sent a telegram to state that the players had been over the ground and picked out the marks from which they would score their goals. We lost heavily (six to one), and it will not be difficult to judge of our consternation when we saw Mr Margoschis's telegram, word for word, in a Glasgow paper after the match.[186]

A Lion's Fun

There was, however, a pleasant surprise in store for the Villa fans in the following November (1884), the occasion of QP's fourth visit to Perry Barr. Archie narrated:

> ...remember that this club [QP] had carried off the Scottish Cup seven times out of a possible ten and that they had only been defeated in the final for the FA Cup by the Blackburn Rovers by two goals to one. And now here was this

---

[185] In those days Queen's Park and Rangers (of Glasgow) competed in the FA Cup. Professionalism having taken over the game, the Scottish FA stopped their members from playing in the FA Cup after 1887.

[186] C.B Fry's Magazine of Action and Outdoor Life Vol 2 Oct 1904 to Mar 1905 from p.44

The Aston Villa Chronicles 1874 – 1924 (and after)

great combination once more opposed to us! The idea of defeating the 'Spiders' was almost too much to imagine... Harvey was now our goal in the place of Vale, but the others were in their usual places, the team being composed as follows:-

Harvey, goal; Riddell and Simmonds, backs; F. Dawson and G. Price, half-backs; Whateley and Albert Brown, right wing; Archie Hunter and Arthur Brown, centres; Vaughton and Davis, left wing.

I do not think that the Scotchmen sent us down their best representatives, for there were several notable absentees - Arnott, Fraser, Kerr and Campbell [major Scottish internationals of that time] among the number. Still they were a grand lot ... They arrived in Birmingham in the small hours of Saturday morning, rather fatigued with their journey.

The contest excited more interest than any other match I remember up to that time. The gate was enormous, over twelve thousand people being on the ground. In the town the excitement was at fever-heat. Buses, brakes, cabs and cars had been carrying down the crowd all the morning and the railway company's special trains were insufficient for the multitude requiring conveyance. Troops of men could be seen in the roads leading to the Villa ground and the one topic of conversation in the town seemed to be the chance we had of beating the yet unbeaten team from over the border. Queen's Park were always favourites with the Birmingham public and as they bowled along in their brake to the field they were cordially cheered by the crowd. Another cheer greeted them as Anderson, with his hands thrust in his pockets, led them from the pavilion. The Villa, naturally, received plenty of encouragement and no sooner had we begun to take up our positions than pigeons could be seen flying from all parts bearing away the news that the battle had begun.

We lost the toss and had to play uphill with a stiff wind against us. I kicked off and we invaded the Queen's Park territory. A corner kick fell to the visitors, but Riddell cleared; a long kick by Miller, however, kept the ball hovering in our quarters. Some fine passing by Whateley and the two Browns made affairs look perilous for the Scotchmen, but McDougall got the ball back and a shot from another player sent the ball into Harvey's hands. He returned the ball into play and Albert Brown went away with a rush, but Harvey in brilliant style tackled him and the ball went out. Simmonds next had some hard work to do and saved some hard shots. Two corners fell to the visitors and the second one made the prospect look dark for us; but Harvey was equal to the occasion and punched the leather out of goal admirably. Whateley took the ball up field and passed to me, but McDougall was waiting

The Aston Villa Chronicles 1874 – 1924 (and after)

and we were again repulsed. A few minutes later a splendid exhibition of passing by Albert Brown, Vaughton and Whateley carried the ball into the enemy's quarters and roused intense enthusiasm. The younger Brown then sent the ball flying into McCullum's hands, but the latter saved his goal and some scientific play which followed drew forth the acclamations of the crowd. Christie next put us on our defence and after some hot shots the visitors gained another corner kick. This was placed right in the mouth of our goal, but Freddy Dawson came to the rescue and the now baffled 'Spiders' came down on us with renewed vigour and attempted to score. A scrimmage ensued and out of this Anderson put the leather through, scoring the first goal, five minutes before half-time.

The spectators greeted the success of the visitors with a loud round of applause as the excitement now reached fever heat. No further score was effected when ends were changed and having the wind in our favour we now played a more aggressive game than before. We were urged on by the shouts of our supporters, who expected us to make a bold bid for success. Davis and Vaughton took the ball down the field and a long and continuous attack on the Queen's Park timbers resulted. Obtaining possession on the right wing I put the ball into McCullum's hands and from his return the ball struck Arthur Brown's knee and rebounded through goal, the score thus being equalised.

The applause was uproarious and hats and sticks were thrown into the air by the enthusiastic crowd. Our hearts beat wildly when the ball was started again. Christie put in a magnificent run and centred which evoked cheers, but Riddell repulsed him. Nevertheless we were severely pressed, for the Queen's Park men were making strenuous exertions to score the winning [goal]. Harvey was kept busy and did his work manfully and the critical nature of the game affected the onlookers considerably. Putting on an extra spurt we took the ball into the opposition territory and were several times within an ace of scoring. Darkness, however, was coming on rapidly and each side played a desperate game. Misjudged kicks were not uncommon, for it was hard to keep cool. At last we secured a corner, the first we had had that day and though it was unproductive, we kept the ball in the opposition territory. A final shot of mine caused the ball to strike the post and it rebounded into play. Vaughton kicked over in self-defence; Eli Davis took the corner grandly and a rush on our part resulted in the ball going through off Albert Brown. This was the winning [goal].

Only a few minutes remained and then Major Marindin sounded the whistle and the Villa had won at last – won by two goals to one. I cannot attempt to describe the scene that followed, the vociferous cheers that greeted us cannot be described in words. The people rushed over the field shouting as long as

The Aston Villa Chronicles 1874 – 1924 (and after)

> they had voices left; they shook us by the hand until our joints were in danger; they patted us on the backs until we were sore. I doubt whether many people went home that day with the same hats they brought out and lost property in the shape of walking-sticks and umbrellas would have made a good stock for a second-hand dealer. At night people went about singing a ballad, with a refrain, 'The Villa have licked Queen's Park' and I was followed home by a multitude roaring as if I had won the battle of Waterloo.

More about being given congratulations:

> ...There was one old gentleman who was in the habit of rushing forward at the end of a game and holding my hand in a tight grip until I had walked off the field. Nothing could induce him to loose it. Then there were those who thought that the highest compliment they could pay us was to deliver thumps upon the back and their aim was not always true, but fell upon the neck or head, or anywhere. I have been carried shoulder-high, too, but how that came about belongs to another occasion.[187]

So, *at last*, a win to the Villa against QP! A return match was played at Hampden Park on New Year's day, 1885. Prior to this, "some of the players spent Wednesday in Edinburgh, while others visited Ayr, the town to which their old captain, Archie Hunter, belonged." This match was played on a pitch that was in a dreadful state, and the Villa found themselves two-down after five minutes! Villa did not allow themselves to be overwhelmed, and Arthur Brown reduced the arrears, but went in at half-time, 1-3 down.

After 60 minutes, Brown again scored, and the Villa's "grand speed and excellent combination delighted the spectators." But though Villa were showing good play, they fell further behind again, before Whateley punished a defensive slip soon after, to make the score, at the finish, a close 3-4 to QP. A Scots reporter observed that Villa "are the speediest team that ever crossed the border" but thought it Villa's folly, arguing that they could not shoot accurately when at such a pace.

In October, 1886, there was another match against QP, reported by Old Fogey:

> Last Thursday's great match at Perry Barr will have become a matter of football history by the time these lines see the light that very little need be written upon it. It becomes us in the first place to very heartily congratulate the Aston Villa on their magnificent victory of three to one. Only a few years ago such a feat would have been deemed simply impossible, and

---

[187] "Triumphs of the Football Field", Birmingham Weekly Mercury, October, 1890 to February, 1891

The Aston Villa Chronicles 1874 – 1924 (and after)

after all the stuff that has been written lately about the decadence of our celebrated eleven, this result is about the best answer that could be given. Granted, if you like, that the home team had an immense amount of luck, and some splendid, goalkeeping in the first half, and they went to work at first in a half-hearted kind of way that did not imbue their supporters with any very great amount of confidence; but they warmed up grandly as the game went on, and certainly played a far steadier and cleverer game after the Queen's Park had scored. Sound, scientific, and good play then set in, and it was pleasing to see the whole team settle down and take matters coolly, after they had been rushed and bothered by the Scotsmen in the first half. Luckily for the Villa, and thanks to the superb goal keeping of Warner, the rushes did not come off, as they have on so many previous occasions, and for once the Villa had quite their share of luck, and a little over.

When the score was one all, everybody on the ground, except the QP themselves and a small band of players who hailed from an adjacent [West Bromwich] borough, and who had a particular and close interest in the match,[188] looked mightily pleased; and when number two was added the smile deepened into a broad grin of honest satisfaction, except as regards the afore-mentioned people, who had cheered themselves almost hoarse when the QP were one ahead; and a round, rubicund little gentleman, who is always around on the Villa enclosure, and who was standing immediately below when the Villa drew to the front, cocked his head on one side, looked up at the quiet faces above him, and said, "Now, then; why don't you durned Throstles shout." Goal number three was kicked just before the end of the game, and the old Villa shout ascended, and let all the neighbourhood know that their favourites had won, and won jolly well, too.

After recalling the history of the start of fixtures between the Villa and QP, Old Fogey went on:

[T]he Queen's Park was a team in those days, and Villa partisans were forced to admit that their men had still a wonderful lot to learn. The Villa team has changed indeed since then, and if my memory serves me rightly Archie Hunter and Simmonds are the only two left who fought in [the first] memorable battle; but though the Scotchmen are an undoubtedly weaker team than the first one which visited us, that is not the only reason for the difference in the result.

---

[188] The West Bromwich Albion team, who were shortly to meet Villa in the Birmingham Cup.

The Aston Villa Chronicles 1874 – 1924 (and after)

We have learnt the science of the game, and can hold our own with the best of them now; and though perhaps old fogies may talk about the degeneracy of the pastime under the professional laws, it cannot be doubted that play has improved very considerably of late years.[189]

More Tartan Stories On Tour

The Villa retained a long and strong association with Scotland, and tours of Scotland (and Scottish teams in England) were a regular fixture in the calendar from 1880 and into the 1890s.

The *Athletic News'* Scottish correspondent reported on a Villa tour of Scotland in early April, 1882:

> At no time could they have been in Scotland in a prettier state than it is at present. They were charmed with the Scottish capital, whose elevated situation and architectural beauties rather surprised them, and on Sunday [they had] a magnificent view of Loch Lomond ... Their delight knew no bounds ... The appearance of the celebrated 'Villans' is an event which cannot be passed over lightly. ...[190]

The Villa met Hearts on this tour, and won 6-2, evoking the following report:

> ... to my recollection, this is the deadliest defeat that has yet been levelled against a Scotch club by English players, and over the Border ... The Hearts, although a very fair club, is not yet on a par with the Villans whom I have always held to be one of the best all-round teams in England. They play the game honestly and artistically, and having great speed amongst their forwards, they can trouble not a few clubs. ... It is not often we find accurate dribbling and speed combined.

However, the following Monday, Villa lost 1-7 to Rangers, but this was generously put down to Villa's shooting being defective! It would appear that defending was a secondary issue in those days!

A Near Disaster

Accidents were not supposed to be part of the plan of a tour, of course, but one serious event occurred during a short tour in April of 1883:

---

[189] Sport and Play, 11 Oct 1886
[190] Athletic News 12 Apr 1882

The Aston Villa Chronicles 1874 – 1924 (and after)

> When within some forty yards of the Trossachs Hotel ... horses, brake and seven prominent members of the team went down the steep bank together ... . 'Quick march' was the order of the day and the alacrity displayed by the occupants was astonishing even to their more fortunate comrades ... . Dawson, in bolting, turned a beautiful Catherine Wheel, dropping on his back, upon which he was promptly sat upon by the daisy-cutter [Ollie Whateley]. Freddy, forgetting the compulsory state of affairs, in an indignant tone, asked 'where are you coming to?'
>
> Apperley, who sat on the box, was unable with anything like safety to get clear off, so with as much Micawberesque philosophy as he could muster on so short a notice, waited for something to turn up. That 'something' was the brake, which decidedly turned-up in the brook, depositing poor Charlie under the wheels and far nearer than was pleasant to the hoofs of the struggling quadrupeds, one of the wheels passing over the half-back's ankle, rendering him *hors de combat*. ...[191]

It was Archie Hunter that carried the sufferer back to the hotel. Somehow, Charlie Apperley was the only serious injury in this mishap; he had a brief footballing comeback after recovery, but did not play again after that. It was observed that virtually an entire Villa team could have been lost – such was the nastiness of the fall!

The 'injured one' – Mr. Apperley himself – kept a diary of that tour, and Archie Hunter also had the full text of that published, including this entry for the last day – the events leading to the mishap at the Trossachs:

> Monday – At 8.30 a.m. we started off in two brakes for the Trossachs. Lochs Vennacher, Achway and Katrine were in turn scanned and admired. Rob Roy's grave near to the Pass of the Trossachs was an object of great interest to all of us (Mac in tears!). The 'Sad and Silent One' ... could not resist the temptation of a plunge into the classic waters of Loch Katrine, while Olly and Alf, not to be beaten, tried a header from the boat-house. I have not hitherto spoken of the grand scenery, of which we were all enthusiastic admirers. The respected descendent of the notorious Highland Chieftain whom Sir Walter Scott immortalised years ago was fairly in his element. His intimate knowledge of all the neighbourhood through which we journeyed made him an invaluable 'illuminator' of the trip. To him every stone and tiny rivulet we passed possessed some historical charm. The beauteous lakes caused him to bubble over with pardonable patriotism and lo, his arms opened to the

---

[191] "Triumphs of the Football Field", *Birmingham Weekly Mercury*, October, 1890 to February, 1891

The Aston Villa Chronicles 1874 – 1924 (and after)

> rugged grandeur of the towering mountain peaks that hemmed us in on all sides. Birmingham lads born and bred caught the contagion and losing sight for the time of their individuality, willingly – nay, joyously – surrendered themselves to the witchery of Bonnie Scotland's glorious landscapes.

After the mishap, the party continued on after arranging replacement transportation and eventually left Stirling at 8.30 p.m. for Birmingham, arriving home at about 6.30 on Tuesday morning.

The party for that tour consisted of "Messrs. Alf Harvey, Tom Riddell, Jim Benson, Fred Dawson, George Price, Charlie Apperley, Arthur and Albert Brown, Olly Whateley, Archie Hunter, Eli Davis, [and club officials] McGregor, Jeffries and Mason".

About what would appear to be an event in the year of 1886, 'Nomad' reported this story:

> They were playing in Edinburgh, and it was the year of the Great Exhibition there. Well, the players were in very high spirits, and while at the Exhibition, some of them were silly enough to purloin some of the exhibits! They did not steal them in the ordinary sense [it was done as a prank], although it would have been stealing in the eyes of the law had they been caught.
>
> They brought the goods to the hotel at night, and Mr. McGregor heard of the freak. He determined to play a joke upon them and at the same time cure them of their propensity for indulging in dangerous pranks. Rushing into the room where they all were, he made the startling announcement that the bar was full of detectives, and that everyone would have to be searched, as there had been a robbery at the Exhibition and some of the culprits had been traced to the hotel.
>
> Oh! what a scuttling about there was! The Villa men rushed to their rooms, searched their pockets and their boxes for every little article that might incriminate them, and then proceeded to get rid of them as best they could. Such a rush to the lavatories you never saw! They did get a fright, but it was all a hoax.[192]

'Nomad' went on to say:

> Football teams [in 1901] are a very sober-minded set of men now, but at the time liberty always meant license, and I remember when three out of four English hotel-keepers would not take in a Scottish touring club... I have seen corridors two inches thick with feathers as the result of pillow fights... [and]

---

[192] Sports Argus 19 Jan 1901

The Aston Villa Chronicles 1874 – 1924 (and after)

every curtain and hanging in every room on a landing, destroyed...

Reporting two weeks later, 'Nomad' went on to describe a situation in Edinburgh mainly revolving round vice-president Fergus Johnstone, who was known as 'Fergie':

> Fergie was a great admirer of purity in sport and nothing elevated his mind so much as to think of the pious principles upon which Scottish football was founded. The picture he painted was that the Scotchmen went leather-chasing because of an instinctive regard for the games of his forefathers, while the management of clubs was undertaken by guileless gentlemen whose honour fortified them against the inroads of professionalism. There were some members of the Villa party who had their doubts about the spotlessness of football management, and, as it happened, the brief sojourn at Edinburgh was destined to throw considerable light on the subject.
>
> The party had scarcely landed in the famous Scotch city when a prominent footballer sought an interview with Albert Albutt, and at its conclusion the latter, approaching Mac and Fergie with the air of a man who had made a great discovery, said: 'What do you think of the purity of Scottish amateurism now? I have just had a talk with one of the best forwards in Scotland who wants to sign on for the Villa if they will give him better pay than he is receiving from the [so-called amateur] Scottish club to which he belongs at present... What price that, Fergie?'
>
> The whole Book of Revelations could not have produced such an aspect of expansive surprise as spread over Fergie's face! He was astonished, enraged, indignant, and doubtful at one and the same time, but he pinned his faith to the integrity of football management in the Land O'Cakes. 'There needn't be any doubt about the business,' said Albutt, 'I will undertake to have the man here, and you shall investigate the matter for yourself.' This had a forcibleness about it that required a lot of resisting, but it was argued with considerable shrewdness that... [by this action] Villa would labour under the imputation of having tried to undermine the Scottish club. This difficulty was quickly overcome, for Albutt suggested that Mac and Fergie should conceal themselves in a pantry in a room into which the player should be invited, and listen [to the proceedings].
>
> This was done and the whole disclosure was made. ... [Then Albutt,] addressing the pseudo amateur, he said: 'Well, now, what do you want to come to the Villa?'
>
> 'I'll take £3 a week and £40 down.'
>
> 'I'll give you £3 a week but I cannot give you more than £20 down.'

The Aston Villa Chronicles 1874 – 1924 (and after)

'That will do!', exclaimed the Scotchman, who had scarcely uttered the last word when Fergie dashed from the pantry, and in his finest Scottish frenzy shouted: 'He has not got permission from the Villa to do it!' The climax was too unexpected and terrible for the poor player, who, without stopping to test Albutt's credentials, bolted from the room in a panic-stricken state!

The above stories were added to by William McGregor,[193] as follows:

Will any of those who participated in their Scottish tours ever forget their experiences? I once took a Villa team on a ten days' tour in Caledonia: at Dundee we had among our committee a pronounced Presbytarian, and he created consternation by refusing to sit near a number of Roman Catholic priests who were on the stand: he would retire to an obscure corner of the structure.

We had a lively experience once when playing the Hibernians. The Scotsmen were badly worsted, and the crowd did not like it. I had acted as umpire for the Villa and as I was walking off the ground when someone from behind partially stunned me. A gentleman was coming to my aid when Freddy Dawson who had not seen what had happened, met the would–be good Samaritan with a straight left in the eye. Immediately there was a free fight: we had to settle a compensation claim over that. It appears that Dawson had struck a pressman; as it was New Year's Day his employers insisted that he should take action in order to prove to them that his eye had been damaged in the manner described by him.

We had another experience on the following day. We were looking at the Forth Bridge when Dawson let a contractor's truck loose, with disastrous results to the wagon. We forgot all about the incident until a policeman asked in broad Scotch:

'What have you done with the bogey?'

'Eh what?', said Teddy, 'and who are you calling names?' [clearly mishearing the word 'bogey'], at the same time squaring up to the officer. We had a job saving Dawson from being arrested.

On the occasion of their first visit to Scotland the players spent the morning in Glasgow inspecting the whiskey distillery. We lost in the afternoon!

We went on to Ayr from Glasgow, and late at night the landlord of the 'King's Arms' refused to supply any more spirits. Of course, there was only one thing to be done; Teddy Lee had a fit, and a bottle of brandy became a necessity. I

---

[193] C.B Fry's Magazine of Action and Outdoor Life Vol 2 Oct 1904 to Mar 1905 from p.44

The Aston Villa Chronicles 1874 – 1924 (and after)

never met anyone who could feign illness better than Teddy Lee. Teddy soon revived under the influence of the spirit, but the players would not give up the remainder of the bottle I don't think anybody slept much that night, and the proprietor swore solemn oaths that no more football teams should stay in his house.

One year we went up to Balloch, Loch Lomond. We started one Thursday night, and arrived on the Friday morning. On the Saturday we encountered Dumbarton. The terms were half the gross gate. Unfortunately, the Villa did not prove a big draw and £5 was all the gate realised. The Dumbarton officials were ashamed to divide it, so they gave us the whole amount and entertained us to tea. That tour cost the club £100.

The Sunday we spent at Callander and I well recall the fact that when we got to the local hotel we were late, and the starchy parsons and honeymoon couples who formed the greater part of the hotel's patrons looked at us askance when the players expressed their disapproval of the regulation that nothing stronger than beer was to be consumed with the meal. Some of the players had their revenge after dinner by getting into the good graces of the servants at one of the big houses in the neighbourhood. They were allowed the run of the cellars, and they returned with a couple of monster pies; these we consumed on the way to Birmingham.

On another of our trips we played the Crusaders, a team got together by Mr John K McDowall, the secretary of the Scottish Football Association. In this match the Villa played a man named W Siddons, a reserve at back. He was in poor form, and gave an inglorious exhibition; so inglorious, indeed, that at the conclusion of the match he ripped up his clothes and sent them with his boots and bag flying all over the Queen's Park ground. After the match we went on to Oban. Most of the men were tired and were lying down, and the sleepy passengers and porters at the stations where we stopped peered into the saloon in amazement when we told them that we were taking a number of lunatics to Oban!

On those old tours we used to have a secret society, with Archie Hunter as the grand master. It was a capital device for keeping the players together. New members could only be admitted by a show of thumbs and if there was one thumb down the intending member either had to pay a fine or be excluded. *But there was always one thumb missing; Arthur Brown had been deprived of one by an accident!* It was a good thing for the funds of the society!

The Aston Villa Chronicles 1874 – 1924 (and after)

8. More Villa Heroes (ca. 1885 to 1891)

James ('Jemmy') Warner (goalkeeper): "It was not uncommon for him to hit the inflated hide with one hand and somebody else's hide with the other ... including a celebrated forward's proboscis!"[194]

Jimmy was a highly capable keeper, but his successful period for the Villa (spread over six years) came to an inglorious end when he was blamed by the fans for the Villa's 1892 Cup Final defeat (as detailed elsewhere). A few years later, he migrated to the USA, which is where he died after a long life.

Frank Coulton ("a fair saxon"):

> Frank was a back of nigh upon the first magnitude, a very safe and powerful kicker, and as fair and gentlemanly a defender as a first-rate knows how to be. He ... feared nothing. He reckoned the ball his every time, and though he would descend to no questionable tricks, he generally got it, and he was a believer in legitimate force to get his own way. [195]

"One of the best Villa backs. Coulton, G. Cox and Howard Spencer [were] the finest defenders so far as 'class' is concerned [by 1908]." [196] Coulton was crippled in a match vs. Small Heath and had to retire. It was thought that perhaps only Spencer was a better back.

Gershom Cox[197] (full-back): From Walsall. He came with the retirement of Joe Simmonds. Just before his advent "a dark-browed defender named Jones" (also from Walsall) had made a good name, but there was a good deal of friction between Walsall and Aston, especially as Richmond Davis had also come from Walsall.

"The Villa was a happy family when Gershom Cox was an active player in it..." and doubt that there was a greater admirer of Denny Hodgetts' ability: "He praised the great left-winger many a time". When Archie Hunter was prematurely retired in 1890, Cox took over the captaincy for a short period.

He joined Villa in 1886; his last match was in 1893. He went to settle in Kent where he acted as coach to Gravesend.

---

[194] Villa News & Record 7 Mar 1908 – "Old Villa Players"
[195] Villa News & Record 2 Apr 1924 – "Some Famous Villa Players"
[196] Villa News & Record 4 April 1908 – "Some Villa Defenders"
[197] Villa News & Record 4 April 1908 – "Some Villa Defenders"

The Aston Villa Chronicles 1874 – 1924 (and after)

A fine Scottish addition was centre-half **Thomas Robertson**.[198] His tenure with the Villa was not long, but "nothing but the most urgent business matters would have induced him to sever his connections with the Villa." As a player he reached his zenith when he joined Queen's Park for whom he played against the Villa when QP won 2-1, in 1888. By 1906, Robertson had returned to the Midlands and was then a highly-respected first-class referee.

Dennis 'Denny' Hodgetts (forward): He essentially came to Villa from Mitchell St. George's at Cape Hill.

> "Many attempts to 'land' him were made and there was great rejoicing at his capture. He was the best inside or outside left I have ever seen, and the manner in which he could conjure a ball with his feet, and his command over it, were delightful things to watch. ... I knew many people who would go to Perry Barr on purpose [just] to see Hodgetts play. ... He was the maker of the reputation of several Villa left-wingers, such as Woolley, Steve Smith and Gray and during the short sojourn amongst us of Archie Goodall. ... When he and Harry Wood played together, England had the best left-wing pair that has ever represented her [prior to 1908]."[199]

Further:

> An adept at drawing a host of opponents around him, he possessed equal facility for steering his way through them all, and as he passed with conspicuous unselfishness, the centre-forward or his partner on the wing had the way paved, to a large extent, for their success.
>
> Hodgetts was known to score goals from near the corner flag with screw kicks that never seemed likely to reach the mouth of goal. His corner kicks were placed with the greatest exactitude, and many a keeper playing against one of those corners for the first time must have found himself wondering why Hodgetts curled the ball so far away from the cross-bar. Then when the spin began to tell, and the ball began to whip back, he would probably cease wondering![200]
>
> [Denny was] A born football player. Remarkably clever with his feet, and possessed many original ideas. Effective in combination, an admirable coach, his skill and unselfishness having the happiest results. [He] shone especially

---

[198] The Sporting Mail 20 Oct 1906 – "Men of Note"
[199] Villa News & Record 17 April 1908 – "A Few of the Old Boys". NOTE: Much earlier there was a Harry Hodgetts playing for Villa – also a left-winger, but was no relation to Dennis.
[200] The Sporting Mail 6 Oct 1906 – "Men of Note"

The Aston Villa Chronicles 1874 – 1924 (and after)

in 'nursing' players lighter and less skilful than himself, many juniors coming into prominence on the strength of his tuition and example.[201]

Old Fogey wrote:

> I once heard Archie Hunter say that Dennis Hodgetts was the cleverest individualist at the game he had ever known. ... When he liked he could steady a game down marvellously, and show that skill and adroitness was always superior to bashing tactics.[202]

Fred Ward (in his 'Aston Villa', 1948) had opportunity to listen to reminiscences from Denny, and one such concerned Denny's approach when playing on frosty ground, to prevent slipping:

> I never had trouble with that. We were our own cobblers, and I would never get put more than one stud near the toe of either boot. I used to soak the discs of leather for a long time and then hammer them so that they set as hard as leather could be.

Fred Ward also relayed a situation when Denny was to play having not fully recovered from a foot injury. Denny knew of the reputation of the back he was to face, and asked for a bandage, which he applied to his *good* foot.

The trainer said, "Dennis, you're putting it on the wrong side."

"Am I?", Dennis replied, "That's my decoy – I know which foot he will go for!"

A Lion's Fun

Albert Brown[203] (forward; brother of Arthur): He was comparatively unknown when he first played at outside-right, against Darwen at Perry Barr in about 1884, scoring two goals. He reigned in that position until Charlie Athersmith came along. The Darwen skipper once said to Vaughton (Villa's skipper for the day), "I say old man, if you have any more youngsters like Brown you might introduce me to some. That young fellow will make a first-rater."

Jack Burton[204] (half-back): One of a famous quartet of brothers who did yeoman service for Aston Villa in the early days. He served with the club from April 1885 to August 1893 and thus was a member of the side in the early years of the League.

He was a terrier-type of player and would 'take a bump' with the same perfect 'sangfroid' as when giving one. He was a shining light in the Villa team and played

---

[201] Villa News & Record (No. 1) 1 Sep 1906
[202] Villa News & Record 7 Jan 1911
[203] Villa News & Record 17 Apr 1908 – "A Few of the Old Boys"
[204] Villa News & Record 9 Jan 1909 – "Makers of Villa History"

in the 1887 Final. He also took part in the famous Preston North End match at Perry Barr (1885) when the crowd broke into the ground.

He represented the Birmingham Association in half-a-dozen matches. It was felt that he would have won a 'cap' but for breaking his leg before he was to have played for the Birmingham Association vs. London, after which the England XI was to have been chosen.

He was known as 'Little Jackie' by the fans. Before he died (Easter, 1914), he asked that he be buried in Villa colours. For some reason this was not practicable, although ribbons in Villa colours were prominent at his funeral.[205]

Harry P. Devey (full-back and half-back):

> Devey never stooped to a mean action. He first played right-back for Aston Clarendon on Potter's Fields and later on at Aston Park, with brother Bob and famous nephew, Jack Devey. He then joined Excelsior at outside-right. They met all the local clubs and Blackburn Olympic, Preston North End, Bolton Wanderers. They used to win most of those matches. Jack Devey joined them [Excelsior] about 1884 and made a big difference to their forward line.[206]

After playing in every forward position, Harry found his best position at centre-half. He played against Aston Villa at Perry Barr when Villa won 2-0. In August 1887 he was approached through Denny Hodgetts and interviewed by Mr. Clamp, chairman of the Villa committee at that time. His first match was vs. Burton United (away) – Villa won 7-1. Fred Dawson kept him out of a regular first-team place to start with, until Fred was injured. Devey played in all the season's remaining matches except the famous cup-tie vs. Preston, when Dawson returned, but Devey was restored the next week. In 1888-89, his best matches then were against Preston and Everton. "All grand games and fought out in real sporting fashion to the bitter end." With the advent of Jas. Cowan, Devey then played at left-half and right-half for several seasons, playing well. He also played full-back for the Villa.

His twin brother Arthur was also on Villa's books, and nephew William played ten games for the Villa after being with Small Heath and Wolves, and the most famous Devey of all – William's brother John (or Jack) – became a legend.

Albert Allen[207] (winger): A light, but most effective wing player, with a good turn of speed. Lack of weight and size did not affect his pluck. Dribbled like an artist and

---

[205] Villa News & Record 18 Apr 1914
[206] Villa News & Record 4 Apr 1908 – "Some Villa Defenders"
[207] Villa News & Record (No. 1) 1 Sep 1906

shot with force and good aim. Always did well in big games and was seen to special advantage in his international. A modest, unassuming, player whom it was a pleasure to meet. Aston born, he scored Villa's first Football League hat-trick in a 9-1 home win over Notts County on 29 September 1888.

'Bat' Garvey (forward): He came to Aston Villa from Aston Shakespeare in 1888 and gave up senior football with the Villa in 1893. He was never one of the 'greats' but nevertheless significantly contributed, and left a tale to tell!

'Bat' first turned out for the Villa in 1888 in a game against Blackburn Rovers. Villa won, 4-2, and he had the satisfaction of marking his début by scoring two of Villa's goals. Another 'first' for him took place at Wolverhampton Wanderers' Dudley Road, ground on September 8, 1888, which was the first English Football League match Villa ever played, and in which Garvey was selected to play and had a significant hand in Villa's first League goal.

In a match against Preston North End in the same season as Garvey's début Blackburn match,[208] Archie Hunter exhorted his team to "do their best to beat North End", then in the heyday of their fame. Garvey wrote about his experiences:

> Whenever our captain felt like that we were always sure to win, and about 20 minutes after we started Archie passed to me and shouted, 'Go all the way with it!'; which I did, and scored the opening goal. A lot of excitement was caused through the Villa scoring the first goal. We won the match sure enough, but I cannot remember what the score was.
>
> I very well remember a match one Christmas with Preston North End, two years later than the one previously mentioned, and when the star of North End had begun to fade.[209] We were all promised a gift if we won - (what would the FA say to this nowadays?) - but we lost the match through the modesty of our umpire. We were winning 2-1 at half-time. In the second half, Jimmy Ross, who played forward, was standing by our goal, and when the ball came to him he kicked it into the net. We appealed for offside, but our umpire took no notice. Sudell, the Preston umpire, appealed for a goal, and as our umpire would not give his opinion, a goal was allowed. About 10 minutes before time, Ross was standing by our goal again, and when the ball came in he

---

[208] In season 1887-88.
[209] It would appear that the match he speaks about here is that on 25 Dec 1889 in season 1889-90 (a League match in this case). Note that the preceding match vs. PNE at Perry Barr that season (in which Garvey did not play) Villa won 5-3. Preston had thought that game would be 'soft', for Villa were supposed not to be fit! – Villa News & Record 11 Apr 1908

The Aston Villa Chronicles 1874 – 1924 (and after)

> deliberately punched it into the net, and it so happened that the referee did not see him do this. We appealed for a foul, and Sudell [appealed] for a goal. Again our umpire would not come up and discuss the matter with him, so a goal was given. We lost the match through our umpire - which was hard luck, as we had much the best of the play, and it took Preston all their time to keep us out.[210]

Whilst narrating stories about Preston, it would be right to include the following story told about Jimmy Ross' brother, Nicholas:

> [Nick Ross was a member of the famed 'Invincibles' side, but went to Everton for 1888-89; it was a move that was "a sensation at the time". But Ross returned to Preston after two seasons when they were in trouble.] He had gained a notoriety for ruthlessness, for at one period of his career his unquestionably firm play was a bit marred by tactics which it would have been flattering to have called 'rough'. As a consequence many of the forwards carefully avoided the meteor-like rush of the famous back.

> [However, on one occasion after Ross returned to Preston, his team met the Villa (probably the match on 25 November, 1893 at Perry Barr; Villa won 2-0).] There played for Villa on the inside-right a young fellow of the name of Charlie Hare, who was not only fleet of foot and keen of eye, but who simply didn't care for hog, dog or devil, and was celebrated for always making a bee-line for his destination. He hadn't played against Ross before, but was warned as to his ruthless rushes and his aptitude for getting the ball. Hare grinned, and said that he would see. Those of us who knew the pair expected to see some fun; we got it!

> The game was barely five minutes old when a pass put the ball midway between Ross and Hare, with both of them going full tilt for it. They arrived at the ball exactly at the same time, with fire in their optics and high resolve in their hearts.

> Everyone expected Hare to be 'rabbitly' lowered, so to speak; but when the shock of battle was over the great Nicholas Ross lay on his back, with quite a comical look of surprise puckering his dour countenance, while Charlie Hare sailed into goal with the ball at his toe, and nearly scored!

> After the shock of surprise, a peal of laughter rippled round the ground, followed by hearty cheers for Hare, who had floored Ross more succinctly than he had ever been grassed before!

---

[210] Villa News & Record January, 1909 – "Portrait : Bat Garvey"

The Aston Villa Chronicles 1874 – 1924 (and after)

Ross spent most of the remainder of the match in hunting Hare, and spoiled a good deal of his play in consequence; but the plucky Hare never shirked the challenge. [Hare] was a brave and goodly youth, and a tremendous favourite with the crowd because he was a 'whole-hogger' and feared no foe. [211]

But Hare played rarely for the Villa after the Preston match before leaving the club in 1896. Nick Ross did not much longer play football either, for in his case he contracted tuberculosis, and died, reportedly, when he was 34.

[Another old Preston player of note was David Russell,] one of the finest centre half-backs, who had a trick of growling fiercely and ominously at the oncoming forward, and many a man was frightened! He tried it on Archie Hunter once, and the old Villa skipper simply] charged him over for his pains! [212]

by Nick Oldham

Dave Russell was abrupt in speech and a big man who was a rock to bump against. As a centre halfback he was quite acrobatic, bringing high balls down to the grass with a foot in the vicinity of an opponent's ear! [213]

Russell was enough to frighten any forwards who were at all timid; [playing] in the scantiest of knickers, jersey flying open, no pads on, no stockings, and boots of such a size that you would think it impossible for him to ever miss the ball! [214]

---

[211] Villa News & Record 25 Mar 1911 – an article by "Old Fogey"
[212] Villa News & Record 8 Apr 1911 – an article by "Old Fogey"
[213] J.A.H. Catton (Tityrus) "The Story of Association Football" (1926) (Classic Reprint)
[214] 'Nomad' in Sports Argus 13 Apr 1901

The Aston Villa Chronicles 1874 – 1924 (and after)

9. Major Crisis Number One

Professionalism

The advent of legalised professionalism helped to bring about a crisis at the Villa in 1885. It was in about January, 1880, that Villa started to pay half railway fare expenses to players, but from such minor payments the situation grew in many clubs to payments being made as cash incentives behind closed doors, and more so as the years passed. The question of professionalism thus came to the fore. Old Fogey wrote:

> Preston North End were said to be responsible for the introduction of professional football in Association football. They may have made the process a good deal faster through Mr. Sudell, who was responsible for the 1888-89 championship-winning side. However, the question had been an agitation for many years before. The trouble originally arose concerning the import of Scottish players – particularly Fergus, Suter and Douglas of the [Blackburn] Rovers during the time of Rovers' Cup successes. [215]

'Tityrus' wrote: "I have even known a chairman give £800 out of his own pocket to a young forward that the Board ardently desired to sign."[216]

It was indeed Preston North End that caused the matter of professionalism to come to a head when, in season 1883-84, Preston were ejected from the FA Cup because they fielded professional players, and admitted as much. But Preston were only carrying on what had been established at Darwen, Blackburn and other clubs – and Preston were not the first Lancashire team to be penalised for paying their players.

Following Preston's exclusion from the FA Cup in 1884, the Lancashire clubs got together and called a 'national' (i.e. the North and the Midlands) meeting of clubs in Manchester. Thirty-one clubs were represented (including, it is said, Aston Villa) and began the creation of a break-away organisation – the British Football Association – but this forced the hand of the FA, who quickly conducted a review of the situation.

In January, 1885, it was Villa's William McGregor, as the only Midland club delegate at a special general meeting of the FA, who had the courage to confirm Preston North End's open admission and to openly advocate professionalism,

---

[215] Villa News & Record 3 Oct 1908 – an article by "Old Fogey"
[216] J.A.H. Catton (Tityrus) "The Story of Association Football" (1926) (Classic Reprint)

knowing that it already existed – 'Mac' did not favour concealment. He and other forthright persons, through their open speaking, thus secured the recognition of professionalism.[217]

McGregor's forthrightness was not entirely welcome, however. Charlie Crump (the Birmingham FA chairman) had been declaring that professionalism would be the first step towards the downfall of football, and on 23 January, Villa held a Special Meeting to discuss a complaint made by Crump, who had spoken shortly before to the FA meeting, prior to McGregor making his now famous open statement, and had said the converse, that there was no professionalism in the Midlands.

'Mac's statement was in clear opposition, and had put the cat amongst the pigeons (to Crump's obvious chagrin), and people assumed that Villa were paying their players. However, the matter ultimately sorted itself out, and professionalism became legalised by July, 1885.

McGregor's position vis-à-vis the Villa is interesting on this issue. At the time of the decision making processes towards professionalism (before July, 1885 at least), 'Mac' was probably not privy to any cash payments to players that might be taking place at Villa, but probably had more than a suspicion that it was taking place. In his tail-piece to his Villa history, produced in C. B. Fry's magazine in 1904, the diplomatic yet honest Scot commented:

> It is interesting to notice that in the season 1883-4 the team's expenses were £364 7s. 11d., and "loss of time to players" took £33 3s. 6d. But in 1884-5 the era of honesty had dawned, and we get "Paid to players, £479 6s. 6d."

'Mac' made this comment expecting the reader to remember that he was elected to the honorary treasurer post at the AGM in 1885 ("the era of honesty had dawned"), and it was he – after weeks of investigation – that arrived at the figures for the 1884-85 season having gone through the books with a fine tooth-comb, despite obstacles that were put in his way by the previous incumbent! This story will be revealed later in the report on the 1885-86 season (below).

There was not a rush to professionalism on the part of all the best players. Archie Hunter made the following remarks:

> Some of the old members, myself among the number, who had been playing as amateurs, had a great reluctance to be paid for our services. Our diffidence may or may not have been reasonable, but it was sincere. When we finally

---

[217] Villa News & Record 29 Feb 1908 – "Portrait of William McGregor"

ceased to be amateurs I may say that we left it entirely with the committee to arrange terms; and I never have much sympathy with players who put pecuniary conditions first and think of the sport afterwards. But professionalism is so strong and competition for good players so great that a 'pro' may ask for a good round sum as a retaining fee [plus] a high salary and stand every chance of obtaining both.[218]

Season 1885-86 : Crunch Time!

The introduction of professionalism caused the management of the club to be turned head-over-heals. The running of the club became vested in nine non-playing members (up to that point, the players had a lot of control over the club), but changes invoked by the new Villa committee seemed odd. It did not take long, for example, in doubling the price of season tickets, and – *very* strangely – talk began of fielding *two first teams*! And in October, the Villa scratched from the Birmingham Cup (the club would have been due to play the Old 'Uns for the umpteenth time). When prompted as to the cause of the withdrawal, a prominent member of the club intimated that Villa were now a recognised professional team; that the ordeal of a series of cup matches with clubs of minor standing would mean upsetting important fixtures and the consequent loss of gate money.

Professionalism was beginning to turn the people's heads in peculiar ways according to those times! In this day and age that observation would perhaps not be a strange one to make, but in 1885, those were different days. Sport, then, was sport, and hard-headed professionalism had not yet been taken on board by the general populace, even though it had now been made legal. Even the football season had become longer – August to May now appeared on the scene, and the Villa's fixtures showed more emphasis on matches with the other top dogs in the sport, particularly those in Lancashire, in order to 'bump up' the gates.

The changed situation caused 'Brum', in the *Athletic News*, to despondently declare: "... within a very few years the wonderful popularity which now attaches to football will wane and fade ... the real merry old days are over, when the fun was rollicking and pleasant ...".

---

[218] "Triumphs of the Football Field", Birmingham Weekly Mercury, October, 1890 to February, 1891

The Aston Villa Chronicles 1874 – 1924 (and after)

The Season's Play

In this season, a stranger picking up the Villa team sheet one week and comparing it with the team sheet of the next week will not have blinked an eye by seeing the name 'Davis' on the wing. He would have been fooled – for very early in the season, Eli Davis finished his career with the Villa, and in came Richmond Davis, from Walsall Swifts. However, if the stranger looked carefully, he would have seen that the Davis name had switched wings! But Mr. R. Davis would prove not to let down the family name!

On the pitch, the Villa started the season on 15 August as though nothing had changed of note. In fact, in beating the current FA Cup holders, Blackburn Rovers, by 2-0, the Villa seemed to be making a statement for the season. That match, however, was a benefit for Arthur Brown, and it was something of an experimental Villa team, with Denny Hodgetts making what appears to have been his first appearance. It would not be long before he became a permanent feature, his shooting being noted as very dangerous.

On 29 August, however, there was a shock. At Bolton, Villa lost 2-7. The Villan's new full-back (Jones) proved to have been a valuable signing, as it was reported that: "[but for Jones] the Villa would have been most decisively beaten!" One wonders when to concede seven goals did not qualify for that description! However, the match report generously stated that it was the Villa that had been wasteful in front of goal – "no end of chances being thrown away." One can only observe that both defences must have been very poor.

Worse was to follow. At Stoney Lane the Villa lost yet again against the Throstles, but this time suffered the ignominy of a 0-5 thrashing. At the Committee meeting on 14 September, it was minuted that the secretary was to write to all players about want of combination and that there had been insufficient attention to individual condition. And, "[to] come to match with all necessary football clothing and in pink of condition."

There was a short respite as Villa won at Walsall Town, 5-0, in the first round of the FA Cup. This was a match in which the Walsall supporters tried to upset the Villa players by jeering at them, but as the Villa responded by 'playing up', those supporters lost their rag, broke in and then stopped the game with six minutes remaining. The result was allowed to stand, however.

The Aston Villa Chronicles 1874 – 1924 (and after)

In the second round of the FA Cup played in November, Villa were drawn to play Derby and had choice of ground. For the prescribed date, Villa were already fixed up to play Queen's Park, and so Villa agreed to forego their home option to go to Derby the week previous. There, Villa lost 0-2. Villa protested that the referee agreed upon (Hon. R. Lyttelton) did not turn up, with the consequence that an official had to be secured from the crowd. It was alleged that the one selected had a bet on the game, but Villa did not prove their case, and the protest was dismissed.[219] To Villa's chagrin, Derby lost heavily to Small Heath in the next round of the Cup! In fact, Small Heath went on to reach the semi-final, only to be beaten by Villa's new Nemesis, West Bromwich Albion.

On 28 November, the Throstles were played yet again – this time at Perry Barr. Villa were now described as "the *once* champions of the Midlands" after the Albion won 5-4.

Shortly after the interval, the score stood at 2-2, and "the enthusiasm was intense." A tremendous yell went up when Villa gained a 3-2 lead, but no sooner had they done that, the Albion established parity yet again. And then added another to make it 3-4 to Albion. And then it was not long before Villa's keeper Hobson made a blunder to enable Albion to score a fifth.

"This continued piling on of the agony raised the enthusiasm of the spectators to the highest pitch, whilst the Villans increased their efforts in every possible way, and strove might and main to avert defeat." However, the Albion defence stood up to all sorts of pressure and just conceded one more goal – to Archie Hunter.

The Lancashire-based *Athletic News* wailed, on 8 December:

> The club, which for several years past has been regarded as the premier football organisation of the Midlands, has receded in the public estimation to such an extent that the time has now arrived when some radical reform is necessary to save the club from utter collapse.

The article went on to cite their local favourites Preston North End as showing the way in how to organise a professional club "in a thoroughly systematic and business-like way" and was disbelieving that the Villa management was able to put the matters right, and hinted that some members of the committee were actually preventing proper management and a policy of considering gate money as the main objective. It was also hinted that a number of amateur players were not doing their part in keeping fit ("attaining proper condition").

---

[219] The 'W. McGregor' column in Sports Argus 29 Jan 1910

The Aston Villa Chronicles 1874 – 1924 (and after)

The Villa's rise to prominence had not come without spiky hurdles to cross on the way, even in their early days at Perry Barr. Very early on, gate receipts very rarely reached £10, but the troubles now experienced proved to be much more deep, to the extent that the club nearly came to be disbanded. They were in such financial difficulties "that numerous writs and other terrible troubles were threatened", wrote 'Mac' in later years.

How Villa came to be in that parlous state has never been properly explained, but at the AGM in 1885, William McGregor – in testimony to his energy and honesty – was appointed not only honorary treasurer but also honorary secretary for the forthcoming year. The club also decided the principle that there should be a full-time treasurer and secretary, but such appointments should be made annually.

It soon emerged by July – after 'Mac' had done some homework – that the club's former honorary treasurer (a player, Tom Bryan) had left the club's finances in a very bad state. There was a cash-in-hand of just £9 12s 2d. An overdraft had to be sought, with 'Mar' Margoschis asked to be surety for £25. Though the club was indebted to the tune of £150, just £50 was needed to keep the most pressing claims at bay.

Oddities having been noted in his financial return, and the club's assets having seemingly plunged from a credit balance of nearly £550 in 1884, Tom Bryan was asked (in early July) to return the club's books – but they remained unforthcoming. On 21 September, it was apparent that there were big question marks with regard to the state of the accounts as inherited, and a special meeting was called for that week, with Bryan called to attend. The perilous matter remained unresolved, with Bryan resisting all calls for a detailed explanation, and return of the books, until the club finally – well into 1886 – sent in the bailiffs to obtain Bryan's piano, in order to settle the issue.[220]

Various other problems now manifested themselves. By September, player training was questioned – that it should contain more than "mere ball kicking for goal", a state that it now appeared to have degenerated into. The committee minutes thus made it apparent that the club at that time had no recognised trainer, and at the meeting of 5 October, it was made known that Billy Gorman had returned from America. He was immediately reinstated as trainer, therefore making it clear that he had been the club's former trainer, perhaps from pre-1882 (before the start of the surviving club minutes).

---

[220] Source: the club's committee minutes.

The Aston Villa Chronicles 1874 – 1924 (and after)

Some of the players (who were now mostly professional) were now either demanding pay that was unreasonable, or asking to be excused from training for unreasonable periods. Drinking was a serious issue and discipline seems to have been lax. Obtaining a quorum at committee meetings also became an issue to the extent that 'Mac' called a special meeting on 7 December (1885) to address that and the other issues.

At that special meeting the issue of drinking was brought up as a primary matter. It was considered that the cause of the players' lack of success could be put down to the drinking, and it was made known that remonstrations with the offending players, and their suspension, had made no difference. It was also urged that committee members should be ready to attend meetings to conscientiously manage the club. Then 'Mac' and the entire committee tendered their resignations.

A Mr. Butler of Smethwick stood up and made a stirring speech in which he "regretted the decline of the popularity of Aston Villa in his district" and linked the cause of that to the losing of so many matches, which, in turn, was put down to drinking and a general lack of discipline.

Following the speech-making, 'Mac' was "most unanimously re-elected" to his two posts – the nine elected members of the committee being Mason, Dawson, Cooke, Punchon, Phil Vaughton, Johnstone, Albutt, Watts, and George Ramsay.

The restoration of order in the club had an immediate affect on the players. In their next match – against Bolton Wanderers at home – 'Brum' reported that their play, "reminded me of the old days. There appeared to be quite a different motive spirit between the players, the amount of real energy and zeal which they infused into the proceedings being truly refreshing" in a match that the Villa won 4-3 after going behind to a Wanderers goal in the first half. In this match, Ritch Davis was described as a lion amongst the Villa forwards, with Jacky Burton the demon of the half-back line. But several other players were also cited for their brilliance in this tremendous struggle of a football match.

Over the Christmas period at Perry Barr, Villa beat Cambridge University 3-1, Acton 13-0 and London Scottish 7-0. These matches were followed by a series of improved performances; not all of them were won, but at least the spirit was back in the team. About an interesting match against Excelsior (the Villa winning 3-0 against a team including three Deveys destined to join the Villa – 'H', 'W' and 'J'!), the crowd was described as follows by *Sport and Play*:

The Aston Villa Chronicles 1874 – 1924 (and after)

"The match at Perry Barr drew together a big crowd, and as both the Villa and Excelsior partisans were there in pretty full strength, no end of fun was knocking about. The chaff among the spectators grew more pointed than polite occasionally, and it was amusing to see sometimes a couple of wordy contestants pause in the middle of a violent personal squabble, to watch a more than usually exciting bit of play in the field."

It was reported that Dawson scored the first goal, "Archie Hunter shoving the keeper out of the way." Arthur Brown was noted as having "his special failing", which was not keeping proper control of the ball.

Villa: *Hobson; Jones, Riddell; Simmonds, Price, Burton;*
R. Davis, Arthur Brown, Hunter, Allen, Dawson.

Though better management control had been instituted, by February the financial position had become so serious that players were requested to take a reduction in pay. Archie Hunter was retained at 30 shillings per week (a reduction of 10 shillings), but the other players had to take 10s 6d for a Saturday match, and 7s 6d for a Monday match.[221]

During that February, there was yet another match against the Albion in front of 7,000 at Stoney Lane on a pitch with a layer of snow. The football proved to be "a contest of exceptionally brilliant and exciting character". Alas, no matter how good Villa's play was (with Archie Hunter playing at half-back), the match went to Albion by three goals to two to register their third win of the season against the Villa. *Sport and Play* reported that the fact Villa were defeated was largely down to a very poor performance by Hobson, their keeper. In fact Villa soon changed him for their remaining games – that keeper was clearly having an unhappy season.

On 13 February, Villa visited Notts County, where they had a fine win of 5-3. "[Villa] delighted even the Nottingham spectators by their brilliant play", reported *Sport and Play*.

> "... in knocking out a shot from the Notts right wing, [Villa's keeper] hugged the upright to save himself from falling, and this, giving way a little, down came the great bar with a bang on his head! ... Being fairly hard-headed, he recovered quickly." There was much mirth in the gallery!
>
> *A Lion's Fun*

The *Athletic News* noted the size of the Notts County team – whose average height was about 5 feet 10 inches, including two players of six feet or more. That, in those

---

[221] The Villa committee minutes of the time. There was also a report about this in the Birmingham Evening Mail in 1968, when Albert Allen's son was interviewed about a letter in his possession that was written to his father by the Villa on this matter.

The Aston Villa Chronicles 1874 – 1924 (and after)

days, was quite unusual – the Villa team was quite small by comparison.

In March, just three weeks after Small Heath's ejection from the FA Cup at the hands of the Albion, Small Heath played the Villa on their own ground.

It was an astonishing match, it being even play for the first 15 minutes until the Heathens scored. Their supporters cheered as though the match was already all over, but immediately down came the Villa forwards, and in went an equaliser, through Archie Hunter.

"Having thus broken the ice, the Villans lost no more time in clearly demonstrating the fact that they were complete masters of the situation, and it was a very rare occurrence indeed for the Heathens to have so much as a look-in…" Villa were 4-1 up by half-time, and went on to win 8-1!

It had to be admitted that Villa fielded a very strong side against the very much below-strength Heathens. In *Sport and Play* it was remarked, about Archie Hunter, that:

> … complaints have now been made of his extreme unselfishness. He is, perhaps, a little too much given to passing the ball when immediately in front of goal. With a pluck and dash which are notorious, he shirks at nothing, but goes ahead from kick-off to time-out at the hardest possible rate – hammer and tongs all the while.

At a time when Villa badly needed income, Preston North End were an expected visitor, but they cried off, alleging that they had too many injuries. "Foul!", cried the press, stating that Preston just didn't want to risk their season's unbeaten record, which at that stage stood at:

P43   W41   D2   L0   F231   A43   Goal Average: 5.37

For the fourth time that season, Villa played the Albion – at home this time. The Albion were fresh from their sad defeat in the 1886 FA Cup Final, and in this match succumbed to the Villa by three goals to one, the Villa registering their first win of the season against them. "Villa showed distinctly better form."

The non-appearance of Preston was not the only calamity. Villa's parlous financial situation became even more desperate. On 13 April, a letter was written to Accrington asking for £15 that was due, "[as] our funds are entirely exhausted."

The Aston Villa Chronicles 1874 – 1924 (and after)

George Ramsay Saves the Day

It was in April (1886) that Queen's Park was expected to fulfil what had then become an annual fixture that would have helped put right Villa's perilous financial state. However, QP wired a few days before the match to say that they could not fulfil the engagement. It was George Ramsay that saved the situation by going post-haste to Scotland to use his good name to raise a team principally composed of Scottish internationals – which named themselves the Scottish Crusaders. They came down and won the match 1-0, but the game generated such interest that a large gate resulted – perhaps as many as 10,000 turned up – and Villa's immediate problems were solved.[222] The club's minutes (29 April, 1886) recorded that over £195 was raised through this match, and more than £100 in two further matches against other important Scottish opposition – Hibernian and Vale of Leven – over the following five days. The minutes went on to give "heartfelt thanks" to George Ramsay for his efforts to save the situation.

At the time of those minutes, there was £187 cash in the bank, but indebtedness still stood at £294. Many years later, William McGregor reported on the state of affairs in the middle 1880s:

> In the 'good old days', it was no uncommon thing for Mr. Sam Richardson[223] to receive a writ either at the offices of the club or his private residence. They were mostly for tradesmen's debts, and these little peeps into the past indicate that Villa were not always in the affluent position they are now [in 1910]. I can recall having to go round with Mr. Jeffries [the hon. treasurer] and make a compromise with the creditors. Some of the debts led to county court proceedings and it was a curious fact, strictly legal, no doubt, that the officers, other than the secretary, were struck out of the summons, being deemed by the judge as mere figureheads.
>
> Mr. Ellis, J.P., was the president of the club, and I was one of the officers. Our names happily were struck out and the secretary held responsible! ... It was not always a pleasant thing to be a club officer, specially a secretary, in the good old days, but despite the money troubles we enjoyed our football.[224]

But, even though the situation had been saved, at least temporarily, the reform of the club was still not complete. What happened next enabled the club to move to a

---

[222] Villa News & Record, Christmas 1907 – taken from an article by "Old Fogey"
[223] A local schoolteacher and hon. secretary prior to Ramsay (1886).
[224] The 'W. McGregor' column in Sports Argus, 22 Oct 1910

The Aston Villa Chronicles 1874 – 1924 (and after)

new level.

In the previous year, the Villa had determined that there should be a paid secretary. They had also determined that there should be a paid treasurer, but this matter was 'shelved' by the new administration in favour of concentration being put on the appointment of a permanent secretary/manager; 'Mac' was to continue as honorary treasurer. Soon after, agreement was reached to appoint a full-time secretary/manager at £100 p.a.

At another special meeting called on 25 June 1886, 'Mac' announced that the club had received 150 applications for the post of secretary/manager, and from this list six were short-listed for presentation at the AGM the following day, including the name of George Ramsay. At the AGM, the short-listed six were brought forward, one-by-one, to be questioned by the membership present (of which there were 45).

George Ramsay – Secretary/Manager

The outcome (perhaps rather predictably) was in favour of George Ramsay, who was voted for by 25 of the members; the next nearest applicant had 9 votes. Thus, at the end of June, 1886, George Burrell Ramsay, at a starting salary of £100 per annum, began 40 years of tenure as secretary/manager of Aston Villa Football Club, a reign which oversaw the most successful period of the club until over 50 years after his retirement. At the same meeting, the club's formal address was given as 6, Witton Road. On 11 October, George Ramsay was asked to move from his residence from William McGregor's home (in Summer Lane) to Alexander's, at 6a, Witton Road.[225]

George Ramsay's first letter in his new post (dated 30 June) was addressed to Queen's Park, about a proposed match the following January:

> ... I feel sure that Aston Villa will force itself this season to a higher position than ever we have obtained, and the time may come when Glasgow people will look forward to our visit in the same spirit as Birmingham do yours.
>
> I know we have to blame ourselves for a good deal, but [it] will ere long be forgotten. Mr. McGregor has just come in and I have told him all I am saying and he agrees with every word.

In that twelve months, from near disaster to the appointment of such capable and honourable men as William McGregor and George Ramsay to the main executive

---

[225] Shown in the club minutes.

posts, and the return of Billy Gorman to instil discipline at training, the Villa were ready to move on. With Archie Hunter still captain they did just that, by immediately winning the FA Cup in their first season under the new administration, and becoming the first Midlands side to achieve that distinction.

But the Villa's growth continued to bring stresses into the club, and the major crisis that arose that season was not the end of the matter. In the seasons from the start of the League (1888) up until 1892-3, beneath-the-surface simmering caused the administration of the club to be looked at again, and more than once.

The Aston Villa Chronicles 1874 – 1924 (and after)

10. Jubilee Year In More Ways Than One

Season 1886-87 : Villa's First FA Cup Success

This was a year that not only had significance for Queen Victoria (her Golden Jubilee)! The Villa's steady progress – massaged by the recent internal crisis of mammoth proportions! – brought them to another stage of achievement.

One significant addition to the Villans for this season was **Jimmy Warner** in goal. He came in as a permanent replacement for Charlie Hobson, who was soon to retire, complaining that the risks of football were not compatible with his married state! Howard Vaughton also returned to play in October.

The Villa's progress in the first two rounds of the FA Cup was easy; they scored nineteen goals in the process – 13-0 at home against Wednesbury Old Athletic (whose standing was now greatly diminished) and 6-1 at home against the once-strong Derby Midland. Archie Hunter, Albert Brown and Denny Hodgetts scored hat-tricks in the debacle against the Old 'Uns, and a man called Loach scored two goals in each of those games, but (in company with the fine Tom Robertson) did not stay with the club, and that is how Albert Allen came to take up Loach's forward spot.[226] Most of the remaining rounds to the final were considerably more testing and the round three tie versus Wolverhampton Wanderers was the first of these tests, and of marathon proportions.[227]

The first match was at Perry Barr – a 2-2 draw. The match was a tough one, with various players injured. The replay was at Ettingshall Road "where the keen and wintry blasts whistled through the intestines of the corrugated iron in a manner that froze our young blood, and caused the tear-drops to start from our weeping eyes." In a match where, reportedly, the Villa "displayed a cautious and scientific mode of aggression which at times completely puzzled their opponents" (but not appropriate for the icy top surface), another draw resulted - 1-1. There was a toss-up for a choice of ground, and Ettingshall Road was the venue once more!

"It was colder and bleaker and more uncomfortable than ever, and a lot of us developed splitting headaches long before the match was over. The roof came down very close to the head and was thus very handy to hit it. Thus, using walking sticks, bottles – anything to hand – "the Wanderers folk started the

---

[226] Loach was mentioned by Archie Hunter as a signing from the Albion and of whom much was expected, but his career was let down by injury.
[227] Villa News & Record 18 Jan 1908

The Aston Villa Chronicles 1874 – 1924 (and after)

game of tintin-nabulation and the Villans from Perry Barr followed suit! This went on for two mortal hours!" But at the end it was a draw again – 1-1. An extra thirty minutes was played, but this only resulted in 2-2. The tie thus took itself to its starting place, at Perry Barr.

The second Perry Barr match was said to have had 12,000 spectators present and was a great game: "very stubbornly and resolutely the Wolves kept the Villa Lions at bay for more than an hour during which the home brigade played exceedingly good football [and] bombarded the Wanderers' citadel, and it was only the gallant defence of the strangers that prevented them taking a long and commanding lead." When another draw was threatening, Howard Vaughton "came careering through the pack of Wolves and whiz went the ball between the posts." The threat remained that Wolves might equalise, but "Archie Hunter gathered the ball, and started in one of his cross-country rushes. Careering down the meadow to within twenty yards of goal, he let fly…" And that was it; 2-0. The match, however, had been played in such blustery conditions that the backs on both sides had been able to kick the ball from goal to goal!

Sportingly, the Wolves captain Charlie Mason said afterwards, to Archie Hunter: 'Well, Archie, old man, you have beaten us at last, though we gave you plenty to do; but yours was the better team today, and you deserved to win. I wish you luck, and hope you win the Cup.' "Archie thanked him, with that bright smile of his, and a handshake that made Charlie Mason wince!"

Old Fogey recollected[228] that the post-match proceedings were spent at the Old Crown and Cushion, with an amusing tale of how the inebriated referee was subsequently despatched home.

Round four resulted in a straight-forward win at home over Horncastle, by 5-0, Albert Brown again obtaining a hat-trick.

In the quarter-final at Perry Barr, the Villa very nearly threw away the match and would thus have ended their cup run. Winning 3-0 at half-time, the Villa team were offered champagne at the break (the Midland Counties Rugby Union Cup being the drinking receptacle), and in the second half faced a fight-back from Darwen, who scored two goals! The Villa, after played some very curious football for half-an-hour, thus won by the much-narrowed margin of 3-2. William McGregor was "a bit wroth" after the match, and delivered "a caustic lecture" to the team.

The Villa were then to meet Rangers in the semi-final, the last year in which Scottish clubs participated in the (English) FA Cup. It was well-known that the Rangers had, for this match, scoured the talent of their country, and put together what was

---

[228] Villa News & Record 14 Feb 1925

The Aston Villa Chronicles 1874 – 1924 (and after)

effectively a Scottish International side. The Scottish game was then still (allegedly) amateur, but it was strongly suspected that the Scottish select did not come along just to play for honour.

"In a good many quarters, the greatness of the Scottish players frightened the nervous ones …", said *Sport and Play*, but the Villa players were reported as being very calm. After all, in friendlies at the New Year, the Villa had won 8-3 vs. Hibs, and were leading 5-1 after three-quarters of an hour's play against the once-great Queen's Park (at QP). QP refused to play the second half on account of very bad weather (so they said), and the match was then hastily abandoned!

The other semi-final was to be between Preston and The Throstles, and those north of the Midlands would have laughed at the suggestion that the two Midland champions would reach the final.

The Training Regime for the Semi-Final

At the end of February, the Villa played a friendly at Notts County (and won, 3-1). Following this match, the Villa left for special training. Archie Hunter wrote an account of this time which deals with how the Villa came to use Holt Fleet as their centre for such training. It continued to be of use for another decade until resorts such as Rhyl and Blackpool began to be favoured:

> We travelled from Nottingham to Birmingham and obtained the necessary apparel for training and went on the same night to Droitwich. Outside the station a brake was waiting for us and on a pitch dark night a dozen of us rode through the quiet country lanes to a little unfrequented place on the river Severn called Holt Fleet.
>
> Here we arrived at midnight and being tired with the day's exertions and drowsy with the ride, we tumbled off to bed. The hotel accommodation in those days at Holt Fleet was of a limited character and the host was not accustomed to such large parties asking for accommodation. He was not prepared for us and the first night we had to rough it. Six of us slept in a top attic in which three beds had been placed. I say we slept, but this is not quite correct. We were put there to sleep, but the pestilence that stalks by night was opposed to us.
>
> All this, of course, was remedied later on by the obliging host, who did his utmost to make us comfortable. But you will wonder why we chose this place for our purpose. It was not our discovery, but was recommended to us by W. G. George, the champion mile-runner. It was his custom to walk, when

The Aston Villa Chronicles 1874 – 1924 (and after)

training, from Bromsgrove to Droitwich and Holt Fleet lies between these two places. The district is very favourable for athletes. There is a fine stretch of open country and there is the river, which affords every facility for boating and swimming. Then the walks all around are delightful and the brine baths at Droitwich are, of course, very convenient.

Since we were there other football teams have experienced its advantages, the Wolverhampton Wanderers in particular. Well, here we stayed for a week with our trainer, Billy Gorman. He was a famous sprint runner and had won a special handicap; and when he ceased to take part in public contests himself he devoted himself to training athletes and a capital fellow he was.

We got up each morning at eight o'clock prompt and breakfasted. Afterwards we strolled about as we pleased for an hour or so. Then we put our uniform on and by permission, which was kindly granted by Lord Dudley's overseer, we were allowed the use of the ground behind the hotel for sprint running and long distance running. It was curious to observe the difference which practice speedily made in some or our physical abilities. There was Dennis Hodgetts, for example, who was called our slow man. Up to this time he was indeed lacking in that desirable quality of fastness which is so serviceable on the field. But after this training he wonderfully developed into one of the speediest of the set and was only excelled by Richard Davis (late of the Walsall Swifts) who had the reputation of being the fastest player for short distances. All the others were very quick: Albert Brown, Joey Simmonds, Jack Burton, Freddy Dawson, Howard Vaughton, Harry Yates and Albert Allen, but the sprint running improved their form tremendously.

As for me, I went in for long distance running, with Warner our goalkeeper, who had no particular need to go in for this training and Coulton, for my companions. Albert Allen, I should here explain, was our reserve man who was in readiness to take Dawson's place if necessary, for Freddy had seriously hurt his knee and we were very uncertain whether he would be able to play. However, when the right time came the question was put to all the team and they decided that he was fit, so Allen was not needed after all.

Well, so the morning went. Sometimes the team walked along the delightful lanes for eight or ten miles, in charge of one or two of the members of the committee and myself and then we returned to dinner.

After dinner we were allowed to lounge about again and then the team were called together for football practice, a gentleman on another side of the river having placed at our disposal a suitable patch of ground. Here we worked hard for an hour and a half, perfecting ourselves in all the science of the game and mastering every trick that could be thought of. It was sport, but we were

The Aston Villa Chronicles 1874 – 1924 (and after)

very much in earnest and though we enjoyed ourselves we spared no pains to learn everything that was to be learnt.

Returning, we were rubbed down and examined by the trainer and then sat down to tea. After partaking of that meal we frequently took a mile and a half walk; and by ten each evening the Villa team were in bed. Such was our training day by day.

For breakfast we had ham and eggs, or fish and we drank tea or coffee. We had no lunch, except perhaps a glass of beer if we were accustomed to it. For dinner we had fish, mostly, salmon or lampreys. Not infrequently our host would bring us in a freshly-caught salmon and on one or two occasions we enjoyed ourselves by going on fishing expeditions also. Sometimes we had a little roast beef or mutton and occasionally fowl; but fish constituted dinner most frequently. Tea consisted of chops and steaks and we went to bed without supper.

Of course, every day was not alike and we had small adventures which formed an agreeable variation to the routine. It was our special delight to come across our fine old trainer [Billy Gorman] seated by the riverside, rod in hand, waiting patiently for the fish that never came, while there was no lack of diversion at night. Pillow-fights were quite the order of the time and as most of us were used to the advantages of town life it was only natural that we should endeavour to find as much amusement as possible in that quiet out-of-the world spot. On some of the nights we were kept at the hotel entertained by the county hop-pickers out of work, who to earn an honest penny dressed themselves up like Red Indians, stuck feathers in their caps, blacked their faces and performed all sorts of wild antics, dancing and singing.

On to the Match at Crewe

We did not travel from Holt Fleet until Saturday, going to Worcester by brake and then proceeding to Crewe without waiting at Birmingham. Our friends mustered in tremendous force and no fewer than five heavily-loaded trains carrying three or four thousand of them started in the morning. One enthusiast, out of work, actually started on Friday night and walked the whole distance of fifty-four miles, determined to see the match. When he got to Crewe he met with a sympathetic friend who paid for his admittance to the ground and his fare home. ...[229]

---

[229] "Triumphs of the Football Field", Birmingham Weekly Mercury, October, 1890 to February, 1891

The Aston Villa Chronicles 1874 – 1924 (and after)

FAC Semi-Final	**vs Rangers (Glasgow)**	**3-1**
5 March, 1887	**at Crewe**	

Old Fogey said (years later, in 1925), "How many the ground held we do not remember, but it was packed so tightly with humans that if you half-closed your eyes the faces of the crowd made a vivid pink sea from which arose little wreaths of smoke as a sort of incense to the game …". In *Sport and Play's* report of the game at the time, Old Fogey stated:

"[After an even start to the semi-final] the match was but ten minutes old when a long fast run by the Villa right wing gave Albert Brown the ball on the goal-line, and a magnificent centre dropped at Archie's foot, who easily made a ring round Gow as he came to meet him with a rush, and a swift shot struck the Ranger's keeper on the left side, hit the upright and bounded through goal. The usual Astonian vociferation took place…"

Villa proceeded to take the upper hand, but Rangers began to get some confidence and then responded with a shot that swerved in flight and bamboozled Warner! It was 1-1. The equaliser put new life into the Rangers, and though Villa continued to 'play up' well, the Rangers had the bit between their teeth, and only the determined play of Coulton, Simmonds and Yates kept them at bay.

There were Rangers' supporters in front of the *Sport and Play* reporter:

> They nearly all of them wore Scotch bonnets of about a yard in circumference, encircled with bright blue ribbon about two inches wide, tied with an immense bow in front, and [following their side's score] these they tossed into the air, uttered Scottish war-whoops altogether impossible to render into English, and generally behaved like madmen. One of them, a tall fine-looking young fellow, with the blood of his forefathers reeling through his veins, shouted at the top of his voice, 'Hey, lads, Bannock-bur-r-en owere again!', whereat his companions were greatly pleased, though their exuberance was somewhat checked as a brawny Brum leaned over and said, 'We'll give ye Bannockburn yet, ye devils!'

A Lion's Fun

The game was level at half-time, but the brawny Brum's prediction came to be true after the break.

Old Fogey wrote, years later:

> I have seen the Villa play hundreds of times, but have never witnessed such dazzling passing and beautiful combination as they displayed that afternoon

The Aston Villa Chronicles 1874 – 1924 (and after)

[– much to the great chagrin of the wee-dram intoxicated Scottish supporters who had expected their favourites to win handsomely having drawn level! Villa went on to score two further goals to make it 3-1].

[Afterwards] the team nearly had their hands shaken off; old gentlemen who ought to have known better capered wildly around them; the young ones cheered themselves hoarse and performed war dances; and everybody was affected with the spirit of triumph and joy! William McGregor ... and Howard Vaughton's father joined hands and did a whirling circle in honour of the occasion [– this in addition to much other merriment, it seems, enhanced when they found that the Albion were to be their opponents in the Final (the news of their beating of Proud Preston brought by telegraph!)]. [230]

About a 'tall and handsome Irish Villa supporter':

[The] Irishman, named Alexander Johnson ... was a great Villan; he'd shout for them anywhere, follow them anywhere, and when he had money (which was pretty often, for he could earn a lot) he'd spend it anywhere.

A fine, upstanding man he was, too; and a tremendous breeder of bulls – the Irish sort, you know!

He could sing a good song, and to hear him dwell on the top note of 'In Happy Moments' made you gasp with wonder, amid fear that something would go; but it never did. He was a most powerful chap in, every way, and could carry as many Old Bushmills as any man in the Army or out of it. A great bhoy, entoirely!

In those days there used to be lilted in every civilised street in the English-speaking world a rippling sort of ditty called 'The Powder Monkey,' and our classic Hibernian started the rousing chorus of

> *'Soon we'll be in London town.*
>
> *'Sing my lads, yo-ho!'*

when the Villa scored their third goal, and it rolled round the big, bright enclosure in ringing waves of sound very pleasant and inspiring to hear, and I think everybody joined in and helped things along.

Anyhow, we had a jovial time, and [he] obliged them with 'Finnegan's Wake' in a big red-brick hotel hard by, after the match, and did it with such fervour that he cleared a whole table-full of glasses with one fell swoop of his big stick when he came to the line — 'Round the room your trotters shake!' [231]

---

[230] Villa News & Record 26 Dec 1906
[231] Villa News & Record 5 Nov 1910 (Old Fogey)

The Aston Villa Chronicles 1874 – 1924 (and after)

Old Fogey also stated he was sceptical that the then modern game [in 1906] was better than that of those early days - and that Villa's performance in that semi-final was "... the cleanest and cleverest ... [they] ever played". "Archie Hunter said (of Howard Vaughton and Dennis Hodgetts) it was the finest example of wing play he had ever seen." Old Fogey's opinion was reiterated in 1925, though he said that the 1897 final was close in quality.[232] The opinion was, therefore, that the more recent finals (before 1925) were not played at the same level.

The *Sport and Play* post-match report noted that the local Crewe supporters were totally behind the Villa, and wore hats with a card stuck in them, with the words written, in chocolate and blue, "Play up Villa", and wandered around town after the match as proudly as though they had won the match!

On coming into New Street station, the Villa supporters hit upon a refrain to the tune of "Marching to Georgia" (the following was followed by three more verses and chorus!):

> *Cheer the good old Villa, boys, we'll sing another song,*
> *Sing it with a spirit that will rouse the game along,*
> *Sing it as we've always sung it, heartily and strong –*
> *The Villa lads have won the match from Scotland.*
>> *Hurrah! Hurrah! the year of Jubilee!*
>> *Hurrah! Hurrah! the final we shall see;*
>> *And so we'll sing the chorus with jolly hearts and free –*
>> *The Villa lads have won the match from Scotland.*

About the Albion (they having also won through to the Final) Archie Hunter had this to say:

> The victory of the Albion over Preston North End was unexpected. We had fully counted upon meeting the North End in the final and it has remained one of the most startling surprises recorded in the history of football how the Albion managed to beat them. The Albion scored the two winning goals just on the call of time and doubtless their victory was due to the famous trick of their forwards breaking away suddenly, pressing the other side hard and unexpectedly rushing the ball through goal. This was always a great feature in the Albion's matches and one that our previous experience had prepared us for. I ought to add ... that on returning from Crewe we were received at every station with cheers in which even the railway officials joined and at one point

---

[232] Villa News & Record 25 Dec 1908 – Old Fogey article about Howard Vaughton – and 25 Feb 1925 about Great Games.

The Aston Villa Chronicles 1874 – 1924 (and after)

a signalman was observed to be making a vigorous demonstration in his lofty box. As for the final reception, it was to be remembered.[233]

Old Fogey wrote:

> Nearly every football critic in the kingdom ... tipped the Albion to be successful and [having conquered Proud Preston] on 'paper form' ... it certainly looked odds-on the Throstles. There were various rumours ... that the Albion folk had made arrangements that the Cup should not even come through Birmingham on its way to West Bromwich!... But there was one writer who believed in Villa, and said so in the *Birmingham Post* on the morning of the match: William Bernard Vince [who sadly died in his youth in 1890].

FA Cup Final	vs West Bromwich Albion at Kennington Oval, London	2-0 2 April, 1887	Attendance: 15,534

Warner
Coulton   Simmonds
Yates   Dawson   Burton
Albt.Brown   Hunter   Vaughton   Hodgetts   R.Davis

It was a sunny and beautiful day at the Kennington Oval and the largest crowd yet to gaze on an Association final. "The turf was in splendid condition and there was hardly any breeze, and I well remember the lilting choruses that went round the ground and floated away over the dingy London houses, while we were waiting for the warriors."

"In the Albion front row of that time was a wandering local star named Tom Green, who had a great reputation ... as a hustler and a goal-getter; but I think the little man in the red cap[234] knocked all the pluck out of him that day, for in the first ten minutes, just as Green was going to head the ball forwards, Simmonds came along like a diminutive avalanche, sprang high in the air, and literally kicked the ball off the bridge of the Albion man's nose! Everybody gasped, while Joe Simmonds smiled, and Green carefully avoided the small Villa defender, for it was a warning that determination of a very dour kind

---

[233] "Triumphs of the Football Field", Birmingham Weekly Mercury, October, 1890 to February, 1891
[234] Joe Simmonds, who was a reputed five feet three inches.

The Aston Villa Chronicles 1874 – 1924 (and after)

had been decided upon! ... [but] it must be confessed that the football in the first half was little better than the usual cup-tie scramble, so that both sets of followers began to grow anxious."

In the second half, Archie Hunter led the Villa team to more attacking purpose and the Albion were kept well in check. But, after 65 minutes, a "long, lofty centre from Richmond Davies went looping into goal" and in went Hunter, Hodgetts and Vaughton, for Hodgetts to guide the ball between the posts, "while Vaughton, Hunter and Albert Brown were making a bee-line for the custodian!"

Claims for offside were dismissed by the fair Major Marindin,[235] "and the critics might have remembered from whence came Hodgetts when he saw the chance of converting a centre, and Master Dennis couldn't half hop it in those days!"

Of the plaudits: "I remember Albert Albutt[236] shouting to William McGregor, 'Now then Mac, pull off your tile and yell,' and the cautious Scot replied, 'It's no time yet; wait a wee, and they'll get anither goal; *then* we'll shout!'"

But for Frank Coulton (the 'Guardian Angel') and his magnificent kicking – well supported by Simmonds, and Warner in goal, the Cup might not have been Villa's. But as the time drew towards a finish, "the Villa were holding something more than the upper hand."

"Then Albert Brown lobbed the ball in a clear space between the backs and the burly Bob Roberts [Albion's keeper] and Archie Hunter made a simultaneous rush for it. *Bang*! They hit one another like two locomotives, and both returned succinctly on their haunches, with the ball lying idly close by; but Hunter was the nimblest, and twisting suddenly on his side... he kicked the second winning goal amidst a perfect whirlwind of cheers."

There were a few minutes left and "the Villa supporters let themselves go in the most reckless style! The father of the Football League made the welkin ring with the McGregor war-whoop, threw his 'bonnet' into the air, and danced about over a lot of imaginary swords... and when brave old Archie arose, his face flushed with football and triumph ... there was a bubbling excitement – such a tempest of cheering as rather staggered the Londoners!"[237]

---

[235] A leading referee and FA man of the time
[236] On the Villa committee at the time, and who was later secretary to Newton Heath – which became Manchester United. Albutt was noted for his enthusiasm as a worker for the Villa.
[237] Villa News & Record 1 Feb 1908

The Aston Villa Chronicles 1874 – 1924 (and after)

> Freddie Dawson was another hero that day – he got badly hurt at the beginning of the second half, and continued to play almost on one leg. He would have died rather than let the side down.

At the end, such was the euphoria that 'Mar' Margoschis was reported to have stood on his head and poised a football on his feet for several minutes!

Old Fogey reported on the London scene:

> It was the first season of the chocolate and blue colours,[238] and the favours were flaunted everywhere, ringing cheers greeting their wearers in Fleet Street, The Strand, around St. Paul's, and even in the regions around Piccadilly Circus and the haunts of the wicked.

Archie Hunter's remembrance of the team's return journey following this historic occasion was as follows:

> It had been originally arranged that we should return on the Monday, but at the last moment our plans were changed and we left London at midnight. At half-past three in the morning, just twelve hours after the great game had begun, we arrived at New Street Station and what a sight met our eyes!
>
> The huge platforms were crowded and as the train steamed into the station a band struck up the jubilant strains of 'See The Conquering Hero Comes.' We could scarcely get out of the carriage for the crowd that surged round, and the deafening cheers which resounded through the station produced a sensation which will never be forgotten by any of us. The enthusiastic multitude followed me home and early the next morning were trooping round again and inquiring for me.
>
> The Bell Inn, where I resided, had been illuminated and all Saturday night the street was blocked. At half-past twelve on Sunday the house was too small to hold the crowd who came and demanded admission and the reception I had was something to remember all my life. Mr. Powell, the proprietor of the Bell, drove over to Mr. Kynoch's, our President, and returned with the FA Cup.[239]

---

[238] These were the colours (as vertical stripes) that were introduced that season, and for years afterwards, Old Fogey referred to Villa as the Chocolate and Blues.

[239] "Triumphs of the Football Field", Birmingham Weekly Mercury, October, 1890 to February, 1891

The Aston Villa Chronicles 1874 – 1924 (and after)

Archie also said:

> As for the Albion, they took defeat rather sorely and their supporters were terribly [upset]. A report was current that many of the Black Country people had sold their pigs and their household goods to back them and the reverse so far affected them that they were obliged to go without their Sunday's dinner.

The Albion had lost in the Final for the second year in succession, and also failed in their opportunity to become the Midlands' first side to win the coveted Cup. However, their trials were to be rewarded the next year, at their third successive Final appearance, thus causing them to receive all kinds of accolades and – despite Villa's success – being regarded by the Lancashire *Athletic News* as the superior Midlands team, even devoting a special weekly column to their exploits!

However, the Villa's capability had been thoroughly demonstrated in both the semi-final and the final of the FA Cup, but it would seem that some jealousy had crept in about it. Fred Ward wrote of the 1886-87 Villa team: "Those players could not only put the ball where they wished to, but where their team-mates wanted them to place it." [240]

Aston Villa – FA Cup Winners, 1887

Back row: F.Coulton, J.Warner (goalkeeper), F.Dawson, J.Simmonds, A.Allen;
Middle Row: R.Davies, Albert Brown, Archie Hunter,
H.Vaughton, D.Hodgetts;
On Ground: H.Yates, J.Burton.

That the Albion had disposed of the Villa in the first round of the Birmingham Cup (0-1, in front of 12,000 fans) back in October of that season, and looking at the

---

[240] In his book on Aston Villa (1948). He was at the Final.

cumulative results of the fixtures between the clubs over the preceding couple of years, there were grounds for giving the Albion their due, but the fact was that it was the Villa that had beaten them in the Cup Final that mattered – and in fine style, too – while the Albion were left with the crumbs of winning the Birmingham Cup against a little club named Long Eaton Rangers (who had removed Small Heath in the semi-final), 1-0 – and in front of only 500 spectators. The status of the Birmingham Cup seemed now to be rapidly falling after ten years of success in what had been (until very recently) a purely amateur sport.

'Brum' of the *Athletic News* wrote a side story to the aftermath of the 1887 Cup Final:

> Outside the Oval gates, when the din of war had ceased, leaning against the wall I noticed two dilapidated care-worn men, with scarcely a shoe to their feet. In each of their brown, faded, ragged caps was stuck a card with the counterfeit representation of the football and the throstle, with the legend 'Play up, Albion!'
>
> 'Hey up, my lads, you seem down in your luck', exclaimed a burly well-to-do looking sportsman, who was wearing the Villa colours.
>
> 'Aye, mester, we are,' explained one of the men. 'We walked all the way from West Bromwich to see t' game, and we canna get back home; we have nowt.'
>
> 'Well, my lads,' replied the Villa man, 'here's a bob[241] each. Get summat inside thee, and turn up at Euston at half-past eleven. You shall have your tickets!'
>
> So shines a good deed in a naughty world! [wrote 'Brum']

A Punishing Conclusion to the Season

On 9 April, the Villa played the Scottish Cup winners, Hibernian – the very side the Villa had beaten 8-3 in a friendly on New Year's day! This match proved to be more difficult, but the Villa did break through to score three goals in the last twenty minutes, to win 3-0.

On Monday, April 11, the Villa beat Notts County 10-1! The next day (the 12th) they played yet another match – against the Scots' side Dumbarton – and won that 4-1. Further matches followed over the next two weeks in what had now become a punishing season (which, early on, had included a 7-0 win over Sheffield Wednesday), against Everton (2-2) and Blackburn Rovers (2-0).

---

[241] a 'bob' was a shilling.

The Aston Villa Chronicles 1874 – 1924 (and after)

This run of matches would be succeeded by a punishing result of its own; what happened next was a *very* severe jab at the Villa's ego!

How Preston North End-ed the Celebrations

> Old Fogey commented:
>
> The Prestonians, who were very wild at the knock received from the Albion, had been looked upon as 'dead snips' for the Cup, and they wanted their revenge ... offering [Villa] a very substantial sum as guarantee.
>
> In a weak and lucre-loving moment, the then Villa management were not wary enough to see the net spread so palpably in sight of their bird, and probably the unfittest that the Villa ever sent out[242] ... went to Preston to meet an eleven that had been specially kept for the occasion ...

The match took place at Deepdale on 7 May, with Villa playing their tired Cup Final team that had probably played a game or two too many over the preceding few weeks.

Astonishingly, the match finished Preston **11** (*eleven*) Villa 1.

It was reported that some Villa supporters went into a swoon when they heard the result, and there were all kinds of attempts to explain away the cause. That the Villa party did not leave Birmingham till the noon prior to the match may have had something to do with it, but it was really impossible to make sense of the debacle that day.

Deeply hurt, the Villa requested a replay at Perry Barr, and on 21 May won the return match 2-1 in front of up to 6,000 spectators. It was reported that the Villa had won deservedly in "the fastest game ever played at Perry Barr."

> One wit of the time suggested that if this 2-1 score were to be written in Roman numerals (II-I), the score would be the same as at Deepdale!

Perry Barr Developments

At the AGM on the 14 June, a cash balance of £135 8s 6d was announced. "Could another association club show such a favourable sheet?" asked the *Athletic News*. The financial recovery was complete, but had all the problems been resolved?

---

[242] The Villa had finished their season with a punishing schedule.

The Aston Villa Chronicles 1874 – 1924 (and after)

Resolved or not, the club found it opportune to invest in a new grandstand.

Back in 1883,[243] the primitive conditions for members and players alike were made apparent by the committee's resolution to "see to get ashes placed in the reserve places and the boards mended", and "to order strips of matting for the dressing tent". It can be imagined how players changed their strip in muddy conditions – worse than the conditions for the parks' players of today.

Later in 1883 (September or October), the committee had a hard look at the possibility of putting up a new stand/pavilion, but decided that because of just £31 being the cash surplus at that time, and with the rent becoming due, the quote of £200 for a new structure was beyond them. It was thus to be nearly another four years before Villa's improved club management made it possible for a new stand/pavilion to be put up. This was coincidental with the first official involvement of Fred Rinder (in 1887), when he was made a member of committee to raise funds for the stand. Daniel Arkell was appointed architect, and he continued to provide services to the Villa to the end of their days at Perry Barr.

Now costing £340, the pavilion was equipped with nine rows of seats, and housed between seven and eight hundred spectators, although with the days of cantilevering some way off, 14 narrow columns supporting the roof slightly restricted the view. A clock donated by a Mr. Wray of New Street was attached to the front of the roof and a large pennant with the initials 'AVFC' fluttered above.

As the *Birmingham Daily Post* pointed out, an ancillary benefit of the new structure was that it blotted out some nearby tramway sheds that had been something of an eyesore.

After the pavilion was built and had been officially opened, a little upset was created when the club's committee found that a plaque had been attached to it without their permission. The committee decided that the inscription was unsuitable and ordered that the plaque be taken down. On 31 October the committee resolved "permission given to builders to fix at the end of the stand a small brass plate on which only the names of the builders and architect shall appear." The Aston Villa club today possess in their archives what is probably the original plaque the committee ordered to be taken down.

---

[243] The Villa minutes from before 1882 have not survived

The Aston Villa Chronicles 1874 – 1924 (and after)

> ASTON VILLA FOOTBALL CLUB
> THIS PAVILION
> WAS FORMALLY OPENED
> 22 OCTOBER 1887

Apparently, the date of official opening of the stand was incorrectly given.

After the Villa moved to Aston Lower Grounds in 1897, that pavilion ended up as part of the terrace cover behind one of the goals at Small Heath's Muntz Street ground, before the 'Heathens', too, moved on to better things.

Later Ground Developments

There were further improvements to the ground as the years passed. In 1893, it was reported that:

> The Villa have erected a fine paddock [the approach to the dressing pavilions and press stand] for the players and only members of the committee and the press can gain admission ... The players are absolutely isolated from the crowd. Then there are 420 yards of substantial iron railings placed in front of the ordinary gaspipe which surrounds the ground.[244]

By that year, banking had been provided on the terraces in order to improve the view of the standing spectators, and then there were the more cosmetic changes. In September, 1894, the *Athletic News* referred to "the gorgeous new flag planted proudly from the centre of the pavilion."

Perry Barr staged an England vs Ireland international in early 1893 (a 10,000 crowd), and its first FA Cup semi-final in 1890, but the second such occasion (in 1896) brought the ground to its peak of utility – immediately prior to its closure. That semi-final was successfully held in front of a then mammoth 30,000 spectators, and required superior ground preparation in the light of the escapade of 1888 – which story is to follow.

---

[244] The Athletic News, 4 Sep 1893

The Aston Villa Chronicles 1874 – 1924 (and after)

11. Defending the FA Cup – and Reputation

The Club's Colours

The Villa's club colours now progressed from the 'Chocolate and Sky Blue' of the club's first glorious Cup-winning season, to the Claret and Light Blue, that has forever since been famous.

However, the 1886-87 colours must have been very similar to the Claret and Light Blue that succeeded them. Old Fogey for many years referred to the Villa as the "Chocolate and Blues".

The shirt/jersey design for the next few seasons would not be the classic design since known by millions (as designed by Ollie Whateley), but, in turn,

Claret and Light Blue quarters
followed by Claret and Light Blue halves.

It is thought that that combination of design and colours was based on that used by Notts County in the early 1880s.

Season 1887-88 : More Cup Exploits

The new season produced the usual spate of changes to the Villa ranks, the main incoming personalities being **Tom Green** from the Albion (who had played in the 1887 Final) and **Harry Devey** (John Devey's uncle) from Excelsior. However, Howard Vaughton – the Villa's remaining first-team amateur – seems to have moved on to (Mitchell's) St. George's where he joined John Devey, late of Excelsior. In the process of moving clubs, Vaughton ran into some hiatus concerning a misunderstood payment to him, and at one stage it appeared that he would have to become a professional. By October, his amateur status was reinstated, and it then emerged that he would continue to play for the Villa in 'important matches', and for St. George's in cup-ties.

The season went very well for the Villa in the period up to December; they played 20 matches with one defeat and no draws, and scored 116 goals as against 18 conceded. That was an average scoring rate of more than 5 goals per match, but it has to be acknowledged that the opposition was not, in the main, of the best quality – none of the Lancashire cracks (Preston, Blackburn Rovers, Bolton Wanderers, nor Darwen) were amongst the opposition. However, the Villa were always happy to shock their supporters, and the one defeat they experienced was a 2-8 result at Notts County! Villa's only excuse was that they had important players on duty for the Birmingham & District FA.

The Aston Villa Chronicles 1874 – 1924 (and after)

In the first three rounds of the FA Cup in this year following Villa's cup success, in 1887-88, Villa scored 17 goals without reply. The first round was a 4-0 win away against an Oldbury Town that included the ex-Villan Tom Riddell. The second round was a 4-0 win at Small Heath, an encounter that was held in direct competition with Buffalo Bill's Wild West Circus on show at the Aston Lower Grounds. A 3,000-capacity stand had been constructed for the 'Circus' display, but their expectations were barely met, whilst perhaps 6,000 attended the Small Heath affair.

"… it was astonishing the easy, nonchalant way in which the Villa people stemmed the tide of [the Heathens early] impetuous rush. Then they went away with a whiz, slipped by man after man in superb style." On scoring their first (through Green) "there was a small kind of yell, which might have been heard at Yardley, and from this point it was really all over bar the shouting."[245]

In the third round, Villa played a team called Shankhouse (an unknown club a little outside of Newcastle-on-Tyne). The Villa had offered £50 to Shankhouse to play the match at Perry Barr, but the offer was refused. In fact, they did not have a hope of being able to play the match on their village ground, and another ground, nearby, was obtained for the match. Their goalkeeper informed a little knot of admirers that they need not be afraid. He said that Aston Villa might shoot as much as they liked, but he would stop the shots. Well, after Villa had won 9-0, he said:[246]

"It's nae guid! They put them this side, even that; they put them where they like!"

> Charlie Johnstone's more expansive account of why the score did not proceed beyond 9-0, and the motivation behind it, was thus:
>
> > As to who Shankhouse were, and where Shankhouse was, we were all profoundly ignorant. At last, it leaked out in the Press that the place was 'up north' somewhere, and that the players were a fine robust lot of men – the dark horse, in a word, of the Competition.
> >
> > The matter was much discussed among the Villa players. At last, Archie Hunter broke out: 'I don't know who they are, or what they are," said he defiantly, "but I'll bet anybody half a sovereign[247] we beat them by ten goals."
> >
> > "It's a bet", said Tommy Green.
> >
> > Towards the finish of the game, when the Villa were winning 9-0, down the

---

[245] Sport and Play 7 Nov 1887
[246] The Sporting Mail 13 Jan 1906

The Aston Villa Chronicles 1874 – 1924 (and after)

> field came Archie with the ball at his toe, intent on winning that half-sovereign. As the back dashed at him, he deftly slipped the ball to Tommy, who went straight for goal, where the poor keeper stood, unmoved. Just as Tommy was about to shoot, some four yards from the post, he suddenly stopped dead, and a doubtful expression came over his face. It had dawned on him that if he scored that goal it would cost him that half-a-sovereign! So, to the amazement and consternation of everyone, he swung round on his left foot and incontinently booted the ball right up the field!
>
> *A Lion's Fun*
>
> When Archie recovered sufficiently to articulate, and the other players grasped the situation, they could hardly kick the ball for laughing![248]

Old Fogey relayed Albert Albut's reminiscences of the occasion:

> [Albert] Albut said he couldn't understand the *patois* — it was so essentially different from Brummagemese, especially when it came to exclamation.
>
> But they were capital sportsmen, and when they found that Aston Villa were as good as, or a little better than they anticipated, they not only orally recognised the fact, but celebrated it in a sort of original way.
>
> About every other man among the crowd — it wasn't very thick, but what it lacked in numbers it made up for in enthusiasm — had a seat consisting of a small keg of liquor, and each one carried a 'tot.'
>
> Every time a goal was scored the majority of the spectators had a refresher, and as the score was 9 to 0 in favour of the Villa, it may be gathered that a good many of the spectators were a trifle merry when the match was over and the dusky night rode down the sky.
>
> The Shankhouse enthusiasts also insisted on the Villa team hobnobbing with them before they left the ground, and I have heard some of the old hands say that for sheer lavish hospitality this was the limit.
>
> The inhabitants had never seen high-class Association football before; and … the Villa had a trick of charming the natives wherever they went.[249]

---

[247] A sovereign was a gold coin, nominally worth £1.
[248] In his column in The Sporting Mail 14 Jan 1911
[249] Villa News and Record 19 Nov 1910

The Aston Villa Chronicles 1874 – 1924 (and after)

> ***'Pets' of a different kind ...***
>
> Archie Hunter kicked a goal of a new sort, last week. A cat was going for his pet canary when the genial Scot came to the rescue. Up went his foot (quite naturally, of course), and what became of poor pussy the deponent sayeth not, but the Villa captain all but dislocated his great toe![250]
>
> *A Lion's Fun*

The next tie in the FA Cup – what proved to be the highly contentious fourth round (January) tie against 'Proud Preston' – was recalled by Archie Hunter:

> As usual, we went into training in our old quarters and Preston North End also made special arrangements. At the end of our week at Holt Fleet[251] we left amid the lusty cheers of the inhabitants and many friends who had assembled to wish us a repetition of the previous year's success. Arriving in Birmingham, we dined in charge of Dr. Jones and then drove in a coach to Perry Barr. Scarcely had we started upon the road than we were surprised at the huge concourse wending their way down towards our ground and when we got on the main road the scene was simply like a Derby day. An endless line of vehicles could be seen slowly moving down and an empty string of vehicles returning; so we had to take our place behind the rest and quietly move along in turn with the rest.
>
> We were soon recognised and amid the exciting hubbub could be heard the encouraging and familiar shout of 'Play up, Villa,' while others singled me out and cheered me all along the way. No one could tell, however, exactly what the fortune of the day would be; certainly no one was prepared for what actually occurred. Preston North End was captained by Nick Ross and the team was much the same as we had met before. The contest between the North End and ourselves had always been keen and everyone anticipated a close match.
>
> Our committee had made tremendous exertions, perhaps almost unparalleled, to secure the convenience of spectators and players. They had gone so far as to ask the local police superintendent to send mounted constables to preserve the field from invasion and to guarantee that the match should be played out without hindrance. The Superintendent said that he would have a sufficient force for our purpose, but he must have under-

---

[250] Athletic News 27 Dec 1887
[251] According to Charlie Johnstone (The Sporting Mail 4 Feb 1911), it is thought that Villa were one of the first clubs to provide "away training" for special and Cup matches, and Holt Fleet was chosen because of Billy Gorman's (the old trainer) love of the Ombersley district, and the brine baths at Droitwich.

The Aston Villa Chronicles 1874 – 1924 (and after)

estimated the crowd. The crowd was, in fact, a source of amazement to us all. Half-a-crown or more was paid willingly for the slightest coign of vantage; trees were climbed, roofs invaded and one enthusiast gallantly perched himself upon the flagpole, where, I think, he was as well off as anybody.

> The *Birmingham Post* added: "We do not remember a football match when such high prices have been charged and cheerfully paid. ... Every house around the grounds showed crowds on the roof and a dozen heads at every window ..."

An hour before the game was announced to commence it seemed impossible to crush any more on to the ground; yet the stream still rolled on[252] and at length the barriers gave way. The forty police were unable to check the rush that followed and Mr. Ramsay at once telegraphed for the Hussars. It was difficult for the officials to prevent the spectators from spreading over the meadow and though the crowd was well behaved, yet their presence on the field had a disturbing effect. Well, having kept them beyond the touch-lines, the two teams emerged from the tent to do battle.

We went on the field amid a storm of cheers, never suspecting that we should be interfered with. Scarcely ten minutes had passed when the game thoroughly warmed up and I received the ball from Allen, shot along with it between the two opposition backs and scored the first goal. It was done so quickly that I well remember the look of surprise and consternation on the faces of the Preston team when they realised all that had happened. But a great shout of jubilation rent the air when the same fact was realised by the spectators and cries of 'Well done, Archie' and 'The Villa wins' could be heard from all parts. A few minutes afterwards, while we were playing a very strong game and had the upper hand of our opponents, we made another attack upon the Preston goal and Tom Green, who was notorious, among other things, for being offside, played the ball when in a position to score a second time. An appeal for off-side followed and to the great disappointment of all, though the decision was perfectly just, judgement was given against us.

But while this had been going on, the crowd had gradually drawn closer and got altogether beyond bounds. They were swarming over the meadow and further play was impossible. The people were breaking through the barriers and those at the back were pushing forward those at the front and encroaching upon the playing ground. The Preston team gathered in a group

---

[252] In fact, the management had set a limit on the number of spectators, but their mood was such that a surfeit was allowed to enter. The crowd probably totalled 27,000 – a figure never heard of before.

and sat on the ground while our players were told to assist the police in clearing the lines. I myself, having some influence with the populace in those days, was particularly requested to speak to the people and induce them to return to their places. I went forward and begged of them to withdraw, pointing out that there was an empty space of a dozen yards or more at the back. But they would not be reasoned with and I next tried to push the multitude back, with the help of a posse of police and I never worked so hard and so ineffectually in my life. I might as well have tried to move a mountain.

All my efforts were unavailing. Two Hussars upon the ground mounted cab horses and careered round as wildly as their dashing steeds would allow them and this did some good. The people retreated a little and we proposed to continue the game. But first, a consultation took place between the two captains, the umpires and the referee and taking into consideration the fact that the game might again be interrupted, both captains agreed that it should be no Cup-tie.

We started again on the full understanding that a friendly game was to be played so as not to disappoint the spectators. But this fact had a depressing effect upon the Villa players; they would not exert themselves and we lost the game by three goals to one. It was a welcome relief to us all when the whistle sounded, for the crowd had again grown unruly and the mounted police arrived too late to be of any use.

How the 'friendly match' agreement was broken ...

Well, I have now to tell you the strange conclusion to this curious episode. The reports of the umpires and the referee were received by the Association and discussed at their meeting at Kennington Oval. But what was our amazement and consternation to find that Preston North End was claiming to have won the match! Considering the definite agreement come to on the field this was startling and we were not prepared for it A vote was taken whether the match should be played again or not and an equal number was recorded on both sides.

Major Marindin then gave his casting vote in favour of Preston North End, blaming Aston Villa for not having made proper provision for the match. I have no great desire to re-open the question now and it has been bitterly discussed on both sides. But I should like to say this: that if fault there were at all it was not on the part of our committee, but on the part of the police superintendent, who declared that he had made sufficient preparations and then left us in the lurch.

The Aston Villa Chronicles 1874 – 1924 (and after)

This then, is how we lost the Cup in 1888 and you will understand how keen our disappointment was in losing under such circumstances.[253]

Sport and Play said that a good number of sportsmen considered that what was done by Preston was "a shabby trick".

> The lady who scampered across the Perry Barr ground amid yells and jeers from some 20,000 throats did the 80 yards in a little more than evens. We saw more of her red stockings than we had paid for and the incident was about the funniest of the afternoon.[254]
>
> *A Lion's Fun*

One further matter occurred on that fateful day against Preston. Friction arose between the club's president, George Kynoch, and a committee member concerning the parking of the president's carriage. The president considered he was not treated with proper respect, and duly resigned!

The committee tried by might and mane to get him to the discussion table, but he remained irascible and sent the message that apart from Archie Hunter, it was he that had done the most to raise the flag of the Villa. He had been president for two years.

At a special meeting, chaired by Billy Mason, his resignation was accepted. It was not very long after that George Kynoch left for South Africa to escape his creditors, and then disappeared into obscurity.

The Remainder of the Season

Villa's performances immediately following that Preston to-do started all kinds of noise about Villa cracking up, that the team had seen its brightest days, and were heading for oblivion. But Villa responded by winning their way through to the final of the Birmingham Cup (vs. Stoke, 4-2), and in their next match – against Mitchell's St. George's on a frozen ground, and opposing players of the ilk of Howard Vaughton and John Devey – Villa showed again their true mettle by winning 5-1. This has to be considered a very good win, as St. George's were then making a bold attempt to achieve parity with the big clubs, and were soon to be considered for inclusion in the Football League. They were no 'pushovers'.

On 18 February, (Glasgow) Rangers came to Perry Barr. The *Athletic News* reporter reminded his readers that the Villa had visited Rangers' ground a few years earlier and

---

[253] "Triumphs of the Football Field", Birmingham Weekly Mercury, October, 1890 to February, 1891
[254] Athletic News 10 Jan 1888

The Aston Villa Chronicles 1874 – 1924 (and after)

were "beaten – nay, demolished – 7-1", though there had been the Villa's glorious Cup semi-final victory against them in 1887. In the match now played, the Villa won 5-1, with Archie and Tom Green both showing wonderful dribbling skills – each beating two or three players on their way to scoring goals.

The Villa then came up against the Albion once more, and, at Stoney Lane, Villa lost 1-4, but they also lost Denny Hodgetts in that match, and played much of it with ten men. This match was supposed to be a warm-up for a more serious match the next week; Aston Villa vs. the Albion in the Birmingham Cup Final at the Lower Grounds on 3 March. The Albion had defeated their worthy local rivals, Wolverhampton Wanderers, 2-0, in their semi-final.

The 1888 Birmingham Cup Final

The previous year, there had been every sign that the Birmingham Cup was quickly losing its reputation, but when clubs such as these two were competing, then it was bound to be that the supporters would come out of the woodwork. An estimated 13,000 turned up to see the Villa attempt to lower the flag of the FA Cup Finalists.

> [Long before the match] there was a continuous stream of vehicles to the scene ... At 3 o'clock, the special grandstand [that had been] erected on the occasion of Buffalo Bill's visit ... was crammed to excess, and the smaller stand running alongside the [skating] rink was equally packed. The switchback railway fairly rocked and creaked under the great burden of supporters ... The top of the rink, roofs of the dining rooms, and the trees and the house tops in the immediate vicinity, all came in for their share of support.

> **Villa**: *Warner; Coulton, Cox; Yates, H. Devey, Burton; Green, Albert Brown, Hunter, Allen, Hodgetts.*

To the reporter, it presented a sight that brought back memories of the Final vs the Old 'Uns in 1880, "only the excitement on Saturday was ten times more intense." It was reported that the sportsmanship was such that any good play by either side was generously applauded by virtually all present.

The weather was fine, but the pitch was almost like a sea of mud following-on from a period of snow and frost, and the subsequent thaw. And in the mud, the Villa appeared in temporarily spotless white kit! After five minues of slipping and sliding ...

> ... Archie again had possession, and after getting round three or four opponents, he plumped the ball nicely into the centre. Allen seized upon it,

The Aston Villa Chronicles 1874 – 1924 (and after)

and without any ceremony, whizzed it past Roberts ... Hats, sticks, handkerchiefs, and pigeons, went up amidst the most deafening thunder of applause, and Albion looked dismayed!

The Albion came back, and not before too long they equalised whilst Warner was distracted in the Villa goal. For the last 20 minutes of the first half, the Albion were playing much better than the Villa.

> Close to half-time, a fox terrier ran onto the pitch to chase the ball, stopping the game. Though he was taken off, he came back and stopped the game once more. This enraged an Albion player to the extent that he kicked a cruel kick, "which drew forth a shower of well-deserved abuse [from the crowd]." The injured dog was carried away by the Albion trainer, with an unknown result.

In the early part of the second period, the Albion continued to look the better team, but then a transformation took place, "with some of the prettiest play of the match" shown by the Villa, resulting in their second goal. Both sides went on to score further goals, one apiece, so that the score finished at 3-2 to the Villa.

The Villa had retrieved something from their season, whilst Albion, on the Villa's behalf (and their own!), went on to put paid to Preston in the FA Cup Final! Albion thus not only won the national Cup in 1888, but also eliminated the great Preston club for the second year in succession.

Important End of Season Matches

The return match to that disastrous early season defeat at Notts County was played in April at Perry Barr, and this time finished 3-3. Again, Villa had important players out – Hodgetts and Allen were both playing for England.

In May, there were a series of matches played off quite close to one another:

12 May: Under the match report heading "Birmingham v Bolton" in the *Athletic News* (the Villa's status clearly having changed in some eyes!), it was reported that the Villa, having led 3-0 in this match at Bolton, lost 3-4. The Villa players, though having lost, were described thus: "... at close passing they showed themselves all round to be superior adepts to the Wanderers."

14 May (Monday): vs. Small Heath Alliance at Perry Barr. It was reported that Albert Allen had broken his ankle and would be out for a long time – some said that he would not be able to play again. Fortunately this fear was unfounded; though a nasty bump, the ankle was not broken. In the match, though Villa were 0-1 down at half-time, they eventually cantered through, 4-1.

The Aston Villa Chronicles 1874 – 1924 (and after)

19 May: The 'revenge' match against 'The Invincibles', at Perry Barr. The *Sport and Play* reporter wrote: "It cannot be said their reception was altogether a friendly one ...". On a swelteringly hot day, Villa won 1-0:

> There was all the old cleverness, the beautiful precision, and 'playing pretty' [about Preston] which are characteristic of them; but for stamina, power and generalship, the Villa were a long distance in front of them ... Deprived of a couple of their best men, they had to meet the full strength of the Proud Prestonians, and the [Villa] victory is all the more meritorious [as the Villa] were practically playing with only ten men, as Albert Brown was only useful when the ball came to him ...

Towards the end of the season, more than one allegation of 'poaching' of players was made – clearly a developing issue. The Unity Gas Company wrote a letter to the *Athletic News* about an attempt on one of their players, complaining:

> Last week the Aston Villa Hon. Sec. paid a visit ... and had the unblushing impudence to tell our captain that he wanted our left-back ... that the Gas club ought to think it a great honour that one of their players was good enough to play for the Villa club.

Hardly a case of *poaching* it would seem – more a case of *bad eggs*! On the other hand, it was also reported that several members of the Villa team had received tempting offers. St. George's were trying to re-sign Dennis Hodgetts, and were tempting him with rich rewards. Allen and Cox had also been sounded.

In March, the club re-engaged most of their leading players at fifteen shillings for each Saturday match and forty shillings for a weekday match. The arrangement for Dennis Hodgetts, however, was thirty shillings per week *all year*, and also £10 down.

End of Season AGM

The balance sheet was not altogether healthy, only £9 4s being carried forward to the next year, but the new pavilion had been built, and had cost £380.

The Villa had 330 members, but were targeting 500. There were 570 season ticket holders, but the club were hoping for 1,000 before next season, which was to be the first season of the Football League. An era had ended.

James Hinks was made president. He replaced George Kynoch, who had earlier resigned in the manner previously reported.

Andy Hunter

By April, 1888, it was well known that Andy Hunter was seriously ill out in Australia. Believing it to be Andy's final days, a fund was set up to bring him home. The gesture proved too late, however, as he died on 19 June.

How poignant that, with the birth of the League and the end of the old era, Andy should now pass away.

He died at the still very young age of 24.

There was a moving tribute to him published in the Sport and Play edition of 11 September, part reproduced in an earlier chapter.

12. Those So-called 'Friendly Matches'

The amount of organised football played during the 1880s increased significantly, and Villa's programme was always one of the most active. The number of matches played by the Villa[255] increased from 18 in 1878-79, to 26 in 1879-80 and then progressively until 40 were played in 1883-84. The 1885-86 campaign – with the onset of legalised professionalism – saw an exponential development, as 59 matches were played that season. In Villa's FA Cup-winning season (1886-87), just 56 matches were played; 44 matches of them were won with a total of 223 goals scored and 62 conceded. However, those statistics (as all of them in those pre-League days) need to be 'read' in conjunction with the kind of opposition played, for although many matches *were* against 'top' opposition, there were a number played against lesser-quality teams where Villa often scored seven, eight or nine goals – sometimes more!

The *Daily Gazette* published[256] an unofficial League table for 1886-87 – two years before the real League was started – of the performances of 20 top-rated clubs. The top seven, based on goal average (because of the large variance in the number of games played by each club), were:

	* a Scottish club	Pld	W	D	L	F	A	Goal Ave.
1	Preston North End	55	46	3	6	251	68	4.32
2	**Aston Villa**	**56**	**44**	**8**	**4**	**223**	**62**	**3.59**
3	West Bromwich A.	43	31	6	6	122	40	3.05
4	Vale of Leven*	34	20	6	8	112	44	2.54
5	Renton*	35	21	9	5	96	43	2.23
6	Wolves	43	25	9	9	131	63	2.07
7	Bolton Wanderers	57	37	8	12	192	105	1.82

Sport and Play published a similar but shorter table for 1887-88, as at 31 March, 1888 (before the actual completion of the season):

---

[255] "Triumphs of the Football Field", Birmingham Weekly Mercury, October, 1890 to February, 1891
[256] On 9 May 1887

The Aston Villa Chronicles 1874 – 1924 (and after)

	* a Scottish club	Pld	W	D	L	F	A	Goal Ave.
1	Preston North End	41	39	1	1	214	44	4.90
2	Renton*	30	27	2	1	135	33	4.90
3	**Aston Villa**	**47**	**40**	**3**	**4**	**232**	**58**	**4.00**
4	West Bromwich A.	42	34	4	4	156	41	3.80
5	Wolves	36	23	6	7	132	38	3.47
6	Arbroath*	33	26	0	7	209	60	3.40

The use of goal average to determine League position– in this case at least – seems to have been a good indicator of a team's worth in view of the variable number of games played, but the reliability of such a table falls down when it is taken into account that it all rather depended on the fixtures that each club had arranged for themselves. In view of their recent successes in the FA Cup, Blackburn Rovers were surprisingly last-but-one in the 1886-87 table. Small Heath Alliance were not shown at all.

It is worth mentioning at this point the now well-known clubs that changed their name over the years:

Arsenal — originally 'Woolwich Arsenal', until they moved to North London in 1913.

Birmingham City — originally 'Small Heath Alliance', then 'Small Heath', then 'Birmingham';

Leicester City — originally 'Leicester Fosse'.

Manchester City — originally 'Ardwick';

Manchester United — originally 'Newton Heath';

Stoke City — originally, simply 'Stoke'.

Sheffield Wednesday — also (formerly) known as 'The Wednesday'.

Villa's local opposition, **West Bromwich Albion,** *have for years had two nicknames – 'the Baggies' and 'the Throstles', or have been known just as 'the Albion'.*

Wolverhampton Wanderers *have usually been known as 'the Wolves', though before the Wanderers came strongly on the scene, the Stafford Road club (of Wolverhampton) were also known as 'the Wolves'.*

The Aston Villa Chronicles 1874 – 1924 (and after)

Notable Foes of the 1880s

Of the pre-League and professional days, Old Fogey wrote: "There was a very healthy sort of rivalry among about a dozen of the best clubs in England – half of which came from Lancashire: and I remember Darwen as one of the big teams that used to draw the crowds."[257] As sports reporter J. H. Stainton stated:

> Who does not recall with rather fearsome thoughts, the ground at Darwen, where, in anything like not good weather, great ponds – not mere pools – were set out all along the playing piece, and good football was practically out of the question.
>
> Brave games used to be played there, nevertheless, and many a hand-fight resulted in the winning team, when it also chanced to be the visiting one, making haste to get to the railway station if safety were to be secured.[258]

At Darwen, a famously fair and scrupulous referee (John Lewis) was surrounded by a mob who knocked him to the ground, then kicked him around mercilessly like a human football. But nothing could faze him, and his fearlessness became proverbial.[259]

Sport and Play described the ground from a different view:

> The ground at Barley Bank seems to be situated high up in the clouds, where one gets a view of nothing but the tops of huge mill chimneys and the roofs of houses, with the smoke curling gracefully into the heavens as the only reminder that we are in the land of the living.[260]

One match the Villa played against Darwen – on their ground – was on 19 November, 1881, at a time when Archie Hunter was back in Ayr, and when Andy Hunter carried the responsibility as captain. The match was a goal-fest – after Villa had taken a 2-1 lead, Darwen drew level, then took the lead at 3-2. Darwen then scored again after half-time (4-2) before Eli Davis brought the score back to 4-3. Not long after, the Villa players disputed Darwen's fifth netting of the day to the extent that they walked off the pitch! After 15 minutes of stoppage, the Villans

---

[257] Villa News & Record 3 Oct 1908 – an article by Old Fogey. Other major Lancashire clubs of that time that have survived into the modern era are Preston North End, Blackburn Rovers and Bolton Wanderers.
[258] Villa News & Record 2 Nov 1907 – an extract from "The Growth of Football". Further, when dressing rooms which had a roof and a wash-basin were regarded as quite up-to-date.
[259] My thanks to author Peter Lupson for providing information on this matter.
[260] Sport and Play 24 Jan 1893

decided to play out the remainder of the match, but as the match finished after Villa had scored a fourth, the Villans decided that 4-4 was the proper result, and not 4-5 as was their opponents' view! The report on this match was taken from the *Daily Gazette* under the banner "How to Fix a Draw"!

The question of which was the superior team of the two was probably settled a little over a year later, on 5 February, 1883, when Villa again visited that outlandish place and won, 5-2, and that with only ten fit men during a portion of the match.

However, Darwen was once a guiding light to the provincial clubs, as a correspondent to the *Sports Argus* wrote:

> Prior to 1883 ... a mapless town, with one main street and a big chimney, for years would whip the world at the 'soccer' game, its club being the first provincial 'trekkers' to the 'Little Village' [London] for the then costly tin pot.
>
> [Blackburn] Olympic, Rovers, [Aston] Villa, and all others were in their infancy when 'the boys of other days' swept the board in most encounters and carried all before them. Their fame was world-wide.
>
> Beardless lads, with heavy clogs doing hard graft week-in, week-out, in factories and foundries, were called upon to journey to London four times in one year, beating Romford in their own dumping ground over a dozen goals; then three weeks' hand running at the Oval against Old Etonians (semi-final) to lead the way for other provincial clubs.
>
> And but for this heavy strain upon them the honour of lifting the Cup from its long rest with Metropolis should have been awarded to Darwen and not to Blackburn, its next door neighbour.[261]

The provincials of Lancashire and Staffordshire took football seriously, very seriously indeed. In the south, it was a game, but the northerners made it almost a way of life. In London, one played football for enjoyment; in Bolton the remark was heard, "We haven't come here for fun; we've come to play football". So much for the term "friendly"!

There was one further matter about Darwen and related to the seriousness of the matter of football in Lancashire, and that was the issue of professionalism. Notably, it was Darwen that made the first moves in this direction before 1880, and whose example was taken on by the other clubs, as referred to earlier.

A series of games that were important at the time were those against Blackburn Olympic, FA Cup winners in 1883, they were the first provincial winners of the Cup.

---

[261] The 'Argus Junior' column in Sports Argus 21 Mar 1903

The Aston Villa Chronicles 1874 – 1924 (and after)

On 28 April, 1883, Villa met the club at Perry Barr (fresh from their Cup victory) and convincingly beat them, 5-1, in a fast and hard-fought game in which Villa had led 3-1 at the break. Dawson excelled himself, playing nearly as well as Apperley. "We have never seen the Villa play so grand a game all-round as they did on Saturday", piped the *Midland Athlete*. Archie Hunter was more generous towards the Olympic, and narrated on what happened:

> [W]e had been fortunate enough to defeat the Blackburn Olympic by five goals to one. As you know, the Olympic were that year particularly strong and our great victory is to be accounted for that we played upon our own ground and that the hard training they had been undergoing had begun to have its effect upon them by the time we met them. But in September, 1883, we went to Blackburn to play the return and by this time the Olympic had picked up again. It was a very hard match indeed and in the end we were defeated by two goals to one. We did not send over our strongest team,[262] I ought to say, while the Cup-holders were in splendid form and the captain, Jack Hunter, played a grand game. The second part of the game was full of excitement and we made a desperate effort to avoid the defeat, but could not succeed in scoring.
>
> [On 13 October, 1883,] we had the pleasure of again meeting the Blackburn Olympic, who came down to Birmingham. A great deal of the interest which this visit excited was due to the fact that the Olympic were the first provincial club to win the English Association Cup. Our previous victory had been taken as a proof, at the time, that we were superior to the Cup holders; then our defeat by the team had given the other side a chance of asserting that they were more than our equals. Consequently, the present encounter was looked upon as being to some extent decisive so far as our rival claims went. The weather was good, it was a splendid October day and the spectators turned up in good number.[263]

He then went on to describe at length how the Villa turned round an apparent defeat to finally win, 3-2, and then said: "The victory created the greatest enthusiasm in the town and after so well-played a game from which we had emerged with flying colours, our hopes of future honours were high."

---

[262] Though, interestingly, both the young Dennis Hodgetts and Albert Brown made an appearance.
[263] "Triumphs of the Football Field", *Birmingham Weekly Mercury*, October, 1890 to February, 1891

The Aston Villa Chronicles 1874 – 1924 (and after)

The *Midland Athlete* considered the match: "One of the finest games ever witnessed at Perry Barr", and described Archie's winning goal in these, more graphic, terms:

> Archie Hunter ... went sailing off at top speed, leaping through the half-back and back division, and keeping command of the ball all the while in the most brilliant fashion. A short quick pass ... [was] instantly returned, and away went the leather through the corner of the goal as if a horse had kicked it! ... To get through such a powerful defence as the Olympic one is a feat that is rarely accomplished. His admirers went almost wild with delight, and the applause was as hearty as I have ever heard, even down on the Villa field.

Of the many other games of great interest, those against Preston North End were often outstanding ones – and often contentious! – as the following description will portray (Archie Hunter again providing the details):

> The North End came down to Perry Barr [the match was played on May 9 1885] and considered purely from the sporting point of view, the game was an excellent one. We were only too pleased to arrange for the visit, for a desire had been expressed in many quarters to have an opportunity of seeing the noted club in Birmingham.
>
> The fixture was hailed with satisfaction and a good crowd was drawn to witness the proceedings, in spite of the boisterous weather. A cordial greeting awaited the visitors and it was soon seen that the Villa were playing a weaker game than their opponents.
>
> The game does not call for much description, though I cannot avoid mentioning that for the first time we had to find fault with our goalkeeper, who seemed either unable or unwilling to defend his charge. Indeed, we and the spectators, were very wroth with Harvey, who was by no means playing up to his usual form; but even if he had been we should have had little chance of winning the match. Finally we were defeated by five goals to none.
>
> The visit of the North End is memorable, however, for other reasons than these and after this lapse of time I can give a dispassionate account of what happened without, I hope, hurting anybody's feelings. One of our players had been kicked and in the heat of the moment he retaliated upon his opponent. The officials intervened and the incident might have ended there and been satisfactorily explained afterwards if the crowd had not interfered and aroused angry feelings at the end of the game.
>
> When the Preston team were leaving the field a number of roughs gathered round them and charged them with using their weight unfairly. Of course, the charge was indignantly denied, but the denial only exasperated the crowd the more and free fights could be seen taking place all over the field. After

dressing, the team prepared to depart, but to our dismay we found an excited and rough gathering round the tent and the appearance of the Preston men was the signal for the renewal of the quarrel. The hostile demonstration continued until the visitors had departed and left a very bad impression upon everybody's mind.

The Preston team not unnaturally were offended, but they freed the Villa Committee of all responsibility and in after-times new fixtures were made which had none of these unpleasant details. [264]

---

[264] "Triumphs of the Football Field", Birmingham Weekly Mercury, October, 1890 to February, 1891

The Aston Villa Chronicles 1874 – 1924 (and after)

13. William McGregor and The League

It was mainly from the time of the legalisation of professionalism (1885) that William McGregor became such a notable spokesman outside the Villa's inner circle, and strove for the proper development and organisation of soccer.

McGregor and his close friend, businessman, pitch official and later football administrator, Joe Tillotson[265] discussed the concerns that clubs in the country had, about how to best organise themselves in a sport that was attracting larger crowds to pay at the turnstiles. And those large crowds were also part of a problem, as the opposition frequently did not turn up! So, it was a question of creating something that would guarantee an organisation of fixtures – a "fixity of fixtures", as 'Mac' liked to call it. It is not that fixtures were currently not present, but the fact that some clubs were lax in keeping to them, especially in the new age of professionalism. As a result, there was a danger of the supporting public walking away from the game for good, and the situation was already causing financial problems for a number of clubs.

It appears that 'Mac' frequently sought opinion from other clubs on the matter of a 'union' (league) a year or two before he resolved to act on the idea, and he would often travel to discuss these issues in the company of Fred Rinder. 'Mac' then sought the counsel of others at the Villa. Charlie Johnstone told of what happened when William McGregor came to present his ideas to his Villa colleague, Fergus Johnstone:

> My father, who was pretty shrewd in reading possibilities, banged the table with his fist. 'Mac, you've got it! You've hit the nail on the head. Work it out, man; work it out – it will be a grand success!'[266]

---

[265] He was a regular Villa supporter who kept a small eating house, or coffee shop as we know them today, and also became involved in the running of the Birmingham and District FA.
[266] Charlie Johnstone's column in The Sporting Mail 23 Dec 1910

The Aston Villa Chronicles 1874 – 1924 (and after)

William McGregor wrote to other Midland and Northern clubs, inviting them to participate in a meeting to take further the proposal of a League. With the full backing of the Villa committee, and authority to act on its behalf,[267] William McGregor succeeded in bringing together the clubs and the matter was decided upon with hardly any delay in meetings held in March and April, 1888. McGregor's own choice of title for the new organisation was the "Association Football Union", but the "Football League" is what it became.

The first season (the League then composed of 12 clubs) started in the autumn of the same year. McGregor was elected the first chairman of the Football League, which post he held (though the title changed to 'president') until he stood down in 1893. *Sport and Play* observed about him, in 1889:

> Up till the last year or two he was not known very much in sporting circles, but latterly he has blossomed out in a marvellous manner, and all who take an interest in matters footballistic cannot fail to have noticed what a name and a fame the great Scotchman has made for himself. One reason for this is that he doesn't exactly hide his light under a bushel; he keeps it steadily burning, and sometimes when a gust of passion moves the serene atmosphere in which it is wont to shine there is a fierce flare whose sputtering scintillations fail not to attract the notice of sportsmen and occasionally a few others as well, and then one is apt to get an insight into the character of the man. And, to tell the plain, unvarnished truth, it is a character that will bear investigation, as the newspaper advertisements say. There is a stratum of sound, honest purpose in it that one cannot help but admire, though now and again it seems to be touched with the baser clay of egotism and self-esteem. In all he says or does he means well, and his influence in the football world has been of a very marked kind, and has nearly always tended in the right direction.

> Aston Villa have a good deal to thank him for in more ways than one, for he saved the vessel a few years ago when it was nearly in a sinking condition – when, indeed, there were rats aboard, and a good many of them, too; and the failings which his detractors are so ready to point out should be put into the balance against his many admirable qualities as a sportsman, and they would easily kick the beam. Perhaps his greatest weakness is his susceptibility to criticism, and yet he not infrequently lays himself open to it.[268]

---

[267] Villa committee minutes 13 Mar 1888
[268] Sport and Play 21 May 1889

The Aston Villa Chronicles 1874 – 1924 (and after)

It is interesting, perhaps, that when the League was formed, it was resolved "… the averages [to determine League position] shall be taken from wins, draws and losses and *not* from the number of goals scored" (my italics). In other words, the now familiar system of points for a win and a point for a draw was *not* the initial system to be followed to determine League position. On 21 November, 1888, however, the League rule was changed so that League position became based upon 2 points for a win and 1 for a draw.

Everton – an initial member of the Football League – were to prove worthy contenders in the League and in the Cup, but, as 'The Father of the League' (William McGregor) recorded,[269] they were not one of the famed clubs before the League, but managed to get extraordinarily high 'gates':

> Everton were not a club with a history when the League was formed, but they were beginning to draw public attention by the number of spectators that found their way to Anfield Road… on Saturday afternoons. They were not asked to the preliminary meeting in London to consider the foundation of a League, but as one of the first suggestions was the pooling of gates, Everton were one of the twelve clubs invited to form the League…[270]

The selection of the original League teams created much "heart-burning at the time, especially up Small Heath and other places where ambition ran higher than ability!"[271] Before the twelve clubs were finally decided upon, the Bolton Wanderers' secretary (J. J. Bentley) wrote to 'Mac' with his suggestions, which included Mitchell's St. George's and Old Carthusians![272] But the main group of clubs were virtually self-appointed; it just required a decision on two or three clubs – and it did not take long to sort out the matter. There were late attempts to change the composition of the League, and on 17 April, there was a meeting of the newly-formed League at Manchester. What would be the twelve original clubs of the League were represented, but there were also late personal applications by another three clubs – Sheffield Wednesday, Notts Forest and Halliwell – who doubtless felt at the eleventh hour that they might be missing a good opportunity after all! But their attempts were to no avail.

---

[269] From his column in Sports Argus 17 Oct 1908
[270] By 1915, Villa, Everton and Blackburn Rovers were the only clubs that had been in the top flight from the start of the Football League.
[271] Villa News & Record 25 Mar 1911 – an article by Old Fogey
[272] 'Nomad' in Sports Argus 19 Jan 1901

The Aston Villa Chronicles 1874 – 1924 (and after)

The twelve teams initially admitted into the League were: Accrington, Aston Villa, Blackburn Rovers, Bolton Wanderers, Burnley, Derby County, Everton, Notts County, Preston North End, Stoke, West Bromwich Albion, and Wolverhampton Wanderers. It was very much a Midlands and north-west concoction.

On the matter of J. J. Bentley's proposed inclusion of Mitchell's St. George's (a team that once had the likes of Denny Hodgetts and John Devey playing for them), that, at the time, would not have been such a surprise, as 'Nomad' related in the *Sports Argus*:

> [With John Devey in their side, St. George's beat the Villa three times one season, and in the third match at Perry Barr, they won 3-0.] In the second half, Jack Devey broke away, and racing uphill in his own inimitable style, reached the backs in front of the Villa goal, and putting his foot on the ball, swung right round (a trick all his own) and was past the defenders, and in the twinkling of an eye the ball was through the posts. [That was for the second goal, and he came up with a second dose later in the half to make it 3-0.][273]

John Devey and St. George's played 'The Invincibles' – Preston North End – in the FA Cup at Deepdale, during the League's first season (1888-89), and came away with a creditable 1-1 result, causing Major Sudell to comment that it was the best game seen at Deepdale. Yes, St. George's had a fair side then, but their standing did not last too long, especially after John Devey left for the Villa. They tried again, however, to win election to the League in 1889, but they were just unsuccessful, being kept out by political voting by the preceding season's bottom four.

The matter of the original selection of twelve clubs in two areas of the country was a lot down to the concern felt about excess travel. In the north-east and in the south, however, there were very few clubs that would be thought of (at that time) as worthy of inviting, together with uncertainties about their 'grounding' – whether they were financially viable. It is also probably true to say that Southern football clubs were not yet developing in the competitive style of their cousins in the Midlands and the North, and did not begin to develop that way until Football League had shown it was not a 'one night wonder'.

One exceptional club, however, was Sunderland (in the north-east). 'Champing on the bit', the club waited on its chance, and in 1890 entered the League at the expense of Stoke. In their first season they finished above Aston Villa, and in their

---

[273] 'Nomad' in Sports Argus 13 Apr 1901, from a recollection of old times by a former St. George's player.

The Aston Villa Chronicles 1874 – 1924 (and after)

second they won the championship with some outstanding results. Until Aston Villa started their glorious run in 1893-94, Sunderland were indeed the 'team of the 1890s' and it was effectively Villa's 'double' success in 1896-97 that lifted the Villa above Sunderland in terms of achievement. Sunderland were a strong competitor to the Villa right until the First World War, in League and Cup, though Sunderland never succeeded in beating Villa in any of the Cup rounds in their many meetings during that time. William McGregor thought highly of Sunderland, calling them "The team of all the talents" in the early 1890s.

It was particularly because professionalism did not catch on in the south that southern clubs did not enter the Football League until the 1900s. It took until 1904 for the first southern representative – Woolwich Arsenal – to enter the top echelon. It was only then that the City of Birmingham ceased to be the southernmost outpost of the League's top division.

Who Was Really Responsible for the Idea of the League?

The *Athletic News*, in their editorial of the 30 October, 1888, claimed that their periodical had advocated the idea of a League some time before! William McGregor – writing from the Villa's official address at 9, Witton Road – responded to the periodical's assertion, questioning the veracity of the claim, and that letter was published in the *Athletic News*.

In reply, the *Athletic News* then pointed to their article printed on 7 June 1887 – nine months before 'Mac' had written to other clubs about the idea – which drew attention to the system of leagues as used in American baseball. The article even suggested the teams that might make up a Football League. However, the periodical continued:

> At the same time, there is no doubt that Mr. McGregor was the means of giving birth to the League. We are only too glad to see that it has been such a success.

Now, it is thought that 'Mac' and Joe Tillotson had worked on the idea of a League as per the American baseball model, but 'Mac' asserted that up until 1888, he had seldom read any athletics' journals. He, therefore, could not have derived the idea directly from such journals. It is possible, of course, that Joe Tillotson had read The *Athletic News'* article – or heard about it from someone else, and influenced 'Mac'. But, as the *Athletic News* rightly stated, whoever was the originator of the idea, 'Mac' still had the right to claim credit for putting the idea into action.

The Aston Villa Chronicles 1874 – 1924 (and after)

In any case, according to Fred Rinder (in "The Story of the Football League", published 1937-8), McGregor started canvassing and counselling advice on the matter of "fixity of fixtures" some two years before the League came about.

Reflections on the League's Success

At the onset of the League in 1888, a writer in *Sport and Play* was moved to write: "The thought often strikes me – whatever did the people do in the old winters when football was not, and the sound of the leather-kicker had not been heard in the land? What a dreary, miserable time the long winters must have been ..."[274] Well, some form of football had in fact been around for a very long time, but doubtless the writer was talking about the degree to which it had developed organisationally, and as a spectator sport.

At the end of September, 1888, the *Athletic News* reported that the fans were acquiring a real taste for League football – the championship having the affect of creating a following not unlike the FA Cup competition, the weekly proceedings now being closely followed. By January, 1889, the *Sport and Play* was also ready to give full credit to 'Mac' and Mr. Lockett (of Stoke, the Football League's first secretary) for the success of the League.

In November, 1895 – seven years since the formation of the League – 'Brum' in the *Athletic News* was able to say, with hand on his heart:

> If we ever have to come back to the old experience of 'friendly' encounters to eke out the season till the Cup ties come on, very very hard it will be for the pastime. That is why I always hail the grand old McGregor's name with thankfulness and feel grateful to his disciples for carrying on so fine a work so ably initiated.

"The Story of the Football League" (1937-8) remarked:

> McGregor's scheme was more ambitious and all-embracing than is generally imagined. ... [H]e had in mind to formulate a subsidiary competition for the twelve teams of the clubs in membership, the idea that later on, many years afterwards in fact, was crystallised in and by the formation of the Central League and the London Combination ...

The Football League continued to grow – eventually into four divisions – and in 1988 it celebrated its 100th anniversary. In 1992, however, the FA created a new

---

[274] Sport and Play 4 Sep 1888

The Aston Villa Chronicles 1874 – 1924 (and after)

league, The Premier League, which ended 104 years of the Football League's monopoly. The Football League's First Division effectively became The Premier League, but the Football League continues to administer the remainder of its former structure.

The Independent newspaper published a table of the 20 teams that had played the most top-flight League games since 1888, as at April 2007. In this table, Everton and the Villa show how well they have survived the rigours of nearly 120 years of League football, and 130 years or more since they were founded. They are the only original members of the Football League in the first 10 clubs in this table:[275]

Everton	4,058 games
Aston Villa	3,724
= Arsenal	3,673
= Liverpool	3,673
Manchester United	3,316
Manchester City	3,159
Newcastle United	3,080
Sunderland	2,960
Chelsea	2,936
Tottenham Hotspur	2,933

---

[275] 17 Apr 2007

The Aston Villa Chronicles 1874 – 1924 (and after)

14. More About Villa – and Their Neighbours

By the mid-1880s, the Villa's most famous neighbours were 'The Albion', who were soon to be followed by 'The Wolves' with the demise of the Stafford Road club, and somewhat later (in terms of fame) 'The Blues' – whose identity went through some transformation before becoming accepted as 'Birmingham' ('City' being a later appendage).

Charlie Johnstone wrote[276] that in 1877 he was at the time secretary of Saltley College F.C., when one day he received a challenge from Small Heath Alliance – an "unknown club" then. Charlie stated that their letter of challenge was headed: "We play on our own ground" – and that this declaration was proudly underlined! Indeed, the Small Heath club had that year opened their ground at Muntz Street.

On the occasion of a visit to St. Andrews by the Villa, on 21st September, 1907,[277] *The Villa News* provided some history about 'The Blues':

> Our neighbours have changed their name twice since Aston Villa first fought with them in the days of long ago. When first the fun began on the old lop-sided meadow off Coventry Road the Villa opposed a club known as the Small Heath Alliance, when Arthur James was a great player and Archie Hunter a footballer with a world-wide reputation.
>
> Later, the club cut off its tail, so to speak,[278] and first became located to the ridge beyond Bordesley. This they stuck to for some years, and a season or two ago still greater ambition dawned upon them and they blossomed out into 'Birmingham', a somewhat inclusive title, and one that seemed a bit large under the circumstances.

What happened here was that in 1903, the local government district of Aston Manor (which included Aston Villa's home) was made a distinct local authority, and it seems that the Small Heath club then decided that they may as well usurp the 'Birmingham' name for themselves!

---

[276] In his column in The Sporting Mail 22 Dec 1906
[277] That particular match turned out to be a fairly-fought classic. Played at high tempo, it was won by the Villa, 3-2. However, Blues were relegated that season but not before beating Villa in the return at Villa Park!
[278] i.e. got rid of the suffix 'Alliance'

The Aston Villa Chronicles 1874 – 1924 (and after)

As their president, Mr. Adams, stated:

> Because Aston Villa are with the newly-made borough of Aston Manor, they are no longer a Birmingham club ... therefore, Small Heath are the leading club in Birmingham.[279]

This remark brought out the following response from *Sports Argus'* 'Argus Junior':

> Aston Villa will never cease to be regarded as the premier Birmingham club all the world over. As a matter of fact, Aston Villa are more essentially a Birmingham team than Small Heath themselves!

Another *Sports Argus* comment was, "What possible benefit can it be to Birmingham, when the Small Heath club will remain the Small Heath club ... ?" Aston Manor's independent status lasted a mere eight years, however, before it was absorbed into Birmingham Corporation, in 1911, and Villa were, officially, again a Birmingham club.

When Villa played their first match against the newly-titled 'Birmingham' team in the 1905-06 season, 'Brum' stated:

> It is an open secret that while there was no local opposition to Small Heath's change of name, a great many people in their inner hearts did not approve the action. Many of the older supporters of the club did not like it because it robbed them of a title they had grown to love, while some of the Villa crowd resented the comprehensive name which Small Heath had assumed.[280]

But, apart from Villa, it was the Albion that were the main runners in the west Midlands area for quite some time, and obtained a number of trophies to prove that point! Villa and Albion, of course, played one another in three FA Cup Finals between 1887 and 1895, with Villa having the slightly better hand. If anything, however, Albion had a better overall record in the Cup between 1885 and 1895, and were famous for twice removing 'The Invincibles' (Preston North End) from the Cup tournament during their heyday. Matches between Villa and Albion, particularly in the Cup, have virtually always raised a great deal of excitement. Old Fogey once commented about the Albion:

> From the very beginning, they seemed to be the natural rivals of the Villa, and ever since they first met the Throstles have almost invariably played right at the top of their form when Aston Villa were the antagonists...

---

[279] Sports Argus 16 Jul 1904
[280] Athletic News 18 Sep 1905

The Aston Villa Chronicles 1874 – 1924 (and after)

> I have been at Stoney Lane and Perry Barr when feeling ran very high indeed, when the excitement was seething, and the sense of tension almost painful, and I have witnessed scenes at both places that were little short of pandemoniums ... [but] generally speaking, the feeling between the clubs has been of the best and most generous kind.[281]

The *Sports Argus* added to Old Fogey's comment:

> No match created such boisterous enthusiasm amongst Black Country footballers as the annual league visit of the Villa to the Albion enclosure [at Stoney Lane]. The meetings between the old rivals form an important page in the history of Association football, and it is as strange as it is true that, despite the times out of number that the clubs have antagonised each other in fair weather and in foul, on their own grounds and on foreign soil, a tussle between them having an important issue depending on it creates just as much – nay, more – excitement than did the fierce emotions of the old days, when bigoted partisanship led to many a spirited argument being settled by fisticuffs, which were in direct variance with the Marquis of Queensbury rules.[282]

The Albion's 'purple period' in the Cup during the late 1880s and early 1890s, and their early entry to the Football League, did not seem to bring them much by way of financial reward, although they had some fine players. One such fine player was winger Billy Bassett, for years an England right-winger and preferred over Villa's Charlie Athersmith. In 1896, they finished their League season in bottom place, and it was only by success in the end-of-season 'test matches' that they remained in the First Division for the next season. In an article in the *Athletic News*, 'Brum' wrote at the time:

> No matter how black the outlook may be, or how groggy the team may be going, they never lose heart, but keep on smiling and coming up round after round and year after year with a cheerful countenance, and with the firm conviction that the Throstles will some day be on the top perch.[283]

In 1899, having attained an average 'gate' of only 5,000 over the previous League season (compared to Villa's average in excess of 20,000), a subscription list was raised to revitalise the club's finances.

---

[281] Villa News & Record 23 Jan 1915
[282] Sports Argus 12 Nov 1898
[283] Athletic News 12 Oct 1896

The Aston Villa Chronicles 1874 – 1924 (and after)

Again, in January, 1905, the Albion were in a financial difficulty of a kind, this time resulting from a stand that was burnt down two months before – the club wanted to build a better replacement. The Villa contributed £105 (100 guineas) to the appeal, eliciting gratitude from the Albion's chairman. The appeal did not totally solve their problems, but by early March the creditors agreed to a stand-off for two years. However, the same month the members of the board resigned, to be replaced by a *pro tem* board including Keys and Bassett.

The Birmingham paper, the *Evening Despatch*, continued an appeal for financial help for the Albion, and the Villa again contributed through that fund, donating the proceeds of practise match attendances before the 1905-06 season.

> In the Autumn of 1894, it was noted that the Wolves were in an unhealthy financial state, and were in need of 1,000 supporters each injecting £1 into the club.

With regard to both the Albion and the Wolves, they had found themselves in Division Two by the time *The Villa News* was launched (in 1906), and *The Villa News* paid them the compliment and hope that both teams would be back to where they rightfully belonged – in the First Division. Birmingham would follow them in relegation within a couple of seasons, although in 1905-06 The Blues had finished marginally higher in the League than The Villa! For quite some seasons, the Villa were the west Midlands only representative team.

From the Villa's Minutes

At the committee meeting on 11 September, 1902, the meeting was informed that the Villa, Wolves and the Albion had agreed that there should be a mutual arrangement to allow free access to the directors and players of each other's clubs. The Board agreed, and asked George Ramsay to make appropriate arrangements for this to take effect.

In season 1906-07, Birmingham protested that Villa had not fielded a strong side in a Lord Mayor's Charity Shield tie. In those days, playing for that Shield was a serious affair, and a matter of local pride. It was a protest which called upon Villa to reply in an appropriate way, and this they did,[284] particularly to emphasise that all players representing the Villa in that match were either playing in the first-team regularly or had played for the first-team at some point in the season, and were selected according to the club's stated policy at the beginning of the season of

---

[284] As reported in Villa News & Record at the time.

The Aston Villa Chronicles 1874 – 1924 (and after)

drawing on 20 specific players.

The Villa News' editor commented: "I am bound to say that I think they [the Villa] did right in keeping particularly disabled men out of their team when they played Small Heath – beg pardon, Birmingham!"

From its inception in 1906 (and lasting several seasons), *The Villa News* maintained a policy of including considerable information about Villa's neighbours' fixtures, results and exploits. In its first edition, *The Villa News* made this comment about The Blues' progress with regard to opening their new ground at St. Andrews:

> It is a real pleasure to be able to comment on the enterprise of the Birmingham Club's directorate, and we trust that the success achieved at Coventry Road will be many times repeated on their new ground.

Having for the first time brought their balance sheet into the black in 1902,[285] Birmingham developed into being a forward-looking club, but perhaps they sometimes over-reached themselves! They opened what was then their new ground at St. Andrews in the middle of the 1906-07 season, but it was not long before the club was relegated. Financial troubles haunted the club once more, and by the end of 1910 the club was £5,000 in debt.[286] It was a case of Birmingham's neighbours having to dig deep into their pockets to provide some relief for the club. Villa donated £250, and George Robey (the entertainer and amateur footballer) and the Birmingham Hippodrome all helped in this regard.

The *Midland Express* in 1902 paid homage to Villa and their accomplishments in trophy-winning, but also wrote:

> Above all, Aston Villa have been famous for their charity and generosity. Rarely has an appeal to them by a sporting organisation in need of funds been made in vain. They have done much for the charities of Birmingham and District ... [and] quite recently the handsome treatment of poor struggling Warwickshire [County Cricket Club] gained favourable recognition.[287]

Edgbaston had been selected as a venue for the forthcoming Test Match between England and Australia in 1902, and the WCCC – wanting to improve the Edgbaston facilities – had visited Villa Park in February, 1902 to view the design of the Villa's stands. As a result of this visit, E.B. Holmes (the designer of those stands) was

---

[285] Sports Argus 21 Sep 1901 (Small Heath's prediction they were to be out of debt)
[286] As oft-stated, these were then big sums of money.
[287] Midland Express 13 Dec 1902

The Aston Villa Chronicles 1874 – 1924 (and after)

appointed by the WCCC to make a design for Edgbaston. Villa also offered WCCC the loan of the moveable seating that Villa used on their cycle track.

In January, 1903, the Villa played the Corinthians to raise money for the WCCC, and succeeded in raising £160.

15. 1888-1891: Finding Their Feet in the League

This was the first season of the Football League. Its commencement had a roll-on affect on a number of sides that had been hanging on to a past reputation; the Old 'Uns – not long-ago Villa's contemporaries – withdrew from professionalism and it was not long before they went out of existence.[288] By the following January, the provincial pathfinders in the FA Cup, Blackburn Olympic, decided on the same strategy: to give up professionalism.

Aston Unity – whose fight for local supremacy began at about the same time as the Old 'Uns, and who were an early opponent of the Villa – simply gave up on football, preferring to concentrate on cricket, with their players migrating to the Villa *en masse*, to play in Villa's reserve team! Walsall Town and Walsall Swifts combined to form Walsall Town Swifts.

More significantly, Small Heath Alliance were worried by an impending financial disaster, and by September became the country's first football club to become a limited company. In the process they became known simply as 'Small Heath' and elected to play in the Football Combination (with Walsall Town Swifts).

Season 1888-89 : Into the League – And another Crisis!
League position: *Runner-up*; **FA Cup:** *3rd Round.*

As a warm-up for their first incursion into the League, the Villa played two matches. The first was against a Birmingham and District FA team on 21 August, when the Villa won through a solitary goal from Green, but the Villa were hampered by a shoulder injury to Archie Hunter that caused him to be absent for most of the second half.

The second preparatory match (on 4 September) was a match against Archie's home town club of Ayr, whom Villa beat, 10-1. That sounds like a happy event for the Villa, but it was the same day that the Villa faithful heard of the death of Andy Hunter, back in June. "The news of his death cast quite a sadness over the Villa ground on Saturday", wrote 'Brum' in the *Athletic News*.

---

[288] Though the club name was reconstituted twice more – "The Old Uns" (Steve Carr)

The Aston Villa Chronicles 1874 – 1924 (and after)

The 'news' had only now filtered through from the other side of the world, and for the moment, the news had an understandable affect on Archie Hunter. He missed the opening League game, and had to be prevailed upon by the committee to start playing.

Villa's season proved to be a good one, finishing runner-up. Proud Preston's season proved to be a lot better, as they went through the whole season without losing, and won the 'double' – League and FA Cup. That was a tremendous achievement in the first season of the League, although the League consisted of only 12 clubs at that stage. It is interesting that the unofficial league tables that had been concocted by the press in the previous two or three years came to resemble – for the first few teams at least – the final position of the League in its first season. Preston and the Villa had been unofficially regarded as being the top two English teams, and here was the official proof of that.

However, no matter how they strove – the Villa even held Preston to a draw on their ground – Villa spent the whole season in second place, and apart from the opening eight or ten games, did not come close to making any impression on Preston's lead. Villa became simply the best of the rest.

The Season's Play

September, 1888

With the news of his brother's death, it is understandable that Archie Hunter did not make an appearance in his side's first League match at **Wolverhampton Wanderers**' ground on September 8, 1888.

Villa: *Warner; Cox, Coulton; Yates, H.Devey, Dawson;*
Albert Brown, Green, Allen, Bat Garvey, Hodgetts.

The Villa were the first to score – but into their own goal, when the ball inadvertently screwed in off Cox's legs – the Villa's first own goal in the League! Villa's equaliser came soon after - *The Midland Athlete* described Villa's goal in the 1-1 draw:

"As half time drew near, Brown, Garvey, and Green broke away, and Garvey again, dribbling well into goal, shot. Green was in the way, but the ball came out to Brown who passed it in the centre, and Green getting it onto the side of his foot sent it against the goal post and it glided through the Wanderers goal, making the score equal."

The Aston Villa Chronicles 1874 – 1924 (and after)

The *Athletic News* declared that "the game was brimful of excitement from first to last…"

As far as individuals were concerned, Bat Garvey was noted as having greatly improved, and Hodgetts and Brown did some clever work; but the severe injury that Albert Allen sustained towards the end of the previous season was clearly still affecting him both physically and in confidence. Green was "too much all over the shop", perhaps missing his captain, who was usually able to keep this temperamental player in line and get the best out of him.

It had been stated in the press that Archie Hunter would not play as frequently, but in fact he was back for the next match, at the expense of Garvey, after the Villa committee had prevailed upon him to play. Archie remained in his customary centre-forward position for virtually the rest of the season.

The first League match at Perry Barr was an apparently decisive win, 5-1, against **Stoke**. A new signing, Dixon (from Small Heath), replaced Dawson.

Villa: *Warner; Cox, Coulton; Yates, H.Devey, Dixon;*
Albert Brown, Green, Hunter, Allen, Hodgetts.

[From the *Athletic News*] It was not long before "Archie Hunter distinguished himself by hopping around about half-a-dozen opponents" before providing Denny Hodgetts with a shooting chance that skimmed the bar. Nevertheless, a hard-fought game found Stoke leading 1-0 at half-time, after taking the lead on 20 minutes.

Dixon, "with a rattling long shot equalised amidst much applause", and the Villa came down yet again to score through Albert Brown. But Stoke were not yet finished and threatened awhile. This danger having passed, "Hunter, with a shot like a streak of greased lightning, scored a third goal." The Villa then went on to win decisively.

The reporter stated how Hunter's presence decidedly re-invigorated Villa's forward play, and he played a game reminiscent of his old style.

The next week, **Everton** played their first game at Perry Barr, and thus started the most frequent competitive fixture between two clubs in the world. In this match, there was in fact a world of difference in the playing style and approach of the two teams, and Villa would have won more convincingly but for the Everton's determined defence, which, however, often incited aggression rather than football. For Villa, Ashmore came into goal as Warner's hand had been injured in the Stoke match.

The Aston Villa Chronicles 1874 – 1924 (and after)

[From *Sport and Play*] Everton had signed the former Preston star, Nick Ross, and he was given quite an ovation on his appearance.

After a while, "a dashing run on the left brought the ball [downfield], Dennis [Hodgetts] centring to Allen, who overran it, but Archie just touched it to the tall forward again, and a regular whizzer caused the dense crowd behind the goal to indulge in an idyllic Perry Barr warble, and everybody knew for a mile around that the Villa were one in front!"

"A good deal of unpleasantness ensued after this, and the referee was shouted at [in protest by the Villa supporters] … What made it worse was that the Everton men were indulging in some mean and paltry tricks … and this roused the ire of some of [the crowd] to an extent that was little short of madness, and at one time the yelling and hooting was simply awful!" Villa's play changed the mood for the better, especially as the Villa had the upper hand.

"From the style of the Villa play it seemed decidedly unlucky for them to cross over with only one goal to the good, and yet it seemed as if that would happen, when a minute or two before the whistle sounded, a splendid run by Tom Green and Albert Brown woke up the spectators". As a result of this movement, "Hodgetts, dashing up at sprinting pace, cannoned through a beauty!"

Two up, the Villa besieged the Everton goal after half-time, five shots in rapid succession being repelled. The Everton keeper (Smalley) was playing out of his skin, and the Villa supporters loved his performance!

"With an occasional break-away by Everton, this sort of thing went on for nearly an hour", until an Evertonian called ("Dirty") Dick took over. "After a bit of a struggle in the corner, Hodgetts had smartly passed the ball to Archie Hunter, and was racing past Dick when the Evertonian deliberately kicked him in the stomach. This was a little too much even for the imperturbability of Master Dennis, and Dick received a crashing right-hander full on the mouth … It was some minutes before the game was resumed."

The incident had a negative affect on the Villa, as their game now fell away and allowed Everton a goal that they scarcely looked like getting earlier on. Indeed, it looked at one stage as though it was a question of how many the Villa would score. However, Villa won, 2-1.

Harry Devey was described as "one of the best half-backs the Villa ever had" – but was hurt in this match.

A third successive home match saw Villa up against an old rival – **Notts County**. Alas, the County were no longer the side they were. Despite the continued appearance of the giant Gunn, they were languishing. Their first problem seemed to be want of urgency, as the match did not start till 4 o'clock, due to their dallying. If they thought that might put off the Villa, then they were sadly wrong as Villa put

The Aston Villa Chronicles 1874 – 1924 (and after)

them out of sight – by 9 goals to 1! Two of the goals were beautiful headers by Hodgetts and Green. "In scoring his", reported the *Athletic News*, "Dennis caught the ball fair and square on his nasal again, but it withstood the shock!" Allen scored a hat-trick in this game, with Archie and Green weighing in with two each.

Villa's first month in the League ended with three wins and a draw in their four matches, scoring 17 goals against 4.

October, 1888

The Villa now made their first trip to **Everton** – at Anfield (as it was then), for their return match. There was a 10,000 gate for this match, as opposed to only 3,000 at leaders Preston, and 3,000 at West Bromwich Albion, but Everton (as 'Mac' had noted) seemed to have a large following since before the League days.

[From the *Athletic News*] "When the Villans appeared, they looked startled at the cordiality of the cheers, which were prolonged until the last of the players had entered the arena." And, before the match, there was an interesting meeting between the extreme antagonists of the previous meeting, Dick (of Everton) and Hodgetts. "Hodgetts looked up Dick, and the two shook hands just as warmly as we may imagine Stanley greeting Livingstone in the wilds of Africa. It fairly fetched the house down, the people cheering to the echo!"

The Villa were surprised by the tenacity of Everton in their determination to win, and it was thanks to Jimmy Warner who kept the score down to an Everton goal in each half. The Villa strove to get back into the game, but it was just not their day, and they lost 0-2.

Whatever was wrong that day, it did cause William McGregor to suggest at the following committee meeting "that the men master the throw-in according to rule". Probably the reason for defeat was a bit more profound, as a letter of complaint published in *Sport and Play* (signed 'A.Member') suggested that the committee did not know what it was doing to send the team to play a friendly at Nottingham on the Thursday, and then to travel to Everton on the Saturday.

Well, the committee seemed to think that it was the team that needed adjusting and not themselves, as they introduced their latest signing, Archie Goodall, a former Preston star, for the next match. He came in at centre-half at the expense of Harry Devey, a move that caused not inconsiderable surprise. This signing actually created a problem with regard to Goodall's status, as it turned out that the rules of the time would not allow him to play for Villa as a professional, and he therefore played this match as an amateur. After a few weeks, the matter was rectified. Burton also came

The Aston Villa Chronicles 1874 – 1924 (and after)

in to make his League début, and became a regular.

Against the great Cup-winning team of the 1880s, **Blackburn Rovers**, they fielding their strongest side at Perry Barr, Villa's team was:

> *Warner; Cox, Coulton; Yates, Goodall, Burton;*
> *Albert Brown, Green, Hunter, Allen, Hodgetts.*

[From the *Athletic News*] It was not until after 20 or 30 minutes that the Villa exerted their authority on this match, and then two goals – a header by Green and a long shot from the wing by Goodall – gave Villa a 2-0 half-time lead.

The second half began with the Villa "storming the Blackburn goal", and this resulted in a Brown header gaining the third goal. Before the cheers had hardly died away, Allen took a delightful pass from Hunter to notch the fourth. Then, despite a goal pegged back by the Rovers, Villa scored two more fine goals through Hunter and Allen, thus running out easy winners, 6-1.

Goodall, despite previous fears about his suitability, "was of immense service to his side."

A Blackburn supporter, before the match started, described his side as "champions of the world", but long before the end, the man had left! However, the Blackburn team declared, prophetically, that they would take it out of the Villa in the return match.

As Archie Goodall's professional status was in query, and his position not resolved till mid-November, the half-back line was re-jigged yet again for the next match (away at **Bolton Wanderers**). Harry Devey was not left out again that season:

> **Villa**: *Warner; Cox, Coulton; Burton, Harry Devey, Yates;*
> *Albert Brown, Green, Hunter, Allen, Hodgetts.*

Thanks to Jimmy Warner and the rest of Villa's defence, Villa won 3-2 after coming back from 1-2 behind. It was described as one of the most exciting matches seen at Bolton's ground.

Apart from the earlier match at Everton, the Villa were piling on the points and the goals in an effort to keep pace with Preston. Villa's next match was at home against **Accrington**, who had just become the first side to take a point off Preston that season, and had also prevented Preston's free-scoring forwards from netting.

A Remarkable Comeback

[From the *Athletic News*] Accrington took the lead after only 5 minutes after a fine bit of passing, but, soon after, Brown planted a corner onto Green's head, the equaliser producing another yell, more vociferous than before. But again Accrington scored, also via a corner, to lead 1-2.

Then the Villa warmed to their game. It was not long before Hodgetts sent in a shot that seemed to have crossed the line before the keeper punched it out, but the referee refused to award a goal, despite "a protracted discussion" about it.

Accrington were playing well, pushing the Villa defence into producing their best performance, and "evoked rounds of applause" for their display.

Still 1-2 down at the start of the second half, Villa's fans thought that with the slope advantage, the match would go Villa's way, but not a bit of it; Accrington scored a third!

With 20 minutes to go, the home team put on all steam, and Brown beat the keeper "with a real beauty." Hodgetts then scored the equaliser "amidst an almost indescribable yell of excitement... [which was] nothing compared with the din that arose a few minutes later, when, out of a surging mass of human frames, Tom Green slid the ball through... [By 4-3] the Villa had won one of the finest games ever witnessed at Perry Barr."

A Canadian Visit

On the following Monday, Villa met a touring Canadian side at Perry Barr. *Sport and Play* noted that a lot of new faces turned up to watch in curiosity. For them, there was none of the feverish interest as held by the regular Villa supporter – these new viewers came to view with calm and deliberate detachment.

At the end of the game "a mild-mannered, meek-eyed old gentleman, who must have learnt the game about the time Napoleon crossed the Alps, came to the reporter's stand at the finish of the game, and said, 'If you please, which is the Villa team, and did the Canadians win?'"

For the record, the Canadians started the match in a very uncertain way, and though losing 4-1 at half-time, they considerably surprised many, though the Villa would hardly have been said to be producing their best.

The Hon. R. Lyttelton was the referee, whose family of players from Frankley were referred to in the history of the early days.

> [He] looked considerably bowed down, and whose walking stick had rather a hard time in propping him up at the finish, and he mopped his aristocratic brow with a grave and thoughtful air, while watching the gambols of the young lambkins under his care.

The Aston Villa Chronicles 1874 – 1924 (and after)

November, 1888

Away games proved to be the Villa's Achilles Heel, as shown in the next match when they met a bottom-but-one **Stoke** side. In driving rain – and not showing good form – they played out a 1-1 draw. In fact, there was some suggestion that Stoke deserved to win.

The following match, however, was a big test – away at leaders **Preston**, who were still unbeaten, and had drawn only one match. They were also fresh from a 7-0 drubbing of Notts County, away from home, the previous week.

A good crowd assembled at Deepdale to witness the clash of the Titans. Archie Goodall was now a fully-fledged professional, and was selected to play against his former club.

Villa: *Warner; Cox, Coulton; Goodall, Harry Devey, Yates; Albert Brown, Green, Hunter, Allen, Hodgetts.*

Holding the Invincibles

[From the *Athletic News*] "The North End started the game uphill, the strong east wind which blew across the ground rather favouring the Villa. Both sides immediately set to with dash and determination, the bulk of the spectators, as a matter of course, working themselves to a high pitch of excitement, which found vent in a mighty roar of applause when, at the end of two minutes, [Archie Goodall's brother John] Goodall (from a throw-in) scored for the Deepdalians, the Villa backs having impeded Warner's view. Some exceedingly clever play ensued by both sides … Archie Goodall came in for a certain amount of chaff from various occupants of the stand.

"In the second half, quite a transformation came over the proceedings. The Villa had now to face the hill, with the disadvantage of the wind, but to the astonishment of the onlookers they showed improved form, while the opponents, in a corresponding degree, deteriorated.

"After a relatively brief period of aggression by Preston, the Villa, in excellent combination, greatly harassed the home defence, and two minutes from the end they were rewarded with a goal, a dropping shot from Archie Goodall being headed through by Green.

"A memorable game [that finished 1-1]. The Villa greatly impressed the Prestonians – every man appeared to be in his right position, and in the passing, which was sometimes long, and sometimes short."

The Aston Villa Chronicles 1874 – 1924 (and after)

This was the status of the top two in the Football League following this match:

Top places in the Football League	Pld	Home W D L F A	Away W D L F A	Overall W D L F A	Pts
1 Preston North End	10	5 1 0 24 6	3 1 0 14 2	8 2 0 38 8	18
2 **Aston Villa**	10	5 0 0 26 7	1 3 1 6 7	6 3 1 30 12	15

From these details, it is clear where Villa's weakness lay – it was their away form. But their achievement at Preston belied that form and for the moment kept Preston within hailing distance. However, at the end of October, and after eight matches, the difference between the two teams had only been two points. Hopes of catching Preston soon evaporated.

The next week, **Blackburn** did to the Villa what they had threatened after the Perry Barr encounter – much to the pleasure of the Lancashire-based *Athletic Times*, whose local reporter asked the printer to *"put the score in heavy type!"* Rovers beat the Villa, 1-5, though it had only been 1-1 at half-time. The Rovers were much improved since the Perry Barr encounter.

The unceasingly good form of Preston, and the (to-date) inconsistent away form of the Villa, had put the championship in the Preston direction. The Villans were not, however, prepared to give up on the matter. The next five matches kept the Villa very much in the hunt.

> *From the Villa's Minutes*
>
> Denny Hodgetts always had an up-and-down relationship with his captain and the Villa committee. Following the Preston match, it was reported that "Hodgettts had changed his position in the Preston match without the captain's sanction, and when asked to go back, he was impertinent." It was also of concern that Hodgetts had a "disinclination to play in Thursday's practise game."

That 'disturbance' between Hodgetts and 'Dirty' Dick in the match against Everton earlier in the season had its consequence. Both players were now suspended – Dick for two months, and Hodgetts for one month. When he arrived at Perry Barr to view the upcoming **Wolves** match, Denny received a sympathetic burst of cheers from the Villa faithful, and was the first man to rush in and give congratulations to the team after they had won, 2-1, in front of a disappointing crowd.

[From the *Athletic News*] To compensate for Denny's absence, Goodall was moved into the forward line, but his ideas and execution did not work at all

The Aston Villa Chronicles 1874 – 1924 (and after)

well, to the extent that the other Archie (Hunter) was continually coaching him. "Keep the ball down!" was the repeated cry of the captain – that being the only way to play in the prevailing small gale.

It was, however, Goodall that scored both Villa's goals (one in each half), but it was not a smooth running Villa performance against a determined and improved Wolves' side, until mid-way through the second half when a fine movement involving virtually all the forwards led to Villa's second goal. This produced "cheers both loud and long."

December, 1888

Essentially the same team then went to bottom-placed **Notts County**. County brought in three new players for this match, and in fact showed improved form, but the Villa cantered through this one, 4 goals to 2, in front of only 1,500 and in miserable weather. The Goodall-Allen left-wing partnership was now settling down a bit.

At **Accrington**, Villa's opponents again performed well, and at half-time the score was 1-1. Green was mentioned for his "circus trick of catching the ball with his heel and kicking it over his head into goal." Despite both sides hitting the woodwork in the second half, the score remained 1-1 at the finish.

The Villa then won their next two home matches 4-2, against **Burnley** and **Derby County**, but it was reported that the Villa looked stale in the Derby match, despite the match result. Perhaps closer to the truth was that the players had been frozen, as it was clearly a very cold day. *Sport and Play* said, "The freezing air seemed to get at you all over, and the stamping of feet went on without intermission."

The unceasingly good form of Preston, and the (to-date) inconsistent away form of the Villa, had long put the championship in the Preston direction. The Villans were not, however, prepared to give up on the matter. The results of the next five matches would in most seasons have kept the Villa very much in the hunt, having lost none and won four, but as 1888 came to an end, the top of the League table now read:

Top places in the Football League	Pld	Home W	D	L	F	A	Away W	D	L	F	A	Overall W	D	L	F	A	Pts
1 Preston North End	18	9	1	0	35	6	6	2	0	29	6	15	3	0	64	12	33
2 Aston Villa	16	8	0	0	36	12	2	4	2	12	15	10	4	2	48	27	24

Despite the Villa's haul of points and goals in December, and that Preston had played two games more, Villa's challenge for the championship was now clearly evaporating against Preston's remorseless surge; they were clearly head and shoulders above the rest of the League members and the League season of 22 matches was nearly finished.

January, 1889

There seemed to be something awry when the Villa next went to **Burnley**. The first hint was a remark made by the *Athletic News*, which stated that the Villa arrived late, that they started play with eight players, but were supplemented by two more within ten minutes. The absentee was Archie Hunter, of all players. *Sport and Play* elaborated a little:

> The Villa went up to Burnley after a wretched scramble for players and received a dreadful hiding of four goals to none [with ten players].

Old Fogey then vented his feelings a little more – the initial arrival of eight Villa players at this match being the matter of special concern:

> Will some kind friend tell me what has come over the Villa? There is evidently something wrong that wants righting, and if they go on much longer in the loose and careless manner they have been doing for the past three weeks, they will come down with a rush from the high position which they, at present, occupy in the football world. I hear of differences between the committee and some of the players and relations between the parties at the present time are reported to be strained ...

The Aston Villa Chronicles 1874 – 1924 (and after)

> ***Trouble in the Committee***
>
> That there were difficulties amongst some Villans became apparent when William McGregor wrote his letter of resignation as hon. treasurer, dated the previous 29 October.[289] He cited medical reasons for the resignation, but there had been an earlier intimation of resignation that presumably must have been withdrawn on receipt of assurances, but this time, using medical reasons, he was clearly determined to withdraw. As was usually the case, his resignation was "left on the table" for a while, but was accepted in November. Mr. Whitehouse replaced him as honorary treasurer.
>
> At a stormy Special General Meeting on 23 November, the following took place:
>
>> Mr. Jeffries, in a lengthy speech, said he feared there were differences between the committee and Mr. McGregor, [then] referred to the newspaper paragraphs and suggested that a commission should be appointed to enquire into the matter.
>>
>> Billy Mason then asked Mr. Clamp [chair of committee] if there were any differences. Mr. Clamp's explanation was "considered satisfactory."
>
> However, 'Mac' certainly was not so unwell that he still didn't have ideas for the future of the Villa, and these plans soon transpired. Clearly they had something to do with the matter of differences of view between members of the committee.
>
> *The ensuing happenings are presented in a section on 'Villa Business' at the end of this season's report.*

In the match against **Bolton Wanderers** at Perry Barr, the Villa's cares were cast away (temporarily, at least):

An Extraordinary Finish

[From the *Athletic News*] Until the last 20 minutes, this was a tight game, but the Villa were invincible in those last minutes. The Villa had opened the scoring, then Bolton equalised and had the best of it up until half-time. Villa then re-took the lead, but thanks to Warner punching a shot onto a forward's chest, Bolton again equalised. Bolton then upset themselves by scoring an own goal, and were so disgusted at this that at one point the team appeared ready to leave the pitch! From this point, the Villa dominated the proceedings, and won 6-2.

---

[289] In the Villa minutes.

The Aston Villa Chronicles 1874 – 1924 (and after)

West Bromwich Albion visited Perry Barr the next week when the Villa won 2-0. The match was not an inspiring one, however, being very much locked up in midfield. The return match was played the following week, but a smaller crowd saw a much more interesting match:

[From the *Athletic News*] Within a few minutes, Albion were two-up, and, before long, three up! "The delight of the Throstles knew no bounds. They warbled in their own sweet way till it must have been awfully tantalising to the Birmingham contingent."

Villa were playing miserably, until Hunter managed to pull a goal back, and 1-3 is how it stood at half-time.

The second half was quite a different story, with Hodgetts' header reducing the arrears again, and this was soon followed by the equaliser from Tom Green – a real beauty. The Villa went all out for a winner, but they were denied, and the match finished 3-3. Goodall and Hunter were brilliant.

February, 1889

The first round of the FA Cup brought down a Lancashire club to Perry Barr that happened to have the name of **Witton**. Clearly feeling close to home, they had the confidence to come back from 2-0 down to tie at half-time, 2-2, before Green scored what proved to be the winner early in the second half.

With the championship decided, **Preston** came to Perry Barr for their return match – Villa's last but one League match of the season. There were great efforts made by the Villa to prevent the crowd trouble of the previous year – security was heavily in evidence. Weather-wise, it was a bitterly cold frosty day, with a thin layer of frozen snow on the pitch.

Villa: *Warner; Goodall, Cox; Burton, Harry Devey, Yates;*
Albert Brown, Green, Hunter, Allen, Hodgetts.

[From the *Athletic News*] After a while adjusting to the playing conditions, there was some brilliant play on each side – "nothing could have been finer than the splendid machine-like movements of the Prestonians and the earnestness with which the Villans went about their business." One clever and dangerous attack by Preston was averted by Goodall, who was by this time playing at full-back (his fifth playing position since joining the Villa). "[Harry] Devey helped the sphere down again, and a fine concerted run between the whole of the Villa forwards drew forth a hearty round of applause and cries of 'shoot', 'shoot', 'shoot' were heard in all directions." But it was not to be against the sound Preston defence.

The Aston Villa Chronicles 1874 – 1924 (and after)

Goal-less at half-time, the second half started with a bang, with Preston scoring almost from the off, Warner being beaten by a fast hot shot. Villa, startled, came back at Preston for some while, but it was Preston who scored next, for their second. The 'goal' was hotly disputed, it being considered offside, but the referee refused to budge.

The Villa had been as good as Preston in the first 30 minutes, but then fell away, with Hodgetts being the biggest disappointment.

> Preston were now considered "the best team in the world" as they continued on, undefeated, for the rest of the season, and won both major tournaments – the first club to win 'the double'. It would not be too long before the Villa would more than equal their achievement.

The second round of the FA Cup was against **Derby County** at Perry Barr.

[From the *Athletic News*] In very wintry conditions, the match turned out to be very exciting. After Villa had opened the account through Hunter, after fine work by Allen and Hodgetts, Derby quickly responded, and before too long had scored twice to take the lead, and it could have been more but for Warner and his defence. Thanks to them, Hunter was able to set matters square before half-time, with a wonderful screw-shot.

The Derby keeper stood in the way of Villa's bombardment in the second half! "Nothing has ever been seen like it at Perry Barr this season. The Villa were shooting and playing with great brilliancy and dash, but there stood the little man (he is only a dot!) with the red cap to stem the tide of all their rushes …"

At length, "Hodgetts was through, along with the leather, the keeper and half-a-dozen other players. A great display of struggling limbs was seen, from which the unfortunate keeper emerged somewhat damaged."

Villa eventually ran out with further goals to win 5-3, Derby's one further score coming from an own goal.

> Albert Brown was selected for England to play in the England vs Ireland match. He was considered[290] to be one of the few consistent Villa players that season, and one of the best right-wingers in the country.

---

[290] *Sport and Play* 19 Feb 1889

The Aston Villa Chronicles 1874 – 1924 (and after)

March, 1889

Having suffered a 1-5 reverse at **Blackburn** in the League earlier that season, Villa were drawn away to meet Blackburn Rovers in the third round of the FA Cup – and proceeded to lose heavily again – *very* heavily, by 1-8! This score remains the Villa's biggest-ever competitive defeat.

Villa: *Warner; Thomas, Cox; Yates, H.Devey, Burton; Albert Brown, Green, Hunter, Allen, Hodgetts.*

Old Fogey recalled that match:

> It was one of the most miserable afternoons I ever spent, and it was the only occasion, I believe, when William McGregor was not known to smile at a football match. 'Twas bitterly cold and before the game started our spirits were below zero, for it was known that, with about two exceptions, the team was a brigade of crocks, while the Rovers were reputed to be in the pink of condition, and they proved beyond question that they were as frisky as young colts, and as clever as they were swift and strong – as you may judge by the aforesaid score ...
>
> If it had not been for strong right arm of that gallant custodian [James Warner] and that splendid centre half-back [Harry Devey] ... the disaster would have been even more prodigious. There were attempts to be merry on the homeward journey but all the efforts in that direction resulted in lethargy and gloom.[291]

According to Archie Hunter, the performance was mainly down to serious foot injuries that he (Archie) and Tom Green had sustained beforehand, and yet they were obliged to play. The team in general, however, was in a dispirited mood.

Villa's last League match of the season, with Hunter missing (unwell), was at **Derby County**, where Derby gained adequate revenge for their Cup defeat by winning 2-5.

On 12 March it was reported that there was a visit of American baseballers, and that they would be playing at Edgbaston. There had been a visit in 1874, which had not left an abiding impression.

By 15 March, the Villa called a halt to all remaining friendly matches, as there had been a number of "accidents" that had befallen the team of late. The Villa did

---

[291] Villa News & Record 22 Feb 1908 (by Old Fogey').

The Aston Villa Chronicles 1874 – 1924 (and after)

continue to compete in the Birmingham Cup, however, but by virtue of the fact that they were a League side, they entered the competition at the quarter-final stage. Villa won the competition yet again – this time beating Wolves 2-0 in the Final, which was – strangely enough – held at Perry Barr. The Villa were entitled by the press as "Champions of the Midlands."

The Football League 1888-89 Top Places	Pld	Home W D L F A	Away W D L F A	Overall W D L F A	Pts
1 Preston North End	22	10 1 0 39 7	8 3 0 35 8	18 4 0 74 15	40
2 Aston Villa	22	10 0 1 44 16	2 5 4 17 27	12 5 5 61 43	29
3 Wolverhampton Wanderers	22	8 2 1 30 14	4 2 5 20 23	12 4 6 50 37	28
4 Blackburn Rovers	22	7 4 0 44 22	3 2 6 22 23	10 6 6 66 45	26

1888-89 League and FA Cup Results			
Sep	8th A Wolves	1-1	
	15th H Stoke	5-1	
	22nd H Everton	2-1	
	29th H Notts County	9-1	
Oct	6th A Everton	0-2	10000
	13th H Blackburn Rovers	6-1	5000
	20th A Bolton Wanderers	3-2	8000
	27th H Accrington	4-3	
Nov	3rd A Stoke	1-1	
	10th A Preston North End	1-1	10000
	17th A Blackburn Rovers	1-5	8000
	24th H Wolves	2-1	5000
Dec	8th A Notts County	4-2	1500
	15th A Accrington	1-1	3000
	22nd H Burnley	4-2	
	29th H Derby County	4-2	
Jan	5th A Burnley	0-4	
	12th H Bolton Wanderers	6-2	
	19th H West Bromwich A	2-0	10000
	26th A West Bromwich A	3-3	6000
Feb	2nd H Witton (FAC)	3-2	
	9th H Preston North End	0-2	
	16th H Derby Cty (FAC)	5-3	
Mar	2nd A Blackburn R (FAC)	1-8	
	9th A Derby County	2-5	

Explanation of this Results table

In this season's table – and in the equivalent table of each subsequent season – the right-hand side column contains the number of spectators present (where a figure has been provided). These figures will usually be an estimate provided by the match report, but in important matches it will be an accurate figure – in which case the figure shown will not be in just thousands; the junior digits will contain a non-zero figure. e.g. 48010 instead of 48000.

End of Season Postscripts

The Villa did finish as League runner-up, but the second half of the season did not have much going for it. Added to that there was clearly some poor feeling running through the club, which perhaps started as one matter and then built up to something more.

The Aston Villa Chronicles 1874 – 1924 (and after)

The Villa had been talking to Archie Goodall about his future at Villa, he having provided valuable assistance to the club, but it transpired that Archie's older brother John (at Preston) had other plans. In partnership, they were to open an inn at Derby, and play for Derby County. Though Archie made some attempt to persuade John to throw his lot in with the Villa, the argument went John's way, so that Villa lost Archie to Derby. On 15 April, the Villa presented Archie with a gold medal for his services.

Also on 15 April, 'Brum' (in the *Athletic News*) wrote a 'call' to Messrs. Albutt, Clamp, Ramsay and Co., the Villa committee. "Why not have an annual dinner? – even the poorest clubs do!"

> At present there is too much exclusiveness about the club's way of doing things, and I am inclined to think that a little less business formality and just a little more sociability would tend to establish a better feeling all round.

The *Athletic News* (on 29 April), reflecting on Villa's play since the preceding Christmas, noted:

> [The Villa] seem to have abandoned that quick close passing which used to be one of their chief characteristics, and adopted an entirely different style of play, which, though it may be ornamental, is by no means objective ...

Villa Business

It will be recalled that there were business matters reported during the season (in January), but on 24 December, 1888, *Sport and Play* had already published the following letter:

> Sir – We beg to state on behalf of the Aston Villa Committee that we know nothing whatever of the proposal to convert the club into a limited company, the committee having first heard of such proposal through the medium of the *Birmingham Daily Mail* of the 21st inst.
>
> (Signed)
>
> Chairman
>
> Hon. Treasurer
>
> Secretary

There – there was clearly something smouldering at the club, and an indication for the resignation of William McGregor the previous October. 'Mac' was clearly determined to bring better organisation and efficiency into the club, as he had done with the formation of the Football League. A development was reported in *Sport*

The Aston Villa Chronicles 1874 – 1924 (and after)

and Play on 29 January:

> Last Monday night, Mr. McGregor attended the meeting of the Committee and explained to them the details of his scheme for converting the Villa into a limited liability company and they were very fully discussed, after which it was arranged that a general meeting should be called and the matter laid before them.
>
> [Until the general meeting,] Mr. McGregor is going to hammer away at his favourite project, and his very persistency will probably carry him through. [Part of the proposal was that no shareholder would hold more than five shares.]

On 5 February, *Sport and Play* reported on the Special General Meeting that had taken place (on 31 January). The journal expressed:

> ... surprise and gratification at seeing so many keen adherents of Aston Villa – gentlemen who appear to be really anxious for the welfare of the club.

The meeting had been chaired by Billy Mason, and George Ramsay soon read a letter from the president, James Hinks, that started: "I cannot see any way to remain connected with the Aston Villa Football Club if converted into a company...", and offered his resignation. Stating that Mr. Hinks' letter lacked appreciation of the opinions of others, Billy Mason called on William McGregor to present his case, stating that the matter coming from such a source was itself a great recommendation. The case was indeed presented, bringing forth all manner of impassioned arguments, but Mr. Joseph Ansell calmed the situation by proposing a sub-committee to look into the matter, a notion that 'Mac' willingly supported.

The Sub Committee soon met and set their function as to decide the benefits (if any) of going limited. 'Mac' was to provide particulars of balance sheets for the last three years and provide details of Small Heath and other incorporated clubs.

In a subsequent meeting in February, Joseph Ansell – then the club's solicitor (and later long-serving president) – as chair of the Sub Committee, declared the "undesirability of introducing speculation with a view to profit."

It was beginning to be clear that the mood of the club was then against the notion of profit making of any kind, as would be implied in limited liability incorporation. Mr. Ansell made the point, however, that under the Companies Act, 1867, the club could be registered without becoming a limited company if the Articles of the club were to prohibit dividends being issued. The club would otherwise enjoy the same benefits as a limited liability company. Halifax was quoted as an example of a football club

The Aston Villa Chronicles 1874 – 1924 (and after)

incorporated in such a way.

At yet a further meeting in February, it was clarified that the previous meeting's suggestion of non-profit incorporation would do little to change the form of management of the club, but would give the Villa status, legal and social position, and allay any want of confidence existing with the members.

A Special General Meeting was called for 22 March to present the case.

Sport and Play stated on 19 March, about an "opposition scheme":

> It seems to me to offer a good middle course between letting things go on in the careless and unsatisfactory mode in vogue at present, and the objectionable idea of the members making a profit out of their sport.

Having implied agreement to the "middle course", the matter went through several more meetings to finalise the details and wordings. At another Special General Meeting on 31 May, a Mr. Bodfish tried to oppose the adoption of the new constitution, but was heavily defeated.

The president (Mr. James Hinks), in moving the adoption of the report, thought there was no football balance-sheet in the world to equal theirs, which showed that the profits for the season would be £210.

All having been agreed, Mr. Ansell was thanked for his assistance. He, in turn, acknowledged the meeting and stated that "the legal costs thereby entailed would be represented by a round **O**!"

At the club's AGM on 6 June, one significant business was that – for the first time – the books would be audited yearly by a professional auditor. William McGregor was one of those who previously held this function on an unpaid basis.

The last meeting of the old committee was held on 16 September, 1889, although the old committee's members were re-elected at a Special General Meeting following a Statutory Meeting (20 September), with the addition of five new members (including Messrs. T. Bates and J. T. Lees). James Hinks was elected president (as before), with Joseph Ansell, William McGregor and Billy Mason vice-presidents. The size of the committee (14, excluding president and vice-presidents) had now gone back to its pre-1886 proportions, over which there had been clamour at the time.

The club – through its name – was now a legal entity in its own right, rather than being a collection of individuals making up a committee, but the club soon found that their new legal standing made no jot of difference to the Perry Barr landlords – they still expected individual members to stand as guarantors for the upholding of the ground lease.

It would not be too many years before the question of limited liability would be revisited; William McGregor was far-seeing in his ideas but at this juncture his colleagues could not see his point.

> The first ever game of baseball played between English and American teams at the Aston Lower Grounds. Playing a team of American Collegians, George Ramsay was captain of Aston Villa and played at first base "in a very commendable manner". Aston Villa were heavily defeated.
>
> *Sport and Play*, 24 August, 1889

Season 1889-90: The End of An Era – Yet another Crisis!

League position: 8th (of 12); *FA Cup:* 2nd Round.

The attention of the Villa supporters was centred on the signing of a new generation of Scots; **James Cowan** and **Billy Dickson**. Jimmy Cowan had come to Birmingham 'under his own steam' to join the ill-fated Warwickshire FC at Edgbaston, but George Ramsay and the committee had other ideas, and duly persuaded Cowan to join the Villa!

Meanwhile, Tom Green had left the Villa.

The Season's Play:

September, 1889

The Villa played a season 'opener' in order to open the Wolves' new ground at Molineux,[292] this being followed by the first League game of the season, at home against **Burnley**, resulting in a 2-2 draw.

[From the *Athletic News*] The opening matches versus Wolves and Burnley were very disappointing, and the inclusion of Garvey instead of Dickson

---

[292] The new Wolves' football ground was – just as the Villa's became a few years later – a development of a pleasure grounds, including the removal of a pool in the centre of what became the football pitch! Archie Hunter was reported as describing that pitch as being "as mooth as a bowling green and as flat as a billiard table." *Courtesy of 'The Wolves (Web) Site'.*

The Aston Villa Chronicles 1874 – 1924 (and after)

provoked "qualms in the region of the waistcoat." In fact, he was in poor form and "was laughed at in a manner that appeared to upset his equilibrium. However, "the Villa have found a treasure in Cowan." It was noted that Hodgetts had increased a lot in weight, but seemed as good as ever.

The next match (against **Notts County** at Perry Barr) saw the following team selection, Garvey's omission being the only change from the Burnley game, except that the two full-backs were switched. A large crowd was present.

Villa: *Warner; Aldridge, Coulton; Clarkson, Jas.Cowan, H.Devey; Albert Brown, Allen, Hunter, Dickson, Hodgetts.*

[From the *Athletic News*] "As usual, Notts were very late – they always are when they come to Perry Barr – it was 4 o'clock before the game started … It took the Villa some time to wake up and make the running, though when they did, the amount of steam they put into their exertions was a caution!" The Villa's midfield play was a treat to watch. Passing the ball around, from wing to wing, the Villa took the game to the County defence and spent some five minutes giving the County defenders an alarming time. The crowd even thought that the Villa had scored at one point.

"Then, a most determined rush by Notts caused a stampede around the Villa goal" and amidst a group of players, the ball was put through to score. 0-1 to County. Villa's appeal for offside was in vain. "That was exasperating, but it was nothing to what followed. Warner stopped two or three excellent shots by Daft and the centre … and then the home team turned towards the bottom goal again, struck the goal-post about three times in about ten seconds, and kept their [keeper] jumping almost like a marionette, saving his goal in all manner of styles …" The game then slackened off after going at a scorching pace, and half-time arrived.

The second half was virtually all Villa, but they could not get past the astonishing keeper, aided by some wayward shooting. With a few minutes to go, the Villa supporters were leaving the ground, grumbling at their wicked luck and bad shooting, "when [Harry] Devey was seen to have robbed Daft of the leather, and running a little forward, that dark-haired half-back sent in a long straight shot which was too hard to knock safely way, and Hodgetts, coming up like a steam train, caught the ball on the bounce and hammered it through the goal amidst a scene of the wildest excitement." Time was called immediately afterwards, the score finishing at 1-1.

The Villa had shown a distinct improvement over the previous week, against an improving Notts team. However, Archie Hunter was noted as being "very slow …". Billy Dickson played a great game, and the half-back line was superb.

Denny Hodgetts was out injured, but the next match (at home) turned out to be **Preston**'s first ever League defeat, after their defeat-free season of 1888-89, and it

The Aston Villa Chronicles 1874 – 1924 (and after)

was against the Villa. From his memory bank, Old Fogey relayed an overview of Villa's feat:

Preston No Longer Invincible!

> It was the initial season of James Cowan; Archie Hunter was still in the team, and Frank Coulton was one of the backs. At half-time the Villa led by 3 goals 1 [after being a goal behind], and the sensation was tremendous. Cowan scored two of the points.
>
> Afterwards the great Nicholas Ross — one of the greatest backs the game has ever known, and long since gone over to the majority — went forward, and by his aid the North End obtained [further] goals; so that the Villa won by 5 to 3, amidst almost feverish exhilaration, and to the wonder of the football world generally.[293]

Old Fogey mentioned an incident concerning Albert Albutt as Villa's umpire in the game:

> He gave a throw-in for the Villa, and the referee went against him; whereupon he spat fiercely upon the ground, smote the palm of one hand with his clenched fist, and otherwise showed his displeasure. The crowd laughed as they took in the situation.

The thrashing which Preston North End received from the Villa has had a curious affect upon most of the football writers of the country ... A few – most of these hail from Lancashire – have been so upset by the news that surprise and consternation have kept them from saying anything at all about it ...

Sport and Play, 1 October, 1889

The predominantly Lancashire portion of the *Athletic News* was strangely silent about this result until *after* the Villa had gone down 0-3 in their next match (away vs. **West Bromwich Albion**), and *then* the Lancashire scribes proceeded to decry the Villa's win against Preston, and dismiss it as an aberration! However, there was definitely a Preston slide in evidence as they lost two further games before the end of October. But it proved a temporary slide – for this season at least.

That match against the Albion attracted – as always – a top gate at the Stoney Lane ground. Archie Hunter was 'rested' by the Villa committee and a defeat ensued as the Villa forwards lost their heads after Albion went into a 0-2 lead after 30 minutes. Without a captain to galvanise them, the Villa failed to take goal chances that would have brought them back into the game. When Coulton had to go off

---

[293] Villa News & Record 19 Nov 1910

injured, Villa's chances also went, and Albion scored a third.

> About Archie Hunter's omission (for which the committee had received criticism), *Sport and Play* prophetically wrote, "... it must be borne in mind that the time is not far distant when they will have to do without his services altogether ..."

October, 1889

The Villa must have been very mindful that their next trip was into Lancashire, home of their greatest critics, to meet **Burnley**. Alas, there was no report to hand of that match, but Archie Hunter was brought back into the fray and scored two goals (with Allen gaining a hat-trick; Hodgetts was the other scorer) in Villa's demolition of Burnley by 6-2. This win was accomplished without Jimmy Warner's help, as the committee left him out; a disagreement over something that he wanted and the way he demanded it, according to *Sport and Play*.

Flushed by their success at lowly Burnley, Villa had **Derby County** next up at Perry Barr, and Derby had been in second place at the end of September. Cox returned for his first game of the season in place of the hurt Coulton, and Villa demolished Derby by half-time, leading 5-0. The Villa won 7-1 and could have won by a greater margin. Allen, Dickson and Brown each scored two, with Hodgetts the other scorer.

Despite the hammering at the Albion, Villa had done well over the preceding month or so, scoring 17 goals in three of the four matches. But, to the great frustration of the fans, Villa's next game – against **Blackburn,** Villa's previous season's scourge – was lost, 0-7.[294]

> At Blackburn, Archie Hunter was "suffering from a violent influenza cold" and if he had acted wisely, he would have stayed at home to be nursed. Duty for the Villa was clearly the priority on his mind, but it naturally affected his game, and he gave nothing like the performance of the previous week.
>
> *Sport and Play*, 22 October, 1889

The next match was versus the **Albion** at Perry Barr. The crowd saw a poor match won by the Villa, 1-0. At this stage in the League proceedings – at the end of October – the Villa's position looked very good, though local rivals Wolves were doing even better! Blackburn Rovers were again looking dangerous with games in hand.

---

[294] Alas, again no match report available.

The Aston Villa Chronicles 1874 – 1924 (and after)

Preston had a poor start, but they were to perform a miraculous turn-a-round and win the championship for the second season.

Leading Positions in The Football League	Pld	Home W D L F A	Away W D L F A	Overall W D L F A	Pts
1 Wolverhampton Wanderers	9	3 1 0 8 4	2 1 2 11 8	5 2 2 19 12	12
2 Everton	9	3 2 0 11 6	1 1 2 10 11	4 3 2 21 17	11
3 Aston Villa	8	3 2 0 16 7	1 0 2 6 12	4 2 2 22 19	10
4 Derby County	8	4 1 0 11 4	0 1 2 4 12	4 2 2 15 16	10
5 Blackburn Rovers	6	4 0 0 22 6	0 1 1 4 5	4 1 1 26 11	9
6 Notts. County	8	2 0 1 8 6	2 1 2 13 6	4 1 3 21 12	9
7 Preston North End	7	2 0 1 15 2	2 0 2 13 9	4 0 3 28 11	8

From the Villa's Minutes

The committee minutes reveal that on 31 October there was a special meeting to discuss the general poor play of the team.[295] Hodgetts was a specific name brought up, and he was summoned to a special meeting on 2 November. At that meeting, Hodgetts declared that he would not be dictated to by the committee, that the more he was talked to the worse he would play, and if Villa were not satisfied then they had better get someone in his place.

The committee then dropped Hodgetts for the next match (vs Wolves), moved Allen to Hodgett's position, and brought in a new player, Moore (signed from Dundee), who then scored both goals in Villa's win!

By 4 November, Hodgetts had regretted what he said and was reinstated. *Sport and Play* remarked (5 November, before they heard of Hodgett's apology): "Dennis is a fearful fellow, they say, when he is on the rampage!"

Also at the 4 November meeting, discussion took place with Archie Hunter about him helping with the coaching and providing a weekly report to the committee. This was to be in an unpaid capacity.

November, 1889

The next match was, then, of great importance. It was against the table-topping **Wolves**, who only the previous match had beaten Preston at Deepdale. The "mutinous" Hodgetts was (as narrated above) left out, and Wolves were favourites to win at Perry Barr.

---

[295] Inconsistency would probably be a more accurate description.

The Aston Villa Chronicles 1874 – 1924 (and after)

[From the *Athletic News*] At half-time, Wolves were winning 1-0, and had played well enough to give confidence to their supporters. But in the first minute of the second half, "from a magnificent run by Hunter and Allen, Brown obtained possession close upon the line, and skimmed a beauty, low and sharp, all across the goalmouth, and Moore popped through the ball …"

Villa enlivened their play now, having equalised, but the pace could not be kept up. This enabled Wolves to come back at Villa, and might well have scored but for Cox and Aldridge, the Villa full-backs.

The Villa once more came back into the game, and with a few minutes to go, with hundreds leaving the ground, Moore scored his second from a pass by Dickson (from another Brown centre). Wolves then made an unsuccessful last ditch attempt to pull the match out of the fire.

Villa should now have gained confidence and be moving on, but the reverse happened. Villa won only 2 League matches in their remaining 13 fixtures! They lost 8 and drew 3. Of the two matches they did win, the second was the last match of the season.

That record does not tell the complete story. The next two matches after the Wolves win were both against resurgent sides, and away from home. The match at **Notts County** ended in a 1-1 draw, whilst at **Bolton**, the Villa came across a side who were "terribly in earnest and apparently astonished the Villa backs by the bull-terrier style in which they hung on to the ball and refused to be shaken off" (*Athletic News*).

The next home match (vs **Everton**) again revealed Villa's waywardness in front of goal, and the better team won, 1-2. Then, away at **Accrington**, with Archie Hunter unable to play, Villa's 2-1 lead was overturned to 2-3 by half-time, and the Villa lost 2-4.

> With baseball seeming to catch on a bit, a National Basketball League was created. William McGregor was one of those elected as a member of the controlling council, together with his friend, Joe Tillotson.

December, 1889

Stoke were next to play at Perry Barr.

Villa: *Warner; Cox, Coulton; Yates, Jas.Cowan, Burton; Albert Brown, Moore, Dickson, Garvey, Allen.*

It was an extraordinary selection, mainly enforced by the selection of Villa players for the Birmingham and District side. In this team, Yates was playing his only game

The Aston Villa Chronicles 1874 – 1924 (and after)

of the season; Moore had been left out after scoring the brace against Wolves and was playing his second match, and Garvey also was playing only his second match of the season, after a poor performance in his first. Yet this Villa side beat Stoke 6-1, with Garvey scoring a hat-trick! However, this would prove to be the last League win till the last game of the season.

The return match at **Wolves** was not a remarkable game, and finished 1-1. But what *was* remarkable is that the committee effectively changed the team back to its selection as before the Stoke match, even though the Stoke selection had been successful, and the previous matches had produced little!

After the Wolves match on 21 December, there was a Christmas sequence of three matches on the 25th, 26th and 28th, all of which the Villa lost. However, in the first of these three – at **Preston** – *Sport and Play* declared "A Fine Show by Villa" as the headline. The following is their complete report of the match:

"Cut it short, and tie it up as close as you can, are my editor's instructions, so please imagine you are seated on the North End stand, and as you look around you see a ground slightly sloping, the top end fairly good, the bottom very heavy and sticky, while the whole circuit of the field of play is surrounded by open stands, tier upon tier. Sharp to time, for the Preston arrangements are A1, the two teams are drawn up in line, the Villa having won the toss and commence playing down hill with the wind. Off they go with a rattle and a bang, a shot by Brown whizzes over the Preston goal bar, while in the same breath Warner has to punch out at the other end; nor is the danger altogether removed, for though Trainer is called upon several times to clear his charge, and it taken him all his time to do so, the balance of play is at the other end, Warner, Coulton, and Aldridge showing a most stubborn defence. In a general scrimmage, a foul is awarded North End close to goal, and from a soft shot, Aldridge kicks over the ball, or slips when about to kick — which of the two is not quite clear — and the ball goes gently through twelve minutes from the start.

"Starting afresh, Preston are soon at the Villa end again, but the visitors are nowise downhearted, and soon remove danger, from this point playing a fine game. Dickson rolls up against a couple with a 'Here, Albert, get away down'; he gives him the ball, and like a greyhound he is off. Graham is powerless to stop him, Holmes has a stern chase, but just on the goal line, Albert gets round his man, a grand centre to Dennis's toe, five yards from Trainer – pop — and you can tell by the Preston peoples' looks that something has gone wrong. Notwithstanding, they give Brown a very hearty cheer for a magnificent bit of play, and the Preston crowd are very fair in their plaudits, besides knowing what good football is, whether from visitors or their own team. The kick from centre is soon pounced on by the Villans, and after North End had paid Warner a

The Aston Villa Chronicles 1874 – 1924 (and after)

visit, Dickson got hold, and setting past the backs, went straight for Trainer, banging the ball hard at him, and the ball being wet and greasy was only partially stopped. Albert Brown was on tho spot, and drove it through to make doubly sure.

"Elated by success, the Villa were fairly bottling North End. A splendid run by Brown, a centre off the line, with no-one but Dickson, Hodgetts, and Moore close in front of Trainer, seemed a 1000 to 1 on a goal; but unfortunately the referee in running up at the time came in contact with the ball, and it went outside off his head, a piece of very hard lines for Villa, but purely accidental. North End were now playing their hardest, but many of their runs were spoiled by Gordon lying offside. From one of those runs, Ross, [junior], went on and 'scored', but as the whistle had gone, and Aldridge stepped on one side, while Warner walked away from goal, it was a pretty effort, but did not count. However, the Preston scribes make a great point of stating they had a goal disallowed — so there you are. Breathing time soon after arrived with the score Villa 2, North End 1.

"After a refresher, the fun began by the home team dashing to the Villa goal, up and down went the ball, neither side having a distinct advantage, till Nick Ross put in a long shot, the ball stuck in the mud close to the goal. Warner only partially cleared with his feet, but quickly punched the ball out, Nick Ross shouted for a goal and the referee allowed it to the disgust of the Villa players. It was a decision to be regretted, the ball was never through, and always in front of the posts, but as the referee was some distance down the field, he must have had Sam Weller's glasses to have seen a goal. However it was the turning point of the game, for the North End now settled down to a steady and persistent pressure, and it was only by the hardest of work the Villa prevented a series of disasters. As it was, from a prolonged scrimmage in front of goal, Nick Ross put on the leading goal, though this would have been disallowed for a foul by Russell, but the Villa umpire was fast asleep and claimed too late.

"For fully twenty minutes the game was a series of tries by Preston to increase their lead but the Villa tackled in a determined manner and broke them up, Dickson and Brown varying the proceedings by dashing away to Trainer — who had several handfuls to dispose of. Fairly beating the North End off, the prolonged siege was removed, and in the last ten minutes Preston were lucky to escape disaster. Once Albert Brown got well down in front of Trainer, the ball butting his legs and coming out, while a minute after, he was awfully lucky in saving another shot from Brown, and just on the stroke of time a pass right in front of Trainer was missed by Garvey by a few inches. Fate was, however, against them and the game ended North End 3, Villa 2."

Villa seem to have either been disheartend or worn out by this match, as over the next three days, they lost 1-2 at home to **Accrington**, and 0-5 at **Derby County**. The

The Aston Villa Chronicles 1874 – 1924 (and after)

committee's meeting on 30 December was a lot focused on the poor play/results recently obtained. "We need to get more players", they said, and George Ramsay was packed off to Scotland to find two forwards and two half-backs.

However, a more real tragedy was about to unfold.

Disaster for Archie Hunter

The conditions at Villa's next opponent's ground – **Everton** – were described by the *Sport and Play* reporter as follows:

"I have, in the course of a pretty long experience seen most of the leading football grounds in the country, but I never saw a ground in such a state in my life. It was totally unfit for football ...

"It was not to be expected that a team used to playing on a dry ground ... would be able to do themselves justice in a veritable Slough of Despond." Everton, on the other hand, "were up to this sort of thing."

Before the game, Archie Hunter formally protested against playing a League match under such conditions. As to the match itself, Everton somehow mastered the conditions and were winning 4-0 at half-time.

"It was at this point in the game that a most dramatic incident occurred. The referee's whistle had scarcely sounded for the interval, when Archie Hunter suddenly dropped like a log of wood into a pool of water. He was speedily raised by his companions ... [and Archie] was removed from the field amidst the sympathies of [the] crowd.

Amazingly, it was reported that though Everton played well, Villa, with 10 men, played much more strongly in the second half. Villa's keeper (Warner) was thought to have been at fault for several goals in Villa's 0-7 defeat.

The committee – at their next meeting – sent a vote of thanks to the Everton club for the very kind help administered to Archie Hunter. After being seen to by the Everton club's physician, Archie was taken in a cab to his hotel.

| Archie Hunter's last match | Archie Hunter's last game was in this away match at Everton on 4 January. The weather was terrible – "all his comrades felt too depressed to play the game, their thoughts being not on the match but with their old captain, whom they all loved

so much."[296] What occurred had been the heart-attack or stroke that brought an end to a Villa era, and was to presage the death of this legend within five years. Hunter soon after applied to the Villa committee to continue playing, but the required medical check-up clearly did not support him; he did not play again.

---

[296] Villa News & Record 4 Apr 1908

The Aston Villa Chronicles 1874 – 1924 (and after)

Archie Hunter's own account, shortly after the Everton event, was as follows:

> The ground was in a fearful condition after heavy rain. Pools of water and masses of mud made play almost impossible and to add to our troubles a biting east wind was cutting us and seemed to pierce us like a knife. I was playing my hardest when I fell into a pool of water. Just before, I had received a severe bruise and with the additional shock to the system I fainted away.[297]

Nevertheless, was illness already affecting Archie before that match, one wonders. Hunter himself stated[298] that his best days were earlier in the '80s - between '82 and '85. By 1889 (aged 30), it would seem he was tiring, and his three brothers had already died before him. Archie had been ill with flu several times in the previous year, and there had been a worrying Villa slide since November. Archie himself had not scored since early October – signs that, indeed, things were not right.

The sports press launched into reflections on the state of the Villa with respect to their performances – Archie Hunter's state of health not being given the time of day! The *Athletic News* stated (6 January, 1890):

> The succession of crushing defeats which have lately been inflicted upon Aston Villa is causing the greatest alarm and consternation to the Perry Barr supporters and the officials of the club. Internal discussion amongst the players is said to be the real secret of the collapse of Villa form ...

Sport and Play joined in, but with a supportive tone (through the pen of 'Veteran', A. G. Taylor):

> Among the thousands who support the Villa may be numbered scores who stand nobly by the club through sunshine and through shade, and who feel their position most keenly just at the present On the other hand, there are scores and scores who may be termed 'fair weather' supporters [who easily criticise] ... [and] some writers have evidently become infected ... Why, to read some of the recent splutterings one would imagine that the Villa players were [a load of duffers] ...

Adding what was, in his view, the real problem:

> The players are there, and have the ability too, let those who deny it who like. In form, they are absolutely first class. But – and here comes the rub! – the earnestness, the loyalty, the enthusiasm and the old Villa fire seem wanting.

---

[297] "Triumphs of the Football Field", Birmingham Weekly Mercury, October, 1890 to February, 1891
[298] "Triumphs of the Football Field", Birmingham Weekly Mercury, October, 1890 to February, 1891

The Aston Villa Chronicles 1874 – 1924 (and after)

> When do we see that close puzzling passing that made the Villa so famous? When do we see that splendid unselfishness, when every man works for his side, and not for individual glory? When do we see the forwards helping the half-backs when pressed and hampered …?

And, prophetically, stated:

> They have had a fair run of success in times gone by, and a little tribulation may do them no harm; the process of refining may be drastic, but it will be effectual, and by and by we shall see the Villa once more singing a triumphant march, and the croaking prophets of evil today trooping at the heels of the players with all the brazenness of gilded weather-cocks!

The journal also reported on the signings that George Ramsay had made in Scotland – including Paton, of the Vale of Leven; "One of the best men in Scotland. … [However], players from the north are never sure until they actually arrive, and if it once leaks out in Scotland who they are, all sorts of practises will be tried to prevent them coming."

George Ramsay in Scotland

James Paton's obituary in a Glossop newspaper (many years later, where he had retired) revealed:

> … [that] he and his brother, Archie Paton, began their football careers with the then famous club, Vale of Leven, one of the oldest clubs in Scotland … At first, James Paton played outside-right … [but] it was when tried as centre-forward that he reached the height of his powers., being a particularly deadly marksman, who hit the ball harder than most … a terror to goalkeepers …

Mr. G. Ramsay brought James Paton from Scotland [further transcription is not possible for a few lines, but it does mention that the 'poaching' of players had dire consequences – the culprit often being tarred and feathered!] … Mr. Ramsay had many unpleasant experiences in Scotland, and especially in the Vale of Leven. He once had to hide in a hayloft for a couple of hours whilst a furious gang of Scotsmen sought his blood.

On the occasion that he secured 'Jimmy' Paton, he got information as to what was awaiting him, and so went to a station other than the one he was supposed to be making for. And a good job too, for at the other station a hostile crowd was waiting for Mr. Ramsay, and that crowd would have stopped at nothing! [Ramsay was successful in obtaining his man and returning with him to Birmingham].

The Aston Villa Chronicles 1874 – 1924 (and after)

The result of George Ramsay's excursions were then made more clear:

> Included in the Villa reserve team, on Saturday, were four fresh players, who were understood to be the recruits which Scotland has furnished for the Perry Barr eleven. But there was an air of mystery about the officials of the club, which was almost comical in its intensity, and unless the bond of secrecy under which they are all confined is pretty soon loosened, I am afraid the tension will be too great for some of them, and disastrous consequences may follow ...[299]

January, 1890

The following Saturday, the Villa were away at **South Shore** in the FA Cup, first round. Playing a non-League side, it might have been an opportunity to try a new team, but none of the new signings participated.

[From the *Athletic News*] At half-time, it looked as though Villa were going to win at a canter, as the score was 2-0 in their favour, the first goal having come as a result of one of Hodgetts' "favourite wing runs", with Allen "cracking the ball through".

"On restarting, there was a revolution.". South Shore, disregarding the wind, played up hard, and were soon working around Warner. After two close efforts, South Shore scored. "This put vim into the game, and cheered on by the spectators, the South Shore boys gave the Villa 'gyp'. Another chance came to them, and following this they scored again: it was now 2-2! The crowd went wild!

However, the Villa clearly had something in reserve, for straight away Hodgetts scored Villa's third, and another Villa score was later added to make it 4-2 to the Villa.

The following week's return to Perry Barr and the League brought **Bolton Wanderers** as the Villa's next opponents, Bolton also having achieved little success that season. This was definitely an experimental side, with Hodgetts out of position and three new signings (Connor, Graham and Campbell) taking their places. However, they were mostly enforced changes, as Dickson was away and Devey was injured.

Villa: *Warner; Cox, Coulton; Burton, Jas. Cowan, Connor; Albert Brown, Hodgetts, Allen, Graham, Louis Campbell.*

---

[299] Athletic News 13 Jan 1890

The Aston Villa Chronicles 1874 – 1924 (and after)

[From the *Athletic News*] "There was a remarkably warm reception which Archie Hunter got when he appeared as umpire for the Villa, and the folks who have watched him perform for so many years seemed delighted to have him amongst them again."

The Perry Barr 'field' was in a shocking state, and there was a high blistering wind that went straight down the slope, and which the Villa had the advantage of for the first half.

As soon as they started, Albert Brown scored from Allen's pass. This gave Villa heart, and they put the Bolton goal under siege. Unfortunately for the Villa, Bolton withstood their attacks, and went so far as to equalise the score. Play then went back to the Bolton end, and for the rest of the half, with one fine Villa 'daisy-cutter' that went in being disallowed for a fractional offside.

Against the wind and against a strident Bolton side, Villa conceded a second goal within five minutes of the restart, and but for the play of Cox and Coulton, they may have conceded more.

February, 1890

The following week, Villa played their old Cup rivals **Notts County** in the FA Cup second round, and lost 1-4.

The *Athletic News* reported: "The Villa team lacked the cohesion which was such a distinguishing characteristic of the Villa in the old days of Archie Hunter. The forwards were somewhat loose, Dickson failing to hold them together." At times, though, their play was "really excellent."

> *Sport and Play* reported, at great length:
>
>> [Concerning a protest lodged by the Villa to the FA] that [the referee] was alleged to have made the remark that if his decision had been asked, he should have allowed one of the goals disallowed against the Villa and disallowed one obtained by Notts ... [the FA disallowed the protest].
>
> But [said *Sport and Play*], Notts were the better team and Villa should have accepted the result with good heart.
>
> The Villa were fined for bringing an action, and *Sport and Play* continued:
>
>> It has long been thought that the Midlands, and Birmingham in particular, have very few friends on the head council board, and now this has been proved to demonstration.

Two weeks later, the Albion came to play a friendly at Perry Barr on a day of a "cold and biting blast and the pitiless rain ... it wasn't fit to turn a tomcat out on such a day ..." Villa, playing on "the vast expanse of mud", lost 0-1, with just 300 to 400

The Aston Villa Chronicles 1874 – 1924 (and after)

spectators braving the weather to watch the game.

March, 1890

On 8 March, Perry Barr was the scene of the FA Cup semi-final between Bolton Wanderers and Sheffield Wednesday, in front of a crowd of 10,000.

The Villa introduced their new centre-forward, Paton, on 15 March, in a friendly match at home against St. George's, which the Villa won 2-1, and should have been won by more. Paton, though he did not score, was pronounced a success: "He will become a big favourite", said the *Athletic News*. "It seems to be many a day since we saw the Villa play with such neatness and resolution combined." Two days later, in an away League match at bottom club **Stoke**, Paton played in a not very inspiring 1-1 draw.

The Villa then followed this up with a 5-1 win over Wolves in the Birmingham Cup semi-final, and this after Wolves had taken the lead. Though Paton was ineligible for this match, Villa, it was reported, were playing in their old style.

The Villa then threatened to carry all before them in an away friendly at the Albion, leading 2-0 at half-time, and Hodgetts showing sparkling form, but the Albion came back with a characteristically late rush, the score finishing 2-2.

While the Villa style is, as perhaps it always has been, more attractive to the spectators, the Albion have a readier method – you may call it rough and ready if you choose – of getting up to goal, and slamming away like mad when they are there.

Sport and Play

There were just some signs, now, of the Villa getting back into shape, and Paton scored in this game. But Paton's troubles started here also, for he received a bad knee injury in the second half which prevented him playing in the final League match of the season and, in the long run, would terminate his career with the Villa before it had barely started.

The Aston Villa Chronicles 1874 – 1924 (and after)

> **A drive to West Bromwich**
>
> The weather being so delightfully fine, and a chance of a drive to West Bromwich by coach presenting itself, we forsook the rail in favour of the road. The drive was not altogether devoid from incident, for after waiting something like half-an-hour while a new whip was provided, we rattled off in fine style, only to be brought up with a jerk somewhere in the vicinity of Key Hill, one of the leaders having got over the trace, and, as the coach happened to be athwart the tram rails, the progress of the cable trams was stayed until there was a string of cars waiting, which threatened to assume the proportions of a Bank Holiday excursion train.
>
> Presently, all was serene again, and without waiting to see the end of an exciting foot-race, which was about to be decided by sprinters in stocking feet on the highway, we pushed towards the Plough and Harrow. What a magnificent reception we had! A score or so of playful young urchins had evidently made arrangements for same, and just as we turned a corner in sight of the ground, a volley of miscellaneous missiles was poured upon us by these horrid young ragamuffins from a bit of waste ground, and we had to go through the process of ducking very considerably to avoid these delicate attentions. Remnants of old shoes, cabbage stalks, pieces of bricks, stones [came their way] ...
>
> *Sport and Play*

Villa had slipped to ninth place (of 12 teams) before the last League game of the season, but a last match win (3-0 vs. **Blackburn**, the new FA Cup holders) raised Villa up one place on goal average above Bolton. "William McGregor's face was adorned with smiles of happiness and contentment", said the *Athletic News*.

> On 12 April, a benefit match in aid of Archie Hunter was played at Perry Barr against a Scottish club, Kilburnie. The devotion towards Archie showed when 7,000 turned up to cheer and see Villa win 7-3. Many tickets were sold that were never utilised.
>
> At the club's AGM on 27 June, Fred Rinder proposed that Archie Hunter be a life member. The idea was welcomed, but members were reminded that a life membership now had a price to it – the sum of £10 10s! A swift whip-round took place to procure the necessary funds!

Villa's season came to a bright end when they played the Albion in the final of the Birmingham Cup – again at Perry Barr – on 19 April. 10,000 saw the Villa win 2-1 to again win this cup for three seasons in a row.

The Aston Villa Chronicles 1874 – 1924 (and after)

Both the Albion and Wolves (both beaten in the Birmingham Cup by the Villa) finished well up in this second season of the League.

The Football League 1889-90	Pld	Home W D L F A	Away W D L F A	Overall W D L F A	Pts
1 Preston North End	22	8 1 2 41 12	7 2 2 30 18	15 3 4 71 30	33
2 Everton	22	8 2 1 40 15	6 1 4 25 25	14 3 5 65 40	31
3 Blackburn Rovers	22	9 0 2 59 18	3 3 5 19 23	12 3 7 78 41	27
4 Wolverhampton Wanderers	22	6 3 2 28 14	4 2 5 23 24	10 5 7 51 38	25
5 West Bromwich Albion	22	8 1 2 37 20	3 2 6 10 30	11 3 8 47 50	25
6 Accrington	22	6 4 1 33 25	3 2 6 20 31	9 6 7 53 56	24
7 Derby County	22	8 2 1 32 13	1 1 9 11 42	9 3 10 43 55	21
8 Aston Villa	**22**	**6 2 3 30 15**	**1 3 7 13 36**	**7 5 10 43 51**	**19**
9 Bolton Wanderers	22	6 1 4 37 24	3 0 8 17 41	9 1 12 54 65	19
10 Notts. County	22	4 3 4 20 19	2 2 7 23 32	6 5 11 43 51	17
11 Burnley	22	3 1 7 20 21	1 4 6 16 44	4 5 13 36 65	13
12 Stoke	22	2 3 6 18 20	1 1 9 9 49	3 4 15 27 69	10

1889-90 League & FA Cup Results

Sep	7th H Burnley	2-2
	14th H Notts County	1-1
	21st H Preston North End	5-3
	28th A West Bromwich A	0-3 10000
Oct	5th A Burnley	6-2
	12th H Derby County	7-1 7000
	19th A Blackburn Rovers	0-7
	26th H West Bromwich A	1-0 12000
Nov	2nd H Wolves	2-1
	9th H Notts County	1-1
	16th A Bolton Wanderers	0-2 8000
	23rd H Everton	1-2

	30th A Accrington	2-4
Dec	7th H Stoke	6-1
	21st A Wolves	1-1
	25th A Preston North End	2-3
	26th H Accrington	1-2
	28th A Derby County	0-5
Jan	4th A Everton	0-7
	18th A South Shore (FAC)	4-2 2000
	25th H Bolton Wanderers	1-2
Feb	1st A Notts Cnty (FAC)	1-4
Mar	17th A Stoke	1-1
	31st H Blackburn Rovers	3-0

End of Season Postscripts

The Villa came very close to having to seek re-election to the League, as the bottom four, according to the rule-book, needed to seek re-election. Although Villa finished outside the bottom four on goal average, it did not prevent Villa being considered for re-election as it was considered that they finished *equal fourth* from bottom, particularly as the goal average separating the two sides was so small. However, on 2 May, 1890, the League passed the following resolution:

The Aston Villa Chronicles 1874 – 1924 (and after)

That in view of the extraordinary circumstances of the case, and in order to arrive at a resolution of the matter, the standing order and rules of the League be suspended. Resolved, that Bolton Wanderers and Aston Villa be allowed places in the League without being elected.[300]

From the Villa's Minutes

At the committee meeting of 19 May, a letter from the Children's Hospital was shown. The position of Hon. Life Governor of the Hospital was offered to William McGregor, which he accepted.

At 5 June meeting, it was reported that negotiations had been taking place with John Devey for him to join the Villa, but there were several financial requirements on his part which the committee felt that they could not accept. The secretary was requested to inform Mr. Devey that "his offer be not entertained."
However, it would only be another year before his signing would be discussed again.

The AGM

At the club's AGM on 27 June, a reduced committee size was proposed, and the scene following the voting was described by the *Saturday Night* periodical:

> It was now 10:30, and a continued murmur of conversation arose from the members waiting anxiously the verdict. The appearance of the scrutineers on the scene was the signal for a general buzz of excitement from the members, cheers and counter cheers rising again as the chairman (Mr. Clamp) read out the names of the successful candidates.

Messrs. Clamp and Whitehouse were voted as hon. sec. and hon. treasurer respectively; other members were: McGregor (74 votes), Archie Hunter (73), Margoschis (65), Dr. V. Jones (61), Cooper (44), Warrilow (44), Lees (39), Albutt (36), Dawson (35).

Albert Albutt declared his intention not to stand again.[301]

The *Athletic News*, observing the reported income of £3,037 and expenditure of £2,895, commented, "what huge financial undertakings football clubs now are! ... Villa seem to have turned the corner."

---

[300] "Linesman" in The Sporting Mail 29 Sep 1906
[301] The next year, Albutt became secretary of Newton Heath, the fore-runner of Manchester United. 'Tityrus' wrote in his "The Story of Association Football" (1926): "Now had there not been Newton Heath and Mr. Albutt, there would not have been Manchester United."

The Aston Villa Chronicles 1874 – 1924 (and after)

Season 1890-91: More Warning Bells!
League position: 9th (of 12); ***FA Cup:*** 2nd Round.

The Villa's prospects for the coming season were certainly dented by Paton's knee injury. Some expectation had been put on him becoming Archie Hunter's replacement at centre-forward: "Looking at the marvellous way in which he was shooting for goal, finer than anything the Villa have had … it is a very heavy loss for the club", said *Sport and Play*. But there was hope that he would be tried again in September. Dickson, who had been recruited as an inside-forward, stood in at centre-forward for much of the season.

Time could not, of course, stand still for the Villa, and the club went out and recruited two more forwards – McNight and Marshall from St. George's. Also Walter Evans, a powerfully-built Welsh full-back, to replace the marvellous Frank Coulton, who would now play a very minor role in the seasons to come.

This was to be another disappointing season as far as the national competitions were concerned, but the season did uncover a diamond or two before the season was over that would be very much central to the club's future successes.

Something, however, seemed to be wrong at the club, as Albert Brown, for several years now one of the club's most consistent forwards, had to be pressed by the committee to continue playing.

The Season's Play

September, 1890

With Hodgetts "ill", the Villa had virtually a new team on show at **Wolves** for the opening League Fixture.

Villa: *Warner; W. Evans, Cox; H.Devey, Jas.Cowan, Connor; Albert Brown, Allen, Dickson, Graham, Marshall.*

The Villa played a good all-round game, and led at half-time through a Wolves' defensive mix-up (Albert Brown the scorer), but Wolves were too strong in the second half. Villa, however, were noted for having given away a number of fouls for holding and tripping. The Villa lost, 1-2.

Against **Notts County** at Perry Barr the next week, Hodgetts returned, and Allen was left out (replaced by McKnight). "Albert Brown gave us one of those queer

The Aston Villa Chronicles 1874 – 1924 (and after)

exhibitions ... I am told that he has a rooted objection to playing alongside a Northerner", reported *Sport and Play*. The *Athletic News* reported the match as being an exciting one, but played in front of less than 5,000 spectators. Villa, 2-1 up at half-time, took a 3-1 lead early in the second half and then slackened off, enabling Notts to score again. Bad temper flared between Brown and a defender, "making a good resemblance to a pack of fighting cocks!"

With Hodgetts and Brown both suspended by the club, yet another forward formation took the field at **Burnley**.

> **Villa**: *Warner; W. Evans, Cox; H.Devey, Jas.Cowan, Connor; Marshall, McKnight, Dickson, Graham, L.Campbell.*

There was a fine footballing game by both sides, Burnley running out the winners, 2-1. Villa had played their best game so far this season, and Dickson, Cowan and Warner were "marvellous", but...

"The services of men who stick their own personality in front of the interests of their fellows had better be dispensed with than that the good name of the club should suffer," exclaimed *Sport and Play* on the matter of the internal trouble causing the suspensions mentioned above.

The same team visited Kidderminster Harriers to play a friendly a few days later, having thrashed the same club 6-0 at Perry Barr the previous week, but this time went under to the Harriers, 1-3!

"shocking ... humiliating," said *Sport and Play*, "Surely there must be something rotten in the state of the team to go along in this way, and no wonder the members and friends of the club are fuming and grumbling about it."

Amazingly, the performance satisfied the committee sufficiently to field the same team yet again against the **Albion** at home (in the League) but were well-beaten, 0-4. Villa's play was "slip-shod", with Cowan and Warner the only Villa heroes.

[From *Sport and Play*] Once upon a time, a win against the Villa was a matter of some pride, but now it's becoming almost everyday. "Never in my recollection [of over 12 years] ... have I seen the club's representatives so helplessly beaten, so completely routed, so palpably outclassed, so utterly demoralised and incapable of effort as they were on Saturday."

The Aston Villa Chronicles 1874 – 1924 (and after)

October, 1890

Virtually the same team (excepting Harley for Marshall) represented the Villa at **Bolton** – and another 0-4 mauling in yet another poor display. However, Paton, Hodgetts and Brown played in a reserve match that day, their team winning 7-0. These three were recalled for the home match against **Everton**.

[From the *Athletic News*] After both sets of forwards opened up with good football, Everton went ahead, and then Warner had to make a couple of very good saves. Everton's play just got better and better, but the Villa came back: "With a swing and a dash they sailed away up the slope, a long pass from Paton giving Hodgetts a chance" – but his shot rebounded off the keeper for a corner.

Soon after, a fine move brought Paton the equaliser – from a long shot. From this time to the interval, it was the Villa that was on the attack, but Everton's defence stood firm. That was how it was till just after the re-start, when the Villa at last got their lead. An exchange of passes between Paton and Cowan and – hey presto – Cowan popped the ball through the goal.

Everton would not lie down, however, and back they came, and strongly, too. The Villa now only managed the occasional breakaway, but with 5 minutes remaining they looked as though they would hold onto their lead. However, after Warner had made a save, the ball went loose and it was kicked against Warner's foot and then it looped into the goal. Or did it? For there was an argument as to whether it went though the woodwork, and to the crowd's chagrin, the 'goal' stood. The Villa even hit the woodwork twice in the remaining time, but a draw was the result (2-2). The Villa had given a good account of themselves in a fine match.

> Presumably finding some difficulty in adjusting to the new condition of his life, Archie Hunter was this week advertising "Weekly Harmonic Meetings" at the Royal Exchange, Six Ways, Aston. *Perhaps this was a 'Barber Shop Quartet' set up?*

Villa's display in the Everton match had buoyed-up the spirits of the Villa supporters, and the team were expected to do better at **Derby**, their next League match. However, the match became something of a disaster, as Paton's leg broke down on 15 minutes. He was carried off and did not play another game for the Villa. *Sport and Play* later declared: "We are not likely to see his superior for many a long day to come" – a statement that proved to be incorrect, but, nevertheless, a fine tribute to Paton.

The Aston Villa Chronicles 1874 – 1924 (and after)

But disaster was turned into something a little miraculous when the skipper then put Cowan to centre-forward! The result was that Cowan was credited with a hat-trick, though the Villa went down 4 goals to 5 after holding Derby to 3-3 at half-time. His second goal was after a brilliant run and shot. "Cowan's display in the front rank was equal to anything he ever did amongst the halves", reported *Sport and Play*. The journal also reported that the referee was a favourite with the Derby crowd, and seemed to show partiality in giving unfair offside decisions against Hodgetts and Brown.

Sport and Play reported that a couple of days later, Villa played Notts Forest in a friendly – and lost 0-3 against the non-League side! The journal commented: "Once they were the most famous club in the Midlands, till Aston Villa rose in its might". The Forest had gradually slipped down the scale until Small Heath scored *twelve* against them in 1888-89, but the club were now on the ascendant.

The next match was the return against **Derby**, with Cowan starting as emergency centre-forward! Two ex-Renton players (James Brown and George Campbell) had been newly signed, and made their débuts at half-back. This team selection included five Scots:

Villa: *Warner; W. Evans, Cox; G.Campbell, H.Devey, Jas.Brown;*
Albt.Brown, Dickson, Jas.Cowan, Graham, Hodgetts.

[From *Sport and Play*] The score was goalless at half-time, and the first half had been poor. Then the skipper moved Cowan to outside-right, Brown to inside-right and himself (Dickson) to centre-forward.

The second half was a transformation! Firstly, Dickson scored from a Brown pass. Then, "Dennis slung in some very nice centres, and from one of these, Cowan put so much steam behind a shot that it first hit one player, then another, then the goalpost, before Cowan followed up to finish the mischief he had begun!" Then Cowan's corner-kick produced the third, via Hodgetts, who also added a fourth.

Both the Goodalls were outstanding for Derby.

November, 1890

The Villa were now eager to get revenge at the **Albion** for the mauling they inflicted at Perry Barr, earlier in the season. The starting team was virtually the same as against Derby, except that Dickson and Cowan swapped positions.

[From the *Athletic News*] A game in which "to and fro the ball hopped and spun, always followed by the greatest excitement and enthusiasm, now one side, now the other playing the upper hand". But as soon as Albert Brown scored, it was the Villa that maintained the upper hand.

The Aston Villa Chronicles 1874 – 1924 (and after)

Going into the second half, Villa's half-backs (and backs, when necessary) dealt with anything the Albion threw against them, Harry Devey playing superlatively. Then Albert Brown was seen careering along the right wing at great pace. He passed Dyer, and then Powell, and then, running at an angle, beat the keeper (Reader) with a beautiful shot.

It was Albert Brown again who supplied a fine centre for Dickson to head through the third in a 3-0 win, the first ever victory for the Villa at Stoney Lane.

An unchanged side then faced Burnley at Perry Barr:

[From the *Athletic News*] "Very rarely indeed have the habituees of Perry Barr been treated to a more exciting contest than that which resulted on Saturday …"

The Villa – aided by indecision in Villa's rear ranks for the first goal – were not long in finding themselves 0-2 down. It was only then that the Villans started to settle about their work! A Dickson header reduced the lead, and then came "two shots from Albert Brown that tested the timbers", followed by a hot one from Dickson that threatened to cut the keeper in two. Subsequently, Cowan scored with a beautiful header to bring the score to 2-2. Not to be outdone, Burnley came back and restored a one-goal lead, to make it 2-3 to them at half-time.

Soon after the interval, the Villa again equalised. The Villa were now playing well – except Hodgetts that is, who didn't seem to exert himself and who regularly missed golden opportunities. Even so, the Villa looked as though they would win, but yet again Burnley scored, to lead 3-4. With little time left, Graham levelled the score for the final time, from a Dickson pass.

Another home match the next week, this time against Accrington. It was the same team again, save that Cowan was not available; Allen substituted for him.

[From the *Athletic News*] Poor shooting ensured that the first half came to a 0-0 conclusion. It was Accrington that scored first after some good movement on their part. Again, the Villa had been slow to rouse themselves, but now they began to play and ran out winners by 3-1. The scoreline should have been greater to the Villa, as Hodgetts had three clear openings that he failed to take.

It caused *Sport and Play* to ask and answer its own question: "Are our Perry Pets coming back again? On the form, I think I may safely say they are!" Well, going by appearances, the drift did seem to be going the Villa's way, but they were currently in seventh place, and that was the highest they were to reach in the League table for the whole season!

The Aston Villa Chronicles 1874 – 1924 (and after)

However, the fun was not to be spoilt just yet as a third home match on the trot – this time against **Bolton** – saw Villa win 5-0. That Bolton were hardly in it was illustrated by the *Athletic News* in this comment:

> [A worrying attack by opposing forwards] is always denoted by Warner waving his arms about in an excited way and appealing for offside. He didn't do it once in the first half ... [and little in the second].

Sport and Play reported, about the ex-Rentonian James Brown:

> The way that young fellow revelled in the fun was pleasant to see, and his sudden dashes, pretty touches, and general all-round excellence was the theme of admiration all around the ground.

But that win proved to be the extent of the Villa's success that season – to all intents and purposes. As happened in the previous season, the Villa, quite suddenly – and seriously – deteriorated. The next League match saw the Villa hammered at **Notts County**, 1-7.

December, 1890

The following match saw yet another mauling, this time at **Blackburn** by 1-5. In fact, after the Bolton match – as happened similarly the previous season – in the remaining 10 League matches, only two were won (and they were the last two of the season), two were draws, and six were defeats. Five of those defeats, however, each involved at least four goals conceded.

The weather conditions at Perry Barr around Christmas and the New Year were atrocious – freezing conditions had been thawing, in fact, making the pitches into mud-baths. The League match against **Sunderland** on Boxing Day (ending 0-0) was played in those conditions, and on 3 January the conditions were so poor that a match that should have been a League game was played against Preston as a friendly, attracting perhaps 7,000 spectators. That was a match which Villa won, 2-1. But, unfortunately, it *was* only a friendly.

January, 1891

The Villa's away form in the League continued very badly. The Villa lost at **Everton** 0-5 on New Year's Day, and in the away defeat at **Sunderland** (1-5), the *Athletic News* reporter stated that the Villa had been "pulverised", and wrote that Sunderland should have scored eight! Only the kicking of Cox and Evans to put the ball way out of touch kept the score down. The Sunderland keeper (Doig) was so unoccupied that he stood the danger of being transformed into a stalagmite! That

The Aston Villa Chronicles 1874 – 1924 (and after)

Villa scored at all was due to the fact that Doig had gone upfield to warm himself up by trying to score!

After this match, the *Sport and Play's* scribe thought that:

> Villa's performers at Perry Barr do not at all match up to their away form. Players do not seem to care enough, though there are still good men and true in the ranks.

Referring to an aggressive stance taken by a Villa committee man in a *Birmingham Mail* debate, *Sport and Play's* reporter wrote:

> ... In the fair days of old, the Villa used to be in the habit of winning nearly all their matches, and to be a member of the great governing body in those halcyon times entitled you to cock your nose in the air, wear a sort of No. 14 smile and be utterly oblivious to the ordinary run of bipeds. But now that other giants have appeared in the land of football, and victory is not so common, a subdued demeanour is necessary [for the committee men].

The journal went on to point out that critics were looking to again see a captain of the character of Archie Hunter. The contribution of Archie over the years had been strongly felt, and perhaps only he, at the Blackburn away game in December, was accepted as having the right – whilst acting for the club as umpire – to coach the players from the touchline. His voice was very distinctly heard, according to the *Athletic News* reporter.

And so the sad story continued. On the occasion of losing 1-4 at **Preston,** only the efforts of Warner kept the score down. Following that match, the previously highly thought of Albert Brown and Harry Devey, as well as Graham, were dropped for the rest of the team's matches that season.

In the FA Cup, the Villa had a very pleasant 13-1 victory against the amateurs, the **Casuals**, but in the second round, Villa played at **Stoke** and were soundly beaten, 0-3. Even though the Villa's recent form had been dire, 1,000 Villa fans still went to Stoke to see the match.

After the Stoke Cup match, there were no further major competitive matches played until March, giving time for the Villa to try new things.

On 21 February, there was another new name on the Villa team sheet. This time, it was not one that was going to make a short-lasting impact; the name was **Charlie Athersmith**. He made his début against Stoke in a friendly at Perry Barr, which the Villa won 2-1, but, apart from his presence, there was only one memorable aspect to it:

The Aston Villa Chronicles 1874 – 1924 (and after)

[From the *Athletic News*] "An adjacent chimney evidently got disgusted at the performances of both teams and suddenly emitted a sulphurous volume of choking, blinding smoke onto the meadow. Play had to be stopped, as it was impossible to see the [players] in the 'smother' which permeated the atmosphere." Play was resumed after some minutes with no improvement in the quality of the play!

Another new – but certainly not unknown – name also signed at this time: one **John Devey**, but he was not to play until the next season.

Aston Villa – Late in the season of 1890-91

Back row: Billy Gorman (Trainer), H Devey, Athersmith, McKnight, Archie Hunter, Warner, Burton, Brown, George Ramsay;
Front Row: Cowan, Dickson, Cox (captain), Hodgetts, L Campbell.

What was strange about the Villa, was that outside the major competitions, the Villa were now having a great time! In the Birmingham Cup they subdued their fellow League members Wolves, by 6-0. And the week after (in a friendly) they beat Derby County 11-0, having led 7-0 at half-time, with Athersmith scoring four.

March, 1891

When the League matches came round again, the Villa immediately lost the replayed home match to **Preston**, 0-1. This was the match when Athersmith made his League début, and played "splendidly" in a match that perhaps they should have won, but Hodgetts and Dickson let their side down.

It was in the penultimate League game of the season (against **Wolves**) that Villa's shooting came back to form. By now the Villa side had achieved quite a transformation, and the club were now playing six Scots:

The Aston Villa Chronicles 1874 – 1924 (and after)

Villa: *Warner; W.Evans, Cox; Jas.Brown, Jas.Cowan, G.Campbell; Athersmith, Dickson, McKnight, L.Campbell, Hodgetts.*

[From the *Athletic News*] McKnight opened the scoring, but the first half was tit-for-tat, with the half-time score at 2-2. This was, however, partly due to Evans having made a tremendous clearance with Warner beaten, and which may have left Wolves ahead at half-time if it had gone in.

The Villa then got the upper hand. Following good chances missed by Athersmith and Hodgetts, Athersmith "slid up and took a good and careful pass, and just slammed it through" to make it 3-2. Villa finally won 6-2, with Athersmith having scored a hat-trick in his second League game. But it was a day when all the Villa forwards did well.

For the final League game of the season (on 21 March), Athersmith was not available, but the Villa upset their own form book by winning away from home, at **Accrington**, by 3-1. This win was a little fortuitous as this match was a replay of that that had been played on 20 December, but which had been converted into a friendly because of the state of the pitch. In that friendly, the Villa had lost 1-6!

Further friendly matches were played in March and April, all at Perry Barr. They included:

28 March	vs. Partick Thistle	10-0
30 March	vs. Wolves	5-2
4 April	vs. Small Heath	5-4

In the Birmingham Cup Final, the Villa came up against their very old foes, Wednesbury Old Athletic, and this time won 3-0, having seen off the Albion in the semi-final. *Sport and Play* felt able to announce that the Villa had now got "a rattling good team."

The Aston Villa Chronicles 1874 – 1924 (and after)

The Football League 1890-91	Pld	Home W D L F A	Away W D L F A	Overall W D L F A	Pts
1 Everton	22	9 0 2 39 12	5 1 5 24 17	14 1 7 63 29	29
2 Preston North End	22	7 3 1 30 5	5 0 6 14 18	12 3 7 44 23	27
3 Notts. County	22	9 1 1 33 11	2 3 6 19 24	11 4 7 52 35	26
4 Wolverhampton Wanderers	22	8 1 2 23 8	4 1 6 16 42	12 2 8 39 50	26
5 Bolton Wanderers	22	9 0 2 36 14	3 1 7 11 20	12 1 9 47 34	25
6 Blackburn Rovers	22	7 1 3 29 19	4 1 6 23 24	11 2 9 52 43	24
7 Sunderland	22	7 2 2 31 13	3 3 5 20 18	10 5 7 51 31	23
8 Burnley	22	7 1 3 33 24	2 2 7 19 39	9 3 10 52 63	21
9 Aston Villa	22	5 4 2 29 18	2 0 9 16 40	7 4 11 45 58	18
10 Accrington	22	5 1 5 19 19	1 3 7 9 31	6 4 12 28 50	16
11 Derby County	22	6 1 4 38 28	1 0 10 9 53	7 1 14 47 81	15
12 West Bromwich Albion	22	3 1 7 17 26	2 1 8 17 31	5 2 15 34 57	12

1890-91 League and FA Cup Results

Sep	6th A Wolves	1-2	8000
	13th H Notts County	3-2	5000
	20th A Burnley	1-2	7000
	27th H West Bromwich A	0-4	
Oct	4th A Bolton Wanderers	0-4	
	11th H Everton	2-2	10000
	18th A Derby County	4-5	
	25th H Derby County	4-0	4000
Nov	1st A West Bromwich A	3-0	
	8th H Burnley	4-4	
	15th H Accrington	3-1	8000
	22nd H Bolton Wanderers	5-0	9000

	29th A Notts County	1-7	5000
Dec	6th A Blackburn Rovers	1-5	4000
	13th H Blackburn Rovers	2-2	
	26th H Sunderland	0-0	8000
Jan	1st A Everton	0-5	
	10th A Sunderland	1-5	5000
	17th H Casuals (FAC)	13-1	5000
	24th A Preston North End	1-4	
	31st A Stoke (FAC)	0-3	
Mar	9th H Preston North End	0-1	
	14th H Wolves	6-2	
	21st A Accrington	3-1	

End of Season Postscripts

The previous season's lowly league position became one position worse this season, and disaster actually loomed very large indeed – at one point, Villa were lying in tenth place. One singular event at virtually the end of the season transformed matters – the signing of Charlie Athersmith, who scored a hat-trick in his second League game, that 6-2 home win over Wolves. Up until then, much of the season had been most discouraging.

The Aston Villa Chronicles 1874 – 1924 (and after)

However, Villa did finish in ninth place and fourth from bottom, and that – under the rules extant – meant that they would need to seek re-election. In fact, this embarrassment was avoided by the fact that the League that year voted to increase the number of clubs to fourteen, re-election being suspended that season.

The club's report to the AGM declared that there was a *deficit* over the year amounting to £125. The press picked up on this and were somewhat incredulous that that should be the case, *Sport and Play* declaring that "[the deficit] had hardly been expected after the hearty and generous support received from the football-loving public", especially during a season that had not risen to great heights. The journal suggested, "Something [must be] radically wrong with the management …". For daring to be so forthright, the journal reported (a couple of weeks later) that "there had been a good deal of indignation and tall talk" received from official sources in connection with those statements, but the journal declared its independence and right to report what it thought fair.

As it happened, the AGM went off reasonably peacefully, except that Charlie Johnstone stood up and made a proposal to reform the committee, that it should have nine members and that the committee be reorganised as three committees, and that the offices of honorary secretary and honorary treasurer should be abolished. Clearly, Mr. Johnstone saw the need to have more focus and objectivity in the management of the club, with fair checks and balances. This led to a defensive speech by Mr. Clamp, not ostensibly of himself (as hon. sec.), it has to be said, but essentially in support of the hon. treasurer, Mr. Whitehouse. His supportive speech led to Mr. Whitehouse's re-election.

A discussion took place about the duties of the manager/secretary, and objections were raised to Mr. Ramsay working on other matters outside his working hours for the Villa; a somewhat tyrannical view, thought the *Sport and Play* reporter. Then, when Albert Albutt formally tendered his resignation from the committee, the *Sport and Play* reporter thought it odd that nothing was said on behalf of him – nor thanks given – for his services to the club, which had been energetically performed. On the other hand, there was an air of self-congratulation (on the part of the committee) that the committee had done so well to create a deficit of *"only"* £125 – despite a successful year in gate receipts.

The methods and practises of the committee would soon be re-visited.

The Aston Villa Chronicles 1874 – 1924 (and after)

16. The Golden Years of the 1890s

William McGregor, in an essay written in 1904, provided an overview of the Aston Villa of the 1890s:

> After 1887, the Villa had some bright and some dismal seasons and it was not until the days of Reynolds, Cowan and Crabtree (prior to the last named Groves was equally brilliant at left-half; Groves, indeed, was one of the greatest half-dozen footballers the world has known) that they came to the fore again. There has been no better trio at half-back than the Villa had in those days. Graham, Davie Russell and Robertson, of North End were possibly its superior, but some will contradict even that reservation.
>
> Prior to this, Tom Robertson, of Queens Park (the [later] talented referee); W. McLeod, of Cowlairs, the baldest footballer I have ever seen – when not wearing a gigantic wig – James Warner, A. Allen, Gershom Cox and Frank Coulton (in their day a rare pair of defenders), Peter Dowds, Baird and Welford, had all served the Villa with distinction. But it was under the guidance of that gentlemanly and talented leader, John Devey, that the golden age of the Villa club was reached.

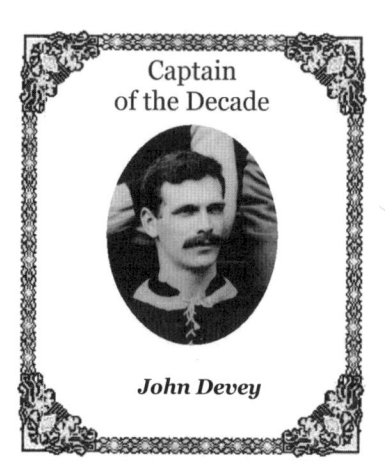

Captain of the Decade

John Devey

> John Devey assumed the captaincy in 1892. Under his leadership the club won the League five times and the FA Cup twice. In 1897 they repeated North End's great feat of winning the Cup and League Championship in one and the same season. Some think the Villa eleven of that year was the greatest side ever got together; personally I do not go quite so far as that; I have an idea that North End at their best were a more talented side, and Sunderland in the early nineties were probably more effective although not so well balanced. But the Villa were a wonderful combination.
>
> John Campbell (of the Celtic) made the team; he was one great pivot the club have had since Archie Hunter's time. His play was peculiarly suited to the Villa's style; he had brains as well as skill in dribbling and shooting. What a line he Athersmith, Devey, Wheldon and Steve Smith made! Supporting them

The Aston Villa Chronicles 1874 – 1924 (and after)

were Reynolds, Cowan and Crabtree, and behind were Spencer and Evans with Whitehouse in goal Oh! It was a great side to watch. Wheldon was pre-eminent in his day, and Athersmith was the fleetest forward seen in modern times. And what of Crabtree, the supremely great footballer of all time, the man who had reduced the game to an exact science! And, prince of centre halves, James Cowan! ... Cowan has not had an equal as a centre half, nor Crabtree as an all-round footballer; and Howard Spencer, too, the man who has been (this is my honest conviction) less generously treated by our [England] team selectors than any player of our day! They won the Cup, and finished eleven points ahead of any other team in the League – eleven points! ...[302]

The great Howard Spencer wrote, years after the 1890s:

The history of Aston Villa for ten years was a continual struggle to remain at the top. Every club used to play themselves out to beat Aston Villa, and whenever they succeeded great was their jubilation.[303]

Spencer's full-back partner in the 'double' year and for a long period, Albert Evans, said that the Villa players of his day adapted their methods to suit the needs of the moment.[304] Villa were then famed for keeping the ball on the ground, and for passing quickly and accurately from man to man. In addition, Villa acquired players who could dribble and create havoc in the opposing defence – players such as Crabtree, Devey, Wheldon and Reynolds – allied to their combination play, and (particularly) the partnership of Devey and the speedy Athersmith.

'Linesman' in *The Sporting Mail* wrote about the great team:

The team ... blended the long and short passing game to perfection. The ball was kept close for a little while [this description sounds a bit like today's patient build-up game], and then when one or other of the wing players, Steve Smith or Athersmith, was unmarked, out it would go to him, and he was off like a deer. Besides it was nothing uncommon to see either Crabtree, from left-half, or Reynolds, from right-half, kick the ball right across to the extreme wing player on the opposite side of the field, and in a twinkling the defenders found themselves up against an entirely different combination of attack.[305]

---

[302] C.B Fry's Magazine of Action and Outdoor Life Vol 2 Oct 1904 to Mar 1905 p.39
[303] Sports Argus 21 Sep 1907
[304] In Peter Morris' *Aston Villa: The History of a Great Football Club, 1874-1960*
[305] The Sporting Mail 24 Sep 1910

The Aston Villa Chronicles 1874 – 1924 (and after)

In the seven-year period from 1893 to 1900, the Villa's accomplishments were astonishing for the time – it would be many years before another team put a string of successes together of such magnitude. Seven trophies were won in that period, but not only that; in all of those seven years, the Villa were the League Division One's top goalscorers, and averaged more than two goals per game in each of those seasons. In 1897-98, the Villa were top scorers whilst finishing in sixth place in the League (thanks to scoring 47 goals at home in 15 matches), and in the last two seasons (1898-99 and 1899-1900), the Villa were each time 14 goals ahead of their nearest scoring rivals (an 18% superiority). This indicates that while defences were generally becoming tighter and more difficult to penetrate, the Villa midfield and attack had the unique ability to unlock such defences and create sufficient scoring chances.

Season	Achievement	League Position	League Games	League Goals Scored	Average Per Game	Scorers' 'League' Position
1891-92	(FA Cup Finalists)	4th	26	89	3.42	2nd
1892-93	(no trophy)	4th	30	73	2.43	3rd
1893-94	League Champions	1st	30	84	2.80	1st
1894-95	FA Cup	3rd	30	82	2.73	1st
1895-96	League Champions	1st	30	78	2.60	1st
1896-97	League Champions & FA Cup	1st	30	73	2.43	1st
1897-98	(no trophy)	6th	30	61	2.03	1st
1898-99	League Champions	1st	34	76	2.24	1st
1899-00	League Champions	1st	34	77	2.26	1st

> With the development of the League to include more teams, and gradually more from parts of the country other than the north-west and the Midlands, the League became more important.
>
> The local competitions that once sustained the Villa – the Birmingham Cup and the Lord Mayor's Charity Shield being the major ones – were no longer to have such importance.

The Aston Villa Chronicles 1874 – 1924 (and after)

Season 1891-92 : The Start of A New Era
League position: 4th *(of 14);* ***FA Cup:*** *Finalists.*

There was one big conundrum that had now been outstanding for more than 12 months: who was to fill Archie Hunter's boots? Gershom Cox first held the captaincy after Archie's retirement for a little while, but results had not gone well. Then Billy Dickson took over the job and kept it till the end of the moderately successful 1891-92 season, **John Devey**'s first season as a player with the Villa.

The Villa still had, in fact, some very talented players, but they needed welding together under a leader who could set the standard. The stars included Denny Hodgetts from old, and also the other two supremos, Cowan and Athersmith.

From the start of the season, John Devey led by example and showed indications of perhaps why he should be considered for the captaincy. Starting the League programme with four successive wins, three of them won by Villa scoring five goals on each occasion; a total of 16 goals scored, 5 conceded in those four matches. Devey himself scored seven of those goals, and he finished the season with 34 goals.

Apart from the signing of Athersmith and Devey towards the end of the previous season, Villa also signed John Baird (full-back) and Percy Hislop (forward), two more Scots for the Villa camp. Charlie Hare (a Brummie) had also been signed. The well-thought-of McKnight had left to make way for Devey.

The Season's Play

September, 1891

The first match of the season was against Cup-holders **Blackburn Rovers** at Perry Barr. This match, at the very least, upheld Devey's reputation. Apart from John Devey and another new signing, Percy Hislop, the season's starting line-up was similar to that that ended the previous season.

Villa: *Warner; W. Evans, Cox; Jas.Brown, Jas.Cowan, Geo.Campbell; Athersmith, Dickson, J.Devey, Hislop, Hodgetts.*

[From the *Athletic News*] The Rovers opened the scoring within ten minutes – "this was very heartily cheered, [but] the cup-holders were at this time playing such a splendid game … Then the Villa also showed glimpses of what they really are capable of, and for just over half-an-hour the folks were simply

The Aston Villa Chronicles 1874 – 1924 (and after)

delighted ... with the brilliant exhibition of football that went on ... When Hislop drew level with a magnificent shot from a pass of Athersmith's, and [when] John Devey followed this up with a real trimmer, the folks were wound up to concert pitch!" Sadly for Rovers, one of their players twisted his knee and had to be carried off, just before half-time. Against ten men, Villa had command of the game, and produced second half goals to win, 5-1. Devey had opened his account with two goals. Cowan and Brown, as providers to their forwards, were "absolutely first-class."

The next match was again at home, and against the **Albion**. As in the previous match, the away team scored in the first ten minutes – after a move in which future Villa player Groves was prominent – to herald a brilliant contest in the first–half, with little to choose between the two sides.

[From the *Athletic News*] As the game developed, Villa's superior condition took over, with Athersmith equalising five minutes into the second half, soon followed by a Devey goal. When Hislop scored a third, that was effectively the end of Albion's chances of getting back into the match, and the Villa ran out 5-1 winners for the second week running.

"I don't believe there is a team in the kingdom who would have held the Perry Barr combination at bay ... James Cowan, as usual, was the shining light, and the plucky and persistent manner in which he tackled Groves was a terrible nuisance to that clever and gentlemanly Scotch player." But all the players did well, and Dickson played better than he had ever done before. Hislop was hurt early on and swapped places with Hodgetts, but was "undoubtedly a good capture, as also Jack Devey, who seems more at home with the Villa team than he did at Cape Hill [St. George's]."

The matter of the Villa team's excellent condition was remarked on again after the Villa's win at **Preston** (1-0):

[From the *Athletic News*] "... their quickness on the ball won them much admiration ... I attribute the Villa success simply to their excellent condition and if a North Ender got a start with the ball, he would quickly be overtaken by an opponent and relieved of his burden ..." Going by their play, the Villa should have had more goals.

In their next match – back at Perry Barr – Villa ran up a 4-1 lead in a one-sided first half against **Sunderland**, but Sunderland rallied in the second half so that the game finished 5-3 to the Villa. Sunderland's Campbell scored a hat-trick – all "rattling good goals."

The Aston Villa Chronicles 1874 – 1924 (and after)

October, 1891

Now top of the table (on goal average), Villa next went to **Derby**. Villa, having gained the lead, were behind by half-time (1-2) in a ding-dong match. However, an injury reduced Derby's numbers, and the play became even, though Villa rode some luck, Villa's woodwork being hit several times. Astonishingly, another injury in Derby's ranks meant that they had only nine fit men on the field (plus one other), yet they scored again before the Villa got their second. Derby scored an excellent fourth late on. The result put Derby level on points with the Villa. Athersmith and Dickson were noted for their magnificent passing runs in this match.

Returning to Perry Barr, Villa's opponents were **Bolton**, who attracted a crowd of less than 4,000, but it was a rainy day. Bolton, however, took a first half lead and the Villa goal also had several close shaves. The game brightened up after the interval, and Hodgetts forced an own goal from the Bolton defence. That was all to no avail, as, despite Villa pressure, they allowed Bolton space to score yet another, and win 1-2 in a not very brilliant game. "Had the Villa bubble burst?", their supporters were beginning to ask, and asked again after losing 1-4 at **Burnley** the following week. The Burnley defeat, however, was unfortunate, as Warner received a bad kick and was lost to the match with the best part of it still to be played.

In the next match, away at **Stoke**, changes were called, though the change of keeper was forced upon the Villa by last week's injury to Warner, who was to be out until January, though part of the reason for that was for coming to loggerheads with the Villa committee.

> **Villa**: *Hinckley; W. Evans, Cox; Jas. Brown, Jas. Cowan, Baird;*
> *Athersmith, Dickson, J. Devey, Hodgetts, Louis Campbell.*

[From the *Athletic News*] After a gradual start, Villa started taking command, and by half-time, they were three-up.

With the wind in Stoke's favour in the second half, the game was transformed. The Villa decided to play a more defensive game by pulling back their forwards, and throughout the half the Villa ventured out from their own half not more than six times! (though one Athersmith shot was headed out.) With Villa 3-1 up with ten minutes to go, Stoke then scored from a penalty (3-2), and went all out for the equaliser, one shot hitting both posts before being cleared. Then the crossbar intervened, and more shots were hurled upon the Villa goal, which somehow withstood further penetration.

The Aston Villa Chronicles 1874 – 1924 (and after)

> Ominously, Sunderland, who had spent the early weeks of the season in bottom place, had now risen to sixth in the League.

Away again, at **Darwen**, Charlie Hare was brought in to replace Dickson. The Villa returned to their 5-goal ways by winning 5-1 after leading 4-0 at half-time, against moderate opposition.

November, 1891

The score against **Notts County** in the next game was the same, 5-1, this time after leading 4-1 at half-time. The County tried hard to come back in the second half, even though they faced a severe deficit ...

[From the *Athletic News*] "... their deft passing and pretty, quick, exchanges being greatly admired by the huge crowd [of 10,000].

"But try as hard as they would, and twist and turn and wriggle and pass as they pleased, they could not break through a defence which could be described as adamantine in character. [For Villa, a] lot of fine runs were made by Hodgetts, Devey and Hare, and Athersmith electrified the spectators [with] his fine bursts of speed and lightning shots. Fed as he was by Devey and Hodgetts, backed up and defended by the unselfish Hare, the brilliant Villa right-winger raised cheer on cheer by his display, whilst on the other wing, little Campbell beetled and dusted along in a style that pleased his clever companion, and enabled the home forwards to have a right good time amongst the Notts defenders."

The Villa's latest little 'bubble' continued with a visit to the **Albion**, where they entertained another 10,000 crowd, half of which had come from Birmingham. The first half was a ding-dong struggle, with the Villa edging it at half-time with a 1-0 lead. In the second half...

[From the *Athletic News*] "... it was simply wonderful the way in which they gained complete mastery of the Albion." Nevertheless, it was 30 minutes into the half before the Villa increased their lead, through "a sort of grass-hopper" by Louis Campbell.

Villa's third was the result of "a bit of work by Devey on the line [which] culminated in a whizzing centre, and Hare put it through on his cranium. Dismay spread all over the Albion countenances."

That win left the Albion stranded at the bottom of the League table, and Villa's next match was against the bottom-but-one team, **Stoke**, at Perry Barr, who put their emphasis on defence, and the saving talents of their keeper. A "huge crowd" saw the Villa take till close to the end of the match to break the final deadlock, and to win

The Aston Villa Chronicles 1874 – 1924 (and after)

2-1. The final goal was thus described:

[From the *Athletic News*] From a corner, "Athersmith rocketed the ball across goal; there was a mixture of arms and legs and leather a-bobbing up and down and which caused a perfect pandemonium of yelling at the top end of the field. [James] Brown, at length, drove the ball into the net and as the players were retiring from goal, it was seen how fierce had been the struggle. Four Stoke players sat solidly on their flatnesses, and the whole team looked disappointed and a little woe-begone."

Then it was on the road again – to **Everton**, who were low down in the table, but were a good home side.

Villa: *Hinckley; W.Evans, Baird; Jas.Brown, Jas.Cowan, G.Campbell; Athersmith, Dickson, J.Devey, Hodgetts, L.Campbell.*

[From the *Athletic News*] There was "an ugly wind blowing nearly from corner to corner", and Everton began the match in command of the game, "when Cowan gave the ball to Devey and he transferred it over to his left-wing. Hodgetts, taking deliberate aim from distance" scored with a fine shot. From hereon in, it was all Everton, yet the interval was reached with the Villa still leading, 1-0. In the second half, the pressure continued until Villa's defence finally caved in. The Villa lost, 1-5.

At the end of November, 1891, there was no particularly outstanding team, and the leading clubs in the League were as follows:

Leading Positions in The Football League	Pld	Home W D L F A	Away W D L F A	Overall W D L F A	Pts
1 Bolton Wanderers	15	6 1 1 19 10	4 0 3 9 12	10 1 4 28 22	21
2 Preston North End	14	6 0 1 21 5	3 1 3 8 11	9 1 4 29 16	19
3 **Aston Villa**	**13**	**5 0 1 23 9**	**4 0 3 16 16**	**9 0 4 39 25**	**18**
4 Sunderland	12	6 0 0 24 6	2 0 4 16 18	8 0 4 40 24	16

Before the Everton match, Villa had been in second place. Sunderland were still quietly mounting the League ladder after that poor start to their season.

The Aston Villa Chronicles 1874 – 1924 (and after)

December, 1891

Villa's first match in December was against **Burnley**, at Perry Barr. Athersmith was not available for selection in this match, and Hare came in on the right-wing.

[From the *Athletic News*] For the first half-hour, there was only one team in it – Aston Villa! But the home supporters were beginning to despair that their team would ever score. However, Hare then put in a smart centre from which Devey "scooped the ball cleverly through the corner", for Villa to take the lead. The pressure continued on the Burnley defence and Villa scored two more in the 15 minutes to half-time.

When the score reached 5-0, the Burnley players started losing their tempers, and resorted to tripping and other heavy fouls to keep the Villa out. Even their keeper started making insulting gestures at the crowd after they jeered him for accidentally hitting Devey in the face.

Ultimately, Burnley pulled a goal back, but then Devey completed his hat-trick. The Villa ran out 6-1 winners and gained adequate revenge for the sound beating the Villa had at Burnley earlier in the season.

The next match was supposed to be a fixture at Accrington, but after seven minutes the match was called off because of a blizzard. The *Athletic News* reporter wrote:

> For 17 miles we travelled through a perpetual fleece, and the outlook was utterly in the extreme ... When I had slid down the descent from Accrington station into the street, I found myself wading through about six inches of slush, whilst a regular blizzard was whizzing through the town ...

The week before Christmas, the Villa met the **Wolves** at Molineux, and in front of 8,000 spectators, lost 0-2, the Villa play being disappointing. On Boxing Day, the weather had changed from bitter frost to soft slush, and the Villa beat **Darwen** 7-0, although: "It was said that the Darwen team had been allowed to travel all the way from Lancashire without refreshments of any description ... [and] long before the finish, the team looked thoroughly flagged and heavy." And they were down to 10 men after 15 minutes.

The 28 December saw the Villa play "one of the best and most exiting games ... at Perry Barr this season", said the *Athletic News* reporter. The match was against **Everton** in front of the biggest crowd of the season at Perry Barr, so far.

"It was a hard race right up to the finish", as Villa made up for earlier shortcomings (particularly in the shooting department) by finishing the match strongly, but it was too late.

The Aston Villa Chronicles 1874 – 1924 (and after)

"Hinckley was as nervous as a kitten", and caused Everton's second by intercepting a ball that was going out and allowing an Everton player to take the ball off him. Everton were leading 0-3 at half-time.

The second half was very different, with Villa on the rampage, and they quickly pulled back two goals, and looked as if they would carry the game. Dickson, however, continued to miss chances, and the Everton defence played strongly. Villa again let in Everton, and Hinckley allowed an easy shot to sneak home. Villa did get another goal, but it was too late, and the score finished at 3-4.

January, 1892

The Villa then travelled to Nottingham to meet **Notts County**, and lost 2-5, having again played disappointingly, with Hodgetts missing a penalty. In the next game, that re-arranged match at **Accrington**, the Villa lost 2-3 after being 0-2 down at half-time, but at least they re-found some method in this match.

The following is a report on the match against **Derby County** at Perry Barr, and sourrounding issues:

[From the *Athletic News*] Villa's considerable up-and-down form of late, and the spate of defeats, brought about a "plan of campaign meeting between committee and players in mid-week."

There had been grave doubts at this match being played. "Oh, how it did freeze. There is a story going about one man at Perry Barr who stood talking to a friend for five minutes, and when he turned to leave, was frozen in so hard that his boots had to be unlaced, and he was lifted out of them and sent home in a cab!"

"The ground had been splendidly prepared by the indefatigable Mr. Secretary Ramsay, several gentlemen of the committee, and a small army of shovel slingers, and the meadow looked like a huge tricoloured flag, with its white undercoat, and its top garment of red tar or gravel dust, and the bright blue lines athwart its surface."

"With Evans having missed his train from Wales, and Cox and George Campbell on the sick-list, Frank Coulton was recalled for the first time in months, and Harry Devey returned also [for Campbell].

"It was soon evident that the experience of the past few weeks had taught the team a lesson. Not only did the half-backs play closer to the heels of their forwards ... but the rearguard have at last come to the decision that an open game is the best one." The result was brilliant – the home team being three-up at half-time. The second half was much of the same vein, except that James Brown had to be taken off after being kicked in the head when bending down to head the ball. Villa won, 6-0.

The Aston Villa Chronicles 1874 – 1924 (and after)

The first round of the FA Cup saw the Villa win 4-1 against **Heanor Town** (at home), but the final score belies the fact that the Heanor colliery team put up a gallant fight, and held the Villa at half-time, 0-0.

The Villa then played a friendly against Notts Forest, and won 3-2 in a fine match with...

> ... the ancient runs of the Villa, their vigorous shooting, and the general go-ahead conduct of the whole brigade a pleasure to behold.

The Forest keeper (Brown) was many times given tumultuous applause for his fine saves, and the Forest team played fine football, and with pluck.

Frank Coulton showed signs of returning to the form of old.

The second round of the FA Cup then came up with a home tie against **Darwen**. The match was won comfortably, 2-0, but the players had to put up with a boisterous wind, and the Darwen keeper did well to keep the score down.

February, 1892

The third round of the Cup was played at Wolves, a match that brought 25,000 to watch these two west Midland foes. It was considered an astonishing 'gate'.

Villa: *Warner; Cox, W.Evans; H.Devey, Jas. Cowan, J.Baird;*
Athersmith, J.Devey, Dickson, Hodgetts, L.Campbell.

[From the *Athletic News*] The match was closely fought, and though Wolves opened the scoring, the Villa gradually took over the game, and Louis Campbell equalised through an overhead kick, that being the score at half-time. The Villa's next goal came through an own goal, but Villa's third came from a "magnificent run by Athersmith [down] half the length of the field, finishing with a splendid centre which J. Devey had little difficulty in converting." Villa won, 3-1.

FAC Semi-Final	vs Sunderland	4-1	*Attendance:*
27 February, 1892	at Bramall Lane, Sheffield		30,000

Villa: *Warner; Cox, W.Evans; H.Devey, Jas. Cowan, J.Baird;*
Athersmith, J.Devey, Dickson, Hodgetts, L.Campbell.

"... [This was] the memorable occasion when the great Northern club were at the top of their form and fame ... and were unquestionably the favourites ... There was a tremendous crowd at Bramall Lane, and the Sheffielders were all agog with excitement.

The Aston Villa Chronicles 1874 – 1924 (and after)

"Sunderland started off with a tremendous rattle, and before one could say 'Jack Robinson', they were [a goal] up, and they shook hands with each other with great gusto. Also, they had the best of the game till nearly half-time, for the Villa couldn't get into their stride, and were dropped about rather mercilessly ... but just before the interval, they came with a swing and a rush, the ball bobbed serenely right under the bar and Billy Dickson nearly pulled Doig's [the keeper's] jersey off his back, what time Jack Devey hummed a rocketing shot past the left-handed protestor. The referee was following the ball with his optic and Dickson knew it! There were wild and whirling words by some of the Northerners, but the goal was allowed, and the Villa skipper smiled wickedly!" [1-1 at half-time]

"When they resumed hostilities ... there was only one side in the running – which wasn't Sunderland. Dennis Hodgetts met a swift cross-shot of Athersmith's, and it bobbed against the meshes while Doig clawed the air. John Devey [later] treated him to a daisy-cutter that scorched the grass as it flew, and [then] Dickson rolled up in his lordly fashion and potted the ball for the fourth time."

This result brought the Villa and Albion to face one another in the final. Old Fogey reported on the joy of the Villa fans:

> At that period, there was a famous music-hall song everywhere ... the idiotic refrain of which was 'Ta-ra—ra-boom-de-ay'; but it had a catchy tune, and was easily sung. Bramall Lane heard it given with tremendous force and volume, and the men from Birmingham had the time of their lives, for the Villa had played a really superb game, and if they could have repeated such an exhibition, no other team would have had a chance in the final. But they didn't ...[306]

March, 1892

The next match was a League appointment at **Blackburn**, where the Villa, without Athersmith, Devey and Hodgetts (on England duty), and Evans (Wales), they led at half-time, 2-1, having led 2-0 till just before interval. Then the Rovers equalised, and their supporters roused their team with continual cheering till they took the lead. Villa equalised with five minutes to go, but, at the 'death', Rovers won the match, 3-4.

12 – 2 ! Only the week before the Final, the Villa achieved their all-time scoring record in the League by beating **Accrington** 12-2 (5-0 at half-time), with 4 apiece for John Devey and

---

[306] Villa News & Record 1 Apr 1926

The Aston Villa Chronicles 1874 – 1924 (and after)

Louis Campbell. The goals came "with a regularity and persistency that fairly drove the cheering spectators wild!"

> About that astonishing result against Accrington, Charlie Johnstone later wrote:
>
> I have always regarded that match as the acme of perfection in the oblique forward passing game, combined with the triangulation combination of the wing half-back and the two forwards in front of him.[307]

In the Accrington match, the Villa played with the same team that had beaten Sunderland so convincingly in the semi-final, so the Villa's expectations were high – and they were the favourites to win the FA Cup.

FA Cup Final	vs West Bromwich Albion at Crystal Palace, London	0-3 19 March, 1892	Attendance. 32,810

Warner
Cox   W.Evans
H.Devey   Jas. Cowan   J.Baird
Athersmith   J.Devey   Dickson   Hodgetts   L.Campbell

In West Brom's first attack, Jasper Geddes sent in a screw shot: Warner received it, but the ball seemed to spin out of his hands, and the first goal was scored for the Albion only three minutes from the start. According to Old Fogey, the shot either hit an indentation in the ground, or had 'side' on it, for it left poor Jimmy groping for the ball – "it twisted out of his hands, ran up his arm [and] over his shoulder [and into the net]."

It was later described in the press as a "terrible blunder" but it looked likely to be academic when Villa swarmed to the West Brom end. Jimmy Cowan put a free-kick straight into the West Brom goal-net - but as nobody touched the ball it didn't count as a goal, such were the rules of the day.

For 20 minutes Villa used the wind to stay on top, then Jimmy Warner had his second chance to shine: Warner partly muffed it, and Nicholls rushed up to send it through the posts. After half-time it was 2-0 to West Brom, against the wind, against the odds.

---

[307] In his column in the Sporting Mail 12 Oct 1912

The Aston Villa Chronicles 1874 – 1924 (and after)

In the fifty-fifth minute, West Brom's 'Baldy' Reynolds[308] shot from 40 yards. Warner was hopelessly out of position; 3-0 to Albion. Although Aston Villa dominated the rest of the game, they could not score.

Reporters chose words like "lamentable exhibition" to describe Jimmy Warner's afternoon's work, and Villa fans started their inquests. Attention switched to the Old College public house at Spring Hill, where Warner was the landlord. That evening supporters sought retribution by smashing all the windows in the pub.

Naturally, this whole affair upset Jimmy Warner after being such a loyal and valiant servant since 1886, and a hero of the '87 Cup-winning side. He immediately left the Villa and soon went to play for Newton Heath (later Manchester United),[309] but in the end he left the country for the United States, where he spent the rest of his days. This was indeed a pity, for Villa were on the verge of true greatness; Jimmy Warner had served Villa well – for the club, it was one more step backwards in order to go forward.

William McGregor went on record to say,[310] "I expressed my opinion that Warner ... did his very best ... and am still of that opinion. The reason that Villa did not score was that the Albion half-backs were too good for the Villa attack ... On that day, Albion were the better side."

Old Fogey reckoned that Albion's first goal had shattered Warner's nerve. All the goals would normally have been saved by Warner.[311] However, Charlie Johnstone put more light on the matter of Warner's performance, reporting that Jimmy had been involved in training a boxer on whom – as Charlie put it – "he had put his shirt", and when the man was defeated on the preceding Friday night:

> Warner simply lost his head. He was more like a madman than anything else when he joined the team [in training] at Worcester; his nerve and judgment had gone completely, and it was a physical impossibility for the man to do himself justice at the Oval on the following day.[312]

Charlie further elaborated about Villa's failure to perform:

> Over-confidence was a great factor in losing that match. We were training at Holt Fleet, near Worcester, and on the Thursday prior to the final the whole

---

[308] Soon afterwards, he was signed by the Villa.
[309] Doubtless through the agency of former Villa committee-man Albert Albutt, who was now secretary of Newton Heath.
[310] The 'W. McGregor' column in Sports Argus 29 Jan 1910
[311] Villa News & Record 30 Apr 1924 – "Some Famous Villa Players"
[312] In his column in The Sporting Mail 19 Apr 1913

The Aston Villa Chronicles 1874 – 1924 (and after)

team followed the hounds for miles, returning to the hotel late at night completely tired out. That was a blunder of which we did not appreciate the full effect until after the battle on the Saturday.

> Those persons who are not in the habit of going to football matches little know the excitement that prevails amongst those who do. The success of the two Midland clubs, the Villa and Albion has caused a floodtide of enthusiasm and the Cup contest today is a very general topic of conversation. Badges of the Villa's colours with the words "Play Up Villa" were being sold in large numbers at the match last Saturday, as were also ivy leaves bearing the same words. The latter form of badge has latterly become very popular and after one-cup tie I was told that Hodgetts, the clever left-wing player of the Villa, was wearing one with "Play up Dennis!" printed on it in large gold letters. It had been presented to him by an admirer and Hodgetts seemed exceedingly proud of it.
>
> *The Birmingham Post,* March 1892

The result of the Final was received in Birmingham with astonishment. Many had turned up at The Oval just to see how many the Villa would score! John Devey wrote that, following the match, "... we all felt our chance of securing FA Cup medals was gone for ever."[313] The reality was far from it, however, although several players had gone by the time 1895 came around!

Back to the League and Villa's next opponents were **Sunderland**, who now were almost certainties for the championship – and they had not dropped any points at home. There was an extraordinary team selection, for the keeper's position was allocated to half-back George Campbell, who, earlier in the season, had gone into goal in a match when Warner was taken off injured. He had played in goal for Renton, his former club.

Villa: *Geo. Campbell; Cox, W.Evans; H.Devey, Jas.Cowan, J.Baird; Athersmith, J.Devey, Dickson, L.Campbell, Hodgetts.*

[From the *Athletic News*] Villa went hard at it in the first half, and the hard fought encounter produced a goal-less first half.

Ten minutes into the second half, "the ball was literally rammed into the [Villa] net, and G. Campbell and Cox with it!" Villa then strove to get back into the game, gaining an equaliser 25 minutes later, through Harry Devey.

With five minutes to go, the spectators were already leaving, when a grand drive was deflected sufficiently to send it into the Villa net for the winner.

---

[313] In his column in The Sporting Mail 20 Jan 1906

The Aston Villa Chronicles 1874 – 1924 (and after)

April, 1892

Against **Bolton Wanderers** – also away – Villa gave the keeper's job to Diver, a Warwickshire cricketer with a seemingly apt surname! He played in goal for the remainder of the season's matches. Hare came in for Hodgetts, who was playing for England against Scotland, and George Campbell now played at full-back in place of Evans. Geo. Campbell played very well until a few minutes into the second half when he received a nasty blow to the face. Badly hurt, he left the pitch for a period, but the applause on his reappearance testified to the excellent game he had played. The Villa won, 2-1.

On 4 April, the Villa played a friendly against Stoke (winning 8-0) to raise funds for Wednesbury Old Athletic and also St. George's. Both clubs' fortunes had dropped alarmingly since the League started. This gesture had the affect of raising the Villa's popularity in the Midlands, but both clubs soon became defunct, though the Athletic were re-formed.

As the Villa came out onto the pitch for the home match against **Preston**, one or two players were given a great ovation by the crowd, and for George Campbell in particular. There was only one team in it in the first half, and the Villa went in at the interval 2-0 in the lead, with the Preston keeper successful in keeping the score down. The second half was not so interesting, but when Preston started playing more like their old style, and pulled a goal back, that had the affect of rousing the Villa, who scored again, and won 3-1. For some reason, the holiday spirit grabbed hold of the Villa players too much, for on the Easter Monday, the Villa were soundly beaten at Perry Barr by the **Wolves**.

Sunderland and the Villa were far ahead of any other team in terms of goals scored, with the Villa treating their Perry Barr faithful to an average 4.8 goals scored per home game.

The Football League 1891-92 Top Places	Pld	Home W D L F A	Away W D L F A	Overall W D L F A	Pts
1 Sunderland	26	13 0 0 55 11	8 0 5 38 25	21 0 5 93 36	42
2 Preston North End	26	12 0 1 42 8	6 1 6 19 23	18 1 7 61 31	37
3 Bolton Wanderers	26	9 2 2 29 14	8 0 5 22 23	17 2 7 51 37	36
4 **Aston Villa**	26	**10 0 3 63 23**	**5 0 8 26 33**	**15 0 11 89 56**	**30**
5 Everton	26	8 2 3 32 22	4 2 7 17 27	12 4 10 49 49	28

The Aston Villa Chronicles 1874 – 1924 (and after)

1891-92 League and FA Cup Results		
Sep 5th H Blackburn Rovers	5-1	9000
12th H West Bromwich A	5-1	12000
19th A Preston North End	1-0	
28th H Sunderland	5-3	10000
Oct 3rd A Derby County	2-4	10000
10th H Bolton Wanderers	1-2	4000
17th A Burnley	1-4	7000
24th A Stoke	3-2	7000
31st A Darwen	5-1	4000
Nov 7th H Notts County	5-1	10000
14th A West Bromwich A	3-0	10000
21st H Stoke	2-1	10000
28th A Everton	1-5	
Dec 5th H Burnley	6-1	8000
19th A Wolves	0-2	8000
26th H Darwen	7-0	5000
28th H Everton	3-4	12000
Jan 2nd A Notts County	2-5	6000
4th A Accrington	2-3	
9th H Derby County	6-0	
16th H Heanor Town (FAC)	4-1	3000
30th H Darwen (FAC)	2-0	
Feb 13th A Wolves (FAC)	3-1	25000
27th N Sunderland (FAC SF)	4-1	30000
Mar 5th A Blackburn Rovers	3-4	5000
12th H Accrington	12-2	8000
19th N West Brom A (FAC F)	0-3	32810
26th A Sunderland	1-2	
Apr 2nd A Bolton Wanderers	2-1	
16th H Preston North End	3-1	10000
18th H Wolves	3-6	

End of Season Postscripts

Apart from a very satisfactory League recovery, Villa also proceeded to the FA Cup Final to meet the once more – but this time the Albion midfield was the better, and Villa's keeper (Jimmy Warner) did not do at all well, as has been discussed.

George Campbell seemed to be gaining hero status, as were some other players, including John Devey, who, in his first season, had shot 34 goals in 30 League and FA Cup matches. Scoring at the rate of one or more per match was (and is) a rare event. Furthermore, Louis Campbell came into the side in November and helped out substantially with the scoring: 15 goals in 18 League matches, and two other players scored 15 or more, while Athersmith weighed-in with another 11.

At the Villa's AGM, the committee were proud to announce a credit balance of £756 – a considerable improvement over the previous year. That, compared with West Bromwich Albion's deficit of £143 (even though they had beaten Villa in the FA Cup Final) showed clearly which club was receiving the better support. As the *Athletic News*' writer remarked in the post-Preston match edition of that journal:

> I do not believe there is such another stick-to-their-own-team multitude in the three kingdoms, and if the players and managers of the club are not proud of their following, they are an ungrateful lot.

The Aston Villa Chronicles 1874 – 1924 (and after)

Season 1892-93: The Crises Reach Their Zenith
League Division 1 position: 4*th* *(of 16);* **FA Cup:** *1st Round.*
The League now consisted of two divisions.

There were several comings and goings (mainly comings) on the signings front. Big Billy Dickson's move to Stoke was the main outgoing, plus the loss (of course) of keeper Jimmy Warner. With the departure of Dickson, John Devey was duly given the responsibility as captain. This season would be a fairly quiet start to his career as captain, but, till the end of the century, Villa would hardly look back!

Not many signings were significant – perhaps the most questionable being the signing of two local full-backs, John Ramsay and Arthur Stokes, and a Scottish forward named James Fleming, all of whom were played at the start of the season. They lasted for a very short time, however, and were gone at the end of the season. The main signings were the keeper **Bill Dunning**, midfielder **Peter Dowds** (who did not stay long but made a *huge* impression) and winger **Albert Woolley** (who did not make his début until late in the season). There was also a welcome return for Albert Brown, after playing no games in 1891-92. The Villa also signed yet another Devey – but he was not to be as successful as his relatives Harry and John.

The acquisition of Peter Dowds was not at all straight-forward, however. Reported as having signed for the Villa in mid-August, the following week he had apparently been "spirited away" by Celtic! Off dashed the Villa's representatives to retrieve the situation, which they clearly succeeded in doing.

A total of 27 players would be tried this season, compared to 20 the season before. The team at the end of the season would be quite different to that which started it and with some painful moments on the way through the season, one of which was another – but major – upheaval of the club management, and the other concerning Sunderland. Old Fogey remembered the matches against Sunderland:

> The worst year the Villa ever had against Sunderland … they were 'bobby dazzlers' and no mistake. They had a dark, dour-looking, black-haired lad in the centre, named [Johnny] Campbell,[314] and the manner in which he could twinkle his feet was bewildering enough to turn any ordinary half-back giddy.
>
> There was also another very forward half-back called Hugh Thomson, and a stolid defender yclept Donald Gow. There were others almost as good, and they were a splashing, dashing, smashing team, who could also play stunning

---

[314] Not the player of the same name who played for Villa later in the 1890s.

The Aston Villa Chronicles 1874 – 1924 (and after)

good football, and some of the brethren couldn't half shoot.

Well, they came down to Perry Barr in the early part of that season, and they waltzed through the Villa defence like you see a circus rider go through a paper hoop.

Sunderland won by six goals to one ... [and] in comparison with their opponents, the Villa were 'very small potatoes' that dreary afternoon. We all went home, and quite expected the deluge.

It came a few weeks later on Wearside, for Sunderland walked through them again by 6 to 0; so that the rather pitiful record of the two clubs that year was 12 to 1 on Sunderland.[315]

Sunderland were then at their greatest, and had replaced Preston as the country's top club. However, both those clubs would soon be replaced by an even greater team whose reign would last much longer.

The Season's Play

September, 1892

The scheduled opening game this year was at the **Albion**. Amazingly, as the scheduled referee (J. J. Bentley) was delayed in the train system, William McGregor at first deputised as referee. That was objected to by the Albion, of course. After a few minutes, Mr. Cooper of Wolverhampton "usurped the League chairman's position".

Villa: *Dunning; Stokes, Ramsay; Dowds, Jas.Cowan, Jas.Brown; Athersmith, J.Devey, Fleming, Hodgetts, L.Campbell.*

[From the *Athletic News*] "Both teams looked wonderfully well, though the visitors had the more robust appearance."

It was an entertaining first half, dominated by both sets of half-backs, with Dowds showing well. It was 0-0 at half-time.

The solitary goal – Villa's winner – came late in the match following a corner involving Hodgetts and Campbell, followed by Devey passing to Athersmith, who hit it first time.

"In Dowds", said the report, "Villa possess an undoubted champion. His tackling, judgment and kicking were little short of wonderful."

---

[315] Villa News and Record 17 Sep 1910

The Aston Villa Chronicles 1874 – 1924 (and after)

> Subsequently, it had been found that Peter Dowds had played illegally against the Albion. He was suspended for a month from the time of the upcoming Sunderland match, and it was ordered that the Albion game had to be replayed on the 19 September.

In what turned out to be the first legitimate League fixture of the season, the Villa then had a good mid-week win at **Burnley** (2-0). Next on the agenda was **Everton** at Perry Barr, and a large crowd turned up for what was expected to be a classic encounter; it did not disappoint.

[From the *Athletic News*] "Taking the game all round, it was most exciting and full of incident. It was not until the last quarter of an hour that the partisans of Aston Villa [could] breathe freely."

After some early Everton pressure, "Athersmith was seen careering off like a greyhound, and, fairly racing past Howarth, had only the keeper to beat. James [the keeper] came out to meet him, but in kicking the ball, sadly strained his leg, and the right-winger scooted it across to Hodgetts, who put it through." This remained the score till half-time, despite a tremendous effort put in by both sides.

The second half also started sensationally, with Fleming extending Villa's lead, before Everton pulled one back. This triggered enormous pressure from Everton, and the Villa faithful, for some time, had their hearts in their mouths. Finally, Villa took over, and Athersmith's fine centre was converted by Devey. Fleming later added a fourth.

Villa's team was now seen to be strong in all departments, with Stokes, Cowan, Athersmith, Dunning and Dowds being the most prominent.

The Villa continued their fine opening to the season with a 1-0 win at **Stoke**, but then the first of the **Sunderland** contests that Old Fogey referred to came about, at Perry Barr. Some 15,000 turned up in high expectation of another Villa victory, but Peter Dowds had been suspended for the next month.

The *Athletic News* reporter reckoned that Sunderland's big win was mainly down to the Villa's defensive give-aways, though he admitted that Sunderland played "exceedingly well". Dunning and Cowan were the only Villa players that came out of the match with any credit.

Dispirited, the Villa then had to replay the opening **Albion** match (away) on the following Monday, and lost 2-3. For that match, Albert Brown returned to the team after his very long absence in place of an unavailable Athersmith, with Brown showing some of his old form. That was the start of a sequence of four away matches, all of which were lost, and the next one at **Bolton** was lost by the margin of 0-5. The Villa had conceded 14 goals in their last three matches.

October, 1892

Next up was the return match at **Everton**. The Villa team by this time had been much revised, and Albert Brown would be virtually a permanent feature at inside-right. Dowds was still suspended.

Villa: *Dunning; Stokes, W. Evans; Jas.Brown, Jas.Cowan, G.Campbell; Athersmith, Alb.Brown, J.Devey, Hodgetts, L.Campbell.*

[From the *Athletic News*] Everton supplied the early pressure, but the Villa defence was on form, and when the Villa found their game, the match swung end-to-end in a "splendid contest", but finished the first half with no score.

The game was not of the same quality in the second half, but the Villa defence remained in form. Everton scored a solitary goal to win the match.

"The recent defeats have sent some panic amongst their supporters", said the report, "and criticism of the committee was rife. Ramsay has been sent to Scotland to find answers."

In heavy rain, the Villa then went to play the **Wolves** on their ground, and lost 1-2. In the meantime, George Ramsay had made some signings that were already playing for the reserves. These were James Logan (centre-forward)[316] and Russell (full-back).

Though the Villa won their next two games at Perry Barr (**Stoke**, 3-2, and **Nottingham Forest**, 1-0) neither win was convincing even though Dowds had made his return, and they then travelled to **Preston**. Though the Villa started the match well, it was not long before Preston scored, and at half-time the Villa were 0-4 down. The fourth goal was something special though:

> ... a piece of wizardry of interplay from Ross and Russell, who passed through half-a-dozen Villa players en route. Even the Villa players could not help expressing admiration. (*Athletic News*)

The Villa's play was "neither pretty nor effective. The exhibition ... not worthy of a third-rate club", though Villa did manage to prevent Preston scoring in the second half, and lost 1-4. It was reported:

> Some of the [players] had been given to understand that unless there was a change for the better, the first team would know them no more. (*Athletic*

---

[316] Not to be confused with another James Logan playing for the Villa ten years later.

The Aston Villa Chronicles 1874 – 1924 (and after)

News)

The next match was at Perry Barr, against lowly **Derby County**. James Brown's absence was accounted for by his being on honeymoon; he missed four matches.

Villa: *Dunning; W. Evans, G.Campbell; Dowds, Jas.Cowan, G.Burton;*
Athersmith, Albert Brown, Logan, J.Devey, Hodgetts.

[From the *Athletic News*] In winning 6-1 (2-0 at half-time), "Villa seemed to have tumbled into their old form, the forwards slinging the ball from one to another in an unselfish fashion seldom seen at Perry Barr nowadays."

Derby were better in the first half, but "Evans, with his big chest, was able to stem the tide time after time with positive relish."

Of Villa: "To give them their fair meed of praise today would be to give one's self away, for we are never certain when the next collapse is likely to arrive … it is something inexplicable how they manage to get thrashed as they do."

After this match the Villa were – amazingly, in view of the recent defeats – lying sixth in the table, but they had played more games than anyone else.

November, 1892

Albion came down to Perry Barr, when the season's best crowd so far came to see the match. Logan was suspended, so Hare came in as a replacement centre-forward.

[From the *Athletic News*] "[Hare] is probably a good a man [as Logan], and if he could only steady down into a cool player, would undoubtedly be a real acquisition to the team."

Albion at first seemed the team more likely to score, but then the Villa got their game going, and Albert Brown scored a nice goal "from a beautifully judged pass by Hodgetts." From that point, there was little doubt as to who would win, with Dowds and Burton having a grip on the Albion wings. Villa led 2-0 at half-time.

After the interval, Villa were all over Albion, and swept though three more goals. Then indifference set in, allowing Albion to score a couple. This mini come-back seemed to re-vitalise the Villa, as they then went back on the attack and spent the rest of the half blazing with all guns until the final whistle, and won, 5-2.

For the match away at **Nottingham Forest**, the Villa selected Burton in favour of Dowds, and a strange but interesting and speedy looking forward line:

Villa: *Dunning; W. Evans, Geo.Campbell; Burton, Jas.Cowan, Stokes;*
Albert Brown, Hare, Athersmith, J.Devey, Hodgetts.

[From the *Athletic News*] "Never, probably, has a team had such a lively time as the Villa had in the first 10 minutes. The shots were literally rained in at

The Aston Villa Chronicles 1874 – 1924 (and after)

the [Villa] goal, and it was marvellous how the Forest were prevented from scoring!"

The Forest's play was "really wonderful" and their play was eventually rewarded with a goal, and they were unlucky in another goalmouth situation. But the Villa got downfield with brilliant passing and Athersmith shot through to equalise. What then followed was unbelievable, as Forest's keeper let through two easy shots from Athersmith and Hare to put Villa 3-1 up at half-time.

After the interval, Forest were still in shock, but recovered after a while, and then a brilliant effort to come back ensued, with the Villa in the end running out winners, 5-4, with Athersmith (the *centre-forward*!) getting a hat-trick.

Villa's forward line did not have a weakness, "but there was one superior to all others, and that one was Athersmith." Stokes shone well as a "stopper", proving more outstanding in that department than Cowan.

The selection of Stokes in the previous game seemed to be a tactical move, as Dowds returned for their first-ever match at bottom-placed Newton Heath,[317] where they were to try their shooting against their old friend Jimmy Warner!

[From the *Athletic News*] Villa's shooting was more frequent and difficult, but they knew Warner was a tough opponent to beat. It was the Heath, however, that took the lead.

"Then Hodgetts and Devey began to be troublesome, and Dowds got in a dinking shot from the half-way line, which Warner saved finely." However, Villa's efforts were in vain – the Heath won 0-2 that day.

The League leaders, Preston North End, then came to Perry Barr. Dunning nor Athersmith were available for this match, and the selectors came up with another interesting choice at centre-forward!

> **Villa**: *Roberts; W.Evans, Stokes; Jas.Brown, Jas.Cowan, Geo.Campbell;*
> *Hare, Albert Brown, Dowds, J.Devey, Hodgetts.*

[From the *Athletic News*] A massive downpour of rain kept the crowd numbers down, but by 2 o'clock the rain had stopped.

With Villa already one-up, Hare's runs on the wing became particularly dangerous, and from one of these Albert Brown scored with a rocket of a shot for the second goal. There was good play by Preston, but their shooting was either wayward or well-covered by the Villa keeper. The Preston runs, at times, were of "amazing brilliancy and correctness".

"Presently, a very deft overhead pass by Devey set Dowds going in fine fashion, and a scorching shot scored the third goal." From that point, the

---

[317] The future Manchester United.

The Aston Villa Chronicles 1874 – 1924 (and after)

Villa were in charge of the match. It was a fine game, with Cowan, Devey and Hodgetts at their best.

December, 1892

The Villa retained Dowds at centre-forward for a visit to **Sheffield Wednesday**, but Athersmith came back at inside-right, and Albert Brown moved out to the wing. Also, Cox returned at left-back after being out for some time.

[From the *Athletic News*] Villa took the lead on 13 minutes when a shot by Dowds was deflected into the net, but this lead was cancelled out shortly before the half-hour mark. Play was mainly around the Villa goal, and by half-time the Villa were 1-3 down. By the 60th minute, Villa were 1-5 down, but, strangely, the game then swung the other way, and a Devey shot then went in off a post. "Then the fight waxed fierce, and there was rather more tripping than was necessary." Another Devey goal was procured, but Villa finally went down, 3-5.

The availability of Logan meant that the centre-forward spot was given to him for the next match, versus **Blackburn Rovers** at Perry Barr, with Dowds returning to right-half. There had been a freezing wind blowing all morning and "hundreds of cartloads" of snow had been removed from the playing surface. Still, 8,000 turned up to watch the match.

[From the *Athletic News*] Rovers opened-up the better side and scored after 10 minutes. The Villa supporters then got a bit anxious and exhorted Villa to "play up!!" It was only after some time that the Villa got their equaliser, a brilliant goal through Athersmith, who had received Albert Brown's cut-back from the goal-line.

The second half started with a bigger wind and snowflakes falling – and John Devey scoring to put Villa ahead. Rovers came back, but again Devey succeeded from an Albert Brown centre. "Ten minutes from the finish, after half-a-dozen good shots had just skimmed the bar or saved by the keeper, Albert Brown got through in fine style, collared a long return of Hodgetts, hopped round two Blackburn bustlers, and planted the ball in the net."

It was a fine Villa team game, with Cowan and Devey again to the fore in their 4-1 victory.

The Villa then travelled to **Derby** with an unchanged side.

[From the *Athletic News*] Derby pressed but, unaccountably, could not score. They were then awarded a penalty when Evans scooped the ball away with his hand on the goal-line. Steve Bloomer's first attempt netted, but the referee ordered a re-take as players had infringed the demarcation line, but this time Dunning saved the kick. Despite Derby being on top, Logan put Villa head

The Aston Villa Chronicles 1874 – 1924 (and after)

just before half-time.

In the second half, the Derby pressure continued, but it was some time before they equalised. When they did score, suddenly the crowd and players were ignited! "They seemed to simultaneously leap into the air!" Bloomer later inspired another move, which Bloomer himself finished off from two yards. 1-2 to Derby is how the match finished.

Derby did not have a good season, but when it came to playing the top clubs, they generally rose above their normal level of play. With Steve Bloomer and the Goodalls in their side they had very good quality, and in their last game of the season, they won at Preston.

Team Morale and Peter Dowds

"We have it on the highest possible authority that a house divided cannot stand, but there has been so much internecine trouble and strife in the Perry Barr household during the last decade, and it has weathered so many storms that the Villa may be said to be still habitable if semi-detached." (the *Athletic News*)

The latest concern was the drinking habits of the players and the general behaviour of four or five of them, with some encouragement (it was said) from some members of the committee. A General Meeting was expected if Margoschis did not revoke his intention of resigning on principle, he being a strong opponent of alcoholic consumnption.

The *Athletic News* then announced that Peter Dowds had been discharged by the club, but he did re-appear in the team in the New Year after he had apologised and agreed to sign a pledge. The *Athletic News* felt that this was a weak stance on the part of the committee – "after [they] took a strong step, which was bound to do the team a lot of good, they wheeled round to the other side again ...". In fact, that the committee "wheeled round" caused Margoschis to carry through his threat of resignation. By March, 1893, the trainer (Dick Oxenbould) wanted to resign because of difficulties with some of the players.

Later, the *Athletic News* said:

> Dowds is one of the greatest and cleverest half-back players who ever crossed the border, and it does certainly seem a pity that a man possessed of so much merit should be lost to the football world through his stupid drnking propensities ...

Sadly, Dowds, was not able to keep to the pledge and his attitude began to affect the team spirit. He left the club after the end of the season.

A below-strength Villa side – they were missing Dowds, Cowan, Evans and Albert Brown (all of whom were probably suspended on account of the drinking issue) – played out a 1-1 draw with **Bolton** at Perry Barr on Christmas Eve, evoking the

The Aston Villa Chronicles 1874 – 1924 (and after)

following comment from the *Athletic News*:

> There was the old Villa failing – too much passing – and the difference is that when Archie Hunter was leading them on they could do it well, but now they do it badly. At that time, it was pleasing to the spectators, for it was very pretty, but now we have got beyond that age, and forwards want energy and determination in addition to scientific passing.

Three days later, the Villa played a friendly against Small Heath at Perry Barr. 10,000 spectators turned up for this 'Christmas Faire'.

[From the *Athletic News*] It was not until after 60 minutes "[before] the fun commenced, and in a very short time the Heathens had scored a couple of goals, at which success their supporters yelled themselves hoarse with delight. [The Villa, however,] pulled themselves together in a wonderful manner, and fairly fetched the game out of the fire. Five minutes from the finish, the scores were equalised, and the excitement was intense, but just on the stroke of time, the Villa scored the [winning] third goal."

Back into the business of the League, **Notts County** were visited on New Year's Eve. Another new Scottish signing – Skea – took his place in the Villa line-up in this 4-1 win (1-1 at half-time). Skea marked his début with a last minute goal, beautifully returning Notts' keeper's clearance back into the net.

Villa: *Dunning; Cox, Stokes; Jas.Brown, H.Devey, G.Campbell;*
Skea, Athersmith, Logan, J.Devey, Hodgetts.

[From the *Athletic News*] "All the Villa front rank played a grand game" and the rest of the team played well, but they were up against a side that did not have an appetite for a hard encounter.

January, 1893

The following week, the Villa faced a **Sheffield Wednesday** team that were third in the League on going into this game. The crowd of 6,000 was disappointing, but the weather was bitterly cold, and the pitch had snow on it that had thawed and then frozen. Even so, the condition of the pitch "[did] the management the greatest credit."

Villa: *Dunning; Cox, Stokes; Dowds, H.Devey, Burton;*
Athersmith, W.Devey, Logan, J.Devey, Hodgetts.

[From the *Athletic News*] Dowds returned to "a very hearty reception … while Will Devey (just transferred from the Wolves) shook his curls with glee as it was plainly evidenced that he has many hundreds of admirers at Perry, judging from the merry things they played on their mouth-organs when his form was

The Aston Villa Chronicles 1874 – 1924 (and after)

observed." Thus, three Deveys were on view - two brothers and their Uncle Harry.

It was only after a few minutes and a couple of hot Villa shots that "from a deft pass from Jack Devey, Logan scored a most brilliant goal, the ball passing the keeper like a flash." Wednesday came back, and Dunning had his work cut out for awhile, but Villa soon went back to the other end to repay the compliment!

"For many minutes, we marvelled at the good judgment, good luck and good kicking of the Sheffield defenders, a series of desperate attacks being carried on by the swarming Villa forwards, the ball being continually returned by the halves and battered about the goal." Though the Wednesday occasionally broke away and looked dangerous, "a second goal fell to the Villa from a nicely placed corner by Athersmith, the ball homing from J. Devey's foot to the more ample one of Hodgetts, and into the net it spun, the heavy-weight left-winger following it home in the most approved style." W. Devey added a third, and the score at half-time was 3-0.

The Villa added two more within five minutes of the re-start, making it 5-0, and then the Villa entertained the crowd to gallery play, the Villa then fooling around with their opponents. In the end, Villa's laxity allowed the Wednesday a consolation goal. The Villa should have won by far more than 5-1.

It was the next week that the second of the **Sunderland** contests took place, at the home of the League-leaders. The Villa's only team changes were at full-back, where Evans was re-instated, and Cox was at left-back. Intermittent blizzards and an icy wind brought out only 7,000 spectators. Once Sunderland had moved into a 0-3 lead within twenty minutes of play, the heart had been knocked out of the Villa.

That an injury reduced Sunderland to ten men is probably the only reason why the scoreline of 0-6 was not increased, and it was reported that in the final minutes of the game, a Sunderland shot hit the crossbar with such force that it was a wonder that the cross-piece did not fall on Dunning's head.

The good temper of Dunning was a feature of the game. He took a lot of heavy knocks in good heart, and caused laughter by the fatherly way he patted (Sunderland's) Campbell on the back.

> ### *How They Coped at Perry Barr*
> Quite a couple of thousand people wended their way to Perry Barr on Saturday – some for the purpose of watching the Villa Reserves perform against Stoke Swifts, while others made the journey more particularly for the purpose of gleaning the earliest intelligence concerning the first eleven at Sunderland.

The Aston Villa Chronicles 1874 – 1924 (and after)

> I need scarcely remark that there were some sad and sorrowful faces when the first wire arrived announcing that Sunderland had scored two goals in the first few minutes. Messrs. McGregor, Margoschis, Aaron Cartwright, and other lights in the Villa Club, tried to look pleasant and consoled one another with the reflection that things would come alright at the finish, as they must be playing against the wind now.
>
> Forthwith they repaired to the bar and regaled themselves – some with Scotch and some with coffee – waiting anxiously for the gladsome news which never came ... and then when the board was paraded around the ground announcing that the game stood Sunderland 4, Villa 0, the crowd commenced to button up their coats, drop their heads into their collars, make a quiet exit, and do a sort of dead march home.
>
> *Sport and Play*

After the League debacle in the north-east, it was now to the north-west to play in the first round of the FA Cup against **Darwen**.

Some more old favourites returned to the Villa line-up:

Villa: *Dunning; Cox, Stokes; Dowds, Cowan, Jas.Brown;*
Alb.Brown, Athersmith, Logan, J.Devey, Hodgetts.

How Villa Lost it but Very Nearly Won it!

[From the *Athletic News*] "The game was a scorcher from first to last" and swung from end-to-end. Within a couple of minutes, a free-kick awarded to Darwen was converted, and a minute later a second was added. But then, "a very considerable interval elapsed, in which there was some magnificent play in the field, before there was any further scoring."

But it was Darwen that were making all the running, and that the Villa did not fall further behind was due to good fortune. Eventually, Darwen did add a third (to make it 0-3), but then "after a fine pice of passing by the Villa forwards, which completely beat the Darwen halves and backs, Hodgetts planted the ball to Athersmith, who, having a clear piece of ground, raced up" and scored with a terrific shot. It was 1-3 at half-time.

The fast play became even faster in the second half, and the Villa came back in remarkable style on seeing that Darwen had resorted to defensive tactics. Their defensive methods were beaten time and time again, so that at one stage the Villa were leading 4-3! But Darwen then changed their tactics, swooped down on the Villa, and emerged with two more goals to run out the winners, 4-5.

The scene at the ground was "almost indescribable; hats and sticks waving, and hundreds almost wild with enthusiasm!"

The Aston Villa Chronicles 1874 – 1924 (and after)

> *Sport and Play* commented:
>
> Finding themselves in front, two at least of the Villa forwards slowed down and began to play with their opponents. The inevitable result followed ...
>
> If Sunderland and Preston North End get into a winning position – do they fool around? *Not they!*

The next Saturday, the Villa welcomed Middlesbrough to Perry Barr for a friendly match. The Villa lost 3-5 in front of 2,000 spectators, the win of the opposition being helped by bad defensive errors and Villa's exhibition was described as mediocre.

> Following the Middlesbrough match, the *Athletic News* commented:
>
> It was a crushing blow to the hopes and aspirations of Birmingham footballers, and it may lead to a revolution in the management of the club before many weeks are over ...The class of players lately engaged have not been high enough, and in many instances the old penny-wise-and-pound-foolish policy has been indulged in, to the very great detriment and lowing of tone of the organisation.
>
> There is very strong talk of a general meeting, and I hear that a requisition has been signed to re-arrange and alter matters.
>
> It is urged by many that things will not take a better turn till a lot of fresh blood is infused into the affair, and some of the oldest and strongest of Aston Villa are very much of that opinion. You may expect to hear of a small revolution pretty soon in regard to their internal affairs, as the members are convinced that the management have not been at all of the high-class character ...
>
> The very mixed reception which the players received from the 2,000 spectators at Perry Barr on Saturday ... convinced even the most rabid supporter of Aston Villa that the patience of the public has become pretty nearly exhausted.

> *Sport and Play* added:
>
> [There was the suggestion] that the present secretary shall be removed. ... Aston Villa members would make a very big mistake if they decided upon the resignation of Mr. George Ramsay ... a better man could not be found for the post, always supposing he had a freer hand. Archie Hunter alone excepted,

The Aston Villa Chronicles 1874 – 1924 (and after)

> George Ramsay has done more than any other man for the Perry Barr organisation and he has never had sufficient credit for the reforms he has instituted, and the able work he has performed.[318]

Careless play also followed in another friendly, this time against the Albion, at Perry Barr, the match ending in a 4-4 draw after the Villa had been leading 4-1.

February, 1893

Back in the League, Villa travelled to **Blackburn**, the side again showing a change of personnel, with Athersmith again tried at centre-forward.

Villa: *Roberts; Baird, Cox; G. Burton, Jas.Cowan, Dowds; Albert Brown, W.Devey, Athersmith, J.Devey, L.Campbell.*

The Villa again let opportunities slip, and a half-time lead of 1-0 continued until mid-way through the second half, when the Rovers equalised. Again the Villa scored, but once more the Rovers came back to equality. It was a game of Villa chances going begging in this 2-2 draw.

The Reformation of Aston Villa (1)

'Brum' in the *Athletic News* reported:

> The affairs of the Aston Villa club have reached an acute stage, and the crisis is near at hand ... the grievance is that the present committee have proved themselves utterly incompetent to control the affairs of the club, and the general body of members feel that a deal of money has been wasted and squandered away by the engagement of high-salaried players that were not worthy of their hire, and the fame and reputation of the club has been trifled with in a manner that has vexed the patrons and supporters of the Villa matches beyond measure ...

A Special Meeting was held on 17 February, "at which some very plain speaking was indulged in." Another meeting was set for 24 February.

Mr. G. B. Ramsay tendered his resignation "so he can be free to speak out in defence of imputations levelled against him."

---

[318] *Sport and Play* went on to devote another three columns addressed to the Aston Villa Committee, suggesting that the committee should look at itself for the faults that lay in the running of the club, and desist from throwing blame at everyone except themselves.

The Aston Villa Chronicles 1874 – 1924 (and after)

Both 'Brum' and 'Lucifer' (Sport and Play) were of the opinion that William McGregor was again needed to pilot the ship to a safe course, as he had done before. "If a plebiscite were taken as to the most popular and able administrator of football regulations and laws, you [McGregor] would head the poll all over the land." *('Lucifer')*

What followed was ...

The Famous Barwick Street (Special) Meeting, 24 February

This meeting – though it was not realised at the time – proved to bring about the final 'clearing of the decks'; the final weeding out of weak individuals and wrong practises in the club, to enable the club to make progress. The 'growing pains' that the club had been suffering since 1885 were about to be finally dealt with – there would be no more serious trouble within the club for another 30 years. This meeting also brought the footballing world to know about Mr. Fred Rinder, "[who] arrived in Barwick Street more in the form of a stormy petrel rather than as a peace-descending dove."[319]

The following is distilled from the reports of the *Athletic News* and *Sport and Play*.

> There was, as I anticipated, a rare old rumpus at the Special General Meeting of the Aston Villa Football Club on Friday last, and the old committee had a very warm time of it. A lot of dirty linen was washed, the grievances of the general body of members were thoroughly aired, and a bold attempt made by 'The Requisitionists' to turn the whole committee out of office and replace them by their own select circles, but the coup did not entirely come off, and the most singular fact about the business is that the ringleader of 'The Requisitionists', *Mr. Rinder*, was not found a seat on the new committee ...
>
> Several times during the evening the assembly looked like becoming uproarious, and had it not been for the calm and judicial manner in which the chairman, Mr. Joseph Ansell, handled the reins, the probability is that the meeting would have resolved itself into a disreputable squabble ...
>
> ... [The] majority of the members had very strong feelings over the undeniable mismanagement of the club's affairs, and the reckless expenditure that has taken place in the engagement of costly players without satisfactory results. *Mr. Rinder* made out a very good case, and was so well up in his facts that the charges made against the committee were beyond contradiction.

---

[319] Villa News & Record 3 Sep 1910 (Old Fogey)

The Aston Villa Chronicles 1874 – 1924 (and after)

> It must be said that [*Mr. Rinder*] handled his brief in a masterly manner, and never attempted to shirk any of the responsibility which he had taken on himself. Without being unnecessarily offensive or personal in his remarks, he stood up to his task and hit out straight from the shoulder. 'There were', he said, 'thirty-four paid players, enough to run three teams, but I would like to know how many of that number were of the slightest use to a first-class team?' [He said] there were no fewer than eight paid [full-]backs, but they had not a single pair of good backs amongst them.

Fred Rinder said much more, including reference to the drink problem amongst some of the players, and finished his speech with the following strongly-worded resolution:

> That the members of the club, having lost all confidence in a majority of the present committee, hereby request the honorary treasurer, the honorary secretary, and other members therof to at once resign their respective offices.

Charlie Johnstone seconded this, and made a speech re-affirming what Fred Rinder had said, and paid tribute to the secretary, George Ramsay.

There then followed a series of statements from some members of the old committee, in defence of themselves, and casting faults to their co-members – a most pitiable state of affairs for them to resort to. This included a reference to Archie Hunter representing the players when 'drink' hearings came up, for which he was criticised. When he stood up to defend himself, Archie – the hero of the club for many a day – was jeered and heckled.[320]

"I confess this incident was the most painful I have experienced for many a day …" said the *Sport and Play* reporter.

George Ramsay also made a speech in which he admitted that he had no chance of seeing any new signing before they were engaged by the club, except Dunning, a statement which rather shocked those present.

> [A] better tone prevailed when *Mr. W. B. Mason* (like the good old war-horse that he is) cautioned the meeting that it was possible they may go from bad to worse, and it was easier to find faults than remedies.
>
> An overwhelming majority, however, carried the resolution mentioned above, and then, amidst a scene of turbulent excitement, Mr. Jenkinson moved that seven members be appointed to act as a provisional committee, and report to

---

[320] In fact, it may well have been this period in the club's history that totally broke Archie Hunter's health. Already unwell, he soon became worse, and by the end of 1894, he had died.

The Aston Villa Chronicles 1874 – 1924 (and after)

> the general meeting ... what alterations in the constitution of the club [were] necessary.
>
> This route being agreed upon, the seven elected – and to report back to the general meeting – were:
>
> > W. McGregor (whose name was received with ringing cheers and without a single dissentient), W. B. Mason, J. Margoschis, J. Dunkley, C. Johnstone, F. Cooper, and V. Jones.

March, 1893

Back to the fray of the Football League, **Newton Heath**'s visit to Perry Barr was unfruitful for them, the Villa winning 2-0, the exact reverse of the score between the clubs earlier that season.

On 11 March, the Villa paid a visit to London to play the Corinthians in a friendly at the Oval. This was a regular fixture that had gone on for some years, and generally the matches were fairly even. Many of the Villa party had never been to London before, and the amount of traffic and the size of St. Paul's amazed them. Old Fogey (for *Sport and Play*) reported:

> The Villa are evidently favourites in the 'Metrolops', for there was a crowd of some six or seven thousand people – at a shilling a head, mind you – with a glorious sprinkling of red coats, and a choice admixture of the fair sex who fairly made your mouth water.

Half-time was reached with the score at 1-1, with the reputation of professional players further tarnished when Dowds made an over-zealous tackle for which he should have been sent off. In the second half, Corinthians had a goal disallowed (to their disgust), and seemed to react to it to such an extent that their lack of concentration helped the Villa run out as 7-2 winners. Athersmith was one of the scorers after he made a single-handed run down three-quarters of the length of the pitch.

The referee of the match against **Notts County** was described as a "genius of the first water" in his conduct of the game – when referees rarely received praise (indeed, neither do they often receive praise today!). Leading 2-0 at the interval, Villa were well on top, but County threatened to come back in the second half. Devey settled matters following a sparkling run by Albert Brown and Athersmith, for Villa to run-out 3-0 winners.

The Aston Villa Chronicles 1874 – 1924 (and after)

> **The Reformation of Aston Villa (2)**
>
> The *Athletic News* reported that: "The new scheme for the Aston Villa management will be laid before the management ... The central idea is to transpose the concern into a limited liability company." Clearly, McGregor's business aspirations for the club were coming to the fore once more. Also:
>
> - Bonuses to players to be withheld and invested until "their play ends" – effectively to be paid as a pension;
> - To establish a sinking fund for provision for a new ground – the lease at Perry Barr was to run out in four years (1897).
>
> All the above proposals were paving the way to what was to happen in a little over two years.

The next League match, against **Accrington** at Perry Barr, was extraordinary, and that only 5,000 turned up to see it meant that a lot missed the amazing turn-a-round in this match! This was the occasion of Albert Woolley's début in the first team.

Villa: *Roberts; Geo.Campbell, Baird; G.Burton, Jas.Cowan, Dowds; Athersmith, Albert Brown, J.Devey, Hodgetts, Woolley.*

[From the *Athletic News*] It was a warm, oppressive day that seemed to have caused a "languid and lackadaisical air" amongst the Villa team, to the extent that at half-time they were 1-3 down. Soon after half-time, Accrington again scored to make the score 1-4!

"Curiously enough the state of affairs rather invigorated than depressed the [Villa] team ... the players got to work with a will" and scored five goals to overhaul Accrington and win 6-4! Woolley scored two on his début.

April, 1893

On 1 April, Villa played the return match against Corinthians, and won 5-2. Injuries meant that Cox, John Devey and Athersmith did not play.

Another five goals then went in against the **Wolves** the following Monday in a League match at Perry Barr, and yet another five were scored when the Villa played against Small Heath in the Birmingham Cup semi-final in front of 16,000 spectators. The Villa might easily have doubled the score in a match where Hodgetts and Woolley were specially singled out for praise.

As has always been the case with the Villa, when things were going well, their fans could suddenly be highly disappointed, and in finishing off their League games, they

The Aston Villa Chronicles 1874 – 1924 (and after)

lost at home to **Burnley**, and drew away at **Accrington**. In the Birmingham Cup Final, Villa went down to Wolves, 1-3.

The Football League Division 1 1892-93 Top Places	Pld	Home W D L F A	Away W D L F A	Overall W D L F A	Pts
1 Sunderland	30	13 2 0 58 17	9 2 4 42 19	22 4 4 100 36	48
2 Preston North End	30	11 2 2 34 10	6 1 8 23 29	17 3 10 57 39	37
3 Everton	30	9 3 3 44 17	7 1 7 30 34	16 4 10 74 51	36
4 Aston Villa	30	12 1 2 50 24	4 2 9 23 38	16 3 11 73 62	35
5 Bolton Wanderers	30	12 1 2 43 21	1 5 9 13 34	13 6 11 56 55	32
6 Burnley	30	10 2 3 37 15	3 2 10 14 29	13 4 13 51 44	30

1892-93 League and FA Cup Results

Sep	5th A Burnley	2-0	
	10th H Everton	4-1	12000
	12th A Stoke	1-0	
	17th H Sunderland	1-6	15000
	19th A West Bromwich A	2-3	
	24th A Bolton Wanderers	0-5	8000
Oct	1st A Everton	0-1	15000
	8th A Wolves	1-2	
	10th H Stoke	3-2	
	15th H Nottingham Forest	1-0	12000
	22nd A Preston North End	1-4	
	29th H Derby County	6-1	6000
Nov	5th H West Bromwich A	5-2	15000
	12th A Nottingham Forest	5-4	
	19th A Newton Heath	0-2	
	26th H Preston North End	3-1	7000
Dec	3rd A Sheffield Wednesday	3-5	6000
	10th H Blackburn Rovers	4-1	8000
	17th A Derby County	1-2	6000
	24th H Bolton Wanderers	1-1	
	31st A Notts County	4-1	3000
Jan	7th H Sheffield Wednesday	5-1	6000
	14th A Sunderland	0-6	7000
	21st A Darwen (FAC)	4-5	7000
Feb	11th A Blackburn Rovers	2-2	
Mar	6th H Newton Heath	2-0	
	18th H Notts County	3-1	9000
	25th H Accrington	6-4	5000
Apr	3rd H Wolves	5-0	
	4th H Burnley	1-3	
	15th A Accrington	1-1	

End of Season Postscripts

Although there had been a bright start to the season of three wins (two of them away), it was followed by a sequence of five successive defeats, resulting in a drop to tenth place in the League, but then Villa pulled themselves together and maintained fourth place for virtually the rest of the season.

The Aston Villa Chronicles 1874 – 1924 (and after)

Villa Business: The Reformation of Aston Villa (3)

The *Report of the Provisional Committee* was presented in May, 1893, and reported in the *Athletic News,* 22 May:

> The legal and business position of the club appears to have been very unsatisfactory, nearly all the leases being drawn in the names of individual members of the club, who had no direct responsibility to the management or other members.
>
> Proposals:
> 1. Reduction of the committee to five;
> 2. Formation of a company separate from the club to secure a ground and lease, *or* formation into a limited company;
> 3. Increase in [member] subscription for the successful and adequate working of the club.

From the *Athletic News,* 29 May, with regard to a subsequent meeting:

> After a pow-wow lasting two hours, the Aston Villa Football Club members decided – subject to approval of the General Meeting next week – that a future working committee of the club shall consist of five only.
>
> They would not have any limited liability business and resolved to gather all the wisdon of the club together in a small compass, so to speak, and see if matters cannot be managed in a better way than was the case for a considerable portion of lase season.
>
> The best speakers at the meeting were Messrs. Margoschis, McGregor and Mason, who tersely and intelligibly put before the meeting what they considered the best thing for the club [and persuaded the meeting to increase the membership subscription from 7s 6d to half-a-guinea (10s 6d)].

[From the *Athletic News,* 5 June and 12 June, with regard to the Annual General Meeting held on 9 June]

> There was a slight attempt to analyse the balance sheet by Mr. F.W. Rinder, but it was rather a mixed-up affair, and Mr. W.B. Mason, who had made himself personally responsible for the figures, very quickly put him right...
> [On the year's working, the club was £273 in *debit*. However, the club also had £400 put aside as security for the ground and other matters].[321]

Mr. James Hinks (president) and Mr. William McGregor (vice-president) would not allow their names to be put forward for office again.

---

[321] On 3 July, the Athletic News reported that Small Heath's financial return showed a loss of £347, while West Bromwich Albion's loss was £1,400.

The Aston Villa Chronicles 1874 – 1924 (and after)

> Consequently, Mr. Joseph Ansell was elected president (a popular choice), but:
>
>> Mr. Ansell made some very hearty and feeling remarks concerning Mr. Hinks, and the meeting enclosed them with a hearty cheer for the rare and good sportsman who has been such a genial and jolly president since the days of Mr. George Kynoch [who resigned in 1888].
>>
>> [Mac's refusal to continue was to do with personal reasons,] and the meeting, while respecting his earnest desire not to become even a vice-president of the club, seemed to look upon his temporary retirement as a wrench which was hard to bear.
>
> Vincent Jones, W.B. Mason, F. Cooper and J. Whitehouse were elected as vice-presidents.
>
> J. E. Margoschis, J. Dunkley, C. Johnstone, F.W. Rinder and J.T. Lees were elected as the five committee members, the number recommended by the Provisional Committee and accepted by the AGM, as was the recommended increase in membership fee.

Celebrating the Past

Aston Villa had now been in existence for 19 years, and it was now recognised that there was much to be remembered and celebrated, particularly in respect of the brotherly spirit that had existed within the club from its earliest days. That spirit had caused the club's on-going growth and developing success.

The following was penned by Old Fogey (in his guise as 'Leather Stocking') as his special report in *Sport and Play* of 11 April, 1893:

> The meeting of 'Old Villans' at Perry Barr on Thursday, supplemented by a dinner at the Old Royal in the evening, was altogether too good a thing to be missed by the present deponent, and as I have had the honour of chronicling many of the victories and defeats and draws of the men who formed the company at both functions, you will, I hope, excuse me if I expatiate a little on the proceedings. The inception of the movement is due in the first instance, I believe, to Mr. W. Cook, who in his day was captain, chief adviser, and a sort of chaperon to what was once known as the Villa First Team, and from the first the idea has been enthusiastically taken up by nearly every one of the old members, notably by Messrs. W. McGregor, W. Sothers, Howard Vaughton, Fred Dawson, Eli Davis, Billy Crossland, Arthur Brown, Joe Simmonds, Tom Fank, Sam Law, Tom Mason, Link Lamsdale, Charlie

The Aston Villa Chronicles 1874 – 1924 (and after)

Johnston, Billy Watts, and a whole host of others. ...

It is intended to make the movement an annual and benevolent one, so that a few of the rare old Villans, whose worldly ways have not been so smooth as some of their more fortunate comrades may benefit by old associations, and all the get-at-able members of the Old Brigade meet once a year to talk over old times and enjoy themselves in the old sweet way. This is an example that may not only be copied by other clubs, but will tend to bring back again the jolly feeling and. good comradeship which used to be such pronounced and pleasant features in the old (and what some people consider the palmiest) days of the pastime. It was a little painful to notice that Archie Hunter was absent through indisposition, and in a letter I have from Olly Whateley, the erstwhile brilliant right-winger, he speaks feelingly of his non-appearance, and also of his own failure (through ill-health) to turn up. He says:

> I was fearfully disappointed in not being able to join all you other 'old crocks,' especially at the dinner, for that's more in my line than foot ball now. Sorry 'Baldie' was not at the match. There is, was, and never will be another captain like Archie. Surely the old Villa fellows are not slighting the grand old man; or is he ill?

That's a plain, outspoken opinion which was never intended for publication, and may help to elucidate things a bit. There is no doubt that the old feeling in the Villa ranks is coming back again, and there is a ring of the ancient form apparent in more than one direction. It will do a lot of good, and all the original members, men who have followed the Perry Barr team from the days of their youth, and who stick to them through fair weather and foul, must have had some curiously blended feelings as they gazed upon the warriors of old, listened to the old battle cries and war-whoops, and noticed with regret and sorrow the gaps in the ranks of the once-famous crews. In the hot broiling sunshine the following teams scampered around:

> First team: *G. B. Ramsay, goal; Joe Simmonds and Frank Conlton, backs; E. B. Lee, Tom Pank, and Sam Law, half-backs; Watts, Will Crossland, Arthur Brown, Howard Vaughton, and Eli Davis, forwards.*
>
> Reserves: *Tom Mason, goal; L. O. Lamsdale and Tom Foster, backs; Fred Dawson, C. Nevill, and W. Cook, half-backs; P. Vaughton, A. Allison, C. S. Johnstone, Harry Hodgetts, and Tom Horton, forwards.*

It would, of course, be superfluous to give any details; but it may be mentioned that two or three of them, notably Frank Coulton, Joe Simmonds, Arthur Brown, and Howard Vaughton, showed surprisingly good form considering their lengthy absence from first-class matches, and I noticed that Tom Pank and Charlie Johnstone could skip pretty nearly as fast as ever, though how they felt next day I leave to the imagination!

The Aston Villa Chronicles 1874 – 1924 (and after)

We bad lots of fun, especially at some of the remarkable saves by George Ramsay; Eli Davis's 'screws', which somehow or other had got a bit loose; Arthur Brown's neat and wholehearted wanderings; Fred Dawson and Joe Simmonds going at one another with all the refreshing vigour and abandon of their most reckless days, and finishing up a battle-royal about six yards off each other, both sitting down and blowing like grampuses; the curious kicking of Teddy Lee and Sam Law; and the sweltering, boiled appearance many of them presented long before the game was over. It was a fearful and a wonderful contest, and George Ramsay's crowd won by four goals to one— Arthur Brown contributing a trio and Eli Davis the fourth with a real old-timer. I wanted to back Howard Vaughton to get a goal somehow (he nearly always managed to scramble one through on state and other occasions), but it did not come off, though I believe he would have been as proud as ever over the performance had he done so. Then they all had their portraits taken, with several ancient ones thrown in (W. McGregor as whistle-blower, and W. B. Mason and W. Sothers as flag-waggers) and a very interesting group they made before a select and admiring crowd of sightseers.

Something like £15 was taken at the gate, and after that they all scooted away to the Old Royal, where Mr. Chartrian not only served up a very bounteous repast but generously gave £10 10s. to the fund.

Back row: F. Cooper, W. Cooke, C. Neville, Phil Vaughton, Tom Mason, Tom Foster, W. Sothers, W. B. Mason, H. Vaughton, Ted Lee, Tom Pank, W. Crossland, W. Jones
Middle Row: Tom Horton, H. Hodgetts, L. Lamsdale, A. Allen, C. S. Johnstone, W. McGregor, F. Coulton, G. B. Ramsay, Joey Simmonds, W. Watt
On Ground: F. Dawson, Arthur Brown, Sam Law, Eli Davis.

This photo reproduced from *The Villa News* (1912).

Mr. W. McGregor of course took the chair, opposite to him was Mr. W. B. Mason, and dotted about all over the room, among others, were:— Messrs. J. Lees, W. B. Mason, F. Cooper, J. Vickerstaff, I. Whitehouse, R. Clucas, E. W.

The Aston Villa Chronicles 1874 – 1924 (and after)

Cox, T. Mason, G. B. Ramsay, L. Lamsdale, T. Foster, F. Coulton, J. Simmonds, E. B. Lee, S. Law, T. Pank, Arthur Brown, Albert Brown, W. Cooke, F. W. Dawson, Howard Vaughton, E. Davies, W. H. Watts, W. Crossland, T. Horton, H. Hodgetts, C. S. Johnstone, P. Naughton, A. Allison, J. Cornwell, W. Light, W. Sothers, W. Jones, and W. H. Rinder. From the very start there was fun galore, but the story would be too long to tell you *in extenso*, and so I will enumerate the chief items.

The chairman's speech was the best I have heard him make, and his touching allusions to Andy Hunter (the rare and radiant right-winger who died in a foreign clime, and whose memory will always be green and fragrant to those who knew him), to Messrs. W. M. Ellis — gentle and useful; G. Kynoch — typical Villan, brilliant, but erratic! – and others who have gone over to the great majority, were greatly appreciated by his audience.

He quoted one of Archie's songs with capital effect, gave a slight sketch of the club, which started from the Aston Villa Wesleyan Sunday School, and from the appreciative way he spoke of the enjoyable journeys to Scotland and other trips, one could almost believe that he was a bit of a roysterer himself instead of the staid Scot that he is. We drank to Andy Hunter's memory in silence, Teddy Lee singing with a good deal of effect one of the right-winger's little ditties which used to fetch ancient Villans in the days of yore. "Phil Blood's Leap," by W. Cook, was most admirably given, and Mr. W. B. Mason, replying to the "Old Villans!" toast, remarked that the pleasure of the re-union was allied with sorrow on account of the absent ones, reminding one of the lines:

Some are gone from us for ever,
Longer here they might not stay;
They have all dispersed and wandered,
Far away, far away.

[After sketching a broader history of the club, Billy Mason] was pleased to note that a benevolent fund was to be started for destitute old Villans, and finished up by saying that he had noticed during the match that while pace had decreased among the old hands, bulk had increased!

... It was pleasant indeed to hear Billy Watts's fine voice in "The Flight of Ages", and when Eli Davies sang "Landlord fill the flowing bowl", we filled it, and drank it round with all the old gusto and heartiness, [to] the ancient refrains of "Bravo; bravissimo", "Here's a health to the laddie who, sang the last song," and other catches being lilted out finely. Tom Horton, Tom Pank, Tom Mason, Sam Law and others treated us to some more music, and Billy Crossland's "Sally in our Alley" was hugely appreciated.

The Aston Villa Chronicles 1874 – 1924 (and after)

> Mr. W. Sothers, in proposing "Absent Old Villans", made some happy and feeling allusions to Archie Hunter, George Copley, Tom Midgeley, Charlie Apperley, Billy Weiss, Llew Summers, Billy Such, and Olly Whateley — all names the old brigade used to swear by; and reiterated the hope that the reunion would be an annual one.
>
> "The Press" was proposed by Mr. W. Jones, and responded to by a *Sport and Play* representative[322] and Mr. S. Gilbert, and after one or two more songs had been given, every Villan went home to bed glad that he had been permitted to take part in such a hearty gathering, and fully convinced that there is not only a lot of life in the old dogs yet, but that the ancient brigade are still capable of greatly enjoying themselves.

Thus ended a report of a unique event – one that acknowledged that time was indeed moving on and that there were veterans that found a need to reproduce old (brotherly) times. The absence of Archie Hunter is mentioned above, but by the end of the following year both he and Billy Mason had 'passed over to the other side', and Eli Davis would follow not long after. However, Joey Simmonds would still be playing in Old Villans' matches twenty years later.

Perhaps it was coincidental that this event occurred at just the time when the Villa were transforming themselves into a leaner and fitter organisation that were more able to deal with the pressures of expansion – and success.

Season 1893-94: Champions for the First Time!

League Division 1 position: Champions; ***FA Cup:*** *3rd Round.*

The time had arrived when all the resources and abilities in the Villa camp came together to produce a defining moment: the Football League Championship for the first time! The running of the club had been sorted out during the club reforms of 1893, and Charlie Johnstone wrote:

> The result on the players was electrical. After a remarkable series of flabby games, they suddenly blossomed forth as a team of skill and illumination.[323]

Added to the club reforms, **Joe Grierson** was acquired that very year from a Middlesbrough club; he was to train Villa sides to so many triumphs prior to World War One. It was Grierson that introduced the players to a new level of fitness – surplus flesh was consigned to the past!

---

[322] Doubtless it was Jack Urry (Old Fogey)!
[323] In his column in The Sporting Mail 2 Nov 1912

The Aston Villa Chronicles 1874 – 1924 (and after)

In addition, there were four signings of significance, which – added to the existing presence of John Devey, Cowan, Athersmith and Hodgetts – made such a great difference and three of these were to remain as successful cogs in Villa teams for some years to come. The new signings were **John Reynolds** and **Wille Groves** from the Albion, **Steve Smith, James Welford** and **Bob Chatt**. Significant departures were Peter Dowds, Louis Campbell, George Campbell and Gershom Cox. Frank Coulton made a very interesting positional move; he was to be, when needed, cover in the goalkeeping department! In fact, on one occasion he was called upon to do so.

In signing Reynolds and Groves – two of the half-backs that caused the Villa considerable problems in the 1892 Cup Final – the Villa had competition from Blackburn and Everton, but then ran into trouble with the FA concerning the signing of Groves. The League found[324] that the Villa had infringed the rule which debarred poaching and fined Villa £25, and also declared that Groves was still an Albion player. The facts as determined by the FA were that he had been registered by the Villa and had not been transferred by the Albion, though Villa maintained that they had been given permission by the Albion. Strangely, Willie Groves was present at Villa's practise match on 10 August, but still the transfer had not taken place.

The Season's Play

September, 1893

The Villa's first League opponents of the season were the **Albion**, at Perry Barr. Although the transfer of Willie Groves to the Villa had only now gone through the formalities, the FA rules still did not allow him to play. The press reported that there was fear there would be crowd disturbances over the matter of the transfer, but the fears proved groundless; the crowd were reasonably behaved.

> **Villa**: *Dunning; Elliott, Baird; Reynolds, Jas.Cowan, Chatt;*
> *Athersmith, Logan, J.Devey, Hodgetts, Woolley.*

[From the *Athletic News*] The Villa, with half their team consisting of new players, did not gel fluently, but the match proved to be interesting and very exciting. The teams were locked at 1-1 at half-time, but Albion took the lead in the second half. The Villa equalised, and then, two minutes from time, "Dunning made a remarkable clearance, and then Woolley got away on the left, dodged about a bit, sent the ball to the centre, and it was in the net!" –

---

[324] Athletic News 5 Jun 1893

The Aston Villa Chronicles 1874 – 1924 (and after)

i.e. the centre had gone straight in. Villa went on to win, 3-2.

The Villa forwards "had the old Villa weakness – passing about in front of goal and never shooting ... It is all very well to pass about and mystify your opponents ..."

The Villa, with an unchanged side, then went to play the mighty **Sunderland**, the scene of last season's twice-over mighty come-uppance! This season, it was quite a different situation.

[From the *Athletic News*] Athersmith supplied Hodgetts for him to score the opening goal on 15 minutes. Later, Dunning shoved Gillespie off the ball to give away a penalty. "For some reason, however, Campbell seemed to think the Villa custodian a target ... there was plenty of room to put the ball through. No; he must land it in Dunning's hands – and he did!"

In the second half, Sunderland continuously sent in shots, but they were repelled, until, after some Dunning heroics, Sunderland got a goal, a header. The match continued as a fine contest, but there was no more scoring; 1-1 is how it finished.

Two days later at Perry Barr, the Villa (again with the team unchanged) were oozing confidence in a 5-1 demolition of **Stoke**, after Stoke had opened the scoring. The Villa now travelled to **Everton** where they found opponents eager to beat the new League leaders, and within 15 minutes, the Villa were 0-3 down! The Villa pulled one back by half-time and played more strongly in the second half, but still lost, 2-4. Everton simply played a more direct style, whereas the Villa's play was at times so pretty that even the Everton supporters were cheering their play.

The Aston Villa Chronicles 1874 – 1924 (and after)

Although the Groves transfer was now officially sanctioned, he was still not played, but both Chatt and Elliott were not well, and replacements for them were necessary for the return match against **Everton** the next week. In addition, Logan had not been playing well, so Will Devey was brought back into the forward line.

Villa: *Dunning; Baird, Welford; Reynolds, Jas.Cowan, Gillian;*
Athersmith, W. Devey, J.Devey, Hodgetts, Woolley.

[From the *Athletic News*] The Villa started brightly, but in time the game swung the other way and Everton opened the scoring, and then came close with further attempts on goal. Hodgetts, however, deserved to score with one terrific shot just before half-time.

Villa came out meaning business in the second half – "[there was] more method and more dash at the finish" – and Villa were 2-1 up in quick time. Woolley scored both, and his second was a very fine cross-shot after a run down the line; the shot was hard enough to have broken the net.

The Villa were now playing very well, but Everton were always in it and two of their shots hit the woodwork. Even when Villa scored a third, Everton were still dangerous. Villa won, 3-1.

"The little outside-left [Woolley] put in some demon shots besides those which he scored." Welford had a good début, but Baird was the more 'finished' player of the two backs.

After this match, the Villa had a disappointing 1-1 draw against **Derby County** at Perry Barr, the Villa being without Athersmith (who remained injured for three League matches), but Groves was brought in for his début at centre-forward. Then Queens Park came down for their annual friendly and Groves was reported as being the best man on the field in the 3-3 draw, he scoring two goals.

October, 1893

At this stage, the Albion were top of the League, having won four and drawn one. However, there were several clubs around the top of the League jockeying for position at this stage, and when Villa were "soundly thrashed" at **Sheffield United** (0-3) in their next match, it was the Sheffield club that momentarily took their position at the top.

> The *Athletic News* reported that the Villa committee issued a caution to the team that matters have to improve, or lose their places. "Better have a good tryer – honest, plucky and true – than a collection of cultured professors whose movements are often animated by personal pique and child-like jealousy"

The Aston Villa Chronicles 1874 – 1924 (and after)

It looks as though the players took the committee's warning to heart, for "Aston Villa were in fine form" in another away match, at **Nottingham Forest**; the Villa won 2-1 against a side that had played Bolton only two days before, and looked affected by their exertions. However, it was reported that Villa's defence was excellent, with Reynolds, Cowan, Groves and Hodgetts also outstanding. However, in two more away games, the Villa disappointingly drew at **Darwen**, and then at **Stoke**.

> William McGregor ceased his duties as president of the Football League. In a circular regarding a testimonial for him, the Football League mysteriously stated: "… in consequence of Mr. McGregor's position in life, having, through no fault of his own, undergone a change which calls for friendly sympathy and help." (The *Athletic News*)

The Villa now had a testing group of three games, all against immediate competition for the League top spot. The first of these was against the **Albion** at Stoney Lane. Welford was now settling in well, and Groves was taken out of the forward line and placed at left-half.

Villa: *Dunning; Baird, Welford; Reynolds, Jas. Cowan, Groves;*
Hare, Athersmith, J.Devey, Hodgetts, Woolley.

[From the *Athletic News*] The Villa won the toss and had the advantage of the slope, wind and sun. Although the Albion started well, the Villa moved ahead, first through a soft goal, and then another goal "with a splendid screw on the part of Athersmith". That afternoon, "the Villa forward line were simply perfection", and before long they were leading 5-0 before Albion pulled one back to make the score 5-1 at half-time.

In the second half, the Albion had the advantages that Villa had before the interval, and quickly pulled back another goal. In fact, the Albion took over the match in some style, but the Villa defence remained cool, although they could not keep out a third goal.

But once more, the Villa came back, and Athersmith's fine centre gave Devey an easy chance. The scoring finished there.

The second of the three 'test' matches was at Perry Barr against **Burnley**. Elliott was brought in for Welford, and the 19-years-old Steve "Tich" Smith made his début, in place of Woolley (stated as being "indisposed").

[From the *Athletic News*] "A desperately determined sort of game" in a high wind, which increased in strength after the interval, at which point the Villa were leading 2-0, with Smith having scored a début goal.

The Aston Villa Chronicles 1874 – 1924 (and after)

After an early period of second half Burnley pressure – and some bad feeling on the part of a couple of Burnley players – the Villa went away in a line, and some beautiful passing ensued which led to Athersmith firing home a third. Burnley were now a "disorganised bunch" but the Villa were at their best.

"Hodgetts raised the enthusiasm of the crowd by a magnificent run … in which he cleverly evaded all opposition, and when well up, transferred to Smith, who waltzed round Crabtree [of future Villa fame] and passed to Devey, who shot the fourth." Villa won, 4-0.

The Villa half-back line was noted for their play, and Smith captured the eye of the spectators. However, the reporter asked, "Why will Athersmith persist in spoiling his good work in that nasty habit of hacking and tripping an opponent?"

'Test' match three was against **Sheffield United**, again at home, and resulted in a 4-1 win for the Villa. The Villa half-backs were again conspicuous; Reynolds, Groves and Cowan "worked with machine-like precision."

In those three matches, then, the Villa had been tried and tested against top opposition, and not only won all of them but did so with an aggregate of 14 goals. Also, they had gone through a run of six games undefeated, four of them away from home.

November, 1893

The Villa were League leaders once more, but the teams below did have games in hand. What could stop the Villa now? The answer proved to be in themselves, as they then went to another highly-placed side (**Blackburn**) and somehow lost in a most "tame and dull" match – the best bit being when the referee called for half-time; he called off all the players, then noted that he had blown five minutes early. They then all trooped back out again to finish the half!

The next potential 'banana skin' was the visit of **Sunderland**. They were not playing at the heights of the previous few seasons, but they had games in hand, and if they could improve their away form, would prove dangerous title contenders.

There was a top attendance at Perry Barr to see what might happen. Athersmith and Woolley could not play as they were away (but "Tich" Smith was in any case doing well in the outside-left slot). Further, John Devey's wife was seriously ill, but he played on – he may have felt he had to, as there would otherwise have been a relatively inexperienced front line. As it was it consisted of *Randle, Hare, Devey, Hodgetts and Smith*.

The Aston Villa Chronicles 1874 – 1924 (and after)

[From the *Athletic News*] Sunderland gave the honour of running the line for them to William McGregor (a testimony to his honesty). Charlie Johntsone was the Villa's 'linesman' – whilst smoking his pipe!

From the start to half-time, the game was predominantly stuck in mid-field – such was the grip that the half-backs had on the game, and there was no score at the break.

Villa broke the deadlock ten minutes into the second period when Groves sent over an adroit free-kick from which Devey scored. This lead was not long after cancelled out by Sunderland. What proved to be Villa's winner came from a penalty, awarded for a foul on Hodgetts. Villa won, 2-1.

Reynolds was outstanding in this match, with Hodgetts, Devey and Smith excellent.

The next match – at **Bolton** – attracted a wind that virtually blew people off their feet, and thus a crowd of only 1,000 came to watch the match. Bolton were fairly low in the division, but perhaps the Villa felt they could afford some 'squad rotation' as the Villa fielded a reduced strength side, leaving out Dunning, Athersmith and Reynolds. The match produced little of interest, but the Villa won.

With the exception of the return of Dunning and Athersmith, Villa fielded an unchanged side against the now-lowly **Preston North End**. The Villa were mostly the masters of this match, but Preston defended well and limited Villa's scoring to a goal in each half. Hare was mentioned as "greatly improved".

> The Villa played Walsall Town Swifts in a friendly. Their keeper was an old friend – Jimmy Warner! He had left Newton Heath and returned to the Midlands. The Villa won 4-1.

December, 1893

Another tricky match came up when the Villa had to visit **Derby**, but the Villa had available what was now their usual side.

[From the *Athletic News*] There was another midfield battle in the first half, with no score at half-time.

After the interval, "within five or six minutes a miskick let in Cowan, who dropped the ball beautifully into the goalmouth. It seemed to hang tremendously in its flight, and to the expectant onlooker it seemed an age on reaching the keeper. When it did arrive, a small crowd of Villa forwards unceremoniously bowled the keeper over and put the ball into the net."

Some fine play ensued from both sides, with both keepers called into action to save their lines. But it was the Derby keeper who made the mistake of

The Aston Villa Chronicles 1874 – 1924 (and after)

trying to kick clear, and missed his kick completely, letting Athersmith's soft shot enter the net! Hodgetts finished off a match that Villa often dominated; they won 3-0.

"The Villa halves were a grand trio," it was reported.

Then **Sheffield Wednesday** visited Perry Barr. Albert Brown was called on to deputise for Hare, but Hare's "indisposition" lasted and Brown continued in his stead for several games. At the start of the New Year, Hare was announced as retired from the game because of ill-health, but although he did not play again that season, he did appear briefly the next season before moving to Woolwich Arsenal. Although not a highly prominent player, he was highly thought of.

A win of 3-0 to the Villa ensued against the Wednesday, after a goal-less first half, but "the Villa were prone to display too much confidence".

At **Newton Heath** (Clayton, Manchester), the Villa found a determined side who threatened to score in the first half, and but for the work by Dunning and the backs, they may well have done so. In a much different second half, the Villa won clearly, 3-1, but thanks to two own goals!

> "There is very little attraction out Clayton [Manchester] way ... except to experience the delights of the perfumes from the neighbourhood chemical works ..."

Wolves were the next opponents (at Molineux) just before Christmas. The Wolves won 3-0, slightly denting the Villa's championship hopes. Again, the Villa's prettiness and scientific football was beaten by dash and energy, and (again) the Villa's shooting was awry. Wolves were then playing well, and on Boxing Day they defeated Blackburn Rovers, 5-1. What happened the following week is hard to say, as the Albion went to Molineux and beat the Wolves, 8-0!

The Christmas period in the Midlands was full of goal-scoring presents for their cold supporters, as on Boxing Day, **Darwen** were thrashed 9-0 by the Villa.

[From the *Athletic News*] "... the Perry Barr brigade made rings round them, the home forwards displaying any amount of confidence, and the way they passed, re-passed, dodged and dribbled was a treat to witness."

Devey, Albert Brown and Hodgetts each scored two, with Smith, Athersmith and Reynolds completing the scoring.

The Aston Villa Chronicles 1874 – 1924 (and after)

January, 1894

On a bitterly cold New Year's day, the Villa played Small Heath in a friendly, and won 4-3. The Villa were over-nonchalant to start with, as they allowed the Heathens to score first before the Villa started to play. But the Villa were made to work hard for their win.

The freezing weather continued, and, back in the League competition, the Villa were again made to work in a draw at **Sheffield Wednesday**. Then the Villa went to play at **Preston** in the League, but the match had to be abandoned ten minutes into the second half, through the bad weather. A week or so later, again the Villa went to play the fixture and again it was called off. Finally, the fixture was fulfilled, and the Villa thrashed Preston 5-2 on 18 January. However, the bad news was that the Football League ruled that Preston should keep the entire gate receipts for the first two (abandoned) matches, and only the receipts for the completed match should be shared. "The Villa committee are dreadfully wild about the matter", said the *Athletic News*.

Wrapped around that final match against Preston were two friendlies played against the Corinthians. The first match was marvellous entertainment for the 10,000 present, the Villa winning at the Oval by 6 goals to 4, after leading 3-0 at half-time. The Corinthians came back strongly in the second half, and levelled at 4-4 before the Villa scored two late goals. At Perry Barr, the Villa lost the return match 2-3, the match report stating that Villa were saving themselves for the FA Cup match versus Wolves.

Wolverhampton Wanderers (h)

The *Athletic News* reckoned that **30,000** spectators were present for the first round Cup match. If that is a true figure, then that easily set the Perry Barr ground record, the previous best being 27,000 in the FA Cup match versus Preston in 1888. The figure was way up on their usual 'good' gates of ten to twelve thousand.

Villa: *Dunning; Baird, Elliott; Reynolds, Jas. Cowan, Groves; Athersmith, Chatt, J.Devey, Hodgetts, Woolley.*

[From the *Athletic News*] The 'gate' "was a splendid sight, and I believe the gentleman who wanted to be first brought his breakfast along with him, and waited patiently until 12 o'clock, when the gates were open."

The Aston Villa Chronicles 1874 – 1924 (and after)

The Villa had learnt from the disorderly affair of the 1888 Preston cup match. "The banking put up … gave everyone a good view of the game, and even had the spectators been so disposed, they would have found it a difficult matter to get over the splendid walls which now surround the playing enclosure."

"The excitement was intense as the two captains went up to toss, and the hearty cheer which rose plainly announced the fact that Devey had won." Villa had the enormous advantage of playing downhill and with the wind.

After only four minutes, "Cowan … crashed the ball through with a shot which threatened to damage the net." Although the Wolves almost immediately equalised with a shot that grazed the post, they were little to be seen in the first half to the extent that the Villa backs stood well over the centre line. Two further goals – both headers – by Devey and Chatt gave the Villa a substantial 3-0 lead at half-time.

Wolves – of course – had the slope and wind advantage in the second half, and they scored within a few minutes, their Griffin bounding past Reynolds and Elliott and screwing the ball home. Dunning looked astonished. And within minutes, a blockbuster from Harry Wood hit the net. It was now 3-2.

Wolves threatened more, but the Villa backs did their job to keep them out, and with 20 minutes to go, "Athersmith, getting hold, sped away and centred right to Woolley's feet" – but he failed with the chance presented. It was not long, however, before Devey received the ball and potted home from two yards. 4-2. "I have heard some cheering in my time, but never anything to equal that goal," wrote the 'Free Critic'. The Villa ran out clear winners against a now disheartened Wolves.

Dunning and Devey were outstanding. Devey was everywhere – one moment clearing from defence, and the next leading his forwards up the field. "He worked like a horse, and gave a display of masterly activity, usefulness and clever play such is seldom witnessed."

February, 1894

A League visit from lowly **Newton Heath** split the first two rounds of the Cup, and the Heath were soundly beaten 5-1, though it took the Villa 30 minutes to get off the mark. The Villa clearly were keeping within themselves, but Devey still managed to collect a hat-trick.

It was a big match at **Sunderland** for the second round of the FA Cup. A **23,000** crowd turned up, including 1,000 Villa supporters, the gate being a new record for the north, despite the westerly gale that blew, and an occasional shower of rain or sleet.

[From the *Athletic News*] Sunderland had the advantage of the wind, and gave the Villa's defence a roasting in the first half; they led at half time by 2 goals

The Aston Villa Chronicles 1874 – 1924 (and after)

to 0. Villa, however, did have the disadvantage in that Reynolds was kicked in the eye early on, but he kept to his post despite the wound continuing to bleed. In between the two goals, Campbell hit the crossbar three times. The second goal was a chance punt at goal from near the grandstand – the scorer being as surprised as everyone else when it went in!

The Villa came back to 2-2 in the second half through a header from Hodgetts and a grand shot from Cowan, and though Sunderland never gave up, the Villa might have won it in the last 10 minutes. Both sides had given their all and did not produce much of note in extra time.

The Villa should, in fact, have been given the game as a Devey shot was entering the net just as the final whistle went – but the referee refused to give the goal! In fact, it would seem that he whistled 20 seconds before due time!

The replay. A match in deplorable conditions resulted in Villa winning 2-0. However, the teams decided from the first to play the match as a friendly, but did not tell the 15,000 crowd that turned up! The fans did not realise until afterwards that the result of the round was still undecided. The following Wednesday, out trooped the teams again to produce exactly the same margin – it finished 3-1 to the Villa.

Sheffield Wednesday (a)

After three strength-sapping Cup matches, the Villa went to play The Wednesday only three days after the last Sunderland match. Another big gate was present.

[From the *Athletic News*] The Wednesday took the lead after ten minutes, but even in that short space of time, the Villa had a trio of efforts on goal, and, at the Villa end, Dunning had made four or five saves in quick succession – the last being "a marvel". Villa's midfield then took over, and Chatt equalised with "a grand low shot" just before half-time.

After the interval, Villa went "on the warpath", but it took 28 minutes for them to score and take the lead, through Chatt. Just three minutes from time, the Wednesday equalised, and extra time was entered into.

In 1911, 'Chicane' in *The Villa News* recalled this match at this point in the game, and his comments are included in the following:

> This was a match where Villa were winning 2-1 with [minutes] to go. The pressmen felt confident to go and wire the 'result', but The Wednesday equalised and then scored a winner in extra time! The referee refused a Villa goal (which would have confirmed Villa's win) in the following way: "The ball came swinging across goal from Charlie Athersmith to where Dennis Hodgetts was waiting to pick up any 'unconsidered trifle'. But Dennis quietly opened his

The Aston Villa Chronicles 1874 – 1924 (and after)

legs – a favourite trick of his – and allowed it to go on". and the ball was put into the net by an awaiting player. Hodgetts, at the time of the 'score', had kept off a defender – the referee saw this as a foul and the 'goal' was disallowed."

Six minutes from the end of extra time, "the Wednesday left wing had brought the ball along with a dash for the Villa goal. Baird went for Spikesley, [with] Dunning rushing out to help him. Spikesley touched the ball back to Woolhouse, and the Wednesday centre lifting it nicely over the heads of several Villans, and [with] no custodian there to stop it, into the net it went."

The reporter declared that The Wednesday "gave us English cup-tie football", while the Villa's "cleverness of their halves and stylishness of their forwards" gained much admiration, but the Villa failed to capitalise on their chances. Chatt was considered "a brilliant forward".

March, 1894

The Wednesday match had taken its toll of Dunning, who was feared as having a fractured cheek-bone, and was now in hospital. Villa's veteran full-back, Frank Coulton, was then selected to deputise – *in goal*! On top of that, John Devey, Reynolds and Hodgetts were called up by England to play against Ireland. Smith was preferred to Woolley and kept his place till the end of the season. The team to play **Bolton** at Perry Barr was:

Villa: *Coulton; Baird, Elliott; G. Burton, Jas. Cowan, Russell; Athersmith, Chatt, W.Devey, Groves, Smith.*

[From the *Athletic News*] The Villa – playing a team that had not had much practise together – pushed Bolton all the way, the score being level at half-time, 1-1. The Villa then took the lead in the second half after they had bombarded the Bolton goal from the start of the half. "It was astonishing how the Bolton goal was saved from falling time after time." Sadly, Bolton equalised, and then took the lead with a few minutes remaining. The Villa lost, 2-3, but it was to be their last League defeat of the season.

On 10 March, the Villa, playing a full side except for Dunning, met Loughborough in the Birmingham Cup – and *lost* 1-2, after extra time! "The match will never be forgotten in Loughborough as the Villa were fairly and squarely beaten", said the *Athletic News*.

> "*The Villa are great favourites everywhere, and are always a big attraction.*
>
> 'En Passent',
> in the *Athletic News*.

The Aston Villa Chronicles 1874 – 1924 (and after)

What made the matter worse was that the Albion thrashed Loughborough 6-1 in the next round!

Blackburn Rovers were the next visitors at Perry Barr. The Villa played their usual side (except that Smith had now taken over from Woolley).

[From the *Athletic News*] Villa started brightly, but the Rovers midfield soon got into their stride, and neither side gained advantage for some time. Rovers scored first, but Chatt converted Reynolds centre just before half-time, when the score stood at 1-1.

"It was warm – very warm – and the players' faces were about the colour of tomatoes as they trooped off the field."

The second half was fairly even – both sides might have scored. However, Smith should have converted an open chance (as, indeed, should have the Rovers), but Smith later made amends when his good wing run ended in him putting the ball across for Chatt to head home the winner, with 15 minutes to go. 2-1 to the Villa.

Two days later (it was Easter), Villa played **Wolves**. A top crowd turned up at Perry Barr, hopeful of a Villa win that would have decided the championship, but were rewarded only with a 1-1 draw. The Villa's shooting was awry that day, and they indulged in too much fancy play.

April, 1894

Next, the Villa visited **Burnley**, who were chasing third place in the League. Even so, only a small crowd turned up, and they were treated to a scoring spectacular. Chatt and Reynolds were called up for the England match (versus Scotland), so Groves moved into Chatt's place, and Burton and Russell were called up to fill the wing-half slots.

[From the *Athletic News*] Burnley had the better of the early exchanges, but, after 25 minutes, "Cowan headed through in such a quiet, easy, manner that the spectators were too surprised to appreciate the point." Right at the end of the half, Dunning could not hold a terrific shot, and it squirmed into the net for the equaliser.

There was quick scoring after the interval, with the score being 2-2 after 51 minutes. The Villa then scored goals three and four via Devey and Hodgetts. However, "the Villa hadn't matters all their own way, though they were showing the prettier football", and Burnley scored a third, and nearly another equaliser before the Villa ran out 6-3 winners with two further goals.

In at last confirming the championship, the Villa won it with style. Captain Devey was reported as "a model centre-forward".

The Aston Villa Chronicles 1874 – 1924 (and after)

The following 'ditty' was sung at the *Theatre Royal* pantomime at the time, to the tune of 'MacNamara's Band':

> *With Chatt, Groves and Welford, Woolley Cowan and Baird;*
>
> *Reynolds, Devey and Athersmith whose names are always heard;*
>
> *And Hodgetts always ready when the ball is on the roll,*
>
> *We must admit that Dunning is a champion in goal!*

On 9 April, the Villa played a friendly against Celtic (the Scottish champions) at home, and won 2-1 in "one of the best games of the season". The return match on the 21st ended with the score being exactly in reverse – 1-2 to Celtic.

In Villa's final League match of the season (against **Nottingham Forest** at Perry Barr) the Villa won 3-1, but had played poorly until the second half. At the interval, they were 0-1 down, and it was only by the encouragement of their voluble supporters that they started playing. Villa equalised in the 60th minute through Athersmith, before the Villa scored two more, through Chatt (a header) and Devey ("a brilliant goal").

The Villa had been at the head of the table for most of the season, and were chased hard, but, in the end, a comfortable margin existed between first and second places.

The Football League Division 1 1893-94 Top Places	Pld	Home W D L F A	Away W D L F A	Overall W D L F A	Pts
1 Aston Villa	30	12 2 1 49 13	7 4 4 35 29	19 6 5 84 42	44
2 Sunderland	30	11 3 1 46 14	6 1 8 26 30	17 4 9 72 44	38
3 Derby County	30	9 2 4 47 32	7 2 6 26 30	16 4 10 73 62	36
4 Blackburn Rovers	30	13 0 2 48 15	3 2 10 21 38	16 2 12 69 53	34
5 Burnley	30	13 0 2 43 17	2 4 9 18 34	15 4 11 61 51	34
6 Everton	30	11 1 3 63 23	4 2 9 27 34	15 3 12 90 57	33
7 Nottingham Forest	30	10 2 3 38 16	4 2 9 19 32	14 4 12 57 48	32
8 West Bromwich Albion	30	8 4 3 35 23	6 0 9 31 36	14 4 12 66 59	32
9 Wolverhampton Wanderers	30	11 1 3 34 24	3 2 10 18 39	14 3 13 52 63	31

The Aston Villa Chronicles 1874 – 1924 (and after)

1893-94 League and FA Cup Results			
Sep	2nd H West Bromwich A	3-2	15000
	9th A Sunderland	1-1	9000
	11th H Stoke	5-1	6000
	16th A Everton	2-4	7000
	23rd H Everton	3-1	12000
	30th H Derby County	1-1	
Oct	2nd A Sheffield United	0-3	
	7th A Nottingham Forest	2-1	12000
	14th A Darwen	1-1	3000
	16th A Stoke	3-3	
	21st A West Bromwich A	6-3	15000
	28th H Burnley	4-0	10000
	30th H Sheffield United	4-1	
Nov	4th A Blackburn Rovers	0-2	
	11th H Sunderland	2-1	15000
	18th A Bolton Wanderers	1-0	1000
	25th H Preston North End	2-0	8000
Dec	2nd A Derby County	3-0	
	9th H Sheffield Wed	3-0	8000
	16th A Newton Heath	3-1	8000
	23rd A Wolves	0-3	10000
	26th H Darwen	9-0	12000
Jan	6th A Sheffield Wed	2-2	
	18th A Preston North End	5-2	
	27th H Wolves (FAC)	4-2	30000
Feb	3rd H Newton Heath	5-1	5000
	10th A Sunderland (FAC)	2-2	23000
	21st H Sunderland (FAC r)	3-1	
	24th A Sheffield Wed (FAC)	2-3	22000
Mar	3rd H Bolton Wanderers	2-3	
	24th H Blackburn Rovers	2-1	12000
	26th H Wolves	1-1	20000
Apr	7th A Burnley	6-3	7000
	14th H Nottingham Forest	3-1	

End of Season Postscripts

In early May, the Villa sent their best team to play Small Heath in aid of their finances, for which Small Heath raised £105. The result was a 3-3 draw. The Albion were also offered Villa's support, which was accepted for a later time.

The reorganisation of the Villa management the year before clearly had its affect. But the management also showed awareness that good communications were necessary, and the necessity of keeping 'tabs' on the atmosphere in the club. The *Athletic News* reported on a meeting held in the clubhouse at Perry Barr, on 1 May:

> All the [players] ... expressed themselves as highly delighted at the treatment they had received from the management, the members of which important body have undoubtedly kept a very high-spirited and gentlemanly set of players splendidly in hand.
>
> They have tempered in business with just sufficient 'softening' to make matters comfortable and happy. This has been talked about among other clubs, and the result is that numerous applications from other players [to join the Villa] have been received.

The Aston Villa Chronicles 1874 – 1924 (and after)

Another pleasing aspect was that there was an indication that football as a popular entertainment was on the increase. Some important matches were now attracting 20,000 or more spectators, a number that was hardly evident before the season just gone.

The *Athletic News*, reporting on the AGM (22 June, 1894), stated that there had been little criticism nor complaint from the membership. Again, however, the 'limited liability' question came up: "A committee was appointed to report upon the advisability of the club being formed into a limited liability company."

W. B. "Billy" Mason

The June AGM received news of the recent sudden death of Billy Mason, aged 39. Charlie Johnstone said that he was one of the best players the Villa ever had; the most honourable of men … A founder-member of the club, he had only the previous year taken such a useful part as a member (and chairman) of the Provisional Committee in order to steer the club through a serious crisis.

It was minuted on 4 October, 1894 that the committee had received a letter from Billy Mason's widow, thanking the committee for the picture of her late husband sent to her. She remarked about a celebratory event that must have occurred after the recent season had ended:

> I will remember on his arrival home his telling me how much he had enjoyed himself and how he regretted he was not well enough to stay longer with you. He was very proud of the Villa's successful season.

Celebrating the Winning of the League Championship

The *Athletic News* reported that on 17 August, 1894, the Villa management were giving a celebratory dinner to the members of the team at a restaurant in Temple Row: "This is the first of a probable series of 'feeds' which probably football followers will remember the Villa were once famous for!"

The Aston Villa Chronicles 1874 – 1924 (and after)

Season 1894-95: Cup Winners Over Albion Again!

League Division 1 position: 3rd *(of 16);* ***FA Cup:*** *Winners.*

A significant new signing for the Villa was Tommy Wilkes (goal). Billy Dorrell (forward) was also a new signing, and played a few games, but the surname is more associated with his son, Arthur, who also played for the Villa, and for England. This season would be most notable for the emergence of **Howard Spencer,** (full-back) who signed as an amateur in 1892, then became professional after coming into prominence in a Junior International at Leamington, in 1894. This man was to become captain of club and country – the first Villa player to captain England.[325]

The previous season, the success of the team hinged a great deal on the half-back line of Reynolds, Cowan and Groves, and, clearly, there was no reason to change that line. However, by 20 August (1894), the *Athletic News* announced:

"What is troubling the committee most just now is the absence of Billy Groves, about the most famous football wanderer in the land."

From the Villa's Minutes

Committee-member Joe Dunkley went up to Scotland to try to seek out the Scot, but came back none the wiser. What became mysterious was that Groves, in the preceding three months, had not applied for, nor received, his salary.

The truth finally emerged just prior to the start of the season. Groves had gone on holiday to the south coast, but was now lying ill with rheumatic fever at Bournemouth. By November, it was learnt that his recovery was a very slow process. Soon after, the bleak news came that his disease had affected his heart to the extent that there was very little probability of Groves again taking any active part in football. The Villa minutes (6 November) reveal that Groves was told that the Villa would keep him on to help in finding new players. He replied that he would be glad to do anything he could for the club.

Groves soon moved back to Edinburgh. He died in 1908, aged only 38.

---

[325] The other England captains supplied by Villa were Frank Moss and Billy Walker in the 1920s.

The Aston Villa Chronicles 1874 – 1924 (and after)

The Season's Play

September, 1894

The first League match of the season was against **Small Heath**, newly promoted to the First Divison, and this was the two teams' first encounter with one another in this competition. Perhaps 20,000 turned out to see this match on a glorious afternoon, the sun shining brilliantly.

Dunning had hurt his finger, thereby giving Wilkes his opportunity in goal, a position he held for a number of matches. John Devey was 'unfit', and, of course, Groves was indisposed at Bournemouth.

Villa: *Dunning; Baird, Welford; Reynolds, Jas.Cowan, Russell; Athersmith, Chatt, Gordon, Hodgetts, Smith.*

[From the *Athletic News*] "The players took to the field to the strains of 'Auld Lang Syne' from a cornet in the unreserved side, and a burst of cheering from the crowd." Small Heath won the toss and selected both the slope and the sun at their backs.

"The start was a sensational one. The Small Heath left winger got away, a smart ... cross to the right wing was followed by a sharp, [angled] shot from Hallam, which Wilkes failed to handle properly, and in a twinkling, the ball was in the net." 0-1 to Small Heath. The Villa were stunned, but it was not long before they rallied and put Small Heath under pressure.

"At last, after 20 minutes play, Athersmith got clean away and centring the ball to Gordon, that player touched it over to Smith, who just squeezed a 'daisy-cutter' inside the post." Within a minute, the compliment was returned, with Gordon receiving from Smith and scoring. 2-1 to Villa.

It was not at all a one-sided contest, and Small Heath were dangerous every time they got to the Villa end, and had two attempts on goal that only just missed their mark.

There was no further score, the second half being the province of the defenders, though Villa did once hit the crossbar.

However, "there never was a time when a better feeling existed between the players and supporters of the two clubs. This is as it should be, and I hope it will continue," wrote the reporter.

In a fund-raising friendly match in aid of the Albion (arranged at the end of the previous season), the Villa went to Stoney Lane the following Monday. They lost 4-5 to Albion, though Villa took the opportunity to try out new players.

The Aston Villa Chronicles 1874 – 1924 (and after)

The Villa tried a new combination for the League trip to **Liverpool**.

Villa: *Dunning; Elliott, Welford; Reynolds, Jas.Cowan, Russell; Athersmith, Chatt, Devey, Smith, Dorrell.*

[From the *Athletic News*] In an even first half, Liverpool took the lead on 18 minutes, and this score remained until half-time.

The Villa got the better of Liverpool in the second half, with Smith scoring with a shot that went in off the post. Chatt later added to Villa's score.

The match was a vigorous one, and it was not until the end that the result was certain.

Further signs of an increasing interest in football came about when the Villa met Sunderland at Perry Barr, the match attracting 20,000. The same day, there were 18,000 at Everton, though a lot of matches were staying at the 5-8,000 level. A resumption of the Hodgetts and Smith left-wing pairing was the only change to the Villa team. [326]

[From the *Athletic News*] Sunderland should have opened the scoring on five minutes, but with the goal at his mercy, their forward missed in "astonishing fashion". "The Villa men then romped up to the other end, and a sharp assault took place right under the bar. It was cleared momentarily, for Cowan dashed in and slipped the ball over to Chatt, who headed straight across goal, Smith having no difficulty in putting it past Doig." Then Chatt netted again, but was given offside.

It was then Sunderland's turn. For a time they pegged away at the Villa goal, but then "Reynolds got the ball away. Smith at once took up the run, and going off at top speed, he beat his back and flew straight for goal, and something very like a huge moan could be heard round the ring as he banged it against the side net."

Sunderland came back again, and when Campbell got possession, he dribbled "with wonderful command of the ball. The Scot wriggled around Welford and, making straight for goal, he let fly and completely beat Wilkes [to equalise]…" Sunderland then missed another fine chance, but nothing more of note occurred before the interval.

Villa started to make mistakes in the second period, but Sunderland showed up well and it was not long before they took the lead with a well-crafted goal. Sunderland now played well enough not to let the Villa back in the game, and ran out 1-2 winners.

---

[326] However, as Dorrell came back in for the next two away matches it would appear that change was because of Hodgetts' unavailability for awhile.

The Aston Villa Chronicles 1874 – 1924 (and after)

Hodgetts and Devey were disappointing, and Athersmith resorted to 'bashing' tactics.[327]

A better-than-usual **Derby County** crowd turned up to see their match against the Villa. Steve Bloomer and the two Goodall brothers were again the quality players amongst the opposition, but Derby were placed at the bottom of the League table, and the Villa were expected to win.

[From the *Athletic News*] From the start, the ball was "travelling with lightning rapidity up and down the ground. Both keepers were called on, and Derby had the best of it for some time.

After 25 minutes, "Reynolds lifted the leather across to the goal, and Chatt headed in. … [After an equal spell,] then commenced one of the most terrific onslaughts on a goal it has ever been my lot to witness … the County literally penned their opponents in …" and players of one side or another got in the way of the Derby shots on goal. The Villa were only relieved when the half-time whistle went.

Into the second period, it was not long before Derby re-commenced their assaults; they cleverly got through time and time again, but their shooting was faulty.

In due course, Derby's pressure was spent, and then Athersmith rattled the posts with a shot. Then Devey got the ball home at the second attempt after Smith's superb shot had been saved. The Villa won 2-0, with Reynolds and Chatt outstanding.

The Villa defence then took a pounding at **Stoke**, where the ex-Villan Billy Dickson led the Stoke forwards to go three-up in the first 20 minutes. The Villa had moments when they got back into the game, and late-on reduced the arrears, but Stoke hit yet a fourth.

October, 1894

Another away game followed at **Nottingham Forest**, and many Villa fans were amongst the crowd. Again, the opponents took an early lead, but the Villa forwards manfully and admirably worked at their task until they at last equalised. Forest did enough, however, and late-on scored their winner.

---

[327] In October, the committee cautioned Athersmith that if he were to be sent off in a match, the Villa would not pay him [during his suspension].

The Aston Villa Chronicles 1874 – 1924 (and after)

> Having managed to win – fortuitously – against the bottom club, and then having lost to two lowly teams, questions were again being asked about the Villa. The *Athletic News* commented:
>
> > ... it is quite evident that there will have to be an overhauling of the machinery and an adjustment of the working parts if the reputation of the Villa club is to be maintained...

The **Albion** were the next opponents, but this time at Perry Barr. The Villa committee responded to the calls for change by bringing out their 'secret weapon' – the 19 years-old Howard Spencer, who had been quietly but effectively learning his trade at full-back in the reserves. 'HS' would provide such a huge contribution to the club over more than forty years, thirteen of those as a player.

Villa: *Dunning; Spencer, Welford; Reynolds, Jas.Cowan, Russell; Athersmith, Chatt, Devey, Hodgetts, Woolley.*

[From the *Athletic News*] The match was full of excitement. "It soon became a scorching-hot game, the Albion certainly showing up best initially, though some sterling back play by Welford and Spencer kept them well at bay, [the wingers] Bassett amd McLeod being very prominent ... Some good gallops were made by Athersmith, and Woolley did several nice things, and presently a rattling centre of the fleet right-wing was finally hooked through by Hodgetts, and there was a great chorus.

"The Albion had hardly time to grow dangerous when the home team were off again, and after Reader had thrice saved superbly, a raking return by Spencer twinkled among the mazy collection of legs, and Devey added the finishing touch ..." 2-0 to the Villa, and it remained that score at the interval.

On the restart, Villa put on a strong fusillade on the Albion goal, with Chatt adding another goal. The Albion men looked unhappy, but a "rare old Albion rush was made by William Bassett and his satellites – for that is what they are – and ... a red-hot shot appeared to burn the fingers of Master Dunning, for he dropped it like a particularly warm potato ...", resulting in an Albion player putting it into the net. This encouraged the Albion, and for a while they looked as though they might turn the game, but their effort soon faded and the Albion goal now had numerous escapes. However, even though Athermith had around six shots, and the other forwards also each had a few, there was no further score. The Villa won, 3-1.

Spencer was included in a list of Villa players who did exceedingly well, "though he strikes one occasionally as being a trifle cool."

The Aston Villa Chronicles 1874 – 1924 (and after)

The Villa now visited **Small Heath** for their return match. Reynolds (scalded foot) and Devey (severe cold) were unavailable.

Villa: *Dunning; Spencer, Welford; G.Burton, Jas.Cowan, Russell; Athersmith, Chatt, Gordon, Hodgetts, Woolley.*

[From the *Athletic News*] The Villa got off to a racing start, with Athersmith hitting the post before Gordon "raced off for goal at top speed and sent in a stinging shot" that brought Villa's first goal. The Villa continued to have the best of it with the Heathens at times looking ragged. Then, right on half-time, they were awarded a penalty, from which they equalised.

The Heathens' forward play improved after the interval but the Villa defence generally kept them at bay, "[but] considering the spirit in which they were playing, it was no wonder to see the Heathens at last get one past the Villa keeper, the ball being headed into the net by Wheldon after every other forward had had a pop. And didn't the people cheer! ... But hardly had the applause died away when a corner was given to the visitors." A scrimmage formed round the Heathens' keeper, and Athersmith was alleged to have been pushed, the referee awarding a penalty to the Villa – to the amusement of Athersmith. Hodgetts thus equalised.

The match was then end-to-end, but culminated in a Villa bombardment of the Heathens' goal, with no further score. 2-2 was the result.

Still without Reynolds and Devey, the Villa then travelled to **Sheffield United**, who were high in the League table. The Villa narrowly lost, 1-2.

> The *Athletic News* reported that, "Many of the Villa supporters are talking of transferring their affections to the Coventry Road organisation unless a material change for the better sets in very quickly, while the Small Heath people are getting very perky ..."

Liverpool were visitors to Perry Barr for the next match. The weather had been so bad that the crowd was only 4,000 at the start of the match, but it got bigger as the weather improved. Devey was still unavailable, giving rise to another strange appearance about the forward line. Wilkes was the preferred keeper.

Villa: *Wilkes; Spencer, Welford; Reynolds, Jas.Cowan, Russell; Athersmith, Smith, Chatt, Hodgetts, Dorrell.*

[From the *Athletic News*] "Villa beat their opponents easily at all points of the game, every department ... being decidedly superior."

Smith and Dorrell received compliments, Chatt was a revelation at centre-forward, Athersmith was outstanding and Hodgetts had never played a better game in the Villa's 5-0 win.

The Aston Villa Chronicles 1874 – 1924 (and after)

At this stage of the season the Villa lay sixth in the table.

November, 1894

With the same side as played against Liverpool, the Villa travelled to **Sheffield Wednesday**, where they lost the game 0-1 thanks to a goal ten minutes from time. It was a game mainly concerned with two good defences.

The visit of third-placed **Preston** brought out a fair number to see the match, but the attendance was again affected by the weather – there was a heavy downpour half-an-hour before the kick-off. John Devey returned to lead the attack, which had a more 'normal' look about it.

Villa: *Wilkes; Spencer, Welford; Reynolds, Jas.Cowan, Russell; Athersmith, Chatt, Devey, Hodgetts, Smith.*

[From the *Athletic News*] For 20 minutes, another reverse seemed likely, but the Villa were the first to score, Devey heading in. This score was deservedly equalised ten minutes later, to provide the interval score of 1-1, although the Villa ended the half well on the attack.

After the interval, "the Villa evidently feeling that a big effort was required from them, metaphorically pulled up their socks and waded into the prey, with the result that the North End had very little chance indeed." Hodgetts won a penalty, but Reynolds' spot kick was well saved. Soon after, however, Hodgetts' pressure caused a defender to concede an own goal.

"Very little relief came to Preston, ere a fine run by Hodgetts and Smith raised the enthusiasm of the crowd, and sweeping down the field in resistless fashion, and passing the ball beautifully from toe to toe, the Villa Vanguard got close in, and Hodgetts, receiving a deft and accurate pass, swiftly scored."

Later, Hodgetts sent in a hot shot that rocketed about among a forest of legs and finally was converted by Chatt. 4-1 to the Villa. More goals seemed imminent, but Preston fought back until, late in the game, Athersmith put in a fine run and "a lightning shot which hit the post."

The reporter ('Brum') advised the committee to leave well alone and give this team selection a prolonged trial.

The Aston Villa Chronicles 1874 – 1924 (and after)

Two days later, the same team thrashed second-placed **Sheffield United** 5-0 at Perry Barr. How the game was ever played, however, was a mystery. Only 500 spectators turned up, and the *Athletic News* reporter described the scene of heavy, chilling rain and mud, and wondered how the referee could have allowed the game to have been played, such were the conditions.

It was in a match versus Sheffield United that Charlie Athersmith is known to have played using an umbrella. This was probably the Match in question.

Cartoon by Norman Edwards in *The Story of Aston Villa*

He wrote: "The keen wind blew the rain in misty driving clouds across the field till you could almost hear the players' scanty clothing flapping in the breeze! ... the players teeth chattered audibly ...".

'Fatty' Foulkes (the Sheffield keeper) was down with stomach cramp for some time. At the end, "players were dithering and shaking as if they had fits of the ague." Some players gave up well before the final whistle and went quickly to the "cheery dressing room".

There was then a slight interruption to the Villa's recovery, as a visit to the **Albion** without Hodgetts produced a 2-3 defeat, but that was after being 0-2 behind at half-time, and at one-time drawing level before the Albion hit their winner. Devey twice hit the post late on.

The Villa again put on their scoring boots in winning 4-1 against **Nottingham Forest**. After scoring the fourth, the Villa slackened off; the Villa then lay in third place.

This last match – in one way – proved to be the end of a great era.

The Aston Villa Chronicles 1874 – 1924 (and after)

Archie Hunter

On 29 November, 1894, Archie Hunter died, aged 35. On the day of his funeral, a crowd six or seven deep lined the route of his last journey – to his place of rest at Witton Cemetary. The pallbearers read like the team-sheet of a great Villa side of yore: Tom Pank, Denny Hodgetts, Howard Vaughton, Frank Coulton, Fred Dawson, Eli Davis, Sammy Law, and (of course) George Ramsay.

At his funeral service, it was stated:

> Would to God that it could be wrote of all men who have made more profession of definite religion that our friend has done. He was always gentle and gentlemanly. If he chanced by sheer superiority to send an opponent to mother earth, he would personally help him to his feet again. ...

The headstone on his grave at Witton reads:

> This monument is erected in loving memory of Archie Hunter, the famous captain of Aston Villa, by his football comrades and the club as a lasting tribute to his ability on the field and his sterling worth as a man.

On 7 January, 1895, the committee resolved to pay Archie Hunter's funeral expenses, and on 23 September, 1895, there was a benefit match played for Archie Hunter's family. The match, at Perry Barr, was played against West Bromwich Albion. Villa won, 2-1.

December, 1894

A "Grand Performance by Aston Villa" took place at **Blackburn** in the next match, resulting in Blackburn's first home defeat of the season.

[From the *Athletic News*] Though Villa played the smarter forward game to start with, it was Rovers that scored on 20 minutes. The Villa came back, but did not gain success until, at length, they gained a corner. The corner reached Devey, who put it to Smith, who, in turn, shot through the keeper's legs. 1-1 was the half-time score.

After the interval, the Rovers played strongly, but Villa kept cool and waited their chance. This came, and Snith scored with a magnificent shot. Again, the Rovers came back, but stalwart play in Villa's defence kept them at bay, and it was Smith again – for his hat-trick – who scored on 75 minutes.

That was the end of the scoring, but "Athersmith was loudly cheered for a brilliant run half the length of the field, finishing with a splendid shot [that was well saved]".

The Aston Villa Chronicles 1874 – 1924 (and after)

Two days later, the Villa played **Sheffield Wednesday** at home, they playing a fine defensive game in the first half, allowing the Villa one shot – from which they scored! The score remained the same for a long time, making the Villa supporters nervous, but then Athersmith gave Devey a fine chance, and he scored. The Wednesday pulled one back, but Reynolds then converted a penalty that gave Villa a 3-1 win. Another home match followed – against **Blackburn Rovers.**

[From the *Athletic News*] After 10 minutes, "the result of some brilliant play by the home forwards enabled Athersmith to get possession, and although having to encounter both backs, successfully scored." The rest of the half was a terrific contest when either side could – and should – have scored. Rovers made one wild miss, and Reynolds' wonderful shot was well saved.

The struggle continued in the second half, with Devey making a mess of one opportunity. Long kicking became the order of the day, with Rovers looking good to take a point from the match.

"In response to cries of 'play up, Villa!', the home brigade put more life into their play, and a passing run by Chatt and Athersmith was nullified by weakness on the part of the home centre-forward [Devey] who seemed dead out of form. However, some pretty passing by the Villa forwards and half-backs culminated in Russell sending on to Devey, who this time cleverly hooked the ball home …

"Now came a change, the home forwards returning to the attack with dazzling brilliancy, and a fast shot by Reynolds, who had backed up well, missed by inches." From here on, the Rovers seemed to deteriorate, but that was more to do with "the superb game the home team played – it was brilliant in the extreme."

Then "[Devey] threaded his way through half-backs and backs, and although much hampered … [scored] … after one of the best individual efforts seen for a long time."

From the Villa's Minutes — At the committee meeting of 15 December, it was communicated that Congreave's Ironworks had sent their thanks to the Villa for "the very ready way they gave their consent for the players to give a benefit match" for those thrown out of work as a result of the closure of the works.

In a high gale (strong enough to partially unroof one of the grandstands), the Villa next beat the **Wolves** 4-0 at Molineux after taking an early lead. The Wolves supporters were seen leaving long before the end, so comprehensively beaten were their team.

The Aston Villa Chronicles 1874 – 1924 (and after)

On Boxing Day, 12,000 saw a one-sided match, with the Villa running out easy winners, 6-0, against **Stoke**; Athersmith scored a hat-trick. The only change to the Villa team in the preceding nine games had been because of the absence of Hodgetts on one occasion, but for the Stoke match, Villa brought Dunning into goal, where he played for six successive matches in place of Wilkes.

The Villa were now on top of the League, but Everton had the same number of points with four games in hand. Sunderland were one point behind with five games in hand.

Leading Positions in Division 1 December 26th, 1894	Pld	Home W D L F A	Away W D L F A	Overall W D L F A	Pts
1 Aston Villa	20	9 0 1 36 7	4 1 5 18 16	13 1 6 54 23	27
2 Everton	16	7 1 0 28 7	5 2 1 24 16	12 3 1 52 23	27
3 Sunderland	15	9 0 0 36 6	3 2 1 10 9	12 2 1 46 15	26
4 Blackburn Rovers	19	7 3 1 26 13	1 2 5 10 19	8 5 6 36 32	21
5 Preston North End	19	4 2 2 14 9	4 2 5 18 20	8 4 7 32 29	20

January, 1895

With **Sunderland** hot on Villa's heels, the match at their ground on 2 January, 1895 had all the expectation of a Cup Final. On a windy day, the match was played on a heavy ground.

[From the *Birmingham Daily Post*] The match was fast and exciting. The Villa opened the scoring on 12 minutes, but this was equalised. Then the Villa scored again, and again the goal was equalised. Villa's third goal of the half (a penalty) meant that the Villa led 3-2 at half-time.

Sunderland equalised yet again on 62 minutes, and then – for the first time – took the lead in the match "amid shouts that could be heard a mile away." The finish was pulsating, and with 10 minutes to go, Devey equalised for the Villa to make it 4-4 at the finish.

The *Athletic News* claimed that Sunderland were "outclassed" and lucky to escape defeat, all their goals being of the soft variety. On the same day, Small Heath were beaten 1-9 at Blackburn, while the Albion lost 4-5 to Preston, at home.

Intensely cold weather meant that 7,000 spectators were at Perry Barr to see the next match, against **Derby County** – again, they not having a good season. The Villa played well within themselves to win 4-0, but "ever and anon they would suddenly wake-up, dart off with a succinctness much relished by the crowd, and give the Derby keeper an immense lot of work to do." (*Athletic News*)

The Aston Villa Chronicles 1874 – 1924 (and after)

Freezing conditions existed at **Preston** for the next match. The ground was so hard that pick-axes had to be used to make holes for the corner flags. The Villa won 1-0, the goal coming in the first couple of minutes, Devey scoring from a Hodgetts corner. Though the first half was evenly-fought, the second half was a defensive one for the Villa, Preston getting through time and time again, only for Dunning always to be in the way.

"The Match for the Championship" was the headline in the *Athletic News*, concerning the Villa's match at **Everton**. 18,000 were present, of which it was thought some 3,000 were Villa supporters. The match was played (very unusually) on a *Thursday*.

After a run of nine games undefeated (eight of them were wins) and no team changes, other than the keeper's position, the Villa were forced to make a change. Chatt went 'lame' in training, so Dorrell was called in to the side, but was "ordered" to play inside-right (Chatt's position) so as not to disturb the successful left-wing partnership.

[From the *Birmingham Daily Post*] Everton scored on two minutes and then proceeded to play brilliantly. They scored another on 10 minutes, and added yet another to make it 0-3 at half-time.

Soon into the second half, Everton added a fourth before a big transformation took place in the game. The Villa had paced themselves better on the heavy ground, and, with Everton tiring, began to play in "irresistible fashion". But had the Villa left it too late?

The Villa scored two goals; then Smith added what appeared to be a legitimate third, but it was not allowed. Right afterwards, a fine move involving Hodgetts and Smith led to Devey having the goal at his mercy – but he shot wide! Everton then put everything into defence, so that the Villa did not get near again, and Villa lost 2-4.

From the Villa's Minutes

The talented left-winger Albert Woolley was transferred to Derby County in January, 1895 for £50, and compensation paid to Woolley for his contract being broken. This matter came back to haunt the Villa, as by October the same year Woolley was taken very ill (with T.B.), and because he could not attend training, Derby refused to pay him his salary. He appealed to the Villa for help; the Villa sent him 5 guineas (£5 5s). *Woolley died early the following year, aged 25.*

The Aston Villa Chronicles 1874 – 1924 (and after)

January 26, 1895 was a suitable frost-bound, snowy day in which to play **Bolton Wanderers** (in their white shirts!), at Perry Barr. However, there had been "ructions" in the Villa camp, and the miscreants relegated to the reserve team; the first team showed a few changes from its normal self:

Villa: *Wilkes; Baird, Elliott; G.Burton, Jas. Cowan, Kinsey; Athersmith, Hare, Devey, Hodgetts, Smith.*

[From the *Athletic News*] Villa's opening goal resulted from an Athersmith corner. The ball struck a Bolton defender, and then glanced into the net in the calmest and most dignified manner. "A little tremor of wonder and laughter thrilled the crowd!"

After the interval, the snow stopped, the sun came out, and this sparked Devey into action. He got onto the ball "like a cock robin on a worm", and "whizzed" the ball into the net. 2-0 to Villa. But then Bolton scored, and this put some fun into the match. Wilkes had to make a few smart saves, "and the folks breathed hard and heavy!" During this time, the Villa's defence was looking most unsafe, but it was not long before Villa were again giving Bolton's keeper something to worry about. He "was cheered again and again by the generous crowd!" Once, Hodgetts and Devey "sat summarily on his chest right under the bar", but still the keeper cleared!

The match finished 2-1 to the Villa, and the reporter commented, "It was good to see the sportsmanlike feeling which prevailed among the players."

It would be another month before the Villa returned to League football, and the situation at the top of League Division One at this point was as follows:

Leading Positions in Division 1 January 26th, 1895	Pld	Home W	L	D	F	A	Away W	D	L	F	A	Overall W	D	L	F	A	Pts
1 Sunderland	22	10	2	0	44	12	5	2	3	20	15	15	4	3	64	27	34
2 Aston Villa	25	11	0	1	42	8	5	2	6	25	24	16	2	7	67	32	34
3 Everton	22	9	2	0	36	10	5	3	3	26	22	14	5	3	62	32	33

February, 1895

The occasion of the FA Cup first round had arrived, and the Villa were drawn against **Derby County** at Perry Barr. Welford and Chatt were unavailable.

Villa: *Wilkes; Spencer, Elliott; Reynolds, Jas.Cowan, Russell; Athersmith, Podmore, Devey, Hodgetts, Smith.*

[From the *Athletic News*] In due course – and without Derby showing much threat – Villa scored "a very fine goal by Devey, most unselfishly worked for by Hodgetts and Russell." On a very treacherous pitch, no more goals ensued

The Aston Villa Chronicles 1874 – 1924 (and after)

before half-time.

"A long kick and rush, with lots of following up" with a little finesse in-between was the type of play adopted in the conditions. It was not long before Bloomer brought the score equal, and Derby began to show how dangerous they could be. The Villa eased their supporters' worries when Smith and Hodgetts combined to give Smith a close-range chance, which he smashed home. Villa led, 2-1.

The game was still not finished by any means. There had to be some clever tackling by Elliott, Reynolds and Cowan as Derby vigorously tried to equalise. However, the Villa made it through, though Derby had played in a manner that belied their League position.

The FA Cup second round, again at Perry Barr, was against Second Division **Newcastle United**. The Villa played Dorrell at inside-right, but the team was otherwise unchanged on a beautifully fine day. Villa were leading 6-1 at half-time in a desperately one-sided match. Easing off in the second half, one more goal was added, the match finishing 7-1 to the Villa.

The FA Cup was interrupted by another League match at **Burnley** on 23 February.

Villa: *Wilkes; Spencer, Elliott; G.Burton, Jas.Cowan, Russell; Athersmith, Chatt, Devey, Hodgetts, Smith.*

[From the *Athletic News*] Though at times an end-to-end game, Burnley started as the most threatening team, and they scored after 25 minutes, from a free-kick. Burnley increased their effort, and and though Wilkes' save went onto the crossbar, the ball came back out and was forced home for a second Burnley goal on 30 minutes. Burnley's play was rewarded with a third goal on 50 minutes, so it was now 0-3 to them. Wilkes kept out more Burnley goal attempts, and the play went on in this manner until 70 minutes had passed, Burnley miraculously failing to score more.

Then the tide changed. Villa were probably the fitter side, and their keeper was forced to make his first saves of the match. Chatt soon scored, and two more goals followed, so that in the final 20 minutes the Villa came back to draw 3-3.

March, 1895

The third round of the FA Cup was against **Nottingham Forest**. Again the tie was played at Perry Barr. Reynolds and Spencer had another enforced absence.

The Aston Villa Chronicles 1874 – 1924 (and after)

Villa: *Wilkes; Elliott, Welford; G.Burton, Jas.Cowan, Russell;*
Athersmith, Chatt, Devey, Hodgetts, Smith.

[From the *Athletic News*] The Villa were always in charge of this match. They scored two early goals, but the Forest's pluck brought them back into it with a goal, before Villa scored again to make it 3-1 at half-time. Wilkes generally had had so little to do "that he got cold and shivered."

Villa continued in like vain after the break, and yet that Forest pluck returned; they scored a second to make it 3-2! What Forest supporters were present "hollered ... and for a time their smile was as expansive as a pancake and as jolly to look at!" However, they might have soon wished that they had never been born. In the next 10 minutes, Villa showed how with "the little twinkling left winger" Smith scoring twice, "and James Cowan, Esq., (he deserves the affix for a really magnificent display!) rocketed through a romper which made the net oscillate and shiver and the Notts keeper to look flabbergasted." Winning 6-2, for the rest of the game, "the home lot simply doddled about".

	Semi- Final	vs Sunderland	2-1	Attendance:
	16 March, 1895	at Ewood Park, Blackburn		15,000

Villa: *Wilkes; Spencer, Welford; Reynolds, Jas. Cowan, Russell;*
Athersmith, Chatt, Devey, Hodgetts, Smith.

William McGregor recorded his memory of this FA Cup semi-final match, played at Blackburn:

> The display of Steve Smith was one of the best I have ever seen. None of Sunderland's defenders seemed able to cope with him. He had one trick which he could do better than any man I have watched. He used to walk past an opponent from practically a stationary position, and rarely did he fail to get right clear. The Villa would not have scored that day but for Smith. On each occasion he got quite near in, but his position was such that to score seemed virtually impossible. Nevertheless, although Doig, the wonderful, wary and vigilant goalkeeper, was on the alert, Smith each time planted the ball into the net with the most wonderful and skilful judgment, two of the finest goals ever scored by one player on the same afternoon. ... He was cheered to the echo by the onlookers; he was feted by his fellow-players, and, what was better, he gained his international cap against Scotland.[328]

Only 15,000 came to see that match – the rest put off by the exorbitant price of entry set for this semi-final.

---

[328] In his column in Sports Argus 20 Feb 1909

The Aston Villa Chronicles 1874 – 1924 (and after)

The referee of that match, John Lewis, later recounted a story – provided by a Villa-supporting Lancastrian – about what probably transformed the outcome of that match:

> It may be news to you that that tie was won in the Aston Villa dressing room. I [the Lancastrian] was there when the teams came off at half-time, the Villa a bit down because the Sunderland halves had been holding Athersmith and Steve Smith with ease. No sooner had they got inside then Dennis Hodgetts shut the door, and, calling the men together, said, 'Now lads, we must change our tactics. You have seen how our wings are being held – well, Chatt, Devey and I will keep the ball to ourselves until we have drawn both halves and backs, and then out the ball will go right or left, and Charlie and Steve must go for all they are worth!' That was agreed upon, and that is how the match was won![329]

Concerning that semi-final, John Devey stated,[330] "It is questionable whether a finer exhibition of football has ever been witnessed than that which this game produced."

So, another Final – the third – against the Albion! However, before that event, there were three League matches to be played out. In the first, at **Bolton**, the Villa went into an early lead, but at half-time they were 1-2 down. Soon after the break, they were 1-4 down, and – as in the Burnley match – the Villa performed a great recovery in which they scored two goals, and so nearly finished level, but this time their effort was not quite enough to equalise. The Villa lost 3-4.

April, 1895

Burnley were an injury-wrecked side when they came to Perry Barr for Villa's next League match, and consequently the Villa won easily, 5-0.

The next match, at home against **Wolves**, was a more important affair, as a win for Villa would take them into second spot, but for Wolves that would mean putting them into the bottom three. Wolves' determination, therefore, was high, and at half-time they were leading 1-2. Villa attacked almost continuously in the second period, but the Wolves defence stood firm against a bombardment. It was not until 12 minutes from time that Spencer's free-kick was deflected in to draw level at 2-2, the final score.

---

[329] In his column in The Sporting Mail 21 Jan 1911
[330] In his column in The Sporting Mail 20 Jan 1906

The Aston Villa Chronicles 1874 – 1924 (and after)

| FA Cup Final | vs West Bromwich Albion
at Crystal Palace, London | 1-0
20 April, 1895 | Attendance.
42,560 |

Wilkes

Spencer Welford

Reynolds Jas.Cowan Russell

Athersmith Chatt J.Devey Hodgetts Smith.

There was great excitement and tension right up to the last minute before the Final started at Crystal Palace. John Devey confided:

> ... there is one respect in which the Palace grounds are most suitable for such occasions. In the dressing rooms each man has a little compartment to himself, and this tends to keep him in a normal state of tranquillity.[331]

John Devey said of the very early winning goal in the Final: "Chatt was under the impression that the ball had gone off the keeper [straight] into the net." To clear up matters about it, Devey stated:

> The [only] goal came in the first minute, and I have never yet seen any accurate description of the way in which it was scored. Most of the players say that it came from the foot of Bob Chatt, but that is not correct. What happened was this (only a player could say with certainty what took place): Chatt was going for goal, and when a few yards away, and quite close to the touch-line, he shot the ball towards Reader at a great pace and struck him [Reader] on the leg. It rebounded from Reader, and as the centre-forward (myself) was rushing up, the ball caught my right knee and shot into the top right-hand side of the net. A big fluke, for I made no effort at the ball.[332]

However, there was another incident early on – a massive head collision between Higgins and Devey.

[From the *Athletic News*] "The Villa captain soon recovered, though he appeared to have some misgivings as to whether his brains had dropped out to assist the cultivation of the new turf!" Higgins was the worse off, and doctors had to see to him. But he continued as best as he could with his

---

[331] In his column in The Sporting Mail 20 Jan 1906
[332] In William McGregor's column in Sports Argus 16 Jan 1909

wound still oozing blood through his bandages, and his football-strip soaked in blood.

The official credit for the early goal was given to Chatt, and such a quick opening score made for a great final. Although neither side managed to add to the scoring, the game was regarded by those who witnessed it as one of the best pre-WW1 finals. Albion were the irresistible force as they attacked in wave after wave in an attempt to equalise. Villa were the immovable object as their defence held firm throughout, as the game was played at break-neck speed.

When Villa did get the ball they set off on lightning counter attacks that constantly left Albion stretched defensively. The two keepers deserve much credit. While Joe Reader of Albion made a string of excellent saves to keep his side in the contest, his opposite number, Tom Wilkes, was equally busy preventing Albion getting an equaliser that on balance they probably deserved on the day. Bassett in particular put in some brilliant work for Albion. However, the Villa held out to win the Cup."

The *Athletic News* reported on the homecoming:

> The Villa party returned to Snow Hill, Birmingham, at noon on the following Monday. "When the train steamed up with a rush, and the members of the victorious brigade were recognised, a cheer loud enough to lift the roof off the station went ringing among the rafters and made the 6 or 7,000 who were thronging Livery Street [aware] that the heroes had come home to be welcomed … Vociferous cheering greeted them at all points of vantage along the route [to Aston].

After the Cup Final, the Villa's last League game of the season was played at Perry Barr, versus second-placed **Everton**. It was a 2-2 draw after Villa had led 2-1 at half-time, but it was Everton's keeper that prevented a thrashing, and Everton were also helped in that Russell was injured and eventually had to leave the field. The Villa thus completed a hard but successful season in third place.

The Aston Villa Chronicles 1874 – 1924 (and after)

How Villa Lost the Cup

Having won it – Villa did not take long in losing it! Aston Villa had to report the loss of the Cup at the FA Committee meeting in November 1895! A villain of another colour stole it from the shop window of William Shillcock, football and boot manufacturer, on a September night. Mr. Shillcock must have regretted signing a letter, residing in the Villa archives, that says: "I hereby agree to return the English Cup in good order and condition …"

The FA meeting in February fined the club £25, which was also the cost of a new trophy "as nearly as possible like the old cup". Howard Vaughton's family business made the replica. In 1910, this replica was awarded to Lord Kinnaird for his services to football, and in 2005 it was purchased for a reported £420,000 by the chairman of the Villa's local rivals, Birmingham City!

In 1958, an octogenarian named Harry Burge told a Sunday newspaper, "We [he and two others] turned the cup into half-crowns and passed some of them in The Salutation pub, which was [then] kept by Dennis Hodgetts, a former Aston Villa player."

There is a delightful story in a letter published by the *Daily Mirror* many years after 1958, from a Staffordshire lady who claimed to have nursed Harry Burge when he was admitted to hospital with a fractured hip, which he had obtained by diving in front of a car to push a child away to safety. It seems that it was after his admission to the hospital that he recounted the story about his part in the cup's disposal.

The story of the how and wherefors of the stealing of the Cup has been gone into great detail over the years, and the Villa's *Claret and Blue* magazine published detailed accounts of stories handed down – with more names quoted of the guilty parties – in two editions of the magazine in 1995 (100 years after the event). The basic story of the melting-down of the Cup as given by Burge was re-iterated in those accounts.

The Football League Division 1 1894-95 Top Places	Pld	Home W D L F A	Away W D L F A	Overall W D L F A	Pts
1 Sunderland	30	13 2 0 51 14	8 3 4 29 23	21 5 4 80 37	47
2 Everton	30	12 2 1 47 18	6 4 5 35 32	18 6 6 82 50	42
3 **Aston Villa**	30	12 2 1 51 12	5 3 7 31 31	17 5 8 82 43	39
4 Preston North End	30	9 3 3 32 14	6 2 7 30 32	15 5 10 62 46	35

The Aston Villa Chronicles 1874 – 1924 (and after)

1894-95 League and FA Cup Results		
Sep 1st H Small Heath	2-1	20000
8th A Liverpool	2-1	4000
15th H Sunderland	1-2	20000
22nd A Derby County	2-0	9000
29th A Stoke	1-4	
Oct 6th A Nottingham Forest	1-2	6000
13th H West Bormwich A	3-1	15000
20th A Small Heath	2-2	15000
22nd A Sheffield United	1-2	
27th H Liverpool	5-0	7000
Nov 3rd A Sheffield Wed	0-1	
10th H Preston North End	4-1	8000
12th H Sheffield United	5-0	500
17th A West Bromwich A	2-3	
24th H Nottingham Forest	4-1	6000
Dec 1st A Blackburn Rovers	3-1	
3rd H Sheffield Wed	3-1	
8th H Blackburn Rovers	3-0	
22nd A Wolves	4-0	3000
26th H Stoke	6-0	12000
Jan 2nd A Sunderland	4-4	12000
5th H Derby County	4-0	7000
12th A Preston North End	1-0	5000
17th A Everton	2-4	18000
26th H Bolton Wanderers	2-1	
Feb 2nd H Derby County (FAC)	2-1	6000
16th H Newcastle Utd (FAC)	7-1	7000
23rd A Burnley	3-3	7000
Mar 2nd H Nottingham F (FAC)	6-2	18000
16th N Sunderland (FAC SF)	2-1	15000
23rd A Bolton Wanderers	3-4	9000
Apr 6th H Burnley	5-0	
15th H Wolves	2-2	
20th N West Brom A (FAC F)	1-0	42560
24th H Everton	2-2	

Villa Business

Committee minutes from December, 1894 indicate that matters were afoot at the Aston Lower Grounds that were of interest to the Villa, stemming from a communication via Charlie Johnstone that Mr. Flower (the Grounds' owner) was anxious to meet the committee. It transpired that Mr. Flower was ready to retire from business and was therefore ready to sell the Grounds. Of course, by that time, the Grounds were no longer viable as pleasure grounds, and that would have been the main cause of his being ready to sell.

This matter seems to have given rise to a look at alternative possible future homes, starting with their present facility at Perry Barr. A Special Meeting was held on the 21 March, 1895, when it was decided to write to the ground trustees to state that the Villa were willing to take on a 14-years lease, with the option of 21 years, if they would also include an adjacent piece of land at £200. The trustees later responded saying they wanted £300 for a 7 or 9 years' lease.

A Special Meeting on the 24 May received a report from the Limited Liability Scheme Sub-committee (which was created at the 1894 AGM).

The Aston Villa Chronicles 1874 – 1924 (and after)

[From the *Athletic News*] "The most concise and lucid speaker of the committee was Mr. C. S. Johnstone" who put the case so well that the meeting clearly understood the situation.

The gist was that with £5,000 that would be raised, the club would either renovate or obtain a new ground – and one of the best in the UK. The Perry Barr ground, however, was unlikely to last for more than two years, and arrangements would be looked to with the proprietors of the Aston Lower Grounds. "The present [situation] is a crisis which may make or mar the club for a very long time to come, though there was enough time at hand to conclude the future."

> At the AGM, Joseph Ansell, the president, stated:
> "*[the Villa] were able to boast that at the present time they were perhaps the foremost football team in the world.*"

About the sadness-tainted move from Perry Barr, Old Fogey remarked:

... Many of the old inhabitants ... hated shifting their quarters (they were 'rooted in' as it were); and they declared with no gentle voice that if they moved 'their tent' their followers would stray into fresh pastures; and they declared that if Perry Barr was deserted the club would never be the same again. There was a black-whiskered and most determined director named Joseph Dunkley ... who moved heaven and earth – [well,] at least Perry Barr, Aston and Birmingham – to prevent the wandering away of the Villa tribe ...

... there were a good many people very sorry for the migration, including the proprietor of Ye Olde Crown and Cushion – Walter Bowen ...[333]

The conclusion at the meeting was that the recommendation would be to wind-up the club as now constituted, and form a new limited liability company. The amazing aspect of it all was that the former president, Mr. Hinks, who had previously been so against the idea (in 1889 and after) was now in favour! The report was passed back to the sub-committee for revision in time for the AGM in June. However, another Special Meeting was called on 10 June where the recommendation was confirmed, that the club would become a limited liability company.

At the AGM (28 June) it was declared that that should be the last AGM before becoming 'limited'.

Various sites were considered for the future location of the club. In addition to Perry Barr and the Aston Lower Grounds, sites considered were at Handsworth, Gravelly

---

[333] Villa News & Record 5 & 6 Apr 1926

The Aston Villa Chronicles 1874 – 1924 (and after)

Hill, Cuckoo Road, Witton Lane, Bristol Road and the New Race Course.

In respect of the possibility of moving to the Aston Lower Grounds, it was stated that Mr. Flower was willing to give a 14 or 21 years lease at £300 p.a., or purchase at £10,000. The AGM felt that the Lower Grounds option sounded the best, but the Perry Barr option was to be pursued for any improvement on terms. By October, committee member Dunkley wanted to hold out for a better offer from the trustees, but by December (1895) there was no change, and Mr. Dunkley was accused of obstructing committee time.

> *From the Villa's Minutes*
> In May, there was a request from South Africa for the Villa to make a 7-week tour, but the Villa committee turned down the request, as insufficient time was given to prepare for the trip.

Season 1895-96: Champions for the Second Time!

League Division 1 position: Champions; *FA Cup:* 1st Round.

There were three significant player acquisitions for the new season. These were **Johnny Campbell** ("a rare dribbler, a good passer and a deadly shot"), from Glasgow Celtic, and who would prove to be the best Villa 'pivot' since Archie Hunter, according to contemporary evaluations. From now on, John Devey's primary position would be at inside-right, where he developed further the famed understanding with Charlie Athersmith, his wing partner.

The other important signings were **John Cowan** (a forward, and James Cowan's brother) from Glasgow Rangers, and **Jimmy Crabtree**. Many years later, in the 1930s, independent observers still hailed Crabtree as the greatest all-round player the game had seen. The way that the Villa acquired him from Burnley is worth telling.

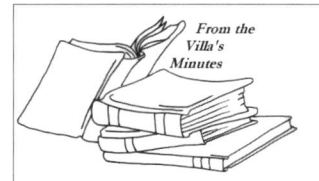

> *From the Villa's Minutes*
> In March (1895), Burnley claimed that they had received offers of five times the sum of £250 that the Villa had offered for Crabtree, and would not give Villa first refusal. A figure of £250 was then considered excessive, let alone one of over £1,000! However, in a neat (coincidental?) twist, by the end of April Crabtree himself wrote to the Villa committee, offering his services to the club. Villa then, in turn,

The Aston Villa Chronicles 1874 – 1924 (and after)

> wrote to Burnley, asking for the transfer fee required.
>
> In May, Burnley asserted – at a League hearing – that the Villa had directly approached Crabtree, which assertion the League dismissed. Being aware that Crabtree would not again sign for them anyway, Burnley now accepted a lower sum of £200, plus the produce of a benefit match with the Villa to be played the next year.
>
> *It turned out that the only declared competitor for Crabtree's signature was Everton, who had offered a mere £175.*

> *From the Villa's Minutes*
>
> In June, the Villa sought the transfer of probably one of England's greatest legends, Worcestershire-born Steve Bloomer, but Derby County would not part with him. *Years later, however, he left for Middlesbrough, but afterwards returned to Derby.*

Having already given the view that their defence was probably the best that the Villa ever had, the *Athletic News*, on 26 August reported:

> The Villa is a most expensive, and supposed to be a very 'classy', team, and it goes without saying that if they fail it will not be because they have not the talent, the money, or the opportunities.

Even the second eleven was expected to be one of the strongest in the country.

The Season's Play

September, 1895

The League opened to midsummer weather. A scorching hot day greeted Villa's first fixture (on a Monday) against the **Albion** at Perry Barr.

Villa: *Wilkes; Spencer, Welford; Reynolds, Jas.Cowan, Crabtree;*
Athersmith, Devey, J.Campbell, Hodgetts, Smith.

[From the *Athletic News*] The only goal came from the boot of John Devey in the first 15 minutes. The match was "a typical Villa and Albion fight" – just as fought many times before. "The Villa always looked like winning on the play, but the Throstles hung on so that the game was never safe until the [final] whistle went."

The Aston Villa Chronicles 1874 – 1924 (and after)

The following Saturday, it was **Small Heath**'s turn at Perry Barr, and it was another hot day. Another member of the Devey family was on the field, as Ted Devey appeared for the Heathens at left-half. Future Villan Fred Wheldon was their centre-forward.

[From the *Athletic News*] With the sun at their backs and the hill in their favour, the Villa sallied forth. Athersmith soon netted, but was ruled offside. "Still, there was no holding the Villans back. Down the hill they came with an irresistible rush, the ball being footed from toe to toe in a masterly manner that boded no good for the wearers of the blue. And this was especially the case when Master Crabtree, with a cleverness that one could not help applauding, deftly tricked two or three Heathens and gave Campbell a fine opportunity in front of goal, which he turned to good account by shooting into the net with a low swift shot that the keeper hadn't a chance of saving. Another followed soon afterwards, and yet another, John Devey being the executant on both occasions … Before the interval, Campbell cleverly back-heeled a fourth, and Smith brought up five."

With sun and slope in Blues' favour, the second half was more equal, and they scored after not too long, and then a second. But this "caused an awakening on Villa's part, with Cowans adding a sixth", only for Blues to score another. The Villa acquired another goal three minutes from the end, to win, 7-3. Johnny Campbell scored four of Villa's goals.

"It is pleasant to be able to say that the game was fought out with the most good temper." The Villa were noted for the power of their half-back line, which now included Crabtree in his new position ("already a prime favourite"), and that Devey and Athersmith played "an irresistible game".

The *Athletic News* stated, "Those onlookers who expected to see the Midland cracks simply step upon the field and win soon found out their mistake" with regard to their away match at **Sheffield United**, which Villa lost 1-2. Villa in fact went ahead after 30 minutes through Hodgetts, after Smith had gone off injured. Smith then returned, though he looked lame for the rest of the match. Villa would have equalised near the end but for a fine save from larger-than-life keeper 'Fatty' Foulkes.

Against **Derby**, Crabtree had his first opportunity to show his skills at full-back with Spencer injured. Burton came in at left-half, and John Cowan came in for his first game in place of the injured Steve Smith. It was another gloriously summer-like day at Perry Barr.

[From the *Athletic News*] "The game opened at a tremendous pace, the Villa … calling forth a round of cheers by some excellent forward play. Cowan

The Aston Villa Chronicles 1874 – 1924 (and after)

hopped in and put Devey and Athersmith on the run, the latter winning and placing a corner kick in great style. Straight across the goalmouth the ball sailed …" but evaded the heads of Devey and Campbell.

Bloomer and Goodall then contrived to set up a chance for Derby, but Wilkes cleared. "Straight from the Villa goal, the players came in a body; a lovely pass by Campbell giving [John] Cowan the ball in a nice position on the left. Running on at a good pace, he got close in and left fly with an [angled] shot which gave the keeper no chance!"

The Villa, having opened the score, now played their best football, "the half-back and forward work being a perfect treat to watch". Reynolds' back-up of the right-wing pair was conspicuous, and those three passed and inter-passed till Devey, "feinting a pass to the outside, ran on into the centre, and instantly sent in a scorcher from a narrow angle, which hit the further post and bounded into the net." 2-0 to the Villa. Despite further good work from Villa, and though Derby's McMillan fluffed four chances, there was no further score in that half.

Derby surprised all by pulling a goal back early in the second half, giving Derby some heart. "Suddenly, the Villa woke up again, Jamie Cowan popping the ball to Campbell, and the latter [passed] across to Athersmith with a beautiful touch. Away flew the Villa sprinter, and from the right corner, the ball sailed across, only for a Derby player to get hold … However, Campbell was again on the scene, and putting in a lovely bit of dodging, he got round … finishing up with a grand shot, beating the keeper all the way." 3-1 to the Villa.

Wilkes, though Villa were winning well, still had some work to do, and from a clearance of his, "Villa romped up to the other end. Athersmith placed another corner most artistically, and the Cowans between them [both] plonked the ball into the net!" Villa won, 4-1, in a highly enjoyable game.

Spencer returned for a hard game at **Blackburn**, that was drawn 1-1, despite Campbell opening the scoring with a grand shot, following a John Cowan shot that rebounded from the crossbar.

The following Monday at Perry Barr, "the weather was too hot for football", but 10,000 witnessed a fine game against **Everton**.

[From the *Birmingham Daily Post*] Campbell scored after only five minutes during a period when Everton were outplayed, but the lead was nullified when Everton's Bell scored from a brilliant individual goal. However, though that equaliser gave Everton some heart, the Villa's defence was unyielding. At the other end, Everton's half-backs and backs could not cope with the home forwards, who scored twice more before the interval, to make the score 3-1.

The Aston Villa Chronicles 1874 – 1924 (and after)

Hodgetts also hit the woodwork.

Bell scored a second for Everton five minutes into the second half, but Campbell then scored for Villa, and then Athersmith hit the woodwork. Amazingly, Bell obtained his hat-trick to make the score 4-3 to the Villa, and in a very exciting finish, Villa's defence had to play their best to keep Everton from scoring again. The *Athletic News* added that at the end of the match, the Everton keeper had to make two scorching saves from Athersmith.

October, 1895

Sunderland were next to come down to Perry Barr, and **20,000** saw the match between the current Cup holders and the League champions. It was a match that generated more interest than any match since the Preston cup tie at Perry Barr in 1888, and the crowd would have been far bigger but for the weather.

[From the *Athletic News*] "Despite the gloomy and threatening outlook, crowds of sightseers could be seen wending their way Wellington Road-wards for at least a couple of hours before the [kick-off]." Rain, in fact, set in just after the kick-off.

For the first 20 minutes, it was the Villa who applied all the pressure, but the Sunderland defence was superb. Then Sunderland got onto the attack, and Wilkes had his work cut out. Then the game swung back the other way, but the interval came up with there being no score.

Only four minutes into the second half, the 'Perry Pets'[334] stormed the opposing goal, and Campbell scored from a scrimmage. "The whole gang of Villans were at this point working with such mechanised precision that the home partisans began to chuckle and anticipate a severe tanning for the League champions!" Their hopes were premature. Within five miniutes, Sunderland's Campbell had a shot that shaved the bar – and then Sunderland equalised.

After a quiet spell, "Johnny Cowan raised the voices of the multitude by scoring a second goal for the Villa from a distance of 30 yards." It was a shot that had plenty of power behind it. The Villa won, 2-1.

The Villa then drew 1-1 at the **Albion** in yet another typical match between the two clubs.

Mid-table **Blackburn Rovers** then visited Perry Barr. Star players Campbell and James Cowan joined Smith on the injury list, so Chatt came in at centre-half, John Cowan moved over to inside-right, and Dorrell came in at outside-left. These moves

---

[334] In referring to the "Perry Pets", Athletic News' reporter commented that when the Lower Grounds migration was to take place, a new term would have to be coined!

The Aston Villa Chronicles 1874 – 1924 (and after)

again demonstrated how many of the players were flexible in the positions they could play in, and with equal affect – particularly Crabtree and Chatt.

[From the *Athletic News*] There was a very fast pace in the first 30 minutes, and "so puzzling and smart was the passing, and so good the backing up of the middle division, that the Rovers were very seldom allowed to get into their stride." Then, "a sharp cross-shot was headed in the air by Crabtree, from whence it curled under the bar, a startling and pleased shout of 'Goal!' being initiated at the top end and taken up in chorus all round the ground." A few minutes later, all that good work was nullified by Welford, who was caught in two minds and succeeded only in deflecting the ball into his own net. The affect of this was to drain confidence from the Villa, and they remained in that state until 20 minutes into the second half.

Whilst the half-backs kept cool, 'pranks' were indulged in by the Villa forwards, and also some curiosities in the way of defence by Welford. This situation caused the crowd to start admonishing their team, and shouted demands to 'play up!' This clearly had some affect, "for in the twinkling of an eye, the Villa ascended in one bound from mediocrity to superiority, and they commenced to go at that Blackburn goal in a style that worked up the people into almost a frantic state of excitement."

It was a while before a score materialised, but some delightful passing was followed by the ball being played across the goal to Hodgetts, who slammed it home. This had the right affect on the Villa, who continued then to bombard the Rovers goal. Dorrell eventually pushed home a rebound to make it 3-1 to the Villa at the finish.

With all players now being fit, the Villa team now reverted to that that had started the season, except that Welford's recent performances had given rise to some anxiety, and Elliott was chosen at left-back for the visit to **Small Heath**. The Heathens were, after eight games, bottom of the table, having lost seven matches and won one. Though the Villa won 4-1, they did not give their supporters much to be pleased about until the latter part of the second half, when they ran rings round their opponents. This match, at the end of October, left the Heathens bottom of the table – and the Villa at the top. The Small Heath supporters were seen demonstrating for the replacement of their club's committee.

The Aston Villa Chronicles 1874 – 1924 (and after)

November, 1895

The Villa completed a trio of successive wins by beating **Burnley** 5-1 at Perry Barr (though a score of 3-1 or 5-3 might have been fairer, it was reported), despite the unavailability of Johnny Campbell.[335] Athersmith, playing inside-right in this match, scored a hat-trick. The *Athletic News* gave a view of Villa's first goal after the interval, when they were leading 1-0 without greatly impressing their supporters. This snippet shows just how keepers could sometimes feel insecure, as they could easily be charged into the net:

> John Cowan whizzed the ball across to Smith, who got his pate violently against it [and towards the keeper's hands]. At the same time, John Devey was making a bee-line for the keeper, who diverted his glance, and the ball bounced over his shoulder and rolled into the net! [Great laughter and cheers followed].

Next up was the return match against **Sunderland** on their ground, and, depite the return of Campbell (but with John Cowan deputising for Smith), the score was an exact reversal of that at Perry Barr, 1-2. Perhaps 1,000 "strong-lunged" Villa supporters were present, and saw Sunderland play very well, the Villa not being able to have any complaints about their defeat.

The win took Sunderland up to fifth place.

> [At Sunderland] ... the sight of ... Athersmith trying to beat level time made the Brummagem partisans shriek themselves hoarse with excitement. Just as the Birmingham idol was preparing to 'put a chalk on', burly Will Gibson stepped into the breach, and presenting to Athersmith his full 14 stones, that young man was brought to a sudden standstill in his wild gallop, and was next seen, to the wonderment of the beholders, trying to emulate the feats of the flying lady, and finally finished by ploughing up a ton of earth with his cranium!
>
> (the *Athletic News* report on the Sunderland match, in which it was added that Athersmith was not discouraged by that experience!)

A Lion's Fun

---

[335] Who was undergoing treatment "at that well-know resort of damaged footballers, Mr. Allison's, Hyde Road, Manchester, for an injured thigh." (Athletic News)

The Aston Villa Chronicles 1874 – 1924 (and after)

In the following home match against **Sheffield United** "the weather was bad, the gate was bad, some of the players' tempers were bad, and the Villa team was bad …" said the *Athletic News*. However, the team had been considerably changed – especially in the forward line – with a bout of fresh injuries to some of its main stars:

Villa: *Harris; Spencer, Welford; Burton, Jas.Cowan, Crabtree;*
John Cowan, Chatt, Devey, Hodgetts, Dorrell.

The Villa were 0-2 down at half-time, and just when defeat seemed inevitable, the Villa scored two goals to equalise. But instead of that giving them the motivation to go on and perhaps win, the Villa only got worse, and with five minutes to go, the Villa passed up a golden chance for a winner. It was a 2-2 draw at the end.

Though most returned for the next match at **Burnley**, Campbell was out injured yet again, and Hodgetts was also on the injury list.

Villa: *Wilkes; Spencer, Welford; Reynolds, Jas.Cowan, Crabtree;*
Athersmith, Chatt, Devey, John Cowan, Smith.

[From the *Athletic News*] Both sides scored within the first six minutes, before Burnley took a 2-1 lead, despite Villa having the best of matters. Then Devey scored on 20 minutes, before Burnley again scored, followed by Reynolds converting a penalty for a reckless hand-ball. It was 3-3, and all the goals had been scored inside the first 30 minutes. Burnley then lost a player through injury.

All watching thought that Villa would run away with the match, but the reverse was true. Burnly gave every bit as good as they got, and it was not until four minutes from the end that Athersmith raced away and scored with only the keeper to beat. 4-3 to the Villa.

Without having played exceptionally well, the Villa continued to be neatly placed at the top of the table by the end of November.

Leading Positions in Division 1 November 23rd, 1895	Pld	Home W D L F A	Away W D L F A	Overall W D L F A	Pts
1 Aston Villa	14	7 1 0 28 12	2 2 2 12 10	9 3 2 40 22	21
2 Everton	15	5 2 1 20 9	3 1 3 14 13	8 3 4 34 22	19
3 Derby County	12	6 0 0 19 6	2 1 3 11 13	8 1 3 30 19	17
4 Bolton Wanderers	13	4 0 1 11 7	4 1 3 11 9	8 1 4 22 16	17

The Aston Villa Chronicles 1874 – 1924 (and after)

> *From the Villa's Minutes*
>
> On 28 November, it was reported that Villa's keeper – Tom Wilkes – had not participated in training, but had instead competed in a professional race at Redditch. He won that race.

On 30 November, the Villa travelled to the Crystal Palace to play the Corinthians in the annual friendly fixture. Without all of the first team, the Villa won 7-3, the score being 2-2 at half-time. On the same day, Small Heath lost 0-8 at Derby, in the League.

December, 1895

With James Cowan (allegedly) unfit, and Hodgetts injured, the Villa again had to re-shape their team for their visit to **Preston**, Chatt again showing his positional versatility.

Villa: *Wilkes; Spencer, Welford; Reynolds, Chatt, Crabtree; John Cowan, Athersmith, Devey, Campbell, Smith.*

[From the *Athletic News*] Despite an early scare to their defence, Preston came back and even took the lead. Back came the Villa, but the Preston defence took a no-nonsense approach against the Villa forwards' science, and kept their lines clear. Despite Villa playing the better football, Preston scored a second, and then a third. At this stage, Devey decided to alter things, and Crabtree and Cowan changed positions. Villa did score before half-time, but it was an own goal. 1-3 to Preston at the interval.

With the wind in the second half, Preston supporters thought that they were safe, "but the Villa soon showed that they had by no means given up the ghost, and I never admired a team more than I did the Villa when they were two goals to the bad … and then they go in and make a gallant effort to pull it off." Despite Villa's efforts, Preston scored again – it was now 1-4!

"[The Villa] went at it in rare style, and Athersmith was in splendid form … continually getting round his opponents – in fact, running straight through them!" Villa then pulled a goal back when Preston's keeper kicked straight to Campbell about thirty yards away. He steadied himself, shot – and scored.

There was still lots of time left, and there was a terrific struggle right to the end. Either side could have scored, in fact, but the Villa succeeded in pulling one more goal back, to make it 3-4 at the finish.

The Villa team was restored to normality (with the exception of Chatt still at centre-half) for the visit of **Bolton**.

The Aston Villa Chronicles 1874 – 1924 (and after)

[From the *Athletic News*] After an evenly contested first half, the second period saw the Villa playing more briskly with the advantage of the slope. Devey and Athersmith in particular sent in a string of shots, and though Bolton came into the match occasionally, the Villa always stormed back and did everything but score. Eventually, the ball "travelled as far as Welford [the left-back] standing well down the field, who put in a long, raking kind of return which fairly mystified the backs and keeper alike, and bounced into the net!" 1-0 to the Villa. That score did much to enourage the Villa and it was not long before Campbell hooked a goal. With Villa finishing the better team, they won 2-0.

> 'Brum' of the *Athletic News* warned that the Villa had better pull their socks up, "[else] the usual crowd of letters from 'disappointed members' will be showered into the local newspapers".

By now, **Everton** had taken over the leadership of Division One, and received the Villa for the next League match in front of a **22,000** crowd. The Villa had a good share of the game, but conceded a goal in each half to lose 0-2. An interesting first half was replaced by one of less interest, but it was not a boring match.

The Powderhall Handicap

The mystery of James Cowan's 'injury' – and absence from the first team – eventually came out.

Cowan was famed for his keenness as a sprinter, and, giving an excuse to the club that he needed to rest an injury, he went to run in an annual professional sprint (the then legendary Powderhall Handicap at Edinburgh). He won the sprint, winning £80, but was found out by the Villa committee!

He was suspended by the Villa for four weeks – until the funny side was appreciated, and the suspension was lifted. Several Villa players are said to have bet on his success in 'the sprint' – and made some money as a result!

As Charlie Johnstone later recounted:

> When the renowned James Cowan was suffering from muscular rheumatism, otherwise 'Powderhall-itis', we immediately [selected] Bob Chatt as his successor, being quite convinced that Jimmy's days were numbered. Chatt was such a pronounced success [in the centre-half slot] that when Jimmy returned, we gave him a rest – just to show our sympathy!

The Aston Villa Chronicles 1874 – 1924 (and after)

The Villa were away again on Boxing Day, and played a hard-fought match at **Wolves** in front of **20,000**. The Villa deserved to win, 2-1, but their second goal was a deflection off the referee's leg! Everyone was surprised by the decision for the goal to be allowed!

Two days later, **Bury** paid their first ever visit to Perry Barr. The rain fell in torrents, but still 8,000 spectators came to see the match. Bury should have taken the lead on 20 minutes, and they played well; it was a long time before the Villa pulled their game together, and then took the lead. Villa's supporters were highly vociferous in urging their team to "get on with it", and their team obliged by adding a second half goal to win, 2-0.

January, 1896

If the Villa were to make a move for the League leadership, and stand a chance of keeping it, then their play needed to become more convincing than of late, and they also needed to take points from other championship contenders. The Villa's first match of 1896 was at **Stoke**, a team that were currently challenging for fourth place. This match would perhaps be a useful indicator as to the Villa's potential. 12,000 attended, despite very poor weather.

Villa: *Wilkes; Spencer, Welford; Burton, Chatt, Crabtree; Athersmith, Devey, Campbell, Hodgetts, John Cowan.*

[From the *Athletic News*] Helped by a free-kick, Stoke "soon swarmed on the Villa stronghold, and had Dickson [the former Villan] taken full advantage of his position, he must have scored. Wilkes, however, fisted away when Brodie put in a splendid swift shot along the turf." A fierce return shot was then turned round the post by Wilkes. From the ensuing corner, Villa broke away and caused problems at the other end, but the Stoke defence was resolute.

It was not long before Wilkes again had to do some work in a game of activity and good football, with Villa – if anything – being outplayed. It was Burton and Spencer who particularly distinguished themselves in keeping the Villa goal safe. "At last, the Villa began to make tracks for Clawley [the Stoke keeper], Athersmith and John Cowan each playing a grand wing game." But again Stoke retaliated.

"The Villa once more raised the siege when John Devey, after passing the centre line, tipped the leather to John Campbell … and displaying great judgment, Campbell wriggled past [their centre-half], and, keeping the ball at his toe, dodged [another back], with the result that he had only Clawley to beat. This he did, with a beautiful shot just under the bar", the goal coming after 30 minutes.

The Aston Villa Chronicles 1874 – 1924 (and after)

Stoke came back, but again the Villans stormed downfield and then Villa were awarded a free-kick. "Crabtree placed well, and in the scrimmage that followed, the ball went in off Devey" – this was after 40 minutes, and Villa went in at half-time being 2-0 up.

Stoke came out in the second half in a very determined fashion, but it was Cowan that came close before Stoke went back and hit a post. "Crabtree was prominent for an extraordinary run on the left wing; he might have been the outside-left! He shot at goal and a corner ensued. Chatt headed in, and another corner followed."

In the last quarter of an hour, Stoke threw everything at Villa, and Wilkes was in action several times, until – at the final stroke of the match – Stoke scored their one goal with a shot from distance.

Villa were seen as being the better team on the day, being strong all-round in a tough fight.

Preston North End were no longer the formidable side they had been a few years earlier, but nevertheless they were expected to be stern opposition, and so it proved, on a beautifully fine day at Perry Barr. Two very good teams played out a goal-less first half, and there was some doubt as to whether the Villa would extract full points from the game. It transpired, however, that John Cowan's deftly headed opener decided the issue, though in the last 30 minutes, Preston came so near to equalising more than once.

The Villa then went to **Sheffield Wednesday**. Again, the Villa's opposition were not easy to break down, but the Villa's staying power – as it had through the season – shone through to bring the Villa's fifth successive win, 3-1.

At Perry Barr, a gloomy outlook for the weather produced less than 7,000 spectators for the visit of **Nottingham Forest**, who were usually popular opponents. Another hard fought match was played, and again a 3-1 result followed, for the Villa's sixth successive win.

February, 1896

The Villa went out at the first hurdle, despite special preparation for the match (mainly at Droitwich and Sutton Park), against the Villa's main competitors in the League, **Derby County**. The match was recalled by Charlie Johnstone:

"Unfortunately, Welford was injured, so [James] Cowan was played left-half and Crabtree at the back. The Derby wing, consisting of John Goodall and Steve Bloomer, were splendidly fed by Archie Goodall at centre-half, and they see-sawed Cowan all down the field. Crabtree, instead of coming up and attending to Bloomer, hugged his goal, and three times in the first half, Steve pounced on a back pass from Goodall, and running for goal, drove the ball in through the top left-hand corner before Crabtree could get at him.

"We were four goals down, and there were ructions at half-time! …" But even though matters were changed (wrote Charlie), the damage was done.[336]

Denny Hodgetts' last match

This match, in which Villa lost 1-4, attracted **27,000**, of which up to 6,000 were from Birmingham. The gates were closed well before the kick-off time. The Notts Forest versus Everton match attracted 18,000, but the next biggest gates in that round were in the order of 12-13,000.

The very next week, the same fixture came up again, but this time as a top-of-the-table clash. The Villa were four points ahead in the table, but **Derby** had two games in hand, so it was vitally important for the Villa to get something from this match. Though 17,000 turned out for this match, the Villa support was notably reduced from the previous week.

The Villa had to ring some changes. Hodgetts had not played at all well of late, and in fact the previous week's cup encounter proved to be Denny's last-ever game for the Villa.

> 'Brum' of the *Athletic News*, on Denny Hodgetts:
>
> The committee have realised the unmistakeable fact that Dennis does not get any younger, and that his activity in the field is getting less pronounced every time he plays … on Saturday week, he couldn't raise a gallop.

Crabtree was ill, but Welford had returned, as did Reynolds.

Villa: *Wilkes; Spencer, Welford; Reynolds, Jas.Cowan, Burton;*
Athersmith, Chatt, Devey, Campbell, John Cowan.

[From the *Athletic News*] Villa had the better of the opening stages, and were determined to show up better than the previous week. "Nothing really seriously happened until James Cowan almost scored with a splendid long shot" – which went wide by a shave. Though Derby were dangerous when given the chance – Wilkes twice having to punch clear in quick succession – Villa continued to have the upper hand. "Athersmith kept swinging some lovely centres from the right" and though the Derby defence coped, there was

---

[336] In his column in The Sporting Mail 4 Jan 1913

The Aston Villa Chronicles 1874 – 1924 (and after)

one scrimmage when they were fortunate not to go a goal down. From this, Derby went upfield; Wilkes partially stopped a shot on the line, "but the force with which it was sent carried it over, and young Bloomer made double sure by dashing up and crashing it into the net."

Villa then visited the other end, but "in a trice Bloomer had left the Villa backs standing still and 'scored' again!" – only for the effort to be disallowed. Then Devey took too long on an opportunity and had the ball taken from him. Again came Derby, and after some fine passing, they scored their second. 0-2 to Derby. On the stroke of half-time, Devey swept in a goal after the keeper had pushed out a Cowan shot, to make it 1-2 at the interval.

Derby made a storming start to the second half, and should have gone further ahead. "At length, the visitors pulled themselves together ... Athersmith (who had a handkerchief tied over one of his eyes through some grit getting into his optic) leading several attacks on the home goal ... Some long passing by the Villans ensued, and Athersmith secured from Campbell and equalised with a superb shot!" It was 2-2. This ignited Derby, but their attacks were repulsed – by giving away corner-kicks! "Most teams know that County are no good whatever at corners!"

"Once, Archie Goodall almost did the trick with a grand overhead kick, and Bloomer nearly took a piece out of the upright with a lightning shot" – but all to no avail. The Villa had got their needed point.

For the rest of the season, until the final two matches, the team selection was:

Villa: *Wilkes; Spencer, Welford; Reynolds, Jas.Cowan, Crabtree; Athersmith, Chatt, Devey, Campbell, John Cowan.*

That is, with the exception that Burton deputised for either Reynolds or Crabtree – one or the other was often absent.

The Villa team was noted as now being a strong one, with Chatt's inclusion notably strengthening it. Smith's absence was prolonged by what turned out to be a displacement of the cartilage behind the knee, but John Cowan had proved to be a fine substitute.

The Aston Villa Chronicles 1874 – 1924 (and after)

The Villa's next opponents – **Stoke**, at Perry Barr – were having quite a good season, but the Villa, having led 2-1 at half-time, ran out 5-2 winners.

March, 1896

Crabtree was playing for England versus Ireland the next week, when the Villa were playing at well-placed **Bolton**. Their supporters were very happy when their side went 0-2 up just after the interval, but one of their backs was then severely hurt and thus was not able to play up to his proper game. This the Villa took advantage of, and Devey scored twice to bring the score to 2-2 at the finish.

One of the most exciting games of the season then took place at Perry Barr against **Sheffield Wednesday**.

[From the *Athletic News*] "[Wednesday's] passing was exceedingly pretty and effective, their defence sound and sure and their whole display very interesting and pleasant to watch. The Villa played with intermittent flashes of brilliance and spasms of dull mediocrity, though it is very fair to them to say that they found the Sheffield keeper a lot more to do than had the professor at the other end."

Wednesday scored first. "A rather long pass should have been easily taken by Spencer, but [though] Reynolds intercepted it, the ball glided off his foot [and] straight to Spikesley, who thereby made a bee-line for goal, with an open meadow and the others in full cry. The speedy Sheffielder made no mistake, but sent in a scorching [angled] shot which struck the further post, and the ball [then] lay comfortably among the meshes. The applause was subdued and decorous …"

This woke up the Villa, and a series of dashing attacks developed. "A long forward pass from Devey came to John Cowan, who careered goalwards in double-quick time. Langley took him amidships just as he was shooting, but the sturdy left wing dropped on his feet, hopped on the ball like a kestrel on a fieldmouse, and whizzed it past [the keeper], while the people hymned him in high hosannas. No more scoring till half-time, but things were very brisk indeed."

Into the second half, and "Villa were now having the best of the deal, especially when it is remembered that Welford had been rendered somewhat unsafe by a violent tumble … and it was easy to see that he was only 'keeping his end up' at the expense of a considerable amount of grief and pain."

"Time was flying fast away … Again and again did the Villa go strongly to the front, only for their efforts to be nonplussed …" A draw seemed likely, and then "a series of corners fell to John Cowan, from the third of which a desperate scrimmage ensued, and Devey netted the ball amid a triumphant yell

The Aston Villa Chronicles 1874 – 1924 (and after)

..."

As the game came to a close, both sides could have added to their score, but the Villa won, 2-1.

On the same day, League challengers Derby lost their first home match – to Sheffield United, who (in the process) won their first away match! The Villa were now five points ahead of Derby, but had played three games more. It seemed it was to be a close finish in the race for the championship.

> ### *The Record Gate at Perry Barr*
> On 21 March, Perry Barr was the scene of the FA Cup semi-final between Derby and Wolves. The Wolves – though low in the League – won, 2-1. Organised by William McGregor, who provided special facilities for a large gate, the crowd was 40,000 – easily the biggest ever crowd at the Perry Barr ground, which would be closed to football twelve months later.

The Villa found themselves with more than they bargained for in their next match, at **Bury**. The Villa's ten-games' unbeaten League run came crashing to an end.

[From the *Athletic News*] Within 11 minutes, Bury were two-up with magnificent shots from one player – Wyllie. The same player scored another – a curling shot – for his hat-trick on 22 minutes, despite Villa attempts at scoring that brought the best out of Bury's keeper, although Devey did pull one goal back to make it 1-3 at half-time.

After the interval, the Villa played a fine passing game, but their shooting was 'off'. This waste was punished by Bury scoring a fourth: it was now 1-4. The score remained unchanged until seven minutes from the end, when Athersmith found Devey, who swept home to make it 2-4, after which Bury scored a fifth, before Spencer's free-kick found John Cowan's head for Villa's third, but a defeat of 3-5.

This defeat made Villa's position vulnerable, but they were lucky – Derby had clearly been dreaming of a great 'double' season (League and Cup), but their dismissal in the Cup semi-final had caused them loss of concentration. They were now losing their League games.

The Villa made a couple of remarkable team changes for their final two games of the season. In an astonishing test of his flexibility, Crabtree was moved to inside-right. It was noted that Smith had returned from successful treatment in Manchester, but would not play again this season.

The Aston Villa Chronicles 1874 – 1924 (and after)

Villa: *Wilkes; Spencer, Welford; Reynolds, Jas.Cowan, Burton; Athersmith, Crabtree, Devey, Campbell, John Cowan.*

With this formation, the Villa obtained a grand 2-0 win over **Notts Forest** – a win that would have been greater but for the Forest's stubborn defence.

By the last game of the season (on Easter Tuesday), the Villa were already League Champions, and as they filed onto the field at Perry Barr for their match against the **Wolves** (the losing Cup Finalists), Villa's supporters cheered again and again.

[From the *Birmingham Daily Post*] Although the Villa had achieved their season's target, they put as much into this match as though the championship depended on it. Two-thirds of the play in the first half was around the Wolves' goal, but stubborn defence kept the Villa out – except on one occasion. On 30 minutes, John Cowan received a beautiful pass from Campbell, raced round the backs, and scored with an angled shot that flashed into the net, just inside the far post. It was one of the goals of the season.

The Wolves' keeper, Tennant, played so well that the crowd generously cheered him, but despite his efforts – and some improvement from his team in the second half – the Villa were dominant all through. The final score was 4-1 to the Villa, including a beautifully shot goal from Crabtree.

The Villa's joy was not shared by their local neighbours, as, though the Wolves reached the Cup Final, they only just escaped relegation, whilst Small Heath were definitely relegated. The Albion survived through success in the deciding 'test matches' (or play-offs) that were played at that time.

The Aston Villa Chronicles 1874 – 1924 (and after)

The Football League Division 1 1895-96 Top Places	Pld	Home W D L F A	Away W D L F A	Overall W D L F A	Pts
1 Aston Villa	30	14 1 0 47 17	6 4 5 31 28	20 5 5 78 45	45
2 Derby County	30	12 2 1 42 13	5 5 5 26 22	17 7 6 68 35	41
3 Everton	30	10 4 1 40 17	6 3 6 26 26	16 7 7 66 43	39

1895-96 League & FA Cup Results

Sep	2nd H West Bromwich A	1-0	15000		14th H Bolton Wanderers	2-0	7000
	7th H Small Heath	7-3	15000		21st A Everton	0-2	22000
	14th A Sheffield United	1-2	10000		26th A Wolves	2-1	20000
	21st H Derby County	4-1	12000		28th H Bury	2-0	8000
	28th A Blackburn Rovers	1-1		Jan	4th A Stoke	2-1	12000
	30th H Everton	4-3	12000		11th H Preston N. E.	1-0	10000
Oct	5th H Sunderland	2-1	20000		18th A Sheffield Wed	3-1	15000
	12th A West Bromwich A	1-1	12000		25th H Nottingham For	3-1	7000
	19th H Blackburn Rovers	3-1	16000	Feb	1st A Derby Cty (FAC)	2-4	27000
	26th A Small Heath	4-1			8th A Derby County	2-2	17000
Nov	2nd H Burnley	5-1	7000		22nd H Stoke	5-2	11000
	9th A Sunderland	1-2	16000	Mar	7th A Bolton Wanderers	2-2	15000
	16th H Sheffield United	2-2			14th H Sheffield Wed	2-1	
	23rd A Burnley	4-3	7000		21st A Bury	3-5	12000
Dec	7th A Preston N. E.	3-4	6500	Apr	3rd A Nottingham For	2-0	
					6th H Wolves	4-1	16000

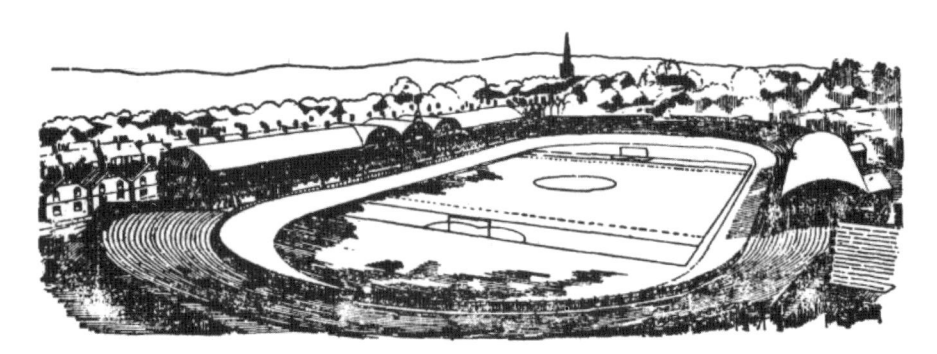

Planning the move to Aston Lower Grounds (Villa Park)

From July until October, 1895, the press and the Birmingham public were given the impression that in just a year's time, the Villa would be playing at a new ground where 40,000 spectators would be accommodated. What 'Brum' stated in his *Athletic News*' column on 7 October, was even more optimistic:

The Aston Villa Chronicles 1874 – 1924 (and after)

> By the time another football season is commenced, it is highly probable that the Perry Barr ground will know the Villa no more. It has been practically settled that an exodus shall be made in the early spring [1896] to the Aston Lower Grounds, where great alterations and improvements are projected and where, for many years, the Villa will have a local habitation, and a name.

Only a week later, however, 'Brum' reported: "There has been some schism at work over the matter." The "schism" was that Joseph Dunkley and his supporters were successful in holding out for better terms with the Perry Barr landlords, but when December came, there was no change, and Mr. Dunkley was accused of obstructing committee time. From that moment, all energy was put to the purpose of the move to the Aston Lower Grounds.

By mid-January, 1896, Aston Villa Limited had been legally established, and a prospectus had been issued; that the purpose of the construction was to fund the new ground on the basis of a 21 years' secured lease. £10,000 share capital in 2,000 £5 shares was required, with call up of half the capital at present, leaving the rest in reserve. Rent was to be £300 per annum, though this was later lowered once the club found that rates and other overheads that were built into the rent had been assessed too high by the freeholder. The Villa then took responsibility for paying those costs.

> [William McGregor's] limited liability company – Lord! How we all jeered at the proposition, and how absolutely necessary it became.
>
> 'Old Fogey', *The Villa News*, Christmas, 1907.

The ground was to hold 40,000 in the unsecured portion; the grandstand to hold 5,500, with standing room for 4,500. The old Aston Lower Grounds buildings were to be converted to offices and recreation areas. With all those improved facilities, the expense of running the new ground was expected to be 40% less than that at Perry Barr.

By early February, the first meeting of the special Joint Committee had been held, consisting of Messrs. Margoschis, Rinder, Johnstone, McGregor, Lees, Whitehouse, Cooper and Lloyd, with George Ramsay in attendance. By that time, 1,698 of the 2,000 shares had already been applied for; the signing of the deeds with Mr. Flower was not far away, and the architect, Mr. E. B. Holmes, had been appointed.

One further aspect of the development was that some revenue would be raised from the provision of a cycling track in the new ground; this was to replace the facility that was previously at the Grounds. The *Athletic News*, on 16 March reported:

The Aston Villa Chronicles 1874 – 1924 (and after)

> A little party consisting of F. W. Rinder, E. B. Holmes and C. Wheelwright were up in London last week inspecting the Catford and Wood Green cycle tracks, for the purpose of getting all the information they could that would be of service to the laying down of the concrete track at Aston.

The periodical heard that the visit had indeed been useful. By 20 April, the delay to the development, and the reality of the closure of Aston Lower Grounds to development over the summer, and therefore its unavailability for sports, had just been realised. The cycling fraternity, in particular, were not pleased!

At the 29 June AGM, the four founding directors of the limited company (Messrs. Margoschis (Chairman), Rinder, Johnstone and Lees) were re-elected and Dr. Jones was taken from the vice-presidents' list and made the fifth director, to meet legal requirements.

Mr. Holmes spent some time examining other grounds that had recently been completed, particularly the one at Sheffield United. It was not until October, therefore, that detailed construction estimates were provided by Mr. Holmes, and when the builders were appointed. Near the end of November, there was alarm at the lack of progress, and then, just after Christmas, the clerk of works had resigned for a better post in London. Not even the offer of a significant pay increase would cause him to change his mind.

These delays severly hampered the completion of the ground, but a quick move was necessary in view of the upcoming ending of the lease at Perry Barr.

Season 1896-97: Winners of Both Trophies – The Double!
League Division 1 position: *Champions;* **_FA Cup:_** *Winners.*

John Devey said, in February, 1897:

"… There is not a man in the team who has the slightest animosity or jealousy against another … You can't have success if the very best feeling does not exist between the men …".

From a playing squad point of view, there were a couple of difficulties to surmount amongst the existing players before matters were settled. The first of these "difficulties" was that in April, Campbell had intimated an agreement to return to Celtic, but then elected to stay with Villa. Then there was a difficulty of agreeing terms with Crabtree, and, finally, a story of Athersmith going to Everton, which was followed by his letter of rejection of the idea.

The Aston Villa Chronicles 1874 – 1924 (and after)

As matters transpired, there was just one significant but sad departure from the Villa. Denny Hodgetts, after ten years' wonderful service in which he had won every honour, left to join Small Heath in their effort to return from the Second Division. He was soon to be joined there by ex-Villan Charlie Hare.

There were three significant incoming members to the team. By May, the signing of goalkeeper **Jimmy Whitehouse** had been completed. He was a Brummie that somehow came to the Villa via Grimsby Town! The Villa already had a good keeper in Wilkes, but Whitehouse had that bit extra. But he was not the only keeper who would soon be lauded – there was a certain **Billy George** that also came onto the books, but he would wait awhile before making his impact.

What followed was the transfer from neighbours Small Heath of a player the Villa had long coveted, the forward **Fred Wheldon**, a signing made easier by the relegation of the Small Heath club. In fact, there was some friction with Small Heath over the matter, but a benefit match for Wheldon between the two clubs was agreed as part of the deal. The match took place at Perry Barr on 1 September, with Villa winning 3-1. Close to his peak when he signed, Wheldon was to have four triumphant years with the Villa.

> There can be no question that great things are expected of Aston Villa during the forthcoming season, and that among their most sanguine supporters they are not only thought capable of retaining their position at the head of the League, but will carry off the English Cup as well ...
>
> 'Brum' in the *Athletic News*, 31 August, 1896

The Season's Play

September, 1896

To open the season, a little over 6,000 turned up at Perry Barr for a 5:30 Wednesday evening kick-off against **Stoke**. A disappointing crowd for the start of the season as reigning League Champions, but it was a mid-week match.

Villa: *Wilkes; Spencer, Welford; Reynolds, Jas.Cowan, Crabtree;*
Athersmith, Wheldon, Devey, Campbell, John Cowan.

[From the *Birmingham Daily Post*] The Villa went in to a 2-0 lead, but what looked like a straightforward win changed its picture towards the end of the first half and in the second half. Stoke came back very strongly and caused the Villa some worry by the end of the match, although the Villa still crept

The Aston Villa Chronicles 1874 – 1924 (and after)

through, 2-1.

The **Albion** – Villa's next opponents – were determined not to be wooden-spoonists again this season! For the Villa, Whitehouse turned out in place of Wilkes in goal in an otherwise unchanged side.

[From the *Athletic News*] Devey left Albion the task of playing downhill, but with wind and rain in their faces, in the first half. The game started with both sides tentatively testing one another out, and after a little while the Villa half-backs exerted their presence – "the Villa trio about this time were about perfect and the Albion forwards were very ragged." However, Whitehouse had to make a save before a move involving Athersmith amd Wheldon then saw the ball going to Devey, "who banged the ball past Reader in splendid style." Albion came back, but the Villa got better without being able to improve on their lead. Villa led 1-0 at half-time.

"[Villa] re-started with a self-satisfied air, and appeared to be content with the lead of one goal." But Albion refused to lie down and were equal to what Villa came up with, with Bassett supplying a centre that was turned in for the equaliser. Villa should have known Albion would fight, and it was not long before Welford was adjudged to have fouled in the penalty area. Albion duly converted the spot-kick. It was 1-2 to the Albion.

Villa then made it hot for the Albion, and Reader had difficult shots to deal with, but again Albion came back and scored with "a clinker". Despite better combination on Villa's part, it is goals that win matches (said the report), and Villa did not score enough!

> It had not been an impressive start, bearing in mind that the Villa had been backed to win everything before them this season. The *Athletic News* reported that already the pessimists were writing in to the newspapers "with fearful and wonderful suggestions to ensure the League champions win every match they play" – but with little agreement between the authors of those letters on how to go about it!

Just to irritate their supporters a little more, Whitehouse and Welford "misbehaved at Grimsby" and missed the next match against **Sheffield United** at home. Added to the absenteeism of those two players, Devey, Campbell and Wheldon "were unaccountably slow on the ball", but, nevertheless, the Villa should have won with ease. Foulkes, however, was in fine form in the United goal in the 2-2 draw.

Whitehouse took his place in goal at **Everton** for what came to be a lengthy stay.

[From the *Athletic News*] "From the very first, two things were evident – that the Birmingham professors did not mean to adhere to their approved

The Aston Villa Chronicles 1874 – 1924 (and after)

scientific method of working the ball up, and that the Everton backs were distinctly lacking in class."

"Eight minutes from the start, Jack Devey got possession, dodged one of the half-backs, stood with the ball waiting for an opening, and then ley fly from long range – a splendid shot."

In fact, Everton had had the best of the opening exchanges, and continued to hold ther own. "Whitehouse saved in a marvellous manner more than once", on one occasion flinging himself full-length to keep out a shot.

In this game, the Villa wingers operated in a very direct style, and it was not long before Campbell scored a second, the quality of the shot being similar to Devey's. 2-0 to the Villa. Just then, down came heavy rain after a sunny start to the game, but Villa coolly kept control, though that control was nearly upset once by Crabtree "through over-indulgence in that smart trick of his – waiting for an opponent and cleverly tipping the ball past him", that this time failed and nearly let Everton score. Close to half-time, Everton threw everything at the Villa, but could not score.

Everton came out in the second half meaning business. "It was a most even game, and fast, too. For one moment, you would see the ball careering around among the Villa backs, and the next moment, it would be taken by the fleet Birmingham forwards to the immediate vicinity of [the opponent's keeper]." But Everton scored first through a free-kick – to a huge roar – only to be followed by the Villa immediately getting away with Campbell's angled shot going in off a defender. 3-1 to the Villa.

Villa continued to play in a cool style, and were always dangerous. "Right to the finish, it was exciting … but we could hardly admire the deliberately slow manner in which Crabtree carried the ball about 20 yards for a free kick …" Clearly, the professional tactic of 'playing for time' was taking root.

Everton scored a second, and then a shot – "one of the best of the day" – threatened to bring the equaliser, but glanced wide.

George Ramsay (speaking in the week preceding the FA Cup Final, in April) saw something in this match that gave him heart:

> … I made up my mind early in the season that we had a great chance of winning the League and the English Cup this year, and I have never had any reason for changing my mind. I based that opinion pretty much on what I saw … when we went to … play Everton. I regarded that match as one of the greatest tests we should have … At the close of the game, I said, 'This form is good enough to win us many of our matches.' My prediction has come true.

The Aston Villa Chronicles 1874 – 1924 (and after)

The crowd were clearly in expectation for the return match after the Villa's promising win at **Everton** the previous week. Spencer was absent, there having been a death in his family, so, as one or other of the full-backs had been out for several weeks, Crabtree dropped back to left-back as he had been doing of late, with Welford at right-back, and Burton deputising at left-half.

[From the *Athletic News*] Though the game had plenty of life about it, it finished with more disappointment for the Villa faithful. The Villa had taken the lead in the first half through Devey's shot hitting the underside of the crossbar before entering the net, but a weak clearance from the Villa defence let in Everton and, under pressure, Welford could do nothing but help the ball into the net.

In the second-half, Villa had the best of it for a long time. In fact there were times when the Everton goal was under great pressure. However, late on, it was Everton that scored again, leaving the Villa with very few minutes to take anything from the game. The Villa tried with great earnestness, but failed to get the equaliser.

> The next match was a benefit at Perry Barr for John Devey, played against Derby County. After a sunny morning, the afternoon saw just rain and more rain. Allied to the team's recent form, instead of the anticipated 6-7,000, just 1,500 turned up.

The end of September had been reached, and the League table did not indicate that the Villa might be world-beaters by any stretch of the imagination!

Leading Positions in Division 1 September 26th, 1896	Pld	Home W D L F A	Away W D L F A	Overall W D L F A	Pts
1 Bolton Wanderers	5	1 1 0 1 0	2 1 0 6 3	3 2 0 7 3	8
2 Liverpool	6	1 1 1 2 2	2 0 1 4 3	3 1 2 6 5	7
3 Blackburn Rovers	5	2 0 1 6 2	0 2 0 1 1	2 2 1 7 3	6
4 Sheffield United	4	2 0 0 4 0	0 2 0 4 4	2 2 0 8 4	6
5 Preston North End	4	2 0 0 10 6	0 2 0 1 1	2 2 0 11 7	6
6 Everton	4	1 0 1 4 4	2 0 0 3 1	3 0 1 7 5	6
7 West Bromwich Albion	5	1 1 0 4 2	1 1 1 3 4	2 2 1 7 6	6
8 Nottingham Forest	4	1 1 0 6 2	0 2 0 3 3	1 3 0 9 5	5
9 Derby County	5	2 1 0 12 6	0 0 2 0 3	2 1 2 12 9	5
10 Aston Villa	5	1 1 1 5 5	1 0 1 4 5	2 1 2 9 10	5

The Aston Villa Chronicles 1874 – 1924 (and after)

October, 1896

> ... another flood of letters into the daily newspapers ...They appear to lose sight of the fact that other clubs beside Aston Villa have been hunting for recruits during the close season and that the Perry Barr management, with all their influence and monetary temptations, cannot command the entire talents of the football world ...
>
> *Athletic News*, 5 October, 1896

The goal-less draw at **Sheffield United** did nothing to brighten the supporters' gloom, though when the season came to its end, Sheffield United's record was seen to be very good. The **Albion** now came to Perry Barr to play their return match.

For the first time for several weeks, both the Villa first-choice backs (Spencer and Welford) were available, and the team now consisted of the same players as in that first match against the Albion, in early September. *But there was one significant difference.* The three inside forwards were the same, but in this (Albion) match they were tried in the formation of *Devey, Campbell* and *Wheldon*. From this point, this combination – and the bonus of the extra understanding that Athersmith and Devey had acquired over the years – paid dividends.

[From the *Athletic News*] Albion started strongly, and got the ball into the net after only a few minutes, only for it to be disallowed. From then, "Villa instituted a series of dashing attacks upon the Albion goal ... Wheldon got in one remarkably fine shot, which the keeper had the greatest difficulty in saving." The Albion then set off, and Welford effected a remarkable recovery after he got back to stop the attack. Then Wheldon (again) and John Cowan forced saves from the Albion keeper. Albion also had a number of attacks on the Villa goal, but, following a free-kick, Villa got in front. Crabtree initiated the movement, and passed forward to Wheldon, and he, "with a beautiful screw shot, sent [the ball] just inside the corner of the goal." There was great cheering.

Albion's attempts to get back were repulsed, and then "Athersmith and Devey had a nice run together, and the latter shot hard for goal, the ball glancing off Campbell's head and going into the net." Albion were not deflated, and Welford twice finely prevented Albion getting through. It was 2-0 to Villa at half-time.

Though Albion continued their attempts into the second period, the wind swung in Villa's favour. Athersmith wasted a chance when he shot wide when

The Aston Villa Chronicles 1874 – 1924 (and after)

a queue of Villa forwards were waiting for a pass into the centre. Then John Cowan ran half the length of the field with the ball before making a complete mess with his shot. The chances continued to come and go, the score remaining the same at the end.

Crabtree was noted as being outstanding against Bassett, and yet he had time to help out in other areas and generally showed his class. Devey and Wheldon were smart in attack, with John Cowan almost as fast with the ball as Athersmith.

Next opponents **Derby County** were injury-hit, and as the game wore on at the Baseball Ground, Villa's pressure increased and the Villa went on to win comfortably, "dribbling and passing in irresistible style."

> In the Derby match, there was an occasion when Crabtree fell and held Bloomer's leg as he was about to shoot. "Strange, however, the referee did not notice it, and surprising, too, to see Crabtree stoop to such a thing and smile at his cleverness."
>
> *Athletic News*

In the home return match against **Derby**, all the scoring was in the second half, with the Villa scoring twice before Derby replied.

> Though the Villa forwards generally played well, Campbell was not, and was described as "a plodder", and his shooting thought no longer reliable. Devey's form was "off", and written of as being "no longer a chicken."
>
> *Athletic News*

The Villa found that their opponents were also injury-hit, so the absence of Crabtree and John Cowan in the Villa ranks at **Stoke** proved not very much of a handicap, particularly as Steve 'Tich' Smith came back into the outside-left slot. Smith scored the second and played well enough to hold his place for some time.

> [Whitehouse] is earning his purchase money. *Athletic News*

Though no-one in the Villa camp were getting ecstatic about their performances, the Villa had been quietly picking up the points during October, and had risen substantially in the League table. Bolton were still going well at the top.

The Aston Villa Chronicles 1874 – 1924 (and after)

Leading Positions in Division 1 October 31st, 1896	Pld	Home W D L F A	Away W D L F A	Overall W D L F A	Pts
1 Bolton Wanderers	10	4 1 0 10 1	2 2 1 8 6	6 3 1 18 7	15
2 Liverpool	12	3 1 1 9 2	3 1 3 10 10	6 2 4 19 12	14
3 Aston Villa	10	3 1 1 9 6	3 1 1 9 6	6 2 2 18 12	14
4 Preston North End	9	4 0 0 14 7	1 3 1 8 6	5 3 1 22 13	13
5 Sheffield United	10	2 3 0 7 3	2 2 1 9 7	4 5 1 16 10	13

November, 1896

At Perry Barr, Villa's thoroughly soaked fans saw their team eke out a 1-1 draw against **Bury** on a slippery pitch. "The wind swept down the rain in drenching gusts." In this match, Albert Evans made his début as substitute for Howard Spencer.

Against the Cup-holders (at **Sheffield Wednesday**), Bob Chatt deputised for John Reynolds at the last minute. Chatt continued to hold a place for a number of games.

Villa: *Whitehouse; Spencer, Welford; Chatt, Jas.Cowan, Crabtree;*
Athersmith, Devey, Campbell, Wheldon, Smith.

[From the *Athletic News*] "A match of rare dash and exciting play was seen" in this fixture. The Villa started in very testing style, and soon went ahead when a midfield free-kick was sent in by Spencer. It dropped in front of goal, and "bobbed about until it came to Wheldon, who just got his head to it."

After some time, the Wednesday got into their stride – after Villa might have increased their lead – and caused a lot of trouble in Villa's goal. But that pressure came to nothing, with the Villa doing better as the interval arrived.

The second half started in similar vein to the first, but then the Wednesday's pressure caused the Villa's backs and half-backs to be over-worked. After 15 minutes of such pressure, Wednesday equalised.

"The Villa now seemed a beaten team, but instead of going to pieces, during the next few minutes they showed up better than ever." They at last played to their reputation, and Campbell scored with a lovely shot. And then the ball was swung across for Athersmith to score a third. And thus the match finished.

The return match against the Wednesday at Perry Barr was a fine exhibition of football.

[From the *Athletic News*] "Immediately the ball was put into motion, it was at once apparent that a fast game would ensue, the forwards on both sides

The Aston Villa Chronicles 1874 – 1924 (and after)

puttiing considerable dash into their movements, and the defence at each end was called upon most frequently to display the utmost vigilance. It was during this period that the visitors' captain showed some of the finest defensive play ever seen at Wellington Road.

"On one occasion, Athersmith, having a clear opening, ran away in his usual style, and the home forwards following up well, he centred right to the mouth of the goal, only to see Wheldon knee the ball over the crossbar. Wheldon, however, was in measure atoned for this a little later by putting in a rasping shot, which was rather luckily cleared. Wednesday also had their misfortune as [they] sent in a magnificent shot which deserved to score, but Whitehouse averted the catastrophe, and a little later, they grazed the side of the post. And so the battle waged with the interval arriving …"

The second half gave the spectators one of the finest displays of modern football ever seen. The ball travelled with lightning-like rapidity, and the home forwards were simply irresistible in their movements. However, the visitors were not idle, and many were the onslaughts brought to bear on the home defence. Whitehouse on one occasion just got the ball away when a score seemed inevitable, whilst another rush of the visiting forwards nearly proved disastrous.

"The scoring, however, was opened at the other end, the Villa forwards taking the ball [downfield] in their well-known and effective style. Smith opened the account by putting through the corner off the [goal] line. The second goal was the outcome of a good run by Devey, who got possession on the half-way line and ran well away, but, being hampered when closing in, shot the ball well forward. Massey [the keeper] came out to clear, but Athersmith, with a lightning sprint, reached the ball first and put it through the undefended goal.

"Nothing daunted, the Wednesday-ites took up the attack, and [they] put in a magnificent shot, which, unluckily for the visitors, hit the crossbar with considerable force."

The scoring continued for the Villa, though. Smith, "who was simply irrepressible", was sandwiched between two players, but still got in his centre for Devey to add the third. This was followed by a score by Wheldon, "after Athersmith had out-distanced his opponent in a race from midfield."

"So ended one of the finest games it has been my good privilege to see." Athersmith's display "was simply magnificent."

At **Blackburn**, Welford was left out, and Albert Evans made his second appearance in a position that he was shortly to make his own.

[From the *Athletic News*] Blackburn had just as many chances as the Villa in the first half, but it was Devey's goal from long range that gave the lead to the

The Aston Villa Chronicles 1874 – 1924 (and after)

Villa at half-time.

Blackburn worked hard to little effect after the interval, and it was Villa that scored a second after an ineffective save by the Rovers' keeper.

"It was from now that we saw the Birmingham gentlemen at their best, for, materially assisted by a weak defence, they simply ran through the Rovers and gave an exhibition of combined play which was delightful to witness."

Subsequent to Villa's third goal, Rovers came back and scored from a free-kick, before the Villa notched a fourth, and then a fifth towards the end of the match, when Villa were playing better than ever.

Wheldon scored a hat-trick, and for the first time this season, the Villa were top of the League.

> There is not a weak spot in the whole team, and Evans ... is endeavouring to imitate Howard Spencer with a fair amount of success.   *Athletic News*

December, 1896

Not very much happened over the next couple of weeks; there was a visit to the Queens Club to play the Corinthians (a 1-1 draw, with the Corinthians equalising in the last minute), and then the League fixture at Burnly (on 12 December) was abandoned because of heavy rain after not much more than 30 minutes, when the Villa were leading 2-1.

> *From the Villa's Minutes*
>
> Having been dropped for the past two matches, for inappropriate behaviour, it was heard on the 26 November that Reynolds had said that he was not happy about playing second team football, and intimated that Blackburn Rovers wanted his signature.
>
> The committee resolved, "We should not part with Reynolds."
>
> *Reynolds was not picked for the match at Blackburn, but was re-instated for the home match with Notts Forest on 19 December.*

On an intensely cold day for the home match against **Nottingham Forest**, Campbell was, in fact, out with – a cold! For this reason, it was one of those occasions when Crabtree was called into the forward line; the previous week he was at half-back, and the next week he would be playing full-back!

Welford had been injured in a junior cup match at Worcester, and Evans continued at left-back. Chatt was at left-half, with Reynolds returning in his customary right-

The Aston Villa Chronicles 1874 – 1924 (and after)

half spot.

[From the *Athletic News*] With a scorching low shot, Reynolds opened the scoring in the first few minutes – perhaps reminding the committee of what he was capable of! But the Forest then equalised. On 15 minutes, Evans sent a well-placed free-kick onto Devey's head, and the ball was truly despatched. "There was no mistaking the really finished play of the Villa team at this period of the match, Chatt at half-back doing many brilliant things."

The Villa had many chances, but the Forest threatened also, and Chatt, "standing under the bar, headed out a shot that certainly deserved to score, a feat for which he was heartily applauded."

It was not long into the second half that Villa sent the ball in time and time again, until "Athersmith dodged for an opening very skilfully, and put one past the keeper very prettily indeed." At 3-1, the Villa looked to have the game, but Forest were not to be denied, and eventually got a second goal. From this point, the game degenerated, although another Forest shot "fairly brought down the house".

> *"For three parts of the match it was as pleasant and exciting as one could wish, full of brilliant bits of play. More skilful overhead kicking it should be difficult to imagine."*

The author's grandfather perhaps chose a good day – Christmas Day – for his wedding. While the Villa were playing away at **Liverpool**, he was kindly allowed the day off by his employer (his own father!) to be married at Trinity Church, Trinity Road. The groom and his bride enjoyed beautiful weather, as did the Villa, who were involved in a grand contest.

[From the *Birmingham Daily Post*] This was a tremendously fast game, but the Villa went behind very early on. Not perturbed, "the Villa men contrived to work with a will", and their promising attacks were stopped only by a determined defence. Liverpool then went so far as to score a second, before Cowan scored from long range, and then Wheldon grabbed an easy goal. With the scores equal, this motivated Villa to create things, and they bombarded the Liverpool goal. Even though Athersmith was constantly dangerous, parity continued to half-time.

A heavy pitch slowed down the play in the second half, and the Villa could not seem to get going properly. In due course, a penalty was given to Liverpool when a Villa defender appeared to punch out the ball from under the crossbar, and this was converted. Athersmith, however, restored parity. The rest of the match saw the Villa battling for the winner, but falling short.

The Aston Villa Chronicles 1874 – 1924 (and after)

Wolverhampton Wanderers (a)

[From the *Athletic News*] Within three minutes, Wheldon had given the Wolves' keeper a taste of three beauties as a result of Athersmith's centres, but not long after, Chatt got the lead for the Villa. This was followed by two opportunities for the Wolves that they should have taken.

"The Villa showed their appreciation of their escapes by putting on the screw with a vengeance. Crabtree, Chatt, Cowan and Reynolds got in some beautiful work and Athersmith's centres were remarkably accurate. Out of an exciting scrimmage, the last-named shot a second."

The game was won and lost in those first 30 minutes, and Villa twice then hit the woodwork, only for the Wolves to snatch one goal back before the interval in a period when Wolves were very dangerous and caused Crabtree and Cowan to make wonderful clearances.

The second half – without seeing more scoring – saw a magnificent battle, with Villa in danger of conceding more goals (Wolves, in fact, were denied a clear penalty), and Villa creating chances at the other end, and once again hit the woodwork. The Wolves deserved a draw.

> *"Not for a very long time has such a brilliant exposition of scientific football been seen on this enclosure."*

At the end of the year of 1896, the reigning League Champions now looked well in control of the League leadership and on course for yet another title. But it had not looked like that until the end of November. It was due to a run of 12 matches undefeated from early October that now put the Villa in this position, a run that was almost certainly mainly due to sorting out the positions of the forward inside trio, Devey, Campbell and Wheldon. But the tactics of those three was also changed – Devey and Wheldon were now doing more 'donkey work', including more tackling, leaving Campbell free to adopt a more direct route to goal. These tactics brought out the best in Campbell.

Leading Positions in Division 1 December 26th, 1896	Pld	Home W D L F A	Away W D L F A	Overall W D L F A	Pts
1 Aston Villa	17	5 2 1 17 9	6 2 1 22 12	11 4 2 39 21	26
2 Bolton Wanderers	16	5 2 0 14 3	4 2 3 14 12	9 4 3 28 15	22
3 Derby County	18	8 1 2 40 18	1 2 4 7 12	9 3 6 47 30	21
4 Liverpool	20	5 3 1 18 6	3 2 6 14 20	8 5 7 32 26	21
5 Preston North End	16	6 2 1 25 15	1 4 2 10 9	7 6 3 35 24	20
6 West Bromwich Albion	19	5 2 4 9 8	2 3 3 9 18	7 5 7 18 26	19

The Aston Villa Chronicles 1874 – 1924 (and after)

January, 1897

The scenario was this; the Villa were riding high in the League table having enjoyed a dozen matches without defeat, and had latterly shown their 'real form', whilst their next visitors, **Burnley**, were languishing at the foot of the table. Granted that Burnley had recently gone out and strengthened their team in an effort to redeem their lowly position, but this match at Perry Barr – to the Villa supporters' eyes – had all the makings of a thrashing. Of Burnley, of course!

For the superstitious ones, that this should be thirteenth successive match without defeat might have have caused some thought that perhaps all was not going to be as it should! And, of course, all *did* go wrong. Burnley scored an early goal, and the Villa – on a treacherous pitch, it should be added – could not get their shooting straight. Even though the game was largely Villa's in the quality of the play (though limited by the pitch conditions), it was Burnley that did the scoring – two more were gained in the second half, aided by indecision in the Villa defence.

"Well," the Villans must have thought, "if we can lose against the bottom team at home, then an away match against the second-bottom team could be a worse proposition!" Well, it was! **Sunderland** were not the team they had been since manager Tom Watson had left them and gone to Liverpool, but they still knew something about how to play, and how to fight. And in typically wintry north-east conditions that they were well used to, set about their job against a Villa side without Reynolds and captain Devey.

Just as in the Burnley match, Sunderland took an early lead, but Villa regained parity (albeit through an own goal) by the interval, and even led straight after the re-start. That was a short-lived joy, as Sunderland equalised and then went on to score two more, and won 2-4.

> *From the Villa's Minutes*
>
> At the meeting on 13 January, it was reported that Villa's was "an indifferent performance [at Sunderland]", and it was thought that Whitehouse should have saved two of the goals. "The effect of the loss seemed to make some of them noisy and quarrelsome in the saloon coming home."

Whitehouse's recent performances not having been to the committee's liking, Wilkes was preferred in goal, and would keep his place for the next few games.

The Aston Villa Chronicles 1874 – 1924 (and after)

The next home match proved to run more to form, but it was a match in which **Sunderland** were definitely playing above themselves in the tradition of matches between these two sides.

[From the *Athletic News*] A ding-dong first half struggle – with the Villa wasting a number of fine Athersmith centres, and Wheldon hitting the bar – left neither side with an advantage at half-time; 0-0.

The second half started with a bang. Devey attacked from midfield and put in a grand shot that Doig saved, but the ball went to Wheldon, who breasted it home. Villa then had the better of the play, but Sunderland – in due course – equalised as a result of a free-kick. Villa then restored their lead – again as a result of a free-kick – and though Sunderland continued with their endeavours, it was Doig that was forced into making the more saves.

Though it took awhile for the Villa to get their shooting sights fixed in the First Round match against **Newcastle United**, they led 4-0 at half-time against their Second Division opponents, and generally showed their class.

The second half was more of a question of going through the motions, though one more goal was added.

A new Birmingham sports journal was born in January, 1897.

Sports Argus.

February, 1897

Bury (a)

[From the *Sports Argus*] The Villa built up their game until "a regular fusilade was commenced on the home goal." Devey grazed the bar with a shot, and then, from a headed clearance by Evans, "Wheldon and Smith carried the ball to the other end of the field, and after smart play by the whole front rank of the Villa, Athersmith finished [the move] with a grand cross to Wheldon", but his shot was cleared.

Bury tried to break out, but after Devey and Athersmith had brought the ball up, a magnificent shot from Smith was saved. After 30 minutes play, Campbell found the net with a low shot, and he scored again three minutes later, from Athersmith's cross.

The second half showed Athersmith displaying "fleetness" and the Villa

The Aston Villa Chronicles 1874 – 1924 (and after)

generally keeping control; "the Villa men always appeared to be in the right place." The game petered out after a while, though Bury tried to produce a goal in the last 15 minutes.

"Crabtree and Athersmith were greatly admired by the Bury folk."

Charlie Johnstone commented that Villa were getting over their bad patch, and the *Argus* acknowledged his prophecy. Though Bury were another lowly side, at least Villa had won away from home against them. Despite the Villa's "bad patch", what helped the Villa a lot was that Bolton – who had hitherto been going strongly – had fallen away from the title race, and no other strong contender for the championship had emerged.

At **Burnley**, the Villa came to gain satisfaction for the previous month's humiliation at Perry Barr, and found the Burnley pitch in a very heavy condition.

[From the *Birmingham Daily Post*] Campbell scored a fine goal on four minutes and it was not long before Devey scored Villa's second and then a third. The Villa dominated the play, but Burnley pulled one back before the interval.

Devey completed his hat-trick soon after the interval, and the Villa should have scored more but for the saves made by their keeper. With Evans limping in the later stages, Burnley pulled two goals back. The Villa won 4-3.

The Villa led the table with advantage over the teams below them in terms of the number of games played. And the Villa had played fewer at home as well.

Leading Positions in Division 1 February 8th, 1897	Pld	Home W D L F A	Away W D L F A	Overall W D L F A	Pts
1 Aston Villa	22	6 2 2 19 13	8 2 2 30 19	14 4 4 49 32	32
2 Derby County	23	10 1 2 43 19	3 2 5 15 19	13 3 7 58 38	29
3 Liverpool	25	6 4 1 19 6	5 2 7 21 28	11 6 8 40 34	28
4 Sheffield United	21	5 4 3 21 11	4 4 1 14 9	9 8 4 35 20	26

Interview With John Devey

When asked what he attributed Villa's success to, John Devey said:

> Without doubt it is the good fellowship and the unselfishness which characterises all the men. There is not a man in the team who has the slightest animosity or jealousy against another ... You can't have success if the very best feeling does not exist between the men ... When the standard drops from what it is now, then the trouble will begin.

Devey went on to point out that Villa had had only 15 "first-class" men to rely on, "with 3 or 4 laid up for the past month, practically." How Villa was to fair,

The Aston Villa Chronicles 1874 – 1924 (and after)

> he said, depended on the best men being fit.
>
> About his own chances of international representation, Devey said:
>
>> ... I am never at my best in a trial match, like the England and Ireland game.[337] I have noticed when playing against Ireland that there always has been a tendency among the Englishmen to think about their Scottish cap, and the result has been that in the forwards they have played in pairs instead of combining as a line. Two men think that if they play together and into each other's hands they will stand a chance of being chosen against Scotland, and the centre is left alone to an extent, which of necessity makes the whole line suffer ...
>
> *Sports Argus*, 13 February, 1897

Against **Notts County** in round two of the FA Cup, Chatt was unable to play because of an injured toe, and, again having been left out for a few matches, Reynolds came in to replace him, and did not miss another match for the rest of the season. Evans, at left-back, had by now settled into that job and took full advantage of Welford's injury. Evans also was not to miss another match until the end of the season.

[From the *Sports Argus*] County chose to have the wind behind their backs, and after three minutes went ahead from a long shot. This inspired the Villa to 'play up', but the County defence played very well. Soon, however, the Villa were level when Wheldon was the one that seemed to have netted during a scrimmage, after a fine run by Athersmith.

County came back strongly, but then play was concentrated for some time on the half-way line. During this period, a contest between Crabtree and a County player resulted in the latter breaking his leg. He was soon taken to hospital, and with the County team re-arranged, County threw great efforts into the match. Nevertheless, Villa's fine efforts twice nearly produced goals.

County continued their hard work after half-time, but Villa's play against the ten men saw the County defence constantly under pressure. Even Evans and Cowan both nearly scored with long shots. Eventually, Villa forced a corner from which Athersmith hit the ball right into the centre of the goalmouth, but just when the ball appeared to be curling into the keeper's hands, up popped Campbell to head in what proved to be the winner, "amid wild enthusiasm".

The match was not all over by any means, and Langham got away, beating both Crabtree and Evans before sending in a pass that looked a fine opening

---

[337] The matches against Ireland and Wales were then considered as preparation matches for the main international, versus Scotland.

The Aston Villa Chronicles 1874 – 1924 (and after)

for County, but the chance was spurned.

> Bob Chatt tried to rest out his injury without success and consequently went to Manchester for treatment.
>
> Chatt was missed; "the assistance he has lent the team at right half-back has been of a very valuable nature indeed ... Reynolds cannot be considered to be the player he once was."
>
> Welford had been "put on the shelf" for breaking training regulations. His absence from the team had been felt.
>
> *Sports Argus*, 27 February, 1897

The result of the next home match (against **Preston**) confirmed the Villa as champions for the second year running, with seven League matches still to play. Also, this match was a prelude to a cup-tie between the two teams in just five days time.

[From the *Birmingham Daily Post*] Preston showed plenty of teamwork and ability, but some of the Villa's play was their very best. As an example, on 15 minutes, just after Devey had put Villa ahead, the report said, "by dint of beautiful passing, they threaded their way up to the North End goal, where Athersmith sent in a terrific shot, but Trainer managed to tip it over the bar …"

"Athersmith had put in any amount of fine screw-kicks", and it was he that supplied Devey with a headed goal on half-time.

Preston were stronger in the second half and pulled back a goal before Athersmith added Villa's third.

> One of the best games seen on that [Perry Barr] ground.
>
> *Sports Argus*, 27 February, 1897

Then came the game at **Preston** in the next round of the Cup.

[From the *Sports Argus*] Preston took the lead on 30 minutes after a see-sawing game had seen Villa have a good number of opportunities of their own. Preston had the game running in their favour until the interval.

In the second half, the Villa upped their game. On 50 minutes, Crabtree was brilliant in his play before feeding Athersmith, who ran and centred. Smith put the ball back, and though the ball was half-cleared, Campbell came in to

The Aston Villa Chronicles 1874 – 1924 (and after)

steer home.

Villa's play was grand, but Preston were also playing well. During the excitement of it all, the pressing crowd caused a barrier to give way, "[and] a huge mass of humanity rolled onto the enclosure. Happily, the police prevented any breaking-in of the crowd." But there was no mention of anyone being hurt!

A hard-fought match, with Wilkes in very good form.

In the first replay at Perry Barr on 3 March, played in front of about 12,000 spectators, there was no score. A strong wind militated against the Villa's style of play, but it was yet another splendid contest between these two great opponents.

In the second replay, Villa brought back John Cowan at outside-left. Played in front of 22,000 at Bramall Lane, Sheffield (on 10 March), there was still no score until after nearly 40 minutes, and it was to the Villa. The entire Preston defence had continued to be in such good form. In fact, both sides had all their players playing on a fine edge, but the Villa were having the best of it. A little while into the second half, Villa went further ahead, but Preston immediately responded with what was thought to be a fortuitous goal to make it 2-1 to the Villa. Those two quick goals seemed to put even more urgency into both sides, and there was a long period of fast, ding-dong play with plenty of action, until Villa gained their third goal. Just when the game seemed all over, Preston scored another, to end it at 3-2 to the Villa, and for the Villa to go through after three pulsating matches.

> John Reynolds was noted as being back to something like his best form in the second replay against Preston.
>
> *Sports Argus*, 13 March, 1897

February, 1897

At the **Nottingham Forest** match, Smith was "a little off colour", and John Cowan was back on the Villa left-wing.

[From the *Sports Argus*] After opening with good attacking play, Devey headed home from Crabtree's free-kick (on 15 minutes). The Villa then "played up in brilliant style". Any Forest shots were not convincingly hit, but at one point they caused the Villa some serious defensive concern.

The Forest did succeed in equalising after the interval, but wonderful combination play involving Wheldon, Campbell and John Cowan saw Cowan giving Villa the lead once more. The effort was "deservedly applauded".

The Aston Villa Chronicles 1874 – 1924 (and after)

Though Villa might have scored again, Forest again equalised, though Wilkes might have saved the shot.

At 2-2, the play became fast and furious, and grand combination again saw the Villa scoring, this time through Devey. The Villa's play remained bright – though Forest had their chances – and towards the end, Wheldon added Villa's fourth, his chipped shot going in over the heads of several players.

Devey and Athersmith were again conspicuous, with Campbell again playing "a rare good game in the centre". Crabtree was again decisive in feeding his forwards and stopping the opposition. Both Villa full-backs were good.

The Villa now met **Liverpool** at home, the team that Villa were also to face the next week in the FA Cup semi-final (it was strange how this fixture arrangement occurred in much the same way as with Preston in the previous round). That Wilkes had been partly at fault in the previous two matches, and that Whitehouse had been agitating for a return to the first team having pronounced his dissatisfaction of playing in the reserves, meant that Whitehouse was restored to his position in goal. The first-choice Villa team was now considered to be:

Whitehouse; Spencer, Evans; Reynolds, Jas.Cowan, Crabtree;
Athersmith, Devey, Campbell, Wheldon, John Cowan.

[From the *Sports Argus*] This proved to be a highly disappointing match, particularly in view of the large crowd that turned up on a fine day. It was considered that Villa had not played so poorly before in that season.

The one moment of interest was when all the Villa players stood in a straight line between the sticks to repel a free-kick!

However, Spencer played the game of his life, and Crabtree was also not to blame as he had to go off injured after trying to do the splits!

The Villa (not for the first time during this Cup run) were to visit Buxton on the Monday, for a change of scenery and preparation for the next week's match.

Coolness and the power to act with lightning speed stamps Whitehouse the superior of the two Villa keepers.

Sports Argus, 13 March, 1897

| FAC Semi- Final | vs Liverpool | 3-0 | Attendance: |
| 20 March, 1897 | at Bramall Lane, Sheffield | | 30,000 |

Crabtree, having been injured in the previous week's encounter with Liverpool, was replaced by Griffiths for this match in an otherwise unchanged side.

The Aston Villa Chronicles 1874 – 1924 (and after)

[From the *Sports Argus*] The good playing conditions produced a match of fine skills. A "hot encounter" was what was expected of this match, and that was what proved to be the case. "Indeed, the game was altogether too vigorous!", stated the match report.

The first goal – to the Villa – came on 35 minutes. "All together!" shouted the Villa supporters, and when Villa scored, there was an almighty yell!

In the second half, Liverpool had their chances, but the fact that Villa went two-up straight after the interval meant that Liverpool had a mountain to climb to get back into the match. John Cowan's second goal – a header from a corner – was a beauty.

Then Athersmith thought it time to show his art. He rushed right through, cleverly dodging the full-back and claimed the third all on his own – "a brilliant effort".

Whitehouse had to save brilliantly on two or three occasions, but in-between, Devey and John Cowan could easily have scored additional goals, and there were other marvellous shots that just missed their target. The Villa finished the match well within themselves.

> The *Sports Argus* contemplated that Joe Grierson was deserving
> "Three cheers for the unobtrusive, yet invaluable,
> part in which he plays …"

The last first-class Game at Perry Barr

This home match against **Bolton** was just two days after the Semi-Final, and not needing to over-stretch some of the first-choice players, not only Crabtree was out, but also Whitehouse and John Cowan.

The match was extraordinary. Bolton were two-up at half-time, and, indeed, were two-up with 30 minutes to go! Once Athersmith scored Villa's first, however, there was only one team in it after Bolton had had their way for the preceding sixty minutes! The Villa then scored another five in the remaining minutes against the side that had been leading the League table for the first part of the season. What a come-back, and what a way to end Villa's term at Perry Barr. This was the last first-class match to be played there before the move to the Aston Lower Grounds, ending 21 years of progressive development and attainment – and no little entertainment!

For the return match at **Bolton**, the Villa played their normal side, apart from Burton deputising for the still-injured Crabtree. This was another extraordinary match in view of the gale behind each team in turn in each of the halves, with Villa

The Aston Villa Chronicles 1874 – 1924 (and after)

scoring their two goals in the first half whilst having the wind behind their backs, and then masterly work by Spencer, James Cowan and Reynolds restricting Bolton to one goal in the second half.

> There were allegations in some quarters concerning Villa's "roughness" in this Bolton match, and suggestions that Villa's reputation was at risk. However, the *Sports Argus* (3 April) observed that:
>
>> The fact of the matter is that Villa can be just as 'rough' as another lot, if they are made to be ... It is generally their opponents who, recognising their lack of success, endeavour to make up for it by the 'bashing' process. And if they are tried and tempted, can you wonder that the Villa men feel constrained to retaliate at times?

> "[In 1896-97, the Villa] played football as if they were playing chess; you were not allowed to interfere with their moves!"
>
> *Bob Holmes, once of Preston North End*[338]

April, 1897

From the Villa's Minutes

On 7 April, the committee resolved that the bonus for a Cup Final win was not to be less than £10 a man.

FA Cup Final	vs Everton at Crystal Palace, London	3-2 10 April, 1897	Attendance: 65,000

The scene in advance of the kick-off was as follows:[339]

3.45 p.m.	A sea of heads and faces; a roar from the crowd, and eleven blue-shirted men bound on the field. "Play up, Everton!"
3.48 p.m.	A bigger and more prolonged roar. The Villans enter the arena. The photographers are busy.
3.54 p.m.	The coin is in the air. Jack Devey wins, and the Villa have a brisk breeze behind them.

The Aston Villa Chronicles 1874 – 1924 (and after)

Ten years after the Villa had won their first FA Cup trophy, the occasion was again one of double celebration - the Queen's Jubilee! Magnificent weather favoured the occasion, and the ground was in perfect playing condition. On both sides, the football was good, and no one could have wished to see better half-back play than that of Reynolds, Cowan – and Crabtree, who had been specially kept away from football since his injury a month before, but here he was, refreshed and eager to be in the fray.

Some interesting and fine early play gave way to an explosion of goals! Campbell, from a magnificent pass by Devey, opened the scoring for the Villa; then Bell – for Everton – shortly afterwards equalised. A few minutes later, a free-kick against Cowan gave Boyle the opportunity of kicking the second goal for Everton. This lead did not last long as, within a few minutes, Crabtree deftly placed the ball for Wheldon to equalise. Then Crabtree headed the third, and winning, goal for the Villa. Although 3-2 behind at the interval, Everton had played a remarkably sound game and there was very little to choose between the two teams

The Villa just had the edge so far, and the second half was also closely contested. However, although strongly pressing towards the finish, Everton could not pierce the Villa defence, despite once hitting the crossbar. The pace was hot throughout, yet the men were going as strongly at the finish as at the beginning.

For the Villa, it was in their half-back line that their real strength lay, and their superiority here gave them the victory. In a match between Villa's combination and Everton's dash, Reynolds displayed marvellous ability in tackling, judgment and heading, whilst James Cowan was perhaps the greatest player in 22 great ones.

> Lord Roseberry, on presenting the Cup to John Devey, described the match as:
> " ... *this splendid Olympic contest* "

That Cup Final against Everton was for many years regarded as the greatest Cup Final – particularly as a contest. The two teams, though of different styles, were of comparable strength, and they came together head-to-head and produced an astonishing match of wonderful football and fair play. The first half was the half of the forwards (all the goals were scored in that half), and the second was the half of the defences.

---

[338] Fred Ward's "Official History of Aston Villa" (1948)
[339] Sports Argus 10 Apr 1897

The Aston Villa Chronicles 1874 – 1924 (and after)

> **A Villa Supporter's View**
>
> "... the best final I've ever seen for sheer skill and delightful football ... I don't remember such an exciting match as that, and though local partisanship must be reckoned for, I think it is still looked upon by old judges as the finest ultimate game for the Cup that has ever been played. For the whole ninety minutes the issue was always in doubt; neither side was ever more than one goal in front, and the lead changed twice. The play was so skilful and telling that the suspense was sometimes almost painful; and I don't mind telling you, after all the years, that I was jolly glad when the last part of the time was over. There was no luck about the Villa win, and what bit of all-round superiority was, the Villa had it, and the fine eleven had no more than its merits; but the teams were so nicely balanced that a mistake on either side might have been fatal, and that slip was made when the Villa scored their first goal and won the match."
>
> 'Jim and Bill', *The Villa News*, 17 April, 1909

> "*As regards combination*, the Villa were certainly superior to their opponents. The Midlanders played in more harmony with each other, the lines working together better, whilst so far as regards individual work the Villa team were more conspicuous when occasion offered than their opponents ..."
>
> *Sports Argus*, 10 April, 1897

What Happened to the Match Ball?

On 15 February, 2009, the Everton match programme (vs Aston Villa at Goodison Park) told the story of how one of the Everton players kept the ball for himself. By a long and indirect route, the ball came into the hands of Everton FC in 1946. Thereupon, the Everton club – in wonderful spirit – not only reconditioned the ball, but returned it to the Aston Villa directors in a ceremony at Liverpool.

The Aston Villa Chronicles 1874 – 1924 (and after)

Double Winners

On the same day as the Cup Final, Villa were simultaneously made League Champions as Derby (the nearest challengers) lost their League match!

This meant one thing – *Villa had won 'the double'!*

An achievement not to happen again for another 64 years.

The *Sports Argus* (27 March, 1897) exclaimed:

"When Preston North End won the championship without losing a single game [in 1888-89], there was nothing like the excitement and sustained interest that there has been shown during the [1896-97] season's campaign. And this, from the simple fact that the strength of teams has been wonderfully improved, and that now the various leading combinations have attained a wonderful level of excellence ..."

'Tityrus' relayed what happened when he visited the Villa team the day after they won the Cup, at Tavistock Hotel, London:

> While I congratulated them, I rashly remarked that I could not help feeling that they had deprived Preston North End of their unique record of having captured both the same honours in 1888-89.
>
> The Villa players objected ... the discussion became heated and even reached the stage of a threat to drop me out of the window into the courtyard.
>
> [Having second thoughts after a while] they did not pitch me out of the window, but one of them ... retorted: 'Preston? Ha! Football was in its infancy then. They had no one to beat!'

The week after, the long-awaited move to the Aston Lower Grounds was accomplished. The season had not only produced a 'double', but a *'triple'*!

The First Match at Aston Lower Grounds (Villa Park)

The Easter Saturday brought **Blackburn Rovers** to an opening event! It was fitting that perhaps the greatest Cup-winning team of the age came for this occasion – the Villa were already League Champions and FA Cup Winners, and were now possessors of perhaps the leading ground in the country at that time. However,

The Aston Villa Chronicles 1874 – 1924 (and after)

although the ground was available for play, the facilities were by no means complete! It was a very wet day, and few of those that came had shelter owing to the fact that the roofing had not been completed. Even the press-men had a hard time recording the game's events in the rain-swept stand! Over the next two or three years, other modifications were needed to modify the terracing on parts of the ground, and also provide crush-barriers.

In a game that did not have any meaning apart from celebrating the ground's first match, the Villa beat the Rovers 3-0, and the *Sports Argus* reported, "The match proved to be very exciting in heavy conditions. Campbell was the first scorer with a lovely goal, and had one of his very best games, where he was more than usually aggressive." Old Fogey remarked, years afterwards, how there was great competition amongst the Villa players to score the first goal at Villa Park!

> George Ramsay himself stated many years later that he was the first and last to kick the ball at Perry Barr, and also the first to kick the ball at Villa Park. However, he added that the last two were "sentimental kicks"!

A truly magnificent 'gate' turned up on Easter Monday to see the Villa play **Wolves**, but doubtless many came for the 'double bill', for the match was preceded by a cycling event, a sport that was then eagerly followed; but the opening was marred by a tragedy.

Tragedy on Easter Monday

One of the competitors at the cycling 'meet' preceding the match was Bert Harris, a Midlander of no mean repute, and who had a substantial following in Australia, where he had planned to emigrate after the 1897 season.

> Prior to a race in Bolton on Easter Sunday 1897, Bert was struck by the premonition that he would die racing. After taking the train with his father, he became so agitated that he disembarked at Derby and rode back to Leicester.
>
> A sense of doom overshadowed the races in Aston on Easter Monday, but Bert was persuaded to participate. In a strange semblance of resignation, he made his farewells to family and friends before the race. When he sustained a puncture, another competitor lent him a front wheel to enable him to take part in the final ten mile highlight of the day.
>
> Four miles in, Bert fell while travelling at around 27 mph. He banged his head on the cement, lay unconscious and was taken to hospital in Birmingham. His borrowed front wheel was very badly damaged and the

> whispers started: would an experienced professional have made such a rudimentary steering mistake? Perhaps he clipped the back wheel of another rider. Rumours were rife around the circuit that he was going to be 'bumped' to fix the race. According to his best friend Will Jordan, he regained consciousness briefly and murmured 'Oh Will, this time I am beat'.
>
> He died at the age of just 23 on 21 April 1897. ... Flowers were sent from all over the world to lament the passing of a hero ...[340]

As far as the football against Wolves was concerned, the Villa opened the scoring after only five minutes through John Cowan. It was Campbell, however, who was again playing above himself as the pivot, dribbling beautifully and scoring two fine late goals as the Villa achieved what looked like an easy win, but belies the fact that Wolves played their part in the match; the Villa defenders made a significant contribution to their side's substantial win.

For the last fixture of the season, it was yet another tight match against **Preston**, the side that had given the Villa such difficulty in the FA Cup (doubtless wanting to prevent the Villa repeating their own 'double' success). Not only was it the last League game of the season but, as it happened, it was the final game for three of Villa's finest players. Both sides played – as before – two strong half-back lines, and, therefore, much of the play was in midfield. Villa's goal was achieved in the first half by Wheldon, who converted an excellent Spencer free kick.

The Football League Division 1 1896-97 Top Places	Pld	Home W D L F A	Away W D L F A	Overall W D L F A	Pts
1 Aston Villa	30	10 3 2 36 16	11 2 2 37 22	21 5 4 73 38	47
2 Sheffield United	30	6 4 5 22 16	7 6 2 20 13	13 10 7 42 29	36
3 Derby County	30	10 2 3 45 22	6 2 7 25 28	16 4 10 70 50	36
4 Preston North End	30	8 4 3 35 21	3 8 4 20 19	11 12 7 55 40	34

> The Villa's success in 1896-97 was much to do with the formidability of the half-back line. As late as 18 June 1908, the *Daily Mail* opined that it was: "... questionable if [these] three have been equalled."

---

[340] The text was obtained from a website devoted to his memory, which appears now to have been usurped for other purposes.

The Aston Villa Chronicles 1874 – 1924 (and after)

1896-97 League and FA Cup Results				
Sep	2nd	H Stoke	2 - 1	6000
	5th	A West Bormwich A	1 - 3	12000
	12th	H Sheffield United	2 - 2	5000
	19th	A Everton	3 - 2	25000
	26th	H Everton	1 - 2	15000
Oct	3rd	A Sheffield United	0 - 0	12000
	10th	H West Bormwich A	2 - 0	20000
	17th	A Derby County	3 - 1	8500
	24th	H Derby County	2 - 1	10000
	31st	A Stoke	2 - 0	6000
Nov	7th	H Bury	1 - 1	6000
	14th	A Sheffield Wed	3 - 1	12000
	21st	H Sheffield Wed	4 - 0	12000
	28th	A Blackburn Rovers	5 - 1	7000
Dec	19th	H Nottingham Forest	3 - 2	10000
	25th	A Liverpool	3 - 3	25000
	26th	A Wolves	2 - 1	18000
Jan	2nd	H Burnley	0 - 3	14000
	9th	A Sunderland	2 - 4	8000
	16th	H Sunderland	2 - 1	15000
	30th	H Newcastle U (FAC)	5 - 1	6000
Feb	6th	A Bury	2 - 0	10000
	8th	A Burnley	4 - 3	5000
	13th	H Notts County (FAC)	2 - 1	4000
	22nd	H Preston North End	3 - 1	20000
	27th	A Preston N E (FAC)	1 - 1	14000
Mar	3rd	H Preston N E (FAC r)	0 - 0	12000
	6th	A Nottingham Forest	4 - 2	8000
	10th	N Preston N E (FAC r)	3 - 2	22000
	13th	H Liverpool	0 - 0	20000
	20th	N Liverpool (FAC SF)	3 - 0	30000
	22nd	H Bolton Wanderers	6 - 2	7000
	27th	A Bolton Wanderers	2 - 1	7000
Apr	10th	N Everton (FAC Final)	3 - 2	65891
	17th	H Blackburn Rovers	3 - 0	15000
	19th	H Wolves	5 - 0	35000
	26th	A Preston North End	1 - 0	3000

End of Season Postscripts

The Villa finished their season with 11 games undefeated in the League, and another 7 in the FA Cup, a total of 18 first-class matches undefeated.

Ten years later, Howard Spencer had this to say about the extent of the achievement of scooping the 'double':

> It is most difficult to bring off the double event for the simple reason that it is no light matter for any club to keep at the top of its form for eight months. ... Several clubs in my time have gone strongly for the double event, but something has always happened, sooner or later, to rob them of the distinction. ... You have to be both brilliant and consistent to win the two major events in one and the same season. [341]

Of course, the number of League games to be played was increasing as the League grew, which added to the difficulty of achieving the 'double'.

---

[341] Sports Argus 21 Sep 1907

The Aston Villa Chronicles 1874 – 1924 (and after)

Aston Villa – League Champions & FA Cup Winners, 1897

Back row: G.Ramsay (Sec), J.Grierson (Trainer), Spencer, Whitehouse (goalkeeper), J.Margoschis (Chair), Evans, Crabtree, J.Lees & C.Johnstone (Directors);
Front Row: V.Jones (Director), Jas.Cowan, Athersmith, Campbell, Devey (Captain), Wheldon, Jno.Cowan, Reynolds, F.Rinder (Director)

By the end of April, Welford's resentment was clearly showing, having been left out of the side for so long and missing the triumphant end of season to 1896-97. All the first-team players had been awarded a wage of £4 per week (all the year-round – then a generous payment in football),[342] but he demanded an increase, and, not getting it, went with John Reynolds to Celtic, to which club Campbell had already returned.

> Charlie Johnstone later explained the circumstances of the Campbell departure. He said that 6 or 7 weeks from the end of the season that he did not intend to sever his connection with Villa, but by the last day of April, seems to have changed his mind, for he then told Charlie that he wanted certain terms. The terms were conceded, but even then he would not sign. On asking for £100 down and £4 10s per week, it was again agreed, but with the papers put in front of him, again he would not sign. Next day, he signed for Celtic.
>
> *Sports Argus*, 4 December, 1897

---

[342] Club Minutes 13 Apr 1897

The Aston Villa Chronicles 1874 – 1924 (and after)

Season 1897-98 : A Rest Year!

League Division 1 position: *6th (of 16)*; **FA Cup:** *1st Round*.

Campbell's departure had not been too much of a shock in view of the fact that he had nearly gone the previous year, but Reynolds' departure was perhaps more surprising. However, he and Welford had been – despite their talents – of some trouble to the Villa administration, and clearly both felt that their future lay in other (dare I say?!) *green* fields.

To replace Johnny Campbell, the Villa brought down another Scot, **Jim Fisher**, a highly-rated 21-year-old that other clubs had been chasing. In addition, two players – brothers – came to the club from Hereford Thistle; **John ('Jack') Sharp**, a 19-year-old forward, and **Bertram Sharp**, a 21-year-old defender. This arrangement with the Hereford club had been agreed early in the 1896-97 season, but the arrangement agreed was that they were to come over for the start of the 1897-98 season.

Jack Sharp was to become famous – but not with the Villa! He joined Everton (with his brother) two years later, and went on to great things with them, as well as becoming an international both in football and cricket.

The Season's Play

September, 1897

The 'gate' was depleted for the home match against **Sheffield Wednesday** owing to it being a weekday and there being continuous rain, but the performance and the result was much brighter! This was the start of the first full season at 'Villa Park'.

Villa: *Whitehouse; Spencer, Evans; Chatt, Jas.Cowan, Crabtree; Athersmith, Devey, Fisher, Wheldon, John Cowan.*

[From the *Birmingham Daily Post*] The match started with a swish as, from a goal-kick, "the ball was passed and re-passed between Devey and Athersmith, and ultimately touched by the former to Fisher, who passed it beautifully to John Cowan, and he scored with a grand shot two minutes from the commencement … The next few minutes saw them constantly on the attack.", with Fisher showing up well.

However, a defensive mistake let in Wednesday, but though it looked offside their goal was given, after 13 minutes. Villa continued to be the more dangerous, with Fisher continuing to be prominent. On one occasion he was

The Aston Villa Chronicles 1874 – 1924 (and after)

tripped when about to shoot. "The free-kick was accurately taken, and Crabtree hit the bar [but] the ball dropped into the corner of the goal[mouth]" before Wednesday managed to scramble it away.

The ensuing play that half was all about Villa, and Wednesday's keeper was frequently tested. However, he failed to hold one, and Wheldon put in the rebound to give a Villa a 2-1 half-time lead.

Fisher was again prominent by drawing opponents to the right wing and then passed to John Cowan, giving him a clear run at goal, but his terrific shot was just wide. After 54 minutes, Athersmith supplied a centre to Wheldon, who notched Villa's third.

"The champions were now playing in fine form, the whole five combining to make an excellent front rank, passing splendidly and displaying great dash. They kept on the attack practically the whole time, Fisher feeding his wings to perfection …" Their keeper had a number of nasty shots to deal with before Athersmith again supplied Wheldon for Villa's fourth, and his hat-trick.

A terrific rainstorm came on, but though playing against it, Villa kept on the offensive. However, despite Villa's superiority, it was Wednesday that broke away to score their second.

After a disallowed goal, John Cowan and Fisher combined to give Athersmith a chance, which he obligingly took to make it 5-2.

Against the Albion at home, it was a warm, bright, day at Villa Park, and the Villa team was unchanged. An exhilirating match enthralled the spectators.

[From the *Sports Argus*] As against Wednesday, the Villa started with a resolve and a result. Hardly had the match started when Fisher smashed in a shot that the keeper could not hold, and in raced Wheldon to bury the ball in the net. Instead of losing heart, however, the Albion fans cheered on their side, and they had the better of it for some time. Then Villa – in one of their breakaways – netted again, but this effort was disallowed for offside. The Villa were inspired to press on, but the game passed back to the Albion, who, in due course, levelled the score.

Fast movements from both sides then developed. Eventually, Athersmith carried on a beautiful bit of passing by providing a centre to Fisher, who again provided an opportunity to Wheldon, who slotted home.

Soon, in the second half, Devey sent Athersmith away, and he provided a centre from the by-line to Wheldon, who volleyed the ball home; 3-1 to the Villa, and Wheldon's second hat-trick in two successive matches. Soon after though, Albion reduced the arrears following a corner, and, scenting possible success, built up their attacks on the Villa goal. Following two unproductive Albion corners, the Villa defence cleared, but only to see the ball thumped back and shooting into the net off the crossbar! It was 3-3!

The Aston Villa Chronicles 1874 – 1924 (and after)

The Villa recomposed themselves, however, and once Fisher scored their fourth from a corner, the Villa finished having the edge.

> Fred Wheldon scored two hat-tricks in the first two games of the season, both at 'Villa Park'. This particular combination is a record that has never been equalled, and has extra significance coming straight after the 'double' season and in starting the first full season at 'Villa Park'.
>
> What is more, both sets of scores were 'pure' hat-tricks – each scored as successive goals without being interrupted by another score from his own side.

Unchanged again, the Villa faced a **Notts County** side (away from home) that included an ex-Villan and brother of John Devey – Will Devey. It was a day of bright sunshine, with a cooling wind, at Nottingham.

[From the *Sports Argus*] For the third successive game, the Villa got off to a storming start. After seven minutes, John Devey sent the ball across. "John Cowan got hold, steadied himself, and then let fly, the ball striking the underside of the bar and cannoning into the net." This reverse to the County only served for them to sharpen their attacks, and, after a while, a tremendous bombardment was inflicted on the Villa goal. "On one occasion, the ball was dangerously near over, and the home side claimed for a goal, but the ball was got down to the centre of the field and play continued for nearly a minute, when – to everybody's surprise – the referee, after consultation with the linesman, allowed [the] goal …" To the Villa's amazement, it was 1-1.

The half was then fought out at tremendous pace, with chances falling to both sides. However, Fisher had one chance to score from about two yards, yet succeeded in putting the ball over the bar!

The County then scored a second, but this goal of theirs also had shades of doubt about it. Instead of playing to the whistle, Whitehouse – Villa's keeper – was busily debating an offside issue when play continued, and the County netted with Whitehouse still arguing! To cap it all, Wheldon – Villa's recent scorer par excellence – unaccountably then missed a wonderful scoring chance! At half-time, the Villa were 1-2 down and it was not looking like their day!

The second half started with the County having the better of things, but as the game wore on, the game went more in Villa's direction. Fisher had one brilliant 'goal' disallowed because of an infringement. Then James Cowan had a 'goal' from a free-kick disallowed; the law then did not allow a direct score from a free-kick!

County were still troubling Villa at times, but, with only two minutes to go, the match produced a twist of its own. Years later, Old Fogey recalled the last few minutes of this match when County were leading 1-2 and there was "plenty of revelry in the fold":

The Aston Villa Chronicles 1874 – 1924 (and after)

Some of the crowd began to move away, and Joe Grierson returned to the dressing-room, feeling just a trifle glum, because the Villa really had been having the best of matters, and it was 'hard-lines' that they should go back home with a thwacking.

Something like this [then] happened on the field: Charlie Athersmith whipped down, got across one of those amazing centres of his, and the ball went through mostly with the assistance of Jimmy Cowan, I think – 2-2! (with shrieks of silence from the Lambs!).

John Devey ... 'grasped the shirt of happy chance' and immediately he got hold of the ball from the kick-off, whacked it away to the speedy right-winger (as he so often and so cleverly did), and sailed away for the centre himself.

He was right! Athersmith didn't stand on the order of being tackled, but lively and smartly lobbed over just the sort of ball Captain John required ... and pop it went among the meshes – with Jimmy Cowan turning Catherine wheels, Charlie Athersmith and the rest of the 'bhoys' with roods of smiles on their counting-houses, and 'thunders of quietude' amongst the multitude.

The most surprised and gratified man that day was Joe Grierson, to whom Cowan conveyed the good news in his quiet way.[343]

At home against **Bury**, the one team change was in goal; Wilkes came in for Whitehouse.

[From the *Sports Argus*] Villa again scored a fairly early goal – Fisher scoring in the eighteenth minute, and although Spencer put through an unfortunate own goal (off his head), another first half goal by Fisher, and then one by Wheldon settled the matter.

Villa were brilliant and on their best form, only the Bury backs and keeper preventing a heavier score. Even so, Villa eased up after going 3-1 ahead. Fisher played his best game yet – and scored two goals – whilst Chatt played much better than of late.

> The skill, the confidence, the flawless combination, and the perfect understanding, which marked the persistent fusillade with which the Villa tested the generally reliable defence of Bury, [affected] even the old stagers among the crowd whom they led in round after round of enthusiastic applause.
>
> *Sports Argus*, 25 September, 1897

---

[343] Villa News & Record & Record 28 Jan 1911

The Aston Villa Chronicles 1874 – 1924 (and after)

The Villa had now accumulated a total of 22 first-class games undefeated since January, and the champions stood at the top of the table looking as though a third title on the trot was feasible. But it was still early in the season!

Leading Positions in Division 1 September 18th, 1897	Pld	Home W D L F A	Away W D L F A	Overall W D L F A	Pts
1 Aston Villa	4	3 0 0 12 6	1 0 0 3 2	4 0 0 15 8	8
2 Sheffield United	4	2 0 0 6 4	1 1 0 4 2	3 1 0 10 6	7
3 Derby County	4	3 0 0 11 4	0 0 1 1 2	3 0 1 12 6	6

At **Blackburn Rovers**, the Villa's 'Waterloo' arrived, but this encounter went right to the 'wire' before Rovers triumphed. After a goal-less first half, but a half containing much that was worth admiring, the crowd were treated to a goal-storm of seven goals, the advantage swinging one way, and then the next. The scores followed in the sequence 0-1 to Blackburn, 1-1, 2-1 to Villa (a penalty), 2-2, 2-3 to Blackburn and then 3-3. Finally, the Rovers scored a late winner.

> In the Blackburn match, a Rovers' forward was making a dangerous bee-line for goal: "A score looked all over a certainty, when Spencer came flying across from the other wing and threw himself full-tilt at his opponent ... The Rover incontinently turned a somersault, and wondered if an avalanche had struck him! The crowd yelled their excretions, but Spencer only smiled, and walked back to his place ..."
>
> *A Lion's Fun*
>
> *Sports Argus*, 2 October, 1897

> The referee of the Blackburn match reported John Devey to the FA as "a fraud and a sneak". Devey was called to attend at the FA to explain himself, where he admitted that he had expressed his dissatisfaction with the referee, but denied the allegation.
>
> *Sports Argus*, 2 October, 1897
>
> "I can't understand it. Devey is not given to saying things to the referee ... He is one of the fairest players who ever went on a football pitch."
>
> John Lewis (leading referee) in the *Sports Argus*, 16 October, 1897

One narrow defeat was about acceptable, but the size of this second successive defeat (away at **Sheffield Wednesday**, 0-3) caused a wave of criticism, particularly pointing out that the Villa had now conceded more goals than any other First Division side, and yet the Villa could not score against the second-highest conceders – the Wednesday themselves!

The Aston Villa Chronicles 1874 – 1924 (and after)

> The *Sports Argus* printed a quote from "a gentleman prominently connected with the Villa":
>
> > ... those two thrashings will do our men a lot of good. They could not have had better proof that other people can play football. Had we tried our best to make the players believe that they had to do more than merely walk on the field to win, we could not have succeeded half so well as by the aid of these two object lessons. Mark my words, the Villa won't be any the worse for their trouncings.
>
> <div align="right"><i>Sports Argus</i>, 2 October, 1897</div>

That the Villa had lost by so much against the Wednesday was partly down to the fact that Howard Spencer had been hurt sufficiently to keep him out for the rest of the season. It was also down to the fact that Evans was not playing that well at this time.

There had been, however, some admission from John Devey that two of the goals at Blackburn should probably have been avoided, and a *Sports Argus* writer felt that Wilkes was at fault for one of the goals, and had fumbled some shots.

> In Wolverhampton, news of the Villa downfall was received with "unalloyed delight". At one function of some description, the announcement of the Villa's state evoked "cheers [that] rent the air and cracked the ceiling right across!"
>
> <div align="right"><i>Sports Argus</i>, 2 October, 1897</div>

> A Villa supporter left his train seat covered with a rug to keep it reserved for himself, and left the train compartment for refreshment. On returning, he found a lady seated there.
>
> *A Lion's Fun*
>
> To his protestations, the lady replied, "Do you know, sir, that I am one of the directors' wives?"
>
> "Madam," replied the enthusiast, "were you the director's *only* wife, I should still protest!"
>
> *The woman kept her seat, though!*
>
> <div align="right"><i>Sports Argus</i>, 2 October, 1897</div>

October, 1897

Helped by the Onion Fair event, another excellent crowd was present for the home **Bolton** match. Several changes had been imposed on the Villa because of injury (Spencer) and illness (Crabtree), but Fisher was also replaced after having a poor

The Aston Villa Chronicles 1874 – 1924 (and after)

match against the Wednesday.

It will be recalled that towards the end of the last season, Bolton's visit saw them leading 0-2, only to succumb to six goals in the last half-hour. Would this be the same kind of match – a *déjà vu*?

Villa: *Wilkes; B. Sharp, Evans; Chatt, Jas.Cowan, Burton; Athersmith, Devey, J.Sharp, Wheldon, John Cowan.*

[From the *Sports Argus*] The Villa's travails continued, when – after just 17 *seconds* play – Wilkes unaccountably miskicked straight back to the Bolton forward, Jack, who returned it into the net – raising "consternation amongst the spectators"!

The Villa then got their game together, and progressively got on top of Bolton, whose keeper several times had great difficulty in keeping the ball out, and robbed Villa of at least one 'certain' goal. Bolton came back, though, and Wright shot from 30 yards for a "splendid goal". But, again, Wilkes was at fault for being late in moving for the shot. Yes, as before, it was 0-2 to Bolton at half-time.

Both sides then threatened the opposing goals. At length, with the Villa defence showing signs of being in calm control, and the halves and forwards starting to play their best game, the Villa imposed themselves. One good move saw Wheldon getting the ball to Jack Sharp, who, though he miskicked first time, he recovered, and put the ball home for his début goal.

The crowd was now behind the Villa, and the Villa had got their game together. The ball was again fed to Jack Sharp, who scored a brilliant equaliser! Then, almost straight away, with the crowd's excitement at fever pitch, Wheldon put Villa ahead! *Three Villa goals in five minutes to come from 0-2 down!*

From then on in, it was a case of close calls at both ends, though Villa perhaps came the closest to adding to their score.

Wilkes was going through some very poor form, and Whitehouse was injured, so it was clear that a drastic measure was required in the goalkeeping department. At the start of the previous season, William George had been announced as a third-choice keeper, but had never played for the first-team. It now turned out that he was not permanently on the Villa's books, and was really available only on a loan basis from Trowbridge Town, his normal club. George was selected to make his début in this match against Albion, at which a record crowd turned out at Stoney Lane.

[From the *Sports Argus*] This was a typical Albion-Villa 'derby'; not a lot of quality, but much over-eagerness. The Villa were reduced to ten men before half-time, when James Cowan had to go off.

The Aston Villa Chronicles 1874 – 1924 (and after)

Jack Sharp scored a "clever goal" on 57 minutes and continued to show promise, but his effort was equalised before the end.

George's first game was a "creditable display", but he was not greatly tested till near the end, when he made a firm impression on the spectators.

From the Villa's Minutes

On 7 October, it was reported that Fred Rinder had tried to permanently sign **William George** from Trowbridge Town. The Trowbridge club had just bought him out of the army and had purchased for him a public house. They therefore asked to be compensated, and agreed only to the loan of George until they had a full team, after which he would be fully available to the Villa.

On 14 October, it was learnt that Fred Rinder had agreed terms for the transfer at £200, with a £10 bonus to George and wages of £4 per week. *The Villa had played George on 9 October, before his permanent signing, but there was clearly an agreement to play him on a loan basis.*

By 25 November, the FA had found Aston Villa guilty of playing an ineligible player, had fined the club £50, and Messrs. Rinder and Ramsay were suspended for one month. "This was unanimously voted a severe and unjust sentence given against the weight of evidence." Ramsay was asked to go to Trowbridge to solicit support for an appeal [but without success.]

The main problem, as it transpired, was that although George had been on the League books for some time, the Villa had failed to submit timely papers to the FA. They were caught out on a technicality, though the FA clearly tried to make out as though the Villa were guilty of massive skulduggery, and applied excessive punishment.

Fred Rinder's Suspension

The suspension that Fred Rinder had inadvertently gained, as a result of his efforts in the William George affair, caused much sympathy from his friends:

A Lion's Fun

> Mr. Rinder's agility has been tested severely in having to climb over mountains of seasonable game, stacks of preserved and crystallised fruits, cases of wine of choice vintage, and bundles of cigars of favourite brand.

Sports Argus, 4 December, 1897

Bob Chatt had not played very well this season, and with the return of Crabtree, Burton was switched to right-half at the exclusion of Chatt for the home match against **Notts County**. 'Tich' Smith came in for the injured John Cowan. Wilkes was back in goal (pending the final transfer of George), and after a shaky start, gave a better display.

The Aston Villa Chronicles 1874 – 1924 (and after)

[From the *Sports Argus*] During the first 12 minutes, the Villa "kept the ball swinging about in front of the County goal, and working gradually nearer and nearer, Devey got an opening and scored a smart goal" and straight from the re-start, Jack Sharp scored a fine individual goal. This dual success was "received with tumultuous applause!" Later, Wheldon scored a third before County pulled one back before the interval.

In the second half, Wilkes was several times in action, but County were awarded a penalty kick – against Evans for holding off an attacker – and it was duly converted. It was now 3-2.

The Villa then pulled themselves together and stepped up their attacks until Jack Sharp scored Villa's fourth. It was Sharp's fifth goal in three games.

Smith disappointed on his return – he was not the player of old. James Cowan was back to his very best, doing the work of five men as he once used to.

In passing ...

The FA Cup was being shown at the Crystal Palace. "Perhaps the Villa people don't want to encourage the burglar any more! " *With implied reference to the 1895 theft.*

At the Everton vs Liverpool match there was further evidence of the sudden increase in interest in football. 40,000 spectators turned up for a League match – a new record!

From the *Sports Argus*, 16 October, 1897

Gates at 'Villa Park' were already beginning to steady at 20,000 and above, whereas at one time (at Perry Barr) 12,000 was thought "good".

From the *Sports Argus*, 6 November, 1897

George was now officially in place in goal, and would play the next few matches until Whitehouse returned from injury.

The away match at **Sunderland** was not of great merit, with Villa being below par, and gave chances to Sunderland that they spurned in the 0-0 draw.

Comments on some of the players (from the *Sports Argus* report of the match):

- George: "A mighty puncher."
- Jack Sharp: Not a strong 'pivot' – Campbell was being missed. *It was probably not helping Sharp's cause that he was played out of position – as he would prove when he went to Everton two years later.*
- Jack Devey: Far from being his old self; slow. *The Villa minutes of this time mentioned the sciatica that he had declared to the committee, doubtless causing his lack of pace.*

The Aston Villa Chronicles 1874 – 1924 (and after)

Spencer had recovered, but yet *another* indisposition kept him out from playing, and the long-term view not being good, it caused the Villa to go out and purchase another full-back – **Tommy Bowman**, from Blackpool. He would give good service over the next four years.

For the visit of **Liverpool**, John Cowan had recovered from injury and replaced Smith.

[From the *Sports Argus*] "The [Villa] ground was in beautiful order" and a large crowd attended, probably attracted more by the first home appearance of Billy George than by the presence of Liverpool. He played a fine game.

The match was not a high-class one, but it was hard-worked, the Villa showing a definite improvement on the previous match.

The first goal came after 25 minutes, Wheldon heading in from an Athersmith cross, and then, just before half-time, Jack Sharp's pass from the right found Athersmith, who scored with a fine shot.

The early part of the second half saw Devey and John Cowan both sending hard drives that skimmed the bar, but then Liverpool pulled a goal back. Athersmith had a hand in Villa's third goal as well – he supplied the centre for Devey to shoot home.

After this result, Villa were still in second place on 16 points, but three points behind the leaders, Sheffield United, after 11 games.

November, 1897

With Wheldon playing for the Football League, Fisher deputised at inside-left in the 1-3 defeat at **Preston**.

[From the *Sports Argus*] The match was an ordinary, plodding game with little to distinguish it from a Villa point of view except that Fisher scored a brilliant goal to equalise the score in the first half. The Villa otherwise gave a "terribly weak and disappointing exhibition", though James Cowan again distinguished himself, and B. Sharp was showing up well as Spencer's deputy.

It was heard that 'carpetings' had been administered to the team after this display.

As at Perry Barr, wet weather frequently affected the **Everton** 'gate', and this day was no exception.

[From the *Sports Argus*] The ground was in a "sodden and holding state" with a wind blowing straight downfield. Despite the conditions, there was a pleasing display of football, as was the usual case between these teams. The Villa had considerably improved and outplayed Everton, scoring two goals in

The Aston Villa Chronicles 1874 – 1924 (and after)

each half.

Chatt came back into the side for the first time for several games, replacing Burton, and he played his best game for some time, well supporting his forwards.

B. Sharp played a grand game from start to finish, and, as a left-footed player (though currently at right-back!) was expected to take over from Albert Evans when Spencer was fit. His brother Jack was kicked badly early on, and was limping through much of the game.

Strangers in Aston Park!

A solemn-looking old gentleman, whilst leisurely walking in Aston Park on a Saturday afternoon, seemed greatly interested by the groups of men hurrying past him. At last, he went up to one and said:

A Lion's Fun

"It is very pleasant to observe the intelligence displayed by the Birmingham artisans. Their week's work finished, see how they flock to the beautiful park to inhale the healthy ozone."

The other man contemporaneously expectorated, pulled his hat a little over his right eye, and replied: "Garn away, old 'Un, they don't come 'ere after no bloomin' ozoned! This is the nighest cut to the Villa's ground!"

Evidently, news of the Villa's move of ground had not yet reached everyone's ears!

Sports Argus 5 February, 1898

Fisher was brought in for the injured Jack Sharp at **Bolton**, but this was another very disappointing performance (0-2). Significant changes were then made for the home match against **Sunderland**, the biggest surprise, perhaps, being the move of B. Sharp from right-back to right-half, with recent signing Bowman selected at right-back. However, John Devey had to bow out because of his sciatica problem, and with Jack Sharp injured and Fisher no longer performing well as a pivot, two reserve players came into the forward line. What could this make-shift team do against Sunderland?

Villa: *George; Bowman, Evans; B. Sharp, Jas.Cowan, Crabtree; Athersmith, Harvey, Suddick, Wheldon, John Cowan.*

[From the *Sports Argus*] The rain was incessant, and the players were slipping and sliding all over the place. However, Harvey opened his Villa account with a goal on 4 minutes, but Sunderland began to get their game together and were level three minutes later. Just before half-time, they went into a deserved lead, and led 1-2 at the interval. The Villa had been ragged in the first half.

The Aston Villa Chronicles 1874 – 1924 (and after)

When John Cowan was fouled a few minutes into the second half, Wheldon converted the penalty, only for Sunderland to re-take the lead within only one minute. 2-3 to Sunderland after 50 minutes.

This prompted Villa into aggression and they then swarmed around Ned Doig, the long-serving Sunderland keeper. It took some while to get past him, but eventually Harvey headed in to equalise.

Now outplaying Sunderland, "in went the Villa again for all they were worth, and yells of satisfaction went up from thousands of throats as from a smart centre by Athersmith, the ball was cleverly hooked into the net by Wheldon!"

A game to be remembered for a long time to come, for, considering the state of the pitch, there was an excellent game of football with plenty of excitement.

Wheldon, Crabtree and James Cowan were the best of the team, and B. Sharp did well, though was considered to be a better back.

From Old Square to Villa Park

Hitherto, cabs had charged sixpence for the journey, but then tried to charge one shilling. If the prospective hirer disagreed he was abruptly told to "get out and walk!" The council intervened, restored the charge to sixpence and made the cab owners display the charge.

At the end of November, the Villa were still in second place, but although Villa had not dropped any points at home, they were being badly let down by their away form.

December, 1897

Blackburn were now due at Villa Park. Whitehouse had returned after injury, and was still regarded as the first-choice keeper, but Jack Sharp and Devey were still unavailable, so Fisher was again tried at centre-forward. Bowman and Evans were continuing a partnership that would continue through nearly the whole of the remaining season.

Villa: *Whitehouse; Bowman, Evans; B. Sharp, Jas.Cowan, Crabtree; Athersmith, Harvey, Fisher, Wheldon, John Cowan.*

[From the *Sports Argus*] After Villa had somehow been unable to score, though the ball was constantly hovering round the Rovers' goal, Rovers broke away and score first. Then, after an average period of play, Athersmith put in several dangerous centres which the forwards failed to convert until one rebound reached Crabtree, and he hit home to bring the scores level. Before the interval, Wheldon headed in to put the Villa into the lead, 2-1, though it was Rovers that had played the better in that half.

The Aston Villa Chronicles 1874 – 1924 (and after)

It was some time in the second half before the Villa made their mark, and not much was expected when Fisher beat some defenders and passed to Athersmith, who, running at full speed, shot home.

Villa remained in the ascendant, and after one shot hit the crossbar and bounced over, James Cowan shot from distance, the ball hitting an upright before settling in the back of the net.

Twice more the Villa came close, and then John Cowan sent a shot that went against the crossbar before going into the net.

> The Villa were now playing with more cohesion – at home at least.
>
> Bowman ("a lithe and sturdy customer") and Harvey were showing up well, Harvey becoming a good partner to Athersmith, who was notoriously difficult to partner on account of his speed.
>
> B. Sharp had developed into a good half-back – superior to either Chatt or Burton.

Three away matches followed. **Stoke** had beaten the leaders Sheffield United the previous week, but this game was spoilt by fog in a goal-less draw. As Stoke wore maroon shirts, they could be barely distinguished from the Villa players; "the way Athersmith disappeared into the fog was very laughable!"

At **Everton**, they had "a spice of luck about their victory" as Villa's attack – with Devey returned to it – deserved more, they hitting the bar five times in the match.

Against **Wolves**, there was another typical 'derby', but the two teams used contrasting styles – the combination play of the Villa against the determined and wing-style play of the Wolves. At 1-1, the result was a fair one, though Athersmith was injured in the middle of the second half and was then unable to "raise a gallop".

The end of the year's League table saw the Villa back at the top, but with Sheffield United having played three games less and being only one point behind, the Villa's ability to stay at the top would be tested in the next two matches. Both of them were to be against Sheffield United!

Leading Positions in Division 1 December 27th, 1897	Pld	Home W D L F A	Away W D L F A	Overall W D L F A	Pts
1 Aston Villa	19	9 0 0 34 15	1 4 5 10 18	10 4 5 44 33	24
2 Sheffield United	16	4 3 0 16 10	4 4 1 18 10	8 7 1 34 20	23
3 Sheffield Wednesday	18	8 0 2 26 7	1 3 4 7 13	9 3 6 33 20	21
4 Wolverhampton Wanderers	18	6 3 1 21 9	2 2 4 11 14	8 5 5 32 23	21
5 West Bromwich Albion	17	6 4 0 18 8	2 1 4 11 16	8 5 4 29 24	21

The Aston Villa Chronicles 1874 – 1924 (and after)

January, 1898

The first of the top-of-the-table clashes against **Sheffield United** was something of a disappointment. The ground was so heavy and slippy that it made it difficult for the players to keep their feet. "Hard kicking [was] more frequently seen than pretty combination", and it was the Villa half-backs and backs that shone the most in the match in which Villa lost 0-1.

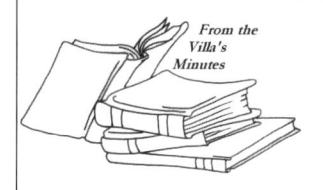

> *From the Villa's Minutes* On 13 January, it was reported to the committee that it had been heard that John Reynolds was not happy at Celtic, and wanted to return to Villa if terms could be arranged. Resolved: To inform John Reynolds, "No opening for a half-back at the moment."

The Villa had relaxed at Droitwich in mid-week in part-preparation for the second battle of the Titans. John Cowan (not in form last week) was rested in favour of Steve Smith.

Villa: *Whitehouse; Bowman, Evans; B. Sharp, Jas.Cowan, Crabtree; Athersmith, Harvey, Devey, Wheldon, Smith.*

[From the *Sports Argus*] The first half was goal-less, though vigorously played, but what followed was amazing in view of the fact that United's centre was injured in the first half and did not re-appear in the second.

In the later stages of the game, United – "with a grand half-back line", including Needham – "overplayed their opponents ... they were the Villa's superiors in the vitally important matters of dash and staying power. ... The home men again exhibiting a tendency towards pretty but ineffective work, which has been the cause of their undoing on more than one occasion this season. I cannot speak too highly of United's play. ... Devey was terribly slow at times and he did not keep his wings going as he used to do ... At half, Cowan stood out head and shoulders above both Crabtree and Sharp ..."

It was the Villa that opened the scoring, however, through a Wheldon penalty, but then the United took over, winning 1-2 despite Wheldon bringing out a marvellous save from Foulkes. Villa's 100% home record was lost – and the Villa effectively lost hope for the championship.

Interestingly, "Athersmith ... appeared to have a roaming commission in this instance, being all over the shop at times."

The Aston Villa Chronicles 1874 – 1924 (and after)

The *Sports Argus* (the following week) produced some statistics on the match – one of the earliest attempts to do so:

		Corners	Shots on goal	Fouls Against	Offside Against
First Half	AV	3	9	4	2
	SU	4	6	2	1
Second Half	AV	2	9	9	3
	SU	6	8	4	1

> ### *About John Devey*
>
> Noting a decided weakness in the Villa front-line shortly after the ball was in motion, I watched him very closely, and with not a little sympathy. He looked anxious and harried, and his inability to go the pace and get the ball was evidently as disappointing to himself as it was to his tens of thousands of admirers among the spectators.
>
> 'Veteran', *Sports Argus*, 22 January, 1898
>
> *Note: 'Sciatica' had previously been referred to as a complaint that Devey was suffering from, but in the next match he was left out as result of rheumatism.*

This was another strange situation of a league fixture being the exact fore-runner to a Cup sequel. Jack Sharp – fit again – replaced the ailing Devey to play at **Derby**. There was a feeling that both sides were saving themselves for the Cup match, but the score belied the fact that Villa had more shooting chances, and, until half-time, it had been an equal match. Villa's goal came as a result of a long high return from Jack Sharp, from just over the half-way line, which the keeper partially saved, but could not prevent from entering the net.

Following this match, the Villa had dropped to fourth place in the League table, and were seven points behind the leaders, Sheffield United.

In the Cup sequel, John Cowan replaced Harvey at inside-right (he "having to stand down"), and James Cowan was noted as being the Villa's captain in the absence of Devey. The 'gate' was a record for **Derby**.

[From the *Sports Argus*] This was an entirely different match to that of the previous week. The Villa were all over the County in the first half and it was estimated that the score should have been three or four in Villa's favour by the interval, instead of the half being goal-less. The Villa's approach play was good, but the shooting was woeful, though the Derby keeper made several saves.

The Aston Villa Chronicles 1874 – 1924 (and after)

Derby scored their goal six minutes into the second half, but the Villa, on occasions, literally swarmed round the Derby goal but could not score. Athersmith and John Cowan even switched places on the right-wing, and that created even more mayhem in the Derby defence. It was just not Villa's day when, towards the end, Crabtree had a shot just tipped over the bar by the keeper.

For the visit of **Preston**, the weather was delightful at Villa Park. Preston were much weaker than the previous season (when they finished fourth and gave the Villa several testing games), particularly in the forward line, and consequently were not regarded as a "good watch". And so it proved in this match; the Preston defenders were heavily worked. The Villa led 3-0 by half-time, and should have won by more than 4-0.

There was no further League football played for another month, but other matches were played. The first was a friendly in near-gale conditions at Sunderland, where Jack Sharp – recognising that perhaps centre-forward was not his real position – was for the first-time tried on the right-wing. This was considered a success, as he gave "the Sunderland backs any amount of trouble", though Villa lost the match, 1-4.

The Villa then had another hiding (at home this time) against Wolves in the Birmingham Cup semi-final. Villa lost 0-5, *but Wolves then lost to Walsall in the Final, 0-3!*

During this time, keeper Tom Wilkes was transferred to Stoke, but apparently on a loan basis. After a good 1895-96 season, "he did not appreciate the rising of Whitehouse, and his chagrin when George appeared on the scene was quite beyond words."

Sports Argus, 5 March, 1898

In the latter half of February, Charlie Johnstone (as a director of the club) organised a playing tour of Norfolk for the team, and after going out in Norwich town and enjoying themselves in the usual way, Charlie recalled:

A Lion's Fun

> About two in the morning I had my lambs safely corralled and in bed – at least, I thought I had! Alas – I was wrong! I hardly began my beauty sleep when the landlord, who, by the way, was a Norwegian and could swear in four different languages, came then erring at my door. The 'boys' were having a beano! Bursting open the [lounge] door – using the foaming landlord as buffer – I found the whole crew holding an assault-at-arms. Crabtree and Devey – stripped to the waist and armed with pillows – were giving a

The Aston Villa Chronicles 1874 – 1924 (and after)

> burlesque display of boxing. The landlord – much to his disgust – was installed as timekeeper, Bob Chatt and Charlie Athersmith being told to see that he did his duty!
>
> Charlie Johnstone's column in the *Sporting Mail,* 9 February, 1907

March, 1898

Winning 4-1 against **Derby** at home, the Villa obtained some satisfaction after losing their FA Cup dual a few weeks before, but it was felt that Derby were saving themselves for their FA Cup semi-final tie. For Villa, Athersmith and Wheldon were away playing for England versus Ireland. The Villa attack were buzzing, however, and "Fisher quite delighted the spectators with his clever tricks with the ball and [his] judicial passing."

At last – another away win! Crabtree and James Cowan kept **Bury** out whilst the Villa forwards played "a very well controlled game". Villa's opening goal followed some very neat forward play, and was beautifully put away by Sharp. The second, by Wheldon, saw him get past two defenders and then "put in a shot that fairly nonplussed [the keeper]."

> On 19 March, the Villa played Small Heath in a friendly – at Muntz Street – before 500 spectators, and won 3-0 without exerting themselves in the second half.

Against **Nottingham Forest**, the Villa, when 0-3 down near the end of the first half, lost an opportunity to pull one back when James Cowan missed a penalty. Forest played a very fast game that took them to their unassailable lead before the Villa could get started. Villa, however, did pull a goal back in the second half.

April, 1898

Relegation-threatened **Stoke** came to Villa Park with a determination to stay up, and included their on-loan keeper, Villa's Tom Wilkes. Villa had several first-team players absent, and two, Athersmith and Wheldon, were on duty for England. Stoke forced a 1-1 draw.

The Villa ground was in a very bad state for the match against **Wolves**. With the Villa losing 1-2, it was commented: "… there is something radically wrong somewhere … a vast improvement will have to be made for next season …"

The 0-4 defeat at **Liverpool** evoked a similar comment to that made following the preceding match. There had been a series of disappointing performances, though the team had been chopped around a great deal of late.

The Aston Villa Chronicles 1874 – 1924 (and after)

Another experimental Villa side was put out for this final game against **Nottingham Forest**, and yet *another* centre-forward. The Villa had newly signed **George Johnson** from Walsall, and he scored on this, his début. Villa won.

The Football League Division 1 1897-98 Top Places	Pld	Home W D L F A	Away W D L F A	Overall W D L F A	Pts
1 Sheffield United	30	9 4 2 27 14	8 4 3 29 17	17 8 5 56 31	42
2 Sunderland	30	12 2 1 27 8	4 3 8 16 22	16 5 9 43 30	37
3 Wolverhampton Wanderers	30	10 4 1 36 14	4 3 8 21 27	14 7 9 57 41	35
4 Everton	30	11 3 1 33 12	2 6 7 15 27	13 9 8 48 39	35
5 Sheffield Wednesday	30	12 0 3 39 15	3 3 9 12 27	15 3 12 51 42	33
6 **Aston Villa**	30	12 1 2 47 21	2 4 9 14 30	14 5 11 61 51	33
7 West Bromwich Albion	30	8 5 2 25 16	3 5 7 19 29	11 10 9 44 45	32
8 Nottingham Forest	30	7 5 3 30 19	4 4 7 17 30	11 9 10 47 49	31

		1897-98 League and FA Cup Results								
Sep	1st H	Sheffield Wed	5-2	8000	Dec	11th H	Blackburn Rovers	5-1	16000
	4th H	West Bromwich A	4-3	20000		18th A	Stoke	0-0	10000
	11th A	Notts County	3-2	15000		25th A	Everton	1-2	
	18th H	Bury	3-1	16000		27th A	Wolves	1-1	
	25th A	Blackburn Rovers	3-4	10000	Jan	8th A	Sheffield United	0-1	
	27th A	Sheffield Wed	0-3			15th H	Sheffield United	1-2	43100
Oct	2nd H	Bolton Wanderers	3-2	20000		22nd A	Derby County	1-3	10000
	9th A	West Bromwich A	1-1	20000		29th A	Derby Cty (FAC)	0-1	
	16th H	Notts County	4-2		Feb	5th H	Preston North End	4-0	15000
	23rd A	Sunderland	0-0	20000	Mar	5th H	Derby County	4-1	15000
	30th H	Liverpool	3-1	25000		12th A	Bury	2-1	
Nov	6th A	Preston North End	1-3	5000		26th A	Nottingham Forest	1-3	
	13th H	Everton	3-0	15000	Apr	2nd H	Stoke	1-1	
	20th A	Bolton Wanderers	0-2	12000		11th H	Wolves	1-2	
	27th H	Sunderland	4-3	15000		16th A	Liverpool	0-4	
						30th H	Nottingham Forest	2-0	

End of Season Postscripts

Of course, the previous season produced the Villa's best possible attainment, so it is possible that whatever happened in 1897-98 may have been seen as a disappointment.

Villa's problems had been a lot to do with the departure of Reynolds and Campbell, who had been such vital cogs in the previous seasons. No proper replacement had come in for either player, although B. Sharp seems to have done better than either Chatt or Burton in the right-half slot. At centre-forward it had been more of a problem, exacerbated by the fact that John Devey – with his rheumatic ailment – did not play in the last ten matches following an earlier absence from a few matches. And the talented wing-man Jack Sharp – mostly tried at centre-forward – was not going to be selected at outside-right while Charlie Athersmith was available. It is quite remarkable today to observe that though Jack Sharp had scored twelve goals in sixteen matches at centre-forward, that that was not seen as his proper position.

The absence of Spencer had also been very problematic. Strangely, it had led to Albert Evans playing in every match of the season at full-back, though the left-footed B. Sharp had been tipped to replace him if Spencer had returned. Conversely, as B. Sharp had been tried at half-back after full-back Bowman had been bought, that move eventually contrived to block Sharp's progress as a first-teamer.

There had been some suspicion in the Press that, owing to the below par performances of the past season, and queries concerning some decisions made by the Board of Directors, there would be an upheaval at the AGM that year. However, no upheaval transpired, although Mr. Margoschis stood down from the chairmanship and the Board, due to poor health. Mr. Rinder was elected in his place as chairman, and W. Cooke became the replacement director. The *Sports Argus* considered Mr. Rinder to be "of the shrewd and far-seeing type and able to give practical advice on keeping one's mouth shut!"

In the spring of 1898, Burnley proposed that the First Division be extended to 18 clubs, and this proposal was carried. The history of Blackburn Rovers – who finished in the bottom-two the previous season – reveals that:

> The news was received with unfeigned joy in Blackburn. ... [It should not be forgotten] that while the issue hung in the balance, the Blackburn club received a letter from Mr. G. B. Ramsay, on behalf of Aston Villa F.C., who after mentioning that the Birmingham club would vote for the extension of the League, said:
>
> > 'If it is carried you will [automatically] come back to the First Division, but if it is not, no one will regret it more than the club I have the honour to represent, and we will be pleased, for bare expenses, to come to Blackburn and play a benefit match in order to help you. Again I assure you of our sincere sympathy.'
>
> All honour to the Villa for their sportsmanlike offer![344]

---

[344] Charles Francis: "History of Blackburn Rovers 1875-1925" (Classic Reprint)

The Aston Villa Chronicles 1874 – 1924 (and after)

Season 1898-99: Champions for the Fourth Time!
League Division 1 position: *Champions;* **FA Cup:** *1st Round.*
The First Division was extended to 18 clubs.

For the new season, the Board had to consider very seriously the situation concerning two of the club's stalwarts of the 'double' campaign, Devey and Spencer, and also had to negotiate quite hard to keep the services of Athersmith and Wheldon, amongst other players. The keeper, Whitehouse, refused to sign, and that seems to have caused Tom Wilkes (who had returned from the loan to Stoke) to re-sign, although earlier he had seemed set to sign permanently for Stoke.

Regarding the matter of John Devey and his unavailability through a good part of the previous season, the Board discussed his matter at length on 21 April, and determined that if his leg broke down, he would be required to help out the club in other ways. As it happened, Devey's career was re-ignited over the next two years, and he would go on to play for another four years in total, though his best years had probably already passed by – he was approaching the age of 32.

At the meeting on 26 April, the Board had to consider the pay claims of Athersmith and Wheldon, Villa's current England internationals. They were both asking for more than the wage usually received by the regular first-teamers, and it would appear that they combined to put pressure on the Board. A three hour meeting was held with those players at the Holte Hotel, and the matter was finally resolved at the meeting on 5 May – as an "emergency decision" – to pay each of them £6 per week all year round, and a bonus each of £12 10s, rather than lose them. At the time, these were thought of as considerable wages, but the retention of these star players proved to be very worthwhile in the next season.

From the Villa's Minutes
At the 26 April meeting a letter was read from William McGregor that suggested a free invitation to matches for all the elementary schools in and around Birmingham. It was agreed, and the matter left to 'Mac'. A suggestion was made that a party should be no more than 20 from each school, accompanied by a teacher. They should view the match from the cycling track.

George Johnson (centre-forward) had been signed near the end of the previous season and was to play a significant part in this upcoming season's campaign. But there were more playing additions to the squad for the start of the season, the most successful being **Albert Wilkes** – a half-back from Walsall (like Johnson), and was Tom Wilkes' brother. The former Sheffield United forward **Richard Gaudie** was

The Aston Villa Chronicles 1874 – 1924 (and after)

bought at no small price, and a certain expensive 19-year-old **Bobby Templeton** also arrived from Hibernian – but he would not yet make his impact.

For Jack Sharp it was going to be an interesting second season – but a diamond that would be lost to the Villa. His departure would prove to be controversial. His co-adventurer and brother, Bertram Sharp, seemed to lose his way in this upcoming season after starting so promisingly as a full-back in 1897-98, but had been moved to half-back.

> *Jack Sharp*
>
> I feel convinced that the Villa have in him an outside-right who is quite good enough to take Athersmith's position without the slightest detriment to his side …
>
> 'Veteran', *Sports Argus*, 10 September, 1898

Bob Chatt had been a stalwart for much of the past five years, but had lost his form and consequently returned to the north-east. Frank Burton, like Chatt was a stalwart over a similar length of time, but never quite being a permanent first-teamer finally left the Villa in the autumn, for Bristol Rovers. Burton was given the rare privilege for a non-regular first-team player of being granted a benefit match, so much did the Board appreciate his attitude. Some players that were tried in the 1897-98 season, such as Fisher and Harvey, were transferred.

Howard Spencer

There was an astonishing stand-off situation that occurred between the Villa and their great full-back, Howard Spencer. When the season started, he still had not signed on. It had been reported in the *Sports Argus,* 6 August, 1898, that because of the last season's lengthy incapacity of Spencer through injury (and from which the specialist had pronounced him recovered), he was to be given two months' trial by the Villa. If the trial was successful, then Spencer would be paid £2 per week to cover the close-season from May to August, and then re-engagement would be at the usual rate. If his knee were to give way, then the close season money would be paid in this situation also, with the addition of a benefit match with a guarantee of £100. At this stage, there was a cloud between Spencer – who wanted an unconditional agreement – and the directorate.

The matter had still not been cleared later in August (just prior to the start of the season), and the *Sports Argus* sent a reporter to Spencer's home, the main parts of the interview being as follows:

The Aston Villa Chronicles 1874 – 1924 (and after)

In opening, Spencer said: "In the first place, I should like to say that my disagreement with the [Villa Board] is not now a question of terms. I don't know where all the facts have come from respecting the terms the Villa offered me, but I must say I don't think the committee ought to be so anxious to give information to the Press on the salaries their players are receiving. Some of the statements that have been made about me are sheer nonsense, and the information Mr. Ramsay gave you is not quite correct."

Q (from the interviewer): "Is it a fact that the [Villa Board] have offered you the same terms as last year?"

HS: "Yes they have, but I have had to refuse them."

Q: "The [Villa Board] stipulated for certain conditions, did they not? [these were the conditions outlined in the *Sports Argus'* report of 6 August, above.]"

HS: "Yes, and I did not feel justified in agreeing to them."

Q: "You did not think that good enough?"

HS: "No, I did not. The [Villa Board] wanted me to take all the risk and have none themselves. When I signed on five years ago, after playing a few matches the season before as an amateur, the [Villa Board] promised that football should not interfere with my business, and I made it quite clear to them that my business would have to stand first. I was not to devote the whole of my time during the season to the club, and we have got on exceedingly well up to now. The [Villa Board] have hitherto placed implicit faith in me, and except when I have been unwell – when no man is in form – I have always turned out fit. In fact, I have never received a single complaint as regards training since I have played for the Villa. The [Villa Board] arranged I should train on Tuesday and Thursday nights instead of during the daytime like the other players, and I have always held to that arrangement and trained regularly."

Q: "Then you think that if the Villa required your services they should have done so without requiring any conditions?"

HS: "I do. I met with the accident whilst I was playing for them, and as a result I have suffered considerably more loss than the club in point of fact. The Villa lost practically nothing over my accident. They made it appear as though they have lost a lot, but it is nothing of the kind, for I was insured, and my salary was therefore paid by the insurance company. At the outside, it did not cost the Villa more than £50.[345] On the other hand, look what it cost me. I was away from my business in Birmingham for three months – six weeks in Manchester and six weeks in London [receiving specialist treatment] – but the [Villa Board] don't take this into consideration. ... I attended a

---

[345] My observation here is that HS was not being totally fair – the club had lost (through innocent injury) the services of probably the best full-back playing at that time, and his absence almost certainly affected the team's below-par results in 1897-98 (i.e. "below par" as against the marvellous preceding 'double' season).

The Aston Villa Chronicles 1874 – 1924 (and after)

[Villa Board] meeting in June and the [Villa Board] then made the offer. I at once told them that I could not possibly accept it. I told them I lost a lot of time at business last year, and as they were not prepared to offer me the old terms without the conditions, I should give up football for this season and devote more time to business. That's how the matter stands and I have heard nothing from the [Villa Board] since. [the interview then went on to discuss the benefit offer, which HS declared he was entitled to anyway – if he wanted it.]

Q: "Then have you quite given up the idea of playing again this season?"

HS: "I think so. I must really devote more time to business this year after what I lost last season. I don't see my way clear at present to play this season and I have told the [Villa Board] so, so you will see the question of terms is not now in it."[346]

[Further questions and answers of lesser importance were reported.]

> 'Argus Junior' commented that he wondered how much the shareholders knew about this matter, and what their opinion would be. He wrote of the outcome of this disagreement: "They have lost the services, this season, of the finest back the club ever had."

The interview with Spencer, however, did illicit the loose training and playing arrangement that Spencer had with the club, that probably would not be possible today, or even (for that matter) ten or twenty years after this incident.

The matter progressed to late October. George Ramsay was then reported[347] as having stated that Villa would give Spencer his own terms provided that Spencer's leg was absolutely sound. Ramsay is alleged also to have said, or implied, that Spencer had always been a little ashamed of being a professional, and was – according to Ramsay – under the impression that he had conferred a great favour on the Villa by condescending to play for them.

Just as the Villa were getting their game together and challenging for the top spot, 'The Veteran' (in the *Sports Argus* of 12 November) wrote, in relation to Spencer, "While the breeze fills the sails of the Villa craft, nobody on board will effect any serious concern for shipmates left behind."

However, by that week, and despite strained relations between Spencer and the Board, Spencer finally agreed to get the requisite medical certificate and to get back into training. By the 26th November, Spencer had signed up once more, and was preparing to play for the reserves as soon as possible. The matter had at last been

---

[346] Printed in Sports Argus, 27 Aug 1908
[347] Sports Argus 29 Oct 1898

resolved, but such had been the success of Villa's play so far that season, and achieved without him (though Villa did have trouble in properly filling the right-back slot), his re-entry to the Villa team was not hurried. He was not to play in the first team until after the best part of February had passed.

> ***Villa's Ground Not Called "Villa Park"?***
>
> The *Sports Argus* asked: "Are we to see the silly attempt to dub the Villa's new home 'Villa Park' wiped out completely this season? Let us hope so."[348]
>
> It was further reported that a concerted opinion of the Villa management was that the ground should be known as 'Aston Villa Grounds' (formerly, of course, named 'Aston Lower Grounds'). This (it was stated) "is sensible and reasonable", and the term was used in subsequent *Sports Argus* reports – though only for a season or so!
>
> *The title 'Villa Park' seems (I suggest) to have better stood the test of time!*
>
> *It should be noted, however, that when the Aston Villa company was formally registered (in 1897), the grounds' address was given as "Aston Villa Grounds", Aston, Birmingham, and remained so registered till well ca. 1969.*

In addition to the loss of Spencer in the early season, Freddie Wheldon committed a misdemeanour and was suspended by the club, as a result of which he would miss the first match. The problem was that Wheldon chose to finish his cricketing commitments in preference to fulfilling his responsibility to the Villa.

The Season's Play

September, 1898

Tommy Wilkes appeared against **Stoke,** the team he was on loan to at the end of the last season, and nearly permanently moved to prior to this season.

The Villa turned out in red shirts, a practice that would be taken up a lot in future opening games, as these shirts (as described in later years) appear to have been light shirts designed for hot conditions – which was the case on this particular day.

Villa: *T.Wilkes; Bowman, Evans; A.Wilkes, Jas.Cowan, Crabtree;*
Athersmith, Devey, Johnson, Gaudie, Smith.

[From the *Sports Argus*] "The sun blazed down on the players, and long before half-time, the men were mopping their foreheads ... It was certainly far too hot for serious play ... [and] it was indeed surprising that they kept up the pace so well."

---

[348] 'The Veteran' in Sports Argus 10 Sep 1898

The Aston Villa Chronicles 1874 – 1924 (and after)

In a very even first half, Athersmith opened the scoring with a "clinking" angled drive, but Stoke equalised soon after to make that the half-time score.

Midway through the second period, "Athersmith, Devey and Johnson were directly responsible for the hot shots that rained upon their keeper", but Villa were held at bay. "At last, Devey, breaking out from the ruck in the centre of the field, raced down in splendid style, and with a well-judged low shot, which gave the Stoke keeper no possible chance, scored the second goal."

"After a period of comparative quietness, the red colours became prominent once more, Crabtree skimming the bar with a long shot."

Evans and Cowan were cheered for their work in breaking up Stoke attacks, "but the Villa were the next to become really dangerous. Smith put in a nice centre which was received by Devey, who unfortunately dallied too long, and was overthrown just in the act of shooting. The disappointment was quickly compensated for a splendid attack by the Villa vanguard [which] ended in Gaudie registering the third goal." Villa pressed to score more, and "excitement ran high."

Although Stoke made efforts to come back into the match, it was Villa who were in the ascendant, with "Devey's final shot – a beauty – being only a little wide."

John Devey looked in "fine fettle!", but "no experienced observer can resist the conclusion that neither the League Championship nor the English Cup can be won with such faulty back play …"

"[Albert Wilkes] will be a useful man ... That he possesses the neck of an ox we can have no doubt about after the quick recovery from as ugly a fall on the head as I have seen on the football field …"

'Veteran', *Sports Argus*, 10 September, 1898

The Villa again turned out in red shirts at **Bury**.

Villa: *T.Wilkes; Bowman, Crabtree; A.Wilkes, Jas.Cowan, Gaudie; Athersmith, Devey, Johnson, Wheldon, Smith.*

[From the *Sports Argus*] "A stiff and stubborn conflict. Villa's short passing often futile because of long tufts of grass." However, there was some fine play by the Villa – and chances missed.

The Villa keeper was at fault for both their goals in the 1-2 defeat.

The Aston Villa Chronicles 1874 – 1924 (and after)

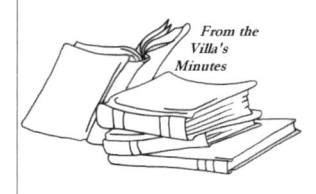

> *From the Villa's Minutes*
>
> Charlie Johnstone's proposal for a bonus scheme, put forward at the 15 September meeting, was approved. It was an accumulated scheme, paid at the end of the season. For wining the championship, it would be 30 shillings for each away win, and 20 shillings (£1) for each home win.
>
> A reducing scale down to sixth finishing place was provided for.

Burnley (a)

[From the *Sports Argus*] George replaced Wilkes in goal, and after Villa went down 0-1 after three minutes play, it was George's brilliant keeping that kept Villa in the game before Johnson sent Smith away, and he finished his run with a fine shot and the equaliser. Then a blocked shot of Wheldon's came back out for Johnson to put Villa ahead. Despite further good work by Villa, Burnley made it 2-2.

"The Villa played up in grand style, and the forwards, racing off at a fast rate, Johnson passed out to Athersmith, and the latter ran in and scored with a brilliant effort." The fast scoring wound up the crowd and the excitement was even greater when Burnley laid siege on the Villa goal, with Cowan clearing from under the Villa bar with George beaten!

The Villa went down the other end, however, and might have scored several more times. It was 3-2 at half-time.

The second half saw more Villa surges and the woodwork being hit. "Then came a beautiful pass by Wheldon to Smith, and the clever little forward ran away from all opposition. Hooking the ball past the full-back, he got in a grand [angled] shot almost from the line, and the twist that was on the ball caused it to swerve out of the keeper's hands and roll into the net! ... Smith's shot was as fine as anything seen from a Villa forward."

At the end, the margin of the win should have been more. There were few faults in the Villa team, but it was Villa's forwards and Cowan and Crabtree that caught the eye, aided by George in goal "who was a decided success ... some of his punches and clearances were master pieces."

> "[Crabtree] was in superb form ..." When dealing with the Burnley captain, Ross, "Crabtree smiled, and actually once laughed outright when he jabbed his foot down and took the ball away from the very toes of the Burnley captain. Ross was fairly mastered, and he didn't like it one bit."
>
> 'Argus Junior', *Sports Argus*, 24 September, 1898

The Aston Villa Chronicles 1874 – 1924 (and after)

Sheffield United (h)

[From the *Sports Argus*] Again, "the sun simply roasted players and spectators alike, and the former had had quite enough of it before the end. After a bright Villa start, the champions played Villa at their own combination game, but were ahead of the Villa in terms of commitment. "Villa had to work desperately hard for their point … a near squeak for them … and the way United held the home side for a good portion of the second half made the crowd very uneasy."

Although the Villa were lying in eighth place after this match, they were only two points off the leaders, Blackburn, and had a game in hand. The League was very open.

October, 1898

Next, away at **Newcastle United**, a 1-1 draw was achieved, but the *Sports Argus* stated that the Villa were guilty of too much fancy work, and the journal made complaints of the referee not looking for the regular use of hands by the home side.

Tootlin' too much!

"The vigorous and hard-working band of tootlers who toot the hard toot on match days are going to be taken in hand by Bandmaster Hughes of the Prince's End Prize Band. … Mr. Hughes, … would you kindly keep your Aston Church E.M.S. pupils from letting themselves go under the shadow of the grandstand? The sounds bang up against the zinc roofing and shoot straight down again in an ear-splitting volume, which makes spectators very wrathful and anxious for gore!"[349]

A Lion's Fun

Preston North End (h)

Villa: *George; Aston, Evans; Bowman, Jas.Cowan, Crabtree;*
Athersmith, Devey, Johnson, Wheldon, Smith.

[From the *Sports Argus*] Bowman was moved to right-half at the expense of Wilkes, and Bowman, Cowan and Crabtree heavily influenced the match outcome. Evans played his best game to date: "not afraid of good honest charging and heavy tackling."

It was Preston that scored after four minutes, with Devey later equalising. The Villa pursued the lead, and they "were not to be denied, for they dashed in again, and Smith, taking the ball away in brilliant style, he got in his centre, though badly hustled by a couple of opponents, and Devey put the finishing touch on amid great enthusiasm. Like the first goal, the second was entirely

---

[349] Sports Argus 8 Oct 1898

The Aston Villa Chronicles 1874 – 1924 (and after)

due to Smith's work, and that player was cheered again and again when he came down the field."

After further Villa attacking, "the ball was sent back to Cowan, and that player, getting round one or two opponents, sent in a ripping shot, which went straight into the net!" Leading 3-1, the Villa increased their attacks, but it was Preston that scored, from a corner, right on half-time.

After sometime in the second half, the game stagnated, and it was only through the shouts of the crowd that the Villa came back to life! The Preston keeper was forced into action a number of times, and then, after further sleep-walking, Johnson scored a fine individual goal to end the scoring.

> *From the Villa's Minutes*
> Charlie Johnstone reported (13 October) that he had visited former Villa full-back Jim Elliott and found him to be in a very weak state. The club agreed to assist in providing more nutritious foods.
>
> *Elliott, who had been playing only two years before, died the following year.*

Liverpool (h)

[From the *Sports Argus*] "A good exposition of football … At times, however, there was rather more illegal work indulged in than was desirable." The referee blew the whistle a lot, and some of his offside decisions "were absolutely contrary to fact."

Villa supporters were present in good numbers to see Smith being monitored by two players, but still "was a very awkward customer to deal with." After the Villa had gone into a 2-0 lead, the reverse caused Liverpool to up their game, but the Villa repulsed anything Liverpool offered. Wheldon added a third shortly into the second half, and Liverpool, though trying their best, were outplayed by the Villa for the remainder of the match.

"It was the greatest game the Villa have played away from home for a very long time." The Villa indulged in short and long passing in a manner which absolutely bewildered the Liverpool team.

For the home match against **Nottingham Forest**, there was a counter-attraction of the Birmingham Races at Castle Bromwich, and this, combined with the weather, affected the Villa's 'gate'. Evans was ill, whilst Athersmith would be out for several games with a leg injury, which provided Jack Sharp with a chance at outside-right.

Villa: *George; Aston, Haggart; Bowman, Jas.Cowan, Crabtree;*

J.Sharp, Devey, Johnson, Wheldon, Smith.

[From the *Sports Argus*] A strong wind was coming from "the City End" (i.e. the Holte End), and it was raining. The Villa were quickly into their stride,

The Aston Villa Chronicles 1874 – 1924 (and after)

and it was not long before Sharp netted when Smith's shot was deflected to him. The Forest warmly responded, and George had to save two or three shots in as many seconds. However, John Devey went on to score a fine goal and then added a simple third before half-time. This actually completed the scoring, yet the second half saw Villa play a better combination game.

> **Billy George**
>
> "... good as he was, has unquestionably developed ... His kicking out and fisting away – and, great Scott, can't he punch the ball! – are more vigorous and precise, and he isn't afraid of all the combined weight of half-a-dozen opponents being hurled at him at once. 'Nerves' are, I should imagine, foreign to him. Those are the little things which upset Wilkes.
>
> *Sports Argus*, 29 October, 1898

The weather again kept down the gate for the home match against **Bolton**, and comments were being made about the need to provide more cover for the spectators! It was Steve Smith's turn to be injured – he had torn knee ligaments – so, as with Athersmith he would be out for a few games, allowing John Cowan to have a period on the left-wing. Evans returned at left-back.

[From the *Sports Argus*] "The game was the best and most evenly contested we have seen on the Aston Villa Grounds this season." Villa's opponents played "capital football", and gave the Villa backs more trouble than they bargained for.

There was good opening football by both sides, then "Villa attacked strongly, and Sharp and Devey started some passing which eventually ended in a score. These two took the ball on and Devey passed to Johnson. The latter tried to get through, but finding himself unable, he sent across the goalmouth to Wheldon, who, being on the run, carried the ball into the net."

Substantial Bolton pressure kept the Villa defence occupied for some time, but the Villa came on again. "Sharp took a beautiful pass from Devey and would probably have got through and scored had not the referee given a rank bad decision in pulling him up for offside." The play then swung from end-to-end, and Johnson ended the half by heading against the crossbar.

More even play eventually resulted in Bolton increasing the pressure, and scored an equaliser. This only caused Villa to up their game, and after sustained attacks, Devey put the ball over the bar, "amidst groans of disappointment from the spectators." But Devey soon atoned, and scored Villa's second soon after a smart centre by John Cowan. Bolton, however, fought strongly to the end.

The Aston Villa Chronicles 1874 – 1924 (and after)

> ***Jack Sharp***
>
> On a day that saw Villa go to the top of the League table, a Bolton journalist declared that "[Sharp] was the best man on the field."
>
> *Scottish Sport* wrote, "Sharp's becoming one of the Aston crowd's biggest favourites …"
>
> The following week, 'Argus Junior', wrote: "One splendid and prominent feature of Sharp's play is that when on the run, he is always boring into goal."
>
> By the 12 November, the *Sports Argus* was declaring that Sharp was "the finest right-wing forward that the Villa have possessed for many a long day … When it comes to football … Sharp is by far the better man [than Athersmith]."

Derby County (h)

The Villa were without Crabtree (on duty for the Football League, together with Bloomer of Derby), so Wilkes deputised. On a day that Villa also continued to be without Athersmith and Smith, the Villa caused havoc amongst the Derby defence.

[From the *Sports Argus*] At the start, it appeared very likely that Derby were going to give Villa a very hard match, but that early sparkle from them went when the game settled down, and it instead became a one-sided match!

It was Devey that opened the scoring on eight minutes, followed by Johnson's "rasper" on 12 minutes, but then Derby pulled one back. However, by 30 minutes, it was 5-1 to the Villa and the game was effectively over, though Villa unsuccessfully pushed to add to their score before the break. Two more were added in the second half to make the score 7-1.

> "The Villa have overcome what has of late years been their besetting sin. They have often sacrificed strenuousness to mere cleverness. Now, science and artistry are excellent things in their place, and there is no crowd which enjoys a pretty piece of passing as the Lower Grounds crowd does, but this does not spell goals. And the Villa have at last realised this."
>
> *Sports Argus*, 12 November, 1898

It was announced that week that the "clever forward", Richard Gaudie (signed just before the start of the season), had been seriously ill and was unlikely to be seen in Birmingham again.

West Bromwich Albion (a)

[From the *Sports Argus*] Albion were lying in 12th place, but it was stated that no matter how much difference there is in league placings between these sides, the Albion invariably raise their game against the Villa. This game was

The Aston Villa Chronicles 1874 – 1924 (and after)

quite in keeping with tradition.

Villa's goal followed a "beautifully concerted movement" in the 36th minute, "Johnson, dashing through, scored with a terrific shot …" Johnson was going at such a pace, in fact, that his momentum caused him to bang into the keeper and floored him. The referee (John Lewis) refused to listen to the keeper's protests!

After that there was a terrible battle, and the Albion not only defended stoutly but could quite easily have equalised. There was also considerable bad temper between the players, requiring some expert handling by the referee.

With Johnson injured, but Athersmith returning, the Villa selectors' job was easier than it might have been for the home match against **Blackburn**.

Villa: *George; Aston, Evans; Bowman, Jas.Cowan, Crabtree; Athersmith, J.Sharp, Devey, Wheldon, Smith.*

[From the *Sports Argus*] Devey put the Villa in front after only two minutes, and this was followed by Sharp's "wonderfully good bit of individual work" that produced a shot that hit the bar. Villa continued to be the better side, and after 19 minutes, "there was some long combination among the forwards, and Athersmith, judging his centre nicely, slung the ball across and Wheldon headed in hard!"

The crowd were now on the best of terms with themselves and they further enjoyed a Crabtree screamer which went just wide. The Villa continued pressing till the break. After the interval, Blackburn eventually came back with a goal. This encouraged them to try again, and caused George some worry. Eight minutes from time, Wheldon put the result beyond doubt.

> *From the Villa's Minutes*
>
> The 24 November meeting heard that there had been an article in the previous week's press reporting that the Villa had enquired into players' dissatisfaction with George Ramsay, and found none. The investigation had been stimulated by a letter in the *Sports Argus* from someone who had signed himself as "A. Player". Fred Wheldon subsequently visited the editor's office and confirmed both that he was satisfied with his treatment at the Villa, and that he was not the writer of the letter.

After seven successive wins, and ten matches undefeated, the Villa's run came sliding to a halt, though it was a well-contested match at **Sheffield Wednesday**'s ground. Jack Sharp had been a prominent reason for the recent good run, but he was left out for this match and another young player – Bedingfield – brought in at centre-forward. Aside from scoring his side's goal, he did nothing else of particular note, nor indicated any promise in this his solitary game. His was an odd selection.

The Aston Villa Chronicles 1874 – 1924 (and after)

Steve Smith returned at outside-left.

The score was 1-3 on the day, but the match finished ten minutes early as reported in the Villa Minutes, below. The Villa were subsequently made to return to Sheffield (by the Football League) to play the remaining ten minutes, and that was when the Villa conceded a further goal. Thus the *official* result became 1-4.

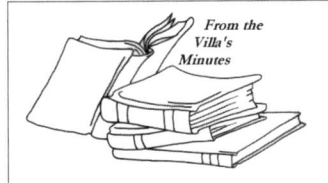

> *From the Villa's Minutes*
> The following week, the committee heard that the Sheffield match had been stopped ten minutes before time as it got dark. It was also said that the match was delayed on account of the referee not turning up till half-time!

When the news was heard in January (that the 10 minutes had to be played), the *Sports Argus* commented: "It has been the cause of really riotous merriment in football circles in Birmingham …"

Those 10 additional minutes were not played until March, 1899.

December, 1898

Sharp was promptly restored for this home match against a resurgent **Sunderland** – with Devey moving to centre-forward to accommodate him at inside-right.

[From the *Sports Argus*] It was Sharp that scored both goals; the first was a magnificent effort, and the second was an easier goal just before the end of the match. In between, Wheldon missed a penalty, but otherwise played a good match. George and the Villa defence were superb. "[Crabtree] again and again averted what appeared to be 'positive certainties' of Sunderland scoring, and he spoiled a score of openings [to Sunderland] …"

The selection decisions appeared to be getting stranger and stranger. Sharp – though he had just scored twice against a top side – was again left out, with the previously out-of-form centre-forward Johnson replacing him at inside-right.

The gate at the home match against **Wolves** was twice as many as the next highest League match that day.

[From the *Sports Argus*] The performance in this match was mediocre at times. "The crowd became very demonstrative, and loudly exhorted the men to 'play up'. The Wanderers went in for heavy and vigorous work, and they showed little inclination to go for the ball instead of the man." A match "best forgotten."

At home, versus **Everton**, Devey resumed at inside-right and Johnson at centre-forward – but there was still no Jack Sharp. His brother Bertram re-appeared at

The Aston Villa Chronicles 1874 – 1924 (and after)

right-back for the injured Aston as Spencer was still not available. James Cowan was out with a rheumatism problem; Albert Wilkes came in as his deputy. Everton were close on Villa's heels (Villa were still leading the League table), and, again, the gate at this match was twice as many as the next highest League match that day.

[From the *Sports Argus*] This match at least saw a return to good football. Wilkes, in his first game at centre-half, caused Cowan not to be missed. In winning 3-0, Johnson was back into his groove, and Wheldon's trickiness and clever control of the ball delighted the spectators, who were, however, no less enthusiastic about Smith's dazzling runs up the line and always-dangerous centres.

> *From the Villa's Minutes*
>
> On 22 December, it was reported that Howard Spencer had not suffered any ill-effects in his first match run-out (in the reserves, against Hereford Thistle).

The conditions at **Notts County** did not suit Villa's short passing game – the tactic they used. They were generally superior in their play, but let themselves down in their shooting, and finally conceded the match (0-1) to County with seven minutes to go.

At home against **Newcastle United**, an Athersmith goal divided the two teams in a close match.

At **Stoke**, there were wretched weather conditions, including ugly puddles scattered here and there. The ball dropped dead whenever it touched a puddle, and it often slipped off the players' toes. The players also found that their feet sometimes slid from underneath them! It was a match where Stoke simply adapted better to the conditions, and won – 0-3.

Despite the recent run of unimpressive results, the Villa were still leading the League table, the other clubs not having mounted a very serious contest. The Villa also had games in hand.

January, 1899

The defence was again re-arranged for the home match against **Bury**. After his few games' run, B. Sharp was left out, and Crabtree was pulled back to fill this position. Albert Wilkes came in at left-half. Crabtree was reported as, "the cleverest man on the field, standing head and shoulders above the other backs." After going into a 3-0 lead on 25 minutes, the Villa then proceeded to let the match very nearly slide away from them, conceding a goal before half-time, and another in the second half.

The Aston Villa Chronicles 1874 – 1924 (and after)

For the match against **Burnley**, Villa's ground did not look at all well. Red sand had been used to sprinkle the turf, and the carts that had been used as a conveyance had left ruts in the turf. They were not only visible but left impossible conditions for good football. However, George was a spectator in a one-sided match that Villa had decided on controlling from the very outset, and perhaps should have won by more than 4-0, against the side who were in third-place at the time.

Sheffield United (a)

[From the *Sports Argus*] The match was played in abominable weather, the rain coming down in drenching sheets.

It was Wilkes that gave the Villa the lead after three minutes, but despite Villa pressing hard, United equalised on 30 minutes, and this remained the score at the interval.

Johnson restored Villa's lead seven minutes into the second half, after Athersmith had beaten the United backs and got in a fine centre. Before the Villa made sure of the result with just ten minutes to go, it looked certain that United would again equalise, until Evans came in and cleared in the nick of time.

At the end, the United players were looking very tired in the poor playing conditions, but Villa – by comparison – finished well, and won the game by grinding down their opponents.

> ### *The Sheffield United Supporters*
> "It didn't matter whether a United man showed good, bad or indifferent form – he had only to touch the ball to make the excited partisans yell until their eyes bulged out and hung over their cheeks. And the number of times that the home players were exhorted to make corpses of their opponents was edifying in the extreme. But one's contempt was turned to disgust to find that the grandstand sheltered a good proportion of the well-dressed blackguardism. How pleasing it is to find such a healthier and more sportsmanlike state of things on the Aston Villa enclosure!"
>
> 'Argus Junior', *Sports Argus*, 28 January, 1899

Nottingham Forest (a)

[From the *Sports Argus*] Villa went behind after four minutes with a peculiar shot which beat George when the Villa custodian was out of his goal. Villa equalised this within three minutes, Johnson heading in a corner. But Forest were well-motivated, and in another two minutes, the Villa's crossbar was rattled, but only to divert the ball into the net. These three goals had been scored in the first nine minutes!

The Aston Villa Chronicles 1874 – 1924 (and after)

For the rest of the half, it was a question of the Forest having misfortune in not adding further goals, with Villa trying to get their game together. Villa had to be thankful for the fine work of Crabtree and Evans in this half.

The Villa were slightly better than Forest in the second half, but towards the end, "there was some very bad blood shown on both sides, there being several cases of men deliberately kicking each other in the most barefaced manner."

February, 1899

Preston North End (a)

[From the *Sports Argus*] A significant step forward was that although Crabtree was injured, Spencer came in for his come-back game. He was not yet showing his old abilities, but he did not do badly.

Severe recent frost did not affect good football, despite the hardness of the ground and the bitterly cold wind. However, though the Villa did not fully adapt to the conditions, they played much better than the previous week at Forest. The match was goal-less at half-time, but Preston – low in the League – did well in the second half, and won 0-2.

Leading Positions in Division 1 February 4th 1899	Pld	Home W D L F A	Away W D L F A	Overall W D L F A	Pts
1 Aston Villa	22	11 2 0 37 10	4 1 4 13 12	15 3 4 50 22	33
2 Liverpool	25	7 3 1 17 7	6 2 6 17 15	13 5 7 34 22	31
3 Everton	24	10 0 3 22 8	2 5 4 13 19	12 5 7 35 27	29

> The Villa played a friendly against the Corinthians, in London, on 11 February, ending in a 1-1 draw. The match evoked the comment (from 'Argus Junior'), "These friendly encounters a very flatulent fizzler nowadays."

Away at **Nottingham Forest**, Crabtree and Athersmith were out on England duty, and the Forest were missing two players for the same reason. This was not a great game, but it did improve after Forest scored their goal on 40 minutes. The Villa were guilty – as was often the case – of playing too prettily and passing in front of goal instead of shooting.

The Aston Villa Chronicles 1874 – 1924 (and after)

March, 1899

From the Villa's Minutes

On the 2 March, Charlie Johnstone submitted his resignation as director of the club, having being on the old committee from 1892, and had then become one of the first directors on the Villa becoming a limited company in 1896.

The reason was put down to failing health, and he had gone to Scotland "for a change of air".

Derby County (a)

[From the *Sports Argus*] "After 25 minutes play, and after some splendid work by Athersmith, the ball was whipped into the centre, and making the most of anything but an easy opening, Johnson scored a lovely goal with a stinging ground shot."

The Villa were back to something like their real form. "Crabtree paid such close attention to Bloomer that the Derby crack had very frequently to take a very backward seat indeed." Villa had numerous goal-scoring chances, but too often the ball was sent straight at the keeper. 1-1 was the final result.

The Villa's poor recent take-up of points allowed Liverpool to take over the League leadership after the 11 March fixtures.

At **Blackburn** Billy Garraty, who had been on Villa's books for eighteen months, but had only signed professional forms the previous summer, was selected in place of the unavailable John Devey. Goal-less, it was not a good match, but the Villa played better in the second half. The Villa then received **Sheffield Wednesday**.

Villa: George; *Spencer, Evans; Bowman, Jas.Cowan, Crabtree;*
Athersmith, Garraty, Johnson, Wheldon, Smith.

[From the *Sports Argus*] Second-from-bottom Wednesday forced Villa into a hard-fought first half, but the Villa broke through just three minutes from the break when Wheldon headed in Garraty's centre.

In the seond half, the Villa took greater control and added two more goals through Garraty and Johnson, before Wednesday pulled a goal back.

The Aston Villa Chronicles 1874 – 1924 (and after)

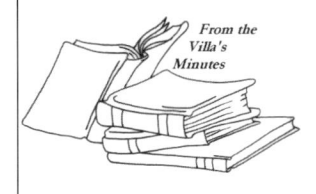

> *From the Villa's Minutes*
>
> At 30 March meeting, a highly poignant letter was read that had been received from Albert Allen, the former Villa stalwart, who had been gravely ill, and was dieing. He firstly stated how grateful he had been to receive a letter of sympathy from the club, and also wrote:
>
> "It shows that although my day is over, I am not forgotten by old comrades and friends ... May the old club still prosper and keep the foremost position in the Football World ..."

April, 1899

A much-changed Villa side was enforced in the visit to **Sunderland** because of Crabtree and Athersmith being on Football League duty (Crabtree was captain and was reported as being "the best man on the field" in the encounter with the Scottish League). Also, Johnson was injured, and would not play again this season; Garraty moved to centre-forward. Though there was opportunity to bring in Jack Sharp at outside-right, the selectors instead chose to give young Bobby Templeton his début.

[From the *Sports Argus*] Sunderland scored first in this encounter, but Devey equalised not long after. Sunderland had to wait until late on in the first half before they added two more goals to lead 1-3 at the break.

Sunderland were pulled-back at the start of the second period when Cowan's shot was not held by Doig, and it skewed into the net, but it was not long before Sunderland restored their two goal margin from a beautiful shot. The Villa pressed, but could not get back into the game, their shooting needing to be better "to put the finishing touches to some clever and smart midfield runs."

Though the Villa returned to something like their normal side, a 0-4 defeat at **Sheffield Wednesday** completed a miserable Easter for the Villa, having conceded eight goals in their two matches, and were in danger of losing their title chance (to Liverpool) after having led the table for much of the season.

> On 8 April, England played Scotland at Villa Park. Crabtree and Athersmith were on duty, with Crabtree again reported as being the game's outstanding player.

The 1-1 away draw at **Everton** was not a good game. Smith's opening score early in the second half was soon equalised by Everton, and at **Bolton**, the Villa again failed to pick up much-needed points and goals, but in fact both sides wasted chances.

The Aston Villa Chronicles 1874 – 1924 (and after)

Bolton played with great determination.

> ### *The Final Run-in*
>
> Over the previous few weeks, the Villa had had to make constant adjustments to the team. Most were mandatory, some not so. But whatever the reason, the results were not those expected from a potential championship-winning side.
>
> The Villa were at a critical juncture. They not only needed to target wins in their last three matches against Notts County, the Albion, and their title competitors – Liverpool – they also needed to score goals. The Villa and Liverpool had both now played 31 matches and were both on 39 points. But whereas Liverpool's goal average was 1.64, the Villa's was 1.53. The goal average would decide the difference if the Villa and Liverpool were to finish on the same number of points.
>
> So, plans were thought out and put into action. The Villa needed a reliable and committed set of players, and, apart from goalkeeper, the right-half and centre-forward, the available team was otherwise much the same as the 'double' winning side of two years previous. Only Garraty was a recent arrival in the team, necessitated by Johnson's injury. Thus, in the run-in, the team was to be:
>
> **Villa:** *George; Spencer, Evans; Bowman, Jas.Cowan, Crabtree;*
> *Athersmith, Devey, Garraty, Wheldon, Smith.*
>
> These last three matches within one week – all at Villa Park and against top-half opposition – were to be treated as the final stages of the FA Cup might have been.

For this series of matches, the club were to undertake a renewal regime in the manner of those taken when big Cup matches came about – there would be visits to Holt Fleet after each of the Notts County and Albion matches, in order for the players to re-charge their batteries.

The first match: Notts County (h)

[From the *Sports Argus*] The match did not start in the way in which it was hoped, though it might have had just the right affect; a stupendous shot from the County full-back, Bull, opened the scoring! However, Devey equalised a few minutes later – "a beauty ... greeted with tremendous cheers!"

Villa gradually stepped up their game, and Wheldon's header on 30 minutes was followed by two more goals within three minutes of half-time, giving Villa a 4-1 lead at the break. The first of these was a Devey volley from Athersmith's centre, and then Garraty headed in. In the process of scoring, Garraty was kicked in the face, but he recovered.

Devey got his hat-trick 15 minutes into the second half – another fine goal after weaving his way through the County defence. Then, it was a grand Smith

The Aston Villa Chronicles 1874 – 1924 (and after)

centre that enabled Garraty to score from a header, to make it 6-1.

Around the second half goals, there were many fine strikes on the County goal, and the crowd was in great humour. But the most pleasing aspect was that the Villa forwards were completely 'on song', with Wheldon and Smith casting off their various indifferent performances of late.

The Villa had made the appropriate start to their 'Cup Final campaign'.

The second match: West Bromwich Albion (h)

[From the *Birmingham Daily Post*] In the first 30 minutes, the Villa obtained a 3-goals advantage, and were well on their way to overhauling Liverpool's goal average. Then Albion scored, and that score gave a fillip to their game so that for a little while there was anxiety amongst the Villa supporters. But Garraty soon scored Villa's fourth, and when Wheldon got the fifth, "the crowd were on the tip-toe of expectation", they knowing full-well that the Villa needed one more goal to equal Liverpool's goal average.

A great cheer went up as Cowan was successful from a corner on 78 minutes. "One more Villa!" the supporters shouted! When Garraty put the ball home for the seventh, seven minutes from the finish, there was wild excitement!

> The Villa had achieved their target, and had played superbly – to the man. At the end of those two matches, Villa had a goal average of 1.775 to Liverpool's 1.75.
>
> Liverpool were due at Villa Park within three days to determine the championship; the Villa just needed a draw to re-gain the title.

> *How come the Albion gave in?*
>
> The Albion were taunted by Liverpool when Albion visited Liverpool before the Villa vs. Liverpool match:
>
> > "However did you let Villa give you a hiding like that?"
> >
> > "*Let?!*", snorted the Throstle: "Don't you talk about 'letting', my lad. Wait till you meet 'em at Aston, and you'll very likely laugh on the other side of your face."
>
> And so it proved![350]

The final act!:   Liverpool (h)

Whichever team won this match was to win the championship. The 'gate' for this match stood as a new League record; the receipts were £1,558 1s 6d.

[From the *Sports Argus*] In the early play, Crabtree was twice cheered for especially good defensive work. Liverpool were pressing, but Smith got the

---

[350] Villa News & Record 8 Apr 1911 – an extract from an article by "Old Fogey"

The Aston Villa Chronicles 1874 – 1924 (and after)

ball and took it down the wing. "[He] sent in a grand centre, from which Devey, rushing in, headed into the corner of the net." This score, on four minutes, was greeted with tremendous cheering!

Though Liverpool came back on terms, on 18 minutes there was a repeat dose of medicine from the Villa involving Smith and Devey – this time Devey finishing the move by shooting home. With only some attempted response from Liverpool, the Villa just got better that half, and before 40 minutes were over, the Villa had scored five! And Devey nearly got a sixth just on half-time.

The Villa had achieved their great success with the backing of a strong wind in the first half, and it came to Liverpool's favour for the second period. Liverpool tried so hard to get back into the game that Wheldon was deputed to help out the Villa half-backs, and this he achieved to great effect, combining well with a great half-back line in which Crabtree played his very best game.

"Garraty was again to the front, and his go-ahead work had ... a great deal to do with the fast and slashing manner in which the men on either side of him travelled. Devey showed superb judgment ..."

The Title was Villa's!

"As soon as the match was over, a vast crowd assembled in front of the grandstand to witness the presentation of the Cup ... Everybody cheered and shouted to his heart's content ... [and when the trophy was handed to Devey, there was] applause that was almost deafening. For some minutes, a great crowd stood cheering and shouting, and dispersed with the consciousness that a brilliant victory had been duly honoured."

The Football League Division 1 1898-99 Top Places	Pld	Home W D L F A	Away W D L F A	Overall W D L F A	Pts
1 Aston Villa	34	15 2 0 58 13	4 5 8 18 27	19 7 8 76 40	45
2 Liverpool	34	12 3 2 29 10	7 2 8 20 23	19 5 10 49 33	43
3 Burnley	34	11 5 1 32 15	4 4 9 13 32	15 9 10 45 47	39
4 Everton	34	10 2 5 25 13	5 6 6 23 28	15 8 11 48 41	38
5 Notts. County	34	9 6 2 33 20	3 7 7 14 31	12 13 9 47 51	37

The Aston Villa Chronicles 1874 – 1924 (and after)

1898-99 League and FA Cup Results

Sep	3rd H Stoke	3-1	20000
	10th A Bury	1-2	
	17th A Burnley	4-2	
	24th H Sheffield United	1-1	25000
Oct	1st A Newcastle United	1-1	
	8th H Preston North End	4-2	20000
	15th A Liverpool	3-0	
	22nd H Nottingham Forest	3-0	18000
	29th H Bolton Wanderers	2-1	17000
Nov	5th H Derby County	7-1	20000
	12th A West Bromwich A	1-0	18000
	19th H Blackburn Rovers	3-1	20000
	26th A Sheffield Wed	1-4	
Dec	3rd H Sunderland	2-0	25000
	10th H Wolves	1-1	20000
	17th H Everton	3-0	28000
	24th A Notts County	0-1	
	26th H Newcastle United	1-0	27000
	31st A Stoke	0-3	
Jan	7th H Bury	3-2	16000
	14th H Burnley	4-0	23000
	21st A Sheffield United	3-1	
	28th A Nottingham F (FAC)	1-2	
Feb	4th A Preston North End	0-2	10000
	18th A Nottingham Forest	0-1	
Mar	4th A Derby County	1-1	
	18th A Blackburn Rovers	0-0	12000
	25th H Sheffield Wed	3-1	12000
Apr	1st A Sunderland	2-4	30000
	3rd A Wolves	0-4	
	15th A Everton	1-1	
	17th A Bolton Wanderers	0-0	
	22nd H Notts County	6-1	20000
	24th H West Bromwich A	7-1	13000
	29th H Liverpool	5-0	43240

End of Season Postscripts

The end to the season had been extraordinary – much more like a Cup Final build up and execution – but that finish belied the fact that for much of the season the Villa had not had much opposition to their leadership of the League, and, in fact, the Villá had only themselves to blame for very nearly throwing away the title opportunity.

The Villa shuffled around their team on so many occasions, and by Easter were being punished for it. Many results in the middle and late part of the season were far from satisfactory until that final three-match push. *But what a glorious push!*

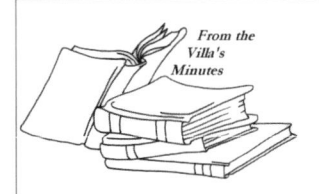

> *From the Villa's Minutes*
>
> On 24 March (1899), it was resolved that a wage of up to £5 per week should be offered to ten players (excluding Tom Wilkes, John Cowan and the Sharp brothers) regarded as 'first-teamers', with the exception that Athersmith and Wheldon should continue to receive £6 p.w. as agreed last season.
>
> On 27 April, trainer Grierson was voted a bonus of £10 "if we win the League" (which was, of course, achieved!). Denny Hodgetts was voted a present of £5 5s for services rendered during that season.

The Aston Villa Chronicles 1874 – 1924 (and after)

The popularity of football was definitely increasing, and the Villa led in the popularity stakes. A list of the clubs and their following was issued; the best-supported clubs were as follows (*Sports Argus*, 29 April):

Club	Total Attendances (17 League games)	Average
Aston Villa	353,000	20,764
Newcastle United	303,000	17,823
Everton	281,000	16,529
Liverpool	243,000	14,294
Sunderland	221,000	13,000

In terms of personnel, it had in the end been proven that the old guard of the 1890s – principally Devey, James Cowan, Crabtree, Athersmith, Smith (who had re-found his old form), and the 'finds' of the 1896-97 season, Spencer, Evans and Wheldon, had yet again shown they were the best players on the Villa's books. However, keeper George, the forwards Johnson and Garraty, and the full-back turned right-half, Bowman, had shown they were more than capable of holding their own in such company.

As for those promising Sharp brothers ... ?

> *From the Villa's Minutes*
>
> The meeting of 6 July received a hand-written letter from the Rt. Hon. Joseph Chamberlain, thanking the club for a donation of £5 to the Birmingham University Fund.
>
> He added his appreciation of "evidence which they have given that the cultivation of athletics does not destroy interest in intellectual pursuits."

Season 1899-1900: Champions for the Fifth Time!
League Division 1 position: Champions; *FA Cup:* 3rd Round.

The goalkeeper Tom Wilkes finally left for Stoke, his "nose put out of joint" by the arrival and displays of Billy George. John Cowan also left, and returned to Scotland. His form came to its peak in time for the finalé to the 1896-97 'double' season, replacing Steve Smith, but in the past season the reverse had taken place, so that Smith was now the recognised left-winger. Though never achieving the fame of his brother James, John was a skilful player who would be remembered by those who saw him at his best. At *his* best, 'Tich' Smith was simply the better player.

The Aston Villa Chronicles 1874 – 1924 (and after)

On 26 April, the Sharp brothers signed for Everton at a joint fee of £450. The reason offered was that they wanted guaranteed football, and this had been denied them. 'Argus Junior' stated: "I am strongly suspicious that there is some other reason." Their treatment looked odd – they were both at one time rated as being very good material, but in Jack Sharp's case there was only one position on the field in which he could be seen at his best, and that was outside-right. The problem for him was that a certain Charlie Athersmith had a hold on that post, virtually *sine die*.

> "... despite the fact that they allowed the brothers Sharp to leave – a doubtful policy, as many think – they have capable reserves to fill almost any position in the field."
>
> *Birmingham Daily Post*, 31 August, 1899

It is probable that Bobby Templeton, who could be played on both wings, was the final cause of the decision to let Jack Sharp go. Unfortunately for Villa, whereas Sharp proved himself to be a sound investment to Everton over a decade, Templeton, though a marvellous entertainer, proved to have more than one drawback for the Villa, and he did not prove to be the solution to Villa's wing hopes.

From the Villa's Minutes

George Ramsay had an assistant working for him for the previous two years, named Homer. Mr. Homer had now resigned (29 June meeting), but was willing to stay if paid an additional ten shillings per week.

However, former player 'Wally' Strange had notified the Board that his job with the School Board was going nowhere, and offered his services at £90 per annum, rising by £10 increments to a maximum of £130 p.a.

Walter Strange was thus appointed, and he remained George Ramsay's assistant for another quarter of a century. His responsibilities included attending away games, and making reports to the directors on the performance of players.

There were no new signings of note for the new season. Billy Garraty had successfully emerged from the reserves during the previous season, and, with George Johnson, provided the main cover for the inside-forward positions. Both wing positions would be covered by another emerging reserve; Bobby Templeton. Albert Wilkes would be the chief cover for the half-back line.

The main issue of concern was whether the fitness of Spencer and Devey would stand up to the season's stresses.

The Aston Villa Chronicles 1874 – 1924 (and after)

> ### Jack Sharp
>
> A talented sportsman, Jack Sharp (1878-1938) achieved international honours in two sporting arenas. Not only did he play football for England, but in cricket he earned three Test caps, and scored a century against Australia in 1909.
>
> Born in Hereford in 1878, Jack Sharp was one of the latest 'sparks' to have been spotted by Villa whilst he was playing for Hereford Thistle. In just a season and a half with Villa, this youngster had accumulated 23 league games and a very high return of 15 goals.
>
> At Everton he appears to have become a winger of extraordinary ability. Over the ensuing Edwardian era, Jack Sharp became a household name, and is recorded as a legend in Everton's history. He was nicknamed 'The Pocket Hercules' by a journalist at the time, the term not only describing Sharp's powerful skill, but also his small stature.
>
> While at Everton he made 342 appearances and scored 80 goals. Everton has recognised his exceptional sportsmanship by making him one of the club's 10 Millennium Giants – the club's greatest footballers. Playing mainly on the wing, Sharp quickly became known for his lightning play and goal scoring ability.
>
> Sharp's fame was an early national sporting phenomenon. In the days before television and sponsorship deals, his popularity was measured by the number of times his picture appeared on cigarette cards.

The Season's Play

September, 1899

For the visit to **Sunderland**, it was the same team that finished the end of the previous season:

Villa: *George; Spencer, Evans; Bowman, Cowan, Crabtree;*
Athersmith, Devey, Garraty, Wheldon, Smith.

[From the *Sports Argus*] Again, the Villa were guilty of too much pretty work and forgetting to shoot! The way to goal learnt in the last three games of the last season seemed to have been forgotten!

It was a game full of incident, and Villa's goal came when Athersmith gave Wheldon a good chance, but his shot was pushed out to Garraty, who took his chance. This winning goal came late in the game.

The Aston Villa Chronicles 1874 – 1924 (and after)

Glossop North End (h)

[From the *Birmingham Daily Post*] New top-flight members Glossop were flush from "a meritorious victory over Burnley on Saturday".

After attacks from both sides that ended with shots into the side netting, "the Villa went away with a swing up the right wing," and Athersmith "sent in one of his characteristic centres." Wheldon was there to head home before the keeper knew what what was coming. "It was soon evident that the visitors were outclassed." Attack after attack followed from the Villa, and a Smith centre found Garraty, who put Villa two-up. Clearly star-struck, Glossop appeared nervous and did not know what to do with the ball, and Villa were consequently always on the attack.

After the Villa reached six goals (Smith (2), Wheldon, Athersmith), George was troubled for the first time, he having three shots to deal with. Glossop gained confidence, and only a referee's consultation with the linesman prevented a penalty kick being awarded against the Villa. Attack after attack followed from Glossop, and it was wondered that Villa did not concede any goals before the interval.

In the second period, Glossop continued to play with improved confidence, but the Villa had many chances to increase their lead. Eventually, "a splendid bit of combination by Athersmith, Devey and Garraty ended in the latter notching a seventh goal"; Garraty and Devey added two more, and the Villa won 9-0, with Garraty scoring four.

> The Villa had scored 27 goals in only their last *four* home matches. This total included a 7-1 trouncing of the Albion at the end of the previous season.

The Villa received **Albion** as the visitors once more, with Villa's supporters thinking back to the slamming of Albion just a few months before. The *Sports Argus* quoted Albion director Keys as saying:

> Some people have told us that the best thing we could do would be to stay at home and allow the game to go by default, the Villa to be credited with, say, ten goals. But we thought we'd come along, you know, and perhaps we may not do so badly after all!

The Albion's kick-and-rush style was designed to spoil Villa's prettier tactics, and the match was by no stretch of the imagination, ' brilliant'. By getting rid of the ball quickly, Albion succeeded in knocking the Villa out of their stride, and also succeeded in scoring two second half goals. Villa's run was decisively halted!

The Aston Villa Chronicles 1874 – 1924 (and after)

At **Everton**, Villa restored their winning theme.

[From the *Sports Argus*] A Wheldon header was adjudged to have crossed the line before being cleared, and so Villa took the lead after early Everton pressure.

Jack Sharp was prominent on the wing against his old team, but the Villa entered a good spell when the ball was pinging around the Everton goal. As the half wore on, however, Everton increased their pressure and the play became faster. Everton equalised after 39 minutes.

The second period started with Everton again strident, but the Villa came back into the game, and an Everton defender had to clear twice from just under the bar, from Wheldon and Smith. Then, after Devey's brilliant shot had been saved, Villa swept back and ten minutes from the end, Garraty slipped the ball home for the winner.

A good match – "fast all through" – with "capital combination from both sides". Spencer was noted as getting back to his best form.

An excellent crowd turned up for the home match against **Blackburn** despite rain showers, and a stiff wind blew across the ground.

[From the *Sports Argus*] Within just 30 *seconds*, a shot from the Blackburn right-wing hit the upright, and following the resulting scrimmage, Rovers took the lead!

The Villa came back and made various swoops on the visitors' goal, only "to be foiled by the keeper and the goal-posts … The spectators groaned with disappointment." Blackburn, however, came back and took paint off the Villa's goalpost!

Blackburn were working hard, but the Villa were having the better of the encounter, and after 30 minutes, Villa equalised when Wheldon "made a brilliant dash through the opposing defence", and scored with a daisy-cutter. A hearty cheer was raised despite the (by now) heavy rain. The half finished with the Rovers backs (including the legendary Crompton) grimly defending. They packed their defence.

To try to confuse Blackburn, Devey and Garraty swapped positions, and after 70 minutes, "Garraty broke away; … his centre was met by Wheldon … [the ball was partly cleared, and then] Devey, running on, banged the ball into the net." This goal opened up the play, and now the Villa were playing at their best. However, it took until the last minute before Devey scored Villa's third.

Devey, despite scoring twice, was in fact carrying an injury that perceptibly affected his play. George did not have a quiet time, "[and] stopped some nasty shots in brilliant style."

The Aston Villa Chronicles 1874 – 1924 (and after)

> *From the Villa's Minutes*
>
> On 21 September, *Sport and Play* – licensees of the Villa Park cycling track – applied for permission to use the track for a *motor* race meeting. Dates were offered to them.
>
> It was heard on 28 September that assistance for the old star Albion and Villa player Willie Groves had been applied for by his proxy. It was resolved, that the club could not give further help – "[the club] has already done more than anyone knows for him."
>
> *The* Sports Argus *had already reported (2 September) that he was in a bad way, and the Players' Union had already decided to pay a grant.*
>
> *The Villa later made a contribution of £5 to a fund that was set up.*
>
> On 28 September, it was heard that John Devey had used insulting language to Mr. Lees at the end of the Albion match, and had previously made remarks to the players in the dressing room. Devey was then left out of the team and suspended until he explains his behaviour.
>
> On 5 October, Devey came in to explain his side. Devey's suspension would be withdrawn if he were to apologise to Mr. Lees. John Devey then suggested that a players' meeting should take place to clear up rumours, and a date in the billiards' room was fixed for that purpose.
>
> *The resulting meeting turned out to be nothing of note – merely "an all's well affair [and] tea party", reported the* Sports Argus.

At **Derby**, Billy Garraty was moved to centre-forward for John Devey, and George Johnson stood in at inside-right. With Derby lying in bottom place, and were yet to score this season, the match looked an easy one for the Villa. But Archie Goodall – after dispute with his club – returned to the Derby ranks, and Steve Bloomer was brilliant. Everything Bloomer did had everything to do with Derby's success. The Villa were disappointing, though Crabtree and Evans had both taken heavy knocks.

The League table now revealed that Sheffield United were setting the pace, and would continue to do so for some time to come. Liverpool, who had made such a strong end-of-season challenge for the title, but had lost so decisively at Villa Park in the final match of last season, were now propping up the division having lost all five of their opening matches!

Leading Positions in Division 1 September 30th, 1899	Pld	Home W D L F A	Away W D L F A	Overall W D L F A	Pts
1 Sheffield United	5	2 0 0 7 0	3 0 0 5 2	5 0 0 12 2	10
2 Sunderland	5	2 0 1 3 2	2 0 0 3 0	4 0 1 6 2	8
3 Aston Villa	6	2 0 1 12 3	2 0 1 3 3	4 0 2 15 6	8

The Aston Villa Chronicles 1874 – 1924 (and after)

October, 1899

For the next home match, Crabtree and Evans had to be replaced by Wilkes and Haggatt due to the knocks received at Derby; Garraty and Johnson swapped positions.

Bury (h)

The Bury keeper and trainer missed their train connection, and so not only did they fail to arrive, *but neither did the playing kit!* Bury had to buy a special set from Shilcock's in New Town Row, and started play with ten men, with a full-back in goal. After twenty minutes play, their keeper arrived.

[From the *Sports Argus*] Bury played with plenty of endeavour, and in fact opened the scoring on 30 minutes, through McLuckie – a player that the Villa fans would come to know much more about in the foreseeable future, when he would join the Villa ranks. He was described as "a big-striding player, [proving] himself a very capable player, and a pivot above the ordinary standard."

To the relief of the fans, the Villa reversed the half-time score with two goals in the first twenty minutes of the second period, but the Villa did not get their game together at all well.

> Fred Rinder was in trouble with the Football League having made a statement that their bonus rules had frequently been broken. An order was made for Rinder to be no longer recognised as Villa's representative to the Football League. (*In fact, that order made no difference – Charlie Johnstone was the Villa's usual representative!*)
>
> *Sports Argus*, 14 October, 1899

At **Notts County**, Devey returned to his usual inside-right position, and Garraty was left out, leaving Johnson as the pivot. Crabtree was still out due to injury.

[From the *Sports Argus*] The report was headed "A Poor Game at Nottingham", but the 4-1 scoreline inferred some better play from the Villa at least. However, it was County that went ahead on 25 minutes after Spencer (of all players!) had put his own goal in trouble. Within two mnutes, Villa were back on terms through Johnson, and he not long after added Villa's second.

The poor play was mainly from County, but the Villa did not take advantage of all the opportunities that were offered to them. Johnson later had to leave the field with what turned out to be a fracture above the ankle, after completing his hat-trick. Devey added another.

The Aston Villa Chronicles 1874 – 1924 (and after)

> **In Passing**
> - Johnson's leg fracture was identified using new X-ray equipment.
> - "The goalposts on the Villa ground have been painted a pinky red."
> - William Shilcock, the sports' outfitters, were being made very busy by supplying footballs to soldiers on their way to the Boer War!
> - Following the death of the ex-Villa player, Jim Elliott, it was heard that the FA had sent his widow £5 from their benevolent fund. The Villa had been sending him a weekly allowance of from 10 to 15 shillings, plus luxuries.
>
> *Sports Argus*, 21 October, 1899

The Villa's injury list had got steadily longer; Johnson, Crabtree and Athersmith were now all out. For the match against **Manchester City**, the situation brought in Bobby Templeton into the outside-right position. Garraty was recalled (to the centre-forward spot). With Billy Meredith showing up well for the City, it was a good game, but the Villa were out of sorts and were missing their absentees. The City scored first, but Wheldon equalised via a penalty shortly before the interval. John Devey scored the winner in the second half.

The Villa were grateful to be able to play Crabtree and Athersmith in this match away against the League pace-setters, **Sheffield United**. The Villa selected the team that opened the season.

[From the *Sports Argus*] The Villa lost the game but deserved a point. In fact, the Villa had the half-time lead after Smith's shot cannoned into the net off the crossbar on 23 minutes. The Villa held that lead till 15 minutes from the end, when United, looking a beaten team, managed to score two, both of them 'odd'. The first was given as an own goal by Spencer; the ball had gone in off his head.

In this match, "There was football of a very high order, at once attractive, bright and clever." Billy George was "more than brilliant at times, and had probably played his best game." Garraty was very short of the mark as centre. The other forwards were good, but Athersmith went lame towards the end. Cowan was on his best form, but Crabtree showed that he had been out for a while.

The Villa were in second place, but now four points behind Sheffield United. Meanwhile, Sunderland were hot on Villa's heels.

The Aston Villa Chronicles 1874 – 1924 (and after)

November, 1899

The home match against **Newcastle United** was played on an overcast day, with a strong wind blowing across the pitch. Athersmith was again out (injured), and would be out for several games; Templeton again deputised for him.

[From the *Sports Argus*] The Villa applied pressure from the 'off', and Devey scored with "a swift, straight, low shot" on four minutes. After 23 minutes, Wheldon made it 2-0 after receiving from Devey, who played well in the first half. Cowan played a fine game, "tricking the United forwards time after time."

Villa led 2-0 at half-time, but United scored five minutes after the interval, and thereafter gave a lot of trouble to the Villa defence. Eventually, to shouts of "Play up, Villa!", the Villa got back into the game, and the match finished with the play being more equal.

Unusually, the crowd voiced their dissatisfaction with the referee's decisions, and Templeton was strangely neglected by Devey, causing the crowd to exhort, "Give Templeton a chance!" Nevertheless, Templeton played well, and showed his speed and centering abilities.

The list of serious Villa absences increased. Apart from Johnson and Athersmith, Crabtree accidentally spiked his heel during the week, and Spencer was also pronounced unfit. James Cowan, however, was now out for a different kind of reason – one related to his 'social life'. He would be replaced by the unknown Christopher Mann, signed from the Albion earlier in the year, who would keep that position for seven matches. Overall, the absence of players of the ilk of Cowan, Crabtree and Athersmith over such a period was a severe test of the team's ability to maintain their League position.

In the goal-less home match against **Wolves**, the players had a tendency to hang on to the ball for too long, though the wings played well. Templeton was badly kicked. Then Villa produced a fine 2-0 win against a fourth-placed **Stoke** in a Monday encounter when Templeton was replaced by a reserve (Garfield), but Spencer returned.

Templeton recovered from his knocks to play at **Liverpool** against a side that were still low in the League table but were slowly recovering. In a match of poor visibility (through fog) at Liverpool, the Villa came back three times from reverses against a Liverpool that was the better side in the first half, to draw 3-3.

The Aston Villa Chronicles 1874 – 1924 (and after)

> Spencer's knee was still giving trouble, but at Liverpool, "he dropped with his knee [onto] a stone. An ugly wound was caused." Examination showed the matter to be severe. He was sent off to be treated at Manchester, and would miss three matches.
>
> *Sports Argus*, 25 November, 1899

It was an interesting, but not an exceptional, game versus **Burnley**, at home. The shooting was "dreadful at times", though the Burnley keeper was kept busy. The match was noteworthy for the first appearance of Michael Noon, as deputy to Howard Spencer. He had been signed earlier in the year as a utility back and half-back. Villa won, 2-0.

Leading Positions in Division 1 November 25th, 1899	Pld	Home W D L F A	Away W D L F A	Overall W D L F A	Pts
1 Sheffield United	15	6 2 0 22 5	5 2 0 10 5	11 4 0 32 10	26
2 Aston Villa	**15**	**6 1 1 20 6**	**4 1 2 13 9**	**10 2 3 33 15**	**22**
3 Sunderland	12	4 0 1 7 2	4 1 2 9 6	8 1 3 16 8	17

> ### *Jimmy Crabtree*
>
> Jimmy Crabtree went on the FA's first ever tour – of Berlin, Prague and Karlsruhe. "All through he played in irresistible style and fair astonished the stolid Germans into quite fierce outbursts of enthusiasm with his finesse and cleverness."
>
> *Sports Argus*, 2 December, 1899

December, 1899

Preston North End (a)

'Proud Preston' were languishing at the bottom of the League table, and they were visited by an almost unrecognisable Villa team (Bowman was now out with flu), apart from the keeper and forwards:

Villa: *George; Noon, Evans; McElery, Mann, Wilkes;*
Templeton, Devey, Garraty, Wheldon, Smith.

[From the *Sports Argus*] Villa having taken the lead on 13 minutes through Garraty, Smith also made his mark. "When in his own half, Smith got hold. He first of all tricked Dunn in midfield, and then went bang for goal, with Holmes scouring after him. When within a few yards of the line, Smith stopped, and Holmes slipped up! The Villa man, cutting across the goalmouth, dribbled close in, and then beat [the keeper] completely!" This goal was greeted with "a rousing cheer!" He was to effectively repeat this goal when scoring his side's fifth near the end of the match. He also scored another before half-time, and so he collected a hat-trick in this match.

Albert Wilkes was badly kicked on the ankle and had to leave the field, shortly before the end.

> *From the Villa's Minutes*
>
> On 7 December, Joe Grierson called in and it was decided that practise matches should be re-introduced instead of "ball kicking".
>
> The 14 December meeting decided that a letter should be sent to James Cowan, along the lines of "we understand he is now well again, and after his long rest hope he will attend to his training and get himself fit as soon as possible."

Bowman returned for the home match against **Nottingham Forest** match, otherwise the team was the same as played at Preston. The match was hum-drum to start with, but after George misjudged the flight of a corner kick and put through his own goal, followed almost immediately by Villa's equaliser, "the play brightened up wonderfully", wrote the *Sports Argus* reporter. He added: "there was [then] plenty of work to keep the crowd fairly agog with excitement." Forest re-gained the lead on 73 minutes, but, "amid deafening applause", the Villa again equalised five minutes from the finish.

To visit **Glossop**, there were more changes to the team; Spencer returned, but Evans was out, and Noon therefore played at left-back. Also, Athersmith returned in place of Templeton. The *Sports Argus* reported: "The Glossop field may fairly be said to be one of the worst, if not the worst, in the First Division." The conditions were treacherous, and the Villa's short passing failed miserably. Villa lost 0-1 against a side that would be relegated and against which the Villa registered a 9-0 win earlier in the season.

At home to **Stoke**, much of the old brigade returned in this match; Cowan (with extra weight!), Crabtree (at left-back) and Johnson at centre-forward, with Garraty taking the absent Devey's position. Noon moved to right-half instead of Bowman. This team selection would last five matches. Despite the scoreline, ex-Villan Tommy Wilkes – in the Stoke goal – did well, in a match of otherwise no great interest, though Villa won 4-1.

The Aston Villa Chronicles 1874 – 1924 (and after)

> *From the Villa's Minutes*
>
> The 28 December meeting decided that Templeton be suspended for two weeks on account of his flouting the club's rules and regulations concerning behaviour – taking into account that this was his second offence.

The match with **Sunderland** was always a popular fixture, and with they being in fourth place and having a couple of games in hand, extra spice was added.

[From the *Sports Argus*] A roar of applause greeted Garraty's strike on 25 minutes, after he burst through a cluster of opponents. Soon after, Johnson received from Athersmith, recovered from stumbling, and returned square across goal. It was almost out of Garraty's reach, but he stretched himself and turned the ball into the net for the second goal.

Soon after the interval, Sunderland pulled a goal back, but one minute after, Garraty secured his hat-trick! While Sunderland were making efforts without achieving a breakthrough, Smith "was earning thunders of applause for his clever wing-play and accurate centres." It was from a Smith corner that Johnson added Villa's fourth goal to make it 4-1.

Later, Sunderland pulled a goal back, and then hit the Villa post with another shot, followed by more shots on and around Villa's goal – but they were repulsed. Sunderland's football – "of the 'clang' order" – was compatible for an entertaining game of football, but the Villa's win was deserved.

Villa were still in second place, but six points adrift of undefeated Sheffield United (but with a game in hand). The Wolves were now making an attempt at getting in on the championship chase.

January, 1900

The *Sports Argus* reporter declared that Villa "came a cropper" at **Bury**. It was the Glossop match all over again; a group of sturdy young athletes resolving to go all the way and coming out triumphant. Villa's form was "too bad to be true." The 0-2 result took Bury to fourth place in the table.

West Bromwich Albion (a)

[From the *Sports Argus*] A day of heavy rain, and in the conditions, wing-work was the only way forward. "The game was to rattle the ball on to the outside, whip it in, and then depend upon rushing work by the men in the centre."

The kind of game that took place, and the enthusiasm it created, is revealed in the report of the early part of the game. "The Villa were the first to become really dangerous. Smith sent across goal. Williams missed his kick ... [and] Athersmith placed the ball nicely into goal, and the left-winger, following it

The Aston Villa Chronicles 1874 – 1924 (and after)

up, Reader [the Albion keeper] had hard work to prevent disaster. Save he did, and raised a loud cheer for doing so. Another onslaught ended in the ball being sent over the line. Richards [of Albion] tried hard to penetrate the Aston defence, but Noon was a stumbling-block, and took the ball from him right smartly.

"The Villa now came perilously near to Reader. Garraty was in the act of shooting when Adams [of Albion] pushed him, and as Athersmith rushed for the ball, Reader treated him in a very summary manner. A penalty kick seemed inevitable, but the referee decided otherwise!"

The game went on much like this, though Albion came to have more of the game, until Garraty opened the scoring with a hot shot on 40 minutes. One minute into the second half, and the conditions caused a defender to slip and the ball to run to Garraty to claim his (and Villa's) second goal.

At the end, the Albion looked well beaten, and the Villa wing-men were tricking the Albion backs time and again, but by that time the Albion were down to nine players, having lost two to injury.

Everton (h)

[From the *Sports Argus*] On a pitch mostly covered in rough sand and offering little grass, Everton gave the Villa a fright.

Jack Sharp had a great reception on this his first return to his former home, and his team took the lead after nine minutes. On numerous occasions in the first half, Spencer saved the Villa goal from threatening Everton attacks. He played some grand football.

Towards the end of the half, a beautiful Sharp centre could easily have produced a further goal, but a combination of George and other bodies somehow cleared the situation. Villa had their chances, but Everton were the more lively, and only George, Spencer and Cowan seemed to be playing their best game. Crabtree, strangely, was off his game at full-back, and tt was notable that the Villa fans were always willing to cheer any good play by Sharp, the player opposing Crabtree!

A very late goal by Athersmith – converting Smith's beautiful cross – brought ultimate relief to the Villa supporters, who let out a great cheer.

In response to a letter of thanks to the *Sports Argus* from a soldier in South Africa, the paper was now organising the sending of thousands of copies of the paper for soldiers on the front line and in hospitals.

Sports Argus, 13 January, 1900

With Evans returning at left-back, Garraty was moved to centre-forward, and Crabtree to inside-right, for the match at **Blackburn**.

The Aston Villa Chronicles 1874 – 1924 (and after)

[From the *Sports Argus*] There was not a great degree of football in this match, in which the Villa scored all their goals in the second half. Both sets of full-backs tended to dominate the proceedings. Although the Villa won by a very comfortable (4-0) margin, it was George that kept the Villa in the match until they had made the score safe. Towards the end, a Blackburn defender was sent off for striking a Villa player.

> At a Lancashire stop on the return from Blackburn, a railway ticket collector popped his head through the players' carriage window and said, "Tha mon gie 'em a reight good beating!"
>
> *Sports Argus*, 27 January, 1900

Devey made a return for the Cup match at **Manchester City**, having returned to training during the week. Crabtree was still absent.

[From the *Sports Argus*] Villa started very brightly, but City opened the scoring in five minutes, Ross scoring following indecision between Spencer and Noon, following a corner.

It was not until 13 minutes into the second half that Devey equalised, following Smith's fine run and centre, but the Villa had had to work hard for that goal. The Villa defence and half-backs (excluding Cowan) were often getting into misunderstandings so that on at least one occasion, Billy Meredith was given a clean run through.

Villa were the clever side, but City played with vigour and generated some bad feeling. James Ross (the old Preston player) "did well for a time, but his methods were execrable, and filled the Birmingham section of the crowd with indignation."

For the replay, the start-of-season team was able to come together once more, all injuries having been sorted out.

[From the *Sports Argus*] "At Aston we saw the Villa almost at their best. Athersmith, well fed this time, was in his old sprinting form, and he made the pace very hot in the opening half. He swung the ball across well, too. Smith and Wheldon made an effective wing; Devey aided the combination excellently, and Garraty was full of dash in front of goal. When Garraty is in a goal-getting mood [he scored two; Wheldon added a penalty], he is a dangerous man indeed; he merely wants a little more coolness … Everyone was glad to see Crabtree and Bowman out once more."

[From the *Birmingham Daily Post*] "Cowan and Spencer were magnificent, with fair play also from Crabtree and Bowman."

In the League, Sheffield United had lost their first match of the season (to Derby), and a two-horse race was developing for the title.

The Aston Villa Chronicles 1874 – 1924 (and after)

Leading Positions in Division 1 February 3rd, 1900	Pld	Home W D L F A	Away W D L F A	Overall W D L F A	Pts
1 Sheffield United	24	8 5 0 31 8	6 4 1 16 11	14 9 1 47 19	37
2 Aston Villa	25	9 3 1 34 14	7 1 4 24 12	16 4 5 58 26	36
3 Wolverhampton Wanderers	23	5 3 2 18 10	6 5 2 16 14	11 8 4 34 24	30

February, 1900

For the home match against **Derby County**, there had been snow. That was cleared from the pitch, which was then covered with a light layer of further snow. The snow later came down without cessation.

[From the *Sports Argus*] Derby opened the scoring in the first half. On 19 minutes, "Bloomer scored a great goal [from a very narrow angle], completely beating George."

Villa attacked hard but could not beat the Derby defenders. At length, Devey changed places with Garraty. "[Then] Smith ran away in gallant style, [the Derby back] evidently determined to stop him at all costs, and so unfair were his methods that the Villa were granted a free kick.", bringing a succession of anxieties on the Derby goal.

Villa went two down three minutes into the second half after sharp Derby play, but this was quickly followed by Smith putting over a beautiful centre to enable Garraty to bang the ball into the net. 1-2. This roused the Villa's game and the spectators' enthusiasm! The Villa started playing more like their true selves, but after some sustained pressure on the Derby goal, Bloomer broke away and netted – the 'score' being disallowed for offside.

Villa's attacks continued. "Play up, Villa!" was the cry from the spectators. Time and time again, the Derby goal escaped. Then Derby broke away again, with Evans conceding a corner, but before this and after, Villa attempts on goal just skimmed the bar. Then a shot from Derby needed George to make a save, and then it was back to the Derby end. More shots skimmed their bar!

At last, and late on, Athersmith put the ball across goal, the ball just requiring a touch from Garraty to score the equaliser! In the next 30 seconds - "amid tremendous excitement" – Wheldon scored Villa's winner!

The Villa's backs and half-backs played without fault, but, in attack, Wheldon was guilty – as he often was – of trying too much finesse. For Derby, Bloomer was "superb", and Archie Goodall was also outstanding.

The home tie against the Southern League side **Bristol City** would have been a lot more even had not the Villa team been playing their best. The Villa eventually coasted through, 5-1.

The Aston Villa Chronicles 1874 – 1924 (and after)

> Steve Smith is showing his best form for four or five seasons in his sharp, sudden, dashes. "The pace he develops the moment he gets the ball is surprising." It was thought his main fault was that his centres were often along the ground.
>
> Smith, Athersmith, Crabtree, Spencer, Evans and George were all now playing up to international form.
>
> 'Argus Junior', *Sports Argus*, 17 February, 1900

For the match against **Notts County,** Villa Park was as good as could be expected, following heavy snow, a thaw and then heavy rains!

[From the *Sports Argus*] Garraty scored for Villa in just 30 seconds, Wheldon nearly adding another straight afterwards. However, the second – from Athersmith – was chalked up on two minutes! The Villa forwards swarmed around the Notts goal, threatening further goals. Perversely, County gradually came back into it, and for a time the play was equal.

"[Then] the Birmingham spectators were glad to see Smith careering down the field with the ball at his foot, and no-one but the keeper between him and the posts. A score seemed almost inevitable, but [a County defender] pursued Smith as though the championship of the League depended on his overtaking him on time. And overtake him he did, and with a vigorous charge, sent the Villa man flying, while his opponent tumbled over him in dubious triumph!"

The County goal was imperilled time and again, but County's forwards were resolute enough to get away and send in a shot that George saved, but the rebound was forced home, and reduced the arrears. Before half-time, both the Villa and County added further goals to make it 3-2 to the Villa at the interval.

Villa then scored two quick early second half goals, and then Smith, for the second time in that match, had a shot hit the post. Smith brought the house down with his ventures down the left, and the County goal was bombarded time and again. Eventually, Garraty added a sixth goal, followed by another goal from County.

> Were it not for Suter, the County keeper, there would have been an avalanche of goals! "The shots which they rained on him were of the shrapnel variety!"
>
> With Sheffield United playing a cup match, the Villa went top of the League for the first time (by one point), but had played two games more.

The Aston Villa Chronicles 1874 – 1924 (and after)

> *From the Villa's Minutes*
>
> At the meeting of 22 February, a letter of thanks was read for the donation of old Villa jerseys to soldiers in South Africa. The Villa were the first club to come forward and offer these to the troops.

Millwall (h) Another encounter with a Southern League side brought the desired start, with the Villa scoring in the first few minutes. However, Millwall came back determinedly and forced a draw in the second half. "A picturesque game", played in good temper. (*Sports Argus*)

In the first replay, "The Villa gave a masterly exhibition of the art of how not to get goals, though they had more good chances of scoring than would fall to the average team in these matches!" (*Sports Argus*)

For the second replay, Crabtree, Wheldon and Cowan were left out, having been found guilty of flouting club rules, and Smith was injured. The side was considerably weakened, but it was another game where Villa failed to translate their play into goals, though there was more than a hint of staleness in their play. Villa eventually won, 2-1. (*Sports Argus*)

March, 1900

It was tit-for-tat in the title race, but the Villa had played more games. The 'crunch' match now came up at Villa Park against **Sheffield United**, Villa's sparring partners for the championship. This match was important for both these top-two sides, with the Villa more needing the points to keep in contention for the title. United were without four of their most important players, including Needham, and keeper Foulkes and another defender were only passed fit at the last minute. Villa, on the other hand, were playing their full team, with the exception of Crabtree (Noon deputised).

> It was an enormous 'gate', and as the teams came out, some seats in the temporary seating on the cycle track gave way. Fortunately, it was not a serious affair, but "the appearance of the carefully-arranged seats was wonderfully changed, being something in the nature of a wreck!" (*Sports Argus*)
>
> At the following Board meeting, the members were informed that the seats had not been put up correctly – the supports were found to be facing all one way instead of each one alternately.
>
> The Board also heard that there were more people on the ground than the receipts figure showed.

The Aston Villa Chronicles 1874 – 1924 (and after)

[From the *Sports Argus*] The Villa went off at a great pace, and had the bulk of the play, yet the visitors were technically better, and scored two minutes before the end of the first half. United had for most of that half been kept in the game by their masterly keeper, Foulkes, as illustrated in this portion of the report:

"… Athersmith was left with a clear run … no-one had a chance of overtaking him. He went straight for the posts, and when within a few yards of Foulkes, flashed in a hard side shot. At the same moment, Garraty made a rush for the giant custodian, but neither man nor ball have any terror for Foulkes, who saved as if he were merely engaged in a little gentle ball practise! … Shooting at Foulkes was almost as futile as kicking against a stone wall!"

> At the interval, the band played 'Rule Brittania', "and the tune was taken up by the vast crowd. It produced a soul-stirring affect, and when the strains ceased, the cheering was loud and prolonged."

In the second half, after an incredible miss by Wheldon, Villa equalised after a goalmouth scramble. The ball was headed in three times before Foulkes was beaten. "What a rending of the air there was! The whole mass of people seemed to rise and shout and wave their hats and sticks!"

"A grand game to watch – full of interest and excitement and teaming with incident. … Villa should have won – yet did not deserve to win."

> Regarding Villa's two preceding performances, against United and in the FA Cup:
>
>> There can be no doubt that the Villa's chances in both these important games were jeopardised by the inconsiderate conduct of certain players who … neglected to keep themselves during the week preceding the matches in that condition so essential to the winning of games.
>>
>> The public have a shrewd idea who the offenders are … their conduct has been spoken of in amazement.
>
> *Sports Argus*, 10 March, 1900

Newcastle United (a) The home side obtained a couple of fortuitous goals, and, with Wheldon missing a couple of fair chances, led by 1-3 till shortly before the end, when Garraty obtained a second for Villa. However, Newcastle always gave the feeling of they being the more dangerous side. (*Sports Argus*)

Fortunately for Villa, on the same day Sheffield United also lost - at Liverpool, 1-2.

> "Bowman is not so resourceful or so nimble as he was last season, and James Cowan is getting slower and slower."

The Aston Villa Chronicles 1874 – 1924 (and after)

Manchester City (a)

[From the *Sports Argus*, 24 March] "The Villa gave a splendid exhibition, and the crowd cheered again and again. The City generally make their opponents go all the way at Hyde Road, but the Villa were always a clear head in front of them. There was excellent understanding between the forwards, and whenever Garraty was left with the ball in the centre, he made a dash for goal.

"The best feature of the forward play was undoubtedly the work of Athersmith. He raced along at top speed, and did not waste a single centre. The ball always dropped straight into the mouth of the goal, although it was not always made good use of. ... Athersmith's show was so good that he was awarded his cap after the match ... but he is still the best outside-right in the country.

"James Cowan surprised all beholders. His play was well nigh flawless, and at times he seemed to be monopolising the ball.

"Their own supporters, as well as the Manchester Pressmen, declared that the Villa had completely outplayed them." Villa won, 2-0.

Liverpool (h) The Villa played exactly the same side that so outplayed Liverpool in the last match of the previous season, but this match was a contradiction of that match – and of the last match at Manchester City. The Villa just pulled through 1-0, although injuries to several players contributed to the disruption of Villa's play. (*Sports Argus*)

With the injuries to Cowan and Smith in the previous match, and Spencer, Crabtree and Athersmith playing in an inter-League match, the Villa team was much changed at **Burnley**, and not for the first time this season. The Villa were, fortunately, playing a team in the bottom reaches of the League table.

Villa: *George; Evans, Aston; Bowman, Noon, Wilkes; Garraty, Watkins, Devey, Wheldon, Templeton.*

[From the *Sports Argus*] Burnley went ahead in eight minutes when George slipped in attempting to save, but Villa drew level two minutes later through Wheldon. At the end of the half, Wheldon's spot kick went high over the bar! The Villa went on to win through a very late Devey goal, resulting from a long free kick.

Templeton was easily the best forward on the field.

Sheffield United had failed to win yet again! This time they lost 0-4 at Nottingham Forest. Villa were now three points ahead with three matches to play, but United still had two games in hand.

The Aston Villa Chronicles 1874 – 1924 (and after)

April, 1900

Preston North End (h) Again, the Villa were much changed, this time with Spencer, Crabtree and Athersmith away with the England party to play Scotland. Again, also, the Villa were playing a team in the bottom reaches of the League table.

Villa: George; Noon, Evans; Bowman, Cowan, Wilkes;
Smith, Garraty, Devey, Wheldon, Templeton.

[From the *Sports Argus*] The Villa scored straight from the kick-off (an own goal), followed by a Templeton goal on six minutes, to put the Villa firmly in charge. However, Smith went off injured after only 15 minutes, and Preston pulled a goal back before half-time. In fact, the Villa should have scored more, even with ten men, but the game was not made safe until Wheldon potted home Villa's third near the end.

Nottingham Forest (a)

Villa: George; Spencer, Evans; Bowman, Cowan, Wilkes;
Athersmith, Devey, Garraty, Wheldon, Templeton.

[From the *Sports Argus*] From Villa's point of view, this match was mostly to do with Templeton. He scored with a wonderful shot that was almost from the touchline, and yet he was also talked about in respect of his temper – "he fires up at every little transgression by an opposing back." A draw; 1-1.

Wolves (a)

Villa: George; Spencer, Evans; Bowman, Wilkes, Noon;
Athersmith, Johnson, Garraty, Wheldon, Templeton.

[From the *Birmingham Daily Post*] The match started in a gale and the most treacherous weather possible; a swishing wind that made it impossible to judge where passes in the air might land.

Templeton scored with a low cross-shot following a long pass by Spencer, and would have scored again but for fine defensive work by the Wolves.

The second half was delayed by heavy rain. Both sides played amazingly well under the conditions. The Villa's programme having completed, Sheffield United were left with needing to win their last two matches (both away), and then the last of these by 9-0, to win the championship. They lost their last match, in fact, 0-1 – a goal in the last minute.

Sports Argus, 21 April, 1900

The Aston Villa Chronicles 1874 – 1924 (and after)

The Football League Division 1 1899-1900 Top Places	Pld	Home W D L F A	Away W D L F A	Overall W D L F A	Pts
1 Aston Villa	34	12 4 1 45 18	10 2 5 32 17	22 6 6 77 35	50
2 Sheffield United	34	11 5 1 40 11	7 7 3 23 22	18 12 4 63 33	48
3 Sunderland	34	12 2 3 27 9	7 1 9 23 26	19 3 12 50 35	41
4 Wolverhampton Wanderers	34	8 4 5 28 16	7 5 5 20 21	15 9 10 44 33	39
5 Newcastle United	34	10 5 2 34 15	3 5 9 19 28	13 10 11 49 40	36
6 Derby County	34	11 2 4 32 15	3 6 8 13 28	14 8 12 45 43	36

1899-1900 League and FA Cup Results

Sep 2nd	A	Sunderland	1-0	
4th	H	Glossop North End	9-0	12000
9th	H	West Bromwich A	0-2	10000
16th	A	Everton	2-1	
23rd	H	Blackburn Rovers	3-1	20000
30th	A	Derby County	0-2	7000
Oct 7th	H	Bury	2-1	20000
14th	A	Notts County	4-1	10000
21st	H	Manchester City	2-1	22000
28th	A	Sheffield United	1-2	20000
Nov 4th	H	Newcastle United	2-1	20000
11th	H	Wolves	0-0	17000
13th	A	Stoke	2-0	
18th	A	Liverpool	3-3	
25th	H	Burnley	2-0	17000
Dec 2nd	A	Preston North End	5-0	7000
9th	H	Nottingham Forest	2-2	
16th	A	Glossop North End	0-1	
23rd	H	Stoke	4-1	9000
30th	H	Sunderland	4-2	20000
Jan 1st	A	Bury	0-2	
6th	A	West Bromwich A	2-0	
13th	H	Everton	1-1	15000
20th	A	Blackburn Rovers	4-0	
27th	A	Man City (FAC)	1-1	
30th	H	Man City (FAC rep)	3-0	15000
Feb 3rd	H	Derby County	3-2	
10th	H	Bristol City (FAC)	5-1	
17th	H	Notts County	6-2	
24th	A	Millwall (FAC)	1-1	
28th	H	Millwall (FAC replay)	0-0	
Mar 3rd	H	Sheffield United	1-1	44010
5th	N	Millwall (FAC replay)	1-2	
10th	A	Newcastle United	2-3	
19th	A	Manchester City	2-0	
24th	H	Liverpool	1-0	12000
31st	A	Burnley	2-1	
Apr 7th	H	Preston	3-1	
14th	A	Nottingham Forest	1-1	
16th	A	Wolves	1-0	15000

The Title was Villa's!

The players were invited for a celebratory dinner at the Holte Hotel on 4 September, when they were to receive their championship medals.[351]

---

[351] From the club minutes.

The Aston Villa Chronicles 1874 – 1924 (and after)

End of Season Postscripts

Villa's title was won by a different process this season – the previous year they had been the pace-setters for most of the season. This time they were in Sheffield United's wake until the very last few games, and thanks to the United having run out of steam, and the Villa's dogged perseverance, the title again went to the Villa. But it was a near run thing.

The great men of the Villa team this season were George (an ever-present), Spencer and Evans – the men at the back. The attack, however, also did its part, as Villa were the only top-flight team to average two or more League goals per match. Wheldon was an ever-present in League matches, whilst Garraty missed one League match.

> "Johnson has lost all his effectiveness. In the previous season, he was compared to the great amateur and captain of England, G. O. Smith, but has suddenly lost all dash and initiative [possibly due to loss of confidence following that serious injury early in the season]."
>
> *Sports Argus*, 28 April, 1900

The Aston Villa Chronicles 1874 – 1924 (and after)

Appendix 1.   The Chief Playing Heroes, 1891 to 1915

Summary of First-class Competitive Appearances

A - G

Player	1892	1893	1894	1895	1896	1897	1898	1899	1900	1901	1902	1903	1904	1905	1906	1907	1908	1909	1910	1911	1912	1913	1914	1915
Athersmith ▶	29	27	29	35	30	37	28	29	30	31														
Bache							7	36	28	29	37	34	31	34	32	35	34	37	41	32	26			
Baird	19	12	33	5																				
Barber																				20	33	15		
Brawn						0	1	21	34	36	15													
Brown, Albert ▶	0	21	6																					
Buckley, C.											22	1	0	27	21	1								
Campbell, J.			27	36																				
Chatt		17	30	18	12	17																		
Coulton (*gk) ▶	5	0	1*	0																				
Cowan, Jas ▶	29	27	34	35	24	37	29	34	30	29	1													
Cowan, Jno				26	18	23	7																	
Cox ▶	20	1																						
Crabtree				29	31	26	32	21	30	31	0	0												
Devey, H. ▶	14	4																						
Devey, Jno	30	31	33	30	31	36	17	31	31	32	4													
Dickson ▶	24																							
Dowds		21																						
Ducat																					4	0	28 ▶	
Evans, Albert					22	31	30	32	31	4	18	15	5	15	0	0								
Garraty					2	9	39	40	28	30	18	37	37	5	10									
George (gk)					7	31	40	38	27	33	27	39	36	38	33	27	4	16						
Groves		26	0																					
Season Ending	1892	1893	1894	1895	1896	1897	1898	1899	1900	1901	1902	1903	1904	1905	1906	1907	1908	1909	1910	1911	1912	1913	1914	1915
Trophy (◊)			◊	◊	◊	◊◊	◊	◊					◊				◊			◊				

481

The Aston Villa Chronicles 1874 – 1924 (and after)

H - W

Player	1892	1893	1894	1895	1896	1897	1898	1899	1900	1901	1902	1903	1904	1905	1906	1907	1908	1909	1910	1911	1912	1913	1914	1915
Hall												11	28	34	27	40	23	28	3	1	16	3		
Halse																				37				
Hampton													29	35	30	31	31	35	35	36	39	35	32	▶
Hardy (gk)																					39	35	39	▶
Harrop																					39	40	34	▶
Hodgetts	▶	29	29	33	30	19																		
Hunter, G.														0	16	35	35	11						
Johnson						1	25	10	24	8	24	13	3											
Leach																					14	33	27	▶
Leake									32	30	36	26	12	4										
Logan, J.										11	30	40	29	16	15	17								
Lyons										0	26	18	38	29	29	36	39	22	▶					
McLuckie							23	24	15															
Miles								0	17	35	7	31	37	35	30	32	28	11	6					
Pearson						6	5	17	26	31	30	3	0											
Reynolds		30	28	22	20																			
Smith, S.		15	31	11	19	10	28	36	34															
Spencer	0	0	27	30	35	6	10	34	22	0	31	25	24	37	0	3								
Stephenson, C.															0	5	20	40	41	39	▶			
Templeton						1	12	21	24	11														
Tranter									0	0	1	30	21	31	38	33	11	9	0					
Wallace										30	35	41	40	38	37	37	32	▶						
Walters									8	27	4	15	14	30	22									
Warner (gk)	▶	16																						
Welford		19	30	24	10																			
Weston																		17	36	33	12	▶		
Wheldon			37	27	34	39																		
Whitehouse (gk)			24	19																				
Wilkes, A.				12	23	31	31	21	20	10	8	1												
Wilkes, T. (gk)	0	25	30	13	5	4																		
Season Ending	1892	1893	1894	1895	1896	1897	1898	1899	1900	1901	1902	1903	1904	1905	1906	1907	1908	1909	1910	1911	1912	1913	1914	1915
Trophy (◊)			◊	◊	◊◊	◊	◊					◊				◊			◊					

482

The Aston Villa Chronicles 1874 – 1924 (and after)

Players' Profiles

Athersmith, Charlie

Born in 1872 at Bloxwich, Staffordshire	England International	
Usual Position: Outside-Right	Appearances: 307	Goals: 85

"One of the fleetest right-wingers of his time. With a working partner he was well-nigh irresistible. Great at touchline play and centred with unerring precision. A trifle wayward and occasionally forgetful of what was due to the game. Played at his best when unruffled. In consequence of his speed, has been penalised for offside play times out of number by unobservant and sometimes incompetent referees. During a long career he has been of splendid service to his country, to Aston Villa and to Small Heath. Possesses a unique record in international matches."[352]

"[He was] very quick in gathering a ball and getting into his stride. He seemed to divine intuitively the exact position for receiving Devey's pass. Then came the electrifying run down the wing, almost invariably culminating in an accurate and beautifully timed centre to Hodgett's foot or Wheldon's head."[353]

Of the Villa players, he could only be classed for pace with Charlie Johnstone and Tom Pank; he could run a 51 seconds' 440 yards. "[Athersmith] could get the ball across at a lightning pace at top speed."[354] "A great walker, he rarely fails to cover ten miles each day."[355]

Many considered Charlie to be just a sprinter, but when a famous full-back (Donald Gow) came up against him, he was so impressed, he said: "And that is the man who is only a sprinter is it? I call him a footballer!"[356]

Charlie was remembered for a prodigious goal from some 50 yards. It occurred when the opposing keeper came out 30 yards to clear a ball, but the clearance came straight to Charlie. Charlie steadied himself and sent in the shot, which sailed over the keeper's shoulder and into the net just as the keeper got back.[357]

Old Fogey wrote: "There was … a feature about Athersmith which some of the latter-day players would do well to copy. He never made a fuss; shamming of any kind was

---

[352] Villa News & Record (No. 1) 1 Sep 1906
[353] Charlie Johnstone in his column in The Sporting Mail 24 Sep 1910
[354] Villa News & Record 17 Apr 1908 "A Few of the Old Boys"
[355] Midland Express 29 Aug 1903
[356] Midland Express 29 Aug 1903
[357] Midland Express 29 Aug 1903

really beneath him; and he would bear really hard knocks with a stoicism that one could not but admire. I have seen him leave the field with some very tell-tale abrasions, and he took it all with cheerful fortitude when the hurts came from honest accident. It was the sly hackings [and the other bad fouls] … which used to anger him …"[358]

Bache, Joe

Born in 1880 at Stourbridge, Worcs	England International
Usual Position: Inside-Left	Appearances: 473 Goals: 184

Club captain from 1908-09. An inside-left, who was re-positioned at outside-left for a time late in his career, in partnership with Clem Stephenson. He previously was the inside partner in another phenomenal left-wing partnership, with Albert Hall. Consistently chosen as a first-team player from 1901-02 to 1914-15, he was thus the main continuity between the great players of the turn of the 20th century (Cowan, Devey, Athersmith and Spencer) and the team of the period immediately before the Great War.

"[In 1913] A veteran with the speed of a lad. He provides object-lessons in what quiet skill with the ball as opposed to the half-hysterical sprints of the ordinary extreme winger will accomplish. He always bears out the truth of the football axiom that it is three to one on the man with the ball. He does by skill what others do by speed, and yet his speed when nothing else will suffice shows itself to a remarkable degree in one so old in the services of the game. He seems to hand rather than kick the ball to his inside colleagues."[359]

"[N]imble, lithe and smart, he had a way of making rings round defenders, and, as a 'pattern-weaver', few have been his equal. … [In 1923,] many Villa spectators will remember Joe Bache with a good deal of admiration, for he was a great favourite with the crowd, and always well worth watching, especially when he started getting the opposing defence in a tangle, and passing the ball to a clubmate in a favourable position."[360]

Particularly in the years preceding his post as club captain, Bache had a tendency to revert to selfish play – by way of trying to do too much on his own – depending on the circumstances of a game, perhaps. Of his early years, this was stated in *The Villa News* in 1906: "[He] has a remarkable control of the ball, can dodge with the best,

---

[358] In his epitaph to Charlie of 24th September, 1910
[359] Villa News & Record 23 Apr 1913 (Portraits of players in the 1913 Cup Final)
[360] Villa News & Record 23 Feb 1924 ("Some Famous Villa Players")

but messes much of his otherwise effective play by his impetuosity in endeavouring to do too much in the zone of the backs. On his day a dangerous shot, but apt to be erratic, as well as a trifle selfish."

This tendency did not entirely go away, but his later years saw much less of that tendency, according to reports. His earlier years with Hall as his outside partner were remembered for the superb partnership and understanding between the two players, particularly in their ability to interchange positions at will. The problem was (as it was oft-reported) that they became so entwined with one another that they sometimes forgot that the forward line composed of three other forwards as well! Both players originated from Stourbridge and they were, for some time (ca. 1905-10), regarded as the best left-wing pair in the country.

"Neither spectators nor players on the other side knew, at times, which was which or where [so clever was their inter-changing and switching of play]."[361]

When Hall's long-standing injury transpired (and even before, from time to time) Bache was forced to play with other wingers such as Walters, Evans, Eyre, Henshall and Edgley, and this, it would seem, caused Bache to play a different game, which was more team-embracing.

Although Bache eventually moved to outside-left to accommodate Stephenson, the departure of Halse after the 1913 Cup win ultimately forced another move-around, with Stephenson moving to inside-right to link with Wallace, and Bache returning to inside-left to partner Edgley.

Baird, John

Born in 1871 at Dumbarton, Scotland
Usual Position: Full-back   Appearances: 69   Goals: 0

"[A] fine back with plenty of pluck and not too much pace, the lack of which he made up for in sound and canny judgment."[362]

Barber, Tom

Born in 1886 at County Durham
Usual Position: Right-Half   Appearances: 68   Goals: 10

An emergency inside-forward or left-half. Signed from Bolton Wanderers in 1912.

---

[361] "All in a Day's Sport" (R. Allen, Ch.3, 1946)
[362] Villa News & Record 18 & 19 Apr 1924 – "Some Famous Villa Players"

The Aston Villa Chronicles 1874 – 1924 (and after)

"It is hard to think of an English half with just the same amount of uprightly skill as Barber has. His tackling is like the thrusting of a rapier. He runs to meet a man and then picks the ball away from his opponent's feet with the adroitness of a footballing pickpocket. He is never at fault after securing the ball, for there is not a better dribbler in the game today. Some suggest that he does too much dribbling, but when that phase of football is indulged in by anyone near as clever as Barber, it is very difficult to have too much of it, for his is dribbling without selfishness – rather it is dribbling in order to make chances for others."[363]

Brawn, Billy

Born in 1878 at Wellingborough	England International	
Usual Position: Outside-Right	Appearances: 107	Goals: 20

"For a period quite the best outside right in the country. Possessing a fine turn of speed, is always a dangerous man when once clear. Centres with force and precision from the line and can shoot with deadly effect when within range. Has scored many fine goals with oblique shots. Brilliant on his day, but somewhat [inconsistent]. Forceful, energetic; has more vim than resource."[364]

"Brawn... reminds me of Billy Gunn (the old Notts man), in his long, raking stride and the manner in which he centres when on the swing."[365]

"Of the many thousands who witnessed his superb display at the Palace last April [1905], there would be a score or two lost in amazement when they learnt of Brawn's transfer [in March, 1906]."[366] He went to play with Steve Bloomer at Middlesbrough.

Brown, Albert: Please see chapter 8.

Born in 1862 at Aston, Birmingham		
Usual Position: Outside-Right	Appearances: 106	Goals: 54

---

[363] Villa News & Record 23 Apr 1913 (Portraits of players in the 1913 Cup Final)
[364] Villa News & Record (No. 1) 1 Sep 1906
[365] 'Argus Junior' in Sports Argus 17 Jan 1903. An opinion also expressed elsewhere.
[366] The Sporting Mail 31 Mar 1906 – "Men of Note"

The Aston Villa Chronicles 1874 – 1924 (and after)

Buckley, Chris

Born in 1886 at Manchester	England Trialist
Usual Position: Centre-Half	Appearances: 143 Goals: 3

A most talented player who would surely have had caps for England but for losing an entire season after injury in a League match, and then also being severely injured in an England trial, a match in which he had been outstanding. It was suggested in various sporting publications that he was the best Villa centre-half since the marvellous James Cowan. Buckley was a thinking player who often stamped his authority on a match. Indeed, that 1909-10 championship half-back line with Buckley at its centre was regarded as Villa's best since the 'double' side of 1896-97.

"No-one is quicker nor more capable of circumventing the best intentions of his opponents, of discovering the weak points in their armour, and of taking full advantage of them … What he makes up his mind to do he does quietly and effectively and without the least ostentation … one of the foremost artists of the day."[367]

His career went seriously awry when he fell into disagreement with the Villa over a benefit payment, for which he was suspended in 1912 for two years (substantiated by both the Football League and Football Association), and did not play for the Villa again. He only re-entered the game with the Arsenal at the end of his suspension, in 1914. However, as a businessman he was eventually elected to the Villa board in 1936 and became chairman in 1955.

He is almost certainly the first Villa player to have possessed a motor-car (ca. 1910), and I understand that after the First World War, he was employed by the Austin Motor Company in a product promotional role.

Originating from Manchester, he and his older brother **Frank Buckley** were farmers during their playing days, and had a farm at Redditch. Frank played for the Villa before Chris, but did not make the first team. However, Frank played for Birmingham at the time Chris was a regular first-teamer with Villa, and in later years became a famous manager of the Wolves.

About Chris Buckley's farming capabilities, it was said: "he has some capital pigs, and only a few days ago sold two Whites for consignment to the King of Italy." Perhaps there are some that never knew that Italy once had a king![368]

---

[367] Villa News & Record, December, 1911, on the occaion of his benefit match.
[368] 'Linesman' in his column in The Sporting Mail 6 Feb 1909

The Aston Villa Chronicles 1874 – 1924 (and after)

Campbell, Johnny

Born in 1871 at Glasgow	Scottish International	
Usual Position: Centre-Forward	Appearances: 63	Goals: 43

"The second greatest centre we have had [to Archie Hunter]. ... He worked for position, and quickly and unobtrusively made openings for the [other] forwards."[369]

"[He was] a rare dribbler, a sure and adroit passer, unselfish, and a fine shot; a stalwart gentleman who played the game because he liked it ..."[370]

Chatt, Bob

Born in 1870 at County Durham		
Usual Position: Half-back or forward	Appearances: 94	Goals: 26

He arrived from the same Middlesbrough Ironopolis club as trainer Joe Grierson, in August, 1893. There are some that spoke well of Chatt's play, but others (whilst accepting that he was a trier and played well at times) thought that he was not up to the 'Villa standard' of high quality. He was, nevertheless, a very useful backup player.

Coulton, Frank: Please see chapter 8.

Born in 1862 at Walsall, Staffordshire		
Usual Position: Full-back	Appearances: 60	Goals: 0

Once played in a League match as an emergency goalkeeper.

Cowan, James

Born in 1868 at Dumbartonshire	Scottish International	
Usual Position: Centre-Half	Appearances: 354	Goals: 26

"For a long period one of the mainstays of Aston Villa as centre half-back. Originally came to the district to play for Warwick County FC, but was attached to Perry Barr [in 1889]. Always a favourite by reason of his untiring energy and skilful tackling. Quick in detecting favourable openings for his side, his prompt backing up and placing of the ball proved of immense value. Undismayed and uncomplaining after the hardest of games, he won a high position amongst the Villa celebrities.

---

[369] Charlie Johnstone in his column in The Sporting Mail 22 Sep 1906
[370] Villa News & Record 9 Feb 1924 – "Some Famous Players"

Occasionally scored, but did not shine as a goal-getter."[371]

He learnt his football, as a boy, from watching the Vale of Leven (then a great side in Scotland), his home team.

Albert Evans, Cowan's full-back colleague in the 'double' team, recalled[372] that it was Cowan that controlled his defence with an iron hand, and decreed that instead of booting the ball from defence (as was the common way, then), Evans should place the ball to his wing-half (Jimmy Crabtree).

"His control of the ball was wonderful, and one particular peculiarity was that he very seldom used his head. [To avoid use of his head, he] would jump a yard and more into the air to gather it by any portion of his body below the shoulders, and he used to say he believed in playing *foot*ball and not bobbing it about in the air with his head." [373]

A celebrated centre-forward once commented: "It's like playing against three men when you meet Jimmy Cowan; he's the most tiresome and tireless half-back I have ever met, and no end of strength to his side."[374]

Howard Spencer wrote: "Then, James Cowan was, and is accepted today, as the greatest exponent of centre half-back play ever seen. A perfect tackler, he was gifted with a remarkable turn of speed for a man of his build, and no-one has ever excelled him in the art of tying-up a centre-forward."[375]

Cowan, John

Born in   1870 at   Dumbartonshire
Usual Position: Outside-Left   Appearances: 74   Goals: 28

Brother of James. Mainly a left-winger, he competed for that spot with Steve Smith in the 'Double' year of 1896-97, and in other seasons, and actually played in the 1897 final. Scorer of some spectacular goals. Otherwise not a highly remarkable player, but one who made few mistakes.

---

[371] Villa News & Record (No. 1) 1 Sep 1906
[372] In Peter Morris' *Aston Villa: The History of a Great Football Club, 1874-1960*
[373] Villa News & Record 12 Sep 1923 – "Some Famous Villa Players"
[374] Villa News & Record 12 Sep 1923 – "Some Famous Villa Players"
[375] In his column in The Sporting Mail 13 Oct 1906

The Aston Villa Chronicles 1874 – 1924 (and after)

Cox, Gershom: Please see chapter 8.

Born in 1863 at Birmingham		
Usual Position: Full-Back	Appearances: 97	Goals: 0

Crabtree, Jimmy

Born in 1871 at Burnley, Lancashire	England International	
Usual Position: Left-Back or Left-Half	Appearances: 200	Goals: 7

Came as a full-back from Burnley in July, 1895. "One of England's greatest players. Shone in any position. Great as a half-back, but greater, possibly, as a back, kicking cleanly and with rare precision. A keen, skilful tackler, clever at close quarters and equally reliable in the open; cool, resourceful, and brainy. Excelled in the finer points of the game, and one of the most versatile players England has boasted. For many seasons unrivalled in his position."[376] He also played in the forward line on occasions.

When he came to Villa, it was because of the current excellence of Spencer and Welford at full-back he was prevailed upon to play at centre-half. He reluctantly agreed but became equally famous as a half-back as a result.[377]

The fee of £250 (then a huge fee) that Villa paid to Burnley for his services was scoffed at by the critics, who said that no player was worth that much. Crabtree proved to be one of the greatest – certainly the most versatile – players of his day. Even in the late 1930s, Crabtree was still thought of as the finest all-round footballer that ever played.[378]

That he was such an outstanding player, and one recognised by many as being good enough to be considered as the best English half-back at least prior to the 1930s, it comes as a surprise to read the following account in a history of Blackburn Rovers:

> When he [Crabtree] began his football career, word reached Blackburn that he was a 'likely lad'. [A scout] was sent to watch him. He returned with the report that the player was 'no good'. This judge of footballers was despatched on the same mission a second and even a third time, but he adhered to his opinion that Crabtree was "not a footballer and never would be!"[379]

---

[376] Villa News & Record (No. 1) 1 Sep 1906
[377] Villa News & Record 5 Sep 1908
[378] Fred Ward, Aston Villa (1948)
[379] Charles Francis "History of Blackburn Rovers 1875-1925" (Classic Reprint)

The Aston Villa Chronicles 1874 – 1924 (and after)

Devey, Harry: Please see chapter 8.

Born in 1860 at Newtown, Birmingham		
Usual Position: Half-Back	Appearances: 84	Goals: 1

Devey, John ('Jack')

Born in 1872 at Newtown, Birmingham	England International
Usual Position: Inside-Right	Appearances: 306 Goals: 186

Club captain from 1892. Inside-right or centre-forward and captain of the side through five League championships and two FA Cup Final wins. Famed for his right-wing partnership with Charlie Athersmith.

"He had for some years been a remarkably able player, and some said his best days were behind him when he came to the Villa. Instead, he became a greater footballer than ever [- he was still only 24 years of age when he joined Villa in March, 1891]. It had been expected he would join Villa (from Excelsior) before, but it was only Archie Hunter's demise that eventually created the opening."[380]

According to John Devey,[381] the move to Villa was not clear-cut:

> [At St. George's] the very people who were loudest in the praise of Devey's play were the first to shout him down when he was 'off colour'. That is why I left the old St. George's, and it was with feelings of regret that I severed the association, for I was leaving one of the best men who ever took an interest in football in Mr. Harry Mitchell.

It was also written: "When the game of baseball was imported from America, John Devey became so proficient that he was probably as fine a player [at that sport] as this country has produced. ..."[382] It is understood that the Villa invited Devey to talk about baseball (see later about his talent in that sport), but when he arrived the topic was quickly switched to football!

It was said of him: "His well-knit figure, his clear, healthy, out-of-door complexion, the fearless, straight-forward glance of his dark eyes, his cheery smile, and his frank, open countenance, would arrest attention anywhere."[383]

---

[380] Villa News & Record 17 Apr 1908 "A Few of the Old Boys"
[381] In his column in The Sporting Mail 13 Jan 1906
[382] Villa News & Record 5 Apr 1912
[383] "Men of Note" in The Sporting Mail 10 Feb 1906

The Aston Villa Chronicles 1874 – 1924 (and after)

After his playing career was over, the following was written: "For one so skilful, thorough, and effective, his merits when in his prime were inexplicably overlooked by the [England] Selection Committee.[384] Could play in most positions in the forward line, and was for many years one of the very best pivots in England. A close dribbler, with good pace, he was alive to every movement on the field, and possessing the rare gift of 'intelligent anticipation', made a splendid leader. Knew the game really well, never lacked initiation, but a strong believer in combination. Exceptionally clever with head and feet in front of goal; a prolific scorer."[385]

"[John Devey] had one marvellously clever habit of tricking a back, and whirling suddenly and sending in a pot shot with the velocity of a cannonball that was [also] generally true to its mark."[386]

The classic publication "Association Football and the Men Who Made It" (1906) wrote of him: "John Devey was equally at home at either inside right or centre, but the former was the position which he made his own. Fast and clever, he could work the ball through the defence at a greater rate than most men, and he usually made a bee-line for the goal. At his best he could dodge and dribble adroitly, and he had a good idea of finding where the posts stood."

However, it was as a team man that he was best remembered: "He didn't aspire to do all the work himself; he was always content to 'sink' his identity. He was unselfish to a fault; he liked to make openings for his partner and the centre-man. In fact, Devey 'made' wing-man Charlie Athersmith. He used to skip along with the ball until the defenders were compelled to go for him, as his progress spelled danger. But the moment that he had drawn the opposition away from Athersmith, the ball used to fly from [Devey's] toe and roll gently towards the touch-line. In a twinkling Athersmith would be on his stride, the half-back was left standing still, and often the full-back was raced past, too. Then there would be either a swinging centre while on the run, or the ball would unexpectedly be tossed back to Devey, and the inside man would be left in an advantageous position for shooting. Devey had a genius for getting the ball out to his partner, and it must be said that he had a partner well worth feeding."

That John Devey scored 186 goals for Villa is testament to the fact that he was not only a play-maker! He is one of only two Villa players (the other being Tom 'Pongo'

---

[384] In particular, he was never selected to play against the key foe – Scotland. This dumbfounded even the Scottish party, who considered Devey (at his best) superior to any other England player in that position.
[385] Villa News & Record (No. 1) 1 Sep 1906
[386] Villa News & Record 17 Apr 1908 "A Few of the Old Boys"

Waring) who scored more goals than the number of games played in a normal season.

He was also a prolific cricketer for Warwickshire, for whom he played until 1907: "As a cricketer, John Devey is invaluable to Warwickshire. The freedom of his batting is remarkable. He never has to play himself in. He is as likely to hit the first ball to the boundary as not, and he can hit a good ball almost as well as a bad one."[387] He once scored over 200 runs in one innings.

As a captain, "He played so hard that he didn't have a lot of breath to give voluminous instructions on the field, but he could (and did) harangue them before and after matches ... [A]n accomplished theorist as well as a most practical and prominent player."[388]

One further tribute to his athleticism at a later age: although he finished his main footballing career by the 1901-02 season, he is recorded as playing in the Villa reserves as late as Easter, 1906, and even scoring a goal![389]

Dickson, Billy

Born in 1866 at Crail, Fife	Scottish International	
Usual Position: Centre-Forward	Appearances: 64	Goals: 34

Captain of the Villa preceding John Devey, and was thus captain of the 1891-92 FA Cup Final side, the defeat at which he was said to be mortified; he thought the Final "a snip" for the Villa. A great character and well-remembered by those who saw him play, though he was not an elegant player. He had ability and was capped for Scotland against England.

Dowds, Peter

Born in 1867 at Johnstone, Renfrewshire	Scottish International	
Usual Position: Half-Back	Appearances: 21	Goals: 3

A Scot from Celtic, Dowds had an extremely short career (he played just 21 matches in 1892-93; he died in 1895, after leaving the Villa), but he was an amazing surprise to all. He is included in this section because of his reputed outstanding talent. "He was a football juggler, and was the only man I ever saw who simply made ducks and

---

[387] 'Nomad' in Sports Argus 28 Jul 1900
[388] Villa News & Record 26 Jan 1924 – "Some Famous Players"
[389] The Sporting Mail 21 Apr 1906

drakes of Mr. Isaiah Bassett's talents. ... At half-back work he was a revelation." [390]
"[Dowds was] thick-set, [with a] large head of the bullet type, and legs like those of a billiards table."[391]

"[H]e showed us tricks and graces in half-back evolution which were, I think, different and more devastating than have been seen before or since his coming. ... [H]e had a way of getting the ball and keeping it as long as he liked that was really uncanny, and he would exasperate his opponents to such a degree that rendered them either furious or flabbergasted – he didn't mind which! Often he would let the other fellow hurt himself by using the ball as an ankle-pad and letting a forward have a 'go' at it that nearly dislocated knee. ... [During that kind of performance] he wore a slow sort of saturnine smile in the manner of Mephistopheles."[392]

'Linesman', in the *Sporting Mail*, wrote:[393]

> [Dowds'] control of the ball was wonderful. It looked sometimes as though he had it glued to the end of his toes.
>
> I can recall a friend of mine, who was an old Yorkshire rugby player, and who was inclined to look despisingly on the Association game, reluctantly consenting to accompany me to see Aston Villa play Blackburn Rovers [at Perry Barr]. I believe he really went to scoff, but he remained to cheer! Peter Dowds above all others – and there were more good ones playing – was the man who took his eye, and before he had been on the ground very long he took off his hat and waved it and vociferously cheered a fine display of mazy dribbling by Dowds.

The Yorkshireman came again to see the Villa; he was well taken with what he saw!

Derby County were the visitors in a match on the old Perry Barr meadow, and Johnny Goodall, the visiting captain, wore, as usual, a close-fitting cap to hide his bald pate. ... Peter Dowds sent down a terrific shot, which was cleverly headed away by Goodall, who, in the effort, had his cap removed and was stunned for a while. Peter stood aghast. 'Megad!', he exclaimed, 'I've scolped the mon!' [394]

A Lion's Fun

---

[390] Villa News & Record 11 April 1908 – "The Middle Line". According to Sports Argus of 29 Dec 1907, Dowds was originally a half-back with Celtic and then converted into a centre-forward, whereupon Celtic achieved a lot of success. It was that position that Villa were concerned about when they brought him to Villa, but after being tried there for two matches he "insisted upon being put in the half-back line." He said, "No more centre-forward for me. I have had enough of it and I don't intend to play there again if I can help it."
[391] Fred Ward's "Official History of Aston Villa" (1948)
[392] Villa News & Record 27 & 31 Oct 1923 – "Famous Villa Players"
[393] 7 Feb 1914

The Aston Villa Chronicles 1874 – 1924 (and after)

Ducat, Andy

Born in 1886 at Brixton, London	England International
Usual Position: Half-Back	Appearances: 87 Goals: 4

He was an outstanding player for Woolwich Arsenal for a number of years, and came to Villa in 1912. His talent was immediately apparent, but he suffered a very bad break in his leg in only his fourth match that not only put him out for the rest of the season, but also the whole of 1913-14. He therefore missed Villa's cup triumph in 1913, but was captain of the side that won the cup in 1920. A cricketer, he played for Surrey and England, and died while playing cricket in 1942. He was a greatly loved sportsman, as became apparent by the number and range of well-wishers when in a lengthy stay in hospital as a result of his accident, in 1912.

Evans, Albert

Born in 1874 at County Durham	
Usual Position: Left-Back	Appearances: 203 Goals: 0

An unfortunate player – on more than one occasion, selection for his country seemed a certainty, but each time accident or illness or precedence given to his club robbed him of the opportunity.

From Barnard Castle in the north-east, he became linked with Aston Villa through his friendship with Bob Chatt, who invited him to spend a holiday in Birmingham one August. Chatt persuaded Evans to turn out in a practice match at Villa, and his performance was such that he was immediately signed up. He played in a very successful Birmingham League Villa team in his first season (1895-96), in which he played in every position except keeper, and then stepped into Welford's position in 1896-97, when Welford became injured. A long and successful partnership with Spencer was thus struck up, but from match reports it looks as though it was not until season 1898-99 that he developed his best play. Before that, he was not seen as an outstanding back.

On various occasions, "his dash and accurate kicking have saved his team from awkward predicaments."

Eventually (in a cup tie at Stoke on 6 Feb 1904), he sustained a fractured right ankle which kept him out of football for some time. Whilst he was out, Miles established himself in Evans' place, and such was Evans' sportsmanship when he returned from

---

[394] The Sporting Mail 16 Mar 1907

injury, he acknowledged Miles to be a great back and was content to play in the reserves. Miles then succumbed to a long period out of the side through blood poisoning, and Evans re-established himself in his old position until he again fractured his right ankle in a match against Birmingham on 20 January 1906. He later broke his leg a third time (during training), and when he recovered from that, he was transferred to West Bromwich Albion, when a fourth (and very serious) breakage brought an end to his playing career. There was also a little known fifth breakage in a friendly match in 1915.

When a youth, Evans had great success on the track and won prizes to the value of £200 in one year (1906 values note!). He was also a good cricketer and golfer, and a "reader of high-class literature."[395]

Evans was a member of the 'double' side of 1896-97, as well as the next two Championship-winning sides. He outlived all other members of those sides, passing away at the age of 92 in 1966, having also actively served in the First World War following a spell as a globetrotter, and as a gold prospector in the Yukon! One-time manager of Coventry City, he was still talent-spotting for Villa when in his 80s.

Garraty, Billy

Born in 1878 at Saltley, Birmingham	England International
Usual Position: Inside-Right	Appearances: 255 Goals: 111

He joined the club as an outside-left, and played some games in that position. Known mainly for his goals in his earlier years (30 goals in his first full season), he became a sound midfield player at inside-right or right-half, and was even tried at centre-half. He gave long and highly valued service.

About his display in the 1905 Cup Final, it was written,[396] "If ever there was a man who earned a distinction by subtle touches, intelligent anticipation, superb endeavour, that man was William Garraty. ... Oh, the beautiful brainy touches ... would that dear old Archie Hunter had lived to see them..."

---

[395] From "Men of Mark" (No. 20) Sports Argus 13 Jan 1906
[396] The Sporting Mail 17 Mar 1906 - "Men of Note"

The Aston Villa Chronicles 1874 – 1924 (and after)

George, Billy

Born in 1874 at Shrewsbury	England International
Usual Position: Goalkeeper	Appearances: 396 Goals: 0

"One of the greatest ... goalkeepers in the history of the club. For many seasons was at the top of his form, after a superb opening display against WBA. Quick on his feet, splendid reach, full of resource, punches the ball with great power, fields well, and a grand kick. A rare good man on a side, and an ornament to the game."[397] One of the rare Villa players of those days who exceeded six feet in height. George was also a capable cricketer and played for Warwickshire.

"It is wonderful what a sense of security one feels with George in goal. There may be more [spectacular] custodians, but all through his long career I know of no-one who has been so consistently safe and reliable [a remark made before the arrival of Sam Hardy]."[398]

Groves, Willie

Born in 1869 at Leith	Scottish International
Usual Position: Half-Back	Appearances: 26 Goals: 3

Said to be a football genius, he was a forward and midfielder who came from West Bromwich Albion in company with John Reynolds in May, 1893. He and Reynolds were two of a famous Albion half-back line responsible for defeating Villa in the Cup Final of 1892. However, Groves significantly contributed for just one season (1893-94) – Villa's first championship win – before he left Villa to return to Scotland, his health being a serious issue.

It was written: "He was one of the most artistic and cheerful of players ... and there is no doubt that to a very large extent he was responsible for the success which crowned the Perry Barr club in their League Championship [in 1893-94]".[399]

---

[397] Villa News & Record (No. 1) 1 Sep 1906
[398] Charlie Johnstone in The Sporting Mail 16 Nov 1907
[399] Athletic News 12 Nov 1894

The Aston Villa Chronicles 1874 – 1924 (and after)

Hall, Albert

Born in 1882 at Stourbridge, Worcs.	England International
Usual Position: Outside-Left	Appearances: 214 Goals: 62

He was brought into the club as an inside-right, but moved to the left-wing. See the profile on Joe Bache. This left-wing pair were at times devastating, and were considered the best left wing pair in the country from about 1905 to 1910. Hall played in every forward position, however, and was capable as a winger on either flank, and at inside-forward, but was at his best on the left with Bache. Acknowledged as a 'brainy' player, it was thought he would be good enough to play with any top inside player.

Hall is said to have had the one fault of over-using the trick of waiting for a back to challenge before dragging the ball back to beat him. When used too much in a match (which was his want), he could get hurt by the back's anticipatory lunge to prevent the drag-back.

Halse, Harold

Born in 1886 at Stratford, East London	England International
Usual Position: Inside-Right	Appearances: 37 Goals: 28

"As an inside-right just about the quickest thing in football, If you do not watch his passes closely you get the impression that he is flighty and undependable. He is not; he is simply amazing by the manner in which, while racing at top speed, he places the ball at the feet of colleagues, or takes a flying shot at goal. One of the most dangerous forwards of his time, he can shoot with either foot, and usually does so at a pace that compels success."[400]

Coming from Manchester United in 1912 – and registering a not remarkable 42 goals in 109 matches for them – Halse only played the 1912-13 season at Villa, but during that time made an indelible mark with his general play and 28 goals in 37 matches, including five in one match when deputising at centre-forward for Harry Hampton. Considering his height (5 feet 5½ inches) he is reported as being an amazingly good header of the ball. His departure to Chelsea helped to cause some unsettling of the Villa team in their performances during the first half of 1913-14, reflecting (possibly) on how perfect a cog he had been in the Villa team during the 1912-13 season.

---

[400] Villa News & Record 23 Apr 1913 (Portraits of players in the 1913 Cup Final)

To add to all that, Charlie Johnstone wrote of him: "Despite his lack of inches, he is a wonderful tackler, and the most scientific charger in the team."[401]

Hampton, Harry ('Appy 'Arry!)

Born in 1885 at Wellington, Shrops	England International
Usual Position: Centre-Forward	Appearances: 376 Goals: 242

He was also a useful emergency centre-half.

Hampton was particularly distinguished by his inclusion – as a 20-year-old – in the renowned four-volume "Association Football and The Men Who Made It", published in 1905. Such was the impact that this player had made on the game in just one season. The three-page section on him included the following:

> He does not make sensational dribbles, but he is always lying in wait ... ready for the ball to come into the centre, and then he takes it on the run, and goes straight for goal with it. He turns neither to the right hand nor to the left. It is his business to get that ball between those posts he sees in front of him, and with that end in view he goes straight on, and if he gets a fair chance of shooting, the odds are that he scores. He has that indescribable dash which no man seems able to acquire unless Nature has planted the instinct in him.

In 1911, the Manchester United Official Programme stated:

> The Wellington youth proved an instantaneous success. He revolutionised the Villa style of attack, and dash and speed became the Villa mode to the exclusion of the older classic methods, which are now almost solely monopolised by Newcastle United and Manchester United.[402]

This comment was enlarged upon two years later:

> No centre-forward of recent years has maintained for so long such splendid form and yet never departed from the injury-inviting style of play that is essential to success in this position. Hampton has the dash of youth combined with the judgment of experience. He is fearless as ever, and capable of much more effective individualisation than used to be the case. When opposed to Hampton, the back who hesitates is lost, and in most cases the goalkeeper is in the same position. He is a man with speed and a fine knowledge of how to use it.[403]

---

[401] In his column in The Sporting Mail 28 Dec 1912
[402] On the occasion of a Villa Cup visit to Old Trafford 4 Feb 1911
[403] Villa News & Record 23 Apr 1913 (Portraits of players in the 1913 Cup Final)

The Aston Villa Chronicles 1874 – 1924 (and after)

Scorer of 242 goals in his career at Villa,[404] he scored five in one match. It was noted at the time that Hampton "has a penchant for the opposing goalkeeper, and likes to have a game of roly-poly with him somewhere in the region of the back netting."

Hardy, Sam

Born in 1883 at Chesterfield, Derbyshire	England International
Usual Position: Goalkeeper	Appearances: 183 Goals: 0

"Saves difficult shots more easily than any other goalkeeper living, never appearing to be at full-stretch to get to the ball. His remarkable intuition is founded upon constant watching of the positions of players and an experience that tells him to which part of the goal-mouth a forward must shoot. ... To realise how good Hardy is you must watch his movements before a shot is made. While forwards are dribbling and manoeuvring for an opening ... you will see Hardy stealing (not skipping and jumping, as is the case with the keeper who is over-anxious to nervousness) from place to place, but is always well-balanced for anything, whether it is the upward spring to the high shot, the downward dive to the ball that is low and wide, or for the catching and hugging of the ball when the rush of an opponent is so well-timed that a shoulder charge must be resisted. The most extraordinary thing about Hardy's play is the fact that he does great things so easily."[405]

Hardy played for Liverpool for a number of years before coming to Villa, and in games against the Villa was usually outstanding. He joined Villa from Liverpool in company with Harrop. Hardy's career with England overlapped his Liverpool and Villa careers. At the close of the 20th century, he was voted one of the League's greatest 100 players.

Harrop, Jimmy

Born in 1884 at Sheffield	England Trialist
Usual Position: Centre-Half	Appearances: 171 Goals: 4

Harrop came from Liverpool in company with Sam Hardy. "In one respect, very much like Barber, inasmuch as always on the move, he never hesitates about a tackle. One of the best halves of the day, he is remarkably clever at meeting and placing a moving ball. Off the side of his foot it can go straight and truly to a colleague at a pace that makes the kick of the nature of a shot. That, however, is only

---

[404] A record eventually narrowly beaten nearly 20 years later by Billy Walker (244 goals).
[405] Villa News & Record 23 Apr 1913 (Portraits of players in the 1913 Cup Final)

The Aston Villa Chronicles 1874 – 1924 (and after)

when something quick is essential to the situation, for with time to place the ball Harrop kicks with an accuracy greater than Harry Vardon's [the champion golfer's] putting shows."[406]

"As cool as the proverbial cucumber."

Hodgetts, Dennis ('Denny')

Born in 1863 at Birmingham	England International
Usual Position: Outside-Left	Appearances: 215 Goals: 91

Please see his profile in Chapter 8. Denny was an extraordinary link between Villa's first FA Cup-winning side and the mid-1890s, when the Villa started to carry off the League and Cup on a regular basis. Denny eventually left Villa to play for Small Heath in te autumn of 1896, fearing that his career with Villa was over. This was a decision he regretted for the rest of his life – Villa won the 'double' that season!

Hunter, George

Born in 1886 at Peshawar, India	
Usual Position: Half-Back	Appearances: 97 Goals: 1

He was previously a soldier. A whole-hearted and robust player, a genuine humourist and a good story-teller. A very good player, he was selected for the Football League before some 'attitude' crept into his game, and he was subsequently sold to Oldham.

Johnson, George

Born in 1871 at West Bromwich	England Trialist
Usual Position: Inside-Right.	Appearances: 108 Goals: 47

An inconsistent player, but on his day could be brilliant.

Leach, Jimmy

Born in 1890 at County Durham	
Usual Position: Half-Back	Appearances: 76 Goals: 3

"A discovery [in 1912-13, from non-league football]; when he went to the Villa, people wondered why. Then he got a chance in the first team, and then people knew

---

[406] Villa News & Record 23 Apr 1913 (Portraits of players in the 1913 Cup Final)

why. He is one of those halves who have the rare quality of being able to show all the dash in the world when tackling, but who change into calm, calculating persons when in a position to touch the ball forward to the advantage of his side. Each of his two styles is an excellent one, and he must be nearly the best new half-back in First League football."[407]

Leake, Alex

| Born in 1871 at Small Heath, Birmingham England International |
| Usual Position: Half-Back Appearances: 140 Goals: 9 |

He joined the Villa rather late in his career (he was over 30), but he nevertheless gave several years good service after finding the Villa to his liking. "A good-tempered, honest worker; safe rather than showy. Hard to beat in a tackle, and good at spoiling an opponent's pass. Alert, keeps his head, and never tires in the hardest matches. His unfailing good humour has made him a general favourite."[408] An import from Small Heath, he became a better player with the Villa.

> Leake was well known as the joker at Villa Park, and the following was written about him in this regard:
>
> *A Lion's Fun*
>
> [In his time at Small Heath] if there was the remotest chance of tickling the humour of 'the gallery' we should see some unrehearsed bit of back-healing, an overhead-kick while in the act of falling down, a gambolling feat in the mud with the ball held between his feet, or, maybe a ludicrously indignant appeal against an opponent after some transgression by himself!
>
> Just take a quiet glance at him as he stands there unfolding some quaint story to his comrades. It might be thought that he was elucidating some mystery of mysteries, so serious is the expression on his earnest face. With a furtive dart of the eyes, first one way, then another, with a little by-play with his hands to give point to the incident being related, he approaches the climax of the anecdote, and as he does, so the eyes begin to twinkle, the expression alters as if by magic. The end comes, there is a burst of laughter from the group, and Alec's face assumes an expression of exquisite drollery which asks quite plainly, 'What is there to laugh about?!'[409]

"With a small rubber ball, [he] could bring the ball back over his head and then, back-heeling to his front again, and catch it on the top of his boot." That was simply playing around, of course, "but could do it effectively in League matches, and would

---

[407] Villa News & Record 23 Apr 1913 (Portraits of players in the 1913 Cup Final)
[408] Villa News & Record (No. 1) 1 Sep 1906

not be asked to 'cut it out'."[410]

Leake also had definite footballing qualities, and England caps to prove it:

> Had I to select a centre half-back to pull a side together through a really big game at any time during the past 7 or 8 years [writing in 1906], Alec Leake would not have been passed over without serious consideration.

Logan, James ("Jock")

Born in 1885 at Glasgow
Usual Position: Half-Back   Appearances: 157   Goals: 4

Also a useful full-back. Not to be confused with another James Logan with Villa in the early 1890s. He came from the famed Queens Park club at the age of 17, and eventually settled in as a worthy half-back (sometimes deputising at full-back), and was captain for awhile following the demise of Spencer. Having had a successful sojourn at the Villa (particularly at centre-half, for which position he competed with Chris Buckley until he settled at left-half), he eventually retreated back to Scotland and signed for Rangers.

A scratch golfer, his brother **Alex Logan** (a forward) also played for Villa for a while during Jock's period at Villa, and a younger brother played for Chelsea.

Lyons, Tommy

Born in 1885 at Hednesford, Staffordshire
Usual Position: Full-Back   Appearances: 237   Goals: 0

"Possessing the drooped head of a man with a set purpose, Lyons plays as he looks. Not a scientist, he knows it and just attempts that which is the obviously best thing for the moment. Never a sign of fear in his tackling, he rushes in with a determination to get the ball, whatever may happen. He appears slow of thought at times, but when that is the case it is merely the hesitation of a man who wants to make sure before he does that which might place him in a false position."[411]

---

[409] The Sporting Mail 20 Jan 1906 - "Men of Note"
[410] Fred Ward's "Official History of Aston Villa" (1948)
[411] Villa News & Record 23 Apr 1913 (Portraits of players in the 1913 Cup Final)

The Aston Villa Chronicles 1874 – 1924 (and after)

McLuckie, Jasper

Born in 1877 at Lancashire		
Usual Position: Centre-Forward	Appearances: 62	Goals: 45

He was very successful in the Bury side that won the Cup by 4-0 in 1900, and scored two goals in that final. Such was his skill that Villa seemed to have been compelled to bring him to Villa Park, and get him they did, although when they signed him he was in the Bury reserves team. In his first season (1901-02) he scored 16 goals in 23 matches, followed the next season by 20 goals in 24 matches. He was top scorer in both those seasons. Three seasons in it was 9 goals in 15 matches. He was then transferred to Plymouth Argyle.

"An adept at clean tackling and smart, tricky work. McLuckie has a command of the ball which many a veteran might envy. ... He is rarely seen bearing down upon the opposing keeper, but he has a neat way of running round the backs, dashing forward at great speed, and firing with tremendous power at the goal."[412]

Miles, Alfred ("Freddie")

Born in 1884 at Aston, Birmingham	England International	
Usual Position: Full-Back	Appearances: 269	Goals: 0

Signed from Aston St. Mary's when 18. He came into the side in the second half of the 1903-04 season as a result of serious injury to Albert Evans, and continued (barring illness and injury) as a back for the next ten years, primarily at left-back. He was thus a member of the 1905 Cup-winning side, and the 1910 Championship-winning side. A genial man, he became club trainer in 1919 and coached the 1920 FA Cup Winning side in his first season as trainer. However, by 1925 he had fallen ill, and died in 1926.

Pearson, Joe

Born in 1877 at Brierley Hill, Staffs.		
Usual Position: Half-Back	Appearances: 118	Goals: 7

"Study Pearson's physiognomy after being pulled up by the referee, and it says as plainly as tongue can speak, 'Rough? What am I here for then?' Watch that glance from Joe's piercing eyes when a peevish disappointed opponent claims a penalty after being legitimately tackled! ... In the 1905 Final, faced by an admittedly clever

---

[412] Sports Argus 19 Oct 1901

and powerful wing – Veitch and Gornell ... - his speed, his watchfulness and following-up must have made the Northerners grow weary of attempting to pass him."[413] He became a leading football linesman, then a referee, after finishing as a player. Even later, he became a headmaster of a school in Stourbridge, and was also Mayor of Stourbridge (1941-43).

Reynolds, John ('Baldy')

Born in 1869 at Blackburn	England (and Irish!) International
Usual Position: Right-Half	Appearances: 110 Goals: 17

Arrived in May, 1893 in company with Willie Groves from West Bromwich Albion – two of the reasons for Villa's defeat by Albion in the '92 Final.

"A remarkably smart half-back. For his inches a perfect wonder. Knew every 'trick of the trade', and usually showed up well in big matches. Had a happy knack of scoring at critical moments. Something of a roamer, he had the unique distinction of representing both Ireland and England in International matches. Had an eye to the humorous side of football."[414]

Howard Spencer wrote: "For a man who was not remarkable for speed – he was ever lacking in that quality – John Reynolds was one of the most successful half-backs that has played. A glance at the cranium gave you the impression that he was in the aged class of footballers, but a wilier being never kicked a ball. He was full of originality, and was one of the most perfect judges of an opponent's intentions I have known."[415]

Smith, Steve ("Titch")

Born in 1874 at Halesowen, Staffordshire	England International
Usual Position: Outside-Left	Appearances: 184 Goals: 42

Arrived in August, 1893 from Hednesford Town. "One of the most effective players on the left wing since the time of Hodgetts [who, by 1893, was playing at inside-left]. A particularly close dribbler, with a fine turn of speed, he was only robbed of the ball with difficulty, and with anything approaching a chance would centre most accurately. Being on the small side, he often suffered from the lungeous opponent, and while with the Villa received more than his share of hard knocks. Quiet and

---

[413] The Sporting Mail 9 Feb 1907 – "Men of Note"
[414] Villa News & Record (No. 1) 1 Sep 1906
[415] In his column in The Sporting Mail 13 Oct 1906

unassuming, he proved a most unselfish partner, and could always be relied upon to do his utmost. A modest winner and a good loser."[416]

Spencer, Howard

Born in 1875 at Edgbaston, Birmingham	England International	
Usual Position: Right-Back	Appearances: 293	Goals: 2

Club captain from 1902-03. "During a long and brilliant career has been one of England's best and fairest backs. Knows and plays the game thoroughly. Came into prominence in a Junior International at Leamington in 1894 [, a match in which he played by accident as he attended as twelfth man and replaced a last-minute absentee]. Afterwards joined Aston Villa and has since played for no other club. Tackles superbly, kicks with precision, and places with judgement; usually at his best when his side is in difficulties. A type of player worthy of emulation by all young players."[417] Captain also of England on three occasions.

His playing career mainly began with Birchfield Trinity, where he was coached under the watchful eye of the famous Villan, Arthur Brown, and from where he was signed for Villa (against opposition from other clubs) through the work of Charlie Johnstone.[418]

A famous Everton left-winger once remarked after a match in which he was up against H.S.: "It isn't natural it isn't! If I had to play against Spencer every week I should give it up. It's too much like running against a brick wall!"[419] When he was beaten, Spencer was known for his powers of recovery for a second try at the opponent, or be on the goal-line to clear a shot.

"[Spencer was] the outstanding example of what Aston Villa tradition on the football field came to mean. I shall never forget that neat-looking, scrupulously clean-playing, solid, safe-looking full-back, tackling crisply, confidently, side-tapping the ball into place for the long, low, raking, perfectly placed clearance. How easy he made it look. It seemed that he retained his control over the ball even after it had left his foot to hover, apparently, in the air, and land right at the foot of the man for whom it was intended."[420]

---

[416] Villa News & Record (No. 1) 1 Sep 1906
[417] Villa News & Record (No. 1) 1 Sep 1906
[418] From "Men of Mark" (No. 25) Sports Argus 10 Feb 1906
[419] From "Men of Mark" (No. 25) Sports Argus 10 Feb 1906
[420] R. Allen, in "All in The Day's Sport" (Chapter 3 on Aston Villa) (1946)

The Aston Villa Chronicles 1874 – 1924 (and after)

A contemporary writer described some aspects of his play:

> It is a superstition of the football world that Spencer *never* charges an opponent ... But Spencer has so many tricks up the sleeve of his jersey that he regards the practise of charging an opponent off the ball as playing the game very low.
>
> There is no finer sight on a football field than to see Howard Spencer falling back on his goal. Your average back will race at breakneck speed to his lines, trusting to luck and his fellow-back to circumvent the oncoming forward. Not so Spencer. If he cannot deprive his man of the ball, he will try to cut him off. And how gracefully he does it! Watching every movement of his adversary, he falls back with the kind of movement known in the army as the 'echelon'. The forward is puzzled. He left Spencer on the midway line; yet here the latter is, waiting to repel borders, right in the goal-mouth!

Referees and critics agreed in describing Spencer as the most gentlemanly player in first-class football.[421] It is recorded that on one occasion, Spencer had been suffering some bad fouling from an opponent. He went up to the player and said, most impressively and distinctly: "Now, don't you do that again. I won't have it; I won't have it!". Spencer did not have any further trouble.[422]

Stephenson, Clem

Born in 1890 at County Durham	England Trialist
Usual Position: Inside-Left	Appearances: 216 Goals: 96

"Has been made by experience. For long it was hard for some to understand why an artist like Bache should be left out [rather, moved to outside-left] for this youth, but some wise head resolved to persevere with the lad until he became as good or better than the English International. When near goal, he has a most deceiving feint, which, when his body sways as if he intends to take the ball wide, is merely the preliminary to a shot. His versatility is astounding for a player so young, and the difficulty which he cannot surmount with one of his many tricks must be a very serious one indeed."[423]

His passes were, according to contemporary observers, "as sweet as stolen kisses". He was regarded by many as of the six greatest Villa inside-lefts in the period up to 1924. One other of those six (Joe Bache) played outside him, making way for his talents in that berth. It is remarkable that while he was at Villa, he did not play for

---

[421] From "Men of Mark" (No. 25) Sports Argus 10 Feb 1906
[422] Sports Argus 22 Dec 1900
[423] Villa News & Record 23 Apr 1913 (Portraits of players in the 1913 Cup Final)

England, though the fact that World War One intervened (just as he was blossoming into his best) must have had a lot to do with it.

After leaving the Villa in 1921, he went on to lead Huddersfield Town (under the managership of Herbert Chapman, who not far in the future was to lay the foundations for Arsenal's success) to a Cup triumph, followed by three League Championships in successive seasons. At the close of the 20th century, he was voted one of the League's greatest 100 players.

Templeton, Bobby

Born in 1879 at Coylton	Scottish International	
Usual Position: Left/Right-sided winger.	Appearances: 71	Goals: 7

"Quite a genius on his day, playing a winning game to perfection. His best efforts came in brilliant intermittent flashes, but he could not always be relied upon to produce his highest form. Speedy and clever, he delighted in showing his tricks against weaker defenders. In big games he was invariably dangerous, possessing as he did the capacity for pulling a match 'out of the fire' at the most unexpected moments. Free and open-handed, he might take the game more seriously with advantage."[424]

"For quite a long time after going to the Villa he held his place as the most popular man in the side amongst the crowd. He had shown sufficient of his best form to make the weekly spectator long for more … Given the humour and the opportunity he would set the crowd in a roar. His cleverness prompted him to the most audacious limits of trickery, and not satisfied with beating his man once, and even twice, he must needs return a third time to the fray often [it seemed] for mere self-gratification and self-glorification. By-and-by, a reaction set in. The crowd wanted goals; the club needed consistency."[425]

It is said that the movement of the crowd to watch Templeton (in the international versus England at Ibrox, 1902) precipitated the collapse of a stand and the deaths and injury of so many spectators.

After serving the Villa, the Scottish international went on to serve Newcastle, then Woolwich Arsenal, and then returned to Scotland to play for Rangers.

---

[424] Villa News & Record (No. 1) 1 Sep 1906
[425] The Sporting Mail 13 Oct 1906 – "Men of Note"

The Aston Villa Chronicles 1874 – 1924 (and after)

Tranter, George

Born in 1887 at Brierley Hill, Staffordshire		
Usual Position: Half-Back	Appearances: 174	Goals: 1

Another player from the Stourbridge club, he was thrown into the fray as a result of a season-long injury to Chris Buckley, followed not long after by the departure of Sammy Greenhalgh, in the early part of the 1907-08 season. It is probable that he was thrown in too early, for his earlier games are noted as being played to the point of exhaustion, so committed was he. He was thus described:[426]

"A tall youth with a turn of speed far above average player, Tranter proved to be also possessed of the most essential qualifications for the position – he had pluck. … His tackling is keen and fearless, his courage of the indomitable order, and his persistency in sticking to his man really admirable."

Wallace, Charlie

Born in 1885 at Sunderland	England International	
Usual Position: Outside-Right	Appearances: 349	Goals: 57

"After leaving the Crystal Palace club [in 1907] he required some time in which to develop the extra skill that was necessary to success in First League football. At the present day, he has all the speed of old, and possesses a number of tricks that enable him to use that speed to the best advantage. Few players can change the direction of their run with the same adroitness. While at top speed for a sprint along the touchline, Wallace will suddenly swerve towards the middle of the field with a facility that leaves defenders wondering what has become of the forward. He centres with almost uncanny exactitude… He puts tremendous power behind his shots, which are exceptionally accurate for an extreme wing player."[427]

In addition, it was said: "He never hesitates to fetch the ball himself, and in this respect is a much more valuable club player than the man who, clever enough that he may be, is purely … content to wait for the ball to be put to him before he shows his mettle."[428] And 'Tityrus' of the *Athletic News* said: "Charlie Wallace stands out as a great player." It was not uncommon for observers who saw Athersmith and Wallace play to opine that Wallace was the better of the two players.

---

[426] The Sporting Mail 23 Nov 1907 – "Men of Note"
[427] Villa News & Record 23 Apr 1913 (Portraits of players in the 1913 Cup Final)
[428] Villa News & Record 26 Oct 1912

The Aston Villa Chronicles 1874 – 1924 (and after)

Although he left Villa in 1921, he not long after – after retiring as a player – returned to Villa Park to work behind the scenes. Wallace was still working at Villa Park when Villa won the Cup in 1957.

Walters, Joey

Born in 1886 at Stourbridge, Worcs
Usual Position: Left/Right-sided winger. Appearances: 120 Goals: 41

Another product of the Stourbridge club. Mostly a fringe player with the Villa during his long stay, he did not make dazzling headlines, though he produced a good games:goals ratio.

Welford, James

Born in 1872 at Glasgow
Usual Position: Left-Back Appearances: 83 Goals: 1

Born in Scotland, he arrived at the Villa in August, 1893 via Mitchell St. George's. He was a good enough player to keep his full-back place when Jimmy Crabtree joined the Villa in 1895, and formed a sound partnership with Spencer until he became injured and the advent of Albert Evans. Welford left for Celtic after the 'double' season.

"[A] man who did not smile overmuch, and was not particularly fast, but he covered a lot of ground, and was a great and stolid stumbling block to opposing forwards. ... [Not] quite in the same class as [Spencer] ... he was an extremely difficult man to pass ..."[429]

He went on to win championship and cup honours with (Glasgow) Celtic, and then went on to play for Belfast Celtic, with whom he won the Irish Cup. Thus he won cup honours in three provinces.

Weston, Tommy

Born in 1890 at Halesowen, Staffs.
Usual Position: Left-Back Appearances: 179 Goals: 0

"At the start of the [1912-13] season, he was somewhat hysterical in his rushes and made mistakes in consequence. Now he has developed the ballast necessary to be sound, and, at the same time, has lost none of his dash. When nothing but a big

---

[429] Villa News & Record 21 Apr 1924 – "Some Famous Villa Players"

effort in the way of a spring at the ball will suffice, he springs with all the confidence of youth, and yet there is that about his play which suggests the judgment of a veteran. He does not place the ball with more than ordinary skill, but he can be no end of a nuisance to opposing forwards."[430]

His absence (through injury in the 1913-14 season) until well into the 1914-15 season was particularly noticeable, and the Villa improved on his return to the fray.

Wheldon, Fred

Born in 1869 at Langley Green, Worcs.	England International
Usual Position: Inside-Left	Appearances: 137 Goals: 74

"One of the select few who have won fame both at cricket and football. At one period of his long and brilliant career, Fred Wheldon's services would have been accepted by any club in the country. When at his best, he was undoubtedly the finest inside left forward England possessed. His command of the ball, his adaptability to prevailing conditions, combined with his dodging, his swerving, and his deadly shooting, made him a great player in the highest company. Brilliant with head and foot alike, he has always been an ornament to the game. Can boast the distinction of having represented Small Heath, Aston Villa, and West Bromwich Albion."[431]

> A Blackburn defender was once telling his friends of his on-the-pitch encounter with Wheldon:
>
> "Why, mon, he kep' runnin' ron' and ron' me in a circle, and for t'life o' me, I could ne'er catch 'im!"
>
> "Well," remarked one of his friends, "if he did, why didn't you turn round and meet him when performing those circles?!"[432]

Another side to Wheldon's play was revealed in the following:

> No man ever helped the half-back behind him better than Fred Wheldon did. He always fell back when he was wanted. ... A born tackler.[433]

---

[430] Villa News & Record 23 Apr 1913 (Portraits of players in the 1913 Cup Final)
[431] Villa News & Record (No. 1) 1 Sep 1906
[432] Sports Argus 19 Feb 1898
[433] Sports Argus 6 Apr 1901

Whitehouse, Jimmy

Born in 1873 at Birmingham
Usual Position: Goalkeeper   Appearances: 43   Goals: 0

Jimmy is mainly remembered as being the keeper in the 'double' season of 1896-97. He had competetition for the spot from Tommy Wilkes, but Whitehouse was considered to be the more reliable and more capable.

Wilkes, Albert

Born in 1875 at West Bromwich, Staffs.   England International
Usual Position: Half-Back   Appearances: 159   Goals: 8

"A player of parts and a worthy follower of past Villa heroes. Scrupulously fair and honest in tackling, a willing worker, and an adept at finding openings for goal in big games. No place in the half-back line comes amiss to him. A quite unostentatious player of the untiring order, he has done his share in raising the tone of football both on and off the field. 'Straight as a die', he is a general and deserved favourite."[434]

He was signed from Walsall just in time for the championship-winning season of 1898-99. By the time he left Villa in 1907, he was already gaining a reputation as a sports photographer, and many Villa photos were produced by his firm in West Bromwich. He later became a director of the Villa.

Wilkes, Tommy

Born in 1874 at Alcester, Worcs.
Usual Position: Goalkeeper   Appearances: 57   Goals: 0

Albert's brother, he was a fine goalkeeper for Villa in the 1890s before continuing his career with Stoke. How Tommy Wilkes came to be signed up is interesting.[435] When he was at Reddich Town the previous season to signing for the Villa, he played in goal with one hand in splints as a result of cutting his hand on glass hours before the match. His performance with, effectively, one hand was so good that the Villa signed him on!

---

[434] Villa News & Record (No. 1) 1 Sep 1906
[435] Athletic News 22 Apr 1895